SOUTHEAST ASIA

Books by Roger M. Smith

Cambodia's Foreign Policy (1965)

Editor of

Bernard B. Fall, Anatomy of a Crisis: The Laotian Crisis of 1960–1961 (1969)

Southeast Asia: Documents of Political Development and Change (1974)

SOUTHEAST ASIA

Documents of
Political Development and Change

Edited by ROGER M. SMITH

CONTRIBUTORS

Clark D. Neher, Josef Silverstein,
Herbert Feith, Alan Smith, J. Norman Parmer,
Marjorie Weiner Normand, Roy Jumper,
Roger M. Smith, David Wurfel

Cornell University Press | ITHACA AND LONDON

First published 1974 by Cornell University Press.
Published in the United Kingdom by Cornell University Press Ltd.,
2-4 Brook Street, London W1Y 1AA.

International Standard Book Number 0-8014-0797-4
Library of Congress Catalog Card Number 73-14062

Printed in the United States of America by York Composition Co., Inc.

Contents

Five: VIET–NAM   306
by *Marjorie Weiner Normand and Roy Jumper*

Preface

During the past twenty-five years, the evolution of politics in the several Southeast Asian states—Thailand, Burma, Indonesia, Malaysia, Singapore, Viet-Nam, Laos, Cambodia, and the Philippines—has been marked by wars, revolutions, coups d'état, and other acts of violence. These and other important, though perhaps less exciting, events have called the world's attention to the area. They have also been the cause for a foreign involvement in Southeast Asia that was not foreseen when, one by one, most of the states wrested their independence from European and American colonial rule. Unfortunately, however, there has been a paucity of published materials reflecting the efforts of Southeast Asian countries in their struggle toward political maturity. Despite the increasing number of monographic studies resulting from the research by both Southeast Asian and Western scholars and such pioneering comparative works as *Governments and Politics of Southeast Asia* (1959 and 1964), edited by George McT. Kahin, and *In Search of Southeast Asia* (1971) by David J. Steinberg *et al.,* a great lacuna in our knowledge of the nine Southeast Asian countries and their more than two hundred million peoples continues to exist. This book attempts to add to our fund of knowledge on their political development. It is to be hoped that, by portraying that evolution through the words and deeds of Southeast Asians themselves, this volume will heighten our understanding and appreciation of them.

Each of the contributors has selected materials which he believes best describe the political thoughts and actions of Southeast Asians and their governments during the past twenty-five years. Most of the materials have originated in Southeast Asia; the few exceptions are joint Southeast Asian–Western statements and agreements, or documents relating to the transfer of power from Western to Southeast

Asian hands. The documents are preceded by brief introductions, designed to place the materials in their proper context and to provide continuity between them. Each chapter is introduced by an essay describing generally the country's political process during the period 1945–1973. A Glossary is located after the last chapter; most of the words in it are Southeast Asian terms found in the documents.

We do not claim to have presented all of the important political documents that have emanated from Southeast Asia during this period. To have done so would require separate and, probably, several volumes on each country. Our selection is intended to illustrate the complexity of the political process in Southeast Asia in the immediate postindependence period and to give rise to further study and research on the region.

The editor and contributors would like to express their gratitude to U Htun Myaing, Orawin Anuwat-Udom, Patcheree Srikanchana, Paveena Kowtrakul, Fernanda LeMonte, and Carol A. Smith for their invaluable assistance in preparing this volume for publication. We are appreciative also of the assistance provided by Harry G. Aveling, Andrew H. Gunawan, Stuart L. Graham, and Mr. and Mrs. Lie Han Koen for the translation of material in the section on Indonesia.

ROGER M. SMITH

Bangkok, Thailand,
  and *Ithaca, New York*

Contributors

HERBERT FEITH (Indonesia), Professor of Politics, Faculty of Economics and Politics, Monash University, Australia

ROY JUMPER (Viet-Nam), Associate Professor of Public Affairs and Director, Division of Professional and Technical Services, School of Public and Environmental Affairs, Indiana University

CLARK D. NEHER (Thailand), Associate Professor of Political Science, Department of Political Science, Northern Illinois University

MARJORIE WEINER NORMAND (Viet-Nam), Specialist on Viet-Nam, New York City; Class of 1975, New York University School of Law

J. NORMAN PARMER (Malaysia and Singapore), Professor of History and Assistant Dean of Faculties for International Studies, Ohio University

JOSEF SILVERSTEIN (Burma), Professor of Political Science, Department of Political Science, Rutgers University

ALAN SMITH (Indonesia), Member of Staff Collective of the Light, Powder and Construction Works, Melbourne, Australia

ROGER M. SMITH (Cambodia, Laos), Visiting Associate Professor of Government and Asian Studies, Southeast Asia Program, Cornell University (1972–1973); Associate Dean of Liberal Studies, State University College of New York at Potsdam (1974)

DAVID WURFEL (Philippines), Professor of Political Science, Department of Political Science, University of Windsor, Canada

SOUTHEAST ASIA

ONE

Thailand

by CLARK D. NEHER

Thailand emerged from World War II considerably more stable and secure than any other nation of Southeast Asia. Although the government, led by Prime Minister Phibun Songkram, had acquiesced to a virtual Japanese occupation during the war, the people suffered few if any real social, economic, or political hardships. The Thai maintained control over the country's internal administration. The mainstay of the economy, rice, was in abundant supply. War-caused damage was slight. Finally, unlike in other countries of the region, Thailand's stability and security were not threatened by a debilitating struggle for independence.

In 1944, when it became evident that Japan would lose the war, the military regime of Phibun Songkram was forced to resign in favor of civilians. Among them the most important were Pridi Phanomyong, the brilliant head of the pro-Allies, underground Free Thai Movement, and Khuang Aphaiwong, an opposition leader who was later to preside as prime minister over four governments. The military was stripped of all effective power, political parties were organized, and the first elections in almost a decade were held. Thailand appeared to be headed toward a constitutional system of parliamentary democracy under Pridi's leadership. Pridi's alleged involvement in the tragic and unexplained shooting of Thailand's young King Ananda Mahidol in June 1946, however, precipitated his downfall. On November 8, 1947, ranking military officers, charging the Pridi regime with failure to cope with severe postwar economic problems, carried out a bloodless coup d'état.

Pridi fled the country; Khuang Aphaiwong was made prime minister of a caretaker government.

Following elections in January 1948, Khuang again formed a government, this time on the basis of a parliamentary majority. Four months later, however, the military once more seized power and the government was turned over to Phibun Songkram. Civilian government in Thailand ended.

Despite a number of attempts to oust him from power, Phibun managed to retain leadership of the government for nine years. His search for a wider base of popular support in the mid-1950's, however, proved to be his undoing: Proclaiming a new "era of democracy" in which freedom of speech and press were encouraged, political parties flourished, and plans were laid for new elections in 1957, Phibun unwittingly unleashed a flood of criticism against his regime, which paved the way for another coup d'état. Capitalizing on Phibun's involvement in the fraudulent February 1957 elections, General Sarit Thanarat, commander of the Bangkok army, seized power in September of that year, suspended the constitution, dissolved the National Assembly, and declared martial law. Phibun fled into exile.

To give an aura of legitimacy to his coup d'état, General Sarit assigned prominent civilians to cabinet posts until the elections in December 1957. He then mobilized a parliamentary majority and set up General Thanom Kittikachorn as prime minister while he went to the United States for extended medical treatment. Thanom's regime, however, was weakened by recurring crises, and when Sarit returned in October 1958 he again seized power. An interim constitution was promulgated giving him unlimited power and establishing an appointive Constituent Assembly with power to legislate and to draw up a new constitution. Sarit died in December 1963 and was succeeded by General Thanom Kittikachorn.

Nearly five years later, Thailand's eighth postrevolution constitution was promulgated, but neither the new charter nor the legislative elections in February 1969 led to a genuinely representative and effective democratic government. Rather, absolute rule returned to Thailand on November 17, 1971, when Prime Minister Thanom Kittikachorn announced that the Revolutionary party had seized control of the government. General Thanom and other leaders of the new party, including General Prapat Charusathien, Police General Prasert Ruchirawongse, Air Chief Marshal Dawee Chulasapya, and Mr. Pote Sarasin, claimed that since the elections a number of attempts had been made to obstruct and sabotage the government. A coup was necessary, they said, because increasing threats to national security required prompt counteraction which was not possible under the constitution.[1] The leaders of the Revolutionary party then formed a National Executive Council, which ruled the country under martial law.

The new military goverment, however, became increasingly corrupt and repressive, and it appeared unable to cope with a number of serious economic problems, including mounting inflation and unemployment, especially among Thailand's burgeoning and restive student population. When the government refused to expedite work on a new constitution, the gap between it and educated youth was widened, and, in October 1973, the military leaders were driven from power as a result of violent, student-led demonstrations in which 200,000 persons were reported to have participated. A new, primarily civilian, government headed by Sanya Thammasak, former chief justice of the Supreme Court and rector of Thammasat University, was formed by King Phumibhol Adulyadej, and the premier announced that a new constitution would be produced within six months. The unprecedented overthrow of the military by citizen protest and the likelihood of the king exercising greater political power in the future were dramatic evidence of fundamental change in Thai political life.

Since the 1932 revolution overthrowing the absolute monarchy Thailand has had a dizzying array of governments. Twelve prime ministers, three for several nonconsecutive terms, have presided over 33 cabinets under nine constitutions. Since World War II the elite groups most successful in aggregating power have come from the military. The coup d'état is well suited to the military: The army's hierarchy is congruent with the organizational pattern of the society as a whole and with popular expectations of what constitutes proper authority. Moreover, Thai cultural emphasis on status relationships has been of immense advantage to the army as it has amassed and exercised power. Political parties, parliament, and public opinion have not had sufficient capabilities in terms of resources, leadership, or unity to challenge

[1] See *The Nation* (Bangkok), November 18, 19, 1971; and *Bangkok World*, November 18, 1971.

the military. However, the frequent use of the coup d'état belies a basic
continuity and stability in post-World War II Thai politics. These ex-
traconstitutional governmental changes have affected only the highest
echelons of the ruling elite. Even among these elites similar objectives
have been pursued: Preservation of internal stability, promotion of development, and prevention of foreign domination.

Once in power governmental leaders have sought legitimization of
their regimes, principally by the holding of elections. Elections, however, have generally served merely to justify and buttress the existing
regime rather than to provide a representative and coequal legislative
branch of government. The National Assembly has been almost totally
ineffective in modifying or influencing executive power. Delegation of
their authority to respected civilian leaders, thus demonstrating the
disinterested nature of their seizure of power, has also been employed
by new ruling groups in their search for legitimization. Finally, the
ruling groups have attempted to win popular sanction for their regimes by promulgating new constitutions. After each major postwar
change of government, institutional structures have been altered to
strengthen the new regimes. The constitutions have also emphasized
the governments' complete loyalty to the monarchy and demonstrated
the king's acceptance of the new rulers.

When compared with her neighbors, Thailand has exhibited a remarkable capacity to cope with the demands made on the political
system. The reasons for Thailand's political stability are inextricably
bound up with traditional cultural patterns. For the Thai peasant, the
legitimacy of a regime stems not only from the elaborate process of
promulgating constitutions, calling new elections, setting up respectable
temporary heads of government, and claiming obeisance to the king,
but also from the regime's very capacity to maintain authority and
retain power. The Thai believe that right behavior leads to prestigious
and powerful positions in the hierarchy. David A. Wilson has developed this idea: "The position of a being, human or otherwise, in this
universe may be measured by the degree to which he is subject to the
will and power of others and the sway of his will and power over
others. This conception is the one which must be referred to throughout [a] discussion of Thai politics, i.e., the necessary and just unity of
virtue and power. Those who have power are good and deserve power.
. . . Power justifies itself. This idea is not to be understood in a cyni-

cal sense which would lead to the view that might is right. It is rather a magico-religious view that right is might."[2]

The Thai government's ability to meet popular demands has been favored by social and economic patterns which permit the absorption, containment, and manipulation of modernizing forces. An open and generally socially mobile society, as well as a history of independence from foreign domination, have given the Thai considerable latitude in accommodating modernizing elements from abroad, thus mitigating social and economic disruption. Thailand's economic policies of recent years have exemplified the government's capacity to cope with new demands and pressures. The First Economic Development Plan, 1961–1966, was essentially conservative in its reliance on private enterprise and in its setting of attainable goals, yet the average growth rate after the plan's inauguration was a phenomenal 7.2 percent per annum. In response to increased Communist insurgency activities in the poverty-stricken northeast provinces, Prime Ministers Sarit and Thanom planned and carried out the Accelerated Rural Development Program, which, supported mainly with United States funds, was designed to hasten economic development in this previously ignored area.

In addition to the government's proven capacity to preserve internal stability and promote development, the Thai are reputed to be brilliant diplomats, their history of independence being cited as proof. Thailand's postwar diplomacy further attests to their diplomatic agility. In less than one year's time, Thailand went from a defeated enemy to a respected and pampered ally of the United States and Great Britain. Following Prime Minister Phibun Songkram's fall from power in 1944, Pridi Phanomyong, in a shrewd maneuver to regain the good favor of the Allies, persuaded the Thai ambassador to the United States, also a distinguished leader of the Free Thai Movement, Seni Pramoj, to become prime minister during the period of negotiations with the United States and Great Britain. The existence of the Free Thai Movement, Pridi's repudiation of Phibun's declaration of war on the Allies, and Seni Pramoj's effective exploitation of his positive relations with the United States all helped bring a swift peace settlement. By December 1946 Thailand was accorded membership in the United Nations.

Thailand and the United States have enjoyed particularly close relations since the war. Although Phibun's military coup d'état against

[2] David A. Wilson, *Politics in Thailand* (Ithaca: Cornell University Press, 1962), p. 74.

a civilian government in 1948 temporarily strained relations, the United States recognized the new regime and accepted Phibun as a leading anti-Communist ally. The political situation in 1948 in Southeast Asia was ominous. Thailand was surrounded by nations torn by wars of independence and threatened by revolutionary guerrilla warfare. The Communist party's growing control over China convinced Phibun that a close association with the Western powers was Thailand's best hope in confronting the perceived Communist threat. Accordingly, in 1950 Thailand and the United States entered into military-assistance and economic-and-technical-cooperation agreements. Phibun's policy of reliance on the Western powers, and especially on the United States, for military and economic assistance was followed by the succeeding Thai governments.

The Laotian crisis in the early 1960's strained Thai-American relations. Thailand, fearing a Communist-controlled Laos on its border, supported the Laotian pro-Western right-wing government, while the United States vacillated in its support between the neutralist and the right-wing government against the leftist Pathet Lao. However, the Thanat-Rusk Agreement in 1962, which pledged American determination to meet any Communist attack muted Thai skepticism of United States' resolve to protect Thailand. In May 1962 in response to the movement of Communist forces into Laos, the United States sent almost 5,000 men to northeast Thailand. This dramatic show of power also helped to refurbish flagging Thai faith in America's commitment.

The Viet-Nam war, in the Thai government's view, became a test of United States' readiness to defend Thailand, just as the Laotian crisis had been previously. President Johnson's decision to intervene in Viet-Nam and his subsequent decision to station some 48,000 American forces in Thailand provided what the Thai government perceived as tangible proof that the American commitment was unconditional. However, the unforeseen political events in the United States in 1968 which culminated in President Nixon's election and his Guam doctrine—Asian wars to be fought by Asians—threatened to undermine the assumptions on which Thai foreign policy was based. Thereafter, the Thai government sought to reshape its foreign relations to meet the new realities, and government spokesmen reiterated two common themes which had been expressed rather perfunctorily in previous years but were now taken increasingly seriously: "We must depend on ourselves," and "We must build Southeast Asian regional alliances."

Thailand since 1945 has proven consistently its capacity to cope with and absorb the changing demands made by both internal and foreign forces on the political system. Economically, the kingdom has enjoyed an extraordinary growth rate without upsetting traditional cultural and social patterns. Politically, Thailand has remained stable except at the highest governmental levels where coups d'état continue to be the means to change governments.

This ability to meet and absorb the heretofore limited needs of the people, however, soon may be severely tested. If the present 3.2 percent rate of population growth continues, for example, Thailand will face a land and rice shortage which could disturb seriously the Thai pattern of socioeconomic organization. The annual urban growth rate of 7.1 percent has already created major pockets of unemployment. Insurgencies in the northern, northeastern, and southern provinces have led to massive aid programs and increased governmental activity in these sensitive areas. As the government imposes itself more directly on the villagers and makes new demands on traditional patterns of behavior, tensions between the villagers and government are likely to increase. Thailand's close alliance with and reliance on the United States could create serious social problems, as the forces of Westernization are increasingly thrust upon Thailand. Adaptation to new challenges may no longer be sufficient to preserve the stability and security Thailand has enjoyed for so long. Its political system must develop an ability not only to cope with change but also to stay in advance of it.

I. Of Coups and Revolution

The promoters of Thailand's revolution of 1932 attempted to replace the absolute monarchy with a Westernized constitutional government comprising an elected parliament, a responsible executive, and a separate court system. Although the promoters of the revolution succeeded in curtailing the king's powers, his authority was largely transferred to a bureaucratic labyrinth controlled by small cliques. King Prajadhipok, the seventh monarch of the reigning Chakri dynasty, quickly assented to the promoters' demands for a constitution, thereby muting their more inflammatory statements as well as preserving the throne and assuring popular acceptance of the revolution. The king's influence, however, was negligible, and in 1935 he abdicated in favor of Ananda Mahidol, a sixteen-year-old grandson of the illustrious King

Chulalongkorn. King Ananda was succeeded by his brother, the present monarch, Phumibhol Adulyadej, following Ananda's death in 1946. For the overwhelming majority of the Thai the king has remained the "King wearing the great crown of the celestial being; royal descendant of the sun who shines like the finest jewel, most excellent of lineage; monarch as supreme as the greatest emperor of the worlds; greatest sovereign of righteousness, supreme King of men."[3]

Ultimatum of the People's Party [June 24, 1932]*

The People's Party consisting of civil and military officials have now taken over the administration of the country and have taken members of the Royal Family . . . as hostages. If members of the People's Party have received any injuries the Princes held in pawn will suffer. . . . The People's Party['s] . . . principal aim is to have a constitutional monarchy. We therefore enjoin Your Majesty to return to the Capital to reign again as King under the constitutional monarchy as established by the People's Party. If Your Majesty refuses to accept the offer or refrains from replying within one hour after the receipt of this message the People's Party will proclaim the Constitutional monarchical government by appointing another Prince whom they consider to be efficient to act as King.

King Prajadhipok's Reply to the People's Party
Ultimatum [June 24, 1932]†

I have received the letter in which you invite me to return to Bangkok as a constitutional monarch. For the sake of peace; and in order to save useless bloodshed; to avoid confusion and loss to the country; and, more, because I have already considered making this change myself, I am willing to cooperate in the establishment of a constitution under which I am willing to serve.

Furthermore, there is a possibility that, if I decline to continue in my office as King, the foreign powers will not recognize the new government. This might entail considerable difficulty for the government.

Physically I am not strong. I have no children to succeed me. My life-

[3] Quoted in *ibid.*, p. 91.

* *Source:* K. P. Landon, *Siam in Transition* (Chicago: University of Chicago Press, 1939), pp. 9–13. Reprinted by permission of the University of Chicago Press.

† *Source: Ibid.*

expectancy is not long, at least if I continue in this office. I have no desire for position or for personal aggrandisement. My ability to advance the progress of the race alone constrains me.

Accept this sincere expression of my feelings.

PRAJADHIPOK

People's Party Announcement to the People [July 1, 1932]*

When the present King came to the throne the people hoped that he would give an equitable administration. Their hopes were unfulfilled. The King was above the law even as his predecessors had been. His relatives and friends, even when without ability, were given the highest government positions. The King allowed government officials to be dishonest. They took personal graft in governmental building projects, in buying supplies, and in the exchange of government money. The King elevated the royal class and permitted them to oppress the common people. The King ruled unwisely and allowed the country to fall into decay, as the present depression proves. The government of the King, who is above all law, is unable to right these wrongs.

The government cannot right the above wrongs because it does not rule for the good of the people as do the governments of other countries. The government regards the people as servants, as slaves, even as animals, not as men. Instead of helping the people, the government oppresses them. The taxes collected are used personally by the King. In a year he receives many millions of the people's money. As for the people, for them to earn even a little money requires them verily to sweat blood. If the people cannot pay taxes their property is seized or they are forced to labour without pay. Royalty sleeps, eats, and is happy. No other nation gives its royal class so much. Perhaps only the Czar and the Kaiser have been so favoured. . . .

Let us have a clear understanding. This country belongs to the people. Where does the money come from that royalty uses? It comes from the people. The country is poor because of this custom of draining off the wealth of the people. Farmers must abandon their fields because they receive inadequate profit. Students graduate from school and find no employment. Soldiers are dismissed from service and must starve. This is the work of a government above the law. It oppresses the lower civil officials and dismisses them with no pension. Money collected by taxation should be used on behalf of the nation and not for the enrichment of royalty. The savings of royalty are sent abroad to foreign banks to await the day

* Source: Ibid.

when a bankrupt nation is abandoned by its rulers who go to live abroad. This is evil work.

For these reasons the people, civil officials, the army, and the navy, have formed a People's Party and have seized the powers of government. The People's Party feels that the way to alleviate conditions is to establish an assembly which can include the best thinking of many minds. This is better than the thinking of one man. . . . The People's Party . . . has invited King Prajadhipok to continue to be King under a constitution. He will not be able to act without the agreement of the assembly. If he refuses, or he does not answer within the time set, he will be regarded as a rebel against his race. It will then be necessary to have a democratic form of government. That is, a president will be a commoner elected by the assembly for a limited period of time. By this system of government the people may hope to prosper and have work. The country is naturally rich. When the taxes are used for the good of the nation then the nation must prosper. The new government will rule with intelligence, not blindly as the old government did. The People's Party has established the following platform:

1. The freedom and equality of the people in politics, in the law courts, and in business, must be maintained.
2. Peace and quiet, with no harm to anyone, must be assured.
3. A national economic policy must be drawn up to guarantee remunerative work to everyone.
4. Equal privilege for everyone must be guaranteed. No one group shall enjoy special privilege at the expense of others.
5. The people shall have freedom and liberty except in those cases where freedom and liberty disagree with the above four points.
6. The people must be given the most complete education possible.

People! Help the People's Party accomplish these aims. The People's Party requests everyone who had no share in seizing the power of government to remain quietly at home, pursuing their usual activities in a peaceful way. Do not interfere with the activities of the People's Party. By helping the People's Party you help the nation, the people, and yourself. . . . Everyone wants peace and prosperity. The People's Party will accomplish these things.

Thailand's highest court ruled in April 1946 that Prime Minister Phibun Songkram could not be held for collaboration with the enemy or for any other war crimes. Neither the Thai people nor the United States government protested the acquittal of the World War II military leaders, and in less than two years the military once again controlled the government. The November 1947 coup d'état clearly pointed out the advantages enjoyed by the military in acquiring power in Thailand. The army controlled the weapons and, therefore, Bangkok. An authoritarian political tradition instilled during military training provided the officers with a philosophical basis for rejecting a less stable liberal constitutionalism. The military rulers retained some democratic elements and temporarily allowed the respected civilian leader Khuang Aphaiwong to rule. But when Khuang's Democrat party won resounding election victories, the military seized complete power in April 1948. The Act to Indemnify Promoters of the Coup d'État states the military's reasons for seizing power.

Act to Indemnify Promoters of the Coup d'État
A.D. *1947* [December 23, 1947]*

Whereas ever since the establishment of the House of Elders and the House of the Representatives following the promulgation of the Constitution of the Kingdom of Siam, A.D. 1946, the internal political conditions of the country have been changing. . . . The economic . . . conditions of the people were affected . . . to a serious degree. Under such circumstances it could have been anticipated that the country would continue to get worse and would finally reach disaster if the situation was not remedied in time. In view of the above a group of persons consisting of members of the armed forces, the police force and civilians decided unanimously to carry out a coup d'état in order to abolish the Constitution of the Kingdom of Siam, A.D. 1946, and to bring into force the Constitution of the Kingdom of Siam (provisional), A.D. 1947. In so doing, events have proceeded in peace and without any show of force. Moreover in effecting the coup d'état, its promoters had no desire other than to remedy and stem the deterioration of the country, as a means of alleviating the hardship of the people and improving the country's security. Their purpose is not one of personal benefit or reward in any way. Therefore it is deemed expedient that indemnity should be granted to the promoters of this coup d'état.

Therefore the King, with the advice and consent of Parliament, commands that an Act shall be enacted as follows: . . .

SEC. 3. Any person who, before this Act comes into force, did any act in connection with the coup d'état in order to abolish the Constitution of the Kingdom of Siam, A.D. 1946, and to enforce the Constitution of

* *Source:* Royal Thai Government *Gazette* (Bangkok), December 23, 1947, pp. 75–76.

the Kingdom of Siam (provisional) A.D. 1947, which shall be an offence against any law, shall not be held liable or responsible for the said act in any manner whatsoever, and any action taken including any notice, notification and order which was issued in connection with the coup d'état as aforesaid shall be deemed to be lawful in every respect.

The "silent coup" of 1951 redistributed the power positions of the 1947 military coup group members. Although Phibun remained as prime minister, his power was drastically circumscribed in favor of Police General Phao Sriyanond and Army General Sarit Thanarat. The bicameral legislature was superseded by an appointed assembly with elections planned for the future. One important reason for the coup, in addition to those listed in the 1951 Amnesty Act, was the imminent return of the king to Thailand after a long absence. An alliance of the royalist-leaning Senate and the king himself was foreseen as a threat to the military's power. Just three days before King Phumibhol's triumphant arrival, the "silent coup" took place, undermining in one stroke the royalists' power and assuring the coup group of continued dominance. It became Phibun's role to balance the newly emerged factions led by Phao and Sarit. Following a period of ruthless suppression of civil liberties under Phao, and an abortive "era of democracy" under Phibun, Field Marshal Sarit Thanarat in 1957 overthrew his two rivals in the triumvirate.

Amnesty Act A.D. 1951 Granted to Persons in the Course of Reviving the Constitution of A.D. 1932 [December 31, 1951]*

. . . Whereas because of . . . world conditions and the threat of communism infiltrating into the Council of Ministers and Parliament, the Government, in spite of tremendous efforts, found itself incapable of averting the danger. Nor could the Government stamp out another danger known as corruption. . . . Consequently political disintegration set in in a manner which has caused grave anxieties for the safety of the nation. Therefore, a party consisting of the Army, Navy, Air Force, Police, promoters of the 1932 coup d'état, promoters of the 1947 coup d'état and members of the public, being imbued with the spirit of patriotism and firmly determined to safeguard the safety of the nation, the Faith, the Throne of the Chakri Dynasty and the constitutional regime, unanimously decided to revive the Constitution dated the 10th of December

* Source: Ibid., December 31, 1951, p. 608.

A.D. 1932 for the welfare and continuity of the state. They, therefore, set up a Provisional Executive Power pending the appointment of a new Council of Ministers under the Constitution. The Provisional Executive Power submitted a petition to His Majesty the King to revive the Constitution of 1932. . . . His Majesty was graciously pleased to grant the petition to revive the said Constitution and enforce the same as from the 29th of November A.D. 1951. Since it appears that what the said party has brought about is motivated mainly by their anxieties concerning the nation, the Faith, the Throne and the constitutional regime and that in carrying out their plan no loss to property or life has been occasioned it is deemed proper to grant them an Act of Amnesty.

His Majesty the King, by and with the advice and consent of the Assembly of the People's Representatives, is graciously pleased to enact the following Act:

. . . SEC. 3. All Acts by any persons committed before the enforcement of this Act in connection with the effort to repeal the Constitution of 1949 and to revive the Constitution of 1932 . . . are hereby declared lawful and free of all offences and liabilities.

Sarit Thanarat's October 1958 seizure of power was total in that he abolished or muzzled every potential institution of opposition: The constitution, the National Assembly, political parties, and the press. Sarit dominated the newly formed cabinet, the appointed Constituent Assembly, and the military. In addition to the office of prime minister, he headed the National Economic Development Board, the National Security Council, the National Research Council, and the National Education Council. He was also the supreme commander of the armed forces and director-general of the National Police Department. The proclamations of the Revolutionary Group remained in force during Sarit's five-year rule and many of them were continued into the early 1970's by his successor, Prime Minister Thanom Kittikachorn. One of the most important of these proclamations is presented below.

Proclamation of the Revolutionary Group, No. 4 [October 20, 1958]*

With reference to Proclamation No. 2 of the Revolutionary Group which informed the people that this seizure of power was necessitated by the tense situation within and outside the country . . . making the seizure of power and revolution in appropriate ways inevitable, the Revolutionary Group clearly gives its reasons as follows:

* Source: Ibid., October 20, 1958, pp. 659–661.

As for the internal situation, the clear infiltration of Communism every-where was the great danger. . . . Infiltration by Communist agents was taking place by all avenues: politically, economically, and socially through the use of propaganda and clever plans, the pouring out of huge sums of money, and the conduct of activities both secretly and openly; the attempt by every means to ruin the country, undermine the throne, annihilate Buddhism, and destroy every institution preserved by the Thai nation with such sacrifice.

Agents and tools of the Communists have disturbed, interfered with, and made difficult the conduct of the affairs of the nation. . . . Negotia-tions with foreign nations encountered obstacles. . . . The Government had no time to marshall thought and strength to improve the nation so taken up was it with meeting internal disturbances and obstacles. . . . Even worse, by secret contacts and open publicity, they tried to cause foreign countries to lose confidence in Thailand, without thinking of how severe the resulting damage to the nation might be.

The Thai people made sacrifices and took risks to establish a constitu-tional system of government . . . but some self-seeking groups took ad-vantage of the constitutional system to destroy the peace, to use their rights and liberties as tools to obstruct progress, create divisions, incite disunity in the nation, persuade the people to be enemies one with an-other, wanting to see only difficulties, deterioration, and final destruction of the nation.

These matters are like a virulent infection which cannot be healed by taking care of each as it comes up, or corrected by changing the govern-ment, the governing, or simply changing the system in some respects. It is comparable to a malignant disease which cannot be cured by medica-tion, only by surgery. Revolution is the only way the said malignant disease of the nation can be treated.

. . . The external situation gives increasing cause for concern, most especially in the areas adjacent to Thailand. If disturbances there reach Thailand at a time when the country is full of destructive thoughts, mu-tual enmity, troublemaking, and the desires of those who wish to see the deterioration of the country, the nation would undoubtedly be extin-guished. The only way to restore the country is to risk coming to grips with such destructive thought, to look for ways to rebuild the stability of the nation on a firm democratic foundation, arrange the economic and social system as may be appropriate to the condition of the nation and Thai people, to establish a lasting plan to benefit the people every-where.

To achieve these aims, the Revolutionary Group was forced to seize power, revoking the Constitution of the Kingdom of Thailand A.D. 1932 amended A.D. 1952 because its provisions were not binding enough to cope with the present situation. For this reason, the government was obliged to resign. A new constitution is necessary, strong enough to fight the dangers that confront the nation. As a result of the revocation of the Constitution, the House of People's Representatives ceases to exist as well. The Revolutionary Group regrets that this must be so, it having harboured no enmity whatsoever for the House. On the contrary, the Revolutionary Group sympathizes with the House of People's Representatives and resigned government which performed to the best of their ability. The obstacles or perils to the state did not arise from having the wrong House of People's Representatives or wrong government but from events which were beyond the power of the House or government to correct with the tools at hand. New tools were necessary to improve the nation as desired.

Apart from the creation of a new constitution, the people will be informed of revolutionary plans in other matters in later proclamations. At this stage, the Revolutionary Group gives a preliminary guarantee:

1. We will respect human rights as set forth in the Universal Declaration of Human Rights passed by the General Assembly of the United Nations doing nothing in violation thereof unless truly necessary to preserve the security of the nation.
2. The independence of the courts will be preserved. The courts will have full freedom to try cases in accordance with law without domination, influence or interference by the Revolutionary Group or the government to be appointed by the Revolutionary Group.
3. International obligations of Thailand as set forth in international agreements will be fully honoured. The Revolutionary Group and the government . . . will strictly conform to and respect international law, whether written or customary, as may be observed by all civilized states. Apart from that, we will fulfill our obligations as a party to the Southeast Asia Mutual Defense Treaty.
4. Most important of all, the Revolutionary Group will always hold that the King and Thai nation are inseparable. The history of the Thai nation from the beginning to the present is founded on the institution of the King as the symbol of the nation and boon of the people. The Revolutionary Group will preserve the basis of this institution with its full strength and ability and will do everything to keep the King in a revered position, permitting no act tortuous to the King, the royal family, or royal traditions which the Thai nation have so long cherished.

The people can rest assured that the Revolutionary Group will keep its four abovementioned pledges to the people. Peace-loving people, those well disposed toward the nation, those not engaging in disruptive, destructive acts, will not be affected in any way whatsoever by this revolution.

FIELD MARSHAL SARIT THANARAT
HEAD OF THE REVOLUTIONARY GROUP

II. Government and Politics

Prime Minister Phibun Songkram's foreign and domestic policies were essentially anti-Communist. The establishment of the People's Republic of China posed a problem for the Thai government because the influential Chinese minority in Thailand were split among three factions: those with primary allegiance to mainland China, to Taiwan, or to Thailand. A solution of the problem was found in the Anti-Communist Activities Act, which General Phao Sriyanond pushed through the National Assembly. The act, passed to intimidate the Chinese community in Thailand, provided a legal basis for the arrest of hundreds of "suspected" Communists, many of whom were not Communists but merely against the Phibun government.

Anti-Communist Activities Act A.D. *1952* [November 13, 1952]*

. . . SEC. 3. In this Act

"Communist organization" means any group of persons or association of persons which has as its object the carrying on of Communist activities, whether directly or not;

"Communist activities" mean

(a) The overthrow of the democratic form of government with the King as the Head of State, or

(b) The changing of the national economic system whereby private ownership or means of production is expropriated to the State by forfeiture or otherwise without payment of just compensation, or

(c) Any act of intimidation, sabotage or deceitful means such as to foment hatred among members of the public if calculated to enforce, assist, support or prosecute the object described in (a) or (b).

SEC. 4. Whoever is engaged in Communist activities shall be punished with imprisonment from ten years up to life imprisonment.

SEC. 5. Whoever incites, advises, encourages, conducts propaganda,

* *Source:* Royal Thai Government *Gazette,* November 13, 1952, p. 489.

holds any secret meeting, joins any association, allows, enters into any agreement with others or makes any preparation with an intent to carry on Communist activities or knowingly of any commission of offence against this Act, present or future, assists in keeping it secret shall be punished with imprisonment from five to ten years.

All printing presses and other properties connected with the commission of any offence under the preceding paragraph shall be forfeited.

SEC. 6. Whoever is a member of any Communist organization shall be punished with imprisonment from five to ten years.

Whoever serves as principal, manager or officer of any Communist organization shall be punished with imprisonment from ten to fifteen years.

SEC. 7. Any Thai national who commits any of the offences punishable under Section 4 or 5 abroad or is a member of any Communist organization established abroad shall be punished with the same penalty therein provided.

SEC. 8. Whoever attends any Communist meeting shall be presumed to be a member of the Communist organization calling the meeting unless he can prove that he did so in ignorance of its nature and object.

SEC. 9. Whoever assists any Communist organization or member of a Communist organization in any of the following manners:

(1) By providing lodging or place of meeting;
(2) By inducing any person to become member or sympathizer;
(3) By giving financial or other assistance;
shall be punished with imprisonment from five to ten years.

SEC. 10. Whenever an offence is committed by a member of a Communist organization in prosecution of the object of the organization the person serving as principal, manager or officer of the organization and any member thereof who is present at the commission of the offence or at the meeting where the commission of the offence was decided upon shall be punished with the penalty prescribed for such offence.

SEC. 11. Whoever, by the use of violence or threat of violence to person, property or reputation or by false imprisonment or threat of false imprisonment or by any other act of intimidation compels another person to carry out the order of a Communist organization or to do any other thing in prosecution of the object of such organization shall be punished with imprisonment from five to ten years.

In June 1968 Thailand promulgated its eighth constitution since the 1932 revolution which replaced the absolute monarchy with a bureaucratic regime. The Thai propensity for changing constitutions (the average life span of a constitution is less than five years) has been referred to as "faction constitutionalism,"[4] whereby each successive draft reflects, legitimizes, and strengthens major shifts in factional dominance. Thai constitutions have not been considered the fundamental law of the land: Rather, they have functioned to facilitate the rule of the regime in power.

Thailand's postrevolution history reflects the direct relationship between power configurations and the content of the successive constitutions. The promoters of the 1932 revolution, for example, drafted Thailand's first constitution in order to enhance their own power and to curtail severely the power of the king and other royalty. The highly trained and educated promonarchist elements did not support the new regime, so in order to regain their support the king was accorded symbolic functions in the second constitution. The promoters assured their own continued dominance of the government by appointing one-half of the legislative body.

Successive constitutions followed the pattern set forth by the 1932 promoters. Regimes whose power emanated from the electorate or from the parliament emphasized the legislative structure in order to ensure their continued rule. Military regimes generally promulgated constitutions which vested power in the executive branch and which called for half-appointed, half-elected parliaments.

Work on Thailand's eighth constitution was begun in 1961. In March 1961 Prime Minister Sarit Thanarat addressed his hand-picked Constitutent Assembly. The speech, excerpts from which are presented below, reflects his rationale for Thailand's faction constitutionalism.

Sarit Thanarat: Speech on the Occasion of the Opening of the Constituent Assembly [March 30, 1961]*

. . . Thailand became a constitutional regime when the Revolutionary Group seized power on June 24, 1932, and declared a temporary constitution on June 27. During the past 29 years, the constitutional regime has had many problems. The constitution which was promulgated on December 10, 1932, and which was expected to be a permanent one, was cancelled after a very short period of time. During the constitutional period, constitutions have frequently been drafted, changed and then

[4] David A. Wilson, *Politics in Thailand,* p. 262.
* *Source: Collected Speeches of Sarit Thanarat* (Bangkok: Government Printing House, 1961).

discarded. Discarded constitutions became the model for new constitutions and in some instances formerly discarded constitutions were accepted as the new constitution. It has been this way for nearly 29 years.

What has been the cause for our unstable constitutional period? It has been argued that the lack of stability stems from the low level of education in Thailand. Some people say it is because we change our regimes too hastily. We don't know or understand enough about freedom. Therefore, we tend to use freedom beyond its limits. Some people say the citizens choose the wrong leaders. Some people say it is the fault of this person or that person. I myself do not blame anyone. However, it is necessary to accept the fact that we formed a constitutional regime without having had the time to lay the basic foundation. We have not been able to do this as other countries have done. The foundations have not yet been made firm. This is why the constitutional period has not been stable.

What is the basis for a constitutional regime? Certainly the education of the citizens is the most important base. In addition to the education base is the need for an economic plan. Whoever forms the regime without an economic plan will form an unstable regime. The constitutional regime of France formed after the great revolution in 1789 was unstable for 30 years, just as in our country, because the framers of the regime emphasized the political more than the economic. We have encountered the very same situation in Thailand. The leaders of the revolution in 1932 had not settled on a coherent economic plan. After they had already seized power, they began to consider in which direction the economic policy would go. A period of disagreement ensued because each person had his own policy. Closest friends became strong enemies and hence Thailand has not had an economic plan for 28 years. Not having had an economic plan for a long time, and working on a day-by-day basis, troubles were bound to arise often. The governments during the constitutional period were heavily criticized for their economic problems. Whoever wished to have political power presented himself as an expert on economic problems. Each time a revolution occurred, the revolutionary leader generally rationalized his part in the revolution by stating his desire to solve the economic problems.

The people who wanted to bring subversive doctrines into Thailand also used the excuse that they were solving economic problems. I suppose that each of you remembers that before the revolution of October 20, 1958, there was so much chaos that we can say that there was no discipline at all in the nation, and it was an open opportunity for dishonest persons to take advantage of the nation. If there had not been a revolution at this time and if the country had not been run strictly with martial law, the country would have encountered even greater dangers.

In order to improve the situation and in order to be rid of harmful influences on the country, I decided to carry out a revolution on October 20, 1958. By using martial law, it has been possible to bring peace to the nation. The orders of the revolutionary leader have been the law. The leader of the revolution has had absolute power. I have held revolutionary power myself for 99 days from October 20 to January 27 before I declared the constitution of January 28, 1959.

Those who have not held absolute power might desire to do so, while those who have held it as I have during those 99 days know that it is not a pleasant task at all. I believe in a constitutional regime. I regard that having a constitution as the principle of control in a country is like having a roof over the heads of the family. Without a constitution the person who has absolute power must be responsible for every mistake made. I alone held this responsibility for 99 days in order to rid the nation of its problems, but there were still many more problems which should have been solved. I wanted to have a protective roof for myself. I, therefore, requested permission from the King to establish a Constituent Assembly in order to draft a constitution and set up a legislative branch and a cabinet. Since that time the burdens I felt from having sole responsibility have been lifted. I thank heaven for having helped me make no mistakes during those 99 days.

. . . The goal of the revolutionary government since its beginning has been to strengthen the foundations for a constitutional regime through educational and economic development plans. For this reason I have established the National Economic Development Board and a National Education Council. In this way I believe that the defects we have had before will be lessened. Education will progress and we won't have to argue about economic policy which has caused delay and disharmony in the past.

I am pleased that the Assembly will begin their work. I believe in the ability of the Chairman, the Vice Chairman and all the Members to draft the best and most appropriate constitution for Thailand. In my position as the leader of the revolutionary government I will have nothing to do with the consideration of the Constitution. You are not to consider yourselves bound to favor the government's line of thought or action, and you are not to be deterred from acting independently by the fear of incurring the displeasure of the revolutionary party or myself. To help you act in a thorough and broad-minded way a Public Opinion Appraisal Committee will present to you a faithful assessment of the attitudes of various segments of the population which will be tantamount to actual public participation.

You will probably be working in two stages, that is to say you will first study the constitutions of 80 countries . . . to acquire an expert knowledge of the constitutions. You will then come to the second phase, that of working out through the process of assimilation and comparison or even pure invention, whatever is suited to the conditions of Thailand and the mentality of the Thai People.

Enquiry into foreign practices will only provide points of reference and will not inordinately influence our thinking. All theories must be put to the test from time to time and in some cases they are found faulty. Even a popular concept such as democracy is differently defined. Even in modern times electoral procedures and suffrage vary from country to country. Surprisingly enough, women are still denied suffrage in some countries regarded as paragons of democracy. This clearly testifies to the relativity of principles and theories. The point I wish to make is that we do not feel diffident about inventing something outright for our own use so long as we are certain it is suitable for our country.

The system of checks and balances puts a curb on any wanton or arbitrary exercise of power. This is the essence of the constitutional regime. In themselves these checks and balances are good but they must be fairly and honestly used. There must be effective safeguards against using the constitution to clog the progress of the nation, destroy others or advance personal prestige or interest. Power must entail responsibility. This is the view that I vigorously maintain. The last thing I would like to mention is that while the Constituent Assembly is working on the constitution, the government and myself will proceed with the work of strengthening the foundations of our constitutional regime, that is to say, we shall go ahead with our work of education and economic development. I wish to say that enough progress has materialized to warrant the belief that the good work will not be undone by the National Assembly convened by virtue of the new assembly.

Prime Minister Sarit Thanarat died in December 1963, two months after delivering the following address on the fifth anniversary of the 1958 revolution. Sarit had claimed to place economic advancement at the forefront of his program for Thailand. His vigorous personality plus his absolute power enabled him to cut through bureaucratic red tape and push forward development programs that former premiers had either ignored or were unable to get enacted. However, following his death it was revealed that through misuse of public funds and by participation on corporation boards, the prime minister had amassed a personal fortune of more than $150 million. Thus, Sarit's admitted accomplishments were tarnished by his own personal corruption.

Sarit Thanarat: On the Fifth Anniversary of the Revolution
[October 20, 1963]*

Today marks the fifth anniversary of the Revolution. . . .

All fellow countrymen will recall the gravity of the crisis facing the nation before the Revolution. We were in very serious financial straits. The Communists had infiltrated and gained a foothold in a great many circles for the ultimate purpose of subverting all our sacred institutions, that is the nation, the religion and monarchy. Furthermore, a number of the people's representatives had openly sold their souls to the Communists. Under these circumstances several patriots agreed among themselves that had such a state of affairs been allowed to go on, national catastrophe would have been inevitable. That was why I staged the Revolution, the purpose of which was to obtain the Revolutionary power in accordance with the principles of political science and jurisprudence in order to root out all these evils and put the country on the path of progress and development.

No sooner had the Revolution been launched than we made a clean sweep of all the ills besetting the nation. Among the measures taken should be cited abolition of the political parties which were the main cause of the prevailing turmoil, drastic suppression of the Communists, all forms of corruption, hooliganism, opium-smoking and prostitution. Meanwhile the Government was speeding up efforts to remedy the financial position of the country through both immediate and long-range measures such as economic and educational development in accordance with the three-year and six-year plans. . . . Within five years since the Revolution and at the completion of the first phase of the National Development Plan so much progress in economic development has been achieved that Thailand can lay claim to being one of the most stable countries in South-East Asia. Credit can also be claimed for an unprecedentedly high rate of development. Thus within five years the Gross National Product has increased by as much as 50 percent. At the same time the living condition of the people has reached a high degree of stability. There is no inflation which is a problem confronting so many countries in the throes of national development today. Furthermore, our currency and foreign exchange reserves have increased to such an extent that we are universally recognized as a financially stable country.

As a highly satisfactory degree of financial stability has been attained, the Government deems fit to announce the par value of the baht . . .

* *Source: Address by Prime Minister Sarit Thanarat on the Fifth Anniversary of the Revolution, October 20, A.D. 1963* (Bangkok: Government Printing House, 1963).

[as] another important step in national economic development. . . . The announcement of the par value will have an immense stabilizing effect on national economic development for it will dispel doubt and uncertainty arising from exchange rate fluctuations. This amounts to laying the foundations of our trade and business transactions with other countries besides giving impetus to investments in local industrial enterprises.

An extensive exploitation of all national resources aimed at increasing the welfare of the people combined with an efficient financial management as set forth above has greatly contributed to the Government's much more favourable financial position.

. . . National income which can reliably be used to assess the economic position of a country [has increased] from 41 billion baht in 1959 to 53 billion baht [in 1962]. [In] the current year 1963, although the figures are not yet available, a fairly close estimate may be made that it will reach a new height of about 55 billion baht. This substantial increase in national income amply reflects the economic position of the country and has made it possible for the Government to expand its budget of expenditure.

As you know, when it came into power the Revolutionary Government established the National Economic Development Board entrusted with economic development planning and supervision and control of governmental economic and financial operations. Last October . . . the Government thought fit to set up the Ministry of National Development for the purpose of centralizing all activities at the national level which are basic to long-range development. This will serve several useful purposes such as greater economy, speedier and more efficient implementation [of economic plans]. . . .

As regards the development of agriculture in which nearly 85 percent of the population is engaged, besides stepping up measures of promotion and assistance . . . the Government has launched an experiment on two-crop paddy farming in some well-irrigated areas with highly encouraging results. This two-crop farming considerably raises the farmer's per rai production which means higher income. . . . [In] areas irresponsive to two-crop farming the Ministry of Agriculture has for the last four years been carrying out a crop rotation project. To date the area brought under the project totals 17,197 rai in 27 provinces and the farmers participating in the project number 6,854. This helps raise each farmer's per rai income to about 700 baht per year. The project is steadily gaining popularity with farmers throughout the country.

One of the factors of prime importance in agriculture is control of water supply. In this connection the Government has . . . expended a considerable amount of money on the construction of irrigation dams.

Apart from the Bhumibol Dam and those at Kang Krajan, Pong River, Lam Plaploeng, and the Chaophya Dam which belong to the earlier period of the Revolutionary Government, the current year . . . will see the beginning of construction work on the dams at Lam Pao and Mae Tang. When completed the two dams together will make available 250,000 rai of irrigated land which will increase the income of a great many farmers of Kalasin and Chiengmai.

[In] education, which is after all a form of development of national manpower, the Government has considerably extended activities in several directions. . . . We are in need of a great deal of skilled labour for national development. To increase the supply of skilled workmen, the Government has taken . . . over the Building Profession Promotion School and raised its status to that of a college of building construction, established seven technical colleges numbering 3,233 students and introduced a new course of agricultural technique in the Northeastern technical college at Nakorn Rajisima. Furthermore, a Thai-German technical college will shortly be set up at Khonkaen with the co-operation of the Federal Republic of Germany. Another technical college is also being contemplated in the North at Tak.

Regarding higher technical schools, great progress has been made. We now have four schools of industrial arts and seven business schools numbering 11,275 students. . . . At present almost all provinces are provided with at least one [trade] school. . . . The six-year project of transforming trade schools into schools of the type conceived and supported by SEATO . . . started in 1968 at the schools of Cha-choeng-sao and Puket. In the current year two more schools at Maha Sarakam and Sakol Nakorn have been brought under the project. It is further planned to offer such courses at the trade schools of Ayudhya and Trang next year. Mention should be made that this training in skilled labour has been given substantial support and assistance by SEATO which is responsible for the establishment of 19 provincial centres of skilled labour training . . . with capacity for 3,700 trainees. . . .

As regards to other aspects of educational development, I should call your attention to teachers training. In the current year students of all teachers training colleges total 3,573 while those working for the certificate and higher certificate of education number 11,734 and 3,342 respectively. . . . This year 121 upper primary schools have been opened bringing the total to 1,610. . . . Extension of compulsory education has been enforced in 394 districts covering 414 schools or 34,760 school children.

. . . 19 [secondary] schools have been opened in the current year bringing the total to 428 with 156,956 students.

As for university education, besides making appropriate adjustments to raise the quality of teaching and research at the five existing universities which number 40,952 students, the Government is pushing on with the construction of Chiengmai University in accordance with the project of spreading higher education to the provinces and stemming the flow of provincial students to the capital. The new university is expected to be completed early next year. As for the projected University of Khonkaen we have reason to expect that it will be ready to take in students at the beginning of 1965.

. . . I would stress that public health is of vital importance in building up the manpower of the nation and guarding against disease and ailments. . . . The Government has devoted a great deal of time, energy and funds to the suppression and prevention of diseases such as liver fluke, leprosy, tuberculosis, cholera and malaria. [It] has just made a resolution to start a new four-year campaign involving 480 million baht against [malaria]. In this connection . . . the number of general hospitals we have exceeds that of the provinces, that is to say, we have altogether 83 provincial hospitals with 7,523 hospital beds. . . .

I cannot help saying with great pride that thanks to the unity and solidarity of Thai nationals and the Government's capability of maintaining law and order, Thailand has won foreigners' praise for being at present the only intrinsically peaceful and happy country in the world. Given such peace and happiness we have been able to devote ourselves with might and main to national development. This is a highly propitious situation unparalleled in other countries. Fellow Thai nationals should therefore be very proud of their country and take advantage of the situation to set their hearts on the task of developing the country.

The last thing I wish to speak about in this report is the progress of the work of national defence. Within the current year I am proud to say that the Government . . . has been able to maintain the present military strength. For economy's sake, no material extension has been made, but a number of adjustments have been effected as regards training and study in such a way that the Thai army has become a highly efficient machinery of defence which is ready at all times to defend the national sovereignty. The strength and efficiency of the national army is of vital importance to the nation both in peace and war time. In peace time a strong army is a great factor in maintaining law and order. It is well known that without political stability a country can hardly keep things in order and devote itself fully to national development. On the other hand when a country is at war the national army is incontestably the most important bastion for the defence of independence and sovereignty.

Fellow Thai nationals, before concluding this rather lengthy report, I wish to reiterate that the most ardent wish of this Government is to achieve for the country maximum stability and advancement. Fellow Thai nationals will surely recall that before we settled down in the Golden Peninsula, the land of our forefathers had been subjected to innumerable incursions and raids. Whenever the Thai people weakened, they were invaded and sometimes even reduced to complete disintegration. Our forbears gave us a lesson of the utmost significance for which they themselves had paid with their blood and even their lives. Thus all Thai nationals with the same blood of their spirited ancestors running in their veins cannot afford to let such calamitous events repeat themselves. Whatever lesson our forefathers learnt with blood and tears must serve as a constant warning to us all. We must always stand united and act in concert to preserve the national independence and sovereignty. Further, we must go full steam ahead with our work of national development. Please do not forget that only a developed nation can provide its people with welfare and happiness and that a country which lags behind in economic advancement is easily exposed to the danger of Communism. I, therefore, implore all Thai patriots to give maximum cooperation to the Government in developing the country by applying yourselves earnestly and with all your might to whatever trades and occupations you are engaged in. Let us vie with one another in doing good to leave footprints in the sand of time and to set examples to the generations to come. As for myself I beg to make a solemn pledge that I will never desert the motherland or fellow Thai nationals. As long as I live, you may rest assured that I am ready to throw in my lot with you, come what may.

Finally, with a heart full of affection and goodwill towards you all, I invoke the Triple Gem and all the sacred things in the universe to shower blessings on all of you so that you may be blessed with long life, happiness, good health, and wealth. Whatever trade or calling you pursue, may you meet with success and prosperity which will assuredly redound to the advancement of the nation as a whole.

Since the 1932 revolution, there has been no regularized or institutionalized means of succession to power in Thailand. The orderly assumption of power by Field Marshal Thanom Kittikachorn following Sarit's death was the first completely peaceful succession in the constitutional era. Sarit's drive for internal security had weakened potential opposition groups. Thanom, as Sarit's designated successor, was able to draw on an established apparatus for controlling the government. In addition, Thanom's experience as prime minister following Sarit's first coup d'état in 1957 was excellent training for his second term. Despite these advantages, most observers saw him as an interim leader with little chance to retain power. First, Thanom's personality was in marked contrast to the aggressive Sarit's. Second, ambitious military generals, most notably General Prapat Charusathien, concurrently deputy prime minister, minister of interior, and commander in chief of the Royal Thai Army, were expected to contend for power. Thanom, however, was able to assimilate potential rivals for power, to use the enormous prestige of the monarchy to strengthen his regime, and to put forward a vigorous program of economic development and national defense.

Thanom's lengthy declaration on "The Administration of the Present Thai Government" is a compilation of published materials pertaining to the constitution, the administrative policy of the government, governmental organization, and problems besetting the administration.

Thanom Kittikachorn: The Administration of the Present Thai Government [March 25, 1967]*

"The Administration of the Present Thai Government" I present here is based upon facts, for the purpose of enabling the reader to have a proper understanding of the government, since mutual understanding is an essential factor which will lead to unity and cooperation in building up the prosperity of the nation."

FIELD MARSHAL THANOM KITTIKACHORN
March 25, 1967

Those who have followed developments in the drafting of the constitution . . . may know the essential points of the new constitution, which has been changed from previous constitutions so that it will better suit national government. For instance, no vote of non-confidence can be passed when the government states its policies to parliament for the first time; members of the House of Representatives cannot concurrently serve as Cabinet members; and a procedure is prescribed to make it more difficult to open debate to advocate a vote of non-confidence against the Cabinet. Generally speaking, these changes have been effected to cut down, to some extent, the power of the legislature, which was disproportionate in the past.

If the reader has examined the comments of individuals and critical articles in newspapers, he will find that these critics want parliament to have much more power than the executive branch, and for people's repre-

* *Source:* Department of Information, Ministry of Foreign Affairs (Bangkok), March 25, 1967.

sentatives to be able to serve concurrently as Cabinet members. They want parliament to be able to overthrow the government easily. Since these principles were used in all of the previous Thai constitutions, and since they caused countless difficulties in political quarters and to the Thai administration, you can decide for yourselves whether it is advisable for us to admit that those principles are not suitable for our country; whether it is advisable for us to replace them with new principles, particularly the principle of cutting down the legislative branch's power in order to maintain a balance with that of the executive branch for the purpose of creating stability in our country. . . . Should we adopt the old principles to comply with those who advocate them, we would not have to do anything new; we could just use the 1949 constitution or any of the others. That would be easy and convenient. Therefore, it can be said that those critics are accustomed to the principles of the British constitution or of the old Thai constitutions, believing that democracy can be achieved if those principles alone are followed. I should like to ask you to recall how chaotic the administration in Thailand was before the revolution of 1958, and you will see for yourselves whether we should again follow the principles of the old constitutions.

Regarding the time taken to draft the constitution, I am aware that many critics say the government intentionally delayed the task so that it could remain in power for a long time. I ask all fair-minded persons to search their memories before making such accusations against the government. Actually, it was three years after the revolution, in 1961, that drafting of the constitution began in earnest, and the people then manifested no reaction. I think the reason the people were not interested in calling for the drafting during that time was possibly because they still remembered how confused politics was during the pre-revolutionary period, and the extensive Communist infiltration and subversion. When the revolution broke out and the constitution was abrogated, the people felt relief, and as they saw a peaceful situation evolve under the administration of the Revolutionary Party, they did not call for the drafting of a constitution. Since the time that I was given a Royal order to form a government on December 9, 1963, I have expedited the drafting of the constitution. Part of the reason for the delay is that the Constituent Assembly has to alternately perform the functions of a legislative body as well. The Assembly can therefore hold only two meetings a month to perform its function as a constituent body. Apart from that, those in the Assembly favoring the principles of old constitutions tried to propose amendments in order to restore those abolished principles and replace them in the constitution. This thus accounted for many reviews and revisions of the resolutions.

The government set forth its policies to the Constituent Assembly on December 19, 1963, and persons interested in the details may study them in official documents such as the Government Gazette. In this article I wish to mention for the reader's understanding, the principles of only four policies which are being implemented by the government. They are:

(1) *National Economic Development Policy.* The government, with a desire to raise the living standard of the people in general, formulated the first economic development plan in 1961. It was divided into two phases—the 1961–1963 and 1964–1966 phases. At present, the National Economic Development Board is in the process of drafting the second economic development plan, for the period 1967–1971, which will cost approximately 56 billion baht.

A survey and assessment of the results of the first phase, 1961–1963 . . . show that the 12 billion baht expended by the government for development may be broken down as follows: 13.3 per cent for agriculture and cooperatives; 11.3 per cent for industries and mining; 20.5 per cent for special projects. The gross national product increased over 10 billion baht in 1963 with per capita income amounting to 2,150 baht. For the most part, development under the first phase came close to the targets.

Work under the 1964–1966 phase came to an end recently, and authorities are now accumulating statistics and figures for evaluation purposes. The National Economic Development Board will report the outcome to the public in the near future. At any rate, if annual budgets are examined, it will be found that in 1964, the government appropriated almost three billion baht or 24.84 per cent of the budget for economic development; in 1965, 3.4 billion baht or 27.7 per cent of the budget; and in 1966, 4.3 billion baht or 28.91 per cent. In 1967, total development expenditure is 5.3 billion baht, the equivalent of 28.97 per cent of the budget total of 18.4 billion baht.

(2) *Social Development Policy.* The government has adopted a social development policy parallel with the economic development plan, and according to the evaluation of the first phase of social and economic development, 22.6 per cent of total expenditure of 12.3 billion baht spent on the plan was used for social development, the majority of which went for the development of education, public health and public utilities.

As for total expenditures for social development in the second phase of the plan, the 1964 annual budget shows that the government spent 1.9 billion baht or 17.30 per cent on education, and 1.6 billion baht, or 14.50 per cent of the budget for public health and public utilities. In 1965, the government expended 2.1 billion, or 17.46 per cent, for education, and

1.8 billion baht, or 14.87 per cent, for public health and public utilities. In 1966, the appropriation for education amounted to 2.4 billion baht, or 16.14 per cent, while the appropriation for public health and public utilities rose to 2.3 billion baht, or 15.31 per cent. In 1967, the appropriation for education totals 2.8 billion baht, or 15.51 per cent, and the appropriation for public health and public utilities is 2.6 billion baht, or 14.05 per cent, of the total expenditure of 18.4 billion baht.

From the above consideration of economic and social development policy, it is evident that the government has laid down definite development plans and objectives and is carrying on national development, as the budget annually permits, in order to attain as many of the objectives as possible. For that reason, newspaper comments asserting that the present government had no aims in national development are not consistent with the facts. As a matter of fact, the government has clearly stated the targets of development, and pertinent documents may be obtained from the National Economic Development Board for examination any time. Additionally, the reader will see from the above figures on appropriations that they are divided proportionately between economic and social development.

Critics have said further that if the government has any aim at all in its economic development plan, that aim is to enable people to "earn" more money; therefore, it would make them become selfish and result in numerous national shortcomings. These comments are not in any way fair to the government. If the reader examines the totals of appropriations I have cited above, he will realize that the government, parallel to economic development, has endeavored to develop education and public health as well as public utilities, so that the nation's youth will have better education and so that the people in general will have perfect health. I regard as unreasonable the criticism that, since economic development is aimed basically at encouraging people to earn money, people have become greedy. . . . Since we today use money as the medium of exchange, it is only natural that everyone has to seek income in the form of money for use in the time of need. That there are some greedy or dishonest men in society is a natural thing, for there are both good and bad men in every country. The government itself has tried to suppress bad men but I still believe that Thailand has more good men than bad ones. That is why we can still live peacefully.

(3) *Policy for Maintenance of Internal Peace.* The government is well aware that internal peace and order is essential to the stability and security of the nation. Without internal peace, the people could hardly be happy, and the pursuance of the above economic and social development

tasks would not be possible. The maintenance of internal peace and order embraces the work of three important branches, namely, the police, the judiciary and the Department of Corrections, for which the government has increased expenditures each year. The expenditures for the three branches are as follows: 850.3 million baht, or 7.44 per cent, in 1964; 929.2 million baht, or 7.48 per cent in 1965; and 1.0 billion baht, or 7.26 per cent, in 1966. In 1967, the appropriation for them is 1.2 billion baht, or 6.47 per cent.

The largest allotment for the task of maintaining internal peace goes to the police, for whom 936.6 million baht is appropriated in 1967. Next, the Department of Corrections receives 146.8 million baht, while the judiciary gets 113.3 million baht. The allocation to the police has been gradually increased because the population of the country has grown, communications are better, and it is necessary to expand the suppression of crimes and banditry. Over the past two years, as the reader may be aware, Communist infiltration has increased in the northeastern and southern regions, necessitating an increase of suppression authorities sufficient to maintain peace and order so that the people may carry on their normal livelihood.

(4) *National Defense Policy.* The defense of national independence and sovereignty constitutes a most vital policy of the government, which must always be in a state of preparedness since the Communist threat has spread and moved closer to Thailand, as evidenced by the fighting which has been going on for many years in neighboring countries. In any event, military appropriations have not been as immense as presumed by some people. In 1964, expenditures for national defense amounted to 1.8 billion baht, or 15.61 per cent; in 1965, 1.9 billion baht, or 15.46 per cent; and in 1966, 2.1 billion baht, or 15 per cent. In 1967, 2.6 billion baht, or 14.17 per cent, of the budget has been set aside for the purpose. If the percentages of national defense appropriations are examined, it will be seen that they have decreased each year, whereas appropriations for economic and social development, as well as other appropriations, have gradually increased. I think our allocations to the military are much lower than those of other countries which are fighting internal wars against the Communists. . . .

That Thailand does not have to increase its national defense expenditures to any great extent, or that the percentage of allocations has slightly declined, is because we are aware that Thailand is a small country. And that is why our policy is to cooperate with neighboring countries such as by joining the Southeast Asia Treaty Organization when it was created. The government has agreed to accept military aid, weapons and military equipment from the United States without concealing it from the people or from other countries, so as to illustrate that we are sincere and a loyal friend; it can be said that we have had the sympathies of the United States throughout. Therefore, in the event of aggression against Thailand, we are confident that all the Allied nations would fully support our fight to protect our independence and sovereignty.

. . . The legislative branch [of the Thai government] is a body charged with the duty of enacting the laws needed for national government and administration. As a rule, parliament forms the most important part of the legislative branch and there may be a single house or two houses depending on the provision of the constitution. To insure the efficient performance of the different sorts of work of parliament there must be a secretariat which runs the parliament's administrative affairs, such as preparing agenda and documents concerning meetings and other administrative work. The secretariat is the responsibility of the Secretary General of the House of Representatives, who answers directly to the Speaker of the House.

The judiciary is made up of the courts whose duties are to settle disputes between parties. In some countries, the work of the court is totally separated from the executive branch in order to permit the judges full freedom in their trial of cases. In some countries, the people are allowed to elect as judges men with legal qualifications. In Thailand, since we adopted a system of trial similar to those abroad at the time when there were not many law graduates, and since the government has had to bear all of the expenses, the courts of justice are still very much connected with the executive branch. That is, all of the judges are still officials of various categories, attached to the Ministry of Justice. Afterwards, the government, being aware of the importance of freedom in the trial of cases by the courts, so as to insure justice to the parties in legal cases, established a Judicial Commission whose duty it is to propose the appointment, removal and transfer of judges as well as to consider their promotions. This is considered to be a good guarantee for the judges. Under this system, the duties of the Minister of Justice are confined to the granting of facilities for the trial of cases, such as the construction of courts, acting upon requests for additional salary appropriations, and the supervision of the administrative officials who are attached to every court. Although the executive branch in Thailand is still closely connected with the judicial branch, it can be said that the government has at all times respected the independence of the courts in their trial of cases and in giving judgments.

The executive branch, which is composed of the ministries and departments which receive policies from the government of the legislative branch for implementation, is considerably larger than the legislative and judicial branches.

Coordination is the responsibility of the Cabinet, the top-level body of the executive branch. The Cabinet holds meetings regularly every Tuesday, to make joint studies of policy matters and problems concerning the functions of the many ministries, as well as other problems which, under the provisions of the law, are within the purview of the duties of the Cabinet. At present, many subjects are brought up for the consideration of the Cabinet and each meeting lasts almost the whole day. At the end of the Cabinet meeting, the Spokesman of the Prime Minister's Office releases to the public, through press reporters, information pertaining to those policy matters on which resolutions were adopted by the Cabinet, and those which deserve public attention.

In each ministry a Cabinet Minister and an Under-Secretary are responsible for the coordination of the functions of the various departments within the ministry. Usually, Directors-General of the ministries hold regular meetings. However, since some of the departments in the ministry confine their attention to their own work and do not have many common interests, they perform their functions separately, until it sometimes takes the form of a competition. This has happened frequently with the result that the press or the people criticize them for a lack of coordination. This therefore is a matter which has to be remedied at all levels and every party should be concerned with common interest rather than competing with one another in order to get things that would only benefit their own work.

Certain activities of the executive branch have been extensively commented upon and criticized by the people and the press, and I should make mention of them here. These are concerned with the operation of state enterprises. The reason the Thai Government must make investment in certain state enterprises is that Thailand is a small agricultural country, and the people in general still lack sufficient income and lack the know-how for conducting large-scale enterprises. Under the circumstances, the Thai Government, being in a better position to mobilize qualified persons in different branches than private individuals and being in possession of capital or being in a position to obtain loans conveniently, has engaged in certain activities such as railway services, the establishment of paper mills, the production of electricity, port and telephone services. Some of these activities bring profits amounting to many millions of baht to the government annually, while some others suffer losses either because they are in the initial stages of operation or because their management is not very satisfactory. At any rate, although it is government policy that it will try not to establish new state enterprises, the government finds it necessary to continue to support the existing state enterprises because their work is connected with the comfort and happiness of the public. Some of the state enterprises also have bearing upon national security and safety.

. . . I will [now] speak of obstacles and pressures connected with four subjects which I think are vital to our nation. They are:

(1) *Finances.* At the beginning I said the government has a policy of accelerating social and economic development for the purpose of raising the standard of living of the people, that it has a policy on the maintenance of internal peace and security aimed at enabling the people to live happily and to carry on their normal livelihood, and that it has also a policy to protect national independence and sovereignty to insure its security and safety. The reader may have noted that the government has to expend many billions of baht annually to achieve the said objectives. It is evident from the budget totals that since 1963, the government's total expenditures each year has been in excess of 10 billion baht. In 1967, this total was raised to 18 billion baht.

The government has nonetheless endeavored to seek adequate income for implementing the various projects. The most important income of the government is derived from taxes and duties collected from the people. In 1964, our estimated receipts from taxes and duties totalled 8.8 billion baht. The total estimated receipts for 1967 were 12 billion baht. Secondary earnings are from the sale of goods and services, the state's trade, and other sources. The total income from taxes and duties, as well as from the other three categories, is still lower than the total of planned expenditures. It is therefore necessary for the government to procure loans from internal and external sources.

(2) *Communist Infiltration.* Another worrisome pressure is communist infiltration and subversion. At the present time, communist doctrine has spread to almost all of the countries around Thailand, and this, as is well known, has brought civil war to those countries. Thailand is another country not overlooked by the communists. At present, the communists have begun to send secret agents here to create disturbances and to subvert the security of Thailand in the northeastern and southern regions.

A successful solution to those problems is dependent upon the cooperation of authorities of all branches, particularly administrative and police authorities in provincial areas, who must try to understand the minds of the people, be on the alert, watch strangers who may be agents sent in by the communists to stir up unrest, and find ways of arresting them. In addition, the government itself has stepped up rural development, especially in the border provinces of the northeastern and northern regions.

The government hopes that when the people are able to live happily, and their standard of living is better, they will not be easily deluded by the communists.

(3) *Public Morals.* This is another cause for concern. Foreign culture based on materialism has flowed swiftly into Thailand, being brought into the country directly by tourists or indirectly by mass media, namely, radio, television and most importantly by motion pictures. These changes are rapid and have, in a short time, shockingly damaged the good morals and culture of certain groups of people. Many people have changed their outlook and are more in favor of materialism, i.e., a life of luxury similar to that of foreigners; but at the same time, they do not have earnings adequate to afford materialistic tastes. In these circumstances, shortcut methods for gaining income have come into being. Pretty girls turn to the business of being mistresses, bar hostesses, masseuses or prostitutes. Young men, being unable to find easy shortcut methods of earning, set up gangs to rob and extort honest persons, thereby accounting for frequent crimes. Some government officials who are unable to resist materialistic charms resort to corrupt practices in order to gain income sufficient for a luxurious life. . . .

. . . These are social phenomena experienced by every society which is moving from the old to new culture. However, the transition is too rapid for Thailand, and, as a result, a vacuum is created while the people are not yet accommodated to the new culture and while they have not yet relinquished the old. Consequently, the good morals of many people have appallingly deteriorated, and if the situation worsens, it may produce unfavorable results, as well as contribute to an increase in crimes.

As for a solution to the above problem, the government is not indifferent, but has tried in every way to make the people understand the difference between right and wrong and to persuade them to do what is proper. For this effort to be fruitful, the public must accord earnest cooperation. Most particularly, the parents and guardians of teenagers should attend to the education of their children so as to prevent them from being led astray by materialistic tastes. Elders should set a good example for the youths if education is to be successful. In this case I wish to place reliance upon any reader who has many children.

(4) *The Quality of the Population.* The last obstacle to national development I will mention here is the quality of the population. When I say the quality of the population I mean the state of physical and mental health of the population.

As far as physical health is concerned, our people now know how to maintain their health much better than previously; this can be gauged from the life expectancy of the Thai people which has increased gradually —from the average age of 40, twenty years ago, to the age of over 50 at the present time. But this is not yet satisfactory. In developed countries, life expectancy is between 60–70 years. It is therefore advisable for us to teach the people to further improve their health.

Malnutrition is the reason why the life span of the people is not yet as long as it should be, and why many die when they are still young, or when they could still be of service to the country. Malnutrition may stem from their poverty which prevents them from buying good food, or from their lack of knowledge of the quality of food. Another important cause is the shortage of modern physicians in rural areas. At present doctors and the people in Bangkok and Thonburi are in the approximate ratio of 1:3,000, which is satisfactory. In provincial areas, however, we have only one physician for every 10,000–20,000 people, which is a low ratio and which also has effects upon life expectancy.

As a matter of fact, the government has been aware of this problem for the past ten years, and it has therefore increased by millions of baht yearly the budget for increasing the output of doctors. The training of doctors is more difficult than the training of other graduates, for the reason that there must be sufficient laboratories and cadavers to be used by the medical students in their studies. I know that the University of Medical Science has been confronted with this serious problem because people in general do not consent to donating the bodies of their deceased parents or relations to the hospitals. The majority of dead bodies received by the medical schools usually are those of persons who have no relatives. This has resulted in limiting the number of physicians. Besides, there is a problem connected with medical graduates: most physicians do not like to stay in the provinces. The Health Department and the Medical Department have dozens of vacant provincial posts to be filled by doctors each year, but nobody applies for the jobs. The problem is aggravated by the large number of doctors going abroad for medical practice each year. The government will give them support if they go abroad for only two or three years and then return to give their service to the country. However, many doctors have gone to foreign countries to work for 5–10 years. Some of them have even moved their families abroad. This is a problem of great importance and for that reason, the government has formed a committee to find remedial measures, otherwise the adverse effects on the community will grow.

In the matter of the intellectual quality of the population, the government has endeavored to raise the level of education of the people. After the change in the form of government to the democratic system in 1932, the literate numbered only 30% of the population above the age of eight. Now, 70% of our population is literate but most of them are those who have only completed Pathom IV [elementary education] and who cannot yet serve the society and the nation to an appropriate extent. At the moment, the government is trying to raise the standard of education of the population in order that they will in the near future complete at least Pathom VII. Further efforts will be exerted in the next step to have them complete Mathayom VI [final grade of secondary education] at the minimum; this will be considered a satisfactory education level.

[The ability of the government to overcome these obstacles depends on] funds needed for national development. I have said we must spend a larger amount of money each year, but we are able to gain an increasing amount of taxes and duties. We have obtained loans only if they are really necessary, and it is within the nation's economic capability to repay them. I think the government will continue to be able to seek adequate money for both short- and long-range projects, since we hope that various constructive investments we have made will yield fruit in increasing amounts every year. The construction of Bhumibol Dam, for example, has made agriculture in areas north and south of the dam more productive and helped to place on sale in the northern provinces a larger quantity of fresh-water fish than in the past. One clearly visible thing is that we in Bangkok, Thonburi and other provinces, where electric lines traverse, are using electricity from Bhumibol Dam. We no longer complain about a shortage of electricity but we, on the contrary, are encouraging people and industrial plants to use more electricity. We have also cut down electric power rates. This is a good example of investment made by the government, which is bringing comfort to the people and enhances the economic progress of the nation. Other dams such as Ubolrat Dam in the Northeast and Kaeng Krachan Dam, in Phetburi, have produced the same good results. Furthermore, when Thapla Dam in Uttaradit and Pattani Dam in the South are completed, people living in the neighboring localities will derive great benefits from them.

Roads and other communication routes on which the government has invested its construction funds, as well as certain roads built with the aid of friendly nations, are bringing economic prosperity to the people and the nation in many respects. For instance, they enable farmers to take their crops for sale at markets more conveniently, extend tourist routes, help to develop rural industries and contribute to moving population to sparsely populated areas. Those are merely an outline of the benefits which the nation is receiving from the construction and maintenance of communication routes which will eventually increase the government's income that can then be expended for other development projects in the future.

I venture to say that as far as seeking funds for national development is concerned, the government is confident that it will be able to raise sufficient income to cope with expenditures, and that in future, loans, as supplementary financing for essential projects, might decrease. Now that I have brought up the subject of loans again, I wish to let all know that the government's credit is excellent. It is able to sell out every issue of government bonds to raise internal loans within a short time, and even foreign countries are always willing to supply loans to Thailand. That our credit is good is because Thailand enjoys both economic and political stability.

As regards the maintenance of internal peace and order, and particularly the prevention of communist infiltration and subversion, I remain confident that the situation will improve with the cooperation of authorities of every branch. I have learned that not long ago the Minister of Interior issued an order for the amendment of the regulations on investigation and interrogation in criminal cases in order to empower Provincial Governors to summon case files for their examination and to expedite criminal interrogation. He further instructed police and administration authorities to cooperate closely with each other. That has rendered the suppression of banditry much more effective.

As for communist infiltration, the government, in addition to ordering authorities of various units to exercise greater vigilance, has carried out its suppression in earnest by establishing a Communist Suppression Headquarters. Apart from that, the government hopes that the policy of accelerated rural development, under which the government has dispatched officials to work actively in various districts, will contribute substantially to mitigating unfavorable situations. When government officials are present near the people, the latter will feel secure and infiltration and agitation by the adversary can only be conducted with great difficulty.

In the matter of public morals, and the quality of public health and education, the government is remedying these problems by increasing schools and teachers as well as by expanding institutions of higher learning to make it possible for them to accommodate a larger number of students each year. The matter of the conduct of youth, however, depends upon the parents and guardians of the youths, who must give full cooperation if success is to be achieved.

Thailand's eighth constitution was promulgated in 1968 amidst splendid ceremonial pomp at the governmental level, but distinct apathy among the overwhelming majority of Thai. The new charter, which assured executive dominance of the legislature, took the government-appointed Constituent Assembly over seven years to draft. The instability of previous regimes, the need for a centralized government to promote development, and the threat from indigenous and external Communism were the reasons set forth by the government to explain the delay in the drafting of the constitution.

At the same time the Thai government, entering its eleventh year of martial-law rule, was eager to legitimize and "democratize" its rule in the minds of the citizenry and in the minds of Western allies. The tenuous Viet-Nam situation and a growing insurgency within Thailand itself made both the Thai and American governments aware of the need for a consensual base. For Thai intellectuals and many bureaucrats, martial law was considered both anachronistic and a distinct embarrassment. But the most important factor assuring promulgation of the constitution was that the regime in power became convinced that the form of the constitution ensured its continued rule. (As noted earlier, however, this constitution was abrogated by the coup d'état of November 17, 1971.)

Following the promulgation of the constitution, the king, on the recommendation of Prime Minister Thanom, appointed 120 members of the Senate. The Senate, which would eventually number 164 members, held the powers and duties of both houses of the bicameral National Assembly during the interim between the enforcement of the constitution and the elections for the lower house. Before election day on February 10, 1969, the Senate was given the responsibility to draft an Electoral Law and a Political Parties Act and to revoke those martial-law provisions which precluded the holding of free elections.

Prime Minister Thanom presented to the Senate the government's proposal for the Electoral Law. In an unexpected display of independence, the Senate ignored the government's position on two of the three most important principles. Whereas the government had requested that all candidates be graduated from secondary school, the Senate fixed the minimum educational qualification at four years of primary school. The government's proposal that party membership be required of all candidates was disregarded by the Senate and replaced by the provision that candidates could seek election independently without membership in a party. The Senate did accede to the government's request that each province be made an electoral constituency and that the number of representatives from each province be based on the population within the constituency. The alternative proposal, only narrowly defeated by the Senate, had called for single-member district constituencies.

The Senate's refusal to accept these two recommendations by the government proved to be a mixed blessing for Prime Minister Thanom's party. The subsequent proliferation and success of independent candidates cut considerably into the strength of the government party. Of the 1,252 candidates, 587 ran without party affiliation. On the other hand, charges by the opposition that the constitution was not democratic were greatly weakened when the Senate reversed the government's proposals. Government party candidates invariably alluded to the Senate action when confronted with accusations that the government party dictated election procedures.

The Electoral Law placed the minister of interior, General Prapat, in charge of administering the election. To avoid charges of favoritism, the general temporarily resigned his position as deputy leader of the progovernment United Thai People's party. Governors, district officers, the police, and other officials were made responsible for the details of election administration throughout the country. District officers, of which there were about 500, appointed election committees for each of the 17,000 voting precincts in the country. The election involved some 250,000 workers and cost 102 million baht.

Act on Election of Members of the House of Representatives [November 4, 1968]*

. . . SEC. 5. The Minister of Interior shall have charge and control of the execution of this Act, and shall have the power to issue Ministerial Regulations for carrying out this Act.

SEC. 6. The election shall be held by the method of representation through multi-member constituency.

In a case of a general election, when the Royal Decree for the election of members of the House of Representatives has been promulgated, it shall be notified by the Ministry of Interior in the Government Gazette as to how many members of the House of Representatives there may be in any Changwad, provided that it will be on the basis determined in the Constitution of the Kingdom of Thailand.

SEC. 7. If, in any constituency, the number of candidates does not ex-

* *Source:* Royal Thai Government *Gazette,* November 4, 1968, p. 437.

ceed the number of members of the House of Representatives to be elected in such constituency, it shall be regarded that the candidates are elected without having to cast votes.

SEC. 8. All employers must render reasonable facilities to their employees in order that the latter may exercise their right to vote and to apply for candidacy.

The provision of the first paragraph shall apply to public bodies, state enterprises under the law on budgetary procedure, and government organizations under the law on retirement of employees in the government organizations, *mutatis mutandis.*

SEC. 9. In no case may an elector be bound to state whether he has voted or for whom he has voted.

. . . SEC. 12. On election day, no person shall make any propaganda to the advantage or disadvantage of any candidate within the radius of thirty meters of the polling-place, and no loud-speaker shall be used nor may any other noise causing disturbance or obstacle to the election be allowed, whether inside or outside the said radius. . . .

SEC. 13. On election day, no person shall sell, distribute or give a drink of liquor within the radius of thirty meters from the polling-place.

SEC. 14. No person of non-Thai nationality shall do anything for the benefit of the election to the advantage or disadvantage of any candidate nor shall he, by any means whatever, participate in the election, except that such doing is to render assistance to the official services, or is an ordinary way of earning his living in good faith.

SEC. 15. Apart from the duties specified in this Act, the Governor of [the] Changwad, Nai Amphur, administrative official and police official shall have the duty to furnish facilities and to keep order in the election.

. . . SEC. 18. A candidate must have a standard of education [equivalent to at least] . . . a primary education according to the syllabus of the Ministry of Education, or have knowledge recognized by the Ministry of Education as equivalent thereto.

SEC. 19. A person of Thai nationality, whose father is an alien, who may become a candidate must possess [educational] qualifications [of at least] the third year of secondary education according to the syllabus of the Ministry of Education, or have knowledge recognized by the Ministry of Education as equivalent thereto, and must possess any of the following qualifications:

(1) serve or have served in the [armed forces] according to the law on military service;
(2) be or have been a government official or local government official of the second class upwards or equivalent thereto; or
(3) be or have been a political government official, member of the As-

sembly of the People's Representatives, member of the House of Representatives, member of the Upper House of the National Assembly, senator, member of the Constituent Assembly, member of the Changwad Assembly or member of the Municipal Assembly.

. . . SEC. 20. A person acquiring Thai nationality by naturalization who may become a candidate must possess the qualifications under SEC. 19 and have domicile in the Kingdom successively for a period of not less than ten years from the date of his naturalization.

SEC. 21. A candidate who offers himself for election in a constituency may not apply for candidacy in any other constituency.

SEC. 22. In applying for candidacy as member of the House of Representatives from any constituency, a candidate must, within the period prescribed by the Royal Decree, in person file his application according to the form determined in the Ministerial Regulation with the Governor of [the] Changwad at the town-hall within whose jurisdiction the constituency for which he offers himself for election is situated.

The Governor of [the] Changwad shall, on the day when the application is received, arrange to have a record made evidencing thereof, and then issue a receipt to the person filing the application. The Governor of [the] Changwad shall make inquiry as to whether or not such candidate is eligible. If he is so eligible, the admission of him as a candidate shall be notified at the town-hall, and the Governor of [the] Changwad shall communicate the admission or non-admission thereof to the candidate forthwith.

SEC. 23. A candidate whose candidacy has been admitted . . . shall, within seven days from the date of receipt of the notification of the admission of his candidacy, pay five thousand baht as security money for candidacy, and submit his photographs, or printed pictures which are as sharp as his photographs . . . to the number of twice the number of electoral districts and the number of Amphurs in that constituency to the Governor of [the] Changwad.

After the payment of money and submission of photographs or pictures by the candidates, the Governor of [the] Changwad shall forthwith publish the names of the candidates and their personal numbers to be used in the voting, and post the photographs or pictures of the candidates at the town-hall, Amphur Offices and every polling-place in the constituency for which they apply for candidacies.

Any candidate who fails to pay the money, or to submit his photographs or pictures to the Governor of [the] Changwad within the period as fixed in the first paragraph, shall no longer be regarded as a candidate, and the Governor of [the] Changwad shall publish the withdrawal of his name from candidacy.

SEC. 24. The security money for candidacy shall, when the election is finished, be returned to the candidate by the Governor of [the] Changwad unless the candidate is not elected and the vote obtained is less than ten percent of the total votes cast in that constituency, or, if the candidate has himself withdrawn his application, it shall be regarded that the candidate consents to have the security money belong to the State.

SEC. 25. If the Governor of [the] Changwad [refuses] to accept the application, the candidate is entitled to file a motion with the Changwad Court within whose jurisdiction the town hall is situated, or with the Civil Court for cases arising in Changwad Phra Nakorn and Changwad Thonburi, without having to pay any Court fees for the proceedings. The Court shall, upon the receipt of the motion, proceed with the examination without delay, and the Civil Procedure Code shall apply *mutatis mutandis*. The Court shall give its decision as to whether or not his application shall be accepted.

The Political Parties Act was passed by the Senate amidst less controversy than occurred during the passage of the Electoral Law. Although political parties had been banned since 1958, thirteen parties managed to organize, register, and engage in campaigning. Of these, the progovernment United Thai People's party (UTPP) and the opposition Democrat party merit particular attention. The organizers of the UTPP were comprised of the persons in the most powerful political institutions of Thailand. In addition to the prime minister, party leaders included the most prominent civilian and military cabinet members and the commanders in chief of the army, navy, and air force. At election rallies in the kingdom's 71 provincial constituencies, the UTPP candidates stressed: 1) the need for strong, centralized leadership to ensure continued stability in the kingdom; 2) the ability of the existing military regime to meet the dangers of Communism; 3) the success of the government's economic development program; and 4) the advantages UTPP candidates would have in terms of access to government funds for local development projects.

The Democrat party, the oldest and most influential of the opposition parties, was led by former Prime Minister Seni Pramoj. In contrast to the UTPP, which fielded a full slate of 219 candidates, the Democrat party ran 192 candidates in only 63 provinces. Again, in contrast to the UTPP candidates, who were generously provided by the party with campaign funds, the Democrats were forced to rely on their own and their supporters' finances. At campaign rallies through-

out the kingdom, the Democrats emphasized: 1) the lack of government support for development projects; 2) corruption among local
officials and the military government leaders; 3) the disproportionate
share of the government budget allocated to Bangkok rather than to
the rural areas; 4) the need for revision of the constitution to make
it more "democratic"; 5) the need for a more flexible foreign policy
with less reliance on the United States; and 6) the oppressive police
power in the rural areas.

A third major group of candidates were the Independents who were
not affiliated officially with any political party. One segment of the
Independents chose deliberately not to join a party because they were
particularly wealthy and famous throughout their provinces. The largest segment of Independents, however, were UTPP supporters who
had hoped to receive the immense advantages, especially financial,
from affiliation with the government party. Having failed to be chosen
UTPP candidates, these Independents requested financial help from
the UTPP in return for support if and when they were elected. Almost
half of the Independent candidates who did win eventually joined the
UTPP.

Forty-nine percent of Thailand's 14,820,180 eligible voters (total
population: 33,000,000) cast ballots for the 219 seats in the House
of Representatives. The number and percentage of seats won by the
parties were as follows:

Parties	Number of seats	Percentage
UTPP	75	35
Independents	72	33
Democrat	57	25
Democratic Front	7	3
Economist-United Front	4	2
People's party	2	1
Others	2	1

Political Parties Act [October 15, 1968]*

. . . SEC. 7. Fifteen or more persons who are of Thai nationality and
not in sympathy with other forms of government which are against the

* *Source:* Royal Thai Government *Gazette,* October 15, 1968, p. 415.

democratic form of government with the King as the head under the Constitution of the Kingdom of Thailand, and not Buddhist priests, novices, holy men or clergies, and have attained the age of not less than twenty years, and who desire to be engaged in political activities, may unite as founders of a political party whose platform is not contrary to law or public order or good morals and send out the party prospectus to those possessing qualification and not being disqualified as aforesaid in order to invite them to subscribe for membership in their political party. In case there are not less than five hundred persons, inclusive of all the party founders, subscribing for membership, the political party may then be formed by filing an application for registration with the registrar at the Ministry of Interior.

. . . SEC. 10. . . . The form of application for registration of the political party shall contain at least the following particulars:

(1) Name of the political party;
(2) Symbol of the political party, if any;
(3) Address of the head office of the political party;
(4) Names, occupations, addresses and signatures of party leader, deputy leader, if any, secretary-general, deputy secretary-general, if any, and other directors appointed at the initial stage by the party founders; and
(5) Names, occupations, addresses and signatures of five hundred members of the political party.

SEC. 11. The party statute shall contain at least the following particulars:

(1) Name of the political party;
(2) Symbol of the political party, if any;
(3) Address of the head office of the political party;
(4) Organization and administration of the political party;
(5) Establishment of branch offices of the political party, if any;
(6) Admission and dismissal of party members;
(7) Selection and retirement at the expiration of the term of offices of the party leader, deputy leader, secretary-general, deputy secretary-general and other directors, determination of power and duty of the board of directors and of each director as well as the holding of meetings;
(8) General meeting of the political party; and
(9) Selection of representatives of branch offices of the political party and the voting of such representatives, if any.

. . . SEC. 19. There shall be a board of directors in the political party consisting of the party leader, deputy leader, if any, secretary-general, deputy secretary-general, if any, and not less than seven other directors to be elected by the general meeting from its members according to the condition and procedure set forth in the party statute, which shall have the duty of carrying on activities in compliance with the political party platform.

The board of directors shall represent the political party in the activities dealing with third persons. For this purpose, the board of directors may delegate its power to one or more directors to act on its behalf.

SEC. 20. Whenever it appears that the board of directors or the director has arranged for the political party to do any act in violation of the political party platform or statute which may be against the democratic form of government with the King as the head under the Constitution of the Kingdom of Thailand, or may be a threat to the national economy, national security, or may be contrary to public order or good morals, the registrar shall have the power to give order in writing to such board of directors or director to refrain from doing such act or to make a rectification thereof within the period determined by the registrar.

If the board of directors or any director fails to comply with the order under paragraph one, the registrar shall have the power to dismiss the board of directors or such director from office. In such a case all such persons may not hold the office of director unless three years have elapsed since the day of being dismissed by the registrar.

SEC. 21. No person shall give money, property or any other benefit to the political party as a return for inducing such political party to do or omit to do any act not conforming to its duties which may be favorable or unfavorable to any person or group of persons, or may cause damage to official services.

SEC. 22. No political party shall receive money, property or any other benefit from any person in order to do or omit to do any act not conforming to its duties which may be favorable or unfavorable to any person or group of persons, or may cause damage to official services.

SEC. 23. No political party shall receive money, property or any other benefit from:

(1) any person being not of Thai nationality;
(2) any juristic person under foreign law being engaged in business or having a branch office registered in Thailand;
(3) any juristic person registered in Thailand with more than twenty-five percent of its capital or shares belonging to foreigners; . . . and
(4) any juristic person whose objective is to carry on activities for the benefit of a foreigner, or having a foreigner as its manager or director.

SEC. 24. No political party shall admit a foreigner to become its member, or to hold any position in its office, or shall allow him to do any act for its own benefit.

SEC. 25. No foreigner shall become a member of or hold any position in the political party, or shall participate in any activity of the political party.

SEC. 26. No person shall become member of more than one political party at the same time.

Resignation from membership of the political party shall be regarded as valid upon being tendered to the leader or secretary-general of the political party.

SEC. 27. No person shall, except in case of applying for the formation or registration of political party, use any name or word in the manner likely to cause the public to misunderstand that a political party has already existed, or, in case a political party has not been formed, use any name with Thai letters to be read as "political party," or use any name in a foreign language to be translated or read in Thai as "political party," in his seal, signboard, letter, notice or any document.

III. Economic Development

The First National Economic Development Plan during 1961–1966 focused on the creation of a basic infrastructure for the Thai economy. As a result, significant changes occurred. The commanding importance of agriculture was reduced in 1966 as a result of a faster growth rate in the nonagricultural sectors. Agriculture's share in the gross national product declined from 38.3 percent in 1961 to 33.7 percent in 1966. Meanwhile, the shares commanded by the industrial and trade sectors increased, with a combined growth of more than 10 percent annually. The high growth rate was attributed to the government's pragmatism and flexibility in seeking these goals, political and monetary stability, and massive external technical and economic assistance, largely from the United States.

During 1967–1971, under the Second National Economic Development Plan, the Thai economy was expected to continue to expand rapidly. Emphasis was given to achieving a more equitable income distribution. An annual growth-rate target of 8.5 percent was established so that the per capita income in the late 1960's of 2,620 baht would be doubled by 1981. Although the agricultural sector, which

employs more than 80 percent of the Thai population, was expected
to maintain at least a 4.3 percent annual growth rate, severe drought
conditions in 1967 and 1968 reduced this low rate to just 2.2 and 0.6
percent, respectively, during those years. Consequently, the overall annual growth rate was revised downward to 7.5 percent. The disparity
in growth rates between the agricultural and industrial sectors was a
source of much criticism for the government's development plans.
Partly as a result, expenditures on agriculture were increased from 14
percent of the total during the first development plan to 20 percent
of the total during the second development plan.

Thailand's First Five-Year Plan [1961–1966]*

Thailand strode forward to another stage of economic development in
1967, after completion of the First Plan period (1961–1966). The year
marks the beginning of the new Five-Year Economic and Social Development Plan. An evaluation of the First Plan shows a considerable achievement. The overall rate of growth, averaging at 7.2 percent a year, is
satisfactorily high. However, on a closer analysis the success appears to be
more illusory than real. That is, the benefits accrued as a result of planning development were mainly gained by the minority. The mass of the
population which is composed overwhelmingly of farmers and agricultural
workers gained unjustifiably little. It is our contention that no success
could be claimed for any planning if it failed to narrow the wide disparity
of income and uplift the standard of living of the masses.

It is quite understandable that a developing country like Thailand
which is basically agricultural has initially to concentrate on infrastruc-
tural development. However, when Thailand sought to change the structure of the economy by directing its planning to accelerate industrialisation, our planners ignored the true condition of the country. It is our contention that emphasis should be laid on the strengthening of the basic
structure, namely agriculture. The development of industries should be
linked firmly with agriculture so that industries which utilize local agricultural produce as raw material would be promoted. Such a policy
would help to stimulate income among the farmers, thereby creating a
built-in market for manufactures.

At present the size of the domestic market is too small for effective
industrialisation because of the generally poor purchasing power among
the masses.

*Source: Bangkok Bank Annual Report, 1967 (printed in the Bangkok Post,
March 20, 1968).

As such no large industries can be developed. Although a large number of private industries have been established since the beginning of this decade, they are mostly small industries and only a few make a real contribution towards the growth of the economy. It seems, however, that was about the best the private sector could do under the circumstances, for without a substantial market, no industries can afford to mass produce. Thus despite years of industrial development, [the cost of] locally manufactured goods [is] unreasonably high and protection of some sort by the government is needed. Take away the special privileges and protection and many industries would collapse.

It is our contention that unless purchasing power among the masses is generated, there are no prospects for real industrialisation to take place. Accordingly, it is suggested that the policy for economic development through industrialisation be reconsidered and necessary adjustments be made in the Second Plan while there is still time. We venture to put forward here proposals which we believe would help to speed up development.

Superficially, the economy of Thailand has been growing at a remarkable rate in recent years and per capita income also appears to have advanced rapidly. In reality, however, income distribution is still marred by a high degree of inequality. . . .

Although [concerted] efforts have been made by the government to revitalize the agricultural sector, the result has been far from satisfactory. This may be substantiated by the fact that while GNP growth under the First Plan averaged at 7.2 percent a year, or an overall growth of 45 percent in six years, agricultural production was increasing at a yearly rate of about 5 percent only. On the other hand, production growth of other sectors averaged at about 10 percent a year. . . . The reason is obvious for there was almost a complete lack of correlation among the different sectors in government planning and development.

We have put forward before an outline of "A New Program for Accelerating the Rate of Economic Growth in Thailand" in the supplement of the 1964 annual report in which we said: "The wealth of the country is concentrated in the hands of a small fraction of the population while the bulk of the people, namely the farmers, remain in utter poverty; to change this situation it would be necessary to give a higher rate of income to the agricultural sector, thus bringing about not only a more equitable distribution of income but also increasing the purchasing power of a large section of our population so that they, in turn, would become a built-in market for the goods produced by our local industries. In other words, if transfer payments from other sectors of the economy can be made to increase the purchasing power of the agricultural sector, all other sectors of the economy would be made to respond to the newly found wealth of the agricultural producers."

. . . A development along this line would help to increase income for the farmers. The fact that our industries would provide a ready market for the agricultural products, would make the farm products less dependent on overseas demand, and thus in turn help to stabilise their prices. Another benefit which may be expected is the diversification in our export trade, as finished or semi-finished goods would have more extensive markets and fetch higher prices. All these would provide incentive for increased productivity. It is, however, necessary that the government take a very active part by laying down a special policy to gear for such a development.

In the initial stage, the agriculture-oriented industries may have to face such problems as high cost of production or [maintaining] the quality of the products. However, this would not be too great a concern, as investors would have to consider these problems beforehand, and special benefits such as tax concessions would enable local products to compete with those imported. Moreover, the availability of low-cost raw material and labor locally should cancel some of the disadvantages. The problems of quality of the products may be solved by usage of modern techniques and machinery.

The next phase of industrialisation should be concentrated on the development of import-substitution industries. This would help to save foreign currencies and enhance our production capacity at the same time. The manufacturing of consumer goods, however, can be developed effectively only if purchasing power among the masses is generated so as to create effective demand. Thus when income is increased and becomes more evenly distributed, the size of the domestic market will be enlarged. . . . In the longer run locally manufactured products will be able to compete freely with imported goods.

. . . [Questions] might be raised about why the development of heavy or key industries is not encouraged at an early stage. The answer is that Thailand is basically an agricultural country and any attempt towards industrialisation should be in support of agriculture. The concept that heavy industry is the fundamental structure and framework for industrialisation may be applicable elsewhere, but not in Thailand. The development of such industries would involve large investment, and capital available locally is very scarce. It is our contention that at this stage it would be more economical . . . for us to import heavy machinery and equipment than to produce them locally.

One concept of industrialisation through agriculture is well supported by Murray D. Bryce in his book *Industrial Development*. We quote: "The most logical way to find new areas for industrial development is to look first for projects which will process further and thereby increase the value of agriculture, mining, and timber products already being produced for export. A second promising approach is to seek projects which can produce economically goods which are already being imported in large quantities. . . ."

For a country like Thailand, industrial development should, therefore, be firstly for agricultural produce-processing industries, secondly for manufacturing industries of import-substitution and finally for heavy industries. But this does not mean that an early development of heavy industries should be completely neglected. As Thailand abounds in natural resources such as tin, copper, and possibly iron and mineral oil, industries producing these minerals may be encouraged.

The Government should allow extra special privileges as incentives for the development of processing industries of agricultural products. Such extra special benefits could be, for example, a longer income tax exemption period; exemption or reduction of business tax and duty on materials which may have to be imported for a specified period. The industries should also be well protected against competition of foreign goods. The Government should also encourage exports of locally manufactured products such as by subsidising the industries and/or by exempting them from export duty. Apart from these incentives the following conditions are also necessary to attract investment:

—political and economic stability.
—government guarantees against nationalisation of and state competition with private enterprises.
—straight forward dealing and efficiency of government officials.
—understanding and cooperation of the government in helping the investors to overcome problems and difficulties regarding laws and regulations.
—genuine interest on the part of the government to solve the problems of capital shortage and marketing.
—protective measures against dumping of foreign goods.
—effective labor laws.
—low-cost, suitable land and other facilities for the setting up of industries, such as a well developed industrial estate.
—availability of trained workers, and also centres for training.
—facilities to repatriate profits of foreign investors.
—relaxed immigration laws to allow foreign entrepreneurs and technical experts to come in.
—temporary exemption (not more than 12 months) of personal income tax for foreign investors.

What are the industrial uses of agricultural commodities? The uses are numerous, directly and indirectly by employing modern technologies. Castor oil, for example, is widely used in industries, including the manufacturing of synthetic products. For this particular product the uses range from pharmaceuticals, toilet articles, cosmetics, dyes, paints, lubricating and hydraulic oils to plastics and other synthetic products. After oil extraction the waste of castor seeds can be manufactured into fertilizer. Castor oil produced in excess of local industrial demand may also be exported. Apart from fetching better prices than seeds, castor oil is also in good demand in the world market.

The underlying objective of our economic development is to raise the general standard of living of the population as a whole. At present not less than 90 percent of the population (of which as much as 85 percent are in the agricultural sector) are still living in poverty. It is, therefore, a matter of greatest importance that the income level of the people be raised as quickly as possible. In this light, it is deemed important that concerted efforts be made to develop our agriculture and also that industrial development be linked more directly with the agricultural sector. It is our contention that if the Government adopts a special policy along this line by taking positive steps to promote processing industries of agricultural produce and increased marketing of agricultural products, by giving undivided attention to solving the problems facing agriculture-industry development, and by providing extra special privileges to industries processing local raw materials, the goal of our development planning could be more easily achieved. Such a development, we believe, would bring about a more equitable distribution of income. This would go a long way towards fortifying us economically against external disturbances which are exploiting the vulnerable spots in our economy.

IV. Foreign Relations

Prime Minister Phibun's foreign policy during 1948–1957 was oriented toward the West, especially the United States. In return for Thailand's support of her international policies, the United States negotiated two far-reaching agreements. The Economic and Technical Cooperation Agreement, signed on September 19, 1950, provided initially $8 million for economic aid to Thailand. By the late 1960's American economic-aid authorizations totalled more than $440 million. The bulk of the aid was for development of agriculture, industry, transportation and communications, education, public health, and public administration. About half of it was used to build and repair roads, for both military and economic development purposes.

The second significant accord was the Agreement Respecting Military Assistance, signed on October 17, 1950. During the next twenty years, military-aid authorizations totalled more than $600 million. As a consequence of the massive influx of weapons, planes, and ships, Thailand's military defense capability was improved immeasurably, and the arms provided Prime Ministers Phibun, Sarit, and Thanom with the means for suppressing internal opposition.

Economic and Technical Cooperation Agreement between Thailand and the United States [September 19, 1950]*

. . . ART. I. The . . . United States . . . will, subject to the terms and conditions prescribed by law and to arrangements provided for in this agreement, furnish . . . Thailand such economic and technical assistance as may be requested by it and agreed to by . . . the United States. . . .

ART. II. In order to assure maximum benefits to the people of Thailand from the assistance to be furnished hereunder by the . . . United States . . . Thailand will use its best endeavors:

A. To assure efficient and practical use of all resources available and to assure that the commodities and services obtained under this agreement are used only for purposes consistent therewith.

B. To promote the economic development of Thailand on a sound basis and to achieve such objectives as may be agreed upon by the two Governments.

C. To assure the stability of its currency and the validity of its rate of exchange and generally to strengthen confidence in its internal financial stability.

D. To take the measures which it deems appropriate, and to cooperate with other countries, to reduce barriers to international trade and to prevent, on the part of private or public enterprises, business practices or business arrangements which restrain competition or limit access to markets, whenever such practices or such arrangements hinder domestic or international trade.

. . . ART. IV. . . . Thailand agrees to receive a special technical and economic mission which will discharge the responsibilities of the . . .

* Source: Royal Thai Government Gazette, September 19, 1950, p. 285.

United States . . . under this agreement, and upon appropriate notification from . . . the United States . . . will consider this special mission and its personnel as part of the Diplomatic Mission of the United States . . . in Thailand. . . . Thailand will further give full cooperation to the special mission including the provision of facilities necessary for observation and review of the carrying out of this agreement including the use of assistance furnished under it. . . .

Agreement Respecting Military Assistance between Thailand and the United States [October 17, 1950]*

... ART. I.

1. Each Government, consistent with the principle that economic stability is essential to international peace and security, will make available to the other, such equipment, material, services, or other military assistance as the Government furnishing such assistance may authorize and in accordance with such terms and conditions as it may agree. The furnishing of any such assistance as may be authorized by either party hereto shall be consistent with the Charter of the United Nations. . . . The two Governments will, from time to time, negotiate detailed arrangements necessary to carry out the provisions of this paragraph.

2. . . . Thailand undertakes to make effective use of assistance received pursuant to paragraph 1 of this Article for the purpose for which such assistance is furnished, and will not, without prior consent of the . . . United States . . . devote assistance so furnished to purposes other than those for which it is furnished.

3. . . . Thailand undertakes to retain title to and possession and control of any equipment, material, or services, received pursuant to paragraph 1, unless . . . the United States . . . shall otherwise consent.

4. . . . Thailand will take appropriate measures to prevent the transportation out of Thailand, including the territorial waters thereof, of any equipment or material substitutable for, or of similar category to, those being supplied by . . . the United States . . . under this Agreement.

ART. II.

1. Each Government will take appropriate measures consistent with security to keep the public informed of operations under this Agreement, and will, at appropriate intervals, consult with the other on the measures to be employed to this end.

2. Each Government will take such security measures as may be requested

* Source: Ibid., October 24, 1950.

by the other to prevent the disclosure or compromise of classified articles, services or information furnished by the other Government pursuant to this Agreement, and to this end will consult with the other as to the measures to be taken.

. . . ART. IV. . . . Thailand will, except as otherwise agreed to, grant duty-free treatment to products, materials or equipment imported into or exported from its territory in connection with this Agreement.

ART. V. . . . Thailand will facilitate the production, transport, export, and transfer to . . . the United States . . . for such period of time, in such quantities and upon such terms and conditions of purchase as may be agreed upon, of raw and semi-processed materials required by the United States . . . as a result of deficiencies or potential deficiencies in its own resources, and which may be available in Thailand. Arrangements for such transfer shall give due regard to the reasonable requirements for domestic use and commercial export of Thailand.

. . . ART. VIII.

1. . . . Thailand will make available to . . . the United States . . . baht for the use of the latter Government for its administrative and operating expenditures within Thailand in connection with assistance furnished to . . . Thailand under this Agreement.
2. The two Contracting Governments will initiate discussions with a view to determining the amount of such baht and agreeing upon arrangements for the furnishing of such baht, taking into account the ability of . . . Thailand to provide such currency.

The Thanat-Rusk Agreement of March 1962 ended a period of strained relations between the United States and Thailand. American military support for Thailand's traditional enemy Cambodia, United States ambivalence toward Laos, and SEATO's refusal to come to Laos' assistance against the Communist threat had been particularly divisive problems. The agreement and the subsequent dispatch of American soldiers to northeast Thailand once again improved Thai-American relations. The joint statement altered significantly the original intent of the SEATO treaty which called for "unanimous agreement" among the member states before action could be taken against "the common danger." In the 1962 statement the United States agreed to defend Thailand without the prior agreement of the SEATO nations. The Thai reaction to the Thanat-Rusk Agreement was enthusiastic. Prime Minister Sarit hailed the American pledge in a special television report to the people. Thanat Khoman, Thailand's minister of foreign affairs, in his statement to the SEATO Council of Ministers pointed out that the SEATO alliance was no longer the basis of Thailand's defense policies. The disinterest of SEATO nations such as Great Britain, France, and Pakistan could no longer preclude unilateral American action in defense of Thailand against Communist aggression.

The Thanat Khoman–Dean Rusk Agreement [March 6, 1962]*

The Foreign Minister of Thailand, Thanat Khoman, and the Secretary of State Dean Rusk met on several occasions during the past few days for discussions on the current situation in Southeast Asia, the Southeast Asia Collective Defence Treaty and the security of Thailand.

The Secretary of State reaffirmed that the United States regards the preservation of the independence and integrity of Thailand as vital to the national interest of the United States and to world peace. He expressed the firm intention of the United States to aid Thailand, its ally and historic friend, in resisting Communist aggression and subversion.

The Foreign Minister and the Secretary of State reviewed the close association of Thailand and the United States in the Southeast Asia Collective Defence Treaty and agreed that such association is an effective deterrent to direct Communist aggression against Thailand. They agreed that the treaty provides the basis for the signatories collectively to assist Thailand in case of Communist armed attack against that country. The Secretary of State assured the Foreign Minister that in the event of such aggression, the United States intends to give full effect to its obligations under the treaty to act to meet the common danger in accordance with its constitutional processes. The Secretary of State reaffirmed that this obligation of the United States does not depend upon the prior agreement of all other parties to the treaty, since this treaty obligation is individual as well as collective.

In reviewing measures to meet indirect aggression, the Secretary of State stated that the United States regards its commitments to Thailand under the Southeast Asia Collective Defence Treaty and under its bilateral economic and military assistance agreements with Thailand as providing an important basis for United States actions to help Thailand meet indirect aggression. In this connection the Secretary reviewed with

* Source: SEATO: 1954–1964 (Bangkok: Southeast Asia Treaty Organization, 1964), p. 62.

the Foreign Minister the actions being taken by the United States to assist the Republic of Vietnam to meet the threat of indirect aggression.

The Foreign Minister assured the Secretary of State of the determination of the government of Thailand to meet this threat of indirect aggression by pursuing vigorously measures for the economic and social welfare and the safety of its people.

The situation in Laos was reviewed in detail and full agreement was reached on the necessity for the stability of Southeast Asia of achieving a free, independent and truly neutral Laos.

The Foreign Minister and the Secretary of State reviewed the mutual efforts of their governments to increase the capabilities and readiness of the Thai armed forces to defend the Kingdom. They noted also that the United States is making a significant contribution to this effort and that the United States intends to accelerate future deliveries to the greatest extent possible. The Secretary and Foreign Minister also took note of the work of the joint Thai-United States committee which has been established in Bangkok to assure effective cooperation in social, economic and military measures to increase Thailand's national capabilities. They agreed that this joint committee and its sub-committees should continue to work towards the most effective utilization of Thailand's resources and those provided by the United States to promote Thailand's development and security. The Foreign Minister and the Secretary were in full agreement that continued economic and social progress is essential to the stability of Thailand. They reviewed Thailand's impressive economic and social progress and the Thai government's plans to accelerate development, particularly Thailand's continuing determination fully to utilize its own resources in moving towards its development goals.

The Foreign Minister and the Secretary of State also discussed the desirability of an early conclusion of a treaty of friendship, commerce and navigation between the two countries which would bring into accord with current conditions the existing treaty of 1937.

Thanat Khoman: Statement at Twelfth Meeting of the Council of Ministers of the Southeast Asia Treaty Organization [April 18, 1967]*

. . . More than twelve years have gone by since the founding of SEATO and with them some of the original hopes and expectations. From the very start, SEATO had to live through many storms blowing

* Source: Collected Statements of Foreign Minister Thanat Khoman, Vol. 3, November 1966–October 1967 (Bangkok: Department of Information, Ministry of Foreign Affairs, 1967).

across the Southeast Asia region where the retreating colonial powers had left a vacuum which the newly emerging communist regimes attempted to fill. The first test came in 1959 when communist forces attempted to overrun a good part of Laos for the purpose of securing a greatly needed staging area for their impending attack on South Vietnam. It became painfully apparent that the Organization was by no means equipped to deal with a crisis of even that proportion. In fact, the collective defense machinery in which many had placed high hopes for the safeguard against communist encroachments never got off the ground. SEATO, for all intents and purposes, did not pass its very first test. It avoided it by shelving for over a month a request for action from a protocol state which it accepted under its protective wings. SEATO's inaction and impotency which reflected the views and policies of many of its members gave the communist expansionists the green light for launching . . . a much bolder adventure in South Vietnam. On the basis of the experience of the past, the latter [the communists] could count on similar inaction and non-interference on the part of the Organization. The worst that could come would be another international conference where a compromise might be arranged which would save the face—and the conscience—of the freedom defenders but would subsequently lead to a communist takeover.

Such a calculation was proven to be both correct and incorrect. The communists were right in their estimate that SEATO would be unable to intervene. . . . They were, however, mistaken in deducing from SEATO's impotence and inactivity that all its members would likewise fail to react. Contrary to their expectation, more than half of the Organization's members saw in the latest communist adventure in South Vietnam a warning of an extensive expansionist campaign which would not be confined to Vietnam alone but would span . . . the whole of Southeast Asia and even beyond. They consequently took the communist challenge with the utmost seriousness. Now after more than twelve years of a rather inactive life, certain well-defined trends have emerged indicating the possible future orientation of the Organization. On the one hand, it is probable that SEATO, as an organization, will continue to lead a sheltered life of almost contemplative nature as far as security actions are concerned. There have been and undoubtedly will continue to be at least two categories of members, the fully active members and the selective ones. The latter will seek the full enjoyment of their rights and privileges but will discharge only those obligations which, they believe, conform to their present foreign and domestic policies.

Thailand, together with certain other members belong to the active category. It has spared no efforts to make the Organization meaningful and effective in spite of the fact that it has not received commensurate return. In 1962, to save SEATO from complete paralysis, it signed with the United States a Joint Communique [Thanat-Rusk Agreement] spelling out that the obligations under the treaty may be both individual and collective. It was fortunate that such an interpretation was subsequently endorsed by many other members. We, in Thailand, do not feel that the cause which brought about the corrosion of the European Collective Defense System, among them the present tendency towards decreasing aggressiveness and expansionism on the part of communist nations, have as yet materialized in Asia. Rather the contrary is true. Indeed, communist nations in Asia continue to pursue a policy of colonial expansionism which is hardly different from the old one. . . . SEATO, therefore, and in spite of its weaknesses, has not completely lost its *raison d'être* or its usefulness, at least as a framework or a legal basis for defense measures to be undertaken, singly or collectively. Indeed SEATO may be more useful for what it cannot do than for what it has actually done.

As far as my country is concerned, it has done and will continue to do what it can to inject life into the Organization so that it may usefully serve the cause of peace and freedom. The decision of the Thai Government recently to allow SEATO allies, particularly the United States, to use military installations and facilities in Thailand, though it affected our national sovereignty, is designed to give meaning to the Organization or otherwise it would be reduced to a useless carcass. Indeed, if today the communist tide is being contained in South Vietnam and has not spilled over into the rest of Asia, we owe it to the gallantry of the dedicated fighters from our freedom-loving countries and, in no small measure, to the willingness of the Thai Government and people to bear the risks involved in the military co-operation with our SEATO allies, especially the United States. In so doing, let me emphasize here that the Thai Nation has been prompted by the determination to deny the aggressors the enjoyment of an undeserved victory, to help shorten the war and alleviate the sufferings and the sacrifices of the victims of aggression as well as their defenders and, most important of all, to ensure that small nations in Asia have the possibility to survive and live in freedom and in honor.

During the course of the Viet-Nam war, Thailand consistently and vociferously supported a strong anti-communist, pro-United States position. The most articulate spokesman of the hard-line exponents was Thanat Khoman. His address in 1967 to the General Assembly of the United Nations exemplified the disdain of the Thai government for those seeking less than a total victory in Viet-Nam. In addition to oral support, the Thai government was host to more than 40,000

American soldiers and airmen for Viet-Nam duty on bases throughout the country. By 1965, 80 percent of American bombing raids on North Viet-Nam emanated from bases in Thailand. By the end of the 1960's, a division of Thai troops was engaged in combat in South Viet-Nam.

Thanat Khoman: Statement at United Nations General Assembly [October 5, 1967]*

. . . Of great importance is . . . the question of the war now raging in Vietnam, for it has given rise to such a campaign of fallacies and aberrations, and about which so many people have unfortunately displayed such lack of candor, that there has been created an abysmal chasm between realities on the one hand and the falsehoods and half-truths that the perpetrators of the war and their sympahtizers have disseminated. North Vietnam and its supporters in the Communist world as well as its Vietcong agents in South Vietnam wanted the outside world to believe that the war of conquest they have been waging for many years against the small and independent country of South Vietnam is a genuine national uprising or, to use their current terminology, a "war of national liberation." This travesty of the truth has convinced neither the South Vietnamese people nor those who live near the scene of the crime and who are directly or otherwise suffering from its nefarious consequences. Only those who are farther away whose minds are less perceptive of the existing realities and those who are always liberal with other people's freedom or are prompted by less than altruistic reasons allow themselves to fall victims of this crude propaganda. But if questions as to what they think of the conflict in Vietnam were directed to those Asians who have their feet firmly on the ground and whose vision has not been clouded by the outlandish ideology of the frustrated author of 'Das Kapital,' they would reply in unison that it is in effect an old-styled colonial conquest with only a few renovated outward trimmings. For this so-called sublime liberation with its accompanying paraphernalia is being directed not solely against the Republic of Vietnam but actually against a dozen other countries in Asia and Africa. Also, the liberation is always forcible, never voluntary. Consequently, it invariably elicits strong resistance against the forceful invitation to be liberated and to join the paradise of Marxist bondage.

The people in our Asian part of the world are presently amazed at the emergence of negative values and logic. They find it particularly difficult to understand the strong advocacies by some quarters that the aggressors

Source: Ibid.

should be appeased and even protected against their crime. Their life and property should not be molested by aerial bombing, while their atrocities in the South and elsewhere evoke hardly any indignation. Thus, for these would-be pacifists and lopsided idealists, the lives of the North Vietnamese and Vietcong attackers seem to have much greater value than the throats and limbs of South Vietnamese and other Asian victims of aggression. That is why they clamour for unilateral and unconditional cessation of bombing, which they contend may bring the aggressive regime of the North to the conference table. It never occurs to them, however, to demand from that regime a positive indication as to what it proposes to do in response to such a gesture. In the meantime, they are acting as unauthorized agents and spokesmen of Hanoi while the latter continues to disdain any prospect of meaningful negotiations except on its own terms. In fact the more the other side shows intransigence and insistence on its unreasonable demands, the more the protagonists of concessions press on with further compromises which ultimately will lead to surrender and delivery of South Vietnam to the North. Indeed, only a few of these advocates have enough courage to admit that South Vietnam is not worth saving but should be handed over to its predators of the North for the sake of temporary peace or even a short-lived truce.

To the millions of suffering people in Asia it seems that the right to call off measures to repel the aggressors such as the bombing of the North should be exercised in consultation with them and not by those apostles of peace who barely suffer at the hands of these cruel enemies of freedom and whose campaign for illusory peace has, twice in a lifetime, led to the tragic disaster of world wars. For those millions of Asians whose life is constantly menaced by the aggressors' guns and terror, the halt in the bombing would gain immediate support and approval if it could lead ultimately to the cessation of hostilities as well as the harrowing reign of terror. Clearly, for them the Vietnam war is indeed unpopular, even greatly more unpopular than in Europe or America which enjoy both safety and abundance. Unlike the Hanoi regime which is unwilling to leave the war-path, they ardently desire to see the war brought to an end provided that in so doing their freedom and independence are not sacrificed, for if peace were to be followed by subjection to alien rule and deprivation of their heritage of liberty, their existence would be without meaning. For them it is deeply painful to watch the agonizing debate stirred up by the instigators of doubt, of confusion and defeatism, who, masquerading as princes of peace, are in fact undermining and damaging the abiding interests of their own countries as well as those of their friends and allies. With a few more grains of wisdom and perspicacity they should be able to realize that the solution to the war in Vietnam can never be found when the defenders of freedom are divided and disunited but only if the latter succeed in closing their ranks and are determined to carry their gallant task to the end. For the aggressive regime of North Vietnam once had the taste of victory snatched from [it] and nothing can dissuade it from thinking that it could [achieve victory] if it manages to sow doubts, dissension, and disruption within and among nations which stand in its way to conquest and domination.

In fact the anatomy of the war in Vietnam can be analysed into various elements. In the first place, hostilities may cease altogether when the aggressors, realizing the hopelessness of their adventure, discontinue their infiltration and intervention against their neighbors. They may be persuaded to adopt this course on finding that the cost of aggression in terms of deterioration of their well-being and even their subsistence is far too high, and on the realisation of the fact that it is not possible for them to achieve their objective through the use of subversion and armed intervention. Indeed, those who are eager to see peace restored in Vietnam should join together in convincing the Hanoi regime of the futility of their venture and that the peaceful approach is actually more beneficial.

Another possibility would appear to be negotiated settlement. Such solution presupposes some form of negotiations and above all the sincere willingness on the part of the parties involved to enter into negotiations. This the parties concerned may directly do on their own, but hitherto the negative attitude of Hanoi has precluded the likelihood of such direct discussion. A further alternative is a larger conference arranged by interested governments for the settlement of this outstanding problem. In particular, the Geneva conference on Indochina may be reconvened to pave the way for negotiated settlement. The first step in this direction would be for both co-chairmen of the Geneva conference to act as true peacemakers by fulfilling their avowed duties as co-chairmen and to forsake their role of ideological partners in the conflict. Instead of adding further fuel to the flames by supplying more arms to the aggressors the co-chairmen would better serve the cause of peace and at the same time perform their part of the obligations by using their influence to persuade Hanoi, the only unwilling party in this case, to come to the conference table. At any rate, the least that should be done would be to show support for the reconvening of such conference.

In all these possibilities, even when negotiations could be initiated either directly or by an internationally arranged conference, a further step would still be to secure a just and durable settlement of the conflict. To achieve this objective either in the process of negotiation or otherwise, one of the prerequisites to be borne in mind by the free nations is for them to remain constantly united and to show their firm determination. Failure to muster such unity or to show firmness may result in superficial settlement entailing transitory peace which is fraught with no less grave danger to peace and security.

The vicious campaigns now being conducted to breed dissension and disunity among us are not completely devoid of usefulness. They opened our eyes to the vagaries of both international and domestic politics in various countries and spurred us to redouble our regional and individual efforts to strengthen our security and defense and to rely more and more on combined endeavours of those who share the same stake and have no doubt as to where their vital interests lie.

That explains why nations in Southeast Asia and in the vast region of Asia and the Pacific have found it necessary to join together in cooperative efforts to bring about greater well-being and progress for our respective peoples. This is our own concept of a revolution in Southeast Asia, a revolution which seeks to fill the stomachs with food and the hearts with realizable hopes for the future, and not the one which throws the starving people into the street to commit depredations and desecration. It is also a revolution to destroy the shackles of past domination and dependency. From now on the nations in the area will be inspired by the spirit of equal partnership and cooperation for the good of each and all. Such efforts would move more swiftly forward were it not for the disruptive Vietnam war which has retarded the development of fuller independence and mutual self-reliance of the nations in the Asian region. That is why all of them without exception earnestly hope that this senseless conflict can be brought to a just and successful conclusion which will open up a new era of greater stability and progress. If South Vietnam is assured of its freedom, smaller nations of the world can look forward to a more secure independence free from interference and encroachment. What smaller nations of the Organization and indeed the whole world should look forward to is not so much the one-sided cessation of bombing which will allow the aggressor to wreak further havoc but rather the ways and means to ensure that there will be no other Vietnams in the future.

TWO

Burma

by JOSEF SILVERSTEIN

Like other Southeast Asian countries, Burma has sought national unity, political stability, and economic progress. Were these goals to be attained, the Burmese would enjoy *pyidawtha,* a term which signifies a peaceful and prosperous country. Unfortunately for the aspirations of her leaders and people, however, these goals have proved to be elusive. Instead, it is the opposite condition, *pyidawcha,* which has been predominant: Disunity has prevailed among her several peoples, political instability has been the rule rather than the exception, and, far from the prosperous, socialist state her leaders have envisaged, Burma has suffered from economic stagnation and decay. At the beginning of the 1970's, Burma appeared to be adrift, and it was uncertain whether her leaders possessed the navigational equipment necessary to plot and follow a course toward the destination they sought. More than anything else, it is this gap between aspirations and the ability to achieve them which has been the distinguishing feature of independent Burma.

At the dawn of independence during 1946–1947, Burma's leaders were supremely confident of their ability to govern the country and to achieve a fairly clear set of political, economic, and social objectives. The negotiation of their country's independence from Britain was successfully concluded in October 1947; a constitution which guaranteed justice to all was agreed upon; and the design for Burma's economic future was drawn. But in their eagerness to take command of Burma, few of the leaders seemed to have anticipated the problems which the attainment of independence would uncover. Perhaps none of these has vexed the Burmese more than that of trying to mobilize and unify the country's several peoples into a single nation.

In Burma, in the area surrounding the Irrawaddy River valley, there are five major ethnic groups—Shans, Karens, Kachins, Chins, and Kayahs—which have never been fully assimilated by the majority Burmans. The situation of these peoples is traceable partly to colonial rule. Burma was conquered in a piecemeal fashion by the British, and it was not treated by them as a single unit. The plains-dwelling Burmans were ruled directly by the British. The peoples of the upland regions generally were protected and controlled through their own hereditary rulers. Largely traditional and conservative in outlook, they had little in common with the young Burman revolutionaries who spearheaded the independence movement. In brief, British colonial rule militated against the formation of a national outlook and, in consequence, Burma began its independence without strong unifying elements to offset the powerful centrifugal forces generated by these divergent groups of people.

Despite their efforts to meet the demands of the minorities for autonomy and protection, the founders of the Union did little to counterbalance these forces. An ostensibly federal constitution gave statehood to the Shan, Kachin, and Kayah frontier regions—and also provided the Shans and Kayahs with the right of secession after 1958—and created a special administrative division for the Chins. A Karen state was created in 1951. The governments of these states, however, were responsible to councils consisting of members of the Union parliament from their areas, not to separate state legislatures. Moreover, all of the state governments were dependent upon subventions from the Union government. In effect, a unitary system of government, domiated by the majority Burmans, was established.

The superiority attitude of the Burmans, and the government's inability to heal rifts between the plains and the upland peoples helped to nourish separatist feelings among the minorities. The subsequent demands for state autonomy and a halt to Burmanization led to the formation in 1960 of a National Liberation Alliance among the Shan and Kayah rebels to which later the Karen National Defense Organization and the Kachin Independence Army joined. Regional disaffection and a growing demand among the minorities for greater autonomy or the right to secede were instrumental in provoking the army to seize power by a coup d'état in March 1962.

The minorities policies of the military government have been similar to those of its civilian predecessors: Each has sought the integration of the minorities with the dominant Burmans. The civilian governments tried to effect Burmanization of the people by fostering the spread of Burman customs and traditions, including language and the Buddhist religion. The military government has employed a more subtle approach, utilizing both persuasion and force in bringing to the minority peoples social and economic improvements. Neither approach has yet been successful, probably because the majority Burmans themselves have yet to convince the minorities that they seek political unity while practicing cultural diversity.

Nor have the alien Indian and Chinese minorities been accepted as full members of the society. Neither has been assimilated, and although the constitution provided for their naturalization, the rules and procedures were so ill-defined and complex that few actually obtained citizenship. As a consequence of this, as well as of the government's economic policies aimed at restricting their activities, there has in recent years been a steady exodus of Indians from Burma. Less tension has existed in the past between Burmese and Chinese, but hostility sprang up between them in the 1960's, particularly as a result of China's support of the Burma Communist party and propaganda among Chinese residents in Rangoon.

Burma's leaders have also been foiled in their pursuit of political stability. At the commencement of independence, their effort to establish stability through parliamentary rule was subjected to a severe test brought on by a Communist-led insurrection in 1948 and minority discontent. Only rivalry among the dissidents and the strong and determined leadership of Prime Minister U Nu preserved the Union in the crucible. The struggle to keep it alive since then has been a costly one.

During 1948–1958, the AFPFL—Anti-Fascist People's Freedom League, a loose federation under the leadership of the men who negotiated independence and the transfer of power from Britain—commanded a substantial majority in the parliament. But, inasmuch as there was no serious parliamentary opposition that could provide the nucleus for an alternative government, it was the party caucus and not the parliament or the cabinet which was the real locus of political power. The AFPFL, however, was not a well-organized and disciplined political group. Although it claimed to be the voice of the people, it developed no grass-roots support, and, many of its members appeared interested only in satisfying their own personal interests. It was, moreover, riddled by powerful personal rivalries, and finally in 1958, it split into "Stable" and "Clean" factions. In consequence, the government was thrown into disarray. When U Nu, prime minister for most of the decade, failed to re-establish harmony between the factions and found himself faced with the prospect of governing with the potentially disruptive support of radical leftists, he stepped aside in favor of an army-run, caretaker government.

The army relinquished its power in 1960 after having established orderly government. In full command of the country for eighteen months, the army had also been able to enforce greater internal security, check hoarders and black marketeers, stabilize the cost of living, increase exports and foreign-exchange reserves, and negotiate a favorable border agreement with China. After the army's retirement from government in 1960, new elections were held in which, much to the officers' dismay, U Nu and his new Union party won an overwhelming victory. The people, it seemed, preferred U Nu's leadership and civilian government to the reforms and discipline which the army had enforced. They may also have backed him because of his promises to make Buddhism the state religion and to grant statehood to the Mons and the Arakanese.

U Nu's new government was no improvement over his old one. The politicians again demonstrated their incapacity to avert national disintegration: The cabinet was neither loyal nor united; corruption led to scandals; a national crisis was provoked when Buddhism was made the state religion; and regional disaffection, especially among the Shans, again posed the threat of insecurity. Once more, popular confidence in the parliamentary system waned.

Thus on March 2, 1962, the army led by General Ne Win carried out a coup d'état: Parliament was abolished, political parties and unions were banned, and most of the politicians, including U Nu, were imprisoned. Parliamentary democracy was rejected because, according to Ne Win, it would never lead Burma to the achievement of its socialist goals. In its place, a military-dominated Revolutionary Council was set up to govern the country; in place of parties, the army formed a national front, a single Burmese Socialist Program party to express the will of the nation, an uncompromising extension of radical nationalism using the slogan, "the Burmese Way to Socialism."

The Revolutionary Council, however, has been no more successful in achieving political stability than the civilian governments. Attempts were made to appease minority discontent through offers of amnesty and negotiation, but by the beginning of 1970, unrest among the minorities remained widespread. The military was equally unsuccessful in suppressing the Burma Communist party. Internal dissension rather than government victories in their struggle kept the Communists from expanding their political power. Contrary to the Revolutionary Council's proclaimed intention to involve the people in a meaningful participation in the country's new socialist system, the military kept a tight grip on political power. Finally, popular discontent was stirred by the army's singularly inept management of Burma's economy: Agricultural production declined, the transportation system deteriorated, and because of frequent breakdowns in the distribution and marketing networks, shortages of food and clothing were common occurrences.

Although the military differ from some civilians in their rejection of parliamentary democracy, they do share a commitment to a socialist economy as the means of attaining economic well-being for all. Immediately after independence was granted, steps were taken by the civilian government toward establishment of a socialist state. A few industries were nationalized. A land nationalization act was passed. But in the face of a severe shortage of skilled managers and technicians and in the absence of development capital, the government was obliged to seek implementation of its economic plans through a mixed economy with private and public sectors participating jointly and independently in agricultural and industrial development. This policy was continued until after the military takeover in 1962 when total nationalization of the economy was effected. Like its predecessors, however, the Revolutionary Council has attempted to manage the economy through a congeries of committees, councils, and corporations, and it has suffered the same results in doing so: Conflict and lack of coordination among government agencies and state enterprises, bureaucratic delays in decision-making, a misallocation of scarce resources, wastage, inflation, a flourishing black market, and shortages of essential consumer goods. As a result, frustration and discontentment have grown in urban areas. In the countryside despite massive aid and welfare programs, low income and indebtedness continue to plague the farmers.

In the early 1970's a crisis of confidence plagued the Burmese. A united national community has not yet been created. As a result of failure to agree on how the country is to be governed and because of the long-term semi-war generated by ethnic factions, Burma does not enjoy political stability. The lack of success in these two areas has made it difficult for the governments to cope with other problems, including especially the problem of economic development.

I. The Pathway to Independence

At the end of World War II, Burma's leaders insisted upon the establishment of their independence and full sovereignty from Britain. Initially, there was wide disagreement between the British and the Burmese nationalists over who should determine the course to and the timetable for independence. A British plan would have given priority to the reconstruction of the badly damaged economy, provided for a British governor with sweeping political power, and continued the colonial policy of political separation of the minority hill peoples from the majority Burmans. The Burmese demanded the immediate creation of a national government vested with real power to plan for independence. It was not until 1946, however, that the British began to display a willingness to meet the AFPFL's political demands. This trend, which helped to pave the way for a smooth transfer of power, is exemplified by the Aung San-Attlee Agreement, which was negotiated by the president of the AFPFL and the prime minister of Great Britain in early 1947. Among its more important features is its provision for unity between the hill peoples and the plains dwellers in the future state of Burma. During that same year, leaders from both of these groups met at Panglong in the Shan states to draw up an agreement on their future cooperation.

The Aung San–Attlee Agreement [January 27, 1947]*

His Majesty's Government and the Delegation of the Burma Executive Council . . . have reached the following agreed conclusions as to methods by which the people of Burma may achieve their independence, either within or without the Commonwealth as soon as possible:

1. The Constituent Assembly. In order that the people of Burma may

* *Source: Burma's Fight for Freedom* (Rangoon: Ministry of Information, 1948), pp. 44–48.

decide on the future Constitution of their country as soon as possible a Constituent Assembly shall be elected instead of a Legislature under the Act of 1935. For this purpose the electoral machinery of the 1935 Act will be used.

The election will take place in April for General Non-Communal, the Karen and Anglo-Burman Constituencies as constituted under the Act of 1935 and for each Constituency two members shall be returned. Any Burma nationals (as defined in Annex A) registered in a General Constituency other than one of those mentioned above shall be placed on the register of a General Non-Communal Constituency.

2. Transitional Form of Government. During the period of transition the Government of Burma will be carried on as at present under the special powers of section 139 of the Act of 1935 and Temporary Provisions Act of 1935 together with any Orders in Council made thereunder.

   If any exceptional circumstances arise which in the opinion of either Government require special treatment H.M.G. will consider what, if any, alteration can be made to meet such circumstances.

3. Interim Legislature. During the interim period there will be a Legislative Council as provided by the Act of 1935. Power will be sought by H.M.G. by Order in Council to increase the numbers authorized from 50 to 100.

   As soon as the elections to the Constituent Assembly are completed the Governor will nominate a Legislative Council of 100. It will be drawn from amongst those elected to the Constituent Assembly with the inclusion of a small number of persons to represent the non-indigenous minorities.

   The powers of the Legislative Council will be identical with those possessed by the recently dissolved Legislative Council of 50.

4. Interim Government. The Executive Council of the Governor will constitute the Interim Government of Burma. While it is not possible to alter the legal powers of the Executive Council or of the Governor which must continue within the frame-work set out in paragraph 2 above the Interim Government will be conducted generally in the same manner as the Interim Government of India at the present time and in particular:

   (a) The Executive Council will be treated with the same close consultation and consideration as a Dominion Government and will have the greatest possible freedom in the exercise of the day-to-day administration of the country. The convention exercised during the currency of the Act of 1935 as to the Governor presiding at the meetings of the Council of Ministers shall be continued in relation to the Executive Council.

(b) His Majesty's Government agree in principle that the Government of Burma shall have financial autonomy. . . .

(c) Matters concerning Defence and External Affairs will be brought before the Executive Council, which will be fully associated with the disposal of business in such matters.

(d) The Governor will depute to his Counsellor for Defence and External Affairs the day-to-day administration of those subjects. Subject only to the limitations inherent in the legal position, the Executive Council will be at full liberty to raise, consider, discuss and decide on any matters arising in the field of policy and administration.

5. External Affairs. There shall be appointed forthwith a High Commissioner for Burma to represent the Burmese Government in London. His Majesty's Government will request the Governments of countries with which Burma wishes to exchange diplomatic representatives to agree to such an exchange.

6. Membership of International Organizations. His Majesty's Government will lend their full support to any application by Burma for the membership of the United Nations Organization as soon as Burma's constitutional position makes it possible for such an application to be entertained. In the meantime His Majesty's Government will explore with the Secretary-General how far it is possible for Burma to be represented at any meetings, or under the auspices of the United Nations Organization.

They will also approach any other International bodies which the Government of Burma may desire with a view to ascertaining whether Burma can be associated with the work of such bodies as a member nation or otherwise.

7. Defence.

(a) In accordance with settled practice all British Forces stationed in Burma will remain under the ultimate control of His Majesty's Government.

(b) All Burmese Forces will forthwith come under the control of the Government of Burma.

(c) His Majesty's Government have agreed in principle that the G.O.C. in Burma shall become subordinate to the Governor and the Government of Burma at the earliest practicable moment, but for the present, until liquidation of Inter-Allied arrangements of Command which cover many countries, the G.O.C. in Burma will remain under S.E.A.L.F. During this period there will of course be close collaboration between the Government of Burma and authorities concerned. . . .

(d) The question of assistance in building up the Defence Forces of Burma will be a matter for discussion between the two Governments. His Majesty's Government wish to do their utmost to help the Government of Burma in this matter but must have regard to their already heavy commitments in other parts of the world.

(e) The question of the retention or use of any British Forces in Burma after the coming into operation of the new Constitution will be a matter for agreement between His Majesty's Government and the Government of Burma.

8. Frontier Areas. It is the agreed objective of both His Majesty's Government and the Burmese Delegates to achieve the early unification of the Frontier Areas and Ministerial Burma with the free consent of the inhabitants of those areas. In the meantime it is agreed that the people of the Frontier Areas should in respect of subjects of common interest be closely associated with the Government of Burma in a manner acceptable to both parties. For these purposes it has been agreed:

(a) There shall be free intercourse between the peoples of the Frontier Areas and the people of Ministerial Burma without hindrance.

(b) The leaders and representatives of the peoples of the Frontier Areas shall be asked either at the Panglong Conference to be held at the beginning of next month or a special conference to be convened for the purpose to express their views upon the form of association with the Government of Burma which they consider acceptable during the transition period: whether

    (i) by appointment of a small group of Frontier representatives to advise the Governor on Frontier Affairs and to have close liaison with the Executive Council, or

    (ii) by appointment of one Frontier Area representative as Executive Counsellor in charge of Frontier Affairs, or

    (iii) by some other method.

(c) After the Panglong meeting or special conference His Majesty's Government and the Government of Burma will agree upon the best method of advancing their common aims in accordance with the expressed views of the peoples of the Frontier Areas.

(d) A Committee of Enquiry shall be set up forthwith as to the best method of associating the frontier peoples with the working-out of the new constitution for Burma. Such Committee will consist of equal numbers of persons from Ministerial Burma nominated by the Executive Council and of persons from the Frontier Areas nominated by the Governor after consultation with leaders of those areas with a neutral Chairman from outside Burma selected by agreement. Such Committee shall be asked to report to the Government of Burma and His Majesty's Government before summoning of the Constituent Assembly.

9. Finance. A number of financial questions have been considered and an agreement has been arrived as to how these matters should be dealt with. . . .

10. Other matters. A number of other questions will arise for settlement between His Majesty's Government and the Government of Burma connected with the change in the status of Burma. These will be taken up as they arise and will be dealt with in the same friendly and cooperative spirit that has marked the present discussions.

Both His Majesty's Government and the delegates of the Burma Executive Council are convinced that by a continuation of the present method of consultation and cooperation smooth and rapid progress can be made towards their common objective of a free and independent Burma, whether within or without the British Commonwealth of Nations, and they have therefore agreed to cooperate in the settlement of all future matters which shall arise between them through the transitional period until Burma's new constitution comes into operation.

C. R. Attlee,   Aung San
10, Downing Street, S.W. 1
January 27th, 1947.

Annex A. A Burma national is defined for the purposes of eligibility to vote and to stand as a candidate at the forthcoming elections as a British subject or subject of an Indian State who was born in Burma and resided there for a total period of not less than eight years in ten years immediately preceding either January 1st, 1942 or January 1st, 1947.

The Panglong Agreement [February 12, 1947]*

A conference having been held at Panglong, attended by certain Members of the Executive Council of the Governor of Burma, all Saophas and representatives of the Shan States, the Kachin Hills and the Chin Hills:
The Members of the Conference, believing that freedom will be more

* *Source:* Burma, *Frontier Areas Committee of Enquiry 1947: Report* (Rangoon: Government Printing and Stationery, 1947), pp. 16–17.

speedily achieved by the Shans, the Kachins and the Chins by their immediate cooperation with the Interim Burmese Government:

The Members of the Conference have accordingly, and without dis-
sentients, agreed as follows:

1. A representative of the Hill Peoples, selected by the Governor on the
   the recommendation of representatives of the Supreme Council of
   the United Hill Peoples, shall be appointed a Counsellor to the Governor to deal with the Frontier Areas.

2. The said Counsellor shall also be appointed a Member of the Governor's Executive Council, without portfolio, and the subject of Frontier
   Areas brought within the purview of the Executive Council by Constitutional Convention as in the case of Defence and External Affairs.
   The Counsellor for Frontier Areas shall be given executive authority
   by similar means.

3. The said Counsellor shall be assisted by two Deputy Counsellors representing races of which he is not a member. While the two Deputy
   Counsellors should deal in the first instance with the affairs of their
   respective areas and the Counsellor with all the remaining parts of the
   Frontier Areas, they should by Constitutional Convention act on the
   principle of joint responsibility.

4. While the Counsellor, in his capacity of Member of the Executive
   Council, will be the only representative of the Frontier Areas on the
   Council, the Deputy Counsellors shall be entitled to attend meetings
   of the Council when subjects pertaining to the Frontier Areas are discussed.

5. Though the Governor's Executive Council will be augmented as agreed
   above, it will not operate in respect of the Frontier Areas in any manner which would deprive any portion of these areas of the autonomy
   which it now enjoys in internal administration. Full autonomy in internal administration for the Frontier Areas is accepted in principle.

6. Though the question of demarcating and establishing a separate
   Kachin State within a Unified Burma is one which must be relegated
   for decision by the Constituent Assembly, it is agreed that such a State
   is desirable. As a first step towards this end, the Counsellor for Frontier Areas and the Deputy Counsellors shall be consulted in the administration of such areas in the Myitkyina and the Bhamo Districts as
   are Part II Scheduled Areas under the Government of Burma Act of
   1935.

7. Citizens of the Frontier Areas shall enjoy rights and privileges which
   are regarded as fundamental in democratic countries.

8. The arrangements accepted in this Agreement are without prejudice
   to the financial autonomy now vested in the Federated Shan States.

9. The arrangements accepted in this Agreement are without prejudice to the financial assistance which the Kachin Hills and the Chin Hills are entitled to receive from the revenues of Burma, and the Executive Council will examine with the Frontier Areas Counsellor and Deputy Counsellors the feasibility of adopting for the Kachin Hills and the Chin Hills financial arrangements similar to those between Burma and the Federated Shan States.

Until he and several of his colleagues were assassinated by a jealous rival in 1947, Aung San, president of the AFPFL, contributed many ideas as well as his leadership to the nationalist movement. As the nation drew closer to the achievement of independence, it was Aung San who spoke out on constitutional issues and gave direction to the men and women who actually wrote Burma's charter. No complete collection of his works exists.[1] Yet, those speeches that have been published in mimeograph form, and others which appeared in the press when they were given, provide background for the range of ideas and institutions that were incorporated in the constitution. The following are excerpts from two speeches in which Aung San considered the problems facing Burma in his time.

Excerpts from the Speeches of Aung San [1946–1947]*

On Leadership. We have still an arduous way to traverse before we reach our goal. And you want me to pilot you safely to that journey's end! I cannot thank you easily for this gesture of trust and confidence you have reposed in me. I must tell you quite frankly from the outset that I cannot dangle any promise of speedy results or sudden windfall of millennium before you. No man, however great, can alone set the wheels of history in motion, unless he has the active support and cooperation of a whole people. No doubt individuals have played brilliant roles in history, but then it is evident that history is not made by a few individuals only. I have already mentioned to you . . . how history develops as the cumulative creation of generations of men responding to the demands of ever

[1] But see Josef Silverstein, comp., *The Political Legacy of Aung San,* Southeast Asia Program Data Paper No. 86 (Ithaca, N.Y.: Cornell University, June 1972).

Source: Aung San, "Burma's Challenge" (Rangoon: mimeo., n.d.), n.p. These speeches were given before AFPFL conventions on January 21, 1946, and May 23, 1947.

growing logical events. I am well aware that there is such a great craving in man for heroism and the heroic and that hero-worship forms not a small motif in his complex. I am also aware that unless man believes in his own heroism and the heroism of others, he cannot achieve much or great things. We must, however, take proper care that we do not make a fetish of this cult of hero-worship, for then we will turn ourselves into votaries of false gods and prophets. And we have had more than enough of such false gods and prophets for this trouble-ridden world.

On Politics. Some of us have been going, consciously or unconsciously, about the same old way of "dirty" politics. But is politics really "dirty"? Certainly not. It is not politics which is dirty but rather the persons who choose to dirty it are dirty. And what is politics? Is it something too high above us to which we can just look up in respectful awe and from which we refrain, because we are just mortal clay in His hands and cannot do it? Is it, as some charlatans, roaming occasionally about in distant nooks of our country, used to prey upon the credulous imagination of some of our people, the kind of thing capable of being set aright only by fanciful tales and legends? Is it a dangerous ground which we must be wary to tread and might as well avoid, if we possibly could? Is it just a question of "race, religion and language" forever, we were once wont to say? What is it, then, really? The fact is that politics is neither high nor low, neither magic nor astrology nor alchemy. Nor is it simply a dangerous ground to tread upon. It is also not a question of bigoted or parochial nationalism either. It must always approximate the truth of marching events. In short, after all is said and done, politics means your everyday life. It is You in fact; for you are a political animal as Aristotle long ago declared. It is how you eat, sleep, work and live, with which politics is concerned. You may not think about politics. But politics thinks about you. You may shun politics, but politics clings to you always in your home, in your office, in your factories. There, everyday you are doing politics, grappling with it, struggling with it. The worker works for his wages, the peasant tills for his living, the clerk and the official toil for salaries, the trader and broker struggle for decent incomes. It is, all, the question of livelihood. The worker wants to have higher wages and live in better conditions. The peasant desires to improve his land and his lot. The clerk and the official want something more than the drudgery of office, something more secure, more complete, more independent. The trader and broker want fair opportunities for trading and business. Thus you have to live and get certain things that are yours for your living, and this is your politics. This is your everyday life; and as your everyday life changes, so changes your politics. It is for you to have such opportunities for your livelihood and better life that we say there must be freedom, freedom to live, freedom to create and develop nationally and individually, freedom which can raise your and our standards without affecting others! And this is politics. Politics, then, is quite human! It is not dirty. It is not dangerous. It is not parochial. It is neither magic nor superstition. It is not above understanding.

On the Separation of Religion and Politics. Politics is religion! Is it? Of course not. But this is the trump card of dirty politicians. In this way, they hope to confuse and befog the public mind, and they hope to slur over and cloud real issues. There is the way of opportunism, not politics. Religion is a matter of individual conscience while politics is a social science. Of course as a social science, politics must see that the individual also has his rights, including the right to freedom of religious worship. But here we must stop and draw the line definitely between politics and religion, because the two are not one and the same thing. If we mix religion with politics, this is against the spirit of religion itself, for religion takes care of our hereafter and usually has nothing to do with mundane affairs which are the sphere of politics. And politics is frankly a secular science. That is it.

On Nationalism and National Unity. What then constitutes nationalism? The main factor is the having to lead together one common life sharing joys and sorrows, developing common interests and one or more common things like racial or linguistic communities, fostering common traditions of having been and being one which give us a consciousness of oneness and the necessity of that oneness. Race, religion, and language are thus by themselves not primary factors which go to the making of a nation but the historic necessity of having to lead a common life together that is the pivotal principle of nationality and nationalism. Nowadays, with the increasing mutual intercourse of nations, there is such a provision in many of the constitutions of the world for naturalisation of foreigners. As I see it, at one time nationalism took a centrifugal turn, as races streamed off from the main stock and family, and now the process seems to be otherwise, it seems to be taking a centripetal course. So our conception of nationalism must move, change and rise with the times. Otherwise we will stew in the juices of parochial nationalism or even jingoism which finally will spell our nation's doom as in the case of Germany.

On Building a True Democracy. Economic principles are the underlying basis of political conception. Politics is inseparable from economics. A capitalist democracy may deny it. But when we study profoundly the constitutions of the world we find economic laws immanent in them. Capitalists may argue that capitalism is the last word in the sphere of economic truth. But no political or economic system can be permanent. They change with circumstances. As for Burma, she has to rise from a position of subjection which is even worse than capitalism. We must first rise from subjection before we can get over capitalism. Meanwhile we can and must control and restrict capitalism. Only by building our economic system in such a way as to enable our country to get over capitalism in the quickest possible time can we attain a true democracy.

How shall we lay the foundations of such a democracy?

(1) Ways must be found that will lead to the nationalisation of important industries and means of production.

(2) Workers must have definite rights regarding their working and living conditions, health, social insurance, etc.

(3) Land must be in the hands of those who work the land and there must be no large-holdings whatsoever.

(4) Various national minorities must be able to enjoy proper rights due to them.

(5) There must be provisions which will enable the people to exercise their power effectively.

(6) There must be provisions for the fundamental rights of citizens irrespective of race, religion or sex.

(7) Defence of the country is the responsibility of the people's State. There should be no necessity for any volunteer organisation to exist apart from the organisations of the State.

(8) The judicial system should be founded on popular conception. Without such fundamental principles no true democracy can be attained. Built on such foundations and in time the noble edifice of true democracy will stand for all the world to marvel.

On Nationalisation and Socialism. Nationalisation means that the state in the name of the people must own major means of production, transit and distribution, such as land, natural resources (forests, mines, oil), electricity, rail transport, air transport, post and telegraphs, telephones, wireless, etc. And as far as possible, co-operative societies must be enabled to own their enterprises. The state should run national enterprises and utilities. Even if it cannot run them yet, they may be leased to others for exploitation on advantageous terms. Foreign trade must be under government control. All this will be to ensure that the benefits of our economy will accrue to the people themselves. Otherwise the capitalists will manipulate business as they please and re-establish the old evils of monopoly and exploitation. If business and commerce, prices and markets are at the mercy of capitalist enterprises it will turn out that we are encouraging monopolist economy, which had but yesterday produced that hateful monster of fascism. Therefore we must clearly prohibit such capitalist and private enterprises as monopolies, cartels, syndicates and trusts.

Now you will want to ask, "Isn't it socialism which you are propounding?" Not quite. In fact, however anxious we may be to set up socialism in our country, her present economic position is such that socialisation at the present stage is by no means possible. Even capitalist enterprise cannot be on a proper basis. We are a step below that stage. That's why we will still have to countenance capitalist enterprises. Naturally, then there will be a certain amount of proprietorship and private enterprise. But where we can, we must control and restrict the operations of such enterprises in the interests of the community. Proprietorship and private enterprises must not harm the masses. Having to countenance capitalist enterprise we have to make sure that provision is made in our draft constitution to give full protection to labour from exploitation by capital, clearly setting out their rights.

In addition to writing a constitution that provided for a parliamentary system of government and a federal pattern which allowed the states the right of secession, one of the last acts performed in 1947 by the Burmese, prior to assuming the burdens of political independence, was to draw up an economic plan for the development of the nation along moderate socialist lines. The inspiration for the plan came from Aung San, and it reflects many of his ideas both about the state of Burma's economy and the mixed approach the nation would have to follow. A number of problems prevented the plan from being implemented, including Aung San's death, rebellion by the Communists, Karens, and several other groups, a shortage of competent administrators, and a lack of knowledge about the real state of the economy. But the plan was important for two reasons: It was the product of Burmese thought, not of foreign economists, and it conveyed the optimism of the nation's leaders at a time when they believed it possible to realize their goals in a reasonably quick and efficient manner.

The Two-Year Plan of Economic Development for Burma [1947]*

During the period in which she formed a part of the overseas dominions of Britain, Burma [was] the scene of intense economic activity in certain

* *Source: Two-Year Plan of Economic Development for Burma* (Rangoon: Government Printing and Stationery, 1948), pp. 1–31.

spheres. Thus, her paddy lands were extended at great speed until within less than half a century she became the biggest exporter of rice in the world. Oilfields of respectable size and production were developed; lead, silver, tin and other minerals were mined in large quantities, and the forests contributed in a great measure to the national wealth. But this period was dominated by the ruling doctrine of laissez-faire, and the nature and extent of the economic development was determined almost exclusively by the self-interest of foreign capitalists and entrepreneurs. Hence the paradox that while the national wealth of the country undoubtedly increased . . . the lot of the villager remained unchanged and he continued to exist just beyond the starvation level and to live in squalor and extreme poverty. While public wealth increased, the material conditions of the people saw little improvement.

Our destiny is once again in our hands and with it the opportunity of developing an economy suited to the needs of the country and the genius of our people. Political independence has been won after hard and prolonged struggle and the supreme sacrifice on the part of many, and it is now the duty of the nation to consolidate that independence and extend it to the economic sphere—to create an economy which will ensure that a fair share of the fruits passes on to the common man. This Plan of Economic Development for the first two years of our independence is drawn with a view not merely to speed our recovery from the devastation caused by war but also to lay the foundations of a balanced economy and increase our national wealth in a manner which will secure for the villager a higher standard of living than has been his lot hitherto.

The lethargy of a hundred years cannot however be shaken off overnight, nor can the pattern of colonial economy imposed upon us for a century be transformed completely within a period of two years. The world-wide shortage of materials and technical personnel will act as a continuous drag on any programme of development that may now be embarked upon, and the full realization of the policy of economic development . . . must thus be preceded by a large amount of preparatory work in the form of economic and scientific research, investigations into the sources and scope of our national wealth, training of personnel and above all the creation in the masses of an attitude of mind inducive [sic] to hard work and whole-hearted co-operation in the task of improving their material condition. The Plan therefore provides for the maximum development which Government consider practicable during the next two years, bearing in mind our limitations of men and resources; and— equally important—for laying the foundations of a planned economy and for transforming Burma into a country where the Welfare of the common man constitutes the main motive of State activity. The Plan is not ambitious, and does not cover every sphere of our economic activity. There are obvious gaps and lack of definiteness in many of the objectives. But conditions essential to the evolution of a comprehensive and fully co-ordinated plan of economic developments—e.g., data relating to our natural resources, expert personnel and knowledge, administrative organization, etc.—are sadly inadequate, and it will take years to remedy these deficiencies. Independent Burma cannot however wait for the removal of these handicaps before stating her main objectives and taking the first steps towards achieving them. The present short-term Plan of Economic Development provides for a programme of activity which if carried out faithfully will not merely secure a substantial increase in our national wealth but start the country on the path to evolving a socialist economy where every son of the soil will have equal opportunity to live a full life and no section or individual will be exploited for the benefit of another. The actual developmental work proposed is important, but the successful completion of the surveys, investigation, research and training provided for is equally essential and vital from a long-term point of view. Both parts require equal emphasis and the same firm determination to see them through no matter what the odds. The Plan defines the initial steps that must be taken for consolidating economically the independence which we have won and for the achievement of which so many of our leaders have laid down their lives, and it is the duty of every section of our people to co-operate in its fulfilment.

The policy of Government in regard to Agriculture is three-fold:

(a) To secure a re-distribution of the agricultural land of Burma with a view to eliminating land-lordism and return alienated land to the peasants and to prevent the peasants from further alienation of land which, if allowed, would fall into a vicious circle.

(b) To evolve an agricultural economy which will ensure that land is cultivated and organized on modern and scientific lines and that the cultivator, who constitutes 65 per cent of Burma's population, gets a fair share of the produce of the land, is protected against the caprices of a fluctuating market and ultimately achieves a standard of living which will enable him to live a full life and enjoy the amenities of modern civilization.

(c) As an immediate target, to increase agricultural production so that Burma will recover her pre-war position as an exporter of rice in the shortest possible time and become self-sufficient in as wide a range of other crops as possible.

The Industrial Development of any country must ultimately be determined by the nature and extent of her natural resources, but the most striking feature in relation to our country is the sad inadequacy of the knowledge we possess thereof. A complete survey of our natural resources is therefore a prime necessity, and our ultimate industrial policy can be formulated only in the light of knowledge acquired by such survey.

Immediate steps must however be taken in regard to the rehabilitation of existing industries and the setting up of such new industries as are feasible on the basis of raw materials already known to exist in economic quantities.

The profit motive and other considerations which usually govern industries in capitalist economy shall not be allowed to determine the development of basic industries in Independent Burma. All such industries shall be established and developed as State enterprise. In regard to consumer goods industries, the profit motive and what is described as "the free choice of Consumers" may be allowed greater freedom—to an extent compatible with the basic features of the Plan. First consideration shall however be given to their development on a state-owned basis, and only if this is not practicable for any reason shall private enterprise be allowed to play a part. It is however essential that development by private enterprise is regulated in a manner which will ensure that it is in consonance with the interest of the country. For this purpose legal powers to control and direct the setting up of industries by private enterprise will be necessary and this question shall be examined and necessary legislation enacted by June 1948. The legislation shall provide for association of indigenous capital, training of indigenous personnel, both technical and administrative, adoption of processes and means of production suited to the genius of the people, avoidance of over-concentration in certain areas leading to unbalanced development, and prevention of undue competition to the detriment of the interests of the country.

The implementation of Government's policy of industrialization with a view to developing a balanced economy in Burma and utilizing to the full our vast natural resources requires as a necessary and indispensable corollary that adequate measures are taken in advance to train in sufficient numbers technicians of all grades to man the industries, and to create amongst the people of Burma a scientific and technical attitude of mind. Foreign experts can of course be obtained for industries and work where highly specialized training and experience is necessary; such experts are in fact essential if industrialization is to be achieved on a sound and scientific basis. But no industrial enterprise can be manned entirely by foreign personnel, neither would it be in the interest of the country to do so. Indigenous personnel must be trained on scientific and adequate lines for all grades and sectors of industries, and the evolution and execution of a scientific plan of technical education must thus form an essential part of our plan of economic development.

II. Problems of National Unity and Political Stability

In the decade following Burma's declaration of independence on January 4, 1948, her leaders were confronted with a series of challenges to their authority, which dimmed their optimism about the benefits to be derived from parliamentary democracy. The Communist party, later known as the White Flags, revolted against the state in March. A large segment of the People's Volunteer Organization (PVO), a paramilitary force created by Aung San during the struggle for independence, joined the Communists. Shortly thereafter, dissident elements among the Karens, Mons, and other ethnic minority groups took up arms against the government and the Communists and the PVO. In an attempt to stem the growth of anarchy, Prime Minister U Nu offered a "leftist unity program," which, if it had been accepted by the rebels, might have paved the way to a rapid adoption of socialism. Perhaps the most controversial element in the program was point 15, which stirred so much unrest that Nu abandoned it when he repeated his offer at a later time. For an appreciation of Burma's policies and plans during the decade of constitutional rule, U Nu's program should be viewed as a pragmatic effort to prevent the disintegration of the Union and not as a rigid manifesto of a dedicated ideologue.

U Nu: Leftist Unity Program [May 25, 1948]*

When pondering over the problem of national unity, I wondered what programme was appropriate and feasible for the welfare of the masses of the people of the Burma Union in the circumstances of the present day, in what way the united strength of Leftism in the country could achieve that programme, and how the unity of the whole people could be built round that Leftist unity. I pondered on these and on other points, bearing in mind always that Leftist unity is not to take the place of national unity but should be the keystone of the arch of national unity.

The chief factor in the problem of unity, I felt, is the determination of a programme . . .

(1) To secure political and economic relations with Soviet Russia and

* *Source:* U Nu, *Toward Peace and Democracy* (Rangoon: Ministry of Information, 1949), pp. 92–94.

the democratic countries of Eastern Europe in the same way as we are now having these relations with Britain and the United States.

(2) To nationalize monopolizing capitalist undertakings, and to administer the resulting national undertakings by partnership between the State and the workers, to secure a living wage, to limit the working day to 8 hours, to ensure the right of association and the right to strike, and to institute old age pensions and other social benefits, the question of compensation to be considered only after these undertakings have been nationalized.

(3) The State to take into its own hands . . . all foreign trade.

(4) The transfer to Burma of the Currency Board now continued in London.

(5) The refusal of any foreign aid of a kind which will compromise the political, economic and the strategic independence of Burma.

(6) To transform the Army of the Union into a People's Democratic Army. . . .

(7) To abolish private ownership of land and to distribute the land only among the tillers of the soil.

(8) To draw up a plan for the industrialization of the country with a time-table and to begin work on it at once.

(9) To establish peoples' governments in the Frontier Areas.

(10) To transform the present bureaucratic machinery of administration into a democratic machinery.

(11) To abolish all repressive laws.

(12) To unite in a counter-attack against the attacks which are being launched by capitalists against the standard of living and the privileges of workers, to make wages commensurate with the high cost of living, and to protect the privileges of employees of Government together with the privileges of other workers.

(13) To unite with and to assist poor town dwellers and oppressed members of the middle classes in securing a reduction of house rents and house taxes, in the securing of house sites, in the formation of co-operative societies and in the destruction of black markets.

(14) The Leftist organizations to secure the assistance of the State, to take the lead and to work with other organizations in the cause of compulsory education, of physical health and of culture.

(15) To form a league for the propagation of Marxist Doctrine, composed of Socialists, Communists, Pyithu Yebaws and others who lean towards Marxism and to read, discuss and propagate the writing of Marx, Engels, Lenin, Stalin, Mao Tse-tung, Tito, Dimitrov and other apostles of Marxism.

[Under pressure from domestic and foreign sources alike, Nu later explained point 15 as follows.*]

(a) In the propagation of the writings of Marxist authors, such as Marx himself, Engels, Lenin, Stalin, Mao Tse-tung, Tito, Dimitrov, the work will not be undertaken either by the Government or the AFPFL Headquarters as such, nor is it intended that Marxism should be forced on the whole of the masses. It will be for the Socialists, the Communists, the Pyithu Yebaws and others who favour the Marxist doctrine to engage themselves on the task of propagating it.

(b) Burma having been established as a democratic country, those who favour anti-Marxist doctrines will have full freedom to propagate their views in the same way as the followers of Marxism will be free to propagate their own views.

I believe now that I have said enough to explain the whole matter. Therefore, in order to be able to build quickly a new world for the masses,
"Let us cease all disorders!
Let us build quickly the edifice of Leftist unity."

In the Korean war, Burma's leaders found still another issue which threatened the country's unity and stability. Burma's policy of neutrality in her foreign affairs is based on several assumptions, including the belief that war does not solve problems between nations, that alignment will compromise a small nation's independence and freedom of action, and that the maintenance of peace is essential for successful development. In keeping with this, Burma has been an active supporter of the United Nations, especially because it serves as a forum for the peaceful settlement of international disputes and has at least the potential to intervene in order to halt aggression. For a number of leftist members of the AFPFL, however, Burma's support of the United Nations' resolution, which approved the Security Council's invocation of collective security measures against North Korea, represented an intolerable departure from nonalignment. Their criticism of this policy resulted in their expulsion from the AFPFL and their formation of the Burma Workers and Peasants party (BWPP), which became the first major opposition the AFPFL had to face in parliament. U Nu's defense of the policy in parliament on September 5, 1950, provides an excellent insight into Burma's position in international affairs.

* Source: Ibid., p. 138.

*U Nu: Why Burma Supported the United Nations
on the Korean Question* [September 5, 1950]*

Both the Union Government and the AFPFL were influenced by three
factors in supporting the United Nations Resolution.

These are: first, the need to protect the Union from aggression; secondly, the Government's policy of non-partisanship; and thirdly, fair
deal. Let me amplify these factors.

Mr. Speaker, Sir, since the regaining of our independence, defence
has been our sole responsibility. . . . It is up to the nationals of the
Union to shoulder this burden. Once it rests on our shoulders, we must
be fully conscious of its magnitude. It will be evident that the responsibility is not small. To begin with, we were left with a depleted force
when the British left. . . .

In the circumstances, it won't do to simply stare at this state of affairs
and tremble. If only we are in right earnest to maintain our independent
status, we must do something to defend our hearths and homes against
aggression. When we seek solution to the problem, we are confronted
with two alternatives.

The first alternative is to expand our fighting forces—land, navy and
air—to cope with our requirements. The second alternative is to join a
world organization which can guarantee us protection in the event of
aggression. It is not an easy task to expand our fighting forces. The first
obstacle is money. Experts in this field will tell us that we need crores
and crores of rupees to augment our fighting strength to the required
standard of efficiency. Even if we spend all our revenues for that sole purpose for a period of twenty years successively, we may have a fairly strong
(I do not mean a really dependable) defence force. Even with such a
force built up for twenty years we cannot expect to feel secure. Of course,
we will be militarily stronger but still our defences will not be strong
enough to stem determined aggression. The explanation is that we are a
nation of only 17 million people. Nations across our borders can boast of
populations ranging from forty to four hundred millions. To think of successfully stemming the aggression from such quarters is simply impossible.

Therefore, it is evident that however much we may expand and
strengthen our fighting forces, we will not be in a position to protect
our independent status effectively.

The second alternative, in the circumstances, is to join an organization
which can come to our aid in time of need. In the present world set-up

* *Source:* U Nu, *Peace in One Year* (Rangoon: Ministry of Information,
1951), pp. 97–100.

there are two blocs: the Anglo-American bloc and the Soviet bloc. Our policy of non-partisanship precludes us from joining any of these two power blocs. The right course and the only course for us to take is to join the United Nations Organization. This organization is not backed up only by one or two countries. It is formed by all those countries which abhor aggression and which are determined to suppress aggression in any part of the globe. By joining this organization, we cannot be dubbed as joining the Anglo-American bloc nor the Soviet bloc. We have joined this organization without prejudice to our declared policy of non-partisanship and with the full conviction that this organization will be able to offer protection to the attacked country in the event of aggression. We lost no time in joining it after we regained our independence. I am sure the Hon'ble member will appreciate our primary objective of joining the United Nations Organization.

Mr. Speaker, Sir, when we joined the great organization . . . what was foremost in our thoughts was the expectation of United Nations assistance when our country is subjected to aggression by a stronger power. We have pinned our faith to the United Nations Organization on that score. With this advantage in view, we felt a reciprocal obligation to contribute our mite to the United Nations when that great organization tackles any aggressor in any place at any time.

Therefore, we have come to realize our responsibility to come to the aid of any attacked country in whatever way we are capable of—morally or physically at any time in any place, because we expect reciprocal help from others in our hour of need. These considerations have compelled us both in the capacity of Government and of the Executive Council of the AFPFL to back up the United Nations Organization in its endeavours to stem aggression.

So far as I can see it will never do for us to try to be too clever and sit on the fence. If we are foolish enough to try that sort of trick, we ourselves will find ourselves face to face with aggression some day. Mind you, aggression now-a-days is no longer the same as the open conquest of the simpler days of old. Aggression has become insidious and subtle. First they will aid and abet their agents among us to stage an armed rising. Then they will have it declared that such and such places have been captured by the insurgents. Then they will have it declared that the people of that place have set up their own government. The next step is to recognize the rebel government and make a secret pact of mutual military assistance. Choosing a favourable moment when the lawful government is preoccupied, the aggressor will publicise some such pretext as oppression by the Government and come to the assistance of the rebels. Their agents, their fifth columnists and their spies will shout loudly that their comrades have liberated Burma and thus put an end to our freedom. That is roughly their procedure. Very practicable. And there are even more subtle methods.

A small, weak nation like ours, how so ever we strengthen our defences, can never successfully defend ourselves alone. Fortunately there is a world organization to prevent aggression, the United Nations, of which we became a member. To be quite frank I was not free from doubts at first although we have become a member. Will the United Nations be a repetition of the League of Nations? Will the member nations only think of their own safety and leave the smaller nations to their fate in the event of aggression by a powerful nation with whom they wish to remain on good terms?

Korea has dispelled these doubts. There may or may not be other motives. But it is a fact that as soon as aggression started in South Korea the United Nations went to its assistance. This has set up a noble precedence. Henceforth, if aggression occurs elsewhere, there too the United Nations must step in. They simply can't get out of this responsibility. This is the great hope, the only hope for small member nations like us. We decided that if Burma was threatened with aggression too the United Nations would come to our help. It is only fitting that Burma wholeheartedly supports the United Nations in the step they have taken in South Korea. That is why both the Government of the Union of Burma and the supreme council of the AFPFL supported the United Nations Security Council Resolution.

The other principle on which we acted was the Government's policy of non-partisanship. To be outspoken, this policy will appeal neither to those who are infatuated with the Anglo-Americans nor to those who are infatuated with Soviet Russia. Nevertheless Government must steadfastly pursue this policy of non-partisanship. . . .

. . . Once Burma has taken sides with either the Anglo-American bloc or the Soviet bloc she must support the side taken in any and everything right or wrong. We will have no choice. That is a position we must never fall into. Our conviction is that in this world there is nobody who is always wrong or always right. To err is human. One will be right sometimes, and sometimes wrong. Nobody can say that the Anglo-Americans are never wrong either politically or economically. Similarly, no one can say that Soviet Russia is never wrong. Therefore we cannot allow ourselves to fall into a position in which we must blindly support any country or countries right or wrong. We do not ever want to be in such a position. If we consider that a right course of action is being taken by a country we will support that country, be it America, Britain or Soviet Russia. If wrong we must object, whichever country it may be, in some way or other. Although a small country, we will support what is right in the world. Let us be destroyed in the effort but let it be said of us by posterity that we were a people who did right. In order to be able to do right we cannot allow ourselves to be absorbed into any power bloc. That is the first point regarding our policy of non-partisanship.

One of the more difficult problems with which the Constituent Assembly dealt while writing the 1947 constitution concerned the future status of the Karens. The Assembly was unable to resolve this problem to everyone's satisfaction, and, in order to complete its work on the constitution, it sought a compromise: It guaranteed the creation of a Karen state at some time in the future when a greater measure of support for one could be found; in the meantime, it accorded the Karens a number of special rights which it hoped would at least temporarily placate them. The Assembly miscalculated, however, for soon thereafter the Karen National Defense Organization (KNDO) revolted. Following a number of unsuccessful attempts to quell the KNDO by military means, the parliament in 1951 acquiesced in the Karen demand for a separate state of their own. Karen dissatisfaction has not been relieved, however, for in their view the state is not economically viable and the dominant Burmans continue to encroach on their way of life. By 1970, the Union army had still not found success from its efforts to suppress the KNDO insurgency completely.

The parliamentary debate in 1951 on the constitutional amendment permitting the establishment of the Karen state provided U Nu with an opportunity to discuss the question of majority–minority relations and to state the government's position on the issue of national unity.

U Nu: The Karen State Constitutional Amendment [October 8, 1951]*

Mr. Speaker, Sir, after this declaration in respect of areas I want to make another clear-cut declaration in respect of rights. And that is: Please choose whichever you like, either the Karen State or the Minority Rights. It is absolutely impossible to choose both.

I have to make this clear-cut declaration despite our wish to treat our Karen brothers liberally, despite our fear of appearing to exercise majority pressure. Far be it from us! But the moment we give the Karens

* *Source:* U Nu, *Burma Looks Ahead* (Rangoon: Ministry of Information, 1951), pp. 14–17.

both a Karen State and Minority Rights we shall be face-to-face with problems impossible of solution in practice.

For instance, Mr. Speaker, Sir, residing within Burma proper are many Shans and Chins. For long they have been agitating for Minority Rights such as the Karens are enjoying in the absence of a distinct Karen State like the Shan States. We have to assuage those Shans and Chins by pointing out that the Karens are enjoying those rights because the Karens have no Karen State such as the Shans already have and the Chins can have very easily. If the Karens continue to enjoy Minority Rights even after a distinct Karen State has been formed, the Shans and Chins will naturally want to know why they cannot do so too. Not only they, the Taungthus, the Was, the Lahus, the Ikaws, the Yawyins, the Nagas, and endless others will start demanding Minority Rights. . . .

. . . So long as we allow this spectre of Minority Rights to continue in our midst, so long shall our efforts to achieve unity and national solidarity be of no avail. Therefore, for the sake of national solidarity, so dear to the hearts of all the nationals within this Union, I appeal to the Karens to relinquish Minority Rights when they accept the Karen State.

. . . Mr. Speaker, Sir, I might explain at this point that the Constitution has made provision for the Rights of Equality and Freedom; Rights relating to Religion; Cultural, Educational and Economic Rights. These Rights will continue to be enjoyed even by the smallest minority. By the term Minority Rights I mean those so-called Rights which entice members of the Union to dismember themselves with separate elections. . . .

Mr. Speaker, Sir, I need hardly say that this Union of Burma belongs equally to all nationals, Shans, Chins, Kachins, Karens, Karennis, Mons, Arakanese, all. Although the Burmese are the majority people they are not a people to misuse their majority. They do not subscribe to ideologies of imperialism, exploitation, violence and banditry. Nowadays it will be hard to find among us even a handful who know no better than to cling to such outdated ideologies. And that handful, I assure you, are now far away from positions of power and authority.

Mr. Speaker, Sir, we Burmans nowadays have learnt our lesson. Our eyes have been opened. We know very well that the Shans, the Chins, the Karens, the Karennis, the Mons, the Arakanese and others—if we can't win them over to our side, they will be won over to THEIR side. We have realized that if we fail to persuade them to look to us, they will look to THEM. Unless we endear them to us, they will be enamoured of OTHERS. From personal experience as well as from lessons of history we have learnt that because of going away from fellow nationals and falling into the arms of strangers we have met the fate of a herd divided when the tiger pounced, of a nation enslaved. We must never let our brother nationals go away from us. And if we do not want our brother nationals to go away from us, we must not try to be clever with our brother nationals. We know that. And we know we must not take advantage of our majority and use any pressure. We want to have and will strive to keep our brother nationals permanently by our side. Only, I appeal to the Karens, who still harbour in their minds any misunderstanding and mistrust of us, to harbour them no more. Whatever we do, I assure you, we shall never do anything that will disunite us and lead us back to slavery. When I say we, I mean we, the whole Burmese people, except that mere handful of traitors who are now looking beyond their natural father for a bastard's father.

During the first decade of her independence, Burma's greatest problem was widespread insurrection of the hill peoples and, consequently, a breakdown of law and order. Perhaps no one was more conscious of this problem than the prime minister, U Nu. He spoke of it frequently, sometimes interpreting it allegorically in the hope that the people would understand better the danger which the absence of stability posed to the country's future.

U Nu: On Revolution [March 27, 1953]*

Once, there was an addle-pated simpleton called Pho Agyi. He was so bereft of intelligence that even Mr. Zeros will have to take off their hats to him. One day Pho Agyi became so hungry that he went in search of a house where he could get some meal. Finding some villagers assembled in a funeral house, he went in and broke into a loud guffaw. When questioned by the relatives of the deceased why he was so merry while they were mourning, Phi Agyi replied that he did so because he wanted a meal. The chief mourner scolded him for his silly indiscretion and told him that if he really wanted a meal he must weep. And he gave Pho Agyi some food to eat. The mourner's intention was to teach him decent ways of human conduct but Pho Agyi, the addle-pated simpleton, took to heart only one lesson: to weep when he wanted a meal, without considering the circumstances. He was elated with the thought that he had got an unfailing open sesame for meals.

At another meal time he walked along the village road and came to a wedding. With the set formula in his head he entered the place and without uttering a single word, he wept. The merry audience at the

* *Source:* U Nu, *Forward with the People* (Rangoon: Ministry of Information, 1955), pp. 10–12.

wedding considered it a deliberate attempt to wreck the auspicious
ceremony and beat him. Pho Agyi explained to them that he wept because
he wanted food. The merry crowd blamed him for his silliness and told
him that he must sing and dance if he wanted a meal. And they fed him.

Pho Agyi had not sufficient intelligence to grasp the meaning of this
lesson. He did not for a moment think why he must sing and dance in a
particular set of circumstances if he wanted a meal. To him a formula
is a formula irrespective of the circumstances and the great lesson he
learned was to sing and dance when he wanted some food.

In another moment of hunger he roamed about the village and came
upon a man and his wife quarrelling furiously. With the newly acquired
lesson firmly fixed in his head, Pho Agyi sang and danced before the
angry couple who suddenly stopped their quarrel, turned on him and
struck him without mercy. Dazed, Pho Agyi explained to them that he
sang and danced because he wanted a meal. The couple told him that if
he wanted a meal he must separate the two who were quarrelling. Pho
Agyi learned a fresh lesson that if he wanted a meal he must separate the
two when they were found quarrelling. Oppressed by hunger he continued
his journey until at last he found two buffaloes furiously goring each
other. In his attempt to separate the two, poor Pho Agyi was gored to death.

I consider that the reason why our country is suffering from one
trouble after another is no other than the fact that it is ridden with Pho
Agyi of all hues who do not attempt to assess a problem with due consideration to circumstances and who have not the ability to assess even if
they want to.

They do not understand the significance of the term "Revolution" and
therefore they fail to see against what ideology or institution the Revolution should be directed. They are also at a loss to understand the actual
method of Revolution. Like Pho Agyi, one set of formula is nailed to their
empty heads: Revolution is armed rising and those who take up arms
"agin" something or somebody are real revolutionaries.

At the outset, I have posed the question "What is Revolution?" I have
given my answer as "Revolution is no other than a sincere effort to uproot
all those factors—ideologies, thoughts, organizations or the machineries
of Government—which are opposed to human progress and mental and
physical well-being of mankind." Who, I wonder, can dispute the correctness of my answer? I am firmly convinced that the correctness of this
answer is indisputable. On this criterion let us examine the correctness or
otherwise of those so-called revolutionaries who consider that their wild
actions are in fact "Revolution."

How can the people of a war-devastated country attain progress and
mental and physical well-being by undergoing insurrection? How can loot-

ing of treasuries, wanton destruction of railways and of bridges, collecting forced "donations" from undefended villagers create human progress and mental and physical well-being? A man cannot just become a saint by merely declaring as such. His work will show him up whether he is a saint or not. Although he may profess to be a saint, if he steals, loots, or plunders, he will be just a thief, a robber or a dacoit. In the same way, those who destroy railways, burn bridges and villages and demand forced "contributions" from defenceless villagers are nothing but the most abominable reactionaries although they may style themselves as revolutionaries.

The third element in the triptych of Burma's problems during 1948–1958, in addition to unity and stability, was the economy. In the midst of a semi-war and majority–minority disputes, her leaders were hardly able to address themselves to the tasks of rebuilding a war-ravaged economy, developing the country's resources, training the people, or coping with an expanding population. The record of economic accomplishment during these years was not a bright one, but, as U Nu reported to the people in 1957, it provided valuable lessons which might be used to avoid errors in the future.

U Nu: Premier's Report to the People [1957]*

Mr. Speaker, Sir, what were the lessons of our experience these past years?

1. First, we have learned that without the complete restoration of law and order our efforts at economic and social development cannot fully succeed. However hard we try, our energy and material resources in large part will be wasted, and go down the drain.
2. Second, we have come to appreciate more clearly the importance of the basic sectors of our economy. Agriculture, timber and minerals must be restored to at least their pre-war output before satisfactory gains in other important sectors of the national economy can be made and sustained.
3. Third, we have learned that new industrial ventures require intensive preparation, organization, supervision and management in order to be successful. Technical and economic studies must be made. Manpower must be found. Careful co-ordination must be provided so that the projects may go forward on all fronts in an orderly way. Skilled man-

*Source: U Nu, *Premier's Report to the People* (Rangoon: Director of Information, 1957), pp. 20–21.

agement must be found for their operation. In many cases domestic raw materials must be developed. . . . Labour must be trained, efficiency must be achieved, proper accounting systems must be introduced, marketing methods must be developed, distribution must be worked out. Our small group of able and trained people, while having to cope with all these tasks in the industries we have already undertaken, have not been able, at the same time, to plan and initiate activities for the further expansion of state-owned and operated industries.

4. A fourth lesson which has come home to us with increasing force in recent years is the fact that the morale of our public servants has deteriorated very considerably, and that until radical steps are taken to improve this morale, all efforts of Government toward economic and social betterment must be badly retarded by this factor.

5. Fifth, for a variety of reasons, efficiency throughout the Government's operations, and particularly in the State-owned Boards and Corporations, is at a very low level. This means that costs are far higher than they should be; that revenues are lower than they should be; that prices to consumers are higher than they ought to be; that where moderate profits should be enjoyed, losses are incurred; and that where large profits might be expected, only very small profits are received. Obviously, strenuous efforts are called for to achieve higher levels of efficiency.

6. Sixth, and closely related to some of the lessons I have already mentioned, is the realization that too much centralization is a bad thing. Over-centralization of authority and responsibility for the Government's far-flung activities means the hopeless overburdening of a relatively small number of people at the very top who cannot give adequate time and attention to the many problems involved, which range all the way from questions of major policy down to the smallest detail. It has become quite clear that if the Government apparatus is to function smoothly, and if our efforts at development are to go forward unhampered, there must be far more decentralization and delegation of authority and responsibility than has been the case till now. At every level of execution and management, there must be exercised that degree of authority and responsibility which is appropriate to the level concerned. Officers at every level must exercise judgment and initiative. We cannot afford to have officers at any level fearful of making decisions appropriate to their office, and passing responsibility for such decisions as these up and up for approval by higher authority before acting, until they reach the very highest levels of Government. This is managerial constipation.

7. Seventh, we have learned that Government just cannot undertake responsibility for everything that needs to be done. Ways and means must be found to permit or encourage or assist the private sector to do things which are necessary, and which the private sector is capable of doing. No Government can do everything. It was our inclination, when we saw a need for something to be done, to think first in terms of having the Government do it. We must change this thinking. We believe the Government should undertake only those tasks which are appropriate for the Government to undertake, leaving other tasks to co-operative organizations and the private sector.

8. The eighth lesson is that if we are to invest for economic and social development, and if we are at the same time to avoid inflation, the people of the country must contribute in reasonable degree to the financing of this investment. Only two-fifths of our capital outlays in the four years ending 1955–56 were financed by taxes and other current earnings of Government. Of the remaining three-fifths, one-fifth was financed (a) by a sizeable reduction in our foreign exchange reserves; and (b) to a limited extent by reparations, loans from abroad and private savings in Burma; and (c) almost two-fifths of the total by an increase in the domestic money supply—in other words, by deficit financing. For the next few years, as matters have stood till now, we could anticipate an even smaller relative contribution toward planned capital expenditure from taxes and other current earnings of Government. We shall have to rely in very large measure on reparations and on foreign loans. But it is also imperative that we contribute more out of current taxes and earnings of Government if we are to avoid inflation. We can do this by improving the efficiency of our Government enterprises and of our tax collections, and by stimulating private savings. To some extent we shall have to do it also by increasing some tax rates or by introducing some new tax measures.

9. Still another lesson we have learned is the importance of a high level of availability of goods for consumers' use both through increased domestic production and increased imports, to counteract the otherwise inflationary influence of large-scale Government expenditures for development, and the need for improved efficiency in the distribution of those goods.

10. Finally, but in a somewhat different category from these lessons I have mentioned, is the recognition that our educational system must be basically improved, that the periodic and costly fire scourge must be eliminated, and that the city of Rangoon must be rehabilitated.

In enumerating thus the lessons learned from experience in recent years, it will be clear that this is equivalent to saying, we have made many mistakes. There will be some, no doubt, who will attempt to make political capital out of this admission. This does not worry me. First, if we have made mistakes, the honest thing to do is to admit them. We will never try to conceal them. Second, it is natural for a young government to make mistakes. Only in this way is it possible to learn. The only way to avoid mistakes is to make no decisions and attempt no improvements. But such a do-nothing policy would be the greatest mistake of all. Third, we are learning from our mistakes, and correcting them. Fourth, we are not the only government which makes mistakes, as can readily be demonstrated.

. . . Those who compare the inefficiency of State Enterprise with the efficiency of private enterprise should remember that not all private enterprise is efficient. The so-called profit system is really a profit-and-loss system, and the system is not free of losses. I do not wish to condone our inefficiency, or our other mistakes. I merely wish to place them in proper perspective. Of course we must correct our mistakes. It is unfortunate that they were made. But let us not regard them as unnatural or calamitous. Let us rather be thankful that we can perceive them, and take vigorous and constructive action to correct them.

Before 1958, the AFPFL dominated Burma's political scene. But as a coalition of ethnic groups, mass organizations, independent members, and at least one party—the Socialist party, which provided it with leadership and ideas—the AFPFL was riddled by long-term personal antagonisms and rivalries, structural defects, and corruption. Moreover, its failure to bring about national unity and political stability had created in the people a weariness and disenchantment with the AFPFL. For a time after the 1956 elections, U Nu relinquished the premiership in order to devote himself to reorganizing the league, purging it of corruption, and restoring harmony among its many factions. In this he failed. The dénouement of the AFPFL came at its third congress in January 1958. In his presidential address, U Nu laid down the goals of the party and what it must do to attain them—principles which had been accepted by all factions prior to the congress. The meeting was dominated, however, by the rivalry of factions for power and control, and four months later the AFPFL split into rival parties, neither of which had sufficient support in parliament to continue to govern.

U Nu: The President's Report to the Third All-Burma Congress of the AFPFL [January 29, 1958]*

. . . So far, there has been no AFPFL Congress at which the Goal of the AFPFL has been stated clearly and approved. Because of this absence of definite statement and approval of "Our Goal," we find that there is increasingly confusion within the AFPFL, as to the ideology or guiding political philosophy that the AFPFL should have. . . . Therefore, I have dealt at length with this point, what should be the Goal of the AFPFL, to wipe out the variety of views on our goal, our policy and our programme. . . .

Comrades, what is the political philosophy, or ideology, of the AFPFL? The AFPFL ideology or political philosophy is neither Communism nor State Capitalism, but Socialism.

What is the Goal of the AFPFL? The Goal of the AFPFL, is to build a Socialist State.

What kind of a State is the Socialist State which is the Goal of the AFPFL? The Socialist State which the AFPFL will create must be a State free from exploitation, injustice and oppression; [and] must be a State which can fully guarantee fundamental rights, economic security, a high standard of living, firm morality, opportunity to practise religion in a positive way over and above mere religious freedom, maintenance and preservation of our traditions, culture and heritage.

What is our policy and our programme for achieving this Socialist State? We have openly and publicly declared that the Socialist State we will create must not be one that is forced on the people of the country, but one which will command the hearty support and co-operation of all the people in the country. Since this is the case, our policy and programme cannot be anything else but to seek a mandate from the people through democratic means, and to build a Socialist State according to that mandate.

. . . Comrades, to make Democracy stand steadfast and lasting, two things above others are needed:

(i) Ability to restrain and discipline oneself, and
(ii) A spirit of sacrifice, which keeps one always ready to make sacrifices for the good of others.

Comrades, the above self-discipline and a spirit of sacrifice are more

* *Source:* Ministry of Information, *Burma Weekly Bulletin* (Rangoon), February 6, 1958, pp. 376, 382.

essential to members of the AFPFL than to others, for as members of the AFPFL, we hold political power. Power is dangerous, especially to its possessors, whom it can fully destroy. Therefore, those who are members of the AFPFL must be extremely careful lest they become fascists and dictators. If the AFPFL which has assumed upon itself the duty of defending democracy should ever become a fascist organization, or a league of dictators, we shall fall from public regard and shall float sorrow-stricken and helpless, in the sea of spit spat out by the people as a gesture of contempt.

Therefore, I exhort all members of the AFPFL to exercise self-discipline beyond all others, and to be ready to make more sacrifices than all others, for the good of all.

Comrades this part of my speech is of great importance to the future of AFPFL. Therefore, I request you to listen with care.

An Editor, whose newspaper always criticizes the Government with furious indignation and bitterness, recently uttered priceless words of wisdom to me and two other leaders of the AFPFL. He said, "Newspapers cannot destroy AFPFL. The opposition cannot destroy AFPFL. Only the members of the AFPFL can destroy AFPFL." In this matter, I am in full agreement with the Editor.

Let me repeat. No newspaper can destroy AFPFL. No opposition member can destroy AFPFL. So long as able men and good men remain in the AFPFL, no one can destroy it.

The AFPFL has been in power for many years now and to make matters worse, it has not been possible to call General Conferences like this regularly. As a result many members of the AFPFL, including myself, have become negligent in character and conduct, perseverance, [and] public relations.

III. The Military Caretaker Government

The fragmentation of the AFPFL in 1958 set the stage for a major political crisis. One of the factions, known as the Stable AFPFL, was eager to topple U Nu's government and take power. In a special session of the parliament in June, Nu and his group, the Clean AFPFL, narrowly won a vote of confidence, but only because they were backed by the National Unity Front (NUF), a coalition of small opposition parties, and the minorities. U Nu was uncertain of this support, however, and felt that when the time came to present his government's budget the tide would turn in his rivals' favor. To avoid this, he persuaded General Ne Win, the head of the army, to form a caretaker government whose task it would be to restore order and prepare for new elections. Ne Win accepted on the condition that the parliament would vote him and his colleagues into office and would continue to sit while the military regime managed the country.

Shortly before the disintegration of the AFPFL, the military had prepared itself for an emergency in which it might have to play the role it was now being called upon to accept. The commanders of the armed forces had formulated their own version of a national ideology in which they expounded on the nation's political and economic goals and the special role of the military. The first of these goals, which are discussed in the following excerpts from the military's exposition, was the restoration of peace and the rule of law, and when the Ne Win government took office in October 1958 its actions were directed immediately to the achievement of this objective.

The National Ideology and the Role of the Defense Services [1959]*

. . . The Union of Burma has passed her eleventh year as a Sovereign Independent Republic and is now entering her twelfth year. In the early days of Independence hopes were bright in the hearts of all citizens of the Union that, free at last, they would enjoy the fruits of this freedom to the utmost. They thought to themselves: "Now free from anxieties over food, clothing and shelter, we shall be able to go in peace to work or to our pagodas and monasteries. Far, far better is our lot now than when we were subjects under imperialist rule." So they hoped and their happiness knew no bounds. But these hopes were soon drowned in a sea of trouble, and a sense of insecurity overwhelmed them.

Having won independence, why were they denied the fruits of freedom? On September 24, 1947, the entire Union, including the Karenni State and Frontier Areas, unanimously adopted and enacted the Constitution of the Union of Burma. Burma was declared a Sovereign Independent Republic on January 4, 1948. Three months later the Burma Communist Party, which earlier had adopted the Constitution along with other political parties, chose to make its bid for power through armed violence. Their fellow-travellers—the Red Flag Communist Party of Burma, the People's Comrade Party, and the racial autonomists like the KNDO's, MNDO's and Mujahids—seized the war's legacy of arms throughout the country to start an armed insurrection. A country-wide struggle began

* *Source: Is Trust Vindicated?* (Rangoon: Director of Information, 1960), pp. 535–537, 539–541.

between the forces of evil, who would set up a one-party dictatorship by force of arms, and the forces of democracy, who would establish a parliamentary government. At the beginning, the forces of evil outnumbered the defenders of the Constitution by more than ten to one. But "Right" proved to be "Might" and one by one the strongholds of the insurrectionists fell to the Defence Services, whose strength was the strength of the people.

The Defence Services are not an upstart organization newly formed after Independence. Neither is their leadership. These Defence Services fought in the vanguard of the pre-Independence struggle, and following Independence they gave an estimable account of themselves against the forces of evil. Under loyal and heroic leadership they have always been staunch defenders of freedom and democracy for the Union. As long as this strength remains, the Constitution shall remain inviolate. The conviction has hardened in the minds of the people that the armed insurrectionists and racial-autonomy rebels shall never be allowed to impair the Constitution. Throughout the struggle for independence the slogan has been:

"Freedom—first,
Democracy—second,
Socialism—third."

Twelve years of our Independence have been dissipated in fighting the evil forces of one-party dictatorship and racial autonomy. Even in the preoccupation of this grim struggle, the Defence Services have recognized the need to discuss and, subsequently, to adopt the National Ideology, which must be their guiding light in the first phase of ideological development. Now the time has come to determine precisely and clearly the Role and the Attitude of the Defence Services in the second phase of ideological development. For the Defence Services simply to accept the National Ideology without giving thought to their Role or defining their Attitude is to develop a strategy without devising the tactics. There is no obscure political meaning in the words "Role and Attitude." What will the Defence Services do in the event of national crisis—what help will they render, what action will they take—what attitude will they adopt? The answer will be determined by the Role and Attitude.

In view of the problems facing the nation, our national objective should be:

To restore peace and the rule of law—first,
To implant democracy—second,
To establish a socialist economy—third.

This too is the objective of the Defence Services—or their Role and Attitude.

The three sections of the above programme are interdependent. To establish a socialist economy, democracy is pre-requisite. For democracy to flourish, law and order is essential. Without peace and the rule of law, no country can be a democratic one. In an undemocratic country, a socialist economy can never be established—a totalitarian government will impose only a rigid economic system which will deny the right of private property.

The most pressing fundamental need of the Union is law and order. A country may possess natural resources and the means of production; and in accordance with the strength or weakness of these, it may prosper or not. Its people, in any case, will desire to live and work in peace and freedom under a lawful government, for no one chooses to live under a reign of violence and lawlessness. As Burma is still an under-developed country, her standard of living, health, education, economy, social services, etc. are all in need of vast improvement. Plans for improvement are recognized as part of the national programme, but our initial efforts must concentrate on the restoration of law and order throughout the country.

In a country where people dare not shout "stop thief," where the wife of a murdered man dare not lament loudly, where a woman being raped dare not scream for help, in such a country to talk of "democracy" would be foolhardy. To talk of a "welfare state" would be empty vaunting. Like in the realm of Pagan, once upon a time, a giant tiger, a giant roe and a giant wild boar had terrorised the population; criminals, dacoits, rapists and armed insurgents had terrorised the people of the country. Taking advantage of the raging insurrection, miscreants had a field day fishing in troubled waters both in towns and villages. Under the circumstances, if one asks a country lad what is it he desires most, his answer can readily be guessed. He would be content if there was peace in the countryside and not having to pay a multiplicity of extortions; if he was able to live without fear of oppression, being injured and insulted, robbed, murdered in bed.

As the Role of the Defence Services, for the moment, is to rally to the help of the country in her most dire need, their first thought should be "What shall we do about it?" To be short and to the point, the Role and the Attitude of the Defence Services today should give first priority to the objective of Peace and the Rule of Law.

Therefore, to conclude and by way of emphasis, the Defence Services have now unanimously adopted, as the second phase of ideological development, the resolution that the National Objective and Programme of the Defence Services are,

(1) To restore Peace and the Rule of Law,
(2) To implant Democracy,
(3) To establish a Socialist Economy.

. . . If the question arises as to "Why a socialist economy?" reference can be made to the Constitution, as has been done in the case of Democracy. The economy as envisaged in the Constitution has all the aspects of a socialist economy.

On January 4, 1948, the day Burma achieved its independence, the President of the Union addressed the Parliament, outlining the national economic policy as set forth in the Constitution: "The primary policy which will be unremittingly pursued is to establish the Union of Burma as a Socialist State which implies prohibition and abolishment of capitalism and the right to ownership of the means of production by the people themselves. This policy, however, does not involve in any way the unlawful expropriation of property from the hands of their owners but is aimed at the happiness and prosperity of every individual without distinction. A country can be said to be truly great if there are no class discriminations and all share alike in harmony in her general prosperity."

The first address of the first President of a new sovereign Republic is a fundamental document of the greatest import. So also is the Constitution and the Declaration of Independence. The Defence Services must cherish and preserve these fundamental documents of the Union of Burma. This is likewise the first duty of every citizen of the Union. Having then established Democracy as a political reality in the Union, with the same zeal and determination shall we strive to develop a socialist economy.

A socialist economy aims to build up a society in which there will be no exploitation of man by man. It hopes to realize, with the direct participation of all free and fair-minded people, a society in which the goal is the happiness and prosperity of every individual without discrimination. It aims at sufficiency for all, solution of the unemployment problem, economic development, productivity, and equitable distribution of the produce of the country.

A socialist economy does not cater to the narrow and selfish interests of a minority group or party or class but directs its productive forces to fulfilling the needs and assuring the contentment of all citizens.

A socialist economy is a "planned economy." Each stage in the nation's economic development is projected with a view to rendering the greatest good for the greatest number.

In the process of developing and consolidating the means of production, it may become necessary to nationalize certain industries and enterprises. Co-operative societies and joint-venture operations will also have their place in a socialist economy.

This does not prohibit private enterprise. On the contrary, it is declared in Sub-section (1) of Section 23 of the Constitution: "Subject to the provisions of this section, the State guarantees the right of private property and of private initiative in the economic sphere."

In fact, any enterprise will be encouraged which does not contravene Sub-section (2) of Section 23 of the Constitution: "No person shall be permitted to use the right of property to the detriment of the general public."

The Union's economy is based on agriculture, but the methods of production are outmoded, and consequently our productive capacity is limited. Small industry is not sufficiently developed to provide adequate consumer goods for all citizens. Therefore, the main feature of the national economic policy should be to modernize the basic agricultural economy and, secondly, to develop local industries commensurate with the natural and human resources of the country. This will require deliberate and thoughtful planning. In the process of development, this State-controlled economy may appear to differ little from state capitalism. But it should be noted, at the same time, that the State will continue to encourage those private enterprises which contribute to increased national productivity.

In sum, the socialist economy of the Union of Burma is to be a productive economy whose goals will be achieved in accordance with respect for individual economic rights and the guiding principles of the Constitution. It will not evolve into a totalitarian form of exploitation.

The goal of a socialist economy is to free men from anxieties over food, clothing, and shelter. The responsibility of a socialist economy is to do so without depriving them of their constitutional rights.

At present such a socialist economy is not yet within reach. The task facing us now is to establish Peace and the Rule of Law so that Democracy may flourish.

Without Peace, without the Rule of Law, without a democratic government, without development of the nation's productive forces, a socialist economy is an impossibility.

But the nation must look forward to the establishment of a socialist economy, for only then will the Union enjoy prosperity for all its citizens. Therefore, having once achieved Peace, and the Rule of Law, and Democracy, and successfully maintaining these, the Defence Services have unanimously resolved to march unswervingly with the nation towards the goal of a socialist economy.

Most commentators on the caretaker regime have remarked its conservative nature and its success in preserving the constitution, contributing to the growth of honest and efficient government, restoring law and order, and cleaning up corruption in the major cities. But few, if any, have given more than passing attention to its efforts to bring the dissident minorities into the national fold. In 1959, one such attempt resulted in an agreement by which the *Saophas* in the Shan and Kayah states surrendered their hereditary powers to the governments of their respective states in exchange for a monetary payment. With this, the military hoped to strengthen resolution of the problem of national unity. A number of these chiefs, however, later tried to recover their powers and a few went into open revolt. Still others organized a political movement advocating greater autonomy for the states within the federal structure, and they threatened to organize a secessionist movement if their demands were not met. The problem grew in scope and intensity after the restoration of constitutional rule under a civilian government in 1960, and it was the major reason for the military's seizure of power in 1962. The agreement between the Shan state government and the *Saophas* and General Ne Win's optimistic commentary on it are reproduced below.

Agreement between the Shan State Government and the Saophas [April 24, 1959]*

This Agreement is made the 24th day of April 1959 between the Government of the Shan State represented by the Head of the Shan State and the Saopha of Mongnai State, hereinafter referred to as the Saopha.

Whereas in the immediate and the best interests of the Mongnai State and its people as well as of the Government of the Shan State, the Saopha of Mongnai State is desirous that the administration of the said State should vest solely in the Government of the Shan State without any reserve of power, authority or jurisdiction in favour of the said Saopha.

And whereas the Government of the Shan State and the Government of the Union of Burma welcome the said transfer of power, authority and jurisdiction.

It is hereby agreed as follows:

ART. 1. The Saopha of the Mongnai State hereby transfers to and vests in the Government of the Shan State all his powers, authority and

* *Source:* Ministry of Information, *Burma Weekly Bulletin,* May 21, 1959, p. 37.

jurisdiction in relation to the Government of his State as from the 24th day of April 1959.

ART. 2. In consideration of the said transfer the Saopha shall be entitled to receive as his commuted pension an outright payment of the sum of K6,62,385 (Kyats Six Lakhs Sixty-two Thousand Three Hundred and Eighty-five only) free of all taxes.

The amount so paid is intended to cover payments by the Saopha to his relatives of such sums of money and in such manner as he may think fit in lieu of pension received by them prior to this Agreement. The said amount is also intended to cover expenses for the maintenance of the Saopha's personal body guards (if any) maintained by him.

ART. 3. Without prejudice to any future amendment of the Constitution of the Union of Burma, the Saopha shall be entitled to enjoy the use of the title of Saopha.

ART. 4. The Saopha shall subject to law be entitled to the full ownership, use and enjoyment of all his private properties . . . belonging to him on the date of this Agreement as distinct from the properties . . . of the Mongnai State. . . .

ART. 5. No enquiry shall be made by or under the authority of the Government of the Shan State and no proceedings shall lie in any court in the Shan State against the Saopha in respect of anything done or omitted to be done by him in bona fide exercise of his powers, authority or jurisdiction as Saopha or under his authority as such during the period of his administration of the Mongnai State.

ART. 6. Except with the previous sanction of the Government of the Shan State, no criminal proceedings shall be instituted against any person in respect of any act done or purported to be done in the exercise of his duties as a servant of the Mongnai State before the day on which the Saopha transfers the administration of the said State to the Government of the Shan State.

ART. 7. (1) The Government of the Shan State hereby guarantees either the continuance in service of the permanent members of the Mongnai State Services on such conditions as are not less advantageous than those under which they were serving before the 1st June 1959 or the payment to them of reasonable compensation.

(2) The Government of the Shan State further guarantees the continuance of pensions and leave salaries sanctioned by the Saopha to members of the Mongnai State Services who have retired or proceeded on leave preparatory to retirement, before the 1st June 1959. . . .

Ne Win: On the Introduction of Popular Government in the Shan State [April 29, 1959]*

Since Independence, the Union has been endeavouring to set up and foster genuinely democratic institutions and ways of life. During the period, the Union has also been attempting to implement the aims and objectives of the Union Constitution. The defence of the Constitution also has been an important preoccupation of the Union since Independence. In thus forging its way ahead on the path of progress through democracy, an obstacle which has been obstructing its course has been removed today. This day therefore deserves to be recorded in the annals of the nation as an especially auspicious day.

The Preamble to the Union Constitution reads:

"WE, THE PEOPLE OF BURMA, including the Frontier Areas and the Karenni States, Determined to establish in strength and unity a SOVEREIGN INDEPENDENT STATE, To maintain social order on the basis of the eternal principles of JUSTICE, LIBERTY AND EQUALITY and To guarantee and secure to all citizens social, economic and political JUSTICE; LIBERTY of thought and expression, belief, faith, worship, vocation, association and action; EQUALITY of status, of opportunity and before the law, IN OUR CONSTITUENT ASSEMBLY this Tenth day of Thadingyut waxing, 1309 B.E. (Twenty-fourth day of September, 1947 A.D.) DO HEREBY ADOPT, ENACT AND GIVE TO OURSELVES THIS CONSTITUTION."

The above terms set down the firm resolution of the Union to accept genuine democracy alone as the basis of its guiding principles.

The time-worn feudal system of rule by hereditary Chiefs in the Shan State has been in existence until today. Therefore in view of the terms of the Preamble to the Constitution which mentions a dedication to democratic principles there would seem to have been a divergence between theory and practice. Sections 154 (2) and 183 (1) of the Constitution under the provisions of which the feudal states have been allowed to exist, also therefore were clearly at variance in spirit with the fundamental concepts underlying the Union Constitution.

These two Sections by the anomalous character of their provisions had made a travesty of the whole Constitution. It is therefore necessary for me to relate the incidents and considerations which had influenced the inclusion of these two Sections in the Constitution.

During the country's struggle for Independence, General Aung San

* Source: Is Trust Vindicated?, pp. 558–559.

and his associates were beset with diverse problems and difficulties. They were confronted with the hardest of these problems when the British attempted to break up the unity of the nation by weaning away the Hill peoples from the peoples of Burma proper.

The British had been planning to grant freedom only to Burma proper and they intended to retain the Hill Tracts under their rule. If this plan should not materialize, their alternate scheme was to attempt to win over the Hill peoples by promising them membership in the British Commonwealth. The British worked assiduously towards those ends. They exploited the comparative lack of political acumen of the Hill peoples and achieved a certain measure of success in alienating the feelings of these people away from the Burmese people of Burma proper.

General Aung San and his associates had to tax their ingenuity considerably in order to remove the suspicions and misunderstandings sown in the minds of the Hill peoples by the British. As a price for achieving unity of all the indigenous races of the country, General Aung San had to concede to the wishes of the Saophalongs and had to guarantee them their accustomed hereditary rights and privileges. Special Sections were included in the Constitution which provided for the exercise of their hereditary rights. Similar arrangements were also made to safeguard the rights and privileges of the Saophas of the Kayah States.

Although the various Chiefs, at that stage, held political concepts which were none too progressive, General Aung San had felt that, given sufficient time, they would learn to adapt themselves to the changing conditions of the times. When that would happen, General Aung San had felt that the Chiefs would of their own accord attempt to remove the offending Sections from the body of the Constitution and they would thus voluntarily divest themselves of their prerogatives.

The resolutions regarding the surrender of hereditary powers by the Chiefs which were passed by the respective State Councils of the Shan and Kayah States during March last, the deliberations of the combined Houses of Nationalities and Deputies in March on the same subject and the splendid co-operation extended by the Chiefs in introducing the new system of Government in the Shan State, all combine to vindicate the decision then taken by General Aung San.

Formerly certain discreditable features of feudal rule and the shortcomings and indiscretions of some of the Chiefs had influenced my attitude towards them. But after witnessing the wholehearted and sincere way in which the Chiefs had set about divesting themselves of their rights and prerogatives, I cannot but entertain great admiration for their spirit. For one thing, had the Chiefs decided differently, various administrative as well as political problems and problems with both administrative and

political implications would have cropped up to poison the relations between the Shan State and the rest of the Union.

Therefore to all the Saophalongs and Saophas who have co-operated in
the introduction of popular Government and who have so magnanimously
given up their powers would belong the full credit for having created the
conditions where the above-mentioned type of problems could not arise.

I would now like to say something about the future of the Shan State.
Now that they have divested themselves of all their hereditary powers and
privileges and have also participated fully in setting up a popular Government, the Saophalongs and Saophas should, in close co-operation with
the people, work diligently for the welfare of the peoples of the Union as
well as the Shan State. I would like to urge them to devote their brains
and their financial resources to the promotion of the social, economic and
industrial development of the Shan State. To the people of the Shan State
also I would like to say this. Because the Saophalongs and Saophas have
given up their powers and are now bereft of all powers you should not
behave disrespectfully towards them on that account.

I would now like to close my speech with the exhortation to you all to
foster and safeguard the Panglong Spirit, to cultivate Union-conscious-
ness, to fight those who would attempt the disintegration of the Union,
to abandon narrow parochial attitudes as regards race and to endeavour
towards the common welfare of the whole of the Union.

IV. National Unity versus Minority Rights

The restoration of constitutional government under civilian guidance
in 1960 did not bring peace and unity to Burma. U Nu's Pyidaungsu
(Union) party won a large parliamentary majority in the national
election in February 1960, and when he took office in April the prospects for his implementing successfully the party's program appeared
to be bright. The program called for the revitalization of democratic
institutions, the establishment of Buddhism as the state religion, the
creation of Mon and Arakanese states, and the elaboration of a plan
for promoting economic and social growth. U Nu's inability to discipline his followers, however, led once again to factionalism, and this
together with a rise in crime and lawlessness weakened his popular
mandate and helped to destroy his position as leader of the party and
prime minister of the government. Moreover, his effort to make Buddhism the state religion stirred grievances among non-Buddhist minorities, which only added to the problems of an already divided nation.

Finally, although he sought to resolve the discontentment of the ethnic minorities, his plan to discuss the future of federalism with the leaders of the minorities appeared to the army as a betrayal of the cause of the nation. Whether in the end U Nu would have been successful in his attempt to unify his countrymen is now a matter for speculation, for on March 2, 1962, General Ne Win and the army overthrew his government by coup d'état.

In the following excerpts from his first address to parliament in 1960, U Nu discusses his government's plans concerning economic development, national unity, and the establishment of Buddhism as the state religion.

U Nu: Address to Parliament [April 5, 1960]*

. . . Burma has just passed through a period in her history which is unique not only in our own experience but that of most other countries in the world.

After long years of suffering and struggling, and the supreme sacrifice on the part of many of our beloved leaders, we emerged as a fully independent nation at the first dawn of that memorable day in 1948. Destiny once again placed complete control of our life and future in our own hands, and we started on our career as an independent nation full of hope for the future. . . .

. . . We achieved much for our people, but failed to achieve much more. We laid the first foundations of a new system of government which would lead our people out of the despondency they had struggled in for many years and help them to find their true stature as a free people, but we failed to complete the structure and to enable that system to spread throughout the entire country and to reach and influence the ordinary lives of our people. Even we who formed the vanguard failed to regulate our own conduct in full accordance with the noble ideals that animated that system.

Then the insurrections intervened, and this great disaster combined with the arrogance, greed and power-madness that gripped many of our leaders, big and small, brought us to the brink of ruin and very close to losing the democratic base of our new Constitution. . . .

Fortunately, however, we survived. As had often happened in our history, we have turned the corner with the essential fabric of our social and political system shaken but unimpaired. The basic ideal of democracy

* Source: Ministry of Information, *Burma Weekly Bulletin*, April 7, 1960, p. 455.

which inspired our Constitution is still alive, ready to be strengthened and developed. . . .

So, Mr. Speaker, we are once again ready to proceed with the task of strengthening the foundations of democracy in Burma, to make it work as a system of government and to make it the sole regulator of our every-day life and conduct. . . .

Mr. Speaker, there are many specific problems in the economic sphere which we must tackle, and . . . we shall carry out our economic policies in accordance with a plan to be evolved on the basis of the following vital considerations:

(a) a proper balance between industry and agriculture;
(b) the extent of direct government participation in economic activity;
(c) protecting the interest of the peasant and the worker;
(d) the ultimate direction of all economic activity to nationals; and
(e) prudent utilization of available resources, both national and foreign, including foreign investment.

We have already given an indication of our attitude to some of these problems, and we have also drawn up certain plans of economic development. . . . We must now enlist the co-operation of all sectors of opinion and we propose therefore to enter into full consultation with all those interested in economic activity—trade and industrial groups, political parties and individuals. We shall submit to them for critical appraisal such plans as we have already evolved. We shall not present them with these plans as something that has already been decided upon. We shall ourselves participate in the discussions with a completely open mind, and we shall accept sound suggestions no matter who submits them. By this democratic process of discussion, consultation and compromise, we shall evolve an economic plan that will satisfy the following six conditions:

(a) a plan that will be in full harmony with our natural resources and available talent—technical, administrative and otherwise;
(b) a plan that will provide full economic security to our people;
(c) a plan that will free national traders and businessmen from the domination of foreigners;
(d) a plan that will fully safeguard the people against profiteering;
(e) a plan that will safeguard the economy against all kinds of smuggling, including foreign currency; and
(f) a plan that will safeguard against the use of economic activity for the aggrandisement of the party, or the personal advantage of politicians.

And we shall implement this Plan to the best of our ability and to the maximum extent possible within the next four years, and in strict accordance with democratic principles.

. . . It will be our constant endeavour to strengthen the ideal of a united Burma which was first evolved at the Panglong Conference and later enshrined in our Constitution—the ideal of a Burma not only of the Burmese but also of the Chins, Kachins, Shans, Karens, Kayahs, Mons and Arakanese—a country where all these elements will be welded into one and in which every citizen will think of himself as a Union citizen, first and last; where every consciousness of a separate race or culture, or of historical differences and animosities, will give way to a consciousness of one's duties and privileges as a citizen of the Union.

Mr. Speaker, a unity of this kind does not require that each group—cultural, national or religious—should sacrifice any of its specific characteristics. In a country with a history, culture and tradition as rich and varied as ours, one must seek unity in diversity, not by making everyone conform to a common pattern. Our Constitution recognizes this fact fully by creating separate States for some of those national groups, and promising Statehood for others provided that there is a true desire for Statehood amongst them. The unity we evolved must be a unity that is in harmony with the desire of the minority groups to retain and develop their special culture and background. A recognition of their special characteristics, and the opportunity to develop their own special culture in full freedom, is in fact essential to the forging of such unity. One can see clear proof of its wisdom if he looks at those minority groups in the Union who already have States of their own, for the sense of unity with other national groups that they now have—the sense of a union consciousness—is much stronger than it has even been before.

Mr. Speaker, we have promised the Arakanese and the Mons separate States, provided there is a real desire for Statehood amongst them. We propose to implement this promise at the earliest possible moment, after ascertaining in a democratic manner whether the people themselves in these areas desire Statehood, and in a manner which will ensure peace, harmony, understanding, happiness and welfare for all who inhabit these areas. We propose to discuss with the leaders concerned the best procedure for ascertaining the wishes of the people.

Mr. Speaker, let me repeat that the creation of a union consciousness amongst all the citizens of the Union—the majority and the minorities alike—is of crucial importance for the stability and the prosperity of the Union, and we pledge to do our utmost in forging such unity and consciousness.

During the ten years that we were in power, we might have omitted to take certain measures in regard to the constituent States which we should have done for their welfare and progress, or we might have taken certain action which we should not have done. I appeal to the constituent States to forgive and forget our past lapses, as we ourselves are determined to forgive and forget any lapses on their part.

We must now get together and work out measures which will promote their maximum welfare and progress, and I promise solemnly from the floor of this House that we shall spare no effort to correct past mistakes and promote the objective I have outlined above. We shall do so in thorough consultation with the peoples and representatives of the constituent States, and in the same democratic spirit of discussion, consultation and compromise that I have emphasized earlier for all our dealings in the future.

. . . We have already promised to make Buddhism the State Religion of Burma in the presence of the Sanghas during the 2,500 anniversary celebration of Buddhism. We propose to implement this promise as speedily as possible. We shall accordingly appoint two commissions—one of Sanghas and the other of laymen—during the present session of Parliament to consider and make recommendations for the achievement of the above objective. The commissions will be required to report before the next session of Parliament, and we shall endeavour to complete action during that session.

Mr. Speaker, let me repeat that the action we shall take to make Buddhism the State Religion will also include measures to protect fully the rights and privileges of the other religions and religious groups in Burma. Their rights are already protected by our Constitution, and I pledge that none of these rights will be infringed by any action we take in order to make Buddhism the State Religion of Burma. The commissions I have mentioned above will be charged with making full recommendations on this subject also.

Among the most important causes of the coup d'état in March 1962 was the military's fear that U Nu's government would not only accord greater autonomy to the dissident ethnic minorities but also grant them the right to secede from the Union. Among the most recalcitrant of the minorities were the Shans, whose leaders met at Taunggyi in February 1961 to formulate their case for greater autonomy. The document they drew up served as a basis for further conferences among the Shans and other hill peoples, which, in turn, led to a federal seminar in February–March 1962 to which leaders from the government and the states were invited to review the workability of the existing federal structure. That seminar was in session when the army staged its coup. The excerpts presented below are taken from a copy of the original document drawn up by the Shans at their meeting in Taunggyi in 1961.

Report of the Union of Burma Constitution Revision Steering Committee for the Shan States [February 22, 1961]*

. . . If we summarize the . . . facts we will see

(1) The Shan peoples had throughout . . . history . . . established a separate independent country publicly.
(2) Because of natural resources in the Shan States they can have economic sufficiency or solvency. It has a separate language and culture.
(3) Because of the 2nd World War experience, the Shan natives had acquired a dynamic political awakening.
(4) Though the Shan States could establish herself as a separate independent State, she joined with Burma proper and wrested Independence. Concluding the Panglong Agreement she laid the foundation for an equal Union.
(5) At the Constituent Assembly, because the representatives from the Shan States were bent on wresting Independence, because their political experience was young, because they had entire confidence in the integrity and sincerity of Burma's political leaders, they gave their assent to the present Union Constitution very lightheartedly.

The present Union Constitution . . . bristles with several defects and grievances. States . . . enjoy no equal rights with Burma proper. If we will analyse the Union Constitution as a whole we will find that there are defects in (1) the pattern of the structure itself (2) in allocation of power and rights (3) in constituting the Parliament and (4) in allocation of the Union revenues and finances. . . . The States are suffering from loss of rights.

. . . According to U Chan Htoon, the Constitution Architect . . .

"The Chapters setting up . . . States with the concession of the right of secession (under stringent safeguards) were inserted to assuage the doubts of the Frontier leaders rather than to meet actual political and administrative requirements; a form of atonement for that age old suspicion of the Burmese, the hill peoples could not at once discard."

The fact that Frontier leaders wish a genuine Union is not because they

---

* *Source:* From a typescript copy of the original document, which was never published (the author has evidence that the typescript in his possession is an authentic copy).

distrust the Burmese . . . but only because they want to exercise the right of self-determination. . . .

A Union pattern means a Union of States on equal terms. . . . In the present Union of Burma, though . . . States such as the Shan states, the Kachin State, the Kayah State and the Karen State had been formed, Burma proper had not come in as one State. Burma proper was made and bound with the whole Central Union Government. This pattern or Structure alone increases the doubts and distrust of the Frontier Areas peoples against the Burmese.

This pattern or Structure can also be a cause for dissolution of the whole Union one day. Hence in revising the present Constitution, Burma proper must be formed as a separate State of the Union so that a strong durable equal Union will be formed.

In the Union Structure there are two kinds of distribution of powers.

(1) In real Union countries, the Central Union Government is given powers for matters concerned with all the States and the States get hold of other residuary powers and rights.

(2) In Moderate Type Union countries, the States are given specified powers and all the other residuary powers are taken over by the Central Union.

The method desired by Frontier Areas leaders is the real Union Structure. And so the distribution of powers by the present Burmese Union Structure is quite against the wishes of the Frontier leaders.

Because the States are given only restricted powers but all the residuary powers are taken over by the Central Union . . . the Frontier Areas peoples are greatly dissatisfied. They believe that the Burmese are monopolizing the whole. So in amending the Constitution the Central Union Government should be given powers for matters concerned with all the States and the States should be entrusted with all the residuary powers.

In Union Parliaments, the tradition is to form a Lower and Upper House. . . . The Lower House is elected based on populations. The States have rights to send Representatives based proportionately on their populations. To the Upper House, however, the States, whether big or small, have the rights to send an equal number of representatives. The Upper House is formed in this manner to act as a check on the Lower House and to prevent big States from torturing the small ones. In other words, the Upper House is . . . formed to make equal all the States in the Union as well as to protect the rights and privileges of the small States. Then again the two Houses are in principle equal in status, powers and privileges.

However, in the present Union of Burma, the Upper House or Chamber of Nationalities has no equal rights and powers like the Lower House.

The States also have no right to send the same number of representatives to it. As the Union Government also is not responsible to the Upper House but only to the Lower House the former lacks prestige. . . . It has no power . . . to protect the rights of the States. Hence in the Constitution, the constitution of the Parliament must be amended. The Upper House should have equal rights and power like the Lower one and all States should have the right to send an equal number of representatives to it.

Under . . . the present Constitution, the revenues allocated to the States are, excepting land revenue and forest royalties, not very significant. These revenues also do not cover even the current expenditure of the States.

. . . The dissatisfaction entertained by the States regarding revenue distribution by the Union starts from the day of attainment of Independence up to now. No distinct Union financial policy could be laid down up to now. So in a future real Union Constitution, special consideration must be given to and policy laid down regarding the Union financial allocations.

There ought to be special provisions in the Constitution for giving autonomy to all the member-States and for non-interference by either the Central Union Government or the States in the internal affairs of member-States like Burma proper.

As the Burma Union that will be newly formed will be a genuine Union, every State should have a . . . State Constitution, not contravening the Central Union Constitution, and also have a separate legislative council, a separate judiciary and a separate executive government. For peoples who have no right to form separate States, National Areas ought to be formed and the Constitution should contain sufficient safeguards for their rights and powers.

To strictly apply these truths and principles it will not be possible by merely making amendments and improvements to defective Sections in the present Constitution. It will be possible only by overhauling the whole of the present Constitution and making amendments removing errors and ushering in a new Constitution based on a genuine Union Structure.

V. The Revolutionary Council Government

On March 2, 1962, the army eliminated the constitutional government by coup d'état. According to Brigadier Aung Gyi, "we had economic, religious and political crises with the issue of federation as the most important reason for the coup."[2] Since then, the army has struck down the constitution and the institutions it supported, and set up a Revolutionary Council to govern the country. To justify these actions and to provide the government with an ideological base, the army-dominated Revolutionary Council promulgated a declaration entitled *The Burmese Way to Socialism*. This statement, reproduced in its entirety below, presents a critique of parliamentary government as it was practiced in Burma and of the economic system it supported. It also offers the military's alternative approach which, however ill-defined, provides the best guide for understanding their thinking and the goals they seek.

The Burmese Way to Socialism [April 30, 1962]*

THE REVOLUTIONARY COUNCIL OF THE UNION OF BURMA does not believe that man will be set free from social evils as long as pernicious economic systems exist in which man exploits man and lives on the fat of such appropriation. The Council believes it to be possible only when exploitation of man by man is brought to an end and a socialist economy based on justice is established; only then can all people, irrespective of race or religion, be emancipated from all social evils and set free from anxieties over food, clothing and shelter, and from inability to resist evil, for an empty stomach is not conducive to wholesome morality, as the Burmese saying goes; only then can an affluent stage of social development be reached and all people be happy and healthy in mind and body.

Thus affirmed in this belief the Revolutionary Council is resolved to march unswervingly and arm-in-arm with the people of the Union of Burma towards the goal of socialism.

In setting forth their programmes as well as in their execution the Revolutionary Council will study and appraise the concrete realities and also the natural conditions peculiar to Burma objectively. On the basis of the actual findings derived from such study and appraisal it will develop its own ways and means to progress.

In its activities the Revolutionary Council will strive for self-improvement by way of self-criticism. Having learnt from contemporary history

[2] *Guardian* (Rangoon), March 8, 1962.
* *Source: The Burmese Way to Socialism* (Rangoon: Director of Information, 1962).

the evils of deviation towards right or left the Council will with vigilance avoid any such deviation.

In whatever situations and difficulties the Revolutionary Council may find itself it will strive for advancement in accordance with the times, conditions, environment and the ever changing circumstances, keeping at heart the basic interests of the nation.

The Revolutionary Council will diligently seek all ways and means whereby it can formulate and carry out such programmes as are of real and practical value for the well-being of the nation. In doing so it will critically observe, study and avail itself of the opportunities provided by progressive ideas, theories and experiences at home, or abroad without discrimination between one country of origin and another.

The fundamental concept of socialist economy is the participation of all for the general well-being in works of common ownership, and planning towards sufficiency and contentment of all, sharing the benefits derived therefrom. Socialist economy aims at the establishment of a new society for all, economically secure and morally better, to live in peace and prosperity.

Socialist economy therefore opposes any pernicious economic system in which man exploits man, and self-interest and self-seeking are the motivating forces.

Socialist economy does not serve the narrow self-interest of a group, an organization, a class, or a party, but plans its economy with the sole aim of giving maximum satisfaction to material, spiritual and cultural needs of the whole nation.

Socialist economy is the planned, proportional development of all the national productive forces.

"Productive forces" is the collective term for natural resources, raw materials, instruments of production, accumulated capital, peasants, workers, intelligentsia, technicians, know-hows and experiences, skills, etc.

Socialist economy proportionally plans, on the basis of the population and productive forces, for sufficiency and abundance of consumer goods. While improving the standard of living and increasing the purchasing power of the nation it also expands production. Socialist economy thus solves the problem of unemployment and ensures security of a means of livelihood for every individual.

In order to carry out socialist plans such vital means of production as agricultural and industrial production, distribution, transportation, communications, external trade, etc., will have to be nationalized. All such national means of production will have to be owned by the State or co-operative societies or collective unions. Amongst such ownerships State ownership forms the main basis of socialist economy. State ownership means ownership by the whole nation itself, whereas ownership by co-operatives or collectives means group-ownership by respective concerns. But as all forms of ownership will have to operate within the framework of socialist national planning they are interdependent.

In building up an economy according to socialist plans every able individual will have to work according to his ability. The material and cultural values that accrue will be distributed in accordance with the quantity and quality of labour expended by each individual in social production.

In our Burmese socialist society equalitarianism is impossible. Men are not equal physically and intellectually in the respective quantity and quality of service they render to society, and differences are therefore bound to exist. But at the same time social justice demands that the gaps between incomes are reasonable, and correct measures will be taken to narrow these gaps as much as possible.

A socialist democratic state will be constituted to build up a successful socialist economy. A socialist democratic state is based on and safeguards its own socialist economy. The vanguard and custodian of a socialist democratic state are primarily peasants and workers, but the middle strata and those who will work with integrity and loyalty for the general weal will also participate.

Parliamentary democracy called "The People's Rule" came into existence in history with the British, American and French Revolutions against feudalism. It happens to be the best in comparison with all its preceding systems.

But in some countries the parliament has been so abused as to have become only the means by which the opportunists and propertied people deceive the simple masses.

In the Union of Burma also, parliamentary democracy has been tried and tested in furtherance of the aims of socialist development. But Burma's "parliamentary democracy" has not only failed to serve our socialist development but also, due to its very defects, weaknesses and loopholes, its abuses and the absence of a mature public opinion, lost sight of and deviated from the socialist aims, until at last indications of its heading imperceptibly towards just the reverse have become apparent.

The nation's socialist aims cannot be achieved with any assurance by means of the form of parliamentary democracy that we have so far experienced.

The Revolutionary Council therefore firmly believes that it must develop, in conformity with existing conditions and environment and ever changing circumstances, only such a form of democracy as will promote and safeguard the socialist development.

These then are the fundamentals of socialist economy.

In marching towards socialist economy it is imperative that we first reorientate all erroneous views of our people.

Fraudulent practices, profit motive, easy living, parasitism, shirking and selfishness must be eradicated.

We must so educate the people that to earn one's living by one's own labour and to see dignity in one's own work comes into vogue. We must educate, lead by example and guide the people away from the base notion that it is beneath one's dignity to work by the sweat of one's brow.

Attempts must be made by various correct methods to do away with bogus acts of charity and social work for vainglorious show, bogus piety and hypocritical religiosity, etc., as well as to foster and applaud bona fide belief and practice of personal morals as taught by ethics and traditions of every religion and culture. We will resort to education, literature, fine arts, theatre and cinema, etc., to bring into vogue the concept that to serve others' interests is to serve one's own.

In our road to socialism the existing bureaucratic administration is a big stumbling block. To achieve our socialist aims with this effete machinery is impossible. Steps will have to be taken to remove this bureaucratic machinery and lay firm foundations for a socialist democratic one.

The existing Defence Services will also be developed to become national armed forces which will defend our socialist economy.

The Union of Burma is an economically backward agricultural country. The national productive forces need to be continually developed to build up socialist economy. That is why various productions that would be compatible with existing conditions and time will have to be planned and developed. While modernizing the agricultural production which forms the main basis of the national economy such industries as would be commensurate with the natural resources and capabilities of the country will also be developed. In doing so national private enterprises which contribute to national productive forces will be allowed with fair and reasonable restrictions.

On the full realization of socialist economy the socialist government, far from neglecting the owners of national private enterprises which have been steadfastly contributing to the general well-being of the people, will even enable them to occupy a worthy place in the new society in the course of further national development.

As the Union of Burma is a country where many indigenous racial groups reside, it is only when the solidarity of all the indigenous racial groups has been established that socialist economy which can guarantee the welfare of every racial group can be achieved. In striving towards fraternity and unity of all the races of the Union we will be guided by what

General Aung San, our national leader, said at the A.F.P.F.L. conference held at the middle terrace of the Shwedagon Pagoda on January 20, 1946:

"A nation is a collective term applied to a people, irrespective of their ethnic origin, living in close contact with one another and having common interests and sharing joys and sorrows together for such historic periods as to have acquired a sense of oneness. Though race, religion and language are important factors it is only their traditional desire and will to live in unity through weal and woe that binds a people together and makes them a nation and their spirit a patriotism."

We, the peoples of the Union of Burma, shall nurture and hug a new patriotism as inspired by the words of General Aung San.

The Revolutionary Council believes that the existing educational system unequated with livelihood will have to be transformed. An educational system equated with livelihood and based on socialistic moral values will be brought about. Science will be given precedence in education.

Our educational target is to bring basic education within the reach of all. As regards higher education only those who have promise and enough potentialities and industriousness to benefit from it will be specially encouraged.

The Revolutionary Council believes that other social services such as Health, Culture, etc., shall flourish in direct proportion to the tides of socialist success like the lotus and the water's height, and will accordingly work towards this end.

The Revolutionary Council recognises the right of everyone freely to profess and practise his religion.

In marching towards the goal of socialism the Revolutionary Council will base its organization primarily on the strength of peasants and other working masses who form the great majority of the nation. It will march also hand-in-hand with those who will work with integrity and loyalty for national interest and well-being of the people.

The Revolutionary Council will therefore carry out such mass and class organizations as are suitable for the transitional period, and also build up a suitable form of political organization.

When political organizational work is carried out socialist democratic education and democratic training will be given to the people so as to ensure their conscious participation. (The Revolutionary Council believes and hopes that there will come about democratic competitions which will promote socialist development within the framework of socialism.)

The aforesaid are in outline the belief and policy of the Revolutionary Council of the Union of Burma.

The Revolutionary Council has faith in the people, and in their creative force.

The Revolutionary Council believes that the people will, with an active awareness of their duties and responsibilities, play their part in full in this national revolutionary progressive movement and programme under the leadership of the Revolutionary Council.

The Revolutionary Council reaffirms and declares again that it will go forward hand-in-hand with the people to reach the goal of socialism.

Let us march towards socialism in our own Burmese way!

One of the first moves made by the Revolutionary Council to implement its new policies was to create a cadre party, the Burma Socialist Program party or Lanzin, which is organized on a nationwide basis. The following document gives the council's reasons for establishing the new party. Since its creation, all other political groups have been banned.

On the Formation of a New Political Party [July 4, 1962]*

In announcing the Burmese Way to Socialism, the Revolutionary Council has already declared that the Burmese Way to Socialism will be the only practical programme to rehabilitate and develop the greatly deteriorating Union, and also that it would be necessary to build up a suitable form of political organization to implement the socialist programme, hand-in-hand with the people.

In this connexion, the Revolutionary Council has, on three different occasions, explained and discussed its conviction and programme with the leaders of political parties, inviting them to strive together in unity. All the political parties unanimously announced their agreement and support of the socialist programme—the Burmese Way to Socialism—but disagreements and discrepancies emerged from among the political leaders on the question of formation of a Party, thereby unavoidably retarding the efforts of the Revolutionary Council to revitalize the fastly dwindling political prestige in the Union.

The Revolutionary Council now realizes that formation of a systematic Party for the entire nation, and unity and understanding among various political parties with strong partisan outlook could not be achieved at once; and also that members of various parties with diverging views could not be accepted in the proposed Party for immediate assignment.

Under these circumstances, the Revolutionary Council considers that

* *Source: Forward* (Rangoon: Director of Information, July 1962).

sufficient time is needed for the formation of the Party, and that it should start from building up the cadre for the proposed Party, Constitution of which is announced herewith.

It must be admitted that successful implementation of the Burmese Way to Socialism cannot be achieved without hardships and difficulties, despite the support to its principles by the political parties. The Revolutionary Council wishes that members of the political parties would be able to discard their partisan feelings and come closer for unity and understanding through intimate exchange of views among themselves.

In establishing the proposed Party, the Revolutionary Council desires quality above quantity, and accordingly will start with the building up of the efficient Cadre Party. In this process, political parties may provide their sincere and constructive criticism, but the Revolutionary Council urges them to refrain from indulging in destructive measures.

It is in the area of economic policy and development that the Revolutionary Council has made a major effort to change Burma. The steps along its self-designed road to socialism, however, have not adhered to a fixed course, but rather have followed the council's ideological guide. Perhaps partly as a result of this unsystematic approach, successful economic development has not been the hallmark of the council's rule: Economic policies generally have been unpopular; production, per capita income, and foreign trade have declined each year.

The Revolutionary Council's first steps were taken in 1963 when nationalization of the economy was begun. The following news account of this move indicates both the direction and the method of the military government.

Announcement of a New Economic Policy [February 14, 1963]*

Announcing the new economic policy of the Revolutionary Government to Burmese businessmen, industrialists and rice millers yesterday, General Ne Win, Chairman of the Revolutionary Council, said that in future the functions of procurement, production, distribution, import and export of goods would be undertaken solely by the Government.

He gave the assurance that this move to socialise all economic enterprises in the country would in no way result in unemployment of businessmen and industrialists, as their services would be used by the Government

* Source: The Nation (Rangoon), February 15, 1963.

in the very trades and industries in which they were skilled and experienced.

. . . General Ne Win disclosed that the socialist programme of the Government envisaged State handling of all work relating to procurement, production and distribution of goods in the country. The Government would of course undertake the work on behalf of the people, and the profits accruing therefrom would be used for the good of the people.

Similarly, import and export of goods would be taken over by the Government.

. . . "Of course you will not be able to make as much personal profit as you do now as private businessmen, but I can assure you that you will be given all the opportunities to give of your best in the service of the country and to enjoy the fruits of your own labor," he told the gathering.

If however all businessmen could not be absorbed thus in State trading agencies, some of them would be given employment in the field of agriculture or industry, on the basis of their personal qualifications and experience. "When we reach the goal of socialism, all these people will find themselves well established in positions for which they are most fitted and will suffer no hardship whatsoever," he pointed out.

General Ne Win said that in future purchase of rice would be undertaken only by the Union of Burma Agricultural Marketing Board [UBAMB]. . . . Rice-millers would receive milling charges for the paddy milled at their rice mills on order by the Board. But these very rice mills would one day become State-owned property. By that time, rice-millers would be employed by the Government as managers or other officials in their former rice mills or in those of others, or in the Board. The Government would certainly make full use of their knowledge of and skill in the rice trade which far surpassed those of the officials of the UBAMB.

He recalled in passing how rice millers last year failed to give wholehearted co-operation to the Government in an emergency. The [Government] suddenly found itself without rice for shipment abroad and therefore appealed to rice millers, who at that time had large stocks of rice in hand, to help it to tide over the crisis. Rice millers insisted that they be paid transport charges for their rice, which the Government had to concede. The matter ended satisfactorily, but he did not think some rice millers gave all the co-operation that they could, or should. In any case, such unhappy episodes would not recur in the future.

As regards private industries General Ne Win disclosed that henceforth no new private industry would be allowed to be set up.

The Revolutionary Government had at one time considered that a certain sector of the industrial field should be left open to private enterprise, because the State would not be in a position to take over and run all industries in the country. It had since found that such a policy would be detrimental to the country. For one thing, industrialists had been found to be anxious to extend their field, and in attempting to do so, often resorted to bribery and graft, thereby corrupting Government officials in the departments concerned. Therefore, setting up new industries would mean giving an added fillip to the prevailing practice of bribery and corruption.

"On top of this, there is our socialist programme, which demands State-ownership of all means of production. Private industries are therefore theoretically incompatible with this programme, while in practice they have proved to be nothing but a hindrance to our progress to the socialist goal."

For these reasons, he added, permission to set up new private industries would not be given.

As regards existing industries, needed facilities would be given in order to keep on operating. But . . . they too would be taken over by the Government in due course. When that time came, the industrialists concerned would be offered suitable posts in the industrial field. They would decidedly not face unemployment.

Although new private industries would ordinarily be disallowed, the Government would welcome proposals for new and worthy projects from "inventive" private individuals. If the proposed industrial projects were found to be really suitable for the country, the Government would take necessary steps to carry them through. The person who made the proposal would then be given a chance to take part in implementing the project, and would be offered a responsible post for this purpose.

General Ne Win explained that he was making an open declaration of the new policy because he wanted to have a straight and honest deal with businessmen and industrialists. The Government could well resort to tricks —for instance it could permit establishment of private industries now and nationalise them after a period of time, or impose price controls over industrial products, fixing prices at a level unprofitable to the industries concerned, and thereby kill them by a process of slow, languishing financial torture. But such dirty tricks were distasteful to the Government.

General Ne Win then explained at length how corruption was rampant among businessmen, industrialists and Government officials, how foreign exchange was smuggled out of the country through collusion among these elements and foreigners. For instance, some time ago, certain importers remitted foreign exchange abroad but received in return, not commodities, but worthless scraps of paper. Similarly, certain exporters declared as the sale price an amount less than was paid for by foreign buyers. The excess foreign exchange was kept in foreign banks, and was sold at black-market prices to foreigners inside Burma through secret deals.

"Corruption is an evil that exists in almost every country. But people in other countries would pause if their act is likely to harm the interests of their motherland. Those countries are rare in which the people are so depraved as to be unconcerned with considerations of national good. But I am afraid Burma is one of those rare countries."

General Ne Win added that steps must therefore be taken to stamp out corruption, and in this work the Government would need the co-operation of the people.

In conclusion, the General repeated his assurance that although trade and industry would in future be the monopoly of the Government, businessmen and industrialists would suffer no loss of employment or of a decent income. Though there would be no chance to get rich quick as in the past, everyone would have the right to enjoy the fruits of one's labour, commensurate with one's physical and mental efforts.

In 1969 political dialogue finally returned to Burma. General Ne Win authorized the formation of a committee, the National Unity Advisory Board, to study the problem of national unity and to report by mid-1969 on how this problem could be solved. The committee was composed of thirty-three former politicians who represented all segments of legal political leadership prior to the coup. In the committee's report, a majority of eighteen, who were former AFPFL and Pyidaungsu officials, recommended a return to the 1948 constitution with slight modifications. Eleven members, representing the National Unity Front (NUF) politicians, argued for a continuation of the socialist programs initiated by the military and a rejection of any effort to revive the parliamentary system. Finally, a minority of three presented their own views on future relations with the hill minorities.

In November General Ne Win, addressing the Fourth Party Seminar of the Burma Socialist Program party, extensively criticized the 1948 constitution and advanced arguments why, in his estimation, it was defective and had to be replaced. Indirectly, therefore, he was criticizing the majority report of the Advisory Board, touching upon their ideas only to dismiss them. That portion of his speech which deals directly with constitutional and political questions is presented below.

Ne Win: Criticism of the National Unity Advisory Body's
Report [November 6, 1969]*

. . . Now I come to my second point, which is the most important one
for this Seminar. The Revolutionary Council has been holding responsibility for the affairs of the State for seven years and more. Democratic
appearances are absent, and it may look as if the members of the Revolutionary Council are responsible only to themselves. We have yet to openly
seek and obtain the people's mandate. We have to assume the responsibility
and the leadership because the Revolutionary Council was not born of
deliberate design and preparation but was brought into being by dire
necessity.

To put the affairs of State on an enduring constitutional basis, however, a constitution must be framed and time is now ripe for that task.
Only when that basis is laid down will the future generations be able
to move forward in orderly manner, guided by the basic principles, even
after we are gone. When we contemplate the constitution, a reflection on
history becomes pertinent. I shall engage in such reflections only to the
extent that it is relevant, for several people have given their versions of
history at very available opportunity. We ourselves wish to face facts
honestly, and in whatever we do we must make our decisions in the light
of the objective facts. . . .

. . . Before the advent of World War II, to take one instance, Burma
was administered under the 91 Departments Scheme in which the Scheduled Areas, namely the frontier regions of Burma, were placed directly
under the Governor. Their explanation for this was that the peoples of
the frontier regions were backward, and that therefore the personal rule
of the Governor was necessary. The actual fact, however, was that they
wanted to divide and rule, and sow the seeds of dissension for the future
as well. The war came, and the resistance against the Japanese Fascists,
and all along, right through the independence struggle, the divide and
rule tactics, so cleverly employed by the British, worked mischief. In fact,
even today, the problem which they created persists. We must tackle
the problem and solve it smoothly and finally. That was a parting shot delivered by the British before they left, or an evil legacy which still gives
us trouble.

With that observation on political matters I shall rest. Turning to the
economic sphere, the majority of our people toiled in agriculture before

* *Source: Official Publication of Speech by General Ne Win at Opening Session of the 4th Party Seminar on November 6, 1969* (Rangoon: Central Press
for the Burma Socialist Programme Party, November, 1969).

the war. Trade in agricultural products was only nominally in the hands of our people. Indian and Chinese traders engaged in wholesale trade in those products, and sometimes, for some products European and British business also came in. Burmans dealt only with the retail trade. Oil, mineral, forest products, especially teak, and such natural resources were largely the monopoly of British business. What the British farmed out the Indians and the Chinese received. Burmans got the crumbs, if at all. In the import and export trade, the Burmans [were] largely excluded. . . .

. . . When war came to Burma in 1942, politically, we organized the Youth League, the Communist Party, the Revolutionary Party, and led by General Aung San, the armed forces, to launch a resistance movement against the Japanese. Behind these organizations, in supportive roles, were the peasants and workers. In this matter, I want to tell you that when history was written after political splits, self-glorification was resorted to by different parties while the role of the other parties was concealed. History should not be written like this. Truth must be brought out in writing history. The fact that all elements had worked together once should be clearly stated. Splits that had occurred later are another matter. As I have told you, these organizations had made secret preparations and had together successfully resisted the Japanese. Look at the economic situation at that time. Before the war, the Burmans could not do anything by themselves. During the war, the peasants were working in their fields and workers were doing what they had to do. Yet they did not get enough to eat. In the latter part of the period, they had not enough to conceal their nakedness. Even in our army, we had to use blankets for making uniforms for the troops.

We had worked, and produced rice and other products, but the Japanese took them away, leaving us little for our use. We were then reduced to destitution. The Japanese currency was worth something at first, but later when the Japanese issued currency notes without limit, prices of commodities rocketed by the hour. The economic situation during the time of the inflation of Japanese currency was the worst. Trade was limited to an exchange of goods in our hands in a small way. Only a few Burmans who had become Japanese agents got something from their hands as compradores.

If the war had not come to an end in 1945, our nation would not have had enough clothing to cover ourselves. During that period we found in the Delta area some young girls of 15 or 16 who did not have enough to conceal their partial nakedness. One of them was fishing by the side of her father. She could not afford to feel ashamed. When strangers passed by their boats, she slipped down into the water to cover herself, leaving only her head exposed above the water.

When the British returned to Burma, after the war, the Japanese currency notes became utterly worthless. The Burmans had been left with no capital. They found it difficult to do trading. But the British came back with the Simla Plan for continuance of their exploitation. The British took hold of the economic reins in the country, and the Chinese and Indians were made their compradores. There might have been a few Burmans among those who got those benefits. As for the political leaders, they had to concentrate on fighting for independence. Their fight had culminated in a situation in which Bogyoke Aung San was called upon to form the government.

We had then reached a stage in which the revolutionary groups had got their places; they were, in other words becoming persons to be reckoned with. At the same time, the British had been sowing seeds of hatred for the Burmese among the people of the frontier areas. To what extent they had worked successfully and openly in alienating the people of those areas can be seen by a telegram which the feudal lords of these people had sent to London, while Bogyoke Aung San was there to negotiate for independence, to the effect that Bogyoke Aung San was not their representative. To counteract this move by the feudal lords of the frontier areas, the young political leaders of those areas had to call a mass meeting to pass a resolution supporting Bogyoke Aung San. These young leaders made this move not to gain independence for their areas alone but to gain independence for the whole country. Thus, we had to set at naught the attempts of the Sawbwas to shove a wedge between the people of the frontier areas and ourselves. Bogyoke Aung San came back from London with a promise for independence. There were then many further actions to take. What had been worrying our leaders was to get the nationalities of the frontier areas to work hand-in-hand with us for achievement of independence. Bogyoke Aung San and others had to cajole and comfort these people, and their efforts culminated in the successful conclusion of the Panglong Agreement. There had been some bargaining in this matter. That bargaining was manifested in a provision in the Constitution for 25 seats for the Sawbwas in the Chamber of Nationalities. Now, it has been glibly said that that was democracy, but is it genuine democracy? We have heard that there were only 9 real Sawbwas before the War. The rest of their crowd were Myosas and Ngwe-khun-hmus. When the provision was made for 25 seats, these lesser lords were turned into Sawbwas and allowed to occupy these seats. It so happened that every time there were general elections, 25 out of the 33 Sawbwas occupied the 25 seats in rotation.

When we were drawing up the Constitution, the British Government conferred with us about the British capital in Burma. We were then green about such things, having no experience in self-government. So we were not able to strike a good bargain. It is something like a young girl wanting to become a film actress. She approaches a film director who is full of experience. He, the regular rake, says: "Well, I will make you a film actress but you must surrender yourself to my desires." The girl has to agree to that deal because she is so eager to become a film actress. So also, we were so eager to gain independence that we made concessions some of which we knew we should not make. We did not then have any bargaining power. We had, therefore, to agree to paying some indemnity which we knew we shouldn't have paid.

So, now, when we draw up a new constitution, we should recall our past experiences. Looking at the past, we find that our political aim was to establish Socialism. In this reference, when I sought out the papers, I found the President's address to the Parliament at 10 A.M. on January 4, 1948. I am not going to read out the entire speech, but I shall read to you the paragraph referring to Socialism. You can look up this reference later if you want to.

"The primary policy which will be unremittingly pursued is to establish the Union of Burma as a Socialist State which means the elimination of capitalism and the ownership of undertakings by the people themselves. This policy, however, does not involve in any way the unlawful expropriation of property from the hands of their owners but is aimed at the happiness and prosperity of every individual without distinction. A country can be said to be truly great only if there are no class distinctions and all share alike in her general prosperity. . . . It is the aim of my Government to promote the interests of the cultivators and to abolish private ownership of land. It is likewise their aim to promote the interests of the workers and to extinguish capitalism."

Then after the assassination of Bogyoke Aung San, U Nu continued with the work of negotiation with the British Government. At this juncture the British Government made demands for protective measures as regards the British capital. The correspondence between the British Government and the Burmese leaders contains a reply by U Nu, from which I will read out the second paragraph:

"I have however to explain that the undertaking given in the preceding paragraph must be read as subject to the provisions of the Constitution of the Union of Burma as now adopted and in particular to the policy of State Socialism therein contained to which my Government is committed. If however, the implementation of the provisions of Articles 23, . . . 218 or 219 of the Constitution should involve the appropriation or acquisition in whole or in part of existing

United Kingdom interests in Burma, the Provisional Government of Burma will provide equitable compensation to the parties affected."

That was a reply to the British Government's letter purporting to seek protection of the British capital. . . . In that reply, it was mentioned that the Constitution was for adoption of the policy of State Socialism. Although we had talked about adopting Socialism, there was no definite provision for such adoption. There was a vague and ambiguous reference to it in the Constitution. On May 19, 1947, Bogyoke Aung San made a speech. As this is important, I shall read fully. "First, the means of production, such as, timber, minerals, natural resources, marine products, electric energy, railway, air traffic, postal, telegraphic and telephonic communications, broadcasting, will have to be stateowned. Other productive agencies should be owned, as far as possible, by people's co-operatives. Only the works the government cannot possibly manage will have to be managed by persons hired by the government."

Article 219 in the Constitution relates to these natural resources. It says: "All timber and mineral lands, forests, water, fisheries, minerals, coal, petroleum and other mineral oils, all sources of potential energy and other natural resources shall be exploited and developed by the Union; provided that subject to such specific exceptions as may be authorized by an act of Parliament in the interest of the Union, the Union may grant the rights of exploitation, development or utilisation of the same to the citizens of the Union or to companies or associations at least sixty per cent of the capital of which is owned by such citizens." Although it had been said on different occasions that Socialism was the aim and that nationalization would be carried out, there were no provisions in the Constitution. There are only articles 23, . . . 218 and 219 relating to economic rights. Yet when it concerns private business, provision was clearly made for sixty per cent share. I shall not dilate on this, but would request that further study be made especially by the members of the Party. The reference to the exploitation of natural resources has been made, as I have pointed out, in article 219.

Bogyoke Aung San then continued: "The government must control foreign trade, and that is in the interests of the people. Otherwise the capitalists will exploit and control the people. If they go farther to bring about monoply and control all the markets, we would be permitting the return of Fascism which had till lately been much disgusted by the whole world." Though Bogyoke had said so, there was not a word in the Constitution about the control of foreign trade by the Government.

Then he said: "We must preclude the possibility of monopolies, cartels, syndicates or trusts by writing clearly about them in the Constitution. It may then be asked whether we will get Socialism by doing that. No.

However much we want to build Socialism in Burma, the economic conditions will not permit us. We don't have what is really capitalism. Our economic system is just one step backward from capitalism. So we may have to permit capitalism entailing the existence of private ownership and private business. But we must control them as much as we can so that these will not affect the interests of the people. We must have foundations open for the State to take over private enterprise in the name of the people, if and when the necessity arises." We have article 23 . . . in the Constitution which says: "Private monopolist organizations, such as cartels, syndicates and trusts formed for the purpose of dictating prices or for monopolizing the market or otherwise calculated to injure the interests of the national economy, are forbidden." As Bogyoke had said, at that time there was no genuine capitalism. I have also said that before the war, there was no real trade in the hands of the Burmans. After the war, too, there was just a meagre trade. So at that time however eager we might be, we could not introduce Socialism. So private business would have to be permitted with controls, and one day we would have to adopt Socialism. That is what Bogyoke said.

In reference to lands, Bogyoke said: "Those who work on the land must have basic right to the land. Landlordism must, however, be abolished by law. The law will have to limit possession of land by the peasants. The law will have to determine how many acres a peasant should own. Otherwise, it would be reviving landlordism. It would be better if all lands could be worked by the state or by co-operatives. Before that stage is reached, however, all those who work the land should own the land they work. At this stage, the government will have to give the middle class and poor peasants all possible help." In spite of the fact that Bogyoke made his wishes known clearly about peasants, there was in the Constitution a casual mention of it, as in Article 30 "(1) The State is the ultimate owner of all lands. (2) Subject to the provision of this Constitution, the State shall have the right to regulate, alter or abolish land tenures or resume possession of any land and distribute the same for collective or co-operative farming or to agricultural tenants. (3) There can be no large land holdings on any basis whatsoever. The maximum size of private land holding shall, as soon as circumstances permit, be determined by law." So far no action has been taken. There is a phrase which gives them an excuse, and that is, "as soon as circumstances permit." If they did not want to take any action, they would say that circumstances did not permit them. I will tell you what I heard at that time. The persons writing the Constitution gave their lands to monasteries as alms for fear of nationalization.

What I mean to say is that Bogyoke Aung San had also had Socialism as his aim but at that time, circumstances did not favour the immediate adoption of Socialism. It was also not possible to stop all the things that were being done. There was also no appropriate machinery. Therefore, Bogyoke said that questions about lands and about capitalism would have to be kept pending. What I want to tell you is that there were in the Constitution some ambiguous provisions relating to economic rights and nothing whatsoever about Socialism. The reason why it was omitted was probably that while the political leaders were negotiating with the British and cajoling and comforting the people of the frontier areas, the so-called legal experts wrote up the Constitution as they liked. Was it so? If it were so, then the political leaders were cheated. Or it might be that the political leaders themselves had been talking glibly about socialism without any sincere belief in it. That is a question for serious consideration. Were the political leaders cheated? Or, did they themselves not want to write socialism into the Constitution? Constitution-making is an important business. There are, however, some points which are referred to in the Constitution, and rules and regulations will have to be made later with reference to those points.

In this connection I shall read to you article 21 of the Constitution which says: "(1) The State recognizes the special position of Buddhism as the faith professed by the great majority of the citizens of the Union. (2) The State also recognizes Islam, Christianity, Hinduism and Animism as some of the religions existing in the Union at the date of the coming into operation of this Constitution. (3) The State shall not impose any disabilities or make any discrimination on the ground of religious faith or belief. (4) The abuse of religion for political purposes is forbidden; and any act which is intended or is likely to promote feelings of hatred, enmity or discord between racial or religious communities or sects is contrary to this Constitution and may be made punishable by law." This is what the Constitution has clearly said.

It says religion must not be abused for political purposes. If anyone did it, he must be punished, and law must be made to punish him. But nobody ever made that law. Not only that, religion was abused for political purposes. The government of that day did not make any law relating to this matter.

Now, there is another thing. Any member of Parliament could be recalled by his constituency. No law relating to it was made. A review of all matters relating to the Constitution reveals the governmental structure as Parliament, the Cabinet, the President, and the Judiciary. In regard to Parliament, there was no law providing for recall of any of its members by his own constituency, although a provision was made in the Constitution for such a recall. As far as I remember, *Widura* Thakin Chit Maung broached this question in the Parliament but nobody paid any attention to him. Parliament is a body of representatives elected by the people. The party commanding the majority is asked to form the government and the Ministers are first the members of Parliament. But the President and Supreme Court judges were appointed by the Parliament; they were not elected by the people. That is, their appointments were submitted to the Parliament which approved of them.

In this connection, I want to tell you this. Although those who wrote the Constitution had been ambiguous elsewhere, they were definite in matters relating to the President and the judges, because these appointments concerned them. As I have told you, it is not certain whether the political leaders were cheated by these Constitution writers. Powers of the President are enormous. Some of them are quite reasonable. For instance, in times of emergency or when a government could not possibly be formed. But there were other powers which I will not mention here for it would make my speech long. But I shall mention one, that is, article 60 which says: "The right of pardon shall be vested in the President." A man was convicted by a court, let us say he was given a death sentence or a life sentence. He could appeal to the President for clemency and the President could do what he liked. Discretion should be used in using this power. . . .

There is yet another provision of the Constitution which is a definite flaw. That is article 62 which says: "The President shall not be answerable to either Chamber of Parliament or to any Court for the exercise or performance of the powers and functions of his office or for any act done or purporting to be done by him in the exercise and performance of these powers and functions." This would make the President a virtual dictator in certain matters. There are other similar provisions relating to the President but this much will suffice.

The Judiciary is also clothed with similar immunities. Article 81 of the Constitution reads: "No discussion shall take place in the Parliament with respect to the conduct of any judge of the Supreme Court or of the High Court in the discharge of his duties, except upon the resolution for the removal of the judge as provided in this Constitution." Now in the affairs of the State, Parliament should be supreme. Yet the judges were not answerable to Parliament. True, there is a provision for their impeachment by a majority of a joint sitting of both Chambers of Parliament, but that was an elaborate and difficult procedure which placed the judges well above disciplinary action. The impeachment provision was probably put in to preserve appearances; for all practical purposes the judges enjoyed full immunity. This is wrong, for Parliament is the supreme body and the maker of all laws which must have the right to comment on the improper goings-on in the State. But restraints on its power are built into the Constitution itself; do not touch the Judiciary; only the difficult process of impeachment may be used to get at the judges.

. . . The politicians had only independence uppermost in their minds and they were at that time prepared to die fighting for it. They had little experience of the legal niceties involved in constitution-making, and they entrusted that task to the so-called legal experts, who, in my view, manipulated things to their own advantage in some matters. The legal experts were nicely vague when they wanted to be, but precise and clear, as in the provisions relating to the President's powers in article 60.

Take another example, that of the issue of an Ordinance. At any time when both Chambers of Parliament were not in session and the President was satisfied that circumstances existed which rendered it necessary for him to take immediate action, he could promulgate Ordinances. The life of an Ordinance was 45 days, during which it could be withdrawn. If it was not, the Ordinance had to be submitted to Parliament within that time, and Parliament could render it void, but whatever had been done under the Ordinance remained. Similarly with rules made under laws. The rules must be laid before Parliament when their constitutionality could be challenged by a member. The rule could be annulled, but that did not affect the validity of anything done previously under the rule. In my view there was a definite defect in these provisions. If an Ordinance was made at the instance of the Government, or a rule, and the Ordinance or the rule was later annulled by Parliament, would that not be tantamount to a vote of no-confidence in the Government? The Constitution was silent on that vital question. Also note that nothing could be done by Parliament if the Ordinance was withdrawn before the prescribed 45 days ran out.

Thus, the legal experts were less than thorough in the drafting of the Constitution. There might have been many reasons for the defects. The politicians, as I said, were engaged in the political struggle, and in negotiations. The legal experts, on the other hand, almost seemed to have done their work light-heartedly. A careful study of the Constitution reveals many serious shortcomings. When we frame a new one, we must be more careful.

I have spoken about the special powers reserved for the President, such as in article 60, and the breach of faith committed by Governments, or the Prime Minister, or the judges. The case of abuse of religion for political purposes was a good illustration of my point. No laws were made, as I have observed before, to prevent the abuses. Leave that alone, if abuses were avoided in fact, it would be well, but no, there were flagrant abuses. These undermined the unity of the nation seriously. When Justice U

Thein Maung and his commission went to Myitkyina to inquire into the matter of the State religion, they excited the people from whose hands the Army had to rescue them.

One more instance. In 1949, U. Ba Pe and other old politicians approached me with a proposal that I should assume power. They said they were ready to support me with money, arms and all I needed. The Indian landlords, the Burmese landlords and British business would finance the venture, they said. What they meant was that I should seize power, be the top man, while they would feed fat on the country; that was to be my share and my lot. I reported at once to the Government that an act of high treason had been committed. To gather evidence I pursued the matter a little further, received them, and tried to get the conversations on record. . . . It was a case of high treason, which called for prompt and deterrent action. But no, the Government did not take any action at all, but waited for three or four years . . . for it was only in 1954, when U Nu became angry with U Ba Pe that he dug up the old case and prosecuted U Ba Pe. I became the star witness in the prosecution, and I even told him, "Kogyi Nu, it is only in the heat of anger that you are prosecuting the case. One day when you are appeased you will withdraw it. On my part, I can only say the truth in Court, no more and no less." I did have my statement recorded, but as I foresaw, the case was finally withdrawn.

I ask you, was that not a case that concerned the entire nation? It was an offence that imperilled the whole country, and must it lie in the hands of the Government to prosecute or not to prosecute? Should not every citizen have the right to set the wheels of the law in motion in such a case? I am told that the sanction of the Home Minister or the Judicial Minister is necessary to institute a prosecution for high treason.

In the new Constitution, we should guarantee certain individual rights, the birthrights, as it were, of citizens. Even there the rights should not be without limits; they should be in consonance with the customs prevailing among the races, and the laws of the State. However, we should write into the Constitution that, by the same token which grants rights to people, those who hold high offices of responsibility such as the President, the Prime Minister or Ministers, shall be amenable to action if they misbehave or abuse their powers. In the past, all they suffered for their misdeeds was defeat at elections.

Our people have yet to learn the value of the vote. So, when the new Constitution is written, it should be provided—though I do not know whether similar provisions may be found in the constitutions of other nations—that while reasonable individual rights will be guaranteed, those who are invested with power will be liable to prosecution if they abuse that power. Hitherto all that might happen to, say, a Minister who committed breaches of trust such as acceptance of bribes was that he might not be returned to office in the following elections. In my view this is not enough. I make these remarks on the basis of what has happened in Burma in the past, and the experiences of our people.

These are points to note when the new constitution is framed. We may be having a one-party system or a multi-party system—it is for the people to decide. If the people should opt for the latter, history may repeat. A party, or a member, if that happens, may again indulge in past practices of making lavish promises to the electors on the eve of the election. All means, in their thinking, justified the end which was the attainment of power. Once they were elected, however, their promises were forgotten. This should not be, for a man who makes a promise in a civil contract comes under a liability which may be enforced in a court of law. Likewise public servants are prone to action on dereliction of duty. In the Armed Forces, examples from which will be more vivid to us for most of us are members of the Armed Forces, this is even more forcefully true. A soldier who takes a nap while on sentry duty is sure to land up before a court-martial. Public servants who fail in their duty are likewise proceeded against departmentally or even prosecuted. Politicians, on the other hand, could promise anything and fail to perform after they were voted into office, or deceive the nation, and they were immune from action other than dismissal from office at elections. This is grossly inadequate. I consider that those who are voted into power should come under similar obligations as public servants and Armed Forces personnel, and they should be liable to discipline and action. Politicians who gave promises at elections should go back to their electors and give an account of their performance. If circumstances did not permit fulfilment of their promises, they should explain them to the people, and get new mandates. This did not happen in the past. For the four years of elective office the politicians could feel free to ignore the people and do what they wanted. Things were ugly. In Parliament, among themselves, the members might resolve on some mild disciplinary action, but beyond that their immunity was complete. In future, even criminal action should be made possible by laws, that is my personal opinion.

We should draw lessons from our past history in considering whether the one-party system or the multi-party system should be adopted. When we speak of multi-parties, there were two or three and Governments did not do what ought to have been done at elections. I shall relate a few instances drawn from experiences of elections for the Constituent Assembly, and for Parliament after independence. The people held the politicians who had led the independence movement in high respect, and it was not difficult for them to get elected to the Constituent Assembly.

Then there were the elections of 1952. Actually the Constitution provided for elections to be held within eighteen months after the Constitution had come into force. But the insurrections, and other circumstances, led to postponements of the elections, first to twenty-eight months, then forty, and yet again forty-eight. Here, if I may remark on legal interpretation, I consider that the Constitution should be strictly observed, and if an amendment was deemed necessary, it should be proposed to Parliament, thoroughly discussed and adopted if the required two-thirds majority was obtained, Now, instead, I find, though I have not looked closely at the papers, that a simple act of legislation was made for each enlargement of the period prescribed by the Constitution for the holding of elections, first to twenty-eight months, then to forty, and again to forty-eight. Thus there were inconsistencies and strange ways in the interpretation of the laws.

I passed over one point which relates to the economic sphere, and may I now return to it. As I have said, the British wanted protection for the capital they had invested in the country, and even the right to continue operations after independence. The Burma Oil Company, the Burma Corporation, the Mawchi Mines and such wanted to continue, but it so happened that the Constitution had a provision which required that at least sixty per cent of the capital in any joint venture in the exploitation of natural resources must be owned by Union citizens. This provision was not complied with in the joint venture with the Burma Oil Company, the Burma Corporation, and so on, perhaps because of lack of capital on our part, or the anxiety to keep the enterprises running. A special law was made in 1949 to permit those joint ventures. The law was lightly made, but the British companies did not take the matter as lightly as our side did. They insisted on having the constitutionality of the law tested.

The 1949 law, incidentally, said that it had retroactivity from the day of independence, namely January 4, 1948. But the British were not reassured by this. They foresaw that if the law was eventually declared to be unconstitutional, they would be in trouble. So the question of constitutionality was referred to the Supreme Court, to which, under the Constitution, questions as to whether a new law fell within the framework of the Constitution or went beyond it could be referred. The Supreme Court found that if they followed the Burmese version of article 219, the article of the Constitution concerned with the matter, they could not be sure that the law was constitutional. Both the English and the Burmese versions were authentic, and the English version of the article gave the Supreme Court some flexibility. The Court therefore resolved to the English text, and stretched it to say, if I may sum up the long opinion written by the Court, that the law was constitutional.

. . . I have omitted to mention that in administration of justice they (the writers of the Constitution) took cover to a great extent. In practice, they acted in such a manner as to excite contempt. Here, I shall cite an instance. It was an ugly act, and there are people who are concerned with it, but I can't help it. I have to make this reference in the interests of the country. Once, a girl prepared to go to compete for the "Miss Universe" title. One of the conditions of the contest was that all contestants must be virgins. But the girl in question was a married woman. She was married to an officer of the Army; she had been married for three or four years. Yet when she went to a court to declare on oath that she was a virgin, the court knowingly issued a certificate to that effect. She went to enter the contest with that certificate. Now, the question is: Will the court accept any false declaration on oath? In this case, what should have been done was to get the girl examined medically. (Laughter). Or, the husband should have been called in for examination by the court. What they uttered must be taken as law, and nobody must question their authority. I have no faith in such a court and administration of justice in this matter. (Applause). We must carefully avoid such defects in the constitution we are going to draw up. Not only that; restrictions must be placed on persons wielding power.

The more power one wields, the greater the restrictions must be. (Applause).

. . . I have all my life believed in Socialism. When the Burma Socialist Party was founded, I was among the founders. In fact, we did not intend to found that Party. When, in 1945, the British came back, we said to ourselves that all the leftist progressives among the politicians should be united, and went to talk over the matter with Communists Thakin Than Tun and Thakin Soe. When we said to them that we would cast our lot with them by joining their Party, they started bargaining tactics. They said that we should join their Party as individuals, and not as a party. They wanted to take me in because they liked me but they didn't seem to like the others. I told them that. I wouldn't join them alone if they didn't allow my friends in. So I came away, and we all started the Socialist Party. When I headed the Caretaker Government, I permitted a policy to issue, to the effect that foreign investments were welcome. There were a lot of concessions for such investments. This Act of Parliament was passed at the time of my premiership. That is a matter causing me a prick of conscience. That is a black mark for me, for I was in a way responsible for that policy. I wasn't happy about it but I had to concede to repeated requests from those around me. Well, if we adopt a multi-party system, we would be having instances similar to the instance I have just cited. . . . Meanwhile, the A.F.P.F.L. Government had issued import licences to Burmese capitalists. You know, the Burmese are mostly lazybones. They sold their licences to the Indians and the Chinese and were quite satisfied with the money they got from such deals. The Indians and the Chinese had thus taken the upperhand in these matters. So, the A.F.P.F.L. Government asked these commercialists, the Burmese, the Indians and the Chinese concerned, to shell out for the election expenses. The practice of this kind got worse during the 1960 elections. So, in the multi-party system, election expenses will have to be asked for from those who have money. A deal is made. It is in this manner: "Now, we have shelled out the money, and you have won the elections. Our turn has come. You have now influence and power as ministers. You will have to do a good turn to us," say those who have helped the politicians with money. So, as they serve each other's interests, the people of the country are reduced to destitution. They have no chance of improving their lot. There is another disadvantage for the multi-party system. The disunity of the people will be in direct proportion to the number of political parties in the country. The worst thing is that the workers and peasants suffered most. They were involved because of their personal attachment, and not because of any political belief. The parties tried to organize people severally. After the 1956 elections, the N.U.F. people got a lot of beatings. Among the workers, clashes occurred between those who followed the N.U.F.'s lead and those who followed the A.F.P.F.L.'s lead. Then, in 1960, after the A.F.P.F.L. split, the clashes were between the followers of the Clean A.F.P.F.L. and of the Stable A.F.P.F.L. This fight between two cocks of the same house disguised from each other by smearing soot, as we say in Burmese, ended only when we came in in 1962. That is one of the defects of a multi-party system. Splits among the people due to the multi-party system would be so serious that it would be difficult to reunite them to meet an emergency. Then, financially speaking, money tells much. Expenses for elections will have to be obtained somehow, and the leaders getting on in years want to provide something for themselves against the evening of their lives. It is different now from their stand when they were young. In those days as they were free of the burden of the family, they did not mind starving or even death. Now, getting old and having no prospects for their future, these erstwhile young adventurous men tried to make hay while the sun shines. Some are rather rakish but others feel compelled to stoop to it. There is yet another defect of that system. At the elections, one party gains majority and becomes the government. That party starts launching its own schemes in accord with its own policy. Then at the next elections, that party goes down, and another party comes up. The winners may continue with the work started by its predecessor, or they may not. So the continuity is disrupted. In some cases, the programmes launched by the former government are in the interests of the people but the next government purposely scraps them simply because they have been started by that party. In the case of a one-party system, as the personnel who have come up are, after all, of the same party, continuity is assured. Then it may be asked: What if the one-party system develops into a dictatorship? Then it would be harmful to the people, so steps must be taken to preclude such a possibility. It must be clearly stated in the constitution that such steps will have to be taken. Not merely that: As I have told you before, restrictions must be placed upon those holding positions of power. Well, these are just some points in general which may be useful when we draw up the constitution. We shall have to make such amendments as are feasible when we have developed into a full-fledged people's party.

In those days, people voted for a person, and once he became the representative, the voters did not have any influence on him. In the Parliament he did what he had to do or what he liked to do. He generally works to gain his share of the profit. Admittedly, there were persons who did something for the people. There were also persons who had done nothing for the people, and they could well afford to remain like that. In the case of elections under the constitution we propose to draw up, there will be direct democracy. Whatever the matter, the representatives must go back to the people and inform them before they take any action. If there are novel ideas, they must discuss them thoroughly with the people. Any of these ideas which the people approve of must be taken back to the assembly and submitted for adoption. For instance, when a measure is decided upon, and the people give it their support, it cannot be implemented only by the people at the top. In the past, there was a common saying about things to be handled by the government since the government was there. What we must do is, whatever has been decided upon and worked out, people must participate in the implementation of it from the time of the decision. People must take part in the implementation by taking roles appropriate to them. The role of the people must be reserved in all matters, political, economic, defence and even judicial. Some persons may not know how to go about it, and in that case, those who know the ropes must guide them. All the affairs must be executed with the participation of the people. Such excuses as, "Oh, there is the Party, there is the Government," or in the case of agriculture, "There is the Department of Agriculture," to do the needful, should not be entertained. All must do these things themselves. We don't know when such a stage will be reached, but this is just what I wish for. As I have said earlier, the worst is the racial question which has made this matter in the old Constitution an un-solved problem. This question was created by the British policy of "Divide and Rule."

The problem was delicate, in reference to the provisions in the Consti-tution. I shall cite here an instance of a snag. According to the Constitu-tion, the leader of the party commanding the majority in the Parliament could submit to the President a list of persons he liked to appoint as ministers, but in the case of the states, he must accept the head of the state council as a member of his cabinet. The states elected their own councils respectively, and the state council elected their own chairman. These chairmen must necessarily be accepted by the Prime Minister as members of his cabinet. For instance, the Chairman of the Kachin State Council must by virtue of his office become a minister in the cabinet. So, although the Prime Minister could select the members of his team, here was a restriction. That would not show up when there existed cordial per-sonal relations between the Prime Minister and these state council chair-men. But when there were differences of opinions and strained personal relations, they could not do real business. There was an instance of this kind. The Chin State Council elected Za Re Lian as its Chairman, and the Prime Minister and he did not hit it off. So there was a little hitch. Then after the split of the A.F.P.F.L., the Clean A.F.P.F.L. became the Government party and the Chairman of the Karen State Council hap-pened to be a member of the Stable A.F.P.F.L. So, the cabinet did im-portant business only when that Karen minister was absent. That was the reason why effective work could not be done.

We should, therefore, give our serious thoughts to the question relating to the states when we draw up our Constitution. I shall tell you what I have omitted earlier. That is about the difficulties we had encountered when the old Constitution was drawn up. We were compelled to include in that Constitution something not quite democratic simply to placate the leaders of the frontier areas who had been somewhat prejudiced. We had not satisfactorily solved all the problems before drawing up that Constitu-tion. We should have solved important problems after we had achieved independence. This we had not done. The British had set us against the frontier people by putting all the Sawbwas, some Duwas and other local rulers of the frontier people under their influence and set them against us. The people of those areas were so backward. Their leaders, these local chiefs, tried to put a spoke in the wheel. But there was one redeeming feature. That was, the young leaders of those areas were at one with us, and had worked with Bogyoke Aung San and us unanimously. The right thing to do is to go to the people and educate them soon after indepen-dence. Burmese should also be given education alongside the people of the frontier areas, for peasants and workers were so inexperienced politically. Chins, Kachins and others of the frontier area are even more backward. The government or the party in power must be able to skilfully handle this problem of the frontier areas, or the same snags could recur. I mean such snags as the clash of powers between the Prime Minister and the State Councils. Similarly, there was a snag relating to budget. The Prime Minister and his cabinet could not interfere with the budget-making of the State Councils, but there was a reservation. That was, according to the Constitution, article 193: "(1) The Head of the State shall prepare or cause to be prepared the estimates of the receipts and of the expenditures of the State for each financial year and shall present them or cause them to be presented to the State Council for consideration." The Head of the State brought the estimates, approved by his Council, to the Parliament. Then sub-para (2) of the same article says: "Subject to any conditions that may be imposed by the Union in respect of any contributions from the Union, the State Council shall have power to approve the budget of the State." This sub-para caused an argument every year between the Heads of States and the Prime Minister. There was dissatisfaction on the part of the former and if the latter felt kindly disposed the contributions increased. The states were dissatisfied because they were not treated by the other side like gentlemen. This problem has become perennial since the achievement of independence. We must solve this problem. How shall we solve it? I must tell you about one thing. In those days when we were fighting for independence, there was no intention on our part of taking office. I know about my colleagues. For instance, Ko Kyaw Nyein and Ko Ba Swe refused in 1948 and 1949 to take office in the government. They said they would work from outside. I understand their sincerity. The same with Thakin Tin. But when they could not refuse any longer and were compelled to get into the cabinet, well, they stayed in it. It was all due to influences of those around them. This is a case supporting the truth of the saying that one can stand hardships but one finds it hard to stand the influence of comfort. So the spirit of the Constitution we are going to draw up does not permit the attitude of serving the interests of the people only in chosen capacities. Our Union is just one homogeneous whole. A Chin, for instance, can go wherever he likes within the Union and stay wherever he likes. So, too, a Burmese. As I have told you before, later everybody will be in the place where he belongs. Everybody can take part in any of the affairs, whether political, economic, administrative or judicial. He can choose his own role. When we come to that stage, we will not need to have separate governments within the Union. So I say, we must solve the problem of the frontier areas satisfactorily: If we retain the names of states such as Karen State or Kachin State, then there is a potential danger. It is all right when we can hit it off, but later, after we are gone, posterity may come to clash over these separate names of states. We will have to give it our serious attention. We must work together, and have power to do the work together. Now, in allocating power, there should not be any attitude that makes one say that he will do it only when he is given the post of a minister or of Head of a State. In those days, the Head of a State distributed the contributions he got from the central government among those near and around him, with only a little for development of his State. I don't mean to say that every one of them did like that. But once I got to a remote area and found a road being constructed. I stopped my car on the way for lunch, and happened to chat with the people on the road. I learned that the contractor for that road was a relative of a leader of that State. That contractor did one-quarter of a kyat's worth and drew one kyat for that work. I have seen such instances so many times. So I repeat that this problem of the frontier areas, of separate states, must be faced squarely and a viable solution found. This problem has been shelved because it was a delicate one, and people felt reluctant to break the ice. The result of keeping this problem pending is that there have been so many hitches in relationships that at last the persons concerned didn't even want to sit face to face with one another.

I have given my general suggestions about the new Constitution. The greatest emphasis I have said is on the question of the states. All I want is to get the Burmese and the people of the frontier areas more and more intimate with one another. It is a two-way traffic, and talks alone will not bring any results. Practical application of the ideas must be made. I said at the Union Day celebrations about the more developed section of the people pulling up those left behind, of course, making certain personal sacrifices for the delay caused in waiting for those lagging behind to come up. Although the Burmese may be ahead here, compared to world standards, they are much behind others. Efforts must be made to make those lagging behind us to come up on level with us.

There are persons who want to seize power. Some of them strike an attitude to the effect that they will do what they like, whatever may be said of them. Well, if they want to fight, let them. We will fight back, for we have been fighting all our lives. That is all about this.

Finally, I shall speak about law and order and general matters. I shall begin with general matters.

Now, there are some who go to seek help from the "red" and others who go to seek help from the "white." Well, among them, I refer to the person who has gone to seek help from the "white." I mean the latest person. I shall tell you about him. When I asked advice of the 33 [the Advisory Board], U Nu said I should become President, and a cabinet would be formed under me. Legislative powers should be given to a body comprising the 33 and, if necessary, a few other persons. I wish to say that I have taken up this position as leader not because I wanted to be a leader. Now, since the time of achieving independence till the time we took over power how much benefit did the peasants and workers enjoy although they constitute the majority in the country? In fighting for independence, these people had to sacrifice their lives. After independence they were left forgotten. I took over power because I wanted to improve the conditions of these people. Alas, to be a leader is a bothersome thing. I lost sleep for two or three nights and couldn't eat well for I had to choose my words carefully for this speech. That's why I am now indisposed. So you see it is not that I take up this position because I feel happy about it, or because I hanker after this position.

About this matter of correct class stance, I shall tell you some persons talk so much about class categorisation. Yes, we should categorise people into classes in general terms, into capitalists, workers and peasants. But that does not mean that all in the capitalist class are bad people. So also, it cannot be said that as they belong to workers' or peasants' classes, they are all good. We must make a thorough examination of individual cases. I shall tell you an instance of exploitation of the proletariat. When we came into power in 1962 and in 1963, workers got much favour. One day, a woman who sold boiled corn on the cob at Theingyizay market put her basket on her head, and was about to go out of the market area when the workers for carrying goods stopped her saying that carrying goods must not be done by anybody other than themselves. They said they would carry the basket, and she must pay the fee. At that time, the workers were not properly instructed. But even today, in spite of whatever education we give them, for instance, the workers handling a box containing chinawares dropped it in a huff. They caused a damage for which they got nothing as personal benefits.

Well, you may blame us if you like. That is because we can't give a job to everybody. There is black-marketeering of cinema tickets. These black-marketeers buy tickets at one kyat and sell them at two kyats. Cinemagoers can buy the tickets by themselves, and these peoples shouldn't have gone in for exploitation. That is why I tell you that it is not enough to look at the class to determine whether each individual in that class is good. Of course, there are more bad elements among the capitalists than among other classes because they have to live their lives by exploitation.

Now, as he (U Nu) said, I must take up the position of President and stop all the work we have now been doing for the benefit of workers and peasants. It was a suggestion for turning the wheel back. I cannot head a system which serves the interests of the exploiting moneyed people. I shall tell you something about the suggestions put up by the remaining 32. That is, two groups of 11 and 21. There is nothing in the suggestions put up by the 21, that is in the interests of workers and peasants. They were not as frank as U Nu, but it is clear what class they meant to serve.

There was nothing in the proposals for the benefit of the oppressed classes. The peasants and the workers are, even now, just beginning to get a little better lot than before. The proposals had nothing in them for these people, and I am not interested in any economic system . . . which did not put the interests of these people first. We must go the way of true Socialism. There are many other things which they wrote in their reports, including suggestions for a new Constitution, and I did say that their suggestions could relate to the Constitution. Taking an overall view of their proposals, economic and general, I must say that they were of a class-orientation which we could not accept.

That is about the proposals made by the 21. Those submitted by the 11 were not too far from what we have in mind. They had the interests of the peasant and worker classes as the core and kernel of their proposals, and their suggestions as to methods contain ideas which we may find useful in the future or even now. I have not been able to meet any of the 11, but to them I wish to say that if they have the good of the country at heart they should serve, in our Party or outside it and in any suitable capacity, to promote the welfare of the peasants and the workers. Here I wish to say why I have not been able to meet any of them. It is not that I am acting high and mighty, but I have had the experience of someone coming to see me, and talking generally, without even touching on politics. Then he would go back and go round saying he had spoken with Bogyoke on such and such matters, spreading stories. Thus has my name been used before, and I now avoid seeing people, except those in whom I may place my trust, even though I do wish to meet people.

THREE

Indonesia

by HERBERT FEITH
and ALAN SMITH

When Indonesia held its first nationwide elections in September 1955, four parties emerged with very large followings. The Indonesian Nationalist party (PNI) obtained 22 percent of the vote. The federation of Muslim organizations, Masjumi, representing mainly the reformist segments of Indonesian Islam, came second with 21 percent. The Muslim Scholars' Association (Nahdatul Ulama), speaking for the more traditional Muslims, obtained 18 percent, and the Indonesian Communist party (PKI) followed with 16 percent. Of the many other parties which contested the elections, none gained more than 5 percent of the vote.

These elections, preceded by two years of vigorous and often tumultuous campaigning, were remarkably free, and their results can be seen as reflecting a more or less settled pattern of communal segmentation, ethnic and religiocultural. Each of the four victorious parties could trace its existence back more than twenty-five years. Each of them had become the organizing center of a matrix of culturally distinctive secondary associations extending from the capital to small and very small towns throughout the country—schools; scouting and theater groups; labor; women's, youth, and student organizations. And each of them had drawn large numbers of village notables into its fold, people who could deliver blocs of votes by a combination of distinctive religious and cultural appeals and long-established patron-client relationships.

The geographical distribution of party strengths was highly significant. The Nationalists, the Communists, and the Nahdatul Ulama emerged as dominant parties in heavily populated Java, and none of them got large numbers of votes in the more sparsely peopled Outer Islands—though the Nationalists and Communists had success in a few relatively small Christian communities, Javanese settler enclaves, and plantation areas. On the other hand, the Masjumi emerged as by far the largest party of the Outer Islands, with relatively few votes from Java, especially from the ethnic Javanese heartland of East and Central Java.

The Communist party attracted widespread support in cities, towns, and plantation communities, but it also proved to have great appeal to village voters, particularly in East and Central Java. It emerged there as a principal spokesman, along with the more conservative PNI, of the religiocultural community of *abangan,* nominal Muslims whose real beliefs owe less to Islam than to Hinduism and Buddhism, the dominant religions of Java before the sixteenth century.

The broad range of ideological themes which has characterized Indonesia's national politics ever since independence from Holland was proclaimed in 1945 is thus neither accidental nor superficial. It is rather the product of cultural legacies going back a long way, and is thus unlikely to disappear quickly, whatever decisions are taken to ban particular parties or ideological streams.

The problem of fashioning consensus had been a central one in the building of the prewar nationalist movement. The various organizations which are retrospectively described as the nationalist movement—cultural regeneration societies, Muslim trading associations, Muslim reform groups, educational movements, ethnic advancement societies, socialist-led organizations of anticolonial protest, and political parties aspiring to independence—were not easily brought together in common endeavor. They eventually came to share the aspiration for early independence from the Dutch and a number of symbols like the national flag and the national anthem. But this communion was never paralleled by organizational cohesion, partly because Dutch repression kept the main nationalist leaders imprisoned and exiled for long periods.

When the Indonesian Republic was declared on August 17, 1945, in the immediate aftermath of the Japanese collapse, its unity rested heavily on the ability of the two long-time leaders of the prewar nationalist movement, Sukarno and Mohammad Hatta, to work closely

together. Sukarno, who emerged as president, was a Javanese of syn-
cretistic religious inclination. Hatta, who became vice-president and
later prime minister as well, is a Sumatran and a thoroughgoing Muslim. Sukarno had worked closely with the Japanese authorities during
their occupation of Indonesia, 1942 to 1945. Hatta, while also holding
high positions under the Japanese, had kept lines open to the pro-
Allied underground. Sukarno, a Bandung-educated architect and a
powerful orator, could rally great popular enthusiasm for the revolutionary struggle against the Dutch, who were in no way prepared to
accept an independent Indonesia. He fashioned compelling images of
a glorious future for the young Republic. Hatta, a Rotterdam-trained
economist, could bring order out of chaos in economic and administrative matters, and could win the respect of the Western world for
his practical and moderate approach to his country's problems.

These two very different men worked together closely during the
four years of armed struggle against the Dutch between 1945 and 1949,
and cooperation between them made it possible for the fledgling Republic, harassed by the Dutch military, to survive a series of major
challenges. The policies Sukarno and Hatta pursued were by no means
popular—especially their preparedness to concede territory to the
Dutch as Dutch military strength grew—and three major attempts
were made to destroy their authority: An abortive coup by national
communists, an unsuccessful revolt by the Communists, and a regional
rebellion led by fundamentalist Muslims, which was not finally crushed
until 1962. But Sukarno and Hatta continued to cooperate closely in
the leadership of the state and their joint prestige made it possible for
the Republic's authority to be maintained.

After the achievement of unchallenged independence in 1949 the
problem of consensus assumed new proportions. Not only was the anti-
Dutch struggle no longer a strong binding force, but in addition the
top leaders of the government found themselves at odds with each
other on major policies. For the first few years, men of Hatta's general
orientation controlled the government. But the policies they pursued—
economic stabilization, protection of Dutch investments, nonalignment
in foreign relations, and placement as a low priority of efforts to free
West Irian from the Dutch—were generally unpopular. President Sukarno, seeing this and fearing lest a large part of the revolutionary
generation should become alienated from the leaders of the Republic,
dissociated himself from them more and more. After 1953, he sup-

ported cabinets with a more militantly nationalist approach. But these were cabinets from which men of Hatta's general orientation were excluded, so the division between the two leaders grew even sharper.

The years of campaigning preceding the 1955 elections gave the consensus problem a new dimension by involving the village masses. The central question of the campaign was deeply divisive: Would the Indonesian state continue to be based on the Panca Sila, President Sukarno's Five Pillars of 1945 which included belief in one's own God, or would it become a "state based on Islam"? When the election results became known, the regional distribution of party strengths made it clear that religious-cum-ideological conflict had a dangerous geographical dimension. With party and ideological disagreements in Indonesia paralleling and aggravating conflicts of interest between the Javanese and the inhabitants of the Outer Islands, a threat of centrifugal politics and ultimate territorial fragmentation came into view; and this seemed all the more acute because the Javanese Sukarno had allowed his name to be used by the Nationalists (and to some extent by the Communists), whereas the Sumatran Hatta had supported the reformist-led Masjumi and its small intellectual ally, the Socialist party.

By this time relations between the two leaders had become highly strained, and in December 1956 Hatta resigned from the vice-presidency. The duumvirate, on which the unity of the Republic had rested thus far, was no more. Sukarno, allying himself with the PNI, and radical nationalist splinter groups, the Communists, and a dominant group in the army, and acting sharply against the Masjumi and the Socialists, moved to establish a new form of government in which "liberal" or "50%-plus-one" democracy would be replaced by "guided democracy."

His moves were not immediately successful. One reaction to them was the rise of army officer-led movements in several of the islands outside Java, movements which combined anti-Communist and anti-Sukarno sentiment with demands for greater autonomy for the outlying areas. But Sukarno persisted, and by the middle of 1958 the rebel officers who had led regional movements and had proclaimed a countergovernment were militarily crushed, the Masjumi and Socialist parties that had sympathized with them had been eclipsed (later to be banned), and a new regime had been established on narrower foundations, with Sukarno sharing power with the leaders of the army. The

new dispensation was formalized in July 1959 with the repromulga-
tion of the 1945 constitution, which replaced the more liberal constitution of 1950 and provided a legal foundation for a strong presidency.

Guided Democracy as a new political order solved a number of the
problems of consensus which had seemed insoluble in the years of open
and pluralistic politics. With the regional rebels defeated and the Masjumi and Socialist parties discredited, it was possible for President Sukarno to suppress all further Islamic debate which questioned the
Panca Sila (and yet maintain the support of the other main Muslim
party, the Java-based Nahdatul Ulama). Moreover he imposed sharp
limits on various other divisive debates by insisting that all who participated in public life should be active adherents of his Political Manifesto.

After 1962 the Guided Democracy regime came under more and
more strain. Sukarno's relations with his coalition partners, the leaders
of the army, grew increasingly tense, as the Communists seemed to
advance by large strides under presidential patronage, and as the president's increasingly militant anti-imperialist foreign policy seemed to
produce little but domestic inflation and international isolation. Communist efforts to implement the government's land reform policy produced unprecedented tension between themselves and the anti-Communists in a politically mobilized peasantry. By late 1964 a sharp
polarization had developed between a Communist and radical-nation-
alist coalition that wanted to follow the president in further "revolutionary intensification" and an army-Muslim coalition that feared this
would lead to a Communist capture of power.

With the pro-Sukarno and pro-Communist coup by Lieutenant
Colonel Untung of October 1, 1965, and its successful suppression by
Major General Suharto on the same day, polarization became rupture. Within a few weeks the army had begun a massive campaign to
destroy the PKI, arresting large numbers of its leaders and cadres and
allowing local anti-Communists to deal with their Communist enemies
as they saw fit. The large-scale massacre of Communists and their
sympathizers which followed in the next six months, when perhaps
500,000 or even as many as a million persons were killed, was a measure of the bitter hatreds that had built up in the peasant population
in preceding years, as well as of the determination of the victorious
army leadership to destroy its archenemy once and for all. The consensus which Sukarno had imposed in the name of Guided Democracy
was shattered.

In March 1966 another attempt to build and impose a consensus was initiated; it became known as the New Order. In that month the predominant student groups in Jakarta and Bandung, allied with army officers who were militantly anti-Communist and anti-Sukarno, succeeded in persuading General Suharto, then army chief of staff, to effect a coup against President Sukarno. Just how important the students' role was in bringing about Sukarno's fall remains in dispute. But they played a role of major importance in 1966 and 1967 as pacemakers in Indonesia's ideological transformation, puncturing the overblown myths of Guided Democracy, and compelling the country to abandon the language of nationalist revolutionary zeal. Their demand that the Suharto government should conceive of its tasks in terms of pragmatic renewal, modernization, and the institution of democracy was never wholly accepted. Stability and order have been more important symbols of the regime than democracy or renewal, and development has tended to eclipse modernization. But the students had established a right to speak as interpreters of the "New Order ideals," which the government wanted to achieve, and they have maintained an important role as critics.

Since 1966 power has been in the hands of the army, or a group of army leaders around General Suharto. Born during the struggle for independence, the Indonesian army has traditionally seen itself as close to the people, called to be custodian of the country's political weal. The leaders of the army have insisted ever since 1945 that the army's national character has enabled it to take political action without succumbing to sectional pressure in the way parties have always tended to do. Accordingly, the army saw its assumption of power in 1966 as an expression, in a moment of crisis, of its long-held sense of political obligation.

As a ruling party, the Indonesian army has not merely provided the country with political direction; it has also had large numbers of its own members controlling the implementation of high-level political decisions at lower levels. In the Guided Democracy period, army men held many key positions in civil administration and economic management, but their role in these positions was greatly expanded after 1966. Members of the armed forces (but especially of the army) came to hold a high proportion of controlling positions; many of them are governors, ambassadors, secretaries-general of departments, and managing directors of state firms, as well as village heads.

Inheriting an economy in nearly catastrophic disarray—characterized by acute inflation, drastic deterioration in the conditions of roads, railways, and shipping facilities, and heavy indebtedness to overseas countries—the army leaders decided in 1966 to concentrate their attention on economic regeneration. To this end, they sought the advice of a number of "technocrats," mainly university economists, who have long been held in high respect in the West. A rescheduling of payments on Indonesia's earlier debts was negotiated and long-term loans and private investment capital were sought from Western countries and Japan. As a result of these policies, within three years inflation had been virtually ended and, by 1973, major improvements in transportation and communications had been achieved, production levels in most areas had been raised, and a spectacular increase in export earnings, particularly from oil, other minerals, and timber, had been produced. At the same time, however, increasing inequalities between the military and civilians, between urban and rural areas, and between landlords and government officials at the local level and the mass of the peasantry, have stirred widespread resentment of the government's policies.

The New Order consensus is in many ways reminiscent of that which prevailed before 1958. The tasks of government are affirmed in Hatta-like terms, with emphasis on good government, effective economic management, symbolism of the rule of law, and internal consolidation rather than foreign-policy activity. The similarities with the period of Guided Democracy are important, too. Suharto has kept the Communists banned as Sukarno did the Masjumi and the Socialists, but the penalties for Communist activity are very much harsher than they were for the Masjumi-Socialist group, and the number of political prisoners is vastly greater. Suharto, like Sukarno, is a Javanese of *abangan* religiocultural orientation who mistrusts most manifestations of activist, political Islam, especially ones originating in the Outer Islands. Similarly, Suharto has at times acted as a centrist balancer in ways quite analogous to Sukarno's. As Sukarno balanced the Communists against the army leaders and the Muslims, so Suharto has balanced the Nationalists, on the one hand, against the Muslims, on the other, and he has balanced the parties in general against the students and the academic-media complex of Jakarta and Bandung.

However, in the final analysis, the New Order regime is more accurately characterized in terms of contrasts with its two predecessors than by similarities with either of them. There are certainly great contrasts with the period of Sukarno's Guided Democracy, when heroic struggle and inspirational leadership were the order of the day, and large sections of the worker and peasant population were mobilized for participation in the government's patriotic causes. The New Order period has in fact been marked by almost unprecedented political passivity in the mass of the population. Unlike the governments of the postindependence and Guided Democracy periods, the New Order regime has maintained a higher degree of continuity in the policies it has espoused and pursued. There has also been greater continuity in personnel than in the earlier periods. While some groups of army men and civilians who were influential in the early Suharto years have seen their power decline, they have rarely been replaced by new influentials. The group of the powerful has grown small, but its core remained unchanged into the early 1970's.

Perhaps the most important contrast with the earlier regimes lies in the government's strength vis-à-vis the parties and other extrabureaucratic groups. Suharto's government, unlike Sukarno's, does not rest on a consensus established among parties. It does not justify itself in terms of a balance between the country's main cultural-cum-ideological streams but rather in terms of a rejection of party politics linked with these streams. This rejection has also been used to justify suppression of opposition, and consequently, balancing parties and cultural streams against each other has been much less important for Suharto than for Sukarno.

Indonesia is today in the hands of a fairly cohesive group of army generals (mainly *abangan* Javanese of lower aristocratic and rich-peasant origin), who have established a degree of control over the society that is unprecedented since the demise of Dutch colonial rule. This control is partly a reflection of the circumstances from which the regime emerged. The shadow cast by the massacres of 1965–1966 was a long one: An estimated 75,000 people who were imprisoned for their Communist and pro-Communist associations before 1965 are still being held, and new arrests of local "troublemakers" for their pre-1965 political involvements have been easily justified. Fear has been a powerful stimulus to political passivity, as has been the postmassacre sense of revulsion against politics.

The Suharto government's enhanced control over society has also resulted from an extended shakedown, streamlining, and militarization of the government's own apparatus. What was previously a heterogeneous, ramshackle, and often stubbornly localistic bureaucracy has progressively been remade into a far more cohesive instrument of control.

The government leaders' control, both over Indonesian society at large and over its bureaucratic machinery, appeared to tighten after early 1970. Ironically, this process was furthered by the country's second nationwide election in July 1971. The decision to hold elections at this time was seen initially as a victory for the parties—especially the PNI, the Nahdatul Ulama, and the Indonesian Muslim party, a government-domesticated successor to the Masjumi—and led them to organize more actively than they had for many years. But this activity prompted a reaction of far greater dimensions from the government: Though it had assured itself of the right to nominate one hundred members to what was to be a parliament of 460, and had subsequently purged most of the parties of their more independent leaders, the government decided to make certain its victory by throwing its weight heavily behind GOLKAR, the Joint Secretariat of Functional Groups, which became in effect an army-run government party.

Because of intensive government pressure on army members and civil servants and, through them, on voters, GOLKAR obtained 236 seats of the elected total of 360. The Nahdatul Ulama emerged as the largest of the nongovernmental contenders with 58 seats. The Indonesian Muslim party followed with 24 seats, while the PNI, the largest of the parties in the 1955 elections, was severely decimated, gaining only 20 seats.

Immediately after the elections were over, pressure on the mass of the people was relaxed. But the government soon made clear that its drive for fuller control over society would be maintained. A central theme of official pronouncements during the next six months was that the luxury of politics could no longer be afforded in what was to be a period of "accelerated modernization." Parties and their affiliated organizations were subsequently denied the right to be active in the villages.

The government also tightened its controls in the 1970–1972 period on protests by small groups of students, who demonstrated repeatedly to persuade the government to take action against the corruptors in its ranks. The students attracted considerable attention in the liberal press for their charges. Moreover, they occasionally accused the armed

forces of "militarism" and "dual function,"[1] specifically raising the
issue of the large number of military men occupying civilian positions.
The students depicted both corruption and militarism as detracting
from President Suharto's and the New Order's goal of economic development. Describing themselves as a "moral force," these students
made no attempt to organize large-scale demonstrations. Their protests, however, came to have political importance because of the support they received from important sections of the Indonesian press
and the widespread sympathy they attracted from the middle classes
in the major cities.

Initially, the government's response to these criticisms was fairly
positive, but by the end of 1970 it appeared unwilling to acknowledge
the substance of the students' demands, especially those relating to corruption, and consequently, it was more disposed to act coercively towards them. The events of the election period evidently heightened
the government's disposition to narrow the limits of student and press
protest. The matter came to a head in late 1971 and early 1972, when
the dissidents launched criticisms of the proposal to build "Beautiful
Indonesia in Miniature," an expensive tourist-attraction project sponsored by the president's wife.

By February 1972, the student critics had been cowed into silence.
Subsequent months saw a further extension of government efforts to
reduce the independence of extrabureaucratic organizations, particularly labor unions and private groups working in the field of community development. Party politics had largely withered in response, on
the one hand, to this restriction and intimidation, and, on the other,
to the manipulation of party leadership positions by the army's intelligence officers. Moreover, the armed forces seemed as capable as in
earlier years of forestalling the re-emergence of an underground Communist movement. Overall, the government was firmly in control.

The Suharto government has sought legitimacy on the basis of its
economic accomplishments, and in order to assure continued economic
progress, it has demanded political passivity from the people. Economic management, however, is not divorced from politics. It is not
only a question of success or failure, but also a question of those who
benefit and those who do not. By 1973, large numbers of Indonesians
had come to resent many of the government's politico-economic poli-

[1] The doctrine under which the armed forces have social and political tasks
to perform as well as ones concerned with defense and security.

cies, which they saw as not merely raising per capita income but also increasing inequalities in both urban and rural areas, with military men and foreigners drawing benefits far greater than they were thought to deserve. The experience of far-reaching political mobilization before 1965, however, and the influence of democratic and anti-imperialist ideologies make it unlikely that the political passivity the Suharto government has created will be long-lasting.

I. The Revolution

The following extract is taken from a now classic speech which the future president of Indonesia made two and a half months before the Japanese surrender to the Allies and the Indonesian proclamation of independence. Sukarno, the most popular of Indonesia's prewar nationalist leaders, who had been exiled by the Dutch to far parts of the archipelago by the mid-1930's, had worked with the Japanese authorities during their occupation and managed to win significant concessions from them: He and his associates were allowed to spread many of the ideas of Indonesian nationalism, and they succeeded in persuading the Japanese to help select and provide military training for a group of Indonesians. In mid-1945 the Japanese allowed the establishment of a Preparatory Committee for Indonesian Independence under the chairmanship of Sukarno, and it was to this committee that he addressed his Panca Sila speech. The Panca Sila, Five Pillars or Five Principles, which Sukarno put forward in this extempore address, have been regarded as the foundation of the Indonesian state ever since, surviving all changes of political climate including the period of de-Sukarnoization after 1966.

Sukarno: The Panca Sila [June 1, 1945]*

We shall establish an Indonesian national state. I ask Ki Bagus Hadi-kusumo and others of the Islamic group to excuse my using the word

* *Source: Toward Freedom and the Dignity of Man: Five Speeches by President Soekarno of the Republic of Indonesia* (Jakarta: Department of Foreign Affairs, 1961). The Panca Sila speech has also been published by the Department of Information in a great many English language editions under the title "The Birth of Pantja Sila."

"Nationalism." I, too, am a man of Islam. But I ask that you do not misunderstand when I say that the first basis for Indonesia is the basis of nationalism. That does not mean nationalism in a narrow sense. What I want is a national state such as I spoke about in the meeting in Taman Raden Saleh several days ago. An Indonesian National State does not mean a state in a narrow sense. As Ki Bagus Hadikusumo said yesterday, he is an Indonesian, his parents are Indonesians, his grandparents were Indonesians, his ancestors were Indonesians. It is upon Indonesian nationalism in this sense intended by Ki Bagus Hadikusumo that we shall base the Indonesian state.

A National State! This matter needs clarifying first, even though I have already said something about it in the mass meeting at Taman Raden Saleh. Let me elaborate and spend a little more time upon the question: What is it that is called a nation? What are the requirements for a nation?

According to Renan, the requirement for a nation is the desire to be united. The people must feel themselves united and want to be united. Ernest Renan said that the requirement for a nation is *le désir d'être ensemble,* the desire to be united. According to the definition of Ernest Renan, it follows that what becomes a nation is a group of people who want to be united, who feel themselves united.

Let us look at a definition by another person, the one given by Otto Bauer in his book *Die Nationalitätenfrage,* where the question is raised *"Was ist eine Nation?"* and the answer is *"Eine Nation ist eine aus Schicksalgemeinschaft erwachsene Charaktergemeinschaft"* (A nation is a community of character which has grown out of a community of shared experience.) That is what a nation is according to Otto Bauer.

But yesterday when Professor Supomo—I think it was he—was quoting Ernest Renan, Mr. Yamin said: "Out of date." Indeed, gentlemen, Ernest Renan's definition is out of date. Otto Bauer's definition is out of date, too. For at the time when Ernest Renan formulated his definition, and at the time Otto Bauer formulated his, there had not yet emerged the new science of geopolitics.

Yesterday, Ki Bagus Hadikusumo—was it he or Mr. Munandar?— spoke about "unity between men and place." Unity between men and place, gentlemen, unity between human beings and the place where they live! Man cannot be separated from place. It is impossible to separate people from the earth under their feet.

Ernest Renan and Otto Bauer looked at people in isolation. They were only concerned with men's feeling of community, with *l'âme et le désir.* They were only thinking of men and their character, not thinking of the earth, the earth those men inhabited, their place. What is their "place"? Their place is a country. That country is one unity. . . .

According to geopolitics, Indonesia is our country. Indonesia as a whole, neither Java alone, nor Sumatra alone, nor Borneo alone, nor Celebes alone, nor Ambon alone, nor the Moluccas alone, but the whole archipelago ordained by God Almighty to be a single unity between two oceans—that is our country.

Therefore, if I recall that there is a relationship between people and place, between men and their lands, then the definitions given by Ernest Renan and Otto Bauer are inadequate. *Le désir d'être ensemble* is inadequate. Otto Bauer's definition, *eine aus Schicksalgemeinschaft erwachsene Charaktergemeinschaft,* is inadequate.

Pardon me, I will take Minangkabau as an example. Among the people of Indonesia who have the greatest *désir d'être ensemble* are those of Minangkabau, numbering approximately two and a half million. These people feel themselves to be one family. But Minangkabau is not a unity, it is only just a small part of a unity. The inhabitants of Jogja [Jogjakarta] also feel *le désir d'être ensemble,* but Jogja also is only a small part of a unity. In West Java the people of Pasundan deeply feel *le désir d'être ensemble,* but Pasundan too is only a small part of a unity.

In brief, the Indonesian Nation is not merely a group of individuals who, having *le désir d'être ensemble,* live in a small area like Minangkabau or Madura or the Sunda region or the Bugis region. The Indonesian Nation is the totality of all the human beings who, according to geopolitics ordained by God Almighty, live throughout the unity of the entire archipelago of Indonesia from the northern tip of Sumatra to Irian. All of them, throughout the islands! Because amongst these seventy million human beings *le désir d'être ensemble* already exists, there is already *Charaktergemeinschaft.* The Indonesian Nation, the Indonesian People, the people of Indonesia, total seventy million persons, seventy million who have already become one, one, once again one!

This is what we must all aim at: The setting up of one National State upon the unity of one Indonesian land from the tip of Sumatra right to Irian! I am confident that there is not one group amongst you, neither the Islamic group nor what is called the nationalist group, which does not agree. This is what all of us must aim at. . . .

Gentlemen, if you accept this, let us take as the first principle of our state: Indonesian Nationalism. Indonesian Nationalism in the fullest sense. Neither Javanese nationalism, nor Sumatran nationalism, nor the nationalism of Borneo, or of Sulawesi, Bali or any other, but Indonesian Nationalism, all of them together, which shall become the basis of one national state. . . .

But, but, there is undoubtedly a danger in this principle of nationalism. The danger is that men may sharpen nationalism to the point where it becomes chauvinism, they may think of *"Indonesia über Alles."* This is the danger. We love one country, we feel ourselves one nation, we have one language. But our country, Indonesia, is only a small part of the world. Please remember this!

Gandhi said: "I am a nationalist, but my nationalism is humanity."

The nationalism we advocate is not the nationalism of isolation, not chauvinism as blazoned by people in Europe who say *"Deutschland über Alles,"* who say that there is none so great as Germany, whose people, they say, are supermen, cornhaired and blue-eyed Arayans, whom they consider the greatest in the world, while other nations are worthless. Do not let us hold by such principles, gentlemen, do not let us say that the Indonesian nation is the most perfect and the noblest whilst we belittle other peoples. We must proceed towards the unity of the world, the brotherhood of the world. We have not only to establish the state of Indonesia Merdeka, we must also proceed towards the familyhood of nations.

It is precisely this which is my second principle. This is the second philosophical principle which I propose to you, gentlemen, which I may call internationalism. But when I say internationalism, I do not mean cosmopolitanism, which does not want the existence of nationalism, which says there is no Indonesia, there is no Japan, there is no Burma, there is no England, there is no America, and so on. Internationalism cannot flourish if it is not rooted in the soil of nationalism. Nationalism cannot flourish if it does not grow in the flower-garden of internationalism. Thus, these two, principle 1 and principle 2, which I propose first of all to you, are closely linked one with the other.

And now, what is the third principle? That principle is the principle of *mufakat,* unanimity, the principle of *perwakilan,* representation, the principle of *permusjawaratan,* deliberation amongst representatives. The Indonesian state shall not be a state for one individual, shall not be a state for one group. . . . But we shall set up a state "all for all," "one for all, all for one." I am convinced that an absolute condition for the strength of the Indonesian state is *permusjawaratan, perwakilan.*

For the Islamic group, this is the best place to pursue the concerns of religion. We are Muslims, myself included. Do excuse me, my Islam is far from perfect, but if you open up my breast and look at my heart, you will find it none but a Muslim heart; and this Muslim heart of Bung Karno's wishes to defend Islam in *mufakat,* in *permusjawaratan.* By means of *mufakat* we shall improve everything, including the safety of religion, that is by means of discussions or deliberations in the People's Representative Body. Whatever is not yet satisfactory, we shall talk over in a *permusjawaratan.* The Representative Body, that is our place for bringing forward the demands of Islam! It is here that we shall propose to the leaders of the people whatever we feel is needed for improvement.

If we are really a Muslim people, let us work as hard as possible so that most of the seats in the people's representative body which we will create, are occupied by Muslim delegates. If the Indonesian people are really a people who are for the greater part Muslim, and if it is true that Islam here is a religion which is alive in the hearts of the masses, let us leaders move everyone of the people to mobilise as many Muslim delegates as possible for this representative body. For example, if the people's representative body has one hundred members, let us work, work as hard as possible, so that sixty, seventy, eighty, ninety delegates sitting in this people's representative body will be Muslims, prominent Muslims. Then, automatically, laws issuing from this people's representative body will be Islamic.

Indeed I am convinced that only if this has actually happened will it be able to be said that the religion of Islam is really alive in the souls of the people, if sixty per cent, seventy per cent, eighty per cent, ninety per cent of the delegates are Muslims, prominent Muslims, learned Muslims. Only when that has happened, will Islam be alive in Indonesia and not given merely lip-service. We say that ninety per cent of us profess the religion of Islam, but look at this gathering, how many per cent here vote for Islam? Forgive me for raising this question. But for me this is proof that Islam is not yet truly alive among the people.

Therefore, I say to you all, to those of you who are not Muslims and especially to those who are, please accept this principle number three, the principle of *permusjawaratan, perwakilan,* the principle of unanimity arising out of deliberation amongst representatives.

In the representative body there will be the greatest possible struggle. No state is truly alive if it is not as though the cauldron of Tjondrodimuko burned and boiled in its representative body, if there is no struggle of convictions in it. Both in an Islamic state and in a Christian one, there is always struggle. Accept principle number three, the principle of *mufakat,* the principle of representation of the people!

Within the people's representative body, Muslims and Christians will work as hard as possible. If, for instance, Christians desire every letter of the regulations of the Indonesian state to conform with the Bible, then let them work themselves to death in order that the greater part of the delegates who enter the Indonesian representative body are Christians. That is just—fair play! There is no state that can be called a living state if there is no internal struggle. Do not think that there is no struggle in Turkey. Do not think that in the Japanese state there is no clash of minds. God Almighty gave us minds so that we might constantly rub against each other in our daily lives, just like the pounding and husking of paddy to obtain rice, in turn to become the best Indonesian food. Accept, then, principle number three, which is the principle of *permusjawaratan.*

I will now propose principle number four. During these three days I have not heard of this principle yet, the principle of well-being. The principle: There shall be no poverty in Indonesia Merdeka. . . .

Do not imagine that if the People's Representative Body is already in existence, we shall automatically have achieved this well-being. We have seen that in European states there are representative bodies, there is parliamentary democracy; but is it not precisely in Europe that the people are at the mercy of the capitalists? In America there is a representative body of the people, but are not people in America at the mercy of the capitalists? Are not people at the mercy of the capitalists throughout the whole Western world?

There is but one reason, namely . . . the people's representative bodies which have been set up there have merely followed the recipe of the French Revolution. What is called democracy there is mere political democracy alone, there is no social justice at all, there is no economic democracy at all.

I remember the words of a French leader, Jean Jaures, who discussed political democracy. "In parliamentary democracy," said Jean Jaures, ". . . every man has equal rights—equal political rights; every man can vote, every man may enter parliament. But is there social justice, is there evidence of well-being amongst the masses?" Therefore, Jean Jaures said further: "A worker's representative who possesses that political right, can act in parliament to bring about the fall of a minister. He is like a king! But in his place of work, in the factory—today he can bring about the fall of a minister, tomorrow he can be thrown onto the street, made unemployed, with nothing at all to eat."

Do we want conditions like that?

Friends, I suggest: If we are looking for democracy, it must not be western democracy, but *permusjawaratan* which brings life, that is politico-economic democracy which is capable of bringing in social prosperity.

The people of Indonesia have long spoken of this matter. What is meant by the *Ratu Adil?* What is meant by the idea of the *Ratu Adil* is social justice. The people want to have enough to eat or enough to wear, the people created a new world in which there is justice under the leadership of the *Ratu Adil.*

Therefore, if we truly understand, remember and love the people of Indonesia, let us accept this principle of social justice, that is not only political equality, but we must create quality in the economic field too, which means the greater possible well-being. Friends, the body for *per-musjawaratan* which we shall establish, must not be a deliberative body for political democracy alone, but a body which, together with the community, will be able to give effect to two principles: Political justice and social justice. We shall discuss these matters together, Brothers and Sisters, in the body for *permusjawaratan*. . . .

The fifth principle should be: To build an Indonesia Merdeka which stands in awe of the One, Supreme God.

The principle of Divinity, of Belief in God. Not only should the Indonesian people believe in God, but every Indonesian should believe in his own God. The Christian should worship God according to the teachings of Jesus Christ, Muslims according to the teachings of the Prophet Mohammad. Buddhists should perform their religious ceremonies in accordance with the books they have. But let us all believe in God. The Indonesian State shall be a state where every person can worship God as he likes. The whole of the people should worship God in a civilized way, that is, without religious egoism. And the State of Indonesia should be a state based on belief in God!

Let us observe, let us practise religion, both Islam and Christianity, in a civilized way. What is that civilised way? It is with mutual respect for one another.

The Prophet Mohammad has given us plenty of examples of tolerance, of respect for other religions. Jesus Christ showed that tolerance, too. So in the Indonesia Merdeka we are building, let us declare that our fifth principle of state is believing in God in a cultured way, believing in God with moral nobility, believing in God with mutual respect for one another.

My heart will feast in delight if you agree that the state of Indonesia Merdeka shall be based on Belief in the One, Supreme God.

Here, then, in the lap of this fifth principle, all the religions to be found in Indonesia today will obtain the best possible place. And our State shall have belief in God, also. Remember the third principle of *mufakat,* of representation—there is the place for each of us to make propaganda for our ideals in a manner that is not intolerant, that is in a cultured way!

Brothers and Sisters: I have already proposed the "Principles of the State." There are five. Is this *Pantja Dharma,* the Five Dharma? No! The name *Pantja Dharma* is not suitable here: *Dharma* means duty, whereas we are speaking of principles. I like symbolism, the symbolism of numbers, too. The fundamental obligations of Islam are five in number; our fingers are five on each hand; we have five senses; what else is five in number? (One of those present: "The five *Pendawa.*") The *Pendawa,* too, are five persons. And now the number of principles: Nationalism, internationalism, *mufakat*, well-being, and belief in God—also five in number. The name is not Pantja Dharma, but I named it with the advice of a linguist friend of ours *Pantja Sila*. Sila means basis or principle. And it is upon those five principles that we shall build Indonesia Merdeka, enduring and age-long.

Or perhaps some of you do not like that number of five? I can compress this number until there are only three. You ask me what are the three products of that compressing?

For decades past I have been thinking about this, that is, the principles of Indonesia Merdeka, our *Weltanschauung*. The first two principles, nationalism and internationalism, nationalism and humanity, I compress into one, which I call socio-nationalism. And democracy which is not the democracy of the West, but together with well-being, I also compress into one; this is what I call socio-democracy. Belief in God with respect for one another is the one principle left.

And so, what was originally five has become three: Socio-nationalism, socio-democracy and belief in God. If you prefer the symbolism of three, then take these three.

But perhaps not all of you like this *tri-sila* and ask for one, one principle alone? All right, I shall make them one, I shall gather them up again to become one. What is that one?

As I said a few moments ago, we are establishing an Indonesian state which all of us must support. All for all. Not the Christians for Indonesia, not the Islamic group for Indonesia, not Hadikusumo for Indonesia, not Van Eck for Indonesia, not rich Nitisemito for Indonesia, but the Indonesians for Indonesia—all for all! If I compress what was five into three, and what was three into one, then I have a genuine Indonesian term, *gotong rojong*, mutual co-operation. The State of Indonesia which we are to establish must be a *gotong rojong* state. How wonderful that is: A Gotong Rejong State!

Gotong rojong is a dynamic concept, more dynamic than the family principle, friends. The family principle is a static concept, but *gotong rojong* portrays one endeavour, one act of service, one task, what was called by Mr. Sukardjo one *karyo*, one *gawe*. Let us complete this *karyo*, this *gawe*, this task, this act of service, together. *Gotong rojong* means toiling hard together, sweating hard together, a common struggle to help one another. Acts of service by all for the interest of all. *Ho-lopis-kuntulbaris!*—One, two, three, heave! for the common interest. That is *gotong rojong!*

The principle of *gotong rojong* between the rich and the poor, between the Muslim and the Christian, between the non-Indonesians and those of foreign descent who have become Indonesians. This, Brothers and Sisters, is what I propose to you.

The Indonesian constitution, which begins with the words below, was promulgated in 1945, one day after Sukarno and Hatta proclaimed the Republic. This constitution was replaced by another at the time of the Indonesian-Dutch settlement in December 1949, but it was promulgated anew on July 5, 1959, as part of President Sukarno's effort to "Return to the Rails of the Revolution."

Preamble to the 1945 Constitution [August 18, 1945]*

Independence being in truth the right of all peoples, colonialism, which does not accord with humanity and justice, must be abolished throughout the world.

The struggle of the Indonesian independence movement has reached the happy stage at which the Indonesian people have been escorted safely to the threshold of an independent Indonesian State which is free, united, sovereign, just and prosperous.

By the Mercy of Almighty God, and moved by the noble desire to live as a free nation, the Indonesian people hereby proclaim their independence.

Further, to establish a Government for the Indonesian state which will protect the whole Indonesian people and fatherland, to promote the public welfare, improve the livelihood of the people and join in establishing a world order based on freedom, everlasting peace and social justice, the Independence of the Indonesian People shall be ordered in a Constitution of the Indonesian State, in the form of a Republic of Indonesia which is based on the sovereignty of the people and on the pillars of the One Deity, just and civilized Humanity, Indonesian Unity and People's rule guided wisely through consultation and representation, in order to achieve Social Justice for the whole Indonesian people.

After the proclamation of independence on August 17, 1945, the new Republic of Indonesia under President Sukarno and Vice-President Hatta proceeded to organize a functioning government. But it was clear that the Dutch would not easily give up their claim to sovereignty. After the Japanese occupation, when the Dutch returned un-

* Source: Let Us Return to the 1945 Constitution (Jakarta: Department of Information, 1959).

der cover of British troops, they were opposed by the Republic's army and harassed by a large array of irregular fighting units. But the principal government leaders of the period, especially Vice-President Hatta and Prime Minister Sjahrir, saw it as important that military resistance be coupled with attempts to win overseas support for the cause of Indonesian independence. The following manifesto, issued in November 1945, reflects the strategy of these leaders, who sought the approbation of the victorious Allies, hoping that the United States and Great Britain in particular could be persuaded to deter the Dutch from attempting to destroy the Republic.

Political Manifesto [November 1945]*

It is two months now since we made clear in every possible way our desire to live as a free people. Today we are entering a new phase in our fight for freedom, and we are conscious that the eyes of the world are on us, with a view to ascertaining what our views and objectives are. It is therefore incumbent on us to afford the world every facility to study us and to realize that not only is our cause grounded on truth, justice and humanism, but also on common sense and sane thinking. . . .

On March 9, 1942, the Dutch Government in Indonesia surrendered to the Japanese in Bandung without offering much resistance to the invaders. As a result of that Dutch defection, the unarmed Indonesian people were delivered to the tyrannical excesses of the Japanese militarists; and for a full three and a half years the Japanese worked their will on the population, subjecting the people to a type of pressure and oppression unknown in the last few decades of Dutch rule here. The Japanese looked upon Indonesians as mere cattle. Not a few Indonesians were sacrificed by them in the interests of Japanese aggression. Forced labour was imposed on the common people, while peasants were intimidated into handing over to the Japanese the fruits or their toil. The intelligentsia was bludgeoned into lying to and deceiving the people, and the entire population was obliged to conform to Japanese military discipline; it was made to drill and carry out orders with soldier-like precision. The Japanese are gone but the little military knowledge they infused into us remains, especially in our youth.

The Dutch must accept the responsibility for what happened. After centuries of so-called "training," on March 9, 1942, the Dutch handed

---

* *Source: Illustrations of the Indonesian Revolution* (Jakarta: Ministry of Information, 1953).

over 70 million people to the Japanese in a condition of military unpre-paredness and intellectual backwardness. Indonesians lacked the where-withal with which to stand up to Japanese might and oppression and fell easy victims to Japanese propaganda. Not trusting us, the Dutch deliber-ately refrained from giving us military training; bent on keeping us ig-norant, the Dutch denied education to the masses.

As they groaned under Japanese excesses our people began to take stock of the Dutch and the consequences of Dutch rule. With sharper insight they were able to perceive how ineffective and valueless the Dutch administration had been. From that moment Indonesians awakened to the true state of affairs and there was a sudden upsurge of nationalism far stronger and deeper than ever before. And that nationalism was height-ened by Japanese propaganda directed towards Asianism. Tyrannical Japanese rule could neither curb nor stamp out the growth of Indonesian nationalism; in fact it was instrumental in fostering the growth of self-respect and patriotism among the masses and in arousing the desire to be rid of Japanese as well as all other forms of foreign domination.

Millions of our peoples died while countless other millions bore every manner of suffering under the three and a half years of Japanese rule: For this the Japanese are responsible but so too are the Dutch for having denied us the mental and material strength needed to stand up to the Japanese. Yet there is one point that must not be overlooked. Although the administration of Indonesia and the management of her industries were nominally Japanese, it was really the Indonesians who—because of the glaring inefficiency of the Japanese—carried out all the functions previously in Dutch hands. This factor is important because it gave us valuable training and self-confidence.

After having handed us bound hand and foot to the Japanese, the Dutch have not even a shadow of moral right to take the virtuous stand that we co-operated with the Japanese; the less so because, generally speaking, the Japanese obtained a greater measure of co-operation from the Dutch men and women in their employ than from the Indonesians. The Dutch willfully ignore the anti-Japanese aspect of Indonesian na-tionalism. Overtly and covertly the Indonesians resisted the Japanese, by sabotage, uprisings and other forms of opposition. Thousands of national-ists fought for this with their lives. Others underwent tortures. Yet others lived like hunted animals. Witness what happened at Blitar, Tasikmalja, and Indramaju, in Sumatra, in West Borneo and in many other places. Other nationalists who worked in the open along constitutional lines in order to strengthen national consciousness were forced into working with the Japanese. They had no option but to march and goose-step and shout out war cries in the approved Japanese manner because they served in the regiments raised by the Japanese for their own purposes.

Despite their enforced presence in the totalitarian camp, the nationalists who worked with the Japanese never for a minute forsook the nationalistic ideals which had for years been their guide. This is evidenced by the constitution they framed for the Republic of Indonesia; although it was worked out during the time of the Japanese occupation, the entire document is entirely democratic in form and spirit. On the 17th of August 1945 the Republic of Indonesia was proclaimed, and it marked the culmination of the political desire of the Indonesian people to attain sovereignty for their nation. Like an irresistible tidal wave, it carried every Indonesian along with it.

Meanwhile the Japanese had begun negotiations for their surrender to the Allies. The world at large, especially those who had helped bring into being the United Nations at San Francisco, was faced with the question of Indonesian sovereignty vis-à-vis the Dutch, whom the United Nations recognised as vested with sovereignty over Indonesia. Whenever they appeared at international conferences the Dutch claimed that they had never looked upon Indonesia as a colony and that, consequently, the Indonesians had nothing but love and affection for the Dutch Government. But for two months now the world has seen how determined the Indonesians are to have nothing to do with Dutch imperialism. In every possible way the Indonesians have manifested their desire to remain a sovereign people. The Dutch want to reimpose their rule on Indonesia; the foisting of Dutch imperialism on us will be nothing but a deliberate violation of the Atlantic Charter and the United Nations Charter; and it will result in endless bloodshed and sacrifice of life, for only by force and force alone can the Dutch try to pull down the Government we have set up.

Nor have the Dutch any moral right to walk into Indonesia to resume their old imperialistic policies on the assumption that they bear no blame for their past sins or for their surrender, which resulted in 70 million Indonesians being delivered to the tender mercies of Japanese militarism. Justice denies the Dutch any say in our affairs, and any sanctioning of their imperialistic aspirations will mean violation of the principles of justice and humanity.

The San Francisco Charter places the responsibility for the welfare of dependent peoples on certain nations, but these nations themselves are not empowered to violate the basic principles of that Charter.

There can be no doubt of the fact that the Dutch have no logical or reasonable answer to offer for the difficulties they are faced with, and this makes their position all the more untenable. Up to now there is no sign of the Dutch having other intentions than restoring the old colonial system, despite their proclamation of a statement made by Queen Wilhelmina in 1942. The Dutch know that they are unequal to the task of imposing their domination on us, but they are buoyed up by the hope of being able to utilize the Allied forces, which are here to disarm the Japanese, to crush the determination of the Indonesians to maintain their sovereignty, and thereby make it possible for the Dutch to colonize all over again. Be that as it may, the Dutch will never be able to make us give up the type of government we have chosen for ourselves because the burning flame of our patriotism will render null and void all Dutch designs on us. So long as the world can see no other way out of the present impasse except that of supporting the Dutch claim on Indonesia, and so long as such action leads to deprivation of the right of Indonesians to decide their own destiny, so long will Indonesia be unable to contribute her material wealth to the enrichment of the world. Such a state of affairs will especially tell on those countries next door to us, chiefly Australia, the Philippines and the United States of America. America must needs be affected because the Indonesians, with the rest of Asia, look forward to generous American assistance in the days to come in the task of reconstructing Indonesia and raising the living standard of her peoples. American credits and technical assistance to our country, plus the purchase of Indonesia's raw material are some forms of help we hope to secure.

In the task of perfecting our social and administrative structure we Indonesians see no necessity for the use of forcible measures. If, however, such force is ever used it will be by the Dutch because of their desire to impose themselves on us. We have no wish to impose our will on other races. All we want is a recognition of our independence and the opportunity to perfect our system of government. . . .

When the Republic of Indonesia is formally recognized we will accordingly take appropriate action regarding a number of important matters. All debts incurred by the Dutch East Indies government previous to the Japanese surrender and fairly chargeable to us we will unhesitatingly take over. All property of foreigners will be handed over to them with one exception—we reserve the right to acquire at fair prices such property as shall be deemed necessary for the welfare of the country. In concert with our immediate neighbours and the rest of the world we intend to take our place in the Council of the United Nations to further and implement the ideals contained in the San Francisco Charter.

Our internal policy will be based on the sovereignty of the people, and we will put into practice all the steps necessary to bring home and evoke in the breasts of the Eurasian and European residents of our country the highest feeling of patriotism and democracy.

In a short while we intend to prove our adherence to democratic ideals by calling a general election, in accordance with the constitutional principles laid down for our country. There is always the possibility that such an election may result in far-reaching changes, both in the composition of the present government and in such constitutional changes as may be called for by the representatives of the people.

Not only will our people enjoy freedom of speech and of religion and freedom from want and from fear, but they will be given every incentive to make themselves healthy in body and progressive in mind by providing all people of all social grades the benefits of modern education and training. Side by side with plans for our internal advancement and well-being, we must go beyond mere trade relations with the outside world. There must in the fullness of time be an interchange of culture and of knowledge, especially with our near neighbors and more so with people such as the Filipinos who spring from a common racial stock.

We can and will make our full contribution to world culture, but that will only be possible when we exist as a free nation on a footing of complete equality with the other peoples of the world.

II. Independence: The Search for Consensus

Having militarily reoccupied a large part of the archipelago but failed to destroy the Republic of Indonesia, the Dutch finally agreed in 1949 to cede sovereignty to a federal Republic of the United States of Indonesia, in which the original Republic of Indonesia became the major constituent state. But this compromise was shortlived: By August 17, 1950, the federation had been dissolved and a unitary state proclaimed. The first prime minister of this new republic was Mohammad Natsir, chairman of the Muslim party, Masjumi, the largest party in the existing parliament. The following is an extract from his statement to parliament when he introduced his cabinet in September 1950. Natsir's cabinet had fallen by the following February, but the central premises of his statement, consolidation and rehabilitation, getting the machines of the state and the economy back into running order, were shared by leaders of the cabinets which followed.

Mohammad Natsir: Consolidation and Reconstruction
[September 1950]*

On September 7, I announced the program of my Cabinet comprising the following eight points:

* *Source:* "A Review of Indonesia's Reconstruction," *Indonesian Review* (Jakarta), 1 (January 1951), 1.

1. To prepare and hold general elections for a Constituent Assembly within the shortest possible time;
2. To consolidate and perfect the structure and apparatus of Government;
3. To speed up the restoration of law and order;
4. To develop and strengthen the economy of the people as a means of realizing a sound national economy, and to promote amity between employers and labour;
5. To assist in building houses for the people and to intensify efforts to raise the standard of health and education of the population;
6. To perfect the organization of the armed forces and to return former army and guerilla members to civilian life;
7. To aim at the settlement of the Irian question within this year;
8. To carry out an independent foreign policy. . . .

I have repeatedly stated that the economic well-being of our community depends largely on certain factors beyond our control. This is in fact a legacy of the colonial economic structure of the past, which is still casting its shadow upon us. Our economic structure is still unbalanced, aimed at the production of agrarian raw materials, mainly for purposes of exporting. Consequently, any fluctuations in world market prices strongly and directly influence the living standards of the members of our community. Establishing a sound national economy means changing the whole structure of the economy. The industrial sector must be expanded and a greater variety of agricultural products must be grown. We must endeavour to achieve a balanced economic structure, a structure which frees us from dependence on incidental foreign factors.

It is quite obvious that such a change will require a long time and can only be realized by hard work and perseverance. The economic changes we seek will not come automatically. To be able to build up a sound national economy, its basis—i.e., the people's economy—must be strengthened and revivified. Otherwise, all schemes and planning will remain mere dreams. It must be emphasized, however, that the desired changes from a colonial to a national economic structure cannot be achieved in one or two years. The endeavour to make Indonesia's economy less dependent upon the world market and to establish an independent economy at home requires not only hard work but also persistence.

Throwing out of foreign manpower and personnel would not bring about a sound national economy but, on the contrary, would mean killing the hen that lays the golden eggs. Let nobody, therefore, expect such foolish steps from the present Government. This Government will only undertake what can be done and completed by its successors in the years . . . to come.

Let us consider the position of our producers, the ricegrowers as well as the export producers. Forming the bulk of our society, they constitute the weakest group. They lack the knowledge, education and organizational skills which present-day conditions require. Their position in relation to other social groups is therefore exceptional. The economic policy of the Government aims at gradually ending this anomaly, at effecting a balance between the economic strength of the people. . . . This is the basis of our economic policy; only thus will it be possible to achieve a healthy economy.

Trade and industry must aim at actively aiding the people's economy. We will pay due attention to trade and industry, but the emphasis in the Government's policy is on achieving equilibrium between the strengths of the various social groups.

Recapitulating, the Government's policy is aimed at improving the living standard of the people on the basis of developing their economic strength, and increasing the stock of goods with which to meet the immediate needs of the people.

This programme will be implemented by:

1. increasing productive capacity, both for home consumption and for purposes of exporting;
2. stimulating the importing of goods, especially capital goods, for the development of small industry;
3. stimulating the growth of popular economic organizations, in particular cooperatives, by means of education, guidance and provision of more credits on more lenient terms of payment; and
4. accelerating the circulation of goods by making use of all facilities.

It is the Government's primary duty to stimulate the activity of our society in all fields, in agriculture, in industry, in commerce, in constructive organization. The Government must emphasize that improvement of conditions, especially economic conditions, can only come about, in the first place, through the activity of society itself. The Government wishes to stress this point because several groups in society cherish the unfounded hope that political independence will automatically be followed by greater prosperity.

Education and guidance to promote economic development will be the main concern of the Government's economic program. Under current conditions, the people have to compete with economically far stronger rivals. In its endeavours to build up the economic strength of the people the Government will pay the greatest attention to remedying two basic deficiencies: The lack of economic knowhow of our producers, and their lack of capital and organization.

In the early 1950's, the Indonesian parliament was widely accepted as a central political institution. Parties bickered and fought, governments lacking cohesion and authority rapidly rose and fell, and disappointment and frustration were rife. But there was little disposition to do away with parliamentary democracy, if only because many Indonesians felt the urge to prove to the Dutch that Indonesia could make a success of self-government in the currently accepted ways. But after elections had been held in 1955 and it became obvious that the Indonesians had not established a stable, authoritative government, dissatisfaction increasingly focused on the parliamentary system itself. By the end of 1956, a variety of challenges to it had appeared: Army-organized smuggling (in the name of local development) in several areas of the Outer Islands, abortive attempts to effect a military coup in Jakarta, and the enunciation of President Sukarno's ideas of Guided Democracy. Hatta was one of the few who, while agreeing that the country's political ills were very serious, sought to defend parliamentary government against its critics. The following extract comes from a speech he delivered at Gadjah Mada University, a few days before resigning from the vice-presidency. Read in conjunction with Sukarno's Independence Day speech of 1959, *Rediscovery of Our Revolution,* below, it shows how the two men had come to stand for antithetical positions.

Mohammad Hatta: Democracy Requires a Sense of Responsibility [November 27, 1956]*

When one looks at recent developments in our country and society, one gets the impression that after the independence of Indonesia had been achieved, with no small sacrifice, our idealistic leaders and freedom fighters were pushed back, while political-economic profiteers came to the foreground. They have used the national movement and its slogans for their ends and have ridden on the backs of the political parties for these same private ends. This has inevitably resulted in political and economic anarchy, followed in its wake by a reign of corruption and demoralisation.

This is the face Indonesia presents today, after having been independent for this number of years. It is clear that it was not this kind of a Free Indonesia that was visualized by our freedom fighters of earlier days.

* *Source: Past and Future* (Ithaca, N.Y.: Cornell Modern Indonesia Project, 1960); reprinted by permission of the publisher.

Everywhere today one finds a feeling of dissatisfaction. It is felt that the reconstruction of our country is not going as it should, that the situation is still far from what we had hoped for, while the value of our money is progressively declining. The gap between the actual state of affairs and our expectations is so great that in disgust people are apt to overlook the constructive things that have actually been accomplished. Just think of our achievements in the fields of education and training programs and in agriculture! However, all these achievements are overshadowed by the many unfinished and neglected projects, which because of their very non-accomplishment are doing untold damage to the state and the livelihood of the people. The depreciation and destruction of capital goods everywhere is even more apparent to the eye. Just look at the deterioration of our roads, of our irrigation system and our harbors, look at the spreading of erosion and all the rest.

The growth of democracy is also being stunted, this by the constant political squabbles. The just Indonesia we are all waiting for is still far away. Establishment of the autonomy of the various territories of Indonesia, on a basis which ensures them their own finances and proper financial arrangements with the central government, has yet to be carried out, in spite of the fact that it is now eleven years since this most important duty of the government was incorporated in the Constitution. . . .

My purpose in presenting this picture, which highlights the tremendous gap between yesterday's ideals and today's realities, is not to spread a feeling of pessimism. I firmly believe in the power of the regenerative process in our community. The demoralization which is rife in all phases of life today may retard this process, but it cannot stop it altogether. Our nation is now undergoing a period of trial for freedom and its responsibility for its own destiny. We are conscious of our freedom, but we do not yet feel our responsibility. In the long run it will be realized that there can be no lasting freedom without self-restraint, without a sense of responsibility to the community to which one belongs.

A thoroughgoing social analysis would show that all our rebellions and our splits, our political anarchy and adventurism, and all the steps taken in the economic field which have created chaos are the result of the fact that our national revolution was not dammed up at the appropriate time. There are those who say that our national revolution is a sudden explosion of society which brings with it an *"Umwertung aller Werte"* (a transvaluation of all values). A revolution shakes the floor and the foundations, it loosens all hinges and boards. Therefore, a revolution should not last too long, not more than a few weeks or a few months. It should then be checked; the time will then have arrived for a consolidation which will realise the results produced by the revolution. What is left unfinished is not the revolution itself, but the efforts to carry its ideals into effect over a period of time after the foundations have been laid. The revolution itself takes only a short time; the revolutionary period of consolidation may take quite a long time, even up to several decades. Thus it was with the French Revolution, with the Russian Revolution, with the Kemalist Revolution of Turkey, and so on.

It is not possible for a revolution to go on for too long, because if it is not checked in time, all the hinges and boards that have come loose will become a jumble and in time new elements will come in and take advantage of the chaotic situation. It will no longer be clear where freedom ends and anarchy begins.

In point of fact our national revolution, having continued for several years, ought to be checked. Its energies should be guided in an orderly fashion so as to teach the mass of the people to become conscious of their responsibilities in democracy. Democracy cannot possibly live without a sense of responsibility. Therefore our people, who have never known democracy at the level of the state, must first be trained in democracy.

But, although we had had no prior training or teaching of responsibility under the sponsorship of a government with authority, we wanted in a great hurry to set up a parliamentary democratic government. We wanted to run a parliamentary democracy without democracy and without a parliament! This resulted in the political anarchy which we have gone through during the last few years. This is why the government has lost its authority. The authority of the government has further declined because party politics introduced and maintained the peculiar custom that power is in fact not vested with the responsible government, but with the party councils which are not responsible. In this way the standing of the government has become that of a messenger boy of the political parties. A further effect of this is the fact that the most prominent party leaders are not members of the cabinet. Those who are appointed as cabinet ministers are not too prominent; sometimes they are second- or third-rate persons, who have no special knowledge of the tasks entrusted to them. This is the reality we have to contend with now as a result of a false interpretation of the course a revolution should follow and the limit of a revolutionary period, and also as a result of a party system which robs the government of the power it should hold in its hands.

The extract below, from an address to the All-Sumatran Congress of Customary Law held in March 1957, expresses some of the central ideas of anti-Jakarta regionalism which had existed in latent and inchoate form since the early 1950's, especially outside Java, and came into great prominence between 1956 and 1958. Shortly before these words were spoken, the military commanders of several areas in Sumatra seized government into their own hands in the name of the regional autonomy movements. In February 1958 several of these movements in Indonesia coalesced to form a countergovernment, the Revolutionary Government of the Republic of Indonesia, which was crushed that same year in a short civil war. Takdir Alisjahbana was trained as a lawyer and won renown as a novelist, essayist, and linguist.

S. Takdir Alisjahbana: Jakarta, a Fat Leech Sucking on the Head of a Fish [March 1957]*

The creation of a unitary state in 1950 signified the achievement of the best possible compromise between national ideals and aspirations and the practical difficulties inherent in any attempt to create a united state and nation in an area as large as Europe. It not only retained the ideal of unity which had fired the minds of Indonesians for 25 years, thereby satisfying those who had sacrificed so much in the name of that ideal, but, in granting the widest possible autonomy to the regions, it opened the way for them to progress and derive satisfaction from their own development, no less than had the Federal State, which had carried the stigma of being a colonial device aimed at keeping the nation divided.

While we have experienced almost seven years as a free and unitary state, in the light of this history and of the present situation of deep crisis we cannot but admit that we have failed to make our Constitution work. Not only have we failed to fulfil the promise of regional autonomy clearly expressed in Article 131 of our Constitution, but we have also misused our slogans of unity to satisfy a whole lot of egotistical desires for power, wealth and position, and even regional advantage. Instead of providing freedom and equality of opportunity to all Indonesians, the central government, under the slogan of unity, now operates in the same centralized fashion as did the Dutch colonial government.

During the stuggle against the Dutch, most of the leaders were dispersed throughout the regions, especially in Jogjakarta. After the transfer of sovereignty they hurried to Djakarta to take over the government of the whole Indonesian state. Then, after all their sufferings in the long and arduous struggle for independence, they were suddenly confronted

* Source: Perdjuangan untuk Autonomi dan Kedudukan Adat didalamnja (The Struggle for Autonomy and the Position of Customary Law Within It) (Jakarta: Pustaka Rakjat, 1957).

with opportunities to gain positions, power and wealth. The outcome was that most of them lost their sense of direction and instead of a concentration of energy and thought upon carrying out the tasks involved in uplifting and advancing the people of all Indonesia who had suffered so much, there has been a scramble for power, position and wealth unparalleled in Indonesia. Leaders flocked to Djakarta to fill top positions in the governmental hierarchy of the unitary state which they had inherited from the Dutch. Alongside this they created various new positions from which to control the whole country.

Not only has most of the revenue of the new State accumulated in Djakarta, but most of it has also been spent there. Djakarta has become the centre where the money collected from the rest of the country is divided up. It is not surprising that anyone who wants to do business of any kind must make his way to Djakarta because only there . . . is there access to finance, only there are decisions made. Consequently the city has expanded at an astonishing rate, far more rapidly than at any time during the colonial period. The pre-war population of half a million has already increased to three and a half million, and along with this population growth has gone a corresponding increase in multi-storied buildings, beautiful villas . . . and fine cars. Due largely to this increased affluence it can be said that Djakarta has grown so as to encompass not only the glittering new satellite town of Kebajoran, but also the large area between Bogor and Tjiandjur, where the Djakarta rich spend their leisure time.

Undeniably Djakarta, as the centre of government and business, has exhibited extremely rapid progress during the last seven years. If Djakarta conditions were a gauge of the condition of the country as a whole, we could well be proud of Indonesia's progress and development. But what are we to say of the real situation, in which Djakarta, with its population of top officials and business leaders who are all tied to each other by a whole range of political and financial connections, is like a fat leech sucking on the head of a fish, the fish being Indonesia. The leech sucks blood from the body of the fish and so grows fatter and fatter while the fish, losing blood, gets thinner.

This is no exorbitant analogy. Djakarta can really only be compared with Chinese cities like Shanghai just before the fall of Chiang Kai-shek. Everybody, even Djakarta people themselves, is aware of the situation, but so many groups and individuals have become involved in this exploitation of the regions during the past seven years, and such a complicated fabric of vested interests has been woven, that it is no longer possible to find a way out. This is principally because the political struggle which called for such great sacrifices during the revolution has been replaced by a scramble to pick the fruits of victory. It is precisely because the politicians have become involved in exploitation of the regions on such a scale, that the crisis now confronting our nation is so grave.

We all know that because Djakarta is the sole centre of power, the political parties playing the game of power have all established their headquarters in Djakarta. The presence of so many political party leaders in Djakarta has increased the total amount of wealth and power there so that it is no longer possible to change the situation by legally proper means. Each new leader who appears in the provinces regards the achievement of a position in the national capital as his goal, and is in fact welcomed to Djakarta with open arms. But his removal to the centre only serves to strengthen the ranks of the rulers at the centre who join in the feast of sharing Indonesia's power and wealth. . . .

In the prevailing atmosphere in the capital of struggle for power, rank and riches, there is no possibility of the problems of the regions receiving a sympathetic hearing.

With all this in mind, we should regard the tumultuous events of the last three months—the actions in Central Sumatra of the Banteng Council and in Medan of Colonel Simbolon,[2] the formation of the Garuda Council in South Sumatra and the announcement of military rule in the 7th military region (East Indonesia)—as evidence that our people in the regions still retain their balance and good sense. They do not want, and will not tolerate, the political game and the financial debauchery in the capital which causes what is potentially one of the world's richest countries to retrogress and decline. . . .

We in South Sumatra are keenly aware of the disparities existing between Djakarta, where construction is on a wasteful scale, and our region, which is one of the chief foreign-exchange producing areas in the country. To say nothing of electrification and factory construction, there is not one stretch of good road in all South Sumatra, an area as large as Java, so that villages become isolated, crops rot in the fields because transport costs are higher than the value of the yield, and economic activity ceases. On all sides the more energetic and spirited young people leave their villages to seek a livelihood elsewhere.

Despite the anger aroused by the sight of such unlimited confusion, incompetence, injustice, corruption and political conflict and despite our vexation at seeing how much work there is to be done, while all our efforts are stultified by the failures, chaos and corruption in the capital, we must, at all costs, approach the problems besetting our nation calmly.

[2] The leader of the unsuccessful attempt to establish rule by an anti-Jakarta regional council in North Sumatra.

We must believe that the present situation is merely a passing mistake, like a sickness in childhood. We must believe that our nation still has the resources to surmount this grave crisis.

I believe that it is this conviction that has endowed all the participants in the anti-government actions in the regions over the last three months with a sense of responsibility and solidarity in stating their grievances against Djakarta. In each case it has been clearly stated that the purpose of such action was to prevent further deterioration in the condition of our nation in order to preserve its unity. In every instance the opportunity for negotiation with the central government has been clearly, indeed eagerly, provided.

III. Guided Democracy

By the middle of 1958 the institutions of parliamentary democracy had crumbled, as a result of the fighting between the central government and the regionalist countergovernment established in West Sumatra; the greatly enhanced political role played by the army after the declaration of martial law; and the wide condemnation of the parties and liberalism by adherents to President Sukarno's ideas of a Guided Democracy. However, the institutions of Guided Democracy did not materialize until 1959. From early in that year, the government pressed for readoption of the 1945 constitution, with its provisions for a strong presidency and a weak parliament, but it failed to gain support from the necessary two-thirds majority of the Constituent Assembly. Then in July 1959 President Sukarno dramatically dissolved the Assembly and decreed the reactivation of the original constitution. In his Independence Day speech of 1959, from which the following extract is taken, the president justified this decisive step. The speech was subsequently schematized as the Political Manifesto (Manipol), the central political doctrine of the Guided Democracy period.

Sukarno: Rediscovery of Our Revolution [August 17, 1959]*

[The year] 1959 occupies a special place in the history of our Revolution. A place which is unique! There has been a year which I named the

* *Source: The Rediscovery of Our Revolution* (Jakarta: Department of Information, 1959), and *Political Manifesto* (Jakarta: Department of Information, 1960).

"Year of Decision." There has been a year which I called the "Year of Challenge." But I shall give the year of 1959 another title: 1959 is the year in which—after almost ten years of bitter experiences—we have returned to the 1945 Constitution, the Constitution of the Revolution. 1959 is the year in which we have returned to the spirit of the Revolution. 1959 is the year of the Rediscovery of the Revolution. 1959 shall be called the "Year of the Rediscovery of our Revolution."

It is for this reason that the year 1959 has a special place in the history of our National Struggle, a unique place.

I have frequently expounded on the stages of our Revolution.

1945–1950 was the stage of physical Revolution. In that stage we seized and we defended what we had seized. That was the power and authority we took out of the hands of the imperialists into our own. We seized and defended that authority with all the spiritual and physical power we had —with the fire of our souls and the fire of our rifles and cannon. The heavens of Indonesia at that time were like the skies ablaze. The earth of Indonesia was a sea of fire. 1945–1950 was then the period of physical Revolution. That period, the period of seizing power and authority and defending it, was the period of political Revolution.

I have called 1950–1955 the stage of survival. Survival means continuing to live and not dying. Five years of physical revolution did not lay us low. Five years of battling, of suffering, of bodily sacrifice, of hunger, of playing dice with death, did not bring us to destruction. Our body was covered with wounds. Where there were holes we mended them, where there were gaps we plugged them. And in 1955 we could say that we had redeemed all the suffering we had gone through in the period of physical revolution.

Beginning with 1956 we sought to enter a new period. We wanted to enter the period of socio-economic Revolution, to realize the final objective of our Revolution. That objective is a just and prosperous society. . . .

It was in this perid, the period of preparation for the socio-economic revolution, that the bad consequences of the compromise of 1949[3] became more and more apparent. It was felt by the whole society—except for that society in which people could touch pitch and not be defiled, that society in which people had "arrived," the society of the sedan leaders and the import-licence grabbing leaders. It was felt by the whole of the People that the spirit, the principles and the objective of the Revolution which we launched in 1945 had now been infected by dangerous diseases and dualisms.

[3] The settlement whereby the Dutch relinquished their claims to sovereignty in Indonesia, and an Indonesian federation, with the Republic of Indonesia as its main constituent, was established.

Where is that spirit of the Revolution today? The spirit of the Revolution has been almost extinguished, has already become cold and without fire. Where are the Principles of the Revolution today? Today nobody knows where those Principles of the Revolution are, because each and every party lays down its own principles, so that there are those who have departed from even the principles of Pantja Sila. Where is the objective of the Revolution today? The objective of the Revolution—a just and prosperous society—is now, for persons who are not sons of the Revolution, replaced by liberal politics and liberal economics. Replaced by liberal politics, in which the votes of the majority of the people are exploited, blackmarketed, corrupted by various groups. Replaced by liberal economics, in which various groups want only to grab wealth at the expense of the People.

All those diseases and dualisms were conspicuous in this period of investment, particularly the four kinds of disease and dualism of which I have several times warned: Dualism between the government and the leadership of the Revolution; dualism in men's perspective on society—a just and prosperous society or a capitalist society; dualism between "the Revolution is over" and "the Revolution is not yet completed"; and dualism as regarding democracy: Shall democracy serve the People, or the People democracy? . . .

When I opened the first sitting of the Constituent Assembly, I began to issue reminders in this direction. I told the Constituent Assembly plainly at that time: "Make a Constitution which is in harmony with the Spirit of the Proclamation; make a Constitution which accords with the Spirit of the Revolution." What I expected of the Constituent Assembly was basically resoluteness, boldness, an ability to use vision. A boldness and an ability to use vision in order that we might leave behind the old sphere of thought altogether, to enter an entirely new sphere of thinking. A boldness and an ability to use imagination which was revolutionary. The whole People felt that the 1950 Constitution dampened the spirit of the Revolution, hampered and slackened the flow of the revolutionary current and killed the revolutionary way of thinking, providing fertile soil for the growth of all kinds of conventional and conservative trends. With emphasis, I reminded the Constituent Assembly that "the Constitution is made for men, and not men for the Constitution," that the Constitution should serve men, and not men the Constitution.

I had indeed hoped that the Constituent Assembly could settle this matter. And I had truly intended to let the Constituent Assembly have a high and honored place in the History of our Revolution, a high and honored place in which it would have been clear that the Constituent Assembly was the saviour of the Revolution.

But what are the facts? The Constituent Assembly proved incapable of settling the questions which faced it. The Constituent Assembly proved incapable of becoming the saviour of the Revolution. Thus, because of that failure of the Constituent Assembly, for the sake of our Country and People, and to safeguard the Revolution, I issued a Decree on July 5th last which runs as follows:

With the Blessing of the One Supreme God,

WE, THE PRESIDENT OF THE REPUBLIC OF INDONESIA, AND SUPREME COMMANDER OF THE ARMED FORCES,

State in all Duty:

That the recommendation of the President and the Government to return to the 1945 Constitution, which was conveyed to all the People of Indonesia in the President's Address of Counsel on April 22nd, 1959, did not result in a decision by the Constituent Assembly on the basis stipulated in the Provisional Constitution;

That in connection with the statement of the majority of members of the Constitution-making Body to the effect that they would not attend sittings again, it is no longer possible for the Constituent Assembly to conclude the task entrusted to it by the People;

That such circumstances give rise to conditions in the institutions of the State which endanger the unity and the safety of the State, the Country and the People, as well as obstructing over-all construction and development to achieve a just and prosperous society;

That we are forced, acting with the support of the majority of the People of Indonesia, and impelled by our own conviction, to follow the one and only way of saving the State of the Proclamation;

That we are convinced that the 1945 Constitution is infused with the spirit of the Djakarta Charter of June 22, 1945, and that the Djakarta Charter is part, with that Constitution, of a single chain of unity.

On this basis, therefore,

WE, THE PRESIDENT OF THE REPUBLIC OF INDONESIA, AND SUPREME COMMANDER OF THE ARMED FORCES,

Decree the dissolution of the Constituent Assembly; Decree that the 1945 Constitution shall be in force again for the whole of the Indonesian People and the entire country of Indonesia as from the date of this decree, and that the Provisional Constitution shall no longer be in force.

The establishment of the Provisional People's Consultative Assembly, (which shall be composed of the members of the People's Representative Council augmented by delegates from the regions and from groups)

and of the Provisional Supreme Advisory Council will be effected in the
shortest possible time.

> Decreed at Djakarta, July 5, 1959.
> In the Name of the People of Indonesia,
> *President of the Republic of Indonesia,*
> *Supreme Commander of the Armed Forces,*
> SOEKARNO.

Yes, Brothers and Sisters after passing through the "Year of Decision"
and the "Year of Challenge," we have now come back to the original basis
of our struggle. We have now arrived at the "Rediscovery of our Revolution."

What is the meaning of this?

Does this mean merely the replacement of the 1950 Constitution with
the 1945 Constitution? No! . . .

Does this mean merely that we are looking for technical perfection and
technical efficiency in our work and all our efforts? No! . . . We are
looking for changes more profound than those. We are looking for a
realization of the deepest possible kind—a realization which penetrates
into the bones, into the soul and the spirit—the realization that we have
deviated from the principles and goals of our struggle. We are looking
for the deepest possible realization of the fact that the basic characteristics of our Revolution cannot be any other than the principles and objectives which we proclaimed on August 17, 1945.

Inner changes, becoming aware of having deviated in this way, will
automatically bring about changes and improvements as regards physical
and material affairs.

People of Indonesia, awaken again now! Rise up again with the spirit
of the Proclamation in your hearts! Abandon the past! But do not complain. Complaints are the signs of a weak soul. Yes, indeed the past has
been wrong. We see that past now as ten years of wasted time. But do not
complain. Be proud and happy that we are now aware of this, and march
on!

The years after 1956 saw a steady rise in President Sukarno's power,
and nowhere was this more obvious than in the field of foreign policy.
He made many extended, overseas trips in these years, seeking attention for the world's fifth most populous country and support for Indonesia's struggle for West Irian. The following extract comes from a
speech Sukarno made before the United Nations General Assembly in
1960. It typifies the terms Sukarno used to speak to the world during

the years before he moved away from active nonalignment to a more radical doctrine of what he called the "New Emerging Forces" (see Sukarno's Independence Day speech for 1963, *The Revolution of Mankind,* below).

Sukarno: Building the World Anew [September 30, 1960]*

Imperialism, and the struggle to maintain it, is the greatest evil of our world. Many of you in this Chamber have never known imperialism. Many of you were born free and will die free. Some of you are born of those nations which have inflicted imperialism upon others, but have never suffered it yourselves. However, my brothers of Asia and Africa have known the scourges of imperialism. They have suffered it. They know its dangers and its cunning and its tenacity.

We of Indonesia know, too. We are experts on the subject. Out of that knowledge and out of that experience, I tell you that continued imperialism in any of its forms is a great and continuing danger.

Imperialism is not yet dead. Yes, it is dying: Yes, the tide of history is washing over its battlements and undermining its foundations. Yes, the victory of independence and nationalism is certain. Still—and mark my words well—the dying imperialism is dangerous, as dangerous as the wounded tiger in a tropical jungle.

I tell you this—and I am conscious of speaking now for my Asian and African brothers—the struggle for independence is always justified and always just. Those who resist that irresistible onward march of national independence and self-determination are blind; those who seek to reverse what is irreversible are dangers to themselves and to the world.

Until these facts—and they are facts—are recognized, there will be no peace in this world, and no release of tension. I appeal to you: Place the authority and the moral power of this organization of States behind those who struggle for freedom. Do that clearly and decisively. Do that now! Do that, and you will gain the full and whole-hearted support of all men of good will. Do that now, and future generations will applaud you. I appeal to you, to all members of the United Nations: Move with the tide of history; do not try to stem that tide.

The United Nations has now and today the opportunity of building for itself a great reputation and prestige. Those who struggle for freedom

* *Sources:* Published under the same title by the Indonesian Department of Information (Jakarta), 1960; also included in *Toward Freedom and the Dignity of Man.*

will seek support and allies where they can; how much better that they should turn to this body and to our Charter rather than to any group or section of this body.

Remove the causes of war, and we shall be at peace. Remove the causes of tension, and we shall be at rest. Do not delay. Time is short. The danger is great.

. . . Humanity the world over cries out for peace and rest, and those things are within our gift. Do not withhold them, lest this body be discredited and deserted. Our task is not to defend this world, but TO BUILD THE WORLD ANEW! The future—if there is to be a future—will judge us on the record of our success at this task.

Do not, I beg of you older-established nations, under-estimate the force of nationalism. If you doubt its force, look around this Chamber and compare it with San Francisco fifteen years ago. Nationalism, victorious, triumphant nationalism, has wrought this change, and it is good. Today, the world is enriched and ennobled by the wisdom of leaders of sovereign nations newly established. . . .

. . . Very definitely, the new and the re-born nations do not present a threat to world peace. We do not have territorial ambitions; we do not have irreconcilable economic aims. The threat to peace does not come from us, but rather from the older countries, from those long established and stable.

Oh yes! There is turbulence in our countries. In fact, turbulence almost seems to be a function of the first decade of independence. Is this surprising? Look here, let me take an example from American history. In one generation we must undergo as it were the War of Independence and the War Between the States. Furthermore, in that same generation we must undergo the rise of militant trade unionism—the period of the International Workers of the World, the Wobblies. We must have our drive to the West. We must have our Industrial Revolution and even, yes, our carpetbaggers. We must suffer our Benedict Arnolds. We are, as I have said very often, compressing many revolutions into one revolution and many generations into one generation.

Do you then wonder that there is turbulence amongst us? To us, it is normal, and we have become accustomed to riding the whirlwind. I understand well that to the man outside, often the picture must seem one of chaos and disorder, of coups and counter coups. Still, this turbulence is our own, and it presents no threat to any one, although, often it offers opportunities to interfere in our affairs.

The clashing interests of the Big Powers, though, are a different matter. There, the issues are obscured by waving hydrogen bombs and by the reiteration of old and worn-out slogans. We cannot ignore them, for they threaten us. And yet, only too often, they seem unreal. I tell you frankly, and without hesitating, that we put our own future far above the wrangling of Europe.

. . . Yes, we have learned much from Europe and America. We have studied your history and the lives of your great men. We have followed your example; we have tried even to surpass you. We speak your languages and we read your books. We have been inspired by Lincoln and by Lenin, by Cromwell and by Garibaldi. And indeed we have still much to learn from you in many fields. Today, though, the fields in which we have much to learn from you are those of technique and science, not those of ideas or of action dictated by ideology.

In Asia and Africa today, still living, still thinking, still acting, are those who have led their nations to independence, those who have evolved great liberating economic theories, those who have overthrown tyranny, those who have united their nations, and those who have defeated disruption of their nations.

Thus, and very properly, we of Asia and Africa are turning towards each other for guidance and inspiration, and we are looking inwards towards the experience and the accumulated wisdom of our own nations.

Do you not think that Asia and Africa perhaps have a message and a method for the whole world?

The following extract from the president's Independence Day speech in 1963 conveys several characteristic features of the late Guided Democracy period, 1962–1965. This was a period when Sukarno's personality overshadowed the polity in higher measure than at any other time, when his revolutionary anti-imperialism was at its shrillest and most strident, when his doctrine of the New Emerging Forces dominated foreign policy, and when he actively encouraged the Indonesian Communist party.

Sukarno: The Revolution of Mankind [August 17, 1963]*

On this day, in this stadium, I speak directly to the People, the People of the whole of Indonesia, even directly to the whole world, from East to West, from North to South. At present I am not in the first place speaking as President-Mandatory, or as President-Prime Minister, or as President-Supreme Commander. I am speaking here as Mouthpiece of the People of Indonesia, as President-Great Leader of the Revolution!

* *Source: The Resounding Voice of the Indonesian Revolution* (Jakarta: Department of Information, 1963).

The Provisional People's Consultative Assembly is an organ of state, the Mutual Help Parliament is an organ of state, the Supreme Advisory Council is an organ of state, but you, you, you, you, you who are present here, you who are everywhere throughout this archipelago, you who are scattered abroad, you are the organs of revolution!

Meeting the People every Seventeenth of August is of the utmost importance to me, not only because this meeting climaxes ceremonies, not only because the Seventeenth of August always arouses a new spirit, new determination, new strength, new inspiration, but also because, to my feeling, the meeting of the Seventeenth of August is a meeting between the Great Leader of the Revolution and the Highest Organ of the Revolution.

In every Seventeenth of August meeting, in every meeting with the Highest Organ of the Revolution as at present, it is as though I was engaged in a dialogue. A dialogue with the People. A two-way conversation between myself and the People, between my Ego and my Alter Ego. A two-way conversation between Sukarno-the-man and Sukarno-the-People, a two-way conversation between comrade-in-arms and comrade-in-arms. A two-way conversation between two comrades who in reality are One!

That is why, every time I prepare a Seventeenth of August address— whether in Jogja, in Djakarta, in Bogor or in Tempaksiring—I become like a person possessed. Everything that is non-material in my body overflows! Thoughts overflow, feelings overflow, nerves overflow, emotions overflow. Everything belonging to the spirit that is in my body is as though quivering and blazing and raging, and then for me it is as though fire is not hot enough, as though the ocean is not deep enough, as though the stars in the heavens are not high enough!

Because the Seventeenth of August address must for me be a dialogue with you. The Seventeenth of August address must really and truly speak with your tongue. O, my sisters and brothers living in shacks, O, my sisters and brothers from the workshops, O, my sisters and brothers in the fields, O, my sisters and brothers whose tongues cannot speak for themselves. The Seventeenth of August address is a dialogue between the Great Leader of the Revolution and the Revolution—your Revolution, my Revolution. It may not be just empty dialogue, it must also cause new thoughts and new concepts to grow which are truly capable of giving guidance to the materialization of the People's aspirations. The Seventeenth of August address should not hesitate to shake up those who are doing things wrongly through carelessness, should not hesitate to twist the ears of those who are making small mistakes, to slap those making bigger mistakes, or to beat and kick those who are seriously in error. Pointers, advice, correction, retooling, recommendations, concepts, self-criticism, information, firing enthusiasm, outlining strategy, determining tactics, encouraging and once more encouraging—all of these must abound in the dialogue I hold with the People every time there is a Seventeenth of August.

And also a stock-taking of the condition of the Revolution! And a sizing up of the further course of the Revolution, that is a looking into the Revolution's future! Do you understand now, my sisters and brothers that I thus become like a man possessed? . . .

Let me be frank: I am not an economist, I am not an expert in economic techniques, I am not an expert in the techniques of trade. I am a revolutionary and I am just a revolutionary in economic matters!

My feelings and ideas about the economic question are simple, very simple indeed. They can be formulated as follows: "If nations who live in a dry and barren desert can solve the problems of their economy, why can't we?"

Then why can't we? Just think about this:

One: Our natural riches, both those that have already been exploited and those that have not, are abundant.

Two: We also have an abundance of labour power, with a population of 100,000,000!

Three: The Indonesian people are very hard-working, and they have great skill; this is recognised by everyone abroad.

Four: The Indonesian people possess the spirit of mutual cooperation and this can be used as the basis for gathering together all funds and forces.

Five: The aspirations and creativeness of the Indonesian Nation are of a very high level—in political affairs, in social affairs, in cultural affairs, and certainly too in the field of economics and trade.

Six: The traditions of the Indonesian Nation are not insignificant. In ancient times we once controlled commerce throughout the whole of southeast Asia. We once ploughed the seas to trade right up to Arabia and Africa and China. What more do you want?

This, then, is how simple my thinking is about this matter. If we are effective in exploiting all the assets and favourable characteristics I have mentioned then the problem of food and clothing, though not simple, will certainly be able to be solved within a short period. . . .

We are a Nation under conditions of a multi-complex Revolution, which includes an economic revolution. Therefore: The economic problem is a part of this Revolution of ours. Therefore: We must tackle the economic problem as a part of the Revolution! Therefore: We must tackle the economic problem as an Instrument of the Revolution. There-fore: We cannot and must not tackle the economic problem in a routine fashion.

There are still people afflicted by the disease of phobias, who pretend not to understand the need for revolutionary national cooperation in the struggle against imperialism. To be specific, there are still people who suffer from communist-phobia. Because they have communist-phobia, they have NASAKOM-phobia! And this despite the fact that I have explained hundreds and hundreds of times that revolutionary national cooperation cannot possibly be effected unless NASAKOM is its core, unless there is unity between Nationalists, Religious People and Commu-nists, the three objective groupings into which the political consciousness of the Indonesian People falls. I have also explained often that being against NASAKOM is the same as being against the 1945 Constitution, the same as being against the Pantja Sila, the same as being against con-centrating our forces, the same as being against the gathering together of all revolutionary groups, the same as being . . . soft in the head!

It is obvious that we have now seized an advantage from imperialism. We have won in our struggle against imperialism in a number of differ-ent fields. We have for instance won in the struggle for the return of West Irian.

Wherein lies our success in winning this advantage from imperialism? World imperialism has unity and alliances, but on the other hand it also has its splits, its quarrels, its inner conflicts. We, on the other hand, do not need to have splits, and if there is a split we must forge unity out of that split. This is our basic point of departure. And so in the struggle against imperialism I always try hard to build up the strength of revolutionary national cooperation, to build up the strength of the gathered assemblage of revolutionary forces, to build up the strength of revolutionary unity based on NASAKOM.

Steer clear of these phobias. Steer clear of nationalist-phobia, steer clear of Islam-phobia, steer clear of communist-phobia, steer clear of NASA-KOM-phobia, steer clear of peasant-phobia, steer clear of worker-phobia and steer clear of all of the other phobias that bring out lack of compact-ness. Because lack of revolutionary national compactness means losing the advantage to imperialism, which means allowing victory to go to im-perialism, which means the failure of our Revolution, which means that we become a nation without significance.

Indonesia's position in the Revolution of Mankind has become clearer as time has gone by. In fact, it stands with others in the front ranks! Indonesia's relations with the outside world are not just based on calcu-lations of material advantage. On the contrary they also involve the relationship between the Indonesian Revolution and the Revolution of Mankind.

In this connection, we are associated together in what I have called the "New Emerging Forces." We are a dynamic and militant member of the association of the New Emerging Forces. What is it that I am calling the New Emerging Forces? The New Emerging Forces are a mighty force consisting of the progressive nations and groups that want to build a New World of justice and friendship between nations, a New World of peace and prosperity, a New World without imperialism and colonialism and without the exploitation of man by man and nation by nation.

The New Emerging Forces are composed of the oppressed nations and the progressive nations. The New Emerging Forces are made up of Asian nations, African nations, Latin-American nations and nations of the Socialist countries and of progressive groups in the capitalist countries. The New Emerging Forces consist of at least two thousand million people on this earth! Is this not a mighty power, so long as it is effectively organised and built up? I am looking forward to the Second Asian-African Conference, I am looking forward to the first Asian-African-Latin-American Conference, I am looking forward to a Conference of the New Emerging Forces!

We are holding GANEFO, that is, the Games of the New Emerging Forces. After they have taken place, let us, God willing, hold CONEFO, a Conference of the New Emerging Forces.

So that the forces of Progressive Mankind can be quickly built up!

So that the Old Established Forces shake, nay, tremble! So that the Old Established Order may quickly collapse!

There are persons who say, why bother about the Old Established Order! Leave them alone, let them be! Live and let live!

How stupid such people are! They do not realize that the world's security is constantly threatened by the Old Established Order. They do not realize that the security of their own nation is constantly threatened by the Old Established Order. Don't they realize that their own nation has been colonised for 350 years, kept in shackles and humiliated for 350 years, oppressed and exploited for 350 years, squeezed for 350 years by the Old Established Order until it became a nation of skin and bones?

Oh yes, to oppose the Old Established Order is to court dangers, to build up the New Emerging Forces is to take risks. But where is there a struggle that is a real struggle that does not bring dangers? Now, are we here a nation engaged in struggle or not? Are we here a fighting nation or not? Are we here a nation of weaklings, or a nation of *banteng,* our own strong bull? If we are a nation that is engaged in struggle, if we are a fighting nation, if we are a nation of *banteng* and not a nation that counts for nothing, then come, let us be bold enough to live dangerously, come, let us be bold to *Vivere Pericoloso!* . . . Long live *Vivere Pericoloso* on the path that is willed by God and blessed by Him.

Apart from it being our duty to oppose the avaricious greed and all the crimes of the Old Established Order, such opposition is also an act of history. The Indonesian Revolution is an act of history; the Revolution of Mankind, too, is an act of history. As I said in Manila, "One cannot escape history." . . . In following the laws of history, we must consult with our friends [and] we must confront our foes. Consultation and confrontation are the essence of the dialectical process by which men and nations act in history, which is always on the march.

IV. The New Order

The transition from Sukarno's Guided Democracy to what became known as the New Order began with the elimination of the PKI after the events of October 1, 1965, and went on to the removal from political power of President Sukarno. On that date, a group of middle-ranking army and air force officers calling themselves the September 30 Movement attempted, through a coup d'état, to force President Sukarno to accelerate the leftward trend of the previous years, and they destroyed the precarious balance of the late Guided Democracy period. The coup group, however, was quickly crushed by the army under the leadership of Major General Suharto, who, asserting that the PKI was involved in the *putsch*, then launched a massive attack on the party and its associated organizations.

By December 1965 PKI activities had been suspended, and thousands of members of the party and its affiliates had been killed or detained. But Sukarno still held out against army pressure to ban the party, and drew more and more hostility from both military and civilian groups. Massive demonstrations in the beginning of 1966 by army-supported student groups, especially in Jakarta and Bandung, finally led Sukarno, on March 11, to sign over most of his executive powers to the army chief of staff, General Suharto. The inception of the New Order is usually dated from this event.

The students who took part in the demonstrations of January to March 1966 feel that their courage and dedication forced the change. The sense of revolutionary purpose and elan of this "1966 Generation" is captured in the following poems. Their simplicity and directness is representative of the poems written during that period to be circulated in mimeographed form and declaimed at large student gatherings.

Three Poems of the 1966 Generation [January–March 1966]*

Tyranny

tyranny is words
which give birth to many means
which say nothing

tyranny is thought
which is changed into slogans
which fetter thought

tyranny is freedom
in the midst of an unbounded desert
which paralyzes freedom

tyranny is power
which reigns over darkness
which breeds more darkness

BUR RASUANTO

Reflections of an Old Fighter

The People's army disarmed Injustice
When they gathered the dust of history
And a group of young men marched
Because today's fight
Is the fight of a pure heart
Never has unity felt so strong
Unless it were twenty years ago.

* *Sources:* "Tyranny" (Tirani) and "Reflections of an Old Fighter" (Refleksi seorang Pedjuang Tua) are taken from H. B. Jassin, ed., *Angkatan 66* (Jakarta: P. T. Gunung Agung, 1968); reprinted by permission of the publishers. An excerpt from "A Petition to Our Lord the Minister" (Sebuah Petisi Kepada Jang Mulia Menteri) is taken from Bur Rasuanto's collection *Mereka Telah Bangkit* (Medan: Cornershop, 1967); reprinted by permission of Bur Rasuanto. The three poems have been translated by Harry Aveling.

Students left their lecture-halls
High-school students ran into the main roads
Soldiers of righteousness rose to set up truth
Again we heard screamed
Your name, Freedom
As twenty years ago.

The circle of history has brought us
To this moment
No tyrant
Dared lift his hand in the middle of the road
And shout: Stop!

None. And were there
He could not.

Because today's struggle
Is the struggle of the pure in heart
Never has unity felt so strong
Unless it were twenty years ago.

                              TAUFIQ ISMAIL

A Petition to Our Lord the Minister

and what of our lord the minister
who cursed the behaviour of the young people
talking about the beauty of our town being destroyed
while as long as we have known
the city has never been beautiful
truly my lord
this city has long lacked beauty
long indeed—has our lord had his eyes closed
for so long
while all the other great lords
besmirched the purity of the city
defiled the history of our race and nation
with their greed, deceit, and various sins
uselessly scattering the fatigue and suffering sweated from the masses
in wasteful banquets and thousands
of meaningless slogans

racing their herds of whores and stirring slanders
antagonism and murder amongst us
providing prison-cells for those who dared question.

BUR RASUANTO

The following extract comes from an editorial of June 1967 in the
influential Bandung weekly, *The Indonesian Student* (West Java
edition). This journal had been founded a year earlier by a group of
Bandung students who were active in the demonstrations of early 1966,
and it had served as a pacemaker in the de-Sukarnoization of the in-
tervening year. But its importance had already begun to recede, as
had that of the student movement as a whole, when President Suharto's rule became more firmly established. The editorial's combination
of disillusionment with military power and optimistic insistence on the
continuing right of the 1966 Generation to shape the New Order,
which it had helped usher in, is perhaps characteristic of student responses to the new situation.

The Holy Anger of a Generation [June 19, 1967]*

On June 19th, 1967, we completed our first year and embarked on a
second. It is not for us to criticise or praise what we have done. Our task
is to do what we promised ourselves we would do and complete what we
have begun; that is what drives us to work. Those whose sleep was disturbed by the sound of our voice and who want us quiet—let them be on
their guard . . . for our voice will continue loud and clear. . . .

We have called for justice a hundred times and we shall call for it
again and again. It is sad when men are locked up like wild animals as a
result of the rule of law, sad to see men forced to live in isolation behind
iron bars or forced to kiss the dust on which they have trampled. But it is
a thousand times sadder when millions of people are cheated, insulted
and exploited, sacrificed to the pleasure of rulers who play at being gods
above the law.

It is not for revenge that we demand an immediate implementation of
justice, but because to delay justice is injustice.

Some say: "Yes, the law must be upheld. But more important still is
order and tranquility." What kind of order and tranquility is this that
would try to postpone justice? Without justice, what sort of order can be

* *Source: Mahasiswa Indonesia* (Edisi Djawa Barat), June 19, 1967.

kept, but one full of complaints and resentments, full of the wrath of men held in contempt. Where can tranquility be found where each mouthful of rice costs men their self respect? Shall this nation which once carved nobility and greatness be allowed to sink further, to become a gang of swindlers, black-marketeers, thieves and pickpockets, spending the rest of their history as a pack of wolves who deceive each other and gobble each other up?

You who have been entrusted by the people to uphold and implement the law, do not look the other way. Answer.

And what of that big word that is tossed about in our country like a toy, democracy. What is democracy, if it is not a symphony of life based on respect for human values and the principles of law? There is no democracy if millions of men are turned into horses for the pleasure of a handful of riders who never pay.

Ah, power, how many rupiahs it can furnish and how much indulgence! And how many there are who obtain it only through cunning, deceit and corruption, by licking the feet of the tyrant!

There are those who say, "Our groups are upholding and implementing true democracy." But we say: Can trees whose only fruit are empty slogans, conflict and tyranny be called trees of democracy? No, indeed, trees like this must be felled and destroyed to the roots and replaced by trees of a new kind. Let those who call themselves the defenders and implementers of democracy get busy with planning and work to produce well-being for the whole people, to put an end to wailing and sighing.

Here we stand, and we voice the holy anger of a generation.

We see before us an Indonesia which is old and broken and poor, bent down by sufferings and foreign debt. If this Indonesia wishes to live on, she must shake off her decrepitude and throw it back into the past. She must absorb new ideas and new values and undergo a complete rebirth.

"But what about our identity?" some people ask. "Must we throw that into the dustbin?" Our reply is: Can a nation go on living with half its body buried in the past? How can any nation pride itself on its identity if it is unable to create anything new? A nation without creative power and capable only of boasting of its past—this is not a nation with identity. It is simply stupidity.

Identity is not a permanent cocoon. Identity is the principle which moves us to surmount one obstacle after another, to smash one form after another in the creation of something new. In the past Indonesia could boast a great identity because she was open to new ideas and new values. Let us too be open to receive all that is new and marvel at inventions and creations. Let us throw off whatever obstructs this renewal as a butterfly throws off its cocoon, to fly high and far and taste life in all its fullness.

Let things new come from any direction whatsoever, for we are not step-children in the world.

. . . How sad the fate of a nation which has yet to learn the ABC's of democracy—after 22 years of independence! How sad the condition of a nation which still has pre-historic vehicles creeping along its countryside, in an age when modern technology is concerning itself with the launching of spaceships, a nation most of whose citizens still live in darkness, un-touched by the progress of civilisation! How sad the state of a nation which, after a quarter century of independence, cannot free itself from the most basic problems of subsistence, with most of its citizens forever forced to worry about food for the next day, their thoughts never rising beyond their bowl of rice!

Let this generation arise then to put an end to this rottenness. Let it arise along with those others whose conscience has not yet been buried under riches and power. When will renewal ever start if not today?

There are those who say, "The earth is a field in which the Devil sows sin. Light the way toward Heaven, ye children of this dark world." But we say: Light up this earthly life, grace it with prosperity and abundance, with a million lights and colors, so that the way to Heaven is broad and bright. Earth is the one place where the spirit can rise through challenge after challenge to ever greater heights. No one can make light of the im-portance of this earthly life without scorning the power of God who is its foundation. How could earth remain solid under our feet but for God's power working in its every atom? How could earth provide us with riches but for God's love acting in and upon it? Men who toil for a new and better life, who wipe the sweat off their brow, know that the earth on which they stand is holy ground.

The following passage comes from a statement by the army leader-ship, issued in July 1967, in answer to rising public criticism of the army's power. Official speeches and government newspapers have con-tinued to support the army against accusations of militarism and dual function. See, for example, Suharto's speech, *Democratic Rights May Not Be Used as Masks,* below.

The Civic Mission of the Armed Services Is Not Militarism [July 1967]*

The adventurist counter-revolutionary September 30 Movement of the PKI created a disastrous national crisis which directly endangered the

* *Source:* Published under the same title by the Department of Defense and Security (Jakarta), 1967,

very foundations and basis of the life of our State and Nation, directly jeopardizing its philosophy, the Pantja Sila.

In serious crises of this kind . . . the Army and Armed Forces have always seen it as their duty to act decisively. . . . On this occasion the Army and Armed Forces, represented in the person of General Suharto, have been directly charged by the People, through the Provisional People's Consultative Assembly, M.P.R.S., the highest political institution of the State, with establishing political and economic stability.

The effort made by the Army and Armed Forces to carry out this task involves equipping itself with able personnel capable of ensuring the implementation of programs decided upon; in other words, putting members of the Armed Forces to work in non-military fields. This is, of course, done on the principle of "the right man in the right place."

With an increase in the number and range of activities of military men in non-military positions, there have been slanderous accusations and expressions of dissatisfaction, including epithets like "the green flow," "the greedy Army and Armed Forces," and "Militarism." Most of these accusations are groundless, cannot be substantiated and should be disregarded.

On October 1, 1965, there was a vacuum of National Leadership, when Dr. Sukarno, who was then President, took the side of the Gestapu/PKI. . . . General Suharto and the Army and Armed Forces . . . took a stand against the attempted coup. They could then have taken power if they had had any such plans. But this was not the case. Democracy and the Constitution were upheld and maintained. There was no seizure of power, but measures were taken to safeguard the Indonesian State and Nation. On March 11, 1966, there was again a situation which could have issued in a military take-over. But again this did not happen. . . .

Ultimately, the People, through the Fourth Plenary Session and the Special Session of the . . . M.P.R.S. expressed their confidence in General Suharto as the representative of the Army and Armed Forces.

The M.P.R.S. Decree No. 9 of 1966 endorsed the Order of March 11, 1966;[4] the M.P.R.S. Decree No. 13 of 1966 empowered General Suharto to form and lead the AMPERA Cabinet; and the M.P.R.S. Decree No. 33 of 1967,[5] issued to eliminate dualism in the Government and the leadership of the nation, expressed confidence in General Suharto as bearer of the responsibility of leadership of the Indonesian Nation.

[4] This order, issued by President Sukarno, empowered General Suharto to "take all steps he deemed necessary to safeguard the security, peace and stability of the Government and the course of the Revolution."

[5] Under this decree President Sukarno was stripped of his remaining powers and General Suharto was named acting president.

The facts can be seen further in the following examples. Wherever a Regional Governor has been appointed from the ranks of the Army or the Armed Forces this has been done according to proper procedures and legal provisions. The man concerned has been chosen by the regional legislature as required under the law. The situation is the same in the case of regional heads at other levels. Everything has been done according to the demands and wishes of the people. The same applies in the case of men appointed to membership of legislative bodies.

Indeed, history will record that in augmenting the membership of the Mutual Help Parliament on the basis of Law No. 10 of 1967, General Suharto and the Army and Armed Forces were in a position to appoint members of the Army and Armed Forces but chose not to use this opportunity. Of the 107 persons chosen as new members of the Mutual Help Parliament, only four were members of the Armed Forces. The other 103 were all civilians, many of them from the Action Commands, representing students, workers, farmers, fishermen and other functional groups, and from the political parties. The criteria whereby members of the Armed Services have been appointed to executive positions at home and abroad are exactly the same as for persons and groups outside the Armed Forces. No exceptions are made and no dispensations granted. The presence of a number of Armed Service members in the AMPERA Cabinet and among the Secretaries General and Directors General should be understood in the light of political and other factors, and particularly of the fact that General Suharto, as Chairman of the Cabinet Presidium and bound by the task entrusted to him in the [MPRS] Decree 13 of 1966, must choose executives who can manage the very complex situation of these times. Indeed, this is only normal personnel policy.

The conclusion can be drawn that the civic mission in which the Army and Armed Services are presently engaged does not constitute militarism in any sense, nor contain elements conducive to militarism. The Army and Armed Services are composed of men from all layers and groups of society in Indonesia, which means that there is no military oligarchy in Indonesia. The political concepts which have been put forward by the Armed Services and are being implemented by them through the duties they are discharging in the executive and legislative fields are all national political concepts which have been delineated and decided upon by the people through the [MPRS]. The military budget makes up only 20% of the State budget, whereas it is common in a military dictatorship or junta government for the appropriation and use of the State Budget to be fully controlled by the military power. The basic thinking of the Army and Armed Services is not military in the conventional sense, but flexible and based on exchanges of opinion or deliberations. The members of the Armed Services . . . are nationally conscious, as are the people in general. . . .

We call upon all members of the Armed Services of the Republic of Indonesia and the people at large to stand shoulder to shoulder in eliminating the issue of militarism, which is no more than a set of slanders aimed at sowing discord amongst the forces of the New Order. We must stand united in fostering and safeguarding the present National Leadership of General Suharto, which is democratic and constitutional, conforming with the [MPRS] Decree 33 of 1967, in order to uphold the Pantja Sila and the 1945 Constitution in all its purity, which has become the ideal of the entire rank and file of the New Order and of the Indonesian People as a whole.

Sudisman, one of five principal leaders of the PKI during 1951–1965, survived the coup and countercoup of October 1, 1965, long enough to analyze their significance. But he was arrested in December 1966, sentenced to death, and executed in 1968. In the following excerpt from his defense speech of July 21, 1967, Sudisman sets forth the reasons for the failure of the coup, staged by the September 30 Movement. Compare his speech to Suharto's Independence Day speech of 1967, *The New Order, the Panca Sila, and the 1945 Constitution*, below.

Sudisman: The Failure of the September 30 Movement
  [July 21, 1967]*

. . . I am aware that failure in struggle is always the result of mistakes. This was the case with the failure of the September 30th Movement, a failure occasioned by the accumulated mistakes of the PKI over a long period of time.

First: In the field of ideology the mistake was subjectivism, originating socially from the ocean of the petty bourgeoisie and based on the narrow-minded working methods of the petty bourgeoisie. This means looking at something from only one point of view, one-sidely, not as a whole, with

* Source: The Trial of Sudisman, Head of the Secretariat and Member of the Executive of the Politbureau of the Central Committee of the Indonesian Communist Party, in relation to the 30 September Movement (Perkara Sudisman, Kepala Sekretariat C.C. P.K.I., Angganta Dewan Harian Politik Biro C.C. P.K.I. dalam Peristiwa Gerakan 30 September) (Jakarta, 1967).

the result that reality is seen not as a coherent totality but as a cluster of discrete fragments. Consequently, at the height of its power, the PKI forgot to be vigilant, forgot that the imperialists and the reactionaries here at home could become consumed by a rage to strike. What was required under such conditions was essentially the Marxist-Leninist skill to calculate scientifically the concrete balance of forces on each side, on the side of the PKI and that of its adversaries. For organizing a movement requires more than just courage; it also requires revolutionary skill in determining the right moment and in leading the movement. These requirements were not fulfilled by the September 30th Movement, and thus were the causes of its failure. Moreover, the movement was totally isolated from any upsurge of the masses. This was true even though the aims of the September 30th Movement, as announced by the Revolutionary Council, were excellent: Preventing military dictatorship, consistently implementing Nasakomization in all areas, and taking action against all abuses in the financial and economic fields. I am in full agreement with the September 30th Movement, because it aimed at defending and maintaining the left-wing policy of the Indonesian Republic

Aside from subjectivism, the PKI leaders were also infected with modern revisionism, which comes from the embourgeoisment caused by attaining official positions in the state. These ideological weaknesses were the origins of certain theoretical conceptions of [cooperation] with the bourgeoisie. One example was the slogan, "Manipol is a common program." This particular formulation was correct, but it became incorrect when it was expanded to run: "If Manipol as a common program is carried out consistently, it will be identical with the program of the PKI." As a common program, Manipol makes room for the interests of the capitalist class (the bourgeoisie), and therefore maintains the existence of exploitation of the working class. On the other hand, the program of the PKI is Socialism, which completely abolishes "l'exploitation de l'homme par l'homme," abolishes the exploitation of man by man. Thus the Indonesian capitalists can not possibly be brought along to Socialism—they will certainly resist Socialism. The proof of this is that after the failure of the September 30th Movement, they demanded the revocation of Manipol, because Manipol declares that the future of the Indonesian Revolution is Socialism, and not capitalism. So much for the question of the PKI's ideological weaknesses, which have already been published in the PKI's Self-Criticism.

Second: In the field of politics, the PKI leadership correctly stressed the importance of "unity and struggle" in carrying out a popular front policy. But in practice the PKI sank deeply into the sea of "unity" and did not pay enough enough attention to "struggle." Working in a front means [working] with other classes; consequently, it is only proper to wage a class struggle in the interests of the driving forces of the revolution—that is, the workers, working peasants and urban petty bourgeoisie. Without struggle, the work of the front is dead; with struggle, the work of the front comes alive. This has been demonstrated by the work of the old National Front, whose decisions were not reached through struggle. As a result, the National Front never really came to life.

Third: In the field of organization, the PKI leadership did not consistently put into practice the proper method of settling contradictions within the Party through criticism and self-criticism. On the one hand, this resulted in liberalism, on the other, in commandism. Without criticism and self-criticism we became uncritical, and criticism from below did not flourish.

These mistakes of the PKI in the fields of ideology, politics and organization are all set out in the PKI's Self-Criticism, which is in the hands of the present military regime.

The positive aspect of the failure of the September 30th Movement is that it has awakened the PKI to study its mistakes and to produce this Self-Criticism. I believe that in the course of history a new generation of the PKI will eventually draw the necessary lessons from this Self-Criticism. This new generation of the PKI will make the PKI a truly Marxist-Leninist party with a revolutionary agrarian program. A PKI of this kind will be able to solve the fundamental problem of the Indonesian People: Armed agrarian revolution by the peasants, supported by a broad national unity front, an alliance of the workers and peasants under the leadership of the working class. A PKI of this kind will certainly be able to integrate itself thoroughly, in word and deed, with the masses of the People, in accordance with the ideals expressed in two stanzas of poetry that I wrote while in the Djakarta Military Prison, which I have called:

The Ocean Adjoins Mount Krakatau

The Ocean adjoins Mount Krakatau
Mount Krakatau adjoins the Ocean
The Ocean may not run dry
Though the hurricane roars
Krakatau does not bend
Though the typhoon rages.

The Ocean is the People
Krakatau is the Party
The two always close together

The two adjoining one another
The Ocean adjoins Mount Krakatau
Mount Krakatau adjoins the Ocean

After March 1966, when he was handed special executive powers from Sukarno, General Suharto sought gradually to consolidate his position, by using the institutions of state, in particular the reactivated but still provisional (i.e., appointed) Supreme People's Consultative Assembly (MPRS). The MPRS met in June–July 1966, endorsing Suharto's position as holder of executive authority and also Sukarno's grant to him in March of sweeping emergency powers. When the MPRS met again in March 1967, Suharto was able to gain its endorsement for a skillfully devised plan whereby he was named acting president, while Sukarno, though left powerless, was not actually removed from the presidency. At its third meeting in March 1968, the MPRS named Suharto full president. By this gradual approach, Suharto had avoided excessively humiliating Sukarno and had averted a new outbreak of violence which might have resulted from a frontal attack on the long-time president.

The following extract comes from Suharto's address to parliament on the eve of Independence Day in 1967, Suharto's first Independence Day as acting president. At that time his government's program of economic recovery and administrative stabilization was well under way but had only just begun to achieve appreciable success. Suharto, in this extract, presents his government's view of itself and its tasks.

Suharto: The New Order, the Panca Sila, and the
1945 Constitution [August 16, 1967]*

The function and object of the New Order is to maintain and purify the manifestation and implementation of the Pantja Sila and the 1945 Constitution. Every Indonesian, every organization, every kind of undertaking whatever that calls itself New Order, must acknowledge these two fundamentals, the Pantja Sila and the 1945 Constitution. And not only must they be acknowledged. They must also be put into practice, must be given full and appropriate substance in a way which maintains their spirit in its pure form.

The New Order is thus no more and no less than the ordering of the

* *Source: State Address of Acting President Suharto on the Occasion of Independence Day, 1967* (Jakarta: Ministry of Information, 1967).

whole life of the People, the Nation and the State with a view to returning to implementation of the Pantja Sila and the 1945 Constitution in all
their purity. I want to emphasize the word "return," because the New
Order developed as a reaction to, and in order to put a complete end to,
all the various aberrations committed under the previous order, the one
now called the Old Order.

The deviations from the Pantja Sila and the 1945 Constitution that
occurred in the period of the Old Order had deep and far-reaching consequences; indeed, they shook the Nation and State to their very foundations.

The Pantja Sila was distorted and defiled as a result of the concept
of NASAKOM, which introduced Communism into its implementation.
Communism, being based on dialectical materialism, is obviously anti-
God, whereas the Pantja Sila includes the principle of The One Divinity.
Religion was abused and distorted for political purposes.

The principle of a just and civilised Humanity was abandoned. Basic
human rights had almost vanished because everything depended on the
will of those in power. Legal guarantees and legal protection were almost
non-existent. All of this happened because what we did came, with or
without our being conscious of the fact, to be part of the strategy of the
Indonesian Communist Party. And the Communist Party accepted the
Pantja Sila simply as a tool, in order later to seize absolute power as part
of a larger plan of international communism.

The principle of Nationalism and national unity were watered down as
far as their implementation was concerned because there were elements
that subjected themselves to other interests and another ideology. The spirit
of unity was destroyed by teachings of contradictions and struggle between
classes. Splits and discord on principles and in action were to be found
among the leaders, who competed with one another by every means available, telling boastful lies to the leadership of the State, slandering their colleagues and scheming to topple them. All these things created opportunities
for the Communists to popularise themselves and to create the impression
that they were on the side of right and the defenders of the interests of the
People.

The Indonesian People know nothing of classes, because indeed we
have no classes and are not going to have classes.

Sovereignty of the People was lost in a haze; what prevailed was sovereignty of the leader.

As for social justice, that receded further and further, because the
wealth of the State was used for personal enrichment and for prestige
projects to make Indonesia a "lighthouse" to the rest of the world,
projects that destroyed the economy of the People and the State. Guided

Economics degenerated into a system of licenses benefiting a handful of persons who were close to those in power.

These were serious deviations from the 1945 Constitution as a result of the concentration of absolute power in one pair of hands, that of the head of state. The principle of a state based on law was gradually abandoned, so that it eventually became a state based on power. Constitutionalism gave way in practice to absolutism. The highest authority of State was no longer that of the People's Consultative Assembly, but rather that of the Great Leader of the Revolution. The President was not subordinate to the Assembly; on the contrary the Assembly was made subordinate to the President. . . .

My aim in detailing these various aberrations which occurred under the Old Order is to issue a reminder that the New Order, determined as it is to introduce a comprehensive change for the better and establish a regular basis for the implementation of the Pantja Sila and the 1945 Constitution, should not repeat these mistakes, should not allow the country to sink once more into the morass of these evil practices. . . .

Let me stress that the New Order has not yet been realized. It will be realized only after the formation of an elected People's Consultative Assembly, an Assembly which will appoint a President who will then form a new Government.

The program of political and economic stabilisation being carried out by the present AMPERA Cabinet is intended to establish a strong foundation for the realization of the New Order. This means that we must persist in our efforts to perfect the way in which the Pantja Sila and the 1945 Constitution are implemented. We have indeed been doing just this, on the firm foundation of shared convictions. . . .

The following extract reflects the sense of achievement felt by the Suharto government since 1968 with the apparent success of its economic policy. The author—a newspaper man, ambassador, and cabinet minister before the 1965 coup—was appointed minister of foreign affairs in 1966.

Adam Malik: The Economic Revival of Indonesia [October 1969]*

The economic conditions prevailing when the new government of President Suharto came to office were dire.

* Source: Adam Malik, "Indonesia's Economic Revival," Pacific Community, 1 (October 1969), 1:108–117. Copyright, 1969, by Pacific Community, the Pacific News Commonwealth, the Jiji Press, Ltd., Tokyo; reprinted by permission of the journal publishers.

The main source of difficulty was the failure of the former government to tackle economic problems. It was always attaching more importance to politics than to improving the economy. The process of deterioration in the economy was seen most clearly in hyperinflation, whose effects penetrated every sector of economic life [and] brought with it many hardships and distortions which seriously affected the whole character of national life. . . .

. . . The old government . . . disregarded the basic principles of realistic and rational economic policy making. Interfering too much in economic activities, it reduced the roles of private entrepreneurs to a minimum. Foreign companies—mostly Western-owned—were nationalized or put under government control. State-owned and State-controlled companies operated in all areas of business activities. . . . The growth of private entrepreneurship, which is essential for economic development, was very clearly hampered, paving the way for unscrupulous adventurers to make a living parasitically from a preferential licensing system. All this was done in the name of Indonesian socialism.

Furthermore, foreign loans amounting to $2.5 billion, which will remain a heavy burden on the balance of payments for years to come, were not used for improving or developing the economy, but rather for unproductive purposes. Where they were used for industrial projects, these were often economically unjustifiable.

As a consequence of government over-involvement in the economy, . . . corruption and abuse of power became the order of the day. There emerged a small group of very rich people amid a mass of poor Indonesians. Those days were for most Indonesians the most difficult period since the proclamation of independence. Their sufferings were aggravated by the feelings of hopelessness engendered by the prospect of a black future.

Accompanying the process of deterioration in the economy was a worsening situation in the area of foreign policy. As a result of the confrontation policy against Malaysia and other countries, Indonesia became more and more isolated from the community of the free world, and in particular from her neighbors. The antagonistic foreign policy followed towards most Western countries created difficulties in economic cooperation with those countries, and their aid to Indonesia was reduced. . . . Reduced economic aid from Western countries led to greater dependence on countries in the Eastern bloc which were willing to give aid to Indonesia for political reasons. The climax of that confrontation foreign policy was reached in 1964 when Indonesia withdrew from the U.N. and other international organizations. At that moment, Indonesia truly isolated herself from the community of nations. Fortunately, this sad state of affairs has ended.

The new government had to start building up and developing the economy from a legacy of ruins. However, the Indonesian people and Government have shown that they are determined to end the process of economic deterioration. They are now working hard to raise the standard of living . . . to at least the level enjoyed by the peoples of neighboring countries in Southeast Asia. Adhering to the decisions of the [MPRS], the new government has embarked upon a policy of overcoming the economic difficulties, according this priority over all other policies. Domestic concerns . . . definitively come before foreign policy interests. The main task has been to work towards economic stabilization and rehabilitation, especially to arrest hyperinflation and to restore price structures. . . . Rehabilitation of the factors of production has also been a matter of immediate concern. In short, everything is being done to awaken the economy into greater activity, to increase employment opportunities and to speed up the rate of economic development so that it overtakes that of population increase.

However, the road to achieving this latter goal is one full of obstacles and difficulties, not least because of the limited means and resources available. Domestic savings and domestic capital were crippled by hyperinflation. Government revenues came to be very low because of the inefficiency of the machinery of taxation. The administrative apparatus of the government functions slowly and inefficiently, hampered by the scarcity of managerial and organizational skills and the very low salaries of government employees.

Nevertheless, thanks to the tenacity and determination of the Indonesian people and Government, and also to generous assistance from friendly countries, great strides have been made over the past three years, especially in the field of monetary stabilization and in the rehabilitation of the production sector. . . . Thus, it has been possible to reverse the process of economic development.

. . . Price levels and market forces are, to a very large extent, no longer controlled by the government, but determined mainly by the private sector. The government now only gives the necessary directions, provides facilities and oversees the turning of the wheel of the economy.

The government is reducing expenditures on the state administration, and is taking steps towards achieving greater efficiency and sound management. Rationalization measures have been taken in state enterprises. The subsidies with which they were . . . provided, . . . have been discontinued except in the case of some vital enterprises. State enterprises which have been sustaining losses over the years have been sold to private businessmen, whereas foreign enterprises which were taken over by the government are being returned to their former owners. As a result of these steps a balanced budget was achieved in 1968.

Since 1968 foreign aid has been used [with few exceptions] only to finance development activities and not for routine expenditures. . . .

In accepting foreign loans, the most important consideration for Indonesia is not the amount of money she receives but rather that the terms not be too burdensome for her balance of payments in the years to come [i.e.] a rate of interest of 3 percent, a grace period of 7 years and repayment over 25 years.

Improvements have also been made in the production sector, especially in . . . rice and other foodstuffs . . . and . . . petroleum.

. . . Due to our limited economic resources and to our determination to build up our economy as soon and as quickly as possible, foreign capital is still needed. It must be utilized to maximum advantage. Indonesia's policy in obtaining foreign aid and . . . investment is in line with the independent and active foreign policy. This means that any foreign aid is welcome . . . as long as it involves no political commitments and adds no further burdens to our balance of payments.

. . . We are convinced that foreign investment can play an important role in speeding up the process of development. From the time of the enactment of the Foreign Investment Law in early 1967 until May 1969, the government has approved requests for investment in Indonesia to the amount of $570 million, covering 121 . . . projects, excluding those in . . . natural oil and gas. These investments cover activities in industry, forestry, fishery, mining and transportation. . . . In the field of oil and natural gas, the government has given its approval to the requests of 21 companies.

The economic situation of Indonesia in 1969 shows that a certain degree of stabilization has been achieved, which will form a strong basis for further implementation of the economic development program.

The Five-Year Economic Development Plan, which commenced on April 1, 1969, is intended to raise the people's welfare. Granted that the needs of the Indonesian people are enormous and the number of possible projects unlimited, and granted also that resources are scarce, it was necessary to allot priority to the most strategic sectors. These strategic sectors are those which concern the life of the entire nation—those which form a basis for other development projects, those whose implementation could be borne with the limited financing available, and those in which it is possible to obtain the maximum participation of the people.

The principal targets . . . are food, clothing, rehabilitation of the economic infrastructure, housing, increased job opportunities and spiritual welfare. The agricultural sector has a central place in it. 70 percent of the people earn their living in this sector, it yields about 65 percent of the national income and it is responsible for providing 65 percent of our foreign exchange earnings. If we succeed in increasing rice production to the point of self-sufficiency—this aim is being given top priority—Indonesia will be able to save $100 million annually in foreign exchange. Other sectors such as industry, services and the infrastructure, are seen primarily as giving support to the agricultural sector.

The student movement born in 1966 fell prey to division in 1967, and after March 1968 its importance in relation to national politics was small. But the movement, or a segment of it, was revived in January 1970 when a wave of protest rose against increases in fuel prices and against corruption.

Arief Budiman, a psychologist and literary critic, was the principal leader of this 1970 movement. He wrote the following article in *Kompas,* one of Jakarta's leading papers since 1966, in July 1970 when the Suharto government was taking the movement's case fairly seriously. Over a year later he was arrested for protesting the "Beautiful Indonesia in Miniature" project. (See Bur Rasuanto, "Is the Government Strong?" below.)

Arief Budiman: A Conversation with Pak Harto [July 20, 1970]*

This was the first time I came face to face with Pak Harto. Mar'ie Mohamad, Jopie Lasut, Didi and I shook hands with him and Pak Harto invited us to sit down. Press photographers were given an opportunity to take our pictures, after which Pak Harto invited us into his study. Pak Harto's aide, Lt. Col. Suroso, followed us, but Pak Harto sent him away. This was a surprise—meeting Pak Harto without a third party being present.

. . . When Pak Harto sent his aide away, we understood what he wanted. The President of the Republic of Indonesia wanted a frank discussion with us and did not want us to be embarrassed by the presence of a third party. I was moved.

I opened the conversation by saying that we had come to submit a document concerning something that could be an act of corruption. I said

* *Source: Kompas* (Jakarta), July 20, 1970.

this because we ourselves had not investigated the problem in detail. We did not claim to present proof of corruption. What we asked was that the problem be investigated by the appropriate authority, namely the prosecutor's office.

[Lengthy discussion of the affair revealed that President Suharto was familiar with it, and, after he promised to examine the case, the interview continued.]

Though our "agenda" was finished, Pak Harto seemed inclined to touch upon other subjects. As for us, we were waiting for such an opportunity. Pak Harto's openness created . . . an atmosphere in which we lost what fears we had had and were prepared to raise whatever was on our minds.

So Mar'ie began to talk about the registration of the wealth of important officials. Pak Harto explained that a bill concerning the registration of private possessions was being prepared. Every year important government officials would have to sign statutory declarations listing their possessions.

If anything suspicious were found, Pak Harto would dispatch people he personally trusts to check the matter. Mar'ie asked why existing agencies would not be used for this task, to which Pak Harto replied that in that case there would be cases of blackmail.

Mar'ie asked further whether the property registers would be made public. Pak Harto said that in the case of certain government officials who were under public scrutiny, he would not hesitate to make the registers public. However, it would not be necessary to publish all of them.

Jopie Lasut asked whether people who were strongly suspected of engaging in corruption would be prosecuted even where clear evidence was lacking. Pak Harto said if evidence was lacking it would not be right to prosecute because the very fact of a man's being brought before a court is damaging to him, even when it results in an acquittal.

I asked, for example, whether such extravagance as General Sutowo displayed when he married off his daughter should not be regarded as evidence of the possibility that this general had been involved in corruption. Pak Harto replied that General Ibnu Sutowo was rich before he assumed office; and that his daughter's wedding had not been paid for by the general himself but by contributions from his friends and relatives.

"I have repeatedly admonished Ibnu Sutowo," Pak Harto said, "and I did when he was planning the wedding of his daughter. But he said that, as a Javanese, he could not reject the offer of his relatives to arrange a large wedding party, and I can understand that."

I said that if that was so, why had charges not been laid against the press for alleging that the general was corrupt. This would help educate the press in responsibility. "And also generally," I said, "I consider that you have provided too few public clarifications concerning the matters on which the press has launched attacks, and so people are not well informed of what the government has been doing. You have always emphasized development, but to work for the country's development, the people must know to where they are being led. You have paid little attention to this aspect of giving idealism to the people."

Pak Harto replied that, in attacking government officials, the press was often looking for sensations. It would be just the sensation the press was after if the government were to bring these officials to court. As for lack of openness on the part of the government, Pak Harto said that to him the important thing was getting things done. This was his nature, he said. "Maybe I am too modest. I do not like talking about things where there are as yet no results to be shown."

I responded to this remark by saying that I did not agree with him, because in an open society as ours now is, the government's silence on the unfavorable press stories about government officials aroused only restless discontent and this was itself an obstacle to development. Pak Harto said that this was probably a personal weakness of his which was exploited by his opponents. "But that is the kind of man I am. I don't like a lot of talking."

Two further points are in my opinion worth noting. The first is Pak Harto's attitude toward opposition. When I raised this Pak Harto said: "I would be happy to have a group opposing me, as long as it is loyal opposition." Loyal opposition, according to Pak Harto, is opposition which does not conflict with the Constitution and the law. "People always say they support me as President, but they have never asked me whether I really like being President. To me, the presidency is a heavy duty. You know I initially had real doubts about accepting it. Only when everyone urged it upon me did I accept it. So when people are not satisfied with my performance, all I can say is that I am doing my best."

"If for example, I did not agree with holding the elections," I asked, "and wrote articles expressing opposition to it and did not vote in it, would I be arrested, or would my position be considered one of loyal opposition?" Pak Harto replied that it was my right to act in all of these ways. The important thing was that I should not resort to unlawful means to sabotage the election or prevent others from voting. So long as my opposition was within the law, that was my basic right. I was very pleased with this answer. . . .

A second point which I considered important was the question of whether Pak Harto considers the actions of the university and high school students a hindrance to development. Pak Harto said he viewed our activities so far as positive. That was why he wanted to respond by holding "consulting hours" on Saturdays. Pak Harto also warned us to be alert against those who would exploit us, and I said that there are indeed too many people and groups exploiting us. However, to us, the important thing was that efforts should be made to eradicate corruption in Indonesia. We did not want to join any group whatsoever. For instance, if Ibnu Sutowo were fired, his enemies would feel they had been vindicated and those replacing him in Pertamina [the State Oil Company] would definitely be favored. But to us, this was not the problem. If the new group engaged in corruption they would be opposed with the same zeal. We cannot afford to be always considering whether others will exploit actions we are contemplating, or we would never act at all.

Receiving Pak Harto's own assurance that he regarded our actions as fair, we thought we had obtained strong moral support directly from the Chief of State with which we could confront government officials who wanted to make arrests or ban our activities completely on the pretext of security. In this respect, Pak Harto apparently understands quite well that security imposed in disregard of the dynamics of society can only be a surface security, feeding tensions which may later find expression in explosions. What Pak Harto is attempting to create is a dynamic security based on links with the living forces of society. I consider this approach correct.

When we left Djalan Tjendana, I felt there were many things, particularly concerning actions against corruption and Pak Harto's attitude of preferring to work silently rather than "propagandize" what he is doing, that I did not agree with. But the impression that Pak Harto is a man of strong principles who knows what he is doing and where he is going was also strongly imprinted in my mind.

For the rest, it remains to be seen whether Pak Harto can find assistants who are capable of working with him to realize his aspirations.

Radical anti-imperialist ideas have found little public expression in the New Order period. But *Merdeka,* one of Indonesia's oldest newspapers, with a fairly large circulation in the New Order period and loose ties with the PNI, has repeatedly denounced the government's dependence on Western business and Western governments. It has done so out of support for the Suharto government and a desire to defend it against criticisms launched by the student groups of the 1966 Generation and their allies in the liberal press. Thus it is understandable that the following editorial includes a defense of General Ibnu Sutowo, the head of the state oil enterprise, who had come under strong attacks from these groups.

Merdeka: *Backward Satellite or Industrial Society*
[December 5, 1970]*

We live in Asia, not in Europe or the United States. Our neighbors are two great nations, India and China, which are already far ahead of us in their efforts to become economically independent. The influence of these two countries and peoples on our political, economic and social life is not inconsiderable. From ancient times to the present the current of their influence has continued to flow as the Solo River has continued to flow to the sea. We are the third biggest nation in Asia after India and China, in terms of both size and population. It is said that we are rich, but our riches have yet to be exploited, by us or with the help of friendly nations. We do, however, have the potential to become rich. And to this end there is need for a government with the courage to look far ahead.

As we look around us, we observe that since 1965 we have really been living under the domination of Western countries. We take pride in the fact that we are the one and only people in the world who defeated a Communist attack on our own, without the help of foreign troops and foreign arms, at a point where the issue was one of life or death for our Pantja Sila state. What we get as "appreciation" from friendly countries is being able to borrow money from them as long-term loans. But the money they provide is for consumer goods and very little of it is in the form of capital goods for our industrialization. Maybe we are wrong, but it seems to us that it is the prevailing mood of the friendly countries to impress us with the notion that we are not yet ready for the industrialization which would give us a sense of being economically independent.

Our economic experts have had their education in the West. That kind of education has not prepared them to see that agricultural nations must also achieve rapid technological progress. They talk of "modernization," but what they mean is slow economic evolution. They are tied to this slow thinking which results in births and poverty increasing more quickly than production.

Notice the kind of advice this group of economic experts has given to President Suharto. Our budget is tied to foreign credits. We just buy consumer goods from the Western world with these credits and at the same time try to "modernize" our agriculture. Modernization in this sense does not mean using heavy equipment and modern technology. It

* *Source: Merdeka* (Jakarta), December 5, 1970.

means using new seeds produced in the Philippines or in the United States.

Let the foreign investors have vast concessions in Indonesia's forests and seas! The credit policy of the Western countries . . . obviously sits well with the ideas of the Western-educated or American-educated economists who hold the key to Indonesia's economy these days. These people refuse to think in terms of general revolution in economic development. That would not please their professors. We must begin to think in terms of establishing basic facilities for an industrial society—synchronizing that with the rapid growth of the Indonesian population. We must think in terms of massive overhead expenditures—to expand our railway system, to build highways, docks, industrial complexes, technical institutions, elementary schools for technical education, power plants, and so on. But they would consider all that too big, costing more money than our creditors would let us have. And that is not the only reason for their reluctance to think in those terms. In addition development of this kind would give our people economic strength, would prevent Indonesia from being used as the foot-mat of those other countries.

Basic projects of the kind we need do not guarantee quick profits for those who proffer the capital for them. Not surprisingly it is areas like consumer goods, where profits can be made fast, which are attractive to foreigners investing in this country. As things stand our position as borrowers has grown weaker because the volume of loans we have contracted has exceeded what President Soekarno was able to obtain in the past. And it is clear that our rate of growth of production has remained low. At the most recent meeting between the Minister of Information and Indonesian journalists, Professor Subroto, one of our economists who believes in what is called "low-keyed" thinking about modernization, said that our annual rate of growth is 6%. This figure is essentially hypothetical because Indonesian statistics continue to be unreliable. But it is clear enough that the rate is low.

We are convinced that President Suharto and his assistants are aware of this situation and we have clear proof that he is concerned with economic problems. He understands what liberating Indonesia as far as the economy is concerned means. His positive appreciation of Dr. Ibnu Sutowo's policy in the oil sector must be seen from this angle. President Suharto has not left all of the economic and financial policy to the low-keyed economic experts, the "modernization" people. Why is it that Ibnu Sutowo's policy has been severely criticized by the group which supports low-keyed "modernization"? It is because Ibnu Sutowo supports rapid technological development for the sake of the progress of the state and the people. His forward-looking ideas will have an impact on the social and economic position of the Indonesian people in a way that should be a lesson to all students of politics, and in particular to our economic experts, the now notorious "Berkeley Mafia."[6]

We who believe that political independence should be accompanied by economic independence understand President Suharto's action in supporting Ibnu Sutowo's policy as regards oil. This is a manifestation of political far-sightedness. The opponents of Ibnu Sutowo's policy are evidently inspired by foreign capital and by the "policy of empire" of the countries which are providing Indonesia with credit and keeping her tied to producing agricultural commodities for their markets. But our oil production is now increasing. With further exploration, it is quite likely that our earnings from oil will far exceed those from our agricultural products.

Therefore, we would suggest to President Suharto that he initiate major changes in the economic and financial area. We believe that we alone must determine the use of the credits we receive. Their use must not be dictated by our creditors.

Moreover, it is important that Dr. Ibnu Sutowo's accomplishments should not be sacrificed in an effort to cover up the weaknesses of that side of our economic policy, the conventional side, which has been determined by foreign economic advisers who want Indonesia to remain backward.

If we cannot catch up with India and the People's Republic of China by modernizing our economy and technology as these two countries have been doing, we will certainly become a satellite of the Western countries, a country without any hope for the future, except as a disguised colony. Was it for that that we crushed the Communists and the "30th September Movement"?

"Overhauling the political structure" was a long-held goal of a group of New Order intellectuals who believed that parties should cease to be linked with particular cultural-cum-ideological streams. Prior to the 1971 elections, this idea was taken up by the government's front, GOLKAR, and used to justify various forms of government pressure on the parties.

Nono Anwar Makarim, a leading intellectual of the 1966 Generation, left his law studies in 1966 to become editor of the student daily, *Harian KAMI* (originally the official organ of KAMI, the Action

---

[6] This term has come to be used for the inner circle of economists in the Suharto period. Several members of this group hold doctorates from the University of California at Berkeley.

Front of Indonesian Students). His editorials and signed articles in *KAMI* for years provided highly stimulating critical comment on political developments. During the pre-election period he maintained a middle position between one group of New Order students who actively supported GOLKAR, another group who urged their supporters to vote for candidates of the parties, and a third group who urged voters to cast blank ballots against government malpractices before the election.

Nono Anwar Makarim: The Overhauling of the Political Structure [April 7, 1971]*

The combination of the Armed Forces, the Government and GOLKAR want something they call the overhauling of the political structure. Let us disregard for the moment the question of what overhauling the political structure means. What we cannot disregard is the way in which this aspiration is being implemented. That is felt concretely and physically. Among other things the GOLKAR–Armed Forces–Government troika is working hard to reduce the room of movement of the Muslim parties and the PNI.

In the all-out effort it is making, the troika is using the slogan "program-oriented and not ideology-oriented." This means roughly that the parties are no longer permitted to organize along religious, traditional or ideological lines, but only on the basis of material, economic and social issues. The [Jakarta] Charter, Marhaenism-Soekarnoism, capitalism, imperialism, and so on—these are forbidden issues.

The machinery the troika is using to achieve the goal of structural overhaul stretches from the President down to the village chief and from the Armed Forces Commander down to the noncommissioned officer in the village.

This machinery is very heterogeneous and different parts of it are out of phase with each other. But it is becoming more tightly organized all the time. Its different parts are coming to function more smoothly and better attuned to commands from the top. This is actually happening. It is not a myth, it is very clearly visible, particularly in the regions, where the pressures of the Government–Armed Forces–GOLKAR troika are most strongly felt. Politics is in the process of being killed, to be replaced by economics. . . .

A military officer goes about his tasks with the support of Indonesia's most modern organization, more modern than any other existing in the

* *Source: Harian KAMI* (Jakarta), April 7, 1971.

country. But if the men of the Armed Forces know that the growth of autonomous and independent social institutions will result in a narrowing of the Armed Forces' Dual Function, will they allow institutions of this kind to grow?

In the past we had Soekarno. For Soekarno's policies to be given effect there was need for a strong Armed Forces and a large government apparatus. As a result of being needed by Soekarno, the Armed Forces and the apparatus of civilian government grew strong. And then Soekarno went and the Armed Forces and the Bureaucracy took over everything.

The mission the Armed Forces have taken on is development. It is development which provides them with the one and only source of legitimacy for the dominant part they are playing. But for the development mission to succeed they will have to allow social, economic and cultural institutions to operate autonomously.

Yes, this is a hypothesis, a myth! But who can live without a myth, without a dream? If there is a nation or a man who can progress without a myth which inspires him to be creative, let us all learn from him.

In the meantime we are watching a drama full of pain and irony. The major changes being introduced are not a product of the scientific work of intellectuals or the political work of charismatic leaders. They are the handiwork of colonels and bureaucrats, men who are usually regarded as mediocre. We can only hope that the result will not be mediocre.

The following editorial from the Catholic daily, *Kompas,* was prompted by a speech by Major General Widodo, the Central Java military commander, who suggested that the village people be depoliticized to become a "floating mass." Acknowledging Indonesia's commitment to accelerated modernization over the next 25 years, General Widodo said there was no need for party organizations or party activity to exist in villages, except in campaign periods preceding elections. *Kompas* has given cautious support to many criticisms of the Suharto government, while eschewing associations with critics whom government leaders see as too strident.

Kompas: *The Concept of the Floating Mass* [September 25, 1971]*

The idea has been proposed before: Organised party activities should be limited to the centre, province and kabupaten. There is no need for them lower than the second level of local government.

* *Source: Kompas,* September 25, 1971.

This opinion has been repeated by the Commander of the VIIth, Diponegoro, Military Command, Major-General Widodo. In Limpung District, Batang, he said it was enough for there to be party organizations in the centre, province and kabupaten. More was not necessary.

We comprehend the good intention behind this concept: Communities outside the kabupaten do not need to be split up by political groupings. Let them live in calm, to work and construct. It is sufficient if there is political activity there when there is a general election.

There are further considerations too. It is not necessary for people to bind themselves organizationally to one of the parties. Just let them choose the one that suits them, the one they consider good, at every general election. In other words, let them form a "floating mass."

We do not reject this concept. But the following questions remain unanswered:

Whatever their deficiencies, the parties (and this goes for GOLKAR as well) serve the function of protecting the interests of the mass of the people. If, for instance, the interests of the majority of the people in the villages are damaged by some individual in authority, to whom shall they turn for political protection?

Moreover, the community of the villages cannot live just to work. They, too, need food for the mind and heart. They, too, have a disposition to think about the common lot. Who is to provide that "food" and how is it to be channeled? If the people are not satisfied with their conditions, who is to channel their dissatisfaction?

In practice, the civil service and its complementary instruments are not able to do all these things alone. Let it not happen that clandestine forces then find a way to the people's hearts and minds through various non-political organizations!

If the political parties (including GOLKAR) are not operating in areas below the kabupaten, this does not mean that there are no political activities there or that the need for political activities has disappeared. Political activities are inherent in the nature of humans as social beings. Parties are only one of the kinds of channels for them.

So thought must be given to the kinds of channels which are to be allowed to develop in areas below the kabupaten. What forms of political creativity should be promoted as something better to take the place of party politics? Farmers' associations, merchants' associations, teachers' associations, other kinds of associations?

Student demonstrations against the "Beautiful Indonesia in Miniature" project brought a sharp threat from President Suharto, noted in a speech, from which the excerpts below are taken. It was unusual because of its informal and personal character, as well as for the anger expressed in it. Several leaders of the anti-project protest were arrested shortly after the speech.

Suharto: Democratic Rights May Not Be Used as Masks [January 6, 1972]*

It is quite unexceptionable for there to be differences of opinion in Indonesia, as long as these remain within the limits dictated by the need to maintain democratic harmony. Differences are the spice of democracy. But they must be kept within the limits of democratic harmony. People should not exercise their democratic rights if the end result is undemocratic. It seems that this sort of thing is happening in Indonesia, particularly in relation to the "Beautiful Indonesia in Miniature" project.

It is actually quite natural that differences of opinion should arise in relation to this project. But these differences should not be blown up to the point where they endanger democracy itself. Conflicts between pro and con factions could come to threaten public security and order and disturb national stability. This would create obstacles for development.

. . . The Beautiful Indonesia in Miniature project has two main functions. The first, outwardly directed, is to act as means of communication, to introduce Indonesia to other nations, to show them the real aspirations of the struggle of the Indonesian people, and the nature of the Panca Sila which reflects their philosophy of life. As I have said before, we cannot isolate ourselves; we must make friends with other countries. Particularly if we want to play a role in building world peace, we have to be trusted by other nations. To be trusted, respected and liked, we must make known the personality of the Indonesian nation which goes back to the eighth century.

Secondly, there is the inwardly directed function. It is impossible for the people of Indonesia to visit all parts of Indonesia—Sumatra, Kalimantan, Sulawesi, the Moluccas, Irian and the Lesser Sunda Islands. That is impossible. But, by visiting this Miniature project they will be able to see the whole country and also have a sense of pride in being a nation, a nation that is really rich in culture, in natural wealth, in flora and fauna, in its various art forms and so on. That will create an awareness of nationhood. And this awareness of nationhood is an absolute neces-

* Source: Address of the President at the Opening of the Pertamina Hospital, 6 January 1972 (Pidato Presiden pada Pembukaan Rumah Sakit Pertamina, Tanggal 6 Djanuari 1972) (Jakarta: State Secretariat, 1972).

sity if we want to live as a nation, to improve our strength as a nation—
ideological, economic and cultural as well as military. Thus, it has the
purpose of teaching us awareness of nationhood by showing us the mag-
nificence of Indonesia.

Moreover it has one further function: Economic development. There are
many people from other countries who would like to see Indonesia, to see it
at close quarters. So we have to exploit this situation. We have to look to
other countries. For development, we need foreign exchange, we need foreign exchange earnings. If we bring in visitors we bring in foreign exchange.
That is what other countries do, like Italy, Spain, Switzerland and Japan.
From tourism alone we could earn more than one billion rupiahs in foreign
exchange. More than from all our exports, oil as well as other goods. Why
shouldn't we get this sort of benefit from the beauty of Indonesia when I
am confident that people of other nations want to see our country? . . .

. . . Another aspect of the Miniature Indonesia project, if it can be
implemented, is its by-product of providing employment, not only
within the project itself, but also in other fields like service to visitors and
the selling of ice cream, peanuts, cigarettes and so on. All these secondary
activities will be opened up for the people, hence the project will contribute to employment. So seen from the point of view of objectives and
ideals, it does not run counter to the strategy of the nation's struggle to
achieve a just and prosperous society based on the Panca Sila. Nor does
it run counter to development strategy as an effort to give body to our
independence and achieve a just and prosperous society. And it will certainly not affect government finances as it will not be financed from the
government budget.

I am quite convinced that this project is important. But I certainly accept that the government must give preference to more important ones.
That is why it has not been made into a government project. But since
development is not the concern of the government alone, and the private
sector has a role to play, I am suggesting to them that they carry out this
project. If the private sector is willing to establish Beautiful Indonesia in
Miniature—without getting favors or special treatment of any kind—
then I say go ahead.

Ladies and gentlemen, I sometimes wonder why this Miniature Indonesia project . . . has become so controversial—mixed up with the issue
of courage to criticize, no different from the Old Order, the exercising
of democratic rights, and so on. If democratic rights are taken too far,
exercised without caution, then democracy is no more, and the strategy
of stability, which is necessary for development, is jeopardised.

Now just what is the principle in doubt? What people are afraid of is
the obstruction of development. As the person responsible for develop-

ment, I can state firmly: I guarantee that this project will not hinder development. Quite the reverse is true, since in no way does it run counter to the development strategy. Secondly, it is said that it will affect government revenues. Again, as the head of government I assure you that the government funds committed for development, to the amount of 231 billion for 1972–73, as I stated before Parliament yesterday, would not be much affected even if the 10 million for the project were to be taken from the development budget. But the government is quite firm on this point: It will not use funds from the development budget. Nor will government revenues be affected.

Well, what is the problem then? Perhaps it is that the Project Officer is Bang Ali[7] and the sponsor Bu Harto, my wife. The impression has been created that the Miniature Indonesia project is a lighthouse project,[8] a project to prolong a term of office. My God! This is just not so! Institutions of this kind just do not exist.

If that is understood it is clear that the project itself is not the real problem at all. Rather, the Miniature project is being used to create a political issue.

Look at the facts. Look at the pattern of controversy since 1968 and 1969. The way issues have been put up has been just the same throughout, always twisting things into their opposites, creating antagonistic opinions and contradictions and confusing the people. The basic aim is to discredit the government. And, as it happens, it is the same people. The actors are the same, and I know that the people behind the screen are the same, too.

What is their real political goal? We know what it is, and it is not the Miniature project. The real goal, in the short term, is to discredit the government, and also, of course, the person responsible, myself, as the head of government and President. And in the long run they want to kick the Armed Forces out of executive activities and eliminate the dual function of the Armed Forces. They want to chase the Armed Forces back into its "stable," that is, limit it to its security function.

If that is the target, it is not up to the Miniature project to answer its critics. The answer must be given by the Armed Forces, and the Armed Forces' answer is quite clear. As I have said repeatedly, the Armed Forces will not relinquish its dual function. On the basis of this dual function, the Armed Forces—together with the other social forces—will be able to safeguard our constitution and our democracy. Together with the other social forces it will occupy executive and legislative positions.

[7] Ali Sadikin, the governor of Jakarta.

[8] Term applied by Sukarno's critics to his plan to build monuments, sports stadia, grand mosques, and so forth.

So it is the Armed Forces which will answer. If the aim is to discredit the government with a view to kicking me out, that can be easily done. That is very easy. It is not necessary to make a lot of fuss about it. I am the head of government in accordance with our constitution. The head of state is elected by the people's representatives, hitherto by the Provisional People's Consultative Congress, henceforth by the People's Consultative Congress. God willing, the elected People's Consultative Congress will assemble next year, in March 1973, to determine the broad outline of state policy and choose a President and a Vice-President. This will give them their opportunity if this is what they want. They can nominate themselves or somebody else in the People's Congress to stand for election as President or Vice-President. It is very simple. Instead of making such a lot of fuss about these things now, let them rather compete with each other in providing their services to the state and let the people choose. Persons with a reputation for service will be the ones trusted by the people and elected in March 1973, just 15 months from now, less a few days.

However, if they cannot wait till March 1973, perhaps because they are disgusted with me, there are things they can do earlier in a constitutional way, that is by holding a special session of the People's Congress. The present parliament, the outcome of the general elections, has been incorporated into the People's Congress by the President. In a short time they will be joined by the representatives of the regions and of the political parties. That means a special session of the People's Congress can be convened at any time if this is what the representatives of the people request. So if they cannot tolerate me until March 1973, a special session can be held to replace me. It is simple, there is no need for fuss.

But let me just remind them of one thing. Everything has to be done in a constitutional way! The purpose of the New Order is precisely to uphold the constitution and democracy. If unconstitutional tendencies arise I will go back to the attitude I took on October 1st, 1965, when I served the people by confronting the P.K.I. who wanted to trample on the constitution and the Panca Sila.

At that time nobody came to me to encourage me. Did the leaders of the political parties offer me support? No. No one of the youth came to me either. No. Nor any of the students. But I didn't care who was behind me. In fact there was only one person, my wife. She said to me simply: "Be strong in your faith." That was my wife's message to me on October 1st. That was my encouragement and it gave me enough strength to urge the people to overcome the P.K.I.

Later, after this had succeeded, the Panca Sila Front and the Generation of '66 were formed and then the movement to hasten the process of overcoming the deviation. And I was urged to act unconstitutionally to speed up the process of correction.

This I firmly rejected. I already knew my mind. Acting according to the constitution was a matter of principle for me. Because all corrections had to be made by constitutional means, the special and general sessions of the Interim People's Consultative Congress were convened, and so on. Everything was done constitutionally, so the people were the ones who took the decisions. My responsibility was to ensure that the changes were not effected by unconstitutional means. And, thank God, I was successful.

After that there was more pressure on me to take steps outside the constitution. But, as I say, thank God, I was successful. If I had acted unconstitutionally in the situation at that time when divisions were so sharp I can just imagine what the picture would have been. There would have been civil war and our situation would probably be very different today.

Thank God, we were able to overcome those difficulties. I have been criticized for doing things too cautiously. I have been abused as a "slow but sure" Javanese, as a Javanese who is like a walking snail, like a snail whose shell is too big and heavy for its body. Never mind. The main thing was to safeguard the state and the nation.

For that reason, if there are now people trying to act in defiance of the constitution, I will go back to the attitude I took on October 1st, 1965. Quite frankly, I will smash them, whoever they are! And I will certainly have the full support of the Armed Forces in that.

And that goes, too, for those who make use of their democratic rights and use those as their masks, who use their rights to excess in any way that suits them. Those rights are like spices: Used excessively, they spoil everything. And if the spoiling of democracy is going to result in the disturbance of order and the general security situation, the disturbance of national stability and the disturbance of development, that is something I will not stand for. Lest you don't understand what I mean by "I will not stand for it" let me say frankly that I will take action. If those people take no notice of warnings and continue to act as they have been I will take action. And if there are legal experts who hold that it is no longer possible for the President to do that, that it would be against the law for me to act against those responsible for these violations—if they want to be stubborn about it—all right, that is simple. In the interests of the state and the nation, I can invoke the Order of March 11, 1966,[9] to declare a State of Emergency. If necessary I can do that even without the existence of an emergency. If those people are going to continue to create chaos I will

[9] See footnote 4.

take it upon myself to act, in my responsibility to the people and to God.

As I said before, it is unexceptionable for there to be differences of opinion in a democratic state, in a democratic environment. But there are limits to differences of opinion. The limits are set by the need for democracy to be in harmony with the calling of our struggle. The calling of our present struggle is to develop, to give content to independence. For development, political and economic stability are essential. And political stability requires order and security.

The following article was published in the Jakarta daily, *Indonesia Raya,* in early 1972 shortly after the arrest of a number of leaders of the movement protesting the "Beautiful Indonesia in Miniature" project. The author is a poet and a journalist of the 1966 Generation.

Bur Rasuanto: Is the Government Strong? [January 31, 1972]*

Is our government strong? For the average citizen today there is no shortage of good reasons for answering this question in the affirmative. In a relatively short period the government has made remarkable progress in the rehabilitation and development of the economy. The government has successfully restored internal security and, within reasonable limits, has created political stability. These achievements alone would seem to be sufficient reason to conclude that the government is now in a strong and secure position.

But since Arief Budiman and his friends were arrested last week it has become apparent that this common assessment of the government is not one that is shared by the government. Those arrests are public evidence that the government is not as powerful or as secure as people have assumed: at least they revealed that the government is not convinced that it is secure. It is frightened of facing criticism. It is nervous at seeing the younger generation and the intellectuals—who, lest it be forgotten, played an important part in giving birth to this government and still support it—demonstrating their support in a critical fashion.

The fear on the part of the government was revealed in the way it reacted to these recent criticisms. The government felt it necessary to call its military intelligence agents into action and to virtually kidnap people like Arief Budiman—a civilian with no other strength than that of his convictions, convictions he has never concealed. The government felt it

* *Source: Indonesia Raya,* January 31, 1972.

necessary to send its loud-mouthed troopers to threaten with their guns the pregnant wife of one of the demonstrators, Jusuf A. R. We can imagine what would happen if anyone dared to treat a soldier's family like that. And the arrests of Arief Budiman and his friends were made after they had called off their protest campaign against what is, after all, supposed to be a private, non-governmental, project, and before there was any official ban on what the authorities call "extra-parliamentary activities."

As I personally witnessed, Arief and Laila Chairani—now his wife— achieved much during that turbulent period. True, he led no armed bands in wiping out communists; the military training he received as a student during [the period of] "confrontation" [of Malaysia] hardly fitted him for that role. But, in his capacity as a civilian, his contribution towards overthrowing the Sukarno regime was second to none.

He is now locked away and not even his family have been informed of his whereabouts. Under the Sukarno regime he was never subjected to interrogation by the authorities, and that regime is regarded as having been "totalitarian." So what's wrong here? The mistake appears to have been Arief's. He believed that the government was strong.

He may well be disappointed to discover that the past and the present are not very different in at least one respect. A strong government can utilize constructive criticism. A weak one must try to conceal its weaknesses behind a screen of bayonets and thereby create an atmosphere of uncertainty and fear. A weak government will ban "extra-parliamentary activities," but at the same time it will take "extra-constitutional" action against its subjects.

So from now on the younger generation and the intellectuals of this country may as well start counting the days until their turn comes. When people are seized in the streets and thrown into secret prisons it is usually a sign that the process of internal rot has set into a regime. Are we now headed in that direction? One thing seems clear: Citizens should not pay taxes to finance the negation of their rights by their government.

Following the massive decimation of the Communist party in 1965–1966, there was some regrouping of surviving cadres in the Blitar area of East Java. But this embryonic base area was discovered and smashed in 1968, and since then PKI activity has apparently been scattered and slight.

Api Pemuda Indonesia (The Fire of Indonesian Youth) is a mimeographed monthly published by a group of Communist émigrés in Tirana, Albania. Its line corresponds roughly with that of several other émigré Communist publications with generally Chinese orientations. In this extract, unlike the *Merdeka* editorial, above, criticisms of the government's economic policies are made in unqualified terms.

A New-Style Colony of U.S. Imperialism [August 1972]*

In the short time that the fascist military regime of Suharto has been in power, Indonesia has been made a new-style colony of U.S. imperialism. All natural resources and sources of Indonesia's wealth . . . have been handed over to be exploited by the foreign monopoly capitalists. The draining of Indonesia's land and sea resources has been left in the first instance to U.S. imperialism. . . . Japanese monopoly capitalism . . . has been active on a large scale. Dutch capitalism has been particularly vigorous in the last couple of years in its efforts to get back its position as a squeezer and exploiter of the Indonesian people, with investments being made in a number of different fields.

The imperialists' endeavour to keep a tight hold over the Indonesian economy is not pursued merely by investments in various branches of industry, but also by what is called economic and financial aid, both direct and through I.G.G.I. [Inter-Governmental Group for Indonesia]. The volume of "aid" granted by I.G.G.I. to the Suharto fascist regime up to 1972 amounts to US$2,988 million, whereas the total of Indonesia's outstanding debt is now more than $5000 million. The more "aid" the fascist regime gets the more it goes on begging for more. I.G.G.I. "aid" rose in 1972 to $723 million as compared with $200 million in 1967. The practical effect of this "aid" has been to fatten the pockets of the bureaucratic capitalist generals and the high-ranking civilian officials who have become the new rich overnight. They are the big-time corruptors who are now increasingly running the whole show in Indonesia. The other side of the picture shows the great mass of the people suffering poverty and misery. Although Indonesia is fertile and rich in natural resources, and despite the fact that its people work hard, shortages of food, clothing, and housing continue to be the ordinary man's lot under the fascist military regime.

Workers' real wages are declining. A family cannot live for ten days on a month's salary. Employment opportunities are narrowing because national firms are folding up in the face of competition from the foreign monopolies which are now flooding the country. Workers and govern-

* *Source: Api Pemuda Indonesia, August 1972.*

ment employees are being sacked en masse in various government firms and agencies. So the number of unemployed is rising. Even certain reactionary Indonesian newspapers concede that their number has risen to 22 million.

The peasants are even worse off than in the past. The number of them who have no land to till is rising all the time. Apart from continuing to suffer feudal oppression and exploitation, the peasants have had new burdens imposed on them in the form of various punishing new taxes. They are forced to make all kinds of "contributions," and in many areas are conscripted to do forced labour, to build roads, bridges, houses for local officials, and even airfields. All of this work is unpaid. People who do not do it are given fines, sometimes money fines and sometimes fines in the form of animals.

Culturally, Indonesia is experiencing unpredecented decadence. The decadent culture of the American and Japanese imperialists has invaded the country, especially the big cities. Young people are madly chasing marijuana and other drugs. Nightclubs, steambaths, brothels and similarly decadent forms of amusement are springing up everywhere, not only officially protected by the fascist regime but also taxed to be a source of government revenue.

The fascist generals' regime headed by General Suharto does not hesitate to use terror to defend its position. It deploys armed force to crush any kind of activity opposed to its policies. To make sure that his position will be strengthened by the bogus People's Consultative Congress when it meets in March 1973, the fascist General Suharto has appointed 155 members of the Armed Forces Functional Group as members of this body. Among them are 47 generals, the important generals, including the Deputy Commander of the Armed Forces, the Chiefs of Staff of the Army, Navy, Air Force and State Police, the commanders of military districts throughout Indonesia and the governors of the military academies. With this series of appointments, 764 of the 920 members of the bogus People's Consultative Congress will be Functional Group members, from either within or outside the Armed Forces. This means that the fascist Suharto will have absolute control over "votes" in the People's Consultative Congress.

Economically and financially totally dependent on the imperialists and especially the American imperialists, the Indonesian fascist regime is naturally loyal in its foreign and defense policies. It loyally serves the global strategy of U.S. imperialism and its efforts to uphold and intensify the colonial oppression of the peoples of many countries. The activities of the regime in the Association of South East Asian Nations, which is described as a body to promote economic cooperation but is in fact a military scheme masterminded by U.S. imperialism, are evidence of how deeply Indonesia has become involved in the aggressive policies of the United States. Suharto's visits to Australia, New Zealand and the Philippines in the first months of this year were part of a policy of military scheming among the satellites of U.S. imperialism. The fascist regime is even intensifying its ties with the Japanese militarists, both in the economic and cultural areas and in the military one.

This then is what the situation in Indonesia is like 27 years after the revolution of August 17, 1945.

Despite obstacles, difficulties and setbacks, the people of Indonesia are continuing to struggle for their liberation. In the words of the November 1967 Program of the Indonesian Communist Party, "The Indonesian revolution is at its present state a bourgeois democratic revolution which is part of the proletarian socialist world revolution or the Revolution of the People's Democracy." The primary task of the Indonesian revolution at this time is to destroy the Suharto fascist military regime, which represents the bureaucratic capitalists, the compradors and the landlords, the classes fully subservient to U.S. imperialism.

The bloody experience of 1965, of the unmatched white terror in which hundreds of thousands of communists and other patriots were killed in most horribly cruel ways, has taught us lessons which must never be forgotten. It has taught us much about the revisionist path, the path of peaceful transition, the parliamentary path—that these are paths which bring disaster to the communists, to the people and to the revolution. Therefore, the way to liberate the Indonesian people is to crush the Suharto fascist military regime by people's armed struggle, to wage a people's war and to establish the power of People's Democracy. It is this path which is now being taken by the Indonesian people under the leadership of the Communist Party of Indonesia.

It is only through people's war that the Indonesian people will win their freedom. There is no other way.

In the following excerpts taken from a lecture Sudjatmoko delivered in Australia in August 1967, he looks at Indonesia's foreign policy as a New Order man sensitive to the continuities which have persisted despite the changes of regime. A leading writer on history, politics, and culture, Sudjatmoko was not a member of the government at the time of his lecture, but subsequently has served as his country's ambassador to the United States.

Sudjatmoko: Indonesia's Place in the World [August 1967]*

The dominating force welding Indonesia together into single nation-hood is nationalism. It is the expression of the will to self determination, to freedom, and to equality and justice in her relationship with the rest of the world. However great the variety of ideological commitments among the various political forces in the country—be they religious, na-tionalist, socialist or communist—all of these can be seen as particular manifestations of nationalism, in the sense that all these ideological com-mitments presuppose and operate within the frame-work of an indepen-dent and strong Indonesian State.

The preservation of national independence is the point where all ideolo-gies meet and the goal to which it is generally agreed all political conflicts should be subordinated.

From its inception the Indonesian nationalist movement saw itself as a part of a world-wide movement against colonial rule. This has instilled Indonesian nationalism with a deep sense of affiliation with the fight for independence everywhere; with any attempt to throw off the colonial yoke in whatever form, under whatever name, and with a readiness to give sympathy and support to such a movement, even at the expense of its national interest narrowly defined. This commitment to freedom and jus-tice expressed itself after the attainment of independence in what seemed a quite natural insistence upon steering clear of ties with the two power blocs into which the world seemed divided at that time. Like other new nations whose struggle for independence was especially difficult, Indonesia did not want to be closely associated with the former colonizing power or its allies; at the same time, it was averse to being included in the then monolithic power system of the communist world with its clear subordina-tion to Soviet hegemony, strategy, and interest. Non-alignment—or in the Indonesian phrase, her independent active foreign policy—is therefore not so much the result of rational calculation of the national interest, but rather the reflection of a basic attitude.

The awareness of the Indonesian nationalist movement of its commu-nity of interest with all struggle against colonialism and the need to orien-tate itself in the world led to a search to define Indonesia's place in the historical processes that were taking place and her relationship to the various interest groupings in the world. From this stems the brief interest in Pan-Islamism in the early days of the Sarekat Islam in the 1920's, and

* Source: Australian Outlook, 21 (December 1967) 3; reprinted by permis-sion of Sudjatmoko and the Australian Institute of International Affairs.

also the influence of Marxism, especially on the pre-revolutionary generation of nationalist leaders.

The role of Marxism was particularly important. Marxism provided
a plausible explanation for one's own colonial status and for imperialism,
and one which could be accepted without harm to a colonial people's
self-respect. It not only provided an explanation, but it also set a goal
and placed the struggle for national independence in relation to that goal.
Equally important, it provided a method, a strategy and the techniques
needed to create power and to use that power in the pursuit of independence. However, the egalitarian claims as well as the eschatological and
utopian elements of Marxist theory regarding the inevitable doom of
capitalism, the source of all evil, and the equally inevitable victory of
socialism, strongly appealing to some traditional patterns of thought, may
very well have been just as much responsible for the popularity of Marxist
notions. . . .

A nation's commitment to being itself, and to defining that self in relation to its own history, in all its varieties, as well as in relation to its own
aspirations and hopes for the future, is a fundamental pre-condition for
its ability to determine its place in the world and to set itself to any major
undertaking. In most nations in Asia and Africa it was the colonial experience that provided the bond and the common frame-work within
which a sense of nationhood grew up, transcending the loyalties of earlier
days to a variety of rival kingdoms or tribes. It was in common hostility to
the colonial ruler that a sense of common identity was first born. This was
then further shaped by the modern concept of the nation state.

It is important to keep this process of growth of colonial nationalism
in mind, lest it be automatically and wrongly identified with some forms
of European nationalism of the nineteenth and early twentieth centuries.
A proper understanding of its origins is particularly important in relation
to the question of to what extent Indonesian nationalism is inherently
aggressive and expansionist.

To impute expansionist tendencies to Indonesian nationalism because
of the existence of traces of nostalgia for the grandeur of the Sriwidjaja
empire of the seventh to the twelfth centuries and the Modjopahit empire
of the thirteenth and fourteenth centuries is to project modern ideas of
territorial control that adhere to the concept of the nation state to an
entirely different historical setting where such notions were alien. And
why should one begrudge a nation a few visionaries like Tan Malaka and
Mohammad Yamin? Every nation has had them at one time or another.
But to infer from their writings that an expansionist element is inherent
in Indonesian nationalism, regardless of particular domestic power con-

figurations, as some Western scholars have done (in ways which delighted the Malaysian Department of Information in the period of confrontation!), seems to me both unfair and unrealistic.

It should be remembered that Indonesia did not deliberately seek a confrontation with Malaysia. She was caught in a chain of events beginning with the Brunei revolt of December 1962, which first her pride, then her suspicion towards the outside world—both elements of nationalism it is true—forbade her to break, leading to a situation from which the pressure of the PKI made it impossible to extricate herself. Moreover, the confrontation campaign was much more directed inwardly than outwardly. At no time did the Indonesian army seriously consider throwing its main force into a major operation against Malaysia. Maintaining the existing balance of power with the PKI within the country remained the major concern of the army throughout the period of confrontation.

Apart from these general features of Indonesian nationalism, its concerns and preoccupations have also been shaped by the impact of its own experiences during the struggle for independence. One of these grew out of the attempts of the Dutch to Balkanize Indonesia through the imposition of a federal system in which a majority of puppet states were to hedge in the barely tolerated Republic of Indonesia and thus render it powerless. The Dutch hoped that such a structure would soon deprive Indonesian nationalism of its military capacity and its political will. This abortive attempt thoroughly discredited the idea of federalism and engendered a continuing fear of Balkanization by an outside power, while also instilling a ready sympathy for all nations threatened by the imposition of such artificial divisions as part of a neo-colonial strategy.

The case of post-Geneva Vietnam comes to mind in this connection.

The second traumatic experience was the series of insurrections and rebellions with various degrees of foreign support which we experienced, starting immediately after 1949 when our independence gained general international recognition. We first had the so-called Westerling affair of 1950 involving remnants of the Dutch East Indies colonial army, then the rebellion of the extremist Muslim group, Darul Islam, which controlled important stretches of West Java and South Celebes and Atjeh in North Sumatra throughout the 1950's and into the 1960's. In 1958 we experienced the largest of all our rebellions, the PRRI attempt to establish a counter-government in Sumatra and the Celebes, and here the evidence of foreign support was particularly clear. There is in Indonesia, therefore, a continuing and deep suspicion towards outside interference, infiltration, and subversion directed both towards East and West, reinforcing a xenophobic tendency already inherent in it, with the result that political change—even desired change—is rejected if the process of bringing about such change involves overt or covert foreign participation.

There is also another set of attitudes, not generally shared but sufficiently widespread to warrant our attention, namely the feeling that, "even now after the communists have been removed as an effective political force, the imperialists are not really willing to help us to develop our economy because of their fear of eventual competition from the new nations." Linked with this is the feeling that "we will remain poor as long as imperialism exists. We will therefore have to fight imperialism before we can properly tackle our problem of poverty."

The prevalence of these attitudes suggests profound fears and suspicions, as well as the deep-seated need for self-assurance and self-assertion. It explains the stridency of much nationalistic language during the period of Guided Democracy, for example.

It would be denying some essential characteristics of Indonesian nationalism to say that Sukarno's foreign policy until its last few years was not widely supported in the country. By taunting and challenging the Western Powers in continuous feats of brinkmanship, Sukarno fulfilled many deeply felt needs—for prestige, for a sense of power, for an honourable position of leadership in what was seen as the inevitable historical process towards a new world—"Let's build the world anew."

But no person and no nation is forever a prisoner of his past experiences. And the lessons drawn from the ultimate failure of our foreign policy of the Guided Democracy period have had a very sobering impact. The dangers of the loss of international goodwill, of international isolation, of pursuing foreign policy goals out of proportion to our real national power are now fully realized. The danger of being misguided by simplistic stereotypes as applied to a complex interrelated world, rapidly changing in its power configuration, is now more clearly seen. We have now also learned that each policy has its price, and that too great a discrepancy between foreign policy goals and the realities of economic life may lead to the destruction of the social and economic foundations of independence. It has become quite clear that for all our claims to international leadership we ended up with an even greater dependency on foreign credits, and with our freedom of action seriously compromised.

Against this background it is worth looking at the guidelines for the conduct of our foreign policy, decided upon by the Provisional People's Congress at its fourth session in 1966. These stipulate that Indonesia's foreign policy should be based:

1. on the ten principles contained in the Bandung Charter, reflecting the solidarity of the Asian and African nations; on the struggle against

imperialism and colonialism in all its manifestations; and on the principle of non-intervention;

2. on the principle that Asian problems should be solved by Asians themselves, and through regional cooperation;

3. on the restoration of the goodwill of other nations and states towards the aims and purposes of the Indonesian Revolution by making more friends than enemies, by avoiding contradictions, and by seeking harmony in accordance with the philosophy of Pantja Sila.

4. These principles are to be applied with flexibility in approach as well as response with a view to furthering the national interest and specifically the economic interests of the people.

With these stipulations in mind, let us now turn to the question of non-alignment.

As I have already indicated, the concept of non-alignment stems from the attitudes towards the world with which many new nations emerged from colonial subjugation. Unable to identify with the West, despite the many political ideas and values they had drawn from that source, unable also to identify with the communist countries, despite the support these countries had given them, and fiercely intent on finding their own way, they found in the concept of non-alignment a vehicle through which to express their dissatisfaction with the state of the world into which they had just emerged, and a hope, ill-defined perhaps, that some better world could be created, and that it should be worthwhile to strive for this. At the same time, the complex and varied patterns of inter-relationships between the new third world and the older two, and the conflicts of interests within the third world itself, soon made it clear that there was no simple formula to guide them in the struggle to gain their rightful place in the world while helping to shape a better one.

This obvious weakness, as well as the brashness and occasional irresponsibility of some new states in the councils of the world, should not close our eyes to the significance of these attitudes in the historical processes that are now taking place and that are gradually changing the world and its order. For all its confusion, internal weaknesses, and internecine conflicts, the third world's attitudes do represent a historical force which eventually must have its impact. We should also be aware that these attitudes are not just irrelevant patterns shaped by the colonial experience, which these countries should outgrow as soon as possible, for their own sake and for the sake of the world at large. There are serious and real problems underlying them, and until these are solved or reduced to manageable or I could almost say, liveable proportions, the third world is in many respects likely to continue to be governed by the thrust of their emotions. Essentially, these problems revolve around the present imbalance in the world between the rich and the poor nations, between the powerful and the weak, the continuously widening gap between the two, and the world's apparent incapacity to deal with them.

FOUR

Malaysia and Singapore

by J. NORMAN PARMER

Malaysia is today one of the most highly developed states in Southeast Asia. Since gaining independence from Great Britain in 1957, the country has enjoyed an able leadership committed to a representative form of government. Administrative, technical, and social services are good. The rates of literacy and life expectancy compare well with those in Japan and the United States. Malaysia's favorable ratio of population to resources and its substantial trade and foreign investment, especially in rubber and tin, have made possible a relatively high living standard and per capita income. In short, there is a semblance of well-being, order, and progress.

Underlying these outward impressions, however, are potentially erosive crosscurrents which flow out of the frustrations and suspicions harbored by each of Malaysia's three major ethnic communities: Malay, Chinese, and Indian. The difficulties facing any single political body that tries to govern these diverse elements were demonstrated in May 1969 when the calm associated with Malaysia was disrupted by racial violence.

It is difficult to exaggerate the importance of racial or communal differences in Malaysia. Yet it is not ethnic diversity per se which underlies the tensions that have marked interethnic relations, in particular those between the Chinese and the Malays, but the fact that tangible differences in socioeconomic status have coincided with and intensified ethnic boundaries.

Malaysia's problem is in large part rooted in the history of British rule in the Malay Peninsula. Britain rationalized its intervention there in the nineteenth century on grounds that the unsettled political and administrative conditions in the Malay states threatened the newly made investments of British subjects who resided in the neighboring Straits Settlements of Malacca, Penang, and Singapore. The investments were then principally in tin; the British subjects were chiefly Chinese; the rulers of the states and the possessors of the land were Malays.

Tin had been mined for centuries in the Malay Peninsula. In the nineteenth century, however, the industrial revolution in Europe created an increased demand for the metal, and the manifold expansion of tin production in the western Malay states by Chinese entrepreneurs led to involved and stormy relations between them and the Malay sultans. The governments of the Malay states, which had been fashioned after the fifteenth-century maritime sultanate of Malacca, had remained virtually unchanged and were unprepared to cope with the new outlook and demands that the rapid development of the tin fields had brought in its wake.

Britain's intervention did not lead immediately to any major changes in the local governments: British rule was indirect and intended to preserve Malay sovereignty. But the practical result of the treaties signed with the Malay sultans was that the British advisers assigned to each sultan became the de facto rulers, and it was with them and their growing staffs that the Chinese entrepreneurs dealt. The Chinese, and other non-Malays who followed, could conform to a growing body of laws drafted to encourage and promote investment and economic growth. Indeed, British imperialism rather quickly developed a modern, efficient framework of government and an administration which functioned largely above and separate from traditional Malay government and administration. It was within this British-created and British-staffed system of government that the major economic achievements were made.

To tin mining was added a rubber-plantation industry of immense value and great political and strategic importance. Roads, railways, telecommunications, modern ports, hospitals, and schools were built and paid for from taxes on exports of raw materials and on imports of food and consumer goods. The importance of these achievements and their consequences cannot be exaggerated: Tens of thousands of individuals prospered. The dollars earned in Malaya helped maintain the British pound as an international currency before and after World

War II. The Malay states became a rich hinterland for the Straits Settlements.

The evolution of a modern system of government and economy, however, proceeded with little or no participation by the Malays: It was the work of the British and the Chinese with some important contributions made by immigrant Indians. Most Malays continued to farm their small plots, and many of them fell victim to those who could successfully manipulate modern concepts of wealth in a monetized economy. The Malay rulers prospered and protested only mildly as they became increasingly ornamental. Only a handful of Malays were brought gradually into minor posts of the elite British Malayan Civil Service, where they adopted the language and some of the values of their imperial rulers.

The Malays were not simply bypassed by their country's headlong plunge into the modern world nor did the British, by some oversight, fail to prepare them for it. The British goal through the 1930's was actually to keep the modern world from the Malays, to assure that they remain rural, pastoral, and traditional. The Chinese and other non-Malays were not similarly dissuaded from entering and competing in a world promising economic rewards, but implicitly, the British assumed they would always be present to protect and intercede for the Malays in their relationships with their more worldly compatriots.

Most Malays, indeed, were contented with Britain's rule. By contrast, Chinese and Indians in the Malay states and the Straits Settlements sought participation in public affairs. They wanted entry into the civil service and greater government support of education in languages other than Malay. Some concessions were made to these demands in the Straits Settlements where the Malay population was small and Malay monarchies were absent. But in the states, the British response was that they, like other non-Malays, were merely guests in Malay houses: The Malay states were sovereign, independent nations with whom the British had treaty arrangements.

British pronouncements in favor of Malay sovereignty were not aimed only at putting off Chinese and Indian demands for political participation. They also were intended to win support for a union of the nine Malay states. Partly as a result of historical circumstances and partly as a reflection of different levels of investment and development, four of the states—Perak, Selangor, Negri Sembilan, and Pahang—had been grouped together under a centralized administration known as the Federated Malay States. The other five states—Johore, Kedah, Trengganu, Kelantan, and Perlis—were administered separately as British protectorates. A union of the states, the British government argued, would pave the way for their further development, which was at the time being hindered by the multiplicity of administrations in the peninsula and the Straits Settlements. Business interests in Malaya in the 1920's and 1930's, however, doubted the capacity of the state governments to administer the country, and this belief was shared by many British officers in the Malayan Civil Service and in the Colonial Office.

In the aftermath of the Japanese occupation of Malaya, however, the British took advantage of unsettled conditions to introduce the Malayan Union in 1946. The nine Malay states lost their sovereignty to Great Britain and were joined to the Straits Settlements of Penang and Malacca. Singapore was declared a separate crown colony. But while Britain's prewar goal of unification of Malaya's administrative structure was thus achieved, the Union attracted little popular support. Instead, it became a catalyst for popular political debate.

Younger-generation Chinese and Indians became more articulate and demanding of the British. Malays, no longer politically quiescent, organized to protest British seizure of sovereignty and to protect themselves against what they saw as the rising political power of the Chinese. The Malayan Communist party, founded in the late 1920's, had played an active military role against the Japanese and now undertook economic and political action against the British. In 1948 it took up arms in what was to become a twelve-year-long, unsuccessful effort to gain political power.

In response, in February 1948 the British replaced the Malayan Union with a new organization. Under the Federation Agreement the nine Malay states regained their sovereignty, but unity was maintained by a central administration in Kuala Lumpur; Singapore remained separate. The new Federation of Malaya was promised self-rule, and once elections were permitted—the first took place on a municipal level in 1951—rapid progress was made toward it.

The problem confronting the imperial power was to find or create a coalition of political forces that could be expected to govern Malaya fairly. The viability of an independent Malayan government would depend on its association with representatives of the major ethnic communities and on its ability to reduce or eliminate the differences among these groups by bringing traditional sectors of the society to an understanding and appreciation of modern values and institutions.

The British thought a solution to the problem had been found when, in 1952, the major communal organizations—the United Malays National Organization and the Malayan Chinese Association—joined forces to form the Alliance party. Advocating the rapid introduction of self-rule and arguing that the only practical Malayan unity was one based on a political rather than a social or cultural community among the races, the politically and economically conservative leaders of the Alliance struck a bargain which was to form the basis of their political paramountcy. Their accommodation, in which the Malayan Indian Congress joined in 1955, involved essentially the reservation for the Malays of their "special position," that is, assurance of their political predominance by preservation of the sanctity of the Malay rulers and by favorable recruitment ratios in certain sectors of the civil service. These provisions, as well as advantages in the allocation of business licenses and scholarships, were designed to compensate the Malays for their inferior economic status. According to the bargain, the Chinese and Indians in independent Malaya would continue to enjoy economic power and would attain limited political strength through liberal citizenship provisions. Over time, it was hoped, this accommodation would foster political cooperation and communal habits thus promoting common bonds. At the same time, the government would undertake other, primarily economic, policies designed to cultivate these bonds. The accommodation was given formal status in the constitution of the Federation of Malaya, which became effective on Independence Day, August 31, 1957.

From 1955 onward, the Alliance won every national election. No opposition party was able to compete successfully with it on a national basis. An important reason for this was that the Alliance leaders were able to persuade their followers that a political community committed to parliamentary democracy was compatible with continued cultural and racial pluralism. Moreover, since most parties were communally-based and since no single ethnic group made up a majority of the population, no party was in a position to overcome the popular attraction of the Alliance forces.

In addition, the Alliance governments tried to provide a strong economic foundation for their political action. The founding of new primary and manufacturing industries, the creation of a national, in place of a colonial, banking system, the doubling of rice-production potential, a huge increase in electric-power capacity, the most productive and efficient natural-rubber industry in the world—all are examples of the Alliance governments' economic achievements. Progress was also made in the provision of social services. In education, for example, all children of primary-school age were placed in schools at no cost to their families; the secondary curriculum was overhauled; and higher education was expanded. A rural public-health program, which brought medical personnel and modern medicines within reach of everyone except perhaps the remotest forest dweller, was completed.

Despite these achievements, there were serious shortcomings in the governments' provision of economic rewards to all people, especially to the Malays. Equitable distribution of wealth and material opportunity had yet to be realized. Unemployment rose steadily after independence, exceeding 7 percent of the total labor force by 1970. An emphasis by the governments on physical construction had little or no effect on incomes and on the standard of living, especially for the Malays, most of whom live in rural areas. In consequence, not a few people in the several communal groups came to doubt whether the accommodation arranged by their leaders would ever produce meaningful results. Their doubts and frustrations were among the reasons for the violent race rioting in 1969 in West Malaysia.

Among these dissatisfied people, a very large number of Malays (probably a substantial majority in both rural and urban areas) who enjoyed only low incomes, retained traditional attitudes and values. But the many Malays who embraced modern values believed, often correctly, that their adoption of a modern economic outlook was hindered by non-Malay control or dominance of many sectors of the economy.

For many non-Malays as well, especially young Chinese, the government and the accommodation on which many of its policies rested were not effective in satisfying their interests. Often very modern in their outlook, young Chinese tended to be very competitive and eager to obtain a share of the new wealth. Merit-oriented, they believed that hard work, self-discipline, and educational achievement should have its rewards. The economy had not expanded rapidly enough to absorb them all into gainful and satisfying employment. The old ways of a generation or two ago, by which young Chinese were taken into business and commerce through family connections, no longer satisfied their aspirations. The special privileges for Malays, though part of a bargain which also provided for the citizenship of the fathers of these young Chinese critics, became a bitter symbol of discrimination and inequality. When coupled with other national symbols, all of which were Malay and Islamic, alienation from the existing system was probably nearly complete for many of these non-Malays.

The incorporation of Sabah and Sarawak, former British dependencies in Borneo, with Singapore and the Federation of Malaya in 1963 to form Malaysia greatly exacerbated the fundamental problem of resolving the differences among and within the ethnic communities. Sabah and Sarawak, although under various forms of British rule since the mid-nineteenth century, were politically and economically traditional and underdeveloped. Singapore, on the other hand, was in the throes of rapid modernization and possessed a high degree of political sophistication. Impatient and demanding, eager and aggressive, Singapore's leaders seemed, to the central administration in Kuala Lumpur, unable or unwilling to understand conditions throughout the country. When the leaders in Singapore sought participation in politics on the peninsula, and attacked the bargain on which the Alliance was based through advocacy of a "Malaysian Malaysia" policy, Singapore was invited to leave Malaysia, and they did in 1965. Sabah and Sarawak have remained in Malaysia, and although their marriage with the peninsular states is not without tensions, their relationship is likely to prove more compatible than did that with Singapore.

Following the racial rioting of May 1969, which was caused by an Alliance setback, though not defeat, in the national election, a state of national emergency was declared, and, for the next twenty-one months, the country was governed by a National Operations Council (NOC), headed by the deputy prime minister, Tun Abdul Razak, who became prime minister in 1970. The NOC, advised by a National Consultative Council (NCC), composed of representatives of most of the country's political parties, sought the re-establishment of peace and order and the restoration of harmony and mutual trust among the races. Although fears were voiced that parliamentary democracy had ended, they proved to be groundless in early 1971 when the parliament was recalled and the NOC and NCC were disbanded.

Of equal importance, however, was the recognition given by the

political leadership to the problem which precipitated the race riots:
The basic cause of discontent was an economy which failed to provide
equal and satisfying material opportunities for all and, in fact, continued to favor the few. In response, the NOC and the NCC formulated a new economic policy, which has sought reduction or elimination of ethnic control of certain economic activities and has recognized, too, that poverty is not a problem restricted to rural people or
to a particular ethnic group. They also devised a national ideology
through which the government will try to promote a stronger sense of
political community, ensure law and order, encourage nation-building,
and lessen existing attachments to race, language, and religion. In
addition, the strength of the military was increased, a plan to establish
Bahasa Malaya as the language of instruction in schools and of communication within the government was introduced, and, in early 1971,
the Sedition Act was amended to enable the government to deal effectively with anyone who questions the Malays' "special position" or
the rights of other cultural communities, the sanctity of the Malay
rulers, *Bahasa Malaya,* or the citizenship of any Malaysian.

By convincing the people of all cultural communities that impartial
attempts are being made to meet their economic needs and aspirations, the Alliance leaders hope to rally grass-roots support for themselves and for a greater sense of nationalism.

I. Constitutional Development

Before World War II, the area now known as Malaysia was largely
free of the interplay of nationalist politics. This remarkable situation
was due, in no small measure, to the efficiency and benevolence of
the British colonial government. There was concern, however, over the
position of the Malays whose culture many British officials felt was in
danger of being submerged by powerful alien and materialistic influences (represented by Chinese and Indian residents) which accompanied British rule. The weight of opinion among British officials before
the war was that the Malays should enjoy paramountcy in the peninsula. One of the most succinct statements of the British position was
made in 1928 by W. G. A. Ormsby-Gore, parliamentary undersecre-
tary of state for the colonies.

W. G. A. Ormsby-Gore: Report on His Visit to Malaya [December 1928]*

It must always be remembered that British influence became established in the Malay States—Federated as well as Unfederated—not as the result of conquest or aggression but at the invitation of the rulers of these several States who realised that the ancient system of administration that had sufficed the Malay people had broken down in the face of 19th and 20th century world conditions, and especially owing to the influx of large numbers of other races. Our position in every State rests on solemn treaty obligations, and, however great the changes may appear to have been since the dates when they were made, these changes have not in any way modified the fundamental status of these countries. They were, they are, and they must remain "Malay" States, and the primary object of our share in the administration of these countries must always be the progress of the indigenous Malay inhabitants at the invitation of whose forefathers we first assumed responsibilities. The States were, when our co-operation in government was invited, Mohammedan monarchies, and such they are to-day. We have neither the right nor the desire to vary this system of government. . . .

. . . We should bear in mind that the Malay people are still strongly bound by ties of sentiment and tradition and by religious feeling to the ruling dynasties of the States. The Malay Sultans are the heads of the national religion in each State, and the traditional protectors of Malay custom. . . . The Courts of the Sultans and Rajahs maintain a measure of dignity and colour loved by the masses.

. . . The maintenance of the position, authority, and prestige of the Malay rulers is a cardinal point of policy.

The British policy of keeping the states "Malay" and of advancing the progress of "the indigenous Malay inhabitants" took more specific form in 1931 when Sir Cecil Clements, the recently arrived governor of the Straits Settlements and high commissioner of the Malay states, announced a policy of decentralizing the Federated Malay States and eventually creating a Malayan union of the nine Malay states and the Straits Settlements of Malacca and Penang.

* *Source:* Great Britain, *Report by the Right Honourable W. G. A. Ormsby-Gore, M.P. (Parliamentary Under-Secretary of State for the Colonies) on his Visit to Malaya, Ceylon, and Java during the Year 1928* (London: H.M. Stationery Office, 1928), Cmd. 3235, pp. 17–18.

Few could dispute the desirability of bringing the separate British-Malay administrations in the peninsula into a national structure, but the policy was vigorously opposed by the Chinese and Europeans, including many British officials. They viewed it as an attempt to dismantle the already national and efficient British administration of the Federated Malay States and hand powers to the state governments which were unsuited to and probably incapable of exercising them. The Chinese had other reasons for opposing the policy; they felt the British were discriminating against them: Tan Cheng Lock, a Chinese spokesman, declared that the policy took no account of the interests or aspirations of the Chinese and other non-Malays who had contributed so much to the economic development of the country. But while some compromises were worked out, decentralization stood, and the Chinese continued to object to the "pro-Malay" and "anti-Chinese" policy of the British.

Rupert Emerson summarized the problem succinctly, when he noted that the old forms of government in Malaya had not evolved as rapidly as the people whom they governed. The anachronism was made worse because of racial differences. An advanced Chinese community, he felt, could not be handed over to Malay monarchies. The Malay political situation could be maintained only so long as these monarchies were merely symbolic and more enlightened elements were permitted to rule.[1]

Although non-Malay and particularly Chinese objections did eventually prevail, when the British returned to Malaya at the end of World War II, they announced a new policy. The following excerpt is from a statement by the secretary of state for the colonies in October 1945, announcing the British intention of establishing the Malayan Union.

Report on a Mission to Malaya [October 1945]*

His Majesty's Government have given careful consideration to the future of Malaya and the need to promote the sense of unity and common

---

[1] Rupert Emerson, *Malaysia* (New York: Macmillan Co., 1937), pp. 338.

Source: Great Britain, Colonial Office, *Report on a Mission to Malaya* (London: H.M. Stationery Office, 1946), Colonial No. 194, pp. 1, 3.

citizenship which will develop the country's strength and capacity in due course for self-government within the British Commonwealth. Our policy will call for a constitutional union of Malaya and for the institution of a Malayan citizenship which will give equal citizenship rights to those who can claim Malaya to be their homeland. . . .

The Malayan Union will consist of nine States in the Malay Peninsula and of the two British Settlements of Penang and Malacca. The Settlement of Singapore at this stage requires separate constitutional treatment and in view of its special economic and other interests provision will be made for it to be constituted as a separate Colony. His Majesty's Government are, however, well aware of the many ties between Singapore and the mainland, and that these ties may well work towards ultimate union. This will be a matter for the governments of the Malayan Union and Singapore to consider in due course.

. . . His Majesty's Government . . . have decided that fresh Agreements with the several Malay Rulers need first to be arranged which will enable His Majesty to possess and exercise full jurisdiction in the Malay States. . . .

There will also be created a Malayan Union citizenship, for which the qualifications will be birth in Malaya or a suitable period of residence. They will be citizens of Malaya, with all the rights and obligations which that term implies. No one must rely upon past privilege, or regard Malaya simply as a source of material wealth. . . .

The Malayan Union was an effort to rationalize the pre-1941 constitutional and administrative structure of the Malay states and the Straits Settlements. Planning for the Union did not, however, take into account the relative political strength of the Malay and Chinese communities, and it failed to anticipate the vigorous Malay reaction in opposition to the Union. The Malayan Union was stillborn in early 1946.

Constitutional Proposals by the British [1947]*

The creation of the Malayan Union brought objections from Malays in all parts of the peninsula. At the basis of the Malay reaction was a

* *Source:* Great Britain, Colonial Office, Federation of Malaya *Summary of Revised Constitutional Proposals* (London: H.M. Stationery Office, 1947), Cmd. 7171, p. 2.

revulsion against what was regarded as a deprivation of sovereignty and a continued fear of non-Malay domination as a result of the proposed new citizenship. His Majesty's government maintained their adherence to two fundamental principles, which were at the root of their whole policy, namely, the establishment of a strong central government with control over all matters of importance to the progress and welfare of the country as a whole, and the introduction of a form of common citizenship open to all those, irrespective of race, who regarded Malaya as their real home and as the object of their loyalty. Attempts were therefore made to bring Their Highnesses the Rulers into consultation and also to consult other leaders of Malay public opinion, in the hope that the Union Scheme could be modified in a way which, while it embodied the two principles mentioned above, met the Malay objections. These approaches met with a favourable response. . . .

The Federation of Malaya replaced the Malayan Union in February 1948. Sovereignty and nationality remained with each of the Malay rulers and, in Penang and Malacca, with the British crown. The chief executive, however, was a federal high commissioner, who resided in Kuala Lumpur. Appointive federal executive and legislative councils were created. The latter, especially, was to advise on and consent to laws made by the high commissioner and "Their Highnesses the Rulers." But the high commissioner was empowered to act without the consent of the Legislative Council and against the advice of the Executive Council if he chose to do so. Provision was also made for state executive and legislative bodies. Federal and state powers were specifically listed.

Although the Federation Agreement awarded the Malays a privileged citizenship position, it by no means excluded non-Malays from citizenship rights. Under the agreement's terms, Malays were given some time to try to improve their economic status vis-à-vis the non-Malays. Various governmental efforts were made to bring the Malays more fully into the modernized economy, but after several years there was little to show for these efforts.

In the meantime, progress was made toward self-rule. A Constitutional Commission chaired by Lord Reid of the United Kingdom met in 1956 to make recommendations for a constitution for an independent Malaya. Among several difficult issues the commission considered was the "special position" of the Malays. Excerpts from the commission's report are presented below.

Report of the Reid Commission [February 11, 1957]*

Our terms of reference require that provision should be made in the Constitution for the "safeguarding of the special position of the Malays and the legitimate interests of other Communities." In addition, we are asked to provide for a common nationality for the whole of the Federation, and to ensure that the Constitution shall guarantee a democratic form of Government. . . . It seemed to us . . . that under a democratic form of Government it was inherent that all the citizens of Malaya, irrespective of race, creed or culture, should enjoy certain fundamental rights including equality before the law. We found it difficult, therefore, to reconcile the terms of reference if the protection of the special position of the Malays signified the granting of special privileges, permanently, to one community only and not to the others. . . .

. . . We found that as a result of the original treaties with the Malay States, reaffirmed from time to time, the special position of the Malays has always been recognised. There are now four matters with regard to which the special position of the Malays is recognized and safeguarded.

(1) In most of the States there are extensive Malay reservations of land, and the system of reserving land for Malays has been in operation for many years. In every State the Ruler-in-Council has the power to permit a non-Malay to acquire a piece of land in a Malay reservation but the power is not used very freely. . . .

(2) There are now in operation quotas for admission to the public services. These quotas do not apply to all services. . . .

(3) There are now also in operation quotas in respect of the issuing of permits or licenses for the operation of certain businesses. These are chiefly concerned with road haulage and passenger vehicles for hire. Some of these quotas are of recent introduction. The main reasons for them appear to be that in the past the Malays have lacked capital and have tended to remain on the land and not to take a large part in business, and that this is one method of encouraging the Malays to take a larger part in business enterprises.

(4) In many classes of scholarships, bursaries and other forms of aid for educational purposes preference is given to Malays. The reason for this appears to be that in the past higher education of the Malays has tended to fall behind that of the Chinese. . . .

We found little opposition in any quarter of the continuance of the

* Source: Great Britain, Colonial Office, Report of the Federation of Malaya Constitutional Commission 1957 (London: H.M. Stationery Office, 1957), Colonial No. 330, pp. 70–72.

present system for a time, but there was great opposition in some quarters to any increase of the present preferences and to their being continued for any prolonged period. We are of the opinion that in present circumstances it is necessary to continue these preferences. The Malays would be at a serious and unfair disadvantage compared with other communities if they were suddenly withdrawn. . . . The Malays should be assured that the present position will continue for a substantial period, but that in due course the present preferences should be reduced and should ultimately cease so that there should then be no discrimination between races or communities. . . . After 15 years there should be a review of the whole matter. . . .

The Reid Commission recommendations were revised in discussion in the spring of 1957: The constitution was made more favorable to the Malays in regard to citizenship, language, religion, and special privileges. The Reid Commission's proposal that privileges be reviewed after fifteen years was rejected, and responsibility for privileges was given to the *Yang di-Pertuan Agong,* the new head of state, rather than to the "appropriate legislature." British rule came to an end, and independent Malaya was proclaimed on August 31, 1957. Excerpts from the constitution are reproduced below.

The Constitution of the Federation of Malaya [August 31, 1957]*

. . . 3. (1) Islam is the religion of the Federation; but other religions may be practiced in peace and harmony in any part of the Federation.

(2) In every State other than Malacca and Penang the position of the Rulers as the Head of the Muslim religion in his State . . . and . . . all rights, privileges, prerogatives and powers enjoyed by him as Head of that religion, are unaffected and unimpaired. . . .

8. (1) All persons are equal before the law and entitled to the equal protection of the law.

(2) Except as expressly authorised by this Constitution, there shall be no discrimination against citizens on the ground only of religion, race, descent or place of birth in any law or in the appointment to any office or employment under a public authority or in the administration of any law relating to the acquisition, holding or disposition of property or the establishing or carrying on of any trade, business, profession, vocation or employment. . . .

* *Source:* Malaya, *Proposed Constitution of Federation of Malaya* (Kuala Lumpur: Government Press, 1957), pp. 1–5, 14, 73–76.

10. (1) Subject to Clause (2)
- (a) every citizen has the right to freedom of speech and expression;
- (b) all citizens have the right to assemble peaceably and without arms;
- (c) all citizens have the right to form associations.

(2) Parliament may by law impose
- (a) on the rights conferred . . . such restrictions as it deems necessary or expedient in the interest of the security of the Federation, friendly relations with other countries, public order or morality and restrictions designed to protect the privileges of Parliament or any Legislative Assembly or to provide against contempt of court, defamation, or incitement to any offence. . . .

11. (1) Every person has the right to profess and practice his religion and, subject to Clause (4), to propagate it. . . .

(4) State law may control or restrict the propagation of any religious doctrine or belief among persons professing the Muslim religion. . . .

32. (1) There shall be a Supreme Head of the Federation, to be called the Yang di-Pertuan Agong, who shall take precedence over all persons in the Federation and shall not be liable to any proceedings whatsoever in any court. . . .

(3) The Yang di-Pertuan Agong shall be elected by the Conference of Rulers for a term of five years. . . .

152. (1) The national language shall be the Malay language and shall be in such script as Parliament may by law provide:

Provided that
- (a) no person shall be prohibited or prevented from using (otherwise than for official purposes), or from teaching or learning, any other languages; and
- (b) nothing in this clause shall prejudice the right of the Federal Government or of any State Government to preserve and sustain the use and study of the language of any other community in the Federation.

(2) Notwithstanding the provisions of Clause (1), for a period of ten years after Merdeka Day, and thereafter until Parliament otherwise provides, the English language may be used in both Houses of Parliament, in the Legislative Assembly of every State, and for all other official purposes.

(3) Notwithstanding the provisions of Clause (2), for a period of ten years after Merdeka Day, and thereafter until Parliament otherwise provides, the authoritative texts. . . .

(b) of all Acts of Parliament and all subsidiary legislation issued by the Federal Government shall be in the English language.

153. (1) It shall be the responsibility of the Yang di-Pertuan Agong to safeguard the special position of the Malays and the legitimate interests of other communities. . . .

(2) . . . The Yang di-Pertuan Agong shall . . . ensure the reservation for Malays of such proportion as he may deem reasonable of positions in the public service . . . and of scholarships, exhibitions and other similar educational or training privileges or special facilities given or accorded by the Federal Government and, when any permit or license for the operation of any trade or business is required by federal law, then, subject to the provisions of that law and this Article, of such permits and licenses. . . .

(4) In exercising his functions . . . the Yang di-Pertuan Agong shall not deprive any person of any public office held by him or of the continuance of any scholarship, exhibition or other educational or training privileges or special facilities enjoyed by him. . . .

(7) Nothing in this Article shall operate to deprive . . . any person of any right, privilege, permit or license accrued to or enjoyed or held by him or to authorise a refusal to renew to any person any such permit or license or a refusal to grant to the heirs, successors or assigns of a person any permit or license when the renewal or grant might reasonably be expected in the ordinary course of events. . . .

(9) Nothing in this Article shall empower Parliament to restrict business or trade solely for the purpose of reservations for Malays.

II. Malaysia

The idea of joining Britain's Borneo dependencies of Sabah (formerly North Borneo), Brunei, and Sarawak to Malaya and Singapore in a single political association had been expressed from time to time in the 1950's. Alliance leaders, however, were dubious of any political union with Singapore. Its large Chinese population and its history of political turbulence were problems which the men in Kuala Lumpur preferred not to have. In fact, Singapore was viewed as a problem for Malaya whether there was political union or not.

The British had established Singapore as a separate crown colony in 1946 for strategic, economic, and racial reasons: It was the bastion of British and Commonwealth armed forces in Asia; its trade was lucrative; and it was feared that if Singapore's predominantly Chinese population was united with the Chinese population on the peninsula, serious racial tensions would be created. Political development was achieved more slowly in Singapore than in Malaya. This was due partly to Britain's interest in maintaining control of the island, but it was also due to the reluctance of many of the people to participate in a political system which placed limitations on their activity. By the early 1950's, however, the campaigns of left-wing trade union organizers, who combined their appeals for support with demands for independence, had begun to stir popular interest in politics. Britain responded to this situation in 1954 by offering constitutional reforms aimed at encouraging the development of parliamentary government and a party system. However, Singaporean political leaders, including Lee Kuan Yew of the radical left-wing People's Action Party (PAP), sought further reforms. Some, like David Marshall, head of the Labour Front, argued strongly for independence. The PAP, which in 1958 captured control of the city council, called for union with Malaya. As a result of further negotiations with Britain, in which all parties were represented, a new constitution providing for local self-government of the State of Singapore was obtained, but foreign relations and defense remained in British hands. Internal security was made the responsibility of an Internal Security Council, composed of an equal number of representatives of Britain and the Singapore government, and one member from the government of Malaya. But Britain reserved the right to suspend the Singapore constitution, so the constitutional future of Singapore was left in doubt.

However, the PAP, which came to power in the state legislative elections of 1959 held under the new constitution, championed merger with the Federation of Malaya as the means by which Singapore could achieve complete independence from Great Britain and from mid-1959 made a concerted effort to identify the island's interests with those of its neighbor to the north. The PAP's purpose was to allay if possible the fears which the Malayan government and the Malayan people had of bringing Singapore's Chinese population into the federation. In this, as well as in their political and social legislation aimed at creating a new society in which the people would have "the opportunity of active leadership," Lee Kuan Yew and the moderates who led the PAP to victory in 1959 were opposed by the party's more militant members. By July 1961, cooperation between the English-educated and the more militant Chinese-educated within the PAP had ended with the formation by the latter of their own organization, the Barisan Sosialis, which was identified as a party of the extreme left. Early in 1962, PAP representatives in the legislature had dwindled from 43 to 26, of a total of 51 popularly elected seats.

At this same time, Malayan leaders began to reconsider their opposition to the inclusion of Singapore in Malaya. As troublesome as Singapore might be in the federation, in their view an independent Singapore ruled by radical leftist leaders would likely prove to be inimical to their interests. The PAP government, which favored a merger, might not long continue in power, and a decision on Singapore's destiny seemed necessary before the island state's next general elections in 1963. An answer to the problem was provided by Malaya's prime minister, Tunku Abdul Rahman.

Tunku Abdul Rahman: The Malaysia Proposal [May 27, 1961]*

Perhaps it would be a good thing for all concerned if the people of Singapore and Malaya could decide to make Malaya what it is—Malaya, our ONE AND ONLY HOME. . . . The Chinese in Malaya, unlike their counterparts in some neighbouring countries, have no reason to be unhappy. They are free to own property, in fact, do own most of the properties and businesses here. The economic life of the country is very largely in their hands and they share political rights with the Malays and others.

Malaya today as a nation realises that she cannot stand alone and in isolation. . . . Sooner or later she should have an understanding with Britain and the peoples of the territories of Singapore, North Borneo, Brunei and Sarawak.

It is . . . inevitable that we should . . . plan whereby these territories can be brought closer together in political and economic cooperation. . . .

Abdul Rahman's remarks were well-received by British and Singapore leaders. Some of Malaya's leaders, however, were cool to the idea of an association with Singapore, and to induce them to accept the proposed merger, it was necessary to provide that the Borneo territories, with their predominantly non-Chinese populations, be included in the new state. Various steps were soon taken to work out the terms on which the new political state called Malaysia would be

---

* *Source:* From a speech by Tunku Abdul Rahman to the Foreign Correspondents Association in Singapore, May 27, 1961, quoted in *Malaysia* (Kuala Lumpur), no. 2 (April 1962), p. 6.

created and to inform the people of the several states involved. A Malaysia Solidarity Consultation Committee was formed in July 1961. Broad agreement was reached between Malaya and Singapore on the terms of the merger of the two states. Similar agreement could not be reached between Malaya and Brunei, and the Sultan of Brunei decided to remain under British protection.

There was also concern over opinion in the crown colonies of Sarawak and Sabah. In both, political experience was limited, colonial administrations were in firm control, and doubts were voiced by local leaders about coming under Malayan rule. A Commission of Enquiry led by Lord Cobbold visited the two colonies early in 1962. Below is part of the commission's report.

Report of the Cobbold Commission [1962]*

. . . Tributes were paid by all communities to the impartiality of colonial administrators and to the progress which has been made since the war. In a multi-racial society . . . belief in such impartiality, is exceedingly important. The present officials, moreover, have an intimate knowledge of the people. . . . Any new arrangements should not cause an exodus of the present officials. . . .

. . . The argument was used by those who opposed the Malaysia proposals that it would be inconsistent with the British Government's obligation to agree to a scheme which did not first grant independence to Sarawak. The Malaysia proposals are regarded in some quarters as an indication that the British Government are no longer prepared to shoulder their responsibilities or honour their commitments. . . .

. . . A very large number of the supporters of Malaysia were influenced by their admiration of the Malayan Prime Minister and his colleagues for their firm leadership and their imaginative policies in rural development. . . . They were anxious that Sarawak should enjoy similar progress within Malaysia. . . . Unfortunate repercussions . . . may follow if these hopes are not realised.

The firm opposition of the present Malayan Government to Communist designs has also won the admiration of many people of all races. . . .

. . . The ideological position of the present leadership in the Federation is also an important factor in the opposition to Malaysia. We have

* *Source:* Malaya, *Report of the Commission of Enquiry, North Borneo and Sarawak* (Kuala Lumpur: Government Press, 1962), pp. 10–13, 49–50.

drawn attention earlier to the threat which Malaysia poses for those Chinese who are emotionally or ideologically inclined to China. . . .

. . . Many people among the native population see no need for the Malaysian proposals and would prefer things to go on as they are. The same is true of a large section of the Chinese business community.

. . . A major strand in the opposition to Malaysia lies in the demand for independence, after the achievement of which there [would be] general readiness to consider the possibility of Malaysia. . . . It springs from a genuine fear of discrimination after [the creation of] Malaysia, a feeling among the Chinese that their status would be reduced to that of "second class citizens" and among the natives that their customary laws and practices would be affected. Similarly there is concern that Malaysia would entail migration from the other territories of the new Federation. . . .

. . . Groups from all native populations expressed a general desire . . . that special privileges should not be given to the natives. They were extremely anxious that their position in the new Federation should be analogous to that of the Malays in the present Constitution of the Federation of Malaya. . . .

Regarding the Head of Sarawak State . . . [t]he natives have insisted that only natives should be eligible to be Head of State, while the non-natives have expressed with equal emphasis their desire that the office should be open to anyone born in Sarawak.

. . . There were differences in attitude towards the acceptance of Islam as the national religion. . . . There were similar differences in attitude towards Malay as the national language. . . .

. . . In assessing the opinion of the peoples of North Borneo [Sabah] and Sarawak we have only been able to arrive at an approximation. We do not wish to make any guarantee that it may not change in one direction or the other in the future. . . .

. . . About one-third of the population in each territory strongly favours early realisation of Malaysia without too much concern about terms and conditions. Another third . . . ask . . . for conditions and safeguards varying in nature and extent. . . . The remaining third is divided between those who insist on independence before Malaysia is considered and those who would strongly prefer to see British rule continue for some years to come. If the conditions and reservations which they have put forward could be substantially met, the second category . . . would generally support the proposals. Moreover, once a firm decision was taken quite a number of the third category would be likely to abandon their opposition and decide to make the best of a doubtful job. . . .

Islam was made the national religion and Malay the national language in the constitution of Malaysia. However, in a number of ways exceptions were made to meet the conditions and preferences of Singapore and the Borneo states. Singapore was permitted the use of Mandarin and Tamil as well as English and Malay in the legislature. Malay special privileges did not extend to Singapore. Singapore was allowed to conduct its own affairs in matters relating to education and labor. Singapore citizenship, valid for purposes of voting and holding elected office in Singapore only, was retained.

In September 1962, after a stormy public debate between PAP and Barisan Sosialis leaders, the Singapore electorate voted overwhelmingly in a special referendum in favor of merger with Malaya. The following document contains Prime Minister Lee Kuan Yew's views on Malaysia, which he expressed in 1961 during the campaign for merger.

Lee Kuan Yew: Malaysia [1961]*

. . . Merger is going to take place not just because it is the desire of the P.A.P. or merely because it is the wish of the Federation Alliance government. It is as inevitable as the rising and setting of the sun. The two territories are so intertwined and so interwoven in their economic, political and military complex that no man can keep up the artificial barrier at the Causeway for long.

If merger does not come with the consent of the people of the two territories, then inevitably it will come by the use of force by one territory over the other, because each is vital to the survival of the other.

Everyone knows the reasons why the Federation is important to Singapore. It is the hinterland which produces the rubber and tin that keep our shop-window economy going. It is the base that made Singapore the capital city. Without this economic base Singapore would not survive.

Without merger, without a reunification of our two governments and an integration of our two economies, our economic position will slowly and steadily get worse. Your livelihood will get worse. Instead of there being one unified economic development for Malaya, there will be two. The Federation instead of co-operating with Singapore will compete

* *Source:* Lee Kuan Yew, *The Battle for Merger*, Vol. V, in *Towards Socialism*, Ministry of Culture Series (Singapore: Government Printing Office, 1961), pp. 3–5.

against Singapore for industrial capital and industrial expansion. In this competition both will suffer.

But Singapore will suffer more, because we have less resources to fall back on. . . .

. . . Now let me tell you why Singapore is vital to the Federation. There is no conceivable way in which Singapore can be completely cut off from the Federation. The Causeway and the Straits of Johore are not the Maginot Line. No iron, rubber or coconut curtain is possible between us. What happens in Singapore must affect the Federation. From Singapore the Federation can be undermined. Singapore is vital to the security and survival of the Federation.

Objections to Malaysia were raised by the governments of the Philippines and Indonesia. The Philippines in early 1962 had formally approached Great Britain with a claim to Sabah, alleging that the terms of the original cession of the Sultan of Sulu's territory had been violated. Indonesia expressed concern over the continued presence of British bases in Malaysia and the right of the people to determine their political future. To meet the Indonesian objection, a special United Nations investigation of opinion in Borneo was undertaken in August 1963; it concluded that a majority of the people in Sarawak and Sabah wanted Malaysia. However, both the Philippines and Indonesia complained that the UN's investigation was too brief and limited to ascertain the real wishes of the people, and both governments withheld their recognition of Malaysia when it was formed on September 16, 1963. Indonesia also decided to resume its policy of "confrontation" with Malaysia.

Within a year of Malaysia's formation, difficulties had arisen: The root of the problem was not Indonesia's decision to oppose Malaysia by force but rather the inability of political leaders in Kuala Lumpur and Singapore to reach accommodation. The Malay legacy of mistrust of Singapore was exacerbated by various activities of the People's Action Party early in 1964, including its decision to enter Malaysia's federal elections. Malay fears of Chinese machinations were inflated by Malay nationalists. Racial rioting occurred in Singapore in July 1964. Although controversy became personal and bitter, Tunku Abdul Rahman was still hopeful that Malaysia would survive.

Tunku Abdul Rahman: The Problems of Malaysia [July 1965]*

. . . Singapore has had no previous experience of working in a federal nation, and due to the fact of being the "New York" of Malaysia it probably feels that its position is far more important than that of the rest of Malaysia. Some of the state's leaders do not realize the great benefit Singapore is already enjoying. . . . They are quick to criticize the central government . . . principally because their own state government is run by an opposition party. This seems to arouse undue apprehension in the minds of some foreign observers, who shake their heads and talk pessimistically about the future of Malaysia. . . . I myself have no doubt that as Singapore continues to make further progress in Malaysia and adapts itself more readily through experience and understanding of the cooperation necessary in a federal structure, these pangs of local pride and wishes for dominance will slowly pass away. . . . The national interest must be the prime overall concern. . . . I am confident that whatever little differences exist at present between the central government and the state government will work out satisfactorily.

Lee Kuan Yew was critical of what he viewed as a trend toward Malay domination, and he called for a "Malaysian Malaysia." Moderate Alliance leaders declared that this, too, was their goal but that Lee, by raising it in a critical context, was in fact provoking communal anxieties and thereby impeding progress toward it. Lee's views are contained in the following document.

Lee Kuan Yew: A "Malaysian Malaysia" [May 3, 1965]†

Some people may wonder why it is that we are not just keeping quiet and allowing people to say what they like, such as "Malays unite." They shout this everywhere. . . . People get worried. If among the Chinese you hear people say, "Hokkiens unite," all the non-Hokkiens will say, "What is it all about? Is it to wallop the non-Hokkiens?" So, when they say, "Malays unite," we say, "What is this all about?" It is a fair question.

You see, the agreement in the Constitution must lead to a Malaysian

* *Source:* Tunku Abdul Rahman, "Malaysia: Key Area in Southeast Asia," *Foreign Affairs,* 43 (July 1965), 4: 659–670; reprinted by permission of the publishers of *Foreign Affairs.*

† *Source:* From an address by Lee Kuan Yew, May 3, 1965, quoted in Lee Kuan Yew, *The Battle for a Malaysian Malaysia,* Vol. 2 (Singapore: Ministry of Culture, 1965), pp. 17–18.

nation—a Malaysian Malaysia, and if they want to stop it they must use unconstitutional methods to stop it. So I say if they want to do that, do it now; better for us; easier for us to make other alternative arrangements. And the alternative arrangements? Well . . . if it is really necessary then I say: Look, all those states which want a Malaysian Malaysia are sure to come together. And I can think of three straight-away: Sabah, Sarawak and Singapore. I can think of a few others like Penang and Malacca. I can even believe that the Sultan of Johore will not want to go and join Indonesia as has been suggested by United Malays National Organization's Malaya Merdeka. Why should he?

On August 9, 1965, Malaysians were stunned to learn that leaders of the central government had decided that Singapore should be separated from Malaysia. The decision was made by Prime Minister Tunku Abdul Rahman and several of his confidants in the cabinet. The following extract is taken from the prime minister's address to the Dewan Ra'ayat or House of Representatives on that date.

Tunku Abdul Rahman: Separation of Singapore from Malaysia [August 9, 1965]*

What I am about to announce to this House will no doubt cause a big surprise and shock to Hon'ble Members. . . . It is the most painful and heartbreaking news. . . . In all the ten years of my leadership of this House, I have never had a duty so unpleasant as this to perform. The announcement . . . concerns the separation of Singapore from the rest of the Federation.

The reasons for this have been many. Since the formation of Malaysia, and this year in particular, there have been so many differences with the Singapore Government and these differences take many forms. . . .

. . . It appeared that as soon as one issue was resolved, another cropped up. Where a patch was made here, a tear appeared elsewhere, and where one hole was plugged, other leaks appeared. So, it does seem completely impossible to arrive at a solution whereby we can hope to pull along together . . . for the common good of Malaysia. . . . There are only two courses of action open to us.

Number one is to take repressive measures against the Singapore Government for the behaviour of some of their leaders and number two to

* *Source:* From *Singapore Breakaway,* a speech by Prime Minister Tunku Abdul Rahman, August 9, 1965 (Kuala Lumpur: Department of Information, 1965), pp. 1–8.

sever all connections with the State Government that has ceased to give even a measure of loyalty to the Central Government. The position of the Central Government not only at Home but worse still abroad has been mocked on many instances.

. . . It is odious for us to take repressive measures against the Singapore Government, for such action is repulsive to our concept of Parliamentary Democracy. Even then it would not solve the problems before us. . . . One that gives us the most concern is [the] communal issue. . . . The peace and happiness of the people in this country depend on goodwill and understanding of the various races for one another. Without it this nation will break up. . . . Contempt, fear and hatred have been sown in Singapore, and even if we try to prevent their growth, I feel that after a time they will sprout up with a more virulent force. The thousands of students abroad have been fed with all kinds of propaganda against the Central Government.

Malaysian Malaysia, in particular, suggests that the Malaysia we have now is bad for it gives all the advantages to one race while depriving others of their rightful place in our society.

Foreign correspondents who approached me on this subject while I was in England and France were under the wrong impression that the Malay-dominated Central Government has not been fair to others, that there has been discrimination against the Chinese in all fields. . . .

It was suggested that our quarrel with the P.A.P. was due to the fact that we are afraid of the far more advanced and enlightened socialist Government of Singapore. They appeared incredulous when I informed them that there are Socialist Parties in the mainland . . . and the P.A.P. contested our election [federal elections in 1964] without success and that the only party that we ban is the Communist Party. I also informed them that most of these parties are made up mainly of Chinese whose number well exceeds that of Mr. Lee Kuan Yew's, and to suggest, therefore, that Mr. Lee Kuan Yew represents the Chinese and at the same time represents the only left-wing party in the country is wrong.

. . . While in London I have had to interview some of the pressmen . . . and explain to them what the position is, but we can't do that all the time. We want to be . . . left alone and to be given the moral support which we deserve to bolster our courage against the communist threat and Indonesian confrontation. We consider ourselves as one of the nations in South-East Asia that has managed not only to fight our enemies but also to provide for our people's need. We are in fact one of the countries that has made a real success of our independence.

. . . There has also been [a] certain inclination on the part of some countries to look upon the Prime Minister of Singapore as an equal partner in the Government of Malaysia. . . . This has made the situation rather awkward for us. In a nation there can only be one national executive head. The illustration which I saw in one of the British papers depicting a cartoon of Lee Kuan Yew and myself over the map of Malaysia, and with the caption "too many cooks" is to the point. . . . There can only be one Prime Minister for the Nation, and so the best course we can take is to allow Lee Kuan Yew to be the Prime Minister of independent Singapore in the full sense of the word.

I was hoping to make Singapore the New York of Malaysia and had begged the politicians in Singapore to give their thought for the fulfillment of this objective. In order to do that it is necessary to place the interest of Singapore above that of their own personal glorification. Unfortunately political rivalry . . . of the various politicians in Singapore had made this impossible. . . . My dream is shattered and so we come now to the parting of ways.

. . . Our relationship with Sabah and Sarawak has been excellent. We are desirous of carrying out [an] extensive development programme in these two States, because we realise that under the colonial rule . . . the two States had been neglected. . . .

They fit into the pattern of administration with the rest of the States of Malaysia so admirably well, and unless we can carry out some development, however small it may be, their hope and trust in us will inevitably lessen. . . .

I hope that the breakaway with Singapore will not cause them undue worry or concern, and that in the circumstances they will agree that the course of action we are taking is the only one open to us in order to maintain peace and harmony in Malaysia, and at the same time to obtain the closest cooperation with Singapore.

III. Political Parties and Issues

The years 1946–1948 constituted the gestation period for Malayan-oriented, organized political life. The United Malays National Organization (UMNO) was formed to oppose the Malayan Union. The Malayan Democratic Union (MDU) was formed to demand that the British make a more demonstrable commitment to self-rule for Malaya. The British authorities granted legal status to the Malayan Communist party (MCP), active among labor and professional groups. But this somewhat permissive attitude toward the Communists was gradually replaced by more restrictive policies.

Subsequent to the formal establishment of the Federation of Malaya in February 1948, Communist terrorist attacks, amounting to armed rebellion, occurred. A state of emergency was declared in June 1948 and remained in effect until 1960. The military undertook draconic measures which served to discourage political activity.

The leaders realized a purely military solution was not possible, however, and steps were taken toward developing democratic processes. Elections for local authorities were first held in 1951. In 1952, the two principal parties, the UMNO and the Malayan Chinese Association (MCA), basing their appeal on communal loyalty, joined to contest the Kuala Lumpur municipal election. The MCA initially was founded to assist in social welfare work among the Chinese and to help in the resettlement of Chinese "squatters."

In August 1953, the UMNO and the MCA met together in a National Convention to demand election of their candidates to the federal Legislative Council in 1954. At the convention, Colonel H. S. Lee, one of the founders of the UMNO–MCA Alliance party and later minister of finance, and Dato Abdul Razak, who became prime minister in 1970, both commented on Malay-Chinese cooperation.

Hon. Colonel H. S. Lee: Malay-Chinese Cooperation
[August 23, 1953]*

. . . This Convention is sponsored by the UMNO and the MCA which are the two biggest political parties and represent the two major communities in this country. These two organizations started working very closely since the beginning of last year in order to obtain the closest cooperation between the Chinese and the Malays. They formed an Alliance to contest the various local elections which by the successful results have amply indicated that the principles of the Alliance have received the overwhelming support of the people of the country. . . . The UMNO and MCA have now reached such an understanding and have accepted the principles of a blueprint for the reform of the Federal Legislative and Executive Councils. . . . It was also alleged that the Alliance was formed on communal lines and was therefore not conducive to the establishment of a United Malaya. The fact that invitations have been sent to other political parties and other communal organizations is, I trust,

* *Source:* Speech by Hon. Colonel H. S. Lee, at the National Convention, August 23, 1953, Hotel Majestic, Kuala Lumpur.

sufficient evidence to show that the real objective of the UMNO and the MCA is to get the co-operation of all the races. . . .

Dato Abdul Razak: Malay-Chinese Cooperation
[August 23, 1953]*

We are assembled here today as representatives of the various political parties in this country in order to give expression to the aspirations of the people whom we represent. These noble aspirations can be expressed in two simple words, "unity and freedom." We desire to bring about unity among the people of the different races who regard this country as their home and home of their children in order that by our united efforts we can establish a united, independent and sovereign state of Malaya.

It is indeed a happy augury that this historic National Convention should have been sponsored by UMNO and MCA—two political organizations which represent the two major communities of this country, Malays and Chinese who comprise nearly 90 percent of the population of this country. No one who has studied the political progress of this country would deny that unity between these two races is absolutely vital to the future peace and progress of this country. The fact that these two races through their respective organizations have decided to sponsor this Convention is a clear evidence of the substantial agreement that they have reached on vital issues affecting the future of this country.

Let, therefore, the unity so far established be the foundation on which to build a bigger and more lasting unity which will ultimately grow into a national solidarity on which the future of this country will be moulded and consolidated. . . .

The Alliance led by Tunku Abdul Rahman won a stunning victory in the first federal elections in 1955. This achievement persuaded the British to negotiate with Alliance representatives on the terms of independence, and power was formally transferred on August 31, 1957. The Alliance, joined by the Malayan Indian Congress (MIC) in 1955, won federal elections in 1959, 1964, and 1969; it represented itself as the party of independence, prosperity, and progress.

Alliance critics have been many, but opposition parties have had difficulty developing strong national organizations. Among them, the revolutionary Malayan Communist party (MCP) has the longest his-

* *Source:* Speech by Dato Abdul Razak, at the National Convention, August 23, 1953, Hotel Majestic, Kuala Lumpur.

tory, but it has failed to escape being labeled a Chinese party. Its efforts, prior to independence in 1957, to effect a Malaysian nationalist appeal also failed; its armed terrorism between 1948 and 1960 alienated many. The Alliance government has viewed the Communists as a continuing threat, as the following report, released in 1959 prior to the federal election of that year, asserts.

The Communist Threat [1959]*

Communism was brought to this country by representatives of the Chinese Communist Party, who set up an organization known as the Nanyang [South Seas] Communist Party in 1928. Two years later this Party was converted into a separate Malayan Communist Party. . . .

In 1948 the Malayan Communist Party, which was then a legal organisation, judged that conditions were favourable for launching an armed revolution. . . . Events proved that the Party's judgment was wrong. . . .

By 1955, the Party was faced with a new situation. It was influenced by another switch of World Communist tactics, and by the fact that in a short time the Federation would achieve its independence. . . .

The Party leaders felt that their position might be redeemed by reaching an agreement with the elected representatives of the people. Thereby the Party could emerge from the jungle with apparent recognition of its claims that its "armed struggle" was a contributory factor in the attainment of independence. Also, it could gain for itself the freedom necessary for it quickly to develop its influence in the changing political conditions of the country. . . .

This then was the nature of the trap being laid in the "peace" overtures of 1955. Chin Peng[2] found his bluff called at Baling. He could not compromise, for only Government's acquiescence in the terms acceptable to the Party would give the Communists the complete freedom necessary for the development of their plot of subversion. . . .

. . . Chin Peng ordained that his followers should remain in the jungle. . . .

. . The current programme of the Party is to offer a political platform which has a popular appeal. At the same time Party executives are directed to infiltrate secretly into non-communist organisations . . . and to lead those organisations into a "united People's Democratic Front." . . .

* *Source:* Malaya, *The Communist Threat to the Federation of Malaya* (Kuala Lumpur: Government Press, 1959), pp. 15–19.

[2] Leader of The Malayan Communist party.

A non-Communist left has had difficulty in forming in Malaya. The explanation appears to be due to several factors: A paucity of able and dedicated leaders; difficulties in attracting support in rural, especially Malay, constituencies; subversion by the Communists; suppression by the government; and difficulty in overcoming communal concern with political appeals. Nevertheless, socialist parties have been a part of the Malayan political scene since 1952. The following extract is taken from a policy statement by the Pan-Malayan Labour party issued in September 1952 when Malaya was still British-ruled.

Pan-Malayan Labour Party: Toward a New Malaya [September 1952]*

The Pan-Malayan Labour Party wishes to be regarded as an instrument of the People in their desire to achieve national independence and social justice. It does not, however, look upon itself as the only party working for the political and economic independence of this country. . . . It is pledged to cooperate with other democratic organisations, but it is determined to give a healthy Socialist orientation to the Mayalan movement for independence.

We firmly believe that independence is not an end in itself. Independence can only be a bridge on the far side of which we want to build a new society. We do not want new masters. We wish to create, through the enterprise of our people, a new age of peace and plenty, with opportunity and justice.

The main choice before the country today is between democracy and socialism on the one hand and totalitarianism and capitalism on the other. . . .

We affirm our belief in democracy, which is the same as putting faith in people. . . . This is virtually an assertion that democracy leads inevitably to Socialism. . . . Therefore, we reject without reservation a single-party system of government.

We assert that armed strength is essential to maintain peace in this country. . . . But we go further. We say that the threat to peace exists wherever mankind lives in poverty, hunger and suffering. It can be no more removed by military force alone than disease can be cured by surgery alone. We seek to remove the fundamental causes. We want to see poverty abolished. We want hunger to be unknown, the sick to be tended,

* *Source:* Pan-Malayan Labour party, *Toward a New Malaya* (Butterworth, Malaya: Information Bureau, 1952), pp. 1–8.

the old folks to be cherished, our children to grow up in a land of opportunity. We want to see at the base of this new structure of liberty a simple thing—a steady job and a living wage for everyone who is willing to work.

. . . We want to be free to speak our minds; free to write and publish what we please; free to organise any sort of activity, short of conspiracy; free to choose our rulers; free to worship the God of our faith.

We require the holding of elections based on universal sufferage for nationals and citizens above the age of 21 years to local councils and the State, Settlement, Federal and Singapore Legislatures. . . .

Socialism rejects any form of racial discrimination. . . . It recognises the value of the different cultures and seeks to promote human dignity everywhere. . . .

We support the principle of *jus soli* in the granting of citizenship and desire that the Malayan citizenship, when created, should be available to all persons born in Malaya and to those who have had a continuous period of ten years residence in this country and declare to have made this country their home and the object of their undivided loyalty. . . .

We . . . call for the implementation of an educational policy which would give free elementary and compulsory education to all. . . .

. . . We require the Malayanisation of the civil service. By Malayanisation we do not mean the immediate replacement of all European civil servants. Technical advisers from overseas may be needed in this country even after we have achieved independence. As a first step towards Malayanisation, the recruitment of non-technical expatriate officers should be discontinued forthwith.

We ask for the establishment of a Public Services Commission. . . .

We seek to improve the social services, leading ultimately to complete social security. We proclaim the right of every man to work. Unemployment destroys human dignity and self-respect. Full employment is essential. . . . A system of social insurance against unemployment should be introduced as soon as possible. . . .

We require a decent standard of life for every man and woman. . . . Essential foodstuffs must be subsidized in order to stabilize the cost of living. Destitution must be abolished. Old-age pensions must be introduced.

Everyone has a right to good health. . . .

We believe that every man and woman has a right to a home. The present state of housing is a challenge to the conscience of the country. . . . The administration must undertake to subsidize the cost of building dwelling houses for the lower income group. . . .

Land must be made available to all who will till. Farmers must be given security of tenure, so that they will have a stake in the country. Agriculture must be encouraged. . . .

We seek to reduce the extreme inequalities of wealth and poverty and to ensure the full fruits of their industry to workers by hand and by brain. In order to achieve this we want to promote and safeguard free trade unionism, and seek to secure for workers a share in the control and management of public services and industries.

We believe that the establishment of social security is only possible through economic democracy. . . .

We assert that the People should collectively control and direct the economic forces which affect their own daily lives and the nation's well-being. . . . The exploitation of man by man must cease.

Socialist planning does not presuppose the public ownership of all the means of production though it maintains that workers must be associated democratically with the direction of their industry. . . .

Those major basic industries which can be most beneficially and efficiently run by the State must be nationalised. Where immediate nationalisation is not possible, the principle of progressive nationalisation must be adopted. . . . We are mindful that nationalisation is a means to an end, not an end in itself.

Those industries which are not of such magnitude as to be turned into public enterprises, but which cannot be left in private hands without being detrimental to the public interest should be brought under the CO-OPERATIVE MOVEMENT. . . .

. . . Such industries as would, for the time being, be most efficiently conducted by Private Enterprise should be allowed to carry on.

It is essential for government to ensure that private industry also works in the public interest. Private industry must conform to the national plan. . . .

. . . No private industry should be expropriated by the State without payment of compensation. We take this stand because we believe in supporting action which will assist the necessary flow of capital to our country during this period of development and transition. . . .

Malaya's economy today depends too much on the vagaries of tin and rubber prices . . . Malaya's agricultural production must be diversified. Manufacturing industries must be energetically encouraged. . . .

Great uneasiness has been caused among Malayan workers by the downward trend in the price of rubber. . . . There is a growing demand for the nationalisation of the rubber industry. . . .

It is contended that only by re-organizing our rubber industry so as to be based on small holdings rather than big capitalist estates owned by absentee shareholders, can we prevent the recurrence of the disaster which visited this country in the 1930's. . . .

We seek a fairer distribution of taxation. We believe in taxation as an instrument for the abolition of the gross inequalities—the great gap between the poverty of the many and the resplendent luxury of the few.

This great gap can only be narrowed by . . . graduated income tax, surtax, excess profits tax, capital gains tax and death duties. . . .

As Democratic Socialists we seek to create between Malaya and Britain friendly relations, with the object of making possible a peaceful and rapid transition to genuine democratic self-government in this country. Through this friendship we hope to expand the area of international cooperation between free peoples. . . .

As Socialists we aim at the liberation of all men from economic, social and political bondage and the creation of a world society based on the rule of law and voluntary cooperation between free peoples. In our present situation we place four things before everything else. The first is peace. The second is to seek equality of rights, opportunities and responsibilities for all people. The third is the right of the people to control the economic forces which shape their lives. And the fourth is democracy. All these we want established in this country as we want to see established the world over.

With the passage of years, democratic socialist parties gained experience and began to focus their criticism on the Alliance. In 1968, a new political party was formed by a number of professional and intellectual leaders. It was the *Parti Gerakan Rakyat Malaysia,* the Malaysian People's Movement, or simply, the *Gerakan.* An excerpt from the *Gerakan's* initial declaration of aims follows.

Parti Gerakan Rakyat Malaysia: Statement of Policy [November 1968]*

. . . We have observed with growing alarm . . . serious deficiencies in the leadership of . . . the Alliance Party. . . .

. . . The Alliance Party . . . will never be able to meet the challenge of the time, such as:

(i) the national integration of our various community interests,

* *Source: Gerakan, Organ of the Malaysian People's Movement* (Kuala Lumpur), 1 (November 1968), 1:1–8.

(ii) the achievement of a just and equitable distribution of wealth and opportunities,

(iii) the tackling of crises and problems in a sober, rational, disciplined manner without panic,

(iv) the use and mobilization of the best talents of our generation, . . .

(v) the creation of an atmosphere of security and genuine concern for the existing communities in Malaysia with their specific problems,

(vi) the radical and vigorous elimination of corruption and inefficiency, and

(vii) the need to uproot the openly cultivated compulsive habit of spending on wasteful projects, festivals and banquets.

The Alliance has failed . . . to improve the condition of the Malays in all fields.

In view of the inevitable decay and downfall of the Alliance Party due to old age and malfunction of its body politic, invaded, as it is, by status-seekers and fortune-hunters . . . we are resolved to . . . provide the only viable, decent, rational, disciplined and humane alternative to the Alliance government.

Our party programme . . . will emphasize the need to uplift the conditions of the workers, the peasantry and the professional classes, based on the principles of democracy, economic and social justice, Malaysian Nationalism, modern scientific outlook and the cultural and ethical values of the Asian civilizations.

. . . We shall strive for a prosperous, just and rational society, uncontaminated by feudalism, corruption, inefficiency, indolence, superficiality, communalism, and the subversion of democracy.

Statements of party policies are one thing; political issues are often another. Of the several important issues in Malaysian politics in the 1950's and 1960's, the most fundamental to an understanding of the country's plural-society problems has been the poor economic circumstances of the great majority of the Malay people. In the early 1920's, British colonial servants had observed that economic development was occurring without the participation of the conservative and traditional Malays. It was the British, the Chinese, and, to a lesser extent, the Indians who appeared to be reaping all the gains.

Political debate in the 1960's focused on the "special position" of the Malays which was enshrined in the constitution. Criticism was leveled at the government's efforts to assist the Malays. These efforts included establishment of the Rural Industrial Development Authority (RIDA), begun in 1950, and the Majlis Amanah Ra'ayat (MARA), which took over and expanded the work of the **RIDA** in the 1960's. In addition, the Ministry for Rural Development was created.

In all of these endeavors the basic aim was to create Malay entrepreneurs. Loans, technical advice, government subsidies, roads, rural health centers, vocational schools, land, and improved communications were provided. Yet, the economic and social condition of most Malays appeared not to have been improved significantly. Some critics doubted that the Malays would ever benefit without fundamental changes in the Malaysian markets, said to be controlled by Chinese and other non-Malays.

The following commentary on the economic position of the Malays was made in 1962 to a United Malays National Organization youth seminar on economic development by Ungku A. Aziz, then a professor of economics and now the vice-chancellor at the University of Malaya.

Ungku A. Aziz: The Economic Condition
of the Malays [December 25, 1962]*

The economic condition of the Malays, I mean those living in the villages, have really worsened while on the whole economic development policies and programmes with regard to rural areas have not shown any benefits to the rural people. Their condition now is like the Malay proverb: *Melukut di-tepi Gantang,* i.e., their existence makes no difference at all.

This position is obvious when the economic conditions of the urban and rural dwellers as a whole are compared, which shows that the gap is widening from time to time.

This is what is called poverty breeds poverty. . . . The rural people are aware and apprehensive of the increasing poverty in their midst. . . .

. . . The attitudes of influential people in our society towards economic betterment of the Malays are not sufficiently deep or informed and firm. Progress cannot be achieved because such attitudes are full of misconceptions, which may be deliberate or stem from lack of knowledge. . . .

In my view, the main question is how to raise the level of income of the rural people. There are two ways to do this: Firstly, abolish exploitation and, secondly, increase the productivity of the farmers.

* *Source:* Address by Ungku A. Aziz to UMMO youth seminar, December 25, 1962, at the Dewan Bahasa dan Pustaka (Language and Literature Agency), Kuala Lumpur.

In order to abolish exploitation it is necessary to re-examine and reorganize the marketing, credit and land tenancy systems under which the farmers live and work.

Only after the necessary changes have been achieved could steps be taken to increase farm productivity.

How do roads, bridges, jetties and community halls that have been constructed in various parts of the country affect the Malays? These efforts could only affect measures to increase farm productivity of rural people provided they are related to the changes in the marketing, credit and land tenancy systems that have been mentioned earlier. . . .

Even in the west today it is realised that the village economy must be protected from all forms of exploitation which can result from the capitalist system and this is effectively controlled by the Government. . . . Almost all the democratic western countries have also established statutory boards to look into the marketing and credit needs of the farmers and fishermen. . . .

It will not be out of place here if I sound a word of caution. . . . This concerns the use of propaganda (a) to weaken and confuse the minds of people, . . . [and] (b) to find ways and means to absolve themselves [the propagandists] from blame if the programmes that they have vehemently proposed should fail to bring the desired results. . . .

In order to prolong the colonial policy of more than 100 years they [the propagandists] also cast aspersions and lies on the Malays which often weakened them morally and also confused their leaders. . . . They said the Malays with all their weaknesses and faults were to be blamed for their backwardness. They themselves will not admit their own faults.

Another point of view has been that Malay values must be changed. A Malay physician, Mahathir bin Mohamad, in a volume published in 1970, discusses Malay attitudes toward work, money, land, time, life, death, and his fellow man, which Mahathir asserts, reveal the Malays as a deeply traditional people.

Mahathir bin Mohamad: The Malay Dilemma [1970]*

. . . Finally, there is the fatalism which characterizes the Malay attitude to life. This fatalism is very much in evidence everywhere. . . . It makes acceptance of everything good or bad possible with unprotesting

* Source: Mahathir bin Mohamad, The Malay Dilemma (Singapore: Donald Moore for Asia Pacific Press, 1970), pp. 158–159, 172; reprinted by permission of the Asia Pacific Press Ltd.

tolerance and resignation. It does not encourage any great effort to change. It does not encourage resistance and certainly does not engender a rebellious spirit. . . . Failure is accepted with resignation. This whole philosophy is contained in the Malay axiom—"Rezeki sa-chupak tak akan jadi sa-gantang" or "One's lot of a quart will never become a gallon." In other words, fate decides all and to strive to better one's lot is useless unless fate wills such betterment.

The effect of this resignation to fate is to relegate the struggle for worldly goods to a low priority. Pride in working to one's utmost ability and capacity is not common. . . . It is no good asking the Malays to go into business if they are not properly motivated and do not understand the functions and value of the monetary system. So long as he is a fatalist, the rural Malay will not struggle hard enough . . . to succeed.

Still another continuing issue of public debate has been the national policy on education. Education was viewed principally as the means of eventually achieving national unity. The form of that unity was to be determined by what was taught in the classroom. Non-Malays, especially Chinese, often expressed their keen desire to keep their own curricula and medium of instruction.

From 1950 onward numerous official studies were made of national education. Fundamental decisions were based finally on the recommendations contained in a report by the 1956 education committee under the chairmanship of Dato Abdul Razak, minister of education, who in 1970 became prime minister. In 1960 another committee reviewed the implementation of the "Razak report."

Report of the Education Review Committee [1960]*

. . . The main objective of the 1956 Report . . . was to establish "a national system of education acceptable to the people of the Federation as a whole which will satisfy their needs and promote their cultural, social, economic and political development as a nation, having regard to the intention to make Malay the National Language of the country, whilst preserving and sustaining the growth of the language and culture of other communities living in the country." This is stated to be the educational policy of the Federation . . . in Section 3 of the Education Ordinance, 1957. . . .

* *Source:* Malaya, *Report of the Education Review Committee 1960* (Kuala Lumpur: Government Press, 1960), pp. 2–3.

Primary education in each of the four main languages of the country [Malay, English, Chinese, and Tamil] is provided in the language-medium of the parent's choice. . . . Faith is thus kept with the promise to preserve and sustain the four main languages and cultures of Malaya.

At the same time . . . common syllabuses and timetables have been promulgated for use in all schools . . . so that whatever language is used, all pupils learn the same things in the same way with the object of fostering a national Malayan outlook.

. . . It would, however, be incompatible with an educational policy designed to create national conciousness . . . to extend and to perpetuate a language and racial differential throughout the publicly-financed educational system.

. . . Therefore, we recommend that education at secondary level paid for from public funds shall be conducted mainly in the medium of one of the two official languages [Malay and English] with the intention of ultimately using the national language as the main medium of instruction. . . .[3]

The establishment of Malay as the *Bahasa Kebangsaan* or national language has also been a serious issue to most Malaysians. The constitutional arrangements in 1957 gave equality to the English language for ten years; this allowed time for non-Malays to acquire a knowledge of Malay and for the further development of the Malay language for modern applications. In 1967, the National Language Act was enacted by parliament. While it established Malay as the sole language of the country, it also allowed important exceptions.

The Use of the National Language [1967]*

. . . Nothing in this Act shall affect the right of the Federal Government or any State Government to use any translation of official documents or communications in the language of any other community of the Federation for such purposes as may be deemed necessary in the public interest.

The Yang di-Pertuan Agong may permit the continued use of the English language for such official purposes as may be deemed fit.

The President of Dewan Negara [Senate], the Speaker of the Dewan Ra'ayat [House of Representatives] or the Speaker of the Legislative As-

[3] Malay is now used as the main medium of instruction in the public schools.

* *Source:* Malaysia, *An Act to Provide for the Use of the National Language* (Kuala Lumpur: Dewan Ra'ayat [House of Representatives], 1967), pp. 1–2.

sembly of any State, or other person performing for the time being the functions of any such office, may permit any member of either House of Parliament or of the Legislative Assembly, as the case may be, to use the English language in addressing, or otherwise participating in the work of, either House of Parliament or the Legislative Assembly:

Provided that nothing herein shall restrict the use of the English language in either House of Parliament by a member for or from a Borneo State.

All proceedings . . . in the Federal Court, the High Court or any subordinate court shall be in the national language or in the English language or partly in the national language and partly in the English language. . . .

Political issues and political parties in Singapore contrasted sharply with those in Malaya. Separated from Malaya in 1946, Singapore moved somewhat more slowly toward popular political participation. Only in 1955 did constitutional reforms expand political opportunities for the people. The socialist People's Action Party (PAP) was the first party to win a majority of seats in the Singapore legislature. Excerpts from the party's 1959 campaign statement follow.

The PAP on the Tasks Ahead [1959]*

. . . Existing conditions are not favourable to the immediate attainment of a socialist society, and . . . a fully-developed socialist economy cannot be achieved as long as Singapore is separated from the Federation mainland. . . . We are only in a period of transition. . . . Nevertheless, we have the important task of preparing the ground, step by step, for the transformation of a feudalistic and conservative outlook to a progressive socialist outlook and so prepare the preliminary ground work for a future socialist society. . . .

. . . The general task of our party will be to infuse into our multiracial society the spirit of belonging to a nation. . . . This work must necessarily be a continuous process. It must be carried out at all levels of our population and through all means available. . . . It must be our aim that within the space of 10 years the basis of nation-building will have been thoroughly and firmly laid.

The other aspect of our general task is to re-organize our economy from a non-productive trading economy to a productive one. . . . Our

---

* Source: The Tasks Ahead: P.A.P.'s Five-Year Plan 1959–1964, Part I (Singapore: People's Action Party, 1959), pp. 7–13.

productive capacity must . . . depend on our ability to utilize all the potential skill of our people. . . .

. . . There will be a revision of the content of the instruction in the schools. More importance will be placed on the subjects that have a relation to the realities of our economic and social conditions. . . . Languages, mathematics and scientific subjects will be emphasized. . . .

. . . Women . . . have an important part to play in our national construction. . . . In order to emancipate them from the bonds of feudalism and conservatism a monogamous marriage law will be passed. Such a law, however, will not apply in those cases where there is a conflict with their religious beliefs.

. . . We shall carry out an extensive education campaign on family limitation and the rights of women. . . . We shall foster the principle . . . that there shall be equality of women with men in all spheres and we shall encourage them to come forward and play a leading role in politics, administration, business and industry, education and other spheres. . . .

. . . We of the People's Action Party are convinced that a Malayan nation must ultimately emerge because that is a historical necessity. . . . The Malays, Chinese and Indians are here to stay. . . . It is inconceivable that they can continue to live here indefinitely as strangers.

. . . Our concern is how this Malayan nation is to be brought into being—whether it is to be brought about painlessly and smoothly or whether it must be attended by . . . bitter communal conflicts. . . . The fatalist may take the attitude that many nations in the past were born after a long struggle between peoples of many races and cultures. . . .

. . . We . . . are not fatalists. As socialists we believe that the people, and not the stars, order human affairs. We believe in the rational organisation of our economic, social and political system. . . .

The biggest obstacle in the way of a Malayan nation today is communalism and political parties based on appeals to racial pride and religious exclusiveness. . . . If these communal political parties are temporary organisations designated to draw their members into the larger Malayan community, then they may be serving a useful purpose.

We should, however, be on guard. . . . A communal political party is more easily tempted to revive waning political fortunes by appeals to racial and religious prejudices.

The "historical necessity" of which the PAP leaders spoke in 1959 became a reality in 1963 with the merger of Singapore with Malaysia. But it was short-lived (see Part II, above). In August 1965 an independent Singapore led by Prime Minister Lee Kuan Yew embarked upon a campaign of economic and political "survival" with a remarkable degree of success.

In the meantime, Malaysia reached what many of her leaders both within the Alliance and without regarded as an important turning point in the country's history. The federal elections of May 1969 were immediately followed by racial rioting in West Malaysia, which resulted in the deaths of many persons and the destruction of much property.[4] The government's views of the May 13 violence were summed up in the preface to a special report.

The May 13 Tragedy: A Report [October 9, 1969]*

May 13, 1969, will go down in our history as a day of national tragedy. On that day the very foundation of this Nation was shaken by racial disturbances whose violence far surpassed any we had known. It was only the firm and prompt action of the Government, together with the loyal support of the Armed Forces and the Police, which quickly brought the situation under control. . . .

. . . We were jolted into a sharp realisation that the racial problem in this country is a serious one and measures taken in the past to cope with it have not proved adequate.

Friction had always existed at the edges of the various communities, but we continued to live in the hope that the heat generated would not reach an explosive level. This faith in the good sense of every Malaysian, and our belief in the virtues of unfettered democratic processes, characterized the conduct of our affairs since Merdeka. We assumed that those who chose to participate in public life would understand the delicate realities of our society and consequently recognise the need for a certain degree of restraint and maturity. . . . It does not take much to realise that there are forces existing in our midst—the Communist agents, the secret societies, the communal extremists—who are out to disrupt our way of life for their own ends.

. . . During the campaign (General Elections of May 1969) a number of opposition candidates attacked the Constitution in racialist terms.

---

[4] Official data on the May 13 disturbances reported 196 persons died and 439 were injured. Of those who died, 25 were Malays and 143 were Chinese. More than 9,000 persons were arrested between May 13 and July 31. The majority were Chinese. (Malaysia, National Operations Council, *The May 13 Tragedy, A Report* [Kuala Lumpur, October 9, 1969], pp. 88–91.)

* *Source:* pp. iii–v from *The May 13 Tragedy* in n. 4 above.

They . . . misrepresented certain provisions. . . . They agitated for the removal of Article 153 which provides safeguards for the special position of the Malays. This caused grave misapprehensions among the Malays. Malay extremist candidates, on the other hand, campaigned on the most far-out and impracticable proposals—of having a purely Malay Government—ignoring the multi-racial realities of our society and thereby caused much worry among the non-Malays. The General Elections went off smoothly and the Government was returned with a comfortable majority. The Opposition parties were returned with a few additional seats. This unexpected success on their part unfortunately made some of them lose all sense of proportion, and their members and supporters went on a rampage of insults and obscenities. . . .

The lesson of the recent disturbance is clear. . . . We must make sure that subjects which are likely to engender racial tensions are not exploited by irresponsible opportunists. We can only guarantee this by placing such subjects beyond the reach of race demagogues, the Communists and other subversives. We need, therefore, to construct a political framework which is realistic and takes full account of the social and economic conditions of our people and which is based on an unshakable and sound foundation. . . .

Another view of the events of May 13 was offered by Mahathir bin Mohamad, a member of parliament and a UMNO leader until he was expelled in 1969 for his criticism of the party and its leadership.

Mahathir bin Mohamad: The Causes of the May 13 Violence [1970]*

. . . There never was true racial harmony. There was a lack of interracial strife. There was tolerance. There was accommodation. . . . [UMNO had become corrupted by power and was held together by] a system of patronage and disguised coercion based on Government rather than party authority. . . . By the time the 1969 elections approached, all sections of the people were disenchanted. . . . The Malays were . . . because in their eyes the Government continually favored the Chinese and failed to correct the real imbalance in the wealth and progress of the races. In airing their grievances they antagonized the non-Malays, especially the Chinese. The Chinese demands increased as Government concessions whetted their appetite. At first, the Chinese moderates thought that the demands of the chauvinists were useful to keep the Malays in check, but soon the moderates became the victims of their own strategy.

* *Source:* Mahathir bin Mohamad, *op. cit.,* pp. 4-5, 9, 13.

To retain their influence they had to fall in line with the chauvinists. Needless to say, this antagonized and revived the distrust of more and more Malays. The cleavage between Malays and non-Malays was thus being continually and inexorably deepened.

Over and above these racial reactions was the increasingly diminishing faith in the ability or desire of the Alliance government to rule and rule well. . . .

As a result of the events of May 13 a state of national emergency was declared and the parliament was suspended. A National Operations Council (NOC) was created to rule the country by decree. To assist it, in early 1970 a National Consultative Council (NCC) was established to provide a private forum where the Alliance and its critics could discuss major issues frankly. Between the two councils, under the leadership of Tun Abdul Razak, a beginning was made on the construction of a new political framework. A number of statutes dealing with sedition, election offenses, local government, and secret societies were altered. When parliament was recalled in February 1971 it legitimized the NOC's decrees by enacting them into law.

Of high importance to the Alliance government was a bill which amended the constitution by extending the ban on public discussion of "sensitive issues" to members of parliament. A sensitive issue was any matter, right, status, sovereignty, privilege, or prerogative protected by the constitution. In addition, the bill made "official purpose" explicit in regard to the use of the national language, and it empowered the *Yang di-Pertuan Agong* to ensure admittance to places of higher education for Malays and the indigenous people of East Malaysia. The amendment bill passed the 144-member Dewan Ra'ayat (House of Representatives) in 1971 by a vote of 125 to 17.

Prime Minister Tun Abdul Razak observed in regard to the amendment bill:

"A new generation has grown to adulthood since independence which is unmindful of the delicate and careful compromises agreed upon by the various races before we attained independence in 1957. . . .

"As we embark now on a new phase in our nation's history, these are the realities which must guide us when we formulate solutions to the many problems which face the nation."[5]

An important aspect of the new political framework devised by the

[5] Quoted in *Malaysian Digest* (Kuala Lumpur), 3 (March 15, 1971), 4:1.

NOC and the NCC was the formulation of a fundamental national ideology, the *Rukunegara,* as a guide for the Malaysian people. The *Rukunegara* called for a greater unity of the people, maintenance of a democratic way of life, creation of a just society in which the wealth of the nation is shared equitably, assurance of a liberal approach to Malaysia's rich and diverse cultural traditions, and construction of a progressive society, oriented to modern science and technology. Attainment of these ends was to be assured by popular acceptance of five guiding principles: Belief in God, loyalty to king and country, support of the constitution, support of the rule of law, and support of good behavior and morality.[6]

Muhammad Ghazalie bin Shafie, minister with special functions and head of the newly created Department of National Unity, described the Rukunegara as ". . . the totality of beliefs and rule, of commitments and principles. It is an integrative force which defines and at the same time confines the framework within which all citizens can have a dialogue . . . which transcends race, class and generation, to realize the Malaysia of our hopes and dreams."[7]

Another commentary on the Rukunegara has been provided by Syed Hussein Alatas, a founder of the *Gerakan Rakyat Malaysia* and chairman of the Department of Malay Studies at the University of Singapore.

Syed Hussein Alatas: The Rukunegara and the Return to Democracy in Malaysia [July 1971]*

. . . The Rukunegara is . . . divided into three parts, an introduction, a declaration, and a commentary. The last part is an explanation of the five objectives and five principles. Most of the objectives and principles are already in the Malaysian Constitution. The Rukunegara spells them out in terms easily understood by everyone. However, there are a number

---

[6] Malaysia, *Rukunegara* (Kuala Lumpur: Di-Chetak Di-jabatan Chetak Kerajaan, 1970), p. 11.

[7] Quoted in *Malaysian Digest,* 3 (March 31, 1971), 5:1.

Source: Syed Hussein Alatas, "The Rukunegara and the Return to Democracy in Malaysia," *Pacific Community,* 2 (July 1971), 4:800–808. Copyright 1971 by *Pacific Community,* the Pacific News Commonwealth, the Jiji Press, Ltd., Tokyo; reprinted by permission of the publishers of *Pacific Community.*

of items which have not been clearly stated in the Constitution. The following extracts will indicate what they are:

(1) "Fundamental liberties and freedom of political activity consistent with the laws of the country are guaranteed by our Constitution, but these rights shall not be abused, in the name of democracy, to promote racialism or to destroy democracy itself."

(Rukunegara, Commentary, A2, p. 16)

(2) "We are dedicated to building a progressive society which will keep in step with scientific and technological advancement while developing spiritual values. The world is now witnessing revolutionary changes in the sciences and in technology. The progressive society to which we are dedicated is one which keeps abreast of the advancements in the fields of science and technology and operates without losing sight of spiritual values."

(Rukunegara, Commentary, A5, p. 17)

(3) "Loyalty constitutes the soul of our nationalism. It is this inherent loyalty to King and Country which binds together our various races into one single, united Nation. Loyalty to other countries is inconsistent with undivided loyalty to this Nation."

(Rukunegara, Commentary, B2, p. 18)

(4) "It is the duty of a citizen to respect and appreciate the letter, the spirit and the historical background of the Constitution. This historical background led to such provisions as those regarding the position of His Majesty the Yang di-Pertuan Agong and Their Royal Highnesses the Rulers, the position of Islam as the official religion, the position of Malay as the national and official language, the special position of the Malays and other Natives, the legitimate interests of the other communities, and the conferment of citizenship. It is the sacred duty of a citizen to defend and uphold the Constitution."

(Rukunegara, Commentary, B3, p. 18

(5) "Individuals and groups shall conduct their affairs in such a manner as not to violate any of the accepted canons of behavior, which include the abhorrence and rejection of any conduct or behavior which is arrogant or offensive to the sensitivities of any group. No citizen should question the loyalty of another citizen on the ground that he belongs to a particular community. Good behavior also includes a high standard of morality in both our personal and public life."

(Rukunegara, Commentary, B5, p. 19)

The danger of communalism, the emphasis on science and technology,

the stress on undivided loyalty, the need for respecting the Constitution
and the appreciation of its historical background, and the insistence on a
high standard of morality in interpersonal and intergroup relations are
elements in the nation's political philosophy which have not been forcefully and clearly formulated in the Constitution. . . . The Rukunegara
fulfills this function. It can be considered as an appropriate introduction
to the Constitution. It reflects the predominant trend in the political and
philosophical thinking of the nation. In order to appraise this accurately,
we should know the background of its birth.

After the May 13 riot of 1969, it became clear to many people that
the pre-election (May 10, 1969) mode of conducting politics cannot be
allowed to continue. A number of politicians agitated along communal
lines, using offensive and inflammatory language, distorting issues beyond
recognition. Whatever the explanation offered for the May 13 riot, the
fact remains that such politicians caused the tragic incident. The existing
grievances and misunderstandings would not have caused an outbreak
unless communal sentiment of the destructive type had been whipped up
by unscrupulous politicians. This fact was recognized by the Rukunegara
in the following words: "Our people had lived together for generations
in peace and harmony sharing the resources with which Nature had
richly endowed our land. Together we had worked for independence and
together we had resisted several encroachments upon our national integrity and independence. Together we were building slowly but surely
the foundations of a society in which there is a place for everyone.

"However, our nation-building efforts were marred by the activities of
destructive elements. These elements are to be found in all communities.
From time to time latent racialist attitudes and racial prejudices were
exploited on various pretexts leading to racial incidents. The most serious
racial incident was the riot of May 13, 1969, in the Federal Capital."
(Rukunegara, Introduction, p. 13)

The need for an agreement on fundamentals was obvious. The Rukunegara was formulated by the National Consultative Council and was
supported by several political parties both inside and outside the government. . . .

It can be asserted safely that the Rukunegara was a national document
upheld by an overwhelming majority. . . .

The Rukunegara was the major achievement of the National Consultative Council. . . .

. . . Both the government and the opposition parties for the first time
established a dialogue beyond the traditional sphere of conflict. Issues
hitherto discussed in public only with embarrassment and misunderstanding between communities were thrashed out meaningfully. The impor-

tant thing is not the extent and volume of the issues discussed but the fact that such a practice had been introduced into the political system. While its role was advisory to the government and to the opposition, it helped to clarify thinking on many problems. When Parliament reconvened in February 1971, the role of the National Consultative Council ended.

The government set up a body, the National Unity Council (*Majlis Perpaduan Negara*) . . . to discuss such matters as the Prime Minister deems fit in relation to national unity and to discuss generally the problems of national unity and recommend measures and programs for fostering racial harmony. Basically it will deal with problems implementing overall national integration. The Rukunegara here will function as the groundwork for major government policies. . . . The National Unity Council will . . . function as a serious forum where problems and solutions could be discussed.

. . . Returning to the Rukunegara, the question now is: To what extent would the government and the people practise its tenets and live up to its spirit, and to what extent would the political parties succeed in influencing their members in that direction? The challenge is greatest for the party in power, the Alliance Party, composed of the UMNO, with 50 seats in the House of Representatives, the Malaysian Chinese Association (13 seats), and the Malayan Indian Congress (2 seats). There are indications that many members of the political parties have not understood the Rukunegara. The problem becomes serious when public utterances in political meetings are of the kind that awaken anxiety. . . .

. . . The particular precept of the Rukenegara, "No citizen should question the loyalty of another citizen on the ground that he belongs to a particular community," must be read in the light of the political background. In the past, certain influential political leaders exploited the issue to ensure support for the ruling party. The theme of loyalty was manipulated in such a way that it almost became identified with support for the Alliance Party. Associated with the accusation of disloyalty was the possibility of withdrawal of citizenship. Thus if individuals or a group were accused of disloyalty, the reaction might be fear of citizenship being withdrawn and out of this fear comes support for the ruling party. The Rukunegara thus is a step forward by preventing the subject of loyalty from being abused.

There are indications that the Rukunegara will exert increasing influence in the future. The government intends to introduce it in the schools. Recently, Television Malaysia began using a quotation from the Rukunegara: "Good behavior includes a high standard of morality in both our personal and public life." The problem remains that the government has not done enough to explain the Rukunegara to the public. It was the Gerakan Rakyat Malaysia, the opposition party controlling the State of Penang, one of the 13 states in the Federation of Malaysia, that first went to the people by organizing special public meetings to explain the Rukunegara. By explaining is not meant a mere reiteration of objectives; the objectives are given in terms of concrete empirical data. These objectives include the following:

(1) "We are dedicated to the creation of a united nation in which all regard themselves as Malaysians irrespective of race or creed. Malaysia is a multiracial society with all its complexities. This situation is further complicated by the fact that certain economic groups are identified with certain racial communities, which in turn are identified with particular geographical locations. This society is further divided horizontally by a distinct generation gap, which makes effective communication even more difficult. Nevertheless, from these diverse elements of our population, we are dedicated to the achievement of a united nation in which loyalty and dedication to the nation shall override all other loyalties."

                                        (Rukunegara, Commentary, A1, p. 16)

(2) "We are dedicated to the creation of a just society in which all members have an equal opportunity to enjoy the material well-being afforded by the Nation. A just society exists where there is fair and equitable distribution of the nation's wealth. To ensure this, it is necessary that the weak and the disadvantaged be assisted to enable them to compete on equal terms. The just society to which we aspire is free from the exploitation of one by another or of one group by another group."

                                        (Rukunegara, Commentary, A3, p. 17)

(3) "We are dedicated to ensuring the existence and growth of a liberal society in which its members are free to practise and profess their own religions, customs and cultures consistent with the requirements of national unity. The Malaysian nation is indeed unique in having rich and diverse cultural traditions and practices. We aspire to a society in which diversity can be an asset and a source of strength."

                                        (Rukunegara, Commentary, A4, p. 17)

The above statements of beliefs and objectives may sound simple. As a document the Rukunegara is meant to be simple and concise. However, much depends upon the detailed explanation of those statements. It is here that the responsibility of the ruling party is greater than that of the opposition, for the ruling party absolutely controls radio and television and to a great extent the press. If the Rukunegara is not comprehensively and forcefully explained to the public in an intelligent and rational manner, its influence will not be as great as hoped for. The Rukunegara resulted from a collective national effort transcending party barriers. It would be consistent with its aim and spirit to allow the opposition parties supporting the Rukunegara to appear on television and radio and contribute their bit to explain its meaning to the people. If this happens, it will create a major impact and generate an atmosphere of national solidarity.

Hardly ever since Independence in 1957 has a member of the opposition been allowed to express the view of his party on any issue on television or radio. Only brief appearances have been allowed in news reports covering elections. On the other hand, government political meetings have been televised at great length. In the UMNO general meeting of January 25, 1971, the speech of Prime Minister Tun Abdul Razak, in his capacity as party leader, was televised for about half an hour. This has been the practise since 1957. But the recent request of Gerakan Rakyat Malaysia to use television and radio to explain the constitutional amendments it intended to support in Parliament was turned down, as in the past. It seems to me that these are examples where the Alliance government has not practised the Rukunegara by failing to co-operate with the opposition where national interests demand it.

Lacking sufficient explanation of what the Rukunegara is, certain critics may regard it as a simple document without grasping the fact that its function is thereby enhanced rather than diminished. The Rukunegara is not an ideology in the sense that it is the fully-worked-out philosophy and program of a political party. Its function resembles that of the United Nations Charter. It is a miniature charter for a single country. Like the U.N. Charter is indicates an agreement on fundamentals upheld by different political systems, parties and ideologies. Though its formulation is simple, the Rukunegara is intended to function like the mariner's chart in a troubled sea. No one can deny the crucial importance of the chart, although from the intellectual point of view one can say that the chart is a simple document. Simplicity in some instances is a great virtue. In a country like Malaysia, an agreement on fundamentals is indeed a vital pre-condition for the continuation of a democracy. The Rukunegara is to perform this function.

The above conception of the Rukunegara in no way eliminates existing problems of interpretation and implementation. There may be differences of opinion regarding the role and function of monarchy between the Alliance Party and certain sections of the opposition, although both uphold constitutional monarchy. There is an increasing number of people who prefer to see the monarchy reformed to keep it in tune with the times. Feudal survivals should be replaced with democratic and modern elements. Certain forms of royal ceremonies may be subjected to reform. The image of the rulers may be better projected. The Dutch, the Danish and the Swedish monarchies may be considered as illustrative examples. The channel for such reform is the Conference of Rulers.

Comparable differences of policy exist between the Alliance Party and certain sections of the opposition regarding ways and means of improving the economic and educational levels of the people. It would be already a great achievement if these differences of policy could be recognized as sincerely motivated. When a country's political life is devoid of the element of sincerity among contending political groups, that country may be considered as morally and intellectually bankrupt. Before the 1969 election, there were some serious breakdowns in communication between the government and the opposition, as well as between the different communities. The most urgent task for Malaysia now is to achieve a reasonable degree of meaningful communication without suppressing policy differences within the context of the national consensus on fundamentals. Both the government and the opposition must perform their roles effectively. The moral and intellectual caliber of political leaders has to be high enough to command sufficient influence. Without this, the Rukunegara will be a dead document.

In the aftermath of the tragic events of May 1969, which called into question the government's effectiveness, the NOC and the NCC recognized the underlying economic problems and appeared determined to correct them. "The unity that we aspire to is not only the unity of the nation," Tun Abdul Razak told the National Press Club of Malaysia on August 20, 1970,[8] "but more so a unity within the nation: It means unity between economic and social groups. . . . We can only achieve that unity if there is a just society in which all members have an equal opportunity to enjoy the material well being of the country." Toward that end, a plan designed to ensure "the survival of our nation" was announced. In early 1971, Muhammad Ghazalie bin Shafie, minister with special functions, described the new policy as having two primary purposes.

[8] Quoted in the *Straits Times* (Singapore), August 21, 1970.

Muhammad Ghazalie bin Shafie: The New Economic Policy [March 5, 1971]*

. . . One is the eradication of poverty irrespective of race. This . . . is a departure from the previous belief that the eradication of rural native poverty alone would conduce towards national unity. The present policy clearly requires that a programme to conquer poverty, to raise income level and employment opportunities, must transcend racial lines. . . .

The second . . . is the restructuring of society through the modernization of rural life, a rapid and balanced growth of urban activities and, above all, the creation of a Malay commercial and industrial community in all categories and at all levels of operation so that over a period of time—in one generation—they can be a full partner in the economic life of a nation. . . .

If this nation is to survive we just cannot afford to fail in this task of restructuring society so that a truly national middle class, modern and creative, would come into being to serve as the stout foundation for the kind of democracy we all want and understand.

The restructuring of the economy must be so designed as to gradually reduce and eventually eliminate the identification of race with economic function. . . .

[Ghazalie bin Shafie also explained the Alliance government's views on the relationship between democracy and a strong middle class.]

. . . What we are concerned with today is the concept of democracy . . . that was transported from Westminster and mindlessly accepted by us in 1957. We did not have . . . the necessary social and economic infrastructure to absorb it. . . . The surgery performed in 1957 was not successful, the transplant did not "take" and unless we take immediate measures the rejection will be complete.

We must now address ourselves to the erection of that infrastructure. We must embark on a bold plan to create a truly Malaysian middle class. . . . We need time, not harrassment; cooperation, not obstacles; enduring devotion to a national objective, not opportunism to promote sectional interests. . . . We may have to practise "undemocracy" and "unfreedom" . . . in order to build an infrastructure here strong enough for us to enjoy the luxury of that democracy and that degree of totally unrestrained freedom of speech.

* *Source:* Muhammad Ghazalie bin Shafie, "Democracy: The Realities Malaysians Must Face," a speech before the Dewan Negara (Senate), Kuala Lumpur, March 5, 1971, pp. 9–14.

. . . Our society suffers not only in that it is economically without a strong foundation, but we are without cohesion because we are of many races, and we are without a stable and cohesive middle class so necessary in any liberal democratic system. We therefore need an industrialisation and urbanisation programme in order that we can build an authentic Malaysian middle class to sustain the kind of democracy we want. . . .

[We must rid our present society] . . . of the little voracious hucksters who are obstacles in the quest for a truly united nation. It is this group of criminally selfish people who would prefer to see the colonial status quo, the continuance of the identification of race with economic functions, supporting their political movements merely to secure for themselves larger slices of the Merdeka cake. It is this group of men, because of their special position, who would acquire a business and then become a mere sleeping partner. It is this group who would take away Colombo Plan scholarships from those who are genuinely willing to serve the nation, who would start a miasma of rumours if such rumours would earn for them a fast dollar, and who would stock their little loot in banks with numbered accounts in a foreign country. . . .

Since 1965, when it was ousted from Malaysia, Singapore has made rapid and impressive progress in its development as an independent state. Its people, more than three-quarters of whom are Chinese, have been called upon to identify themselves with a nation in which modernity, economic development, and racial harmony have been singled out as the essential values on which peaceful evolution of the state must rest. In the following document, Singapore's prime minister Lee Kuan Yew discusses the objectives of the People's Action Party (PAP) and its frankly multiracial policies, which have been designed "to protect and advance the interests of everyone in Singapore."

Lee Kuan Yew: Toward a More Integrated Society [August 1969]*

Every serious political party sets out to achieve certain ideological, economic or social objectives. To achieve these objectives, it must achieve power.

The organisation of a political party must muster support for its aims and objectives. And it must formulate a strategy to achieve majority support for its programmes and policies.

* *Source:* From Prime Minister Lee Kuan Yew's speech to the People's Action Party's executive committee and cadre members at a closed meeting in August 1969 (published in the *Straits Times* [Singapore], December 15, 1970).

This enables it to achieve power under a system of representative government in order to carry out its policies which more or less reflect the ideology or philosophy of the party.

We formed the P.A.P. in 1954. The objectives were enshrined in the constitution. The party was formed to enable us to achieve power to implement our beliefs as set out in the constitution. We did not set out immediately to achieve all the objectives.

By assembling together the highest common factors amongst anti-colonial and Socialist-minded activists, we set out to get majority support, to get into power.

They were first, anti-colonialism and freedom, second, merger with Malaya, third, within the context of a merged Malaya and Singapore, to achieve a more equal and a more just society, where education, employment, social and economic opportunities are more equitably distributed.

The Communists and the Socialists in the P.A.P. formed a united front to achieve independence and merger. We knew, and so did the Communists, that the moment freedom was achieved, the question which would divide us and them was, what kind of independence would it be. We knew that ultimately we had to be on different sides.

We achieved self-government in 1959. By 1961, the united front broke. The British contrived an issue which made the Communists come out openly against us, before freedom was achieved. It was tactically a crucial mistake for the Communists.

They believed that the British would allow them to achieve power, limited power in a self-governing Singapore. So they broke off and attacked us, since we refused to follow their line.

Through Dr. Lee Siew Chon, they tried to assume power with a majority of 26 assemblymen. Then there would be no merger.

They made an error. They could not get 26 assemblymen. We stayed in office and achieved merger. General elections took place in September 1963. We won.

From 1963 to 1965 marked the next phase. Riots took place in Singapore on the Prophet Mohamed's birthday. They were the result of a deliberate and sustained campaign. We put in a huge bundle of documents to prove this before the Commission of Inquiry. But it never sat.

A turning point within Malaysia was the formation of the Malaysian Solidarity Convention. We got many groups together, all those who were prepared to fight communalism, in this case Malay communalism.

We had quite a number of the educated and forward looking Malays with us. The convention was formed in late May 1965. Singapore was pushed out of Malaysia in early August 1965.

. . . We had sought independence from Great Britain and consciously formulated our policies to avoid seeking majority support on the basis of race, language and culture. We did not believe that the way forward was through solidarity within races. We sought merger in Malaysia—in a Malaysian Malaysia. We failed to get this accepted and were asked to leave.

What has happened in the years before and since August 1965 has left its imprint on us and our policies.

You cannot look at a Malay and know that this is a Singapore Malay and therefore different. But we must, for there will be a difference even though in appearance there is none.

Living in Singapore and going to schools with non-Malays, his attitudes may become more and more like all the others, as he strives to improve himself like all the others.

We can influence tomorrow if our educational and social policies are structured intelligently towards a more integrated society.

Yesterday is over and done with. You can rewrite the textbook and pretend that what took place did not happen. But it has happened. It has affected peoples' minds and attitudes.

Our problem is to prevent a reaction to what has happened, inter-racial riotings and murders. We are fools if we let ourselves react emotionally, even though it is a very natural thing to do. Our Malay MPs and party cadres should make a conscious effort to get Singapore Malays to demonstrate that they are Singaporeans.

We must together establish a separate identity, a separate outlook. This will make it easier to persuade the majority of non-Malays to support our programmes and policies designed to help Singapore Malays. These policies, which all cost money, must be clearly seen to be in aid of multi-racial ends.

If the money spent is seen to be in aid of communal ends, then no party governing on the basis of one man one vote, will be in a position to go out of its way to give more to a group which says it is going to be more loyal to its ethnic ties than to Singapore society.

What we do in the next few years will determine the shape of things for the next few decades. Unless we prepare ourselves for all the possible and probable shocks which are coming within a few years, we shall be caught up in a crisis, which will mar all that we have created in multi-racial living and make our past policies completely irrelevant.

There is a relentless logic in communal politics. The logic and dynamics of racial-religious politics have been demonstrated in so many other new countries.

As members of the central executive and as party cadres, we are more politically aware of the next stage of communal religious politicking. We must be faced with a ground hardened and polarised, in communal groups.

P.A.P. policies are to protect and advance the interests of everyone in Singapore, regardless of race or religion. It is unlikely that we can be defeated in the next elections due in 1973.

Nobody can produce 58 candidates more competent, and put up a programme or policy likely to give Singapore a better future.

Our problems are more external than internal.

If we, as a party, mobilise support on the basis of race and religion we shall easily fragment.

I am a Hakka, you are a Hokkien, he is a Hainanese. And there are Indians, Malays, and others. We can break up into little bits and pieces.

So we have pursued the other course. We must find common denominators, the maximum common ground.

We must resist the temptation of reacting in a communalist way to communalist policies being pursued around us.

Then we have a very good chance to solve the problems of the next decade.

We now have to implement the programmes we had planned for the middle of the 70's quicker, to meet all possible contingencies.

FIVE

Viet-Nam

by MARJORIE WEINER NORMAND
and ROY JUMPER

In no country have the two phenomena of war and politics been more closely intertwined than in Viet-Nam. War has been almost a way of life in contemporary Viet-Nam and a constant theme in the country's politics. Most adult Vietnamese have experienced three great wars, beginning with Japan's effort in World War II to exploit the fall of France in Europe by expanding the war in Asia to French Indochina: Viet-Nam was brought into Japan's sphere of influence in June 1940 and was formally occupied by the Japanese in March 1945. The end of this war in August 1945 signaled the beginning of still another conflict: The Vietnamese rebellion led by Ho Chi Minh against France's attempt to restore its control.

The war against France was ended in June 1954. Viet-Nam was split into two rival entities, the Communist-dominated Democratic Republic in the north and the traditionalist monarchy in the south. A year later, after brisk fighting in the Saigon area, the monarchy was overthrown by rivals, and the Republic of Viet-Nam in the south was proclaimed with Ngo Dinh Diem as its president. Coincident with the establishment of the Republic, the United States took over from France the responsibility for training and equipping the country's armed forces. It also initiated a program of aid for economic development.

The Democratic Republic of Viet-Nam (DRVN) established in the north was built upon a strong political base composed of a mobilized peasantry and modernizing intellectuals in the cities. In the south, however, the rival Republic of Viet-Nam (RVN) failed to implant itself in the rural areas of the south where Communist forces were able to foment a guerrilla war. The DRVN encouraged this revolt and eventually intervened openly on the side of the guerrilla forces. The United States, in turn, expanded greatly its position in South Viet-Nam in early 1962 by the establishment there of a "command outpost," sustained by antiguerrilla special forces and modern airpower. The American military command eventually assumed responsibility for direction of the war which it prosecuted until the early 1970's with a large expeditionary force.

Neither side was able to achieve a military victory, however, and an end to the stalemate between them was sought through diplomacy. An agreement on a ceasefire was reached on January 13, 1973, and on January 27 in Paris an accord was signed by which North Viet-Nam and the United States agreed that South Viet-Nam's destiny should be determined by a political contest among the Vietnamese.

The documents in this chapter are not entirely chronological; instead they are arranged under four headings. In the first part, the documents deal with the Vietnamese "war of resistance" against the French; the documents in the second part trace the socialist development of the DRVN in the north. Part III presents extracts descriptive of the development of the RVN in the south; and the extracts found in Part IV deal with the struggle for reunification of Viet-Nam.

I. The War of Resistance

After the fall of France in 1940, the Vichy-appointed high commissioner for Indochina, Jean Decoux, in an attempt to preserve French sovereignty, acceded to Japanese demands for military bases in Viet-Nam, Laos, and Cambodia. In return for granting the Japanese forces important military concessions and use of Indochina's raw materials, Decoux retained control over local administration and security. French authority and prestige were damaged, however, and in the countryside a newly organized political force, the *Viet Nam Doc Lap Dong Minh Hoi* (League for the Independence of Viet-Nam), popularly known as the Viet Minh, began in 1941 to wrest political control from the colonial power. Ho Chi Minh was secretary-general of this coalition of nationalist groups and individuals, but leadership was vested in a small inner circle of political figures drawn largely from the Indochinese Communist Party (ICP).

The Viet Minh sought to mobilize both the peasantry and the urban masses in Viet-Nam with an anti-French appeal based on nationalism. Political discipline and direction were provided by cadres of the Communist party, who began to infiltrate and indoctrinate the northern hinterland far from Japanese and French influence. After securing a territorial base in the mountain provinces lying on the Chinese border, they gradually extended their perimeter of activity into the populous Red River delta. From these early propaganda and guerrilla units, Vo Nguyen Giap organized a small, effective armed force in December 1944, a forerunner of the Viet-Nam People's Army (VPA). During this period the Viet Minh provided espionage and intelligence services for the Allies, rescued downed fliers, and courted Allied recognition.

The year 1945 proved crucial to the course of this revolutionary movement. On March 9, the Japanese put a forcible end to French (Vichy) rule throughout Indochina. The Viet Minh capitalized swiftly on the sudden elimination of the French colonial administration by setting up national liberation committees to govern locally in Viet-Nam and by working to achieve de facto political power on a country-wide basis before the French could return. Immediately following the Japanese surrender to the Allies on August 13, 1945, a hastily assembled national congress, convened by the Viet Minh Central Committee, issued an order for general insurrection against the Vietnamese monarchy and established a provisional government headed by Ho Chi Minh. Forces from Vo Nguyen Giap's People's Army quickly entered Hanoi and occupied key government buildings. Faced with this determined and militant organization claiming to lead a national revolution, Viet-Nam's emperor Bao Dai abdicated on August 26 in favor of the new regime and urged his countrymen to rally to the cause of independence. He also provided the provisional government with royal consecration as the legitimate government of all Viet-Nam by accepting a post in it as political adviser. On September 2, President Ho Chi Minh appeared before a rally in Ba Dinh Square in Hanoi to deliver the Declaration of Independence and to proclaim the birth of the Democratic Republic of Viet-Nam.

The course of the "August Revolution" had been decisively influenced by a decision made by the Allies at the Potsdam Conference during the summer of 1945: Chiang Kai-shek was invested with the task of occupying Viet-Nam north of the sixteenth parallel, while the British were assigned to the south. The Chinese forces, which began to arrive on September 9, 1945, and were to remain for some seven months, were not unsympathetic to Vietnamese nationalist aspirations and were, in fact, hostile to France's hopes of re-establishing its colonial regime. But the Chinese attempted to promote the fortunes of two other Vietnamese nationalist groups, the *Cach Menh Dong Minh Hoi* (Viet-Nam Revolutionary League) and the *Viet-Nam Quoc Dan Dang* (Viet-Nam Nationalist Party), and to dislodge the Viet Minh from its position of leadership. Nevertheless, the Viet Minh proved flexible enough to arrive at an accommodation with these two groups, at least until the withdrawal of the Chinese troops, and on the whole the cause of Vietnamese self-rule was strengthened during the Chinese occupation. By leaving the Chinese free to pursue their immediate aim of enriching themselves at the expense of the Vietnamese economy, the Viet Minh government earned the time to institutionalize its administrative apparatus.

The Viet Minh won its revolution in the north by the vigor of its response to unusually favorable circumstances. But in the south, the pattern of revolution differed sharply. Historically a frontier region built up by territorial expansion, southern Viet-Nam was ruled directly by the French during the colonial period. Its elite was therefore less traditionally educated, less bound to the accepted Vietnamese cultural and political centers of Hué and Hanoi, and more vulnerable to the conflicting claims of European ideologies. Clandestine nationalist political and religious groups proliferated, many basing their hopes and ideological doctrines on violent revolution as the only means of effecting political change under colonial rule. During the Japanese interregnum, some of them acquired a military arm and a territorial base, as well as a popular following. These militant forces, such as the Hoa Hao, Cao Dai, and Trotskyists, offered the Viet Minh stiff competition in the struggle for control of the nationalist movement, especially since most of them were more extreme in their opposition to France. They only reluctantly joined the Viet Minh in an uneasy united front, the Provisional Executive Committee of the South, whose administration of Saigon was weakened by internal dissension and regional rivalry.

But the Provisional Executive Committee failed to maintain military

and political control in Saigon not because of local problems but because of the hostility of the British who came to relieve the Japanese
in the south. Unlike the Chinese in northern Viet-Nam, the British,
under the command of General Douglas D. Gracey, were sympathetic
to French aims and facilitated French efforts to re-establish their position in their former colony. Under the guise of helping to maintain
order, General Gracey rearmed French forces previously interned by
the Japanese and permitted them to wrest control of the administration buildings in Saigon from the Vietnamese during the night of September 22–23, 1945. Violence in Saigon was increased by the use of
terror on both sides, and a short-lived truce was definitively broken
off when, in early October, enough French reinforcements had arrived to begin the "pacification" of the countryside. Subsequent Vietnamese history was shaped by this initial failure to establish the Viet
Minh revolution in southern Viet-Nam.

French military forces in Viet-Nam operated on the basis of a declaration by the French Provisional Government issued in Paris on March
24, 1945, defining in very general terms the future status of Indochina. It contained the outline of a constitutional formula to salvage
French interests and prestige and, at the same time, to provide for a
degree of self-government by establishing an Indochinese federation,
composed of Tonkin, Annam, Cochinchina, Cambodia, and Laos,
within the French Union and setting up provisional governments under the authority of a French governor-general. The declaration, however, did not take into account the new political realities in Viet-Nam,
and as a result, French officials failed to agree upon a strategy for
dealing with the Viet Minh government in the north. General Philippe
Leclerc, supreme commander of French troops in the Far East, feared
the consequence of imposing French reoccupation by force of arms
on a recalcitrant population. He proposed instead to acknowledge the
legitimacy of the Viet Minh regime by negotiation of a formal agreement to establish a political community between France and Viet-
Nam. Because the Viet Minh was fearful of dissipating its energies
struggling on a triple front—against the Chinese, the French, and
Vietnamese opposition groups—it decided to come to terms with
France. The French and the DRVN representatives reached a compromise agreement in Hanoi on March 6, 1946, recognizing the
DRVN as a "free state" with its own government and army but per-

mitting the return of French armed forces to relieve the Chinese occupation.

The March 6 accord was unsatisfactory to the militants of both Viet-Nam and France, and it left the pivotal issue of reunification unsolved, providing an excuse for future disagreement. The French high commissioner for Indochina, Admiral Georges Thierry d'Argenlieu, was an uncompromising foe of negotiation. He sought the restoration of French sovereignty, by military force if necessary, and undertook to vitiate the March 6 accord. On June 1, 1946, acting on his own initiative without authority from Paris, he sponsored a rival Republic of Cochinchina in the south, dominated by colonial functionaries and landowners. Since about 60 percent of the total French economic investment in Indochina was in Cochinchina, its political detachment from the DRVN would safeguard French economic interests.

D'Argenlieu was able to impose on Paris his views on policy-making, in part because of the confused, conflicting, and vacillating lines of authority between the French government and Saigon. His Republic of Cochinchina formed the nucleus for both the State of Viet-Nam, established in 1949, and its successor in 1955, the Republic of Viet-Nam. The establishment of the State of Viet-Nam removed any possibility of French accommodation with the DRVN, for whom the issue of reunification was and still is crucial. It was only a matter of time before a stream of minor clashes in the north led to a French confrontation with the Viet Minh. On November 22, 1946, fighting broke out in the port of Haiphong, and the following day French bombardment of the city resulted in six thousand Vietnamese deaths by the French count. On December 17, French authorities demanded that the Viet Minh militia lay down its arms as a sign of peaceful intentions. The Viet Minh responded two days later by unleashing a coordinated attack against French military positions all over Viet-Nam. This marked the beginning of the "war of resistance."

The following letter, widely circulated by the Viet Minh during 1945 and 1946, was an effective instrument for the mobilization of Vietnamese opinion in favor of the "August Revolution." It called on all Vietnamese to rise up and claim their independence under the banner of the Viet Minh Front. Ho Chi Minh is believed to have written it at the National Congress convened in Tuyen Quang Province on August 16, 1945, to approve an order for insurrection previously issued by the Viet Minh Front on August 13 and to establish a provisional government.

Appeal for General Insurrection [August 16, 1945]*

Dear compatriots,

Four years ago in one of my letters I called on you to unite together. Because unity is strength, only strength enables us to win back independence and freedom.

At present, the Japanese army is crushed. The National Salvation movement has spread to the whole country. The Revolutionary Front for the Independence of Viet Nam (Viet Minh) has millions of members from all social strata: intellectuals, peasants, workers, businessmen, soldiers, and from all nationalities in the country: Kinh, Tho, Nung, Muong, Man, etc. In the Front our compatriots march side by side without discrimination as to age, sex, religion or fortune.

Recently, the Viet Minh Front convened the Viet Nam People's Congress and appointed the National Liberation Committee to lead the entire people in the resolute struggle until national independence is won.

This is a great advance in the history of the struggle waged for nearly a century by our people for their liberation.

This is a fact that enraptures our compatriots and fills me with great joy.

However, we cannot consider this as good enough. Our struggle will be a long and hard one. Because the Japanese are defeated, we shall not be liberated overnight. We still have to make further efforts and carry on the struggle. Only a united struggle will bring us independence.

The Viet Minh Front is at present the basis of the struggle and solidarity of our people. Join the Viet Minh Front, support it, make it greater and stronger!

At present, the National Liberation Committee is so to speak in itself our provisional government. Unite around it and see to it that its policies and orders are carried out throughout the country!

In this way, our Fatherland will certainly win independence and our people will certainly win freedom soon.

Dear compatriots,

The decisive hour in the destiny of our people has struck. Let us stand up with all our strength to free ourselves!

*Source: Breaking Our Chains: Documents on the Vietnamese Revolution of August 1945 (Hanoi: Foreign Languages Publishing House, 1960), pp. 71–72.

Many oppressed peoples the world over are trying with each other in the march to win back their independence. We cannot allow ourselves to lag behind.

Forward! Forward! Under the banner of the Viet Minh Front, move forward courageously!

On September 2, 1945, the following Declaration of Independence was delivered by Ho Chi Minh, then president of the provisional government of the Democratic Republic of Viet-Nam, to the people of Hanoi. It followed the abdication of the emperor Bao Dai, who had specifically handed over "the rule of the country" to the democratic republican government, thus providing it with an important token of legitimacy and continuity. The text obviously borrows from the American Declaration of Independence and the French Declaration of the Rights of Man, and was issued at a time when the DRVN was assiduously courting Allied support.

Declaration of Independence of the Democratic Republic of Viet-Nam [September 2, 1945]*

"We hold truths that all men are created equal, that they are endowed by their Creator with certain unalienable Rights, among these are Life, Liberty and the pursuit of Happiness."

This immortal statement is extracted from the Declaration of Independence of the United States of America in 1776. Understood in the broader sense, this means: "All peoples on the earth are born equal; every person has the right to live to be happy and free."

The Declaration of Human and Civic Rights proclaimed by the French Revolution in 1791 likewise propounds: "Every man is born equal and enjoys free and equal rights."

These are undeniable truths.

Yet, during and throughout the last eighty years, the French imperialists, abusing the principles of "Freedom, equality and fraternity," have violated the integrity of our ancestral land and oppressed our countrymen. Their deeds run counter to the ideals of humanity and justice.

In the political field, they have denied us every freedom. They have enforced upon us inhuman laws. They have set up three different politi-

* *Source:* Information Service, Viet-Nam Delegation in France, *The Democratic Republic of Viet-Nam* (Paris: Imprimerie Centrale Commerciale, 1948), pp. 3-5.

cal regimes in Northern, Central and Southern Viet Nam [Tonkin, Annam, and Cochinchina] in an attempt to disrupt our national, historical and ethnical unity.

They have built more prisons than schools. They have callously ill-treated our fellow-compatriots. They have drowned our revolutions in blood.

They have sought to stifle public opinion and pursued a policy of obscurantism on the largest scale; they have forced upon us alcohol and opium in order to weaken our race.

In the economic field, they have shamelessly exploited our people, driven them into the worst misery and mercilessly plundered our country.

They have ruthlessly appropriated our rice fields, mines, forests and raw materials. They have arrogated to themselves the privilege of issuing banknotes, and monopolised all our external commerce. They have imposed hundreds of unjustifiable taxes, and reduced our countrymen, especially the peasants and petty tradesmen, to extreme poverty.

They have prevented the development of native capital enterprises; they have exploited our workers in the most barbarous manner.

In the autumn of 1940, when the Japanese fascists, in order to fight the Allies, invaded Indochina and set up new bases of war, the French imperialists surrendered on bended knees and handed over our country to the invaders.

Subsequently, under the joint French and Japanese yoke, our people were literally bled white. The consequences were dire in the extreme. From Quang Tri up to the North, two millions of our countrymen died from starvation during the first months of this year.

On March 9th, 1945, the Japanese disarmed the French troops. Again the French either fled or surrendered unconditionally. Thus, in no way have they proved capable of "protecting" us; on the contrary, within five years they have twice sold our country to the Japanese.

Before March 9th, many a time did the Viet Minh League invite the French to join in the fight against the Japanese. Instead of accepting this offer, the French, on the contrary, let loose a wild reign of terror with rigour worse than ever before against Viet Minh's partisans. They even slaughtered a great number of our "condamnés politiques" imprisoned at Yen Bay and Cao Bang.

Despite all that, our countrymen went on maintaining, vis-à-vis the French, a humane and even indulgent attitude. After the events of March 9th, the Viet Minh League helped many French to cross the borders, rescued others from Japanese prisons and, in general, protected the lives and properties of all the French in their territory.

In fact, since the autumn of 1940, our country ceased to be a French colony and became a Japanese possession.

After the Japanese surrender, our people, as a whole, rose up and proclaimed their sovereignty and founded the Democratic Republic of Viet Nam.

The truth is that we have wrung back our independence from Japanese hands and not from the French.

The French fled, the Japanese surrendered. Emperor Bao Dai abdicated, our people smashed the "yoke" which pressed hard upon us for nearly one hundred years, and finally made our Viet Nam an independent country. Our people at the same time overthrew the monarchical regime established tens of centuries ago, and founded the Republic.

For these reasons, we, the members of the Provisional Government representing the entire people of Viet Nam, declare that we shall from now on have no more connections with imperialist France; we consider null and void all the treaties France has signed concerning Viet Nam, and we hereby cancel all the privileges that the French arrogated to themselves on our territory.

The Vietnamese people, animated by the same common resolve, are determined to fight to the death against all attempts at aggression by the French imperialists.

We are convinced that the Allies who have recognised the principles of equality of peoples at the Conferences of Teheran and San Francisco cannot but recognise the Independence of Viet Nam.

A people which has so stubbornly opposed the French domination for more than 80 years, a people who, during these last years, so doggedly ranged itself and fought on the Allied side against Fascism, such a people has the right to be free, such a people must be independent.

For these reasons, we, the members of the Provisional Government of the Democratic Republic of Viet Nam, solemnly declare to the world:

"Viet Nam has the right to be free and independent and, in fact, has become free and independent. The people of Viet Nam decide to mobilise all their spiritual and material forces and to sacrifice their lives and property in order to safeguard their right of Liberty and Independence."

Hanoi, September 2nd, 1945

Signed: Ho Chi Minh, *President*

A compromise agreement reached in Hanoi between French and DRVN representatives in March 1946 accorded the DRVN official recognition as a "free state" within the French Union, but it left unsolved the difficult problem of reuniting Cochinchina with the DRVN. It also permitted unimpeded entry of French troops into northern

Viet-Nam. But the accord (excerpts of which appear below) proved too fragile to prevent the outbreak of hostilities in December 1946.

Preliminary Franco-Vietnamese Agreement [March 6, 1946]*

1. The French Government recognizes the Republic of Viet-Nam as a free state, with its own government, parliament, army and finances, belonging to the Indochinese Federation and to the French Union.

Concerning the unification of the three ky [Tonkin, Annam, and Cochinchina], the French Government undertakes to carry out the decisions of the population consulted by referendum.

2. The Government of Viet-Nam declares itself ready to receive the French army amicably when, in conformance with international agreements, it relieves the Chinese troops. . . .

3. The stipulations formulated above shall enter into force immediately. Directly after the exchange of signatures, each of the high contracting parties shall take all necessary measures to end hostilities immediately, to keep troops in their respective positions and to create the favorable climate necessary to the immediate opening of friendly and frank negotiations.

These negotiations shall deal particularly with the diplomatic relations of Viet-Nam with foreign states, the future status of Indochina, and French economic and cultural interests in Viet-Nam. . . .

Signed at Hanoi, March 6, 1946

SAINTENY, HO CHI MINH, and VU HUNG KHANH

The "war of resistance" can be divided roughly into two periods. Until 1950 it was essentially a local war, with French forces controlling most cities and towns, while Viet Minh guerrillas gradually established "liberated zones" in the countryside. In December 1949, the Chinese Communists arrived on the Tonkinese border; the DRVN now began to receive increased military and economic aid, and its struggle for survival was transformed into a push for victory. In January 1950 both the People's Republic of China and the Soviet Union recognized the DRVN, while in the following month the United States and the United Kingdom accorded recognition to France's protégé,

* *Source:* France, Direction de la Documentation, "Documents Relatifs aux Problèmes Indochinois I—Accords entre la France et le Viêt-Nam," *Notes Documentaires et Etudes* (Série France d'Outre-Mer. XIX), No. 548 (February 15, 1947), p. 4.

the Bao Dai regime (see Part III below). But the outbreak of the Korean war in June 1950 brought the United States into direct confrontation with Communist powers in the area and forced the Vietnamese into the cold-war arena. The war in Viet-Nam ended in 1954 after an epic battle at Dienbienphu: The Viet Minh emerged victorious; its hegemony in Viet-Nam, north of the seventeenth parallel, subsequently was sanctioned at an international conference in Geneva.

A paramount factor contributing to the Viet Minh's success in driving France from Viet-Nam was its ability to gain and retain leadership of the nationalist revolution, especially in the north. In order to rally to its cause Vietnamese of all political and religious persuasions and social classes, the Viet Minh made no mention, in its program, of the key Communist doctrines of social revolution and agrarian reform; instead it emphasized the ouster of French forces, national independence, and the formation of a broadly based government. After fighting broke out with France in 1946, the Viet Minh problem of rallying the Vietnamese people became simplified: Given the choice of being pro-French or pro-independence few genuine nationalists among them opted for France.

When they took to the hills in 1946, the Viet Minh claimed to possess two of the keys to a modern democratic state: A written constitution guaranteeing fundamental individual rights, and a popularly elected national assembly. In reality, the constitution was considered more of a propaganda façade than a working plan of government: It was adopted in 1946 when the Viet Minh was seeking Allied support against France, and therefore it contained many features of the American constitution. Moreover, effective legislative power was lodged, not with the National Assembly as a whole, but with its Permanent Committee and with the executive branch. Ho Chi Minh held both the positions of president and prime minister. He governed together with a cabinet (Council of Ministers) and the Permanent Committee of the National Assembly, most of whose members also held positions of commensurate importance in the Viet Minh Politburo, which held the effective decision-making power.

Until 1950, DRVN leadership placed primary emphasis on the coalition nature of its government. The Viet Minh remained the popular organization of the masses. Its influence extended throughout the countryside by a network of grass-roots committees and organizations, representing a multiplicity of interests and identifications, social, religious, economic, and political. These mass organizations permitted the peasantry to share local power by entering the political structure at the lowest levels, thereby ensuring them avenues of upward mobility. Thus the popular base of political support was expanded without forcing the Viet Minh Politburo to relinquish any control of the political hierarchy.

Although the Indochinese Communist party (ICP) was supposedly dissolved in 1945 in an effort to disguise the Communist affiliation of many Viet Minh leaders, subsequent Communist literature has claimed for the party an unbroken command of the Vietnamese revolutionary movement since 1931. A favorable international climate permitted the ICP to re-emerge in 1951 as the Workers' party (*Dang Lao Dong*) and again to assume overt direction of the DRVN. The structure of the Lao Dong party was highly centralized, extending down through zone and region, province and village, to the basic unit of organization, the cell group. The party's trained propaganda agents or cadres provided direct links between the government, the party, and the people. The influence of these cadres in any given region varied in direct proportion to the government's control over the political and administrative machinery of that particular village or region. Sent out in propaganda teams to villages not completely secure, the role of these cadres gradually evolved to that of developing front groups into which most popular efforts could be channeled; these groups then formed hierarchical organizations joined together in the Viet Minh Front, with the Lao Dong party at the apex. As a village was brought securely into the Viet Minh camp, party cadres were instrumental in recruiting for local guerrilla forces and regional militia. The DRVN's primary concern, especially in the early years before 1950, was military survival, and all its vast political machinery was geared to the overriding goal of building an army and mobilizing the country for its political and military support.

The Viet-Nam People's Army (VPA) was conceived and used as a political army, and it remained a reliable instrument of government as the DRVN's military organization developed and expanded. But the armed forces were not merely politically oriented; they were in fact organizationally linked to the Lao Dong party. Party cells existed at all levels of the VPA's hierarchy, and the VPA's own political commissars supervised the political education of the soldiers. Basic to this education was the importance attached to promoting cordial relations between the military and civilian populations, for the military tactics on which the guerrilla forces depended for survival and success required intelligence and reconnaissance services from the local people. These military tactics and strategies were adapted to the VPA's fundamental principle that it was fighting a "liberation war" in which to win the minds of the people was more important than to win their land. Under the guidance of Commander in Chief Vo Nguyen Giap, VPA commanders and political commissars paid the same painstaking attention to detail in planning propaganda campaigns—ranging from the training of hard-core, ideologically militant guerrillas to the broad indoctrination of the masses—that they did in planning military campaigns.

The ideological underpinnings for the kind of revolutionary, politicomilitary war waged by the Viet Minh were initially provided by the theories of Mao Tse-tung. In *On Protracted War,* Mao envisioned a long-term struggle of resistance against an "imperialist" army, characterized by three phases of warfare: The first phase, one of defensive action and struggle for survival; the second, a period of active guerrilla warfare; and finally the terminal stage, when military initiative passes to the revolutionary forces which launch a general counteroffensive. Giap so skillfully modified Chinese theory to fit the Vietnamese experience that he succeeded in driving the French to the conference table at Geneva in 1954.

The concept of a "people's war" and the development of the VPA into a politicomilitary organization capable of waging that kind of total war explain the tactics that were taken by the People's Army. The following excerpts from a series of articles written by General Vo Nguyen Giap and first published in Hanoi in 1961 deal with the importance of the relationship of the Lao Dong party and the VPA and their espousal of the strategy of the liberation war.

Vo Nguyen Giap: The Viet-Nam People's Army [1959]*

The Vietnamese people's war of liberation was a just war, aiming to win back the independence and unity of the country, to bring land to

* *Source:* Vo Nguyen Giap, "The Vietnamese People's War of Liberation Against the French Imperialists and the American Interventionists (1945–1954)" and "People's War, People's Army," *People's War, People's Army* (New York: Frederick A. Praeger, Inc., 1962), pp. 27–28, 54–55; reprinted by permission of Praeger Publishers, Inc.

our peasants and guarantee them the right to it, and to defend the achievements of the August Revolution. That is why it was first and foremost a *people's war*. To educate, mobilise, organise and arm the whole people in order that they might take part in the Resistance was a crucial question.

The enemy of the Vietnamese nation was aggressive imperialism, which had to be overthrown. But the latter having long since joined up with the feudal landlords, the anti-imperialist struggle could definitely not be separated from anti-feudal action. On the other hand, in a backward colonial country such as ours where the peasants make up the majority of the population, a people's war is essentially *a peasant's war under the leadership of the working class*. Owing to this fact, a general mobilisation of the whole people is neither more nor less than the mobilisation of the rural masses. The problem of land is of decisive importance. From an exhaustive analysis, the Vietnam people's war of liberation was essentially a people's national democratic revolution carried out under armed form and had a twofold fundamental task: the overthrowing of imperialism and the defeat of the feudal landlord class, the anti-imperialist struggle being the primary task.

. . . The Viet Nam People's Army has been created by the Party, which ceaselessly trains and educates it. It has always been and will always be under the *leadership of the Party* which, alone, has made it into a revolutionary army, a true people's army. Since its creation and in the course of its development, this leadership by the Party has been made concrete in the organizational plan. The army has always had its political commissars. In the units, the military and political chiefs assume their responsibilities under the leadership of the Party Committee at the corresponding echelon.

The People's Army is the instrument of the Party and of the revolutionary State for the accomplishment, in armed form, of the tasks of the revolution. Profound awareness of the aims of the Party, boundless loyalty to the cause of the nation and the working class, and a spirit of unreserved sacrifice are fundamental questions for the army, and questions of principle. Therefore, the political work in its ranks is of the first importance. *It is the soul of the army.* In instilling Marxist-Leninist ideology into the army, it aims at raising the army's political consciousness and ideological level, at strengthening the class position of its cadres and soldiers. During the liberation war, this work imbued the army with the policy of long-drawn-out resistance and the imperative necessity for the people and the army to rely on their own strength to overcome difficulties. It instilled into the army the profound significance of mass mobilisation in order to achieve rent reduction and agrarian reform, which had a decisive effect on the morale of the troops. In the new stage entered upon since the restoration of peace, political work centres on the line of socialist revolution in the North and of struggle for the reunification of the country.

But that is not all. Political work still bears upon the correct fulfillment in the army of the programmes of the Party and Government, and the setting up of good relations with the population and between officers and men. . . . The Viet Nam People's Army has always seen to establishing and maintaining *good relations with the people*. These are based upon the identity of their aims of struggle: in fact, the people and army are together in the fight against the enemy to save the Fatherland, and ensure the full success of the task of liberating the nation. The people are to the army what water is to fish, as the saying goes. . . . The Vietnamese fighter has always taken care to observe point 9 of its Oath of Honour:
"In contacts with the people, to follow these three recommendations:
—To respect the people
—To help the people
—To defend the people . . . in order to win their confidence and affection and achieve a perfect understanding between the people and the army."

In the following excerpt from his pamphlet *The Resistance Will Win*, published in Hanoi in 1947, Truong Chinh, leading theoretician of the Lao Dong party, expounded the doctrine, borrowed from Mao Tse-tung, of waging a long-term resistance against a stronger enemy. In making this a basic tenet of his military strategy, Vo Nguyen Giap recognized that it required "a whole system of education, a whole ideological struggle . . . a gigantic effort of organization in both military and economic fields." The ability to coordinate such an effort brought victory to the VPA.

Truong Chinh: The Resistance Will Win [1947]*

The guiding principle of our whole resistance strategy must be to wage a prolonged war.

To protract the war is the key to victory. Why must the war be protracted? Because if we compare our forces with those of the enemy, it is obvious that the enemy is still strong, and we are still weak. The enemy's country is an industrial one—ours is an agricultural country. The enemy

---

* *Source:* Truong Chinh, *The Resistance Will Win* (Hanoi: Foreign Languages Publishing House, 1966), pp. 36–37, 41.

has planes, tanks, warships; as for us, we have only rudimentary weapons. The enemy troops are well-trained, ours are not inured to war. If we throw the whole of our forces into a few battles to try and decide the outcome, we shall certainly be defeated and the enemy will win. On the other hand, if while fighting we maintain our forces, expand them, train our army and people, learn military tactics, strive to secure in sufficient quantities the things of which we are short, strengthen our weak points and at the same time wear down the enemy forces, we shall weary them and discourage them in such a way that, strong as they are, they will become weak and will meet defeat instead of victory. In short, if we prolong the war, thanks to our efforts, our forces will grow stronger, the enemy forces will be weakened, their already low morale will become still lower, their already poor finances will become still poorer. The more we fight, the more united our people at home will be, and the more the world democratic movement will support us from the outside. On the other hand, the more the enemy fights, the more the anti-war and democratic movement in France will check his hands; the revolutionary movement in the French colonies will oblige the enemy to divide his forces; and he will find himself in a position of isolation in the international arena. To achieve all these results, the war must be prolonged, and we must have time. Time works for us—time will be our best strategist, if we are determined to pursue the resistance war to the end.

Under the Tran dynasty, our people had to fight three times within thirty-one years to defeat the Mongol invaders. Under the later Le dynasty, it took them ten years' resistance to drive out the cruel Ming troops. The Chinese people carried out resistance for eight years to free themselves from Japanese occupation. The lesson of those long resistance wars is very clear. Those who want "to fight rapidly and win rapidly," to bring the whole of our forces to the battle-front so as to win a speedy victory and achieve a quick decision, do not profit from the invaluable experiences of history; nor do they understand anything of the strategy that our people should follow in this resistance war. They do not believe in the capacities of the masses. All that they would achieve would be the premature sacrifice of all our forces in a few adventurous battles; they would commit heroic but useless suicide. They pretend to under-estimate the enemy, yet they are actually afraid of him and of a long resistance war. . . .

Guerilla warfare must be the tactic of the people as a whole, not of the army alone.

To achieve good results in guerrilla and mobile warfare, we must mobilize the people to support our armed forces enthusiastically and to fight the enemy together with them. The people are the eyes and ears of the army, they feed and upkeep our soldiers. It is they who help the army in sabotage and in fighting. The people are the water and our army the fish. The people constitute an inexhaustible source of strength for the army. To increase their numbers, the troops must recruit new fighters from among the people. That is why the entire people must be armed, guerrilla movement must be initiated, the actions of the regular army, people's militia and guerrilla forces must be coordinated. We must act in such a way that wherever the enemy goes, he meets the resistance of the entire Vietnamese people who, arms in hand, fight against him, ready to die rather than return to slavery.

The following platform of the Lao Dong party was written to rally the Vietnamese to their cause of "resistance." After a recapitulation of Viet-Nam's relations with the world since World War II and of the growth of the national liberation movement, the platform identified the party's interests with the worldwide struggle of liberation movements. Chapter 3 of the platform, with a total of fifteen points (six are printed below), offered something for everyone connected with the resistance: Peasants, minorities, religious groups, and so forth. The platform deliberately rejected radical land reform in favor of minor adjustments to speed up production and help the war effort without alienating landlords.

Platform of the Lao Dong Party [March 19, 1951]*

Chapter 3: "Policy of the Viet-Nam Lao Dong Party"—The Viet-Nam Lao Dong Party is determined to complete the liberation of the Viet-Nam people, to curb the influence of feudalism, to advance toward the eradication of feudal and semifeudal vestiges, to develop people's democracy, to build an independent, unified, democratic, prosperous, and powerful Viet-Nam, and to lead it toward socialism. During and immediately after the liberation war, the Viet-Nam Lao Dong Party plans to carry out the following policy, aimed at bringing an early and complete victory to the resistance and at laying the basis for the building up of a prosperous and powerful state:

1. Fighting until complete victory—The entire Viet-Nam people are resolved to fight to the end in order to wipe out the French colonialists,

* *Source:* Democratic Republic of Viet-Nam, Radio *Voice of Viet-Nam*, March 19, 1951.

defeat the American interventionists, punish the traitors, and gain complete independence and unity for the Fatherland.

The liberation war of the Viet-Nam people is a people's war, a nationwide, total, and long-drawn-out war. It must pass through three stages: A defensive stage, an attrition stage, and a counteroffensive.

The central task of the Viet-Nam people from now until the final victory of their resistance is to complete preparations for a general counteroffensive and to launch a victorious general counteroffensive. In order to win complete victory, they must at the same time mobilize their manpower, their material and financial resources for the liberation war in accordance with the slogan, "All for the front, all for victory," and continually recoup their fighting power. They must bear in mind the following strategic principles of the resistance: All political, economic, and cultural works must aim to insure military victories and the military struggle must be coordinated with the political, economic, and cultural struggle. Frontal fighting against the enemy must be closely coordinated with guerrilla fighting and sabotage work in the enemy's rear. The liberation war of the Viet-Nam people must be closely coordinated with the armed resistance of the people of Laos and Cambodia and with world-wide struggle for peace and democracy.

2. Consolidating the people's rule—The political power in our country is a democratic power of the people, that is, of the workers, peasants, petty bourgeois, national bourgeois, patriotic and progressive personages and landlords. The form of this regime is the People's Democratic Republic. Its essence is the people's democratic dictatorship—democratic toward the people, dictatorial toward the imperialist aggressors and the reactionaries.

The people's rule relies on the National United Front on the basis of the alliance between the workers, peasants, and intellectual workers under the leadership of the working class.

The principle of organization of the people's rule is democratic centralism. . . . In order to consolidate our people's rule we must continually strengthen the relations between the state power and the popular masses; increase the participation of workers, peasants, and women in the Government organizations, particularly in the People's Councils; put into use a genuine people's democratic constitution; enhance the Party's leadership in Government organizations of all levels; and strengthen the relations between Viet-Nam, the Soviet Union, China, and other People's Democracies.

3. Consolidating the National United Front—The National United Front of Viet-Nam united all political parties, people's organizations, and patriots, irrespective of class, nationality, religion, and sex, in the com-

mon struggle for liberation and national construction. The National United Front is one of the pillars of the people's power. It has the task to mobilize, organize, educate, and lead the people, to implement the policy of the Government, and to inform the Government about the wishes and initiative of the people.

The Viet-Nam Lao Dong Party cooperates closely with all the political parties, people's organizations, and personages in the National United Front. . . .

4. Building up and developing the People's Army—The Viet-Nam Army is a People's army organized by the people, entertained and assisted by the people, and fighting for the people. It has a national, popular, and democratic character. Its discipline is a very strict and self-convinced discipline.

While fighting, it carries on widespread political work, strengthening the single-mindedness between the rank and file and between the Army and the people and strives to carry out propaganda work among the enemy with a view to shattering their morale.

In order to build up and develop the People's Army we must develop the local people's forces, militia, and guerrillas in the village and select the draftees captured by us or who crossed over to our side, so as continually to recoup our regular army. Also, we must capture the enemy's arms, munitions, and food supplies, so as partly to solve the equipment and supply problems.

5. Developing the economy—Our economic policy is now to increase production, so as to meet the demands of the liberation war and to raise the living standard of the people, benefiting both the Government and the private individuals, both labor and capital. Attention must be paid at present to the development of agriculture, industry, handicrafts . . . to lay a basis for State economy and for the development of a cooperative economy.

With regard to the national bourgeoisie our Party seeks to encourage, assist and guide it in its enterprise.

In the financial field we urge the raising of income through production increases, reduction of expenses and economy, and the implementation of democratic contributions. In regard to the enemy economy we urge planned sabotage and blockade in a way beneficial to the liberation war and the people, confiscation of the properties of the imperialist aggressors and traitors to be put at the disposal of the people's power.

6. Carrying out agrarian reform—Our agrarian policy mainly aims at present in carrying out the reduction of land rent and interest. . . .

Following the Geneva Conference in 1954, DRVN leaders had the unhappy task of justifying to their people, especially those south of the seventeenth parallel, their acceptance of a partition of Viet-Nam in return for sovereignty in the north and provisions for future countrywide elections.

Ho Chi Minh: Appeal on the Signing of the Geneva Agreements [July 22, 1954]*

At the Geneva Conference, thanks to the struggle of our Delegation and to the assistance of the two delegations of the USSR and the People's Republic of China, we have scored a great victory; the French Government has recognized the independence, sovereignty, unity and territorial integrity of our country and accepted to withdraw French armed forces from our land. . . .

To carry out the cease-fire, it is necessary to regroup the armed forces of the two sides into two separate zones, that is to readjust the military areas.

The readjustment of military areas is a temporary and transitional measure to realize the armistice, restore peace and progress toward national unification by means of general elections. [It] . . . does not mean by any way a partition of our country nor a division of powers. . . .

This is a necessary measure. But, North, Central and South Vietnam are integrant [sic] parts of our territory, our country will surely be unified and our compatriots throughout the country will certainly be emancipated.

Our compatriots in the South were the first to wage the patriotic war and are highly awakened. I am confident that they will place the interests of the whole country above the local interests. . . . The Lao Dong Party and the Government and myself are always following the efforts of our compatriots in the South and are confident that they will win success. . . .

We are determined to carry out faithfully the provisions of the agreement we have signed with the French Government, and at the same time we demand the French Government should implement faithfully the provisions of the agreement it has signed with us.

* Source: Statement by President Ho Chi Minh after the Geneva Conference (Hanoi: Foreign Languages Publishing House, 1955), pp. 3-7.

II. The Road to Socialism

For more than ten years, from the signing of the Geneva agreements in July 1954 to the first United States bombing of North Vietnamese territory on February 7, 1965, the DRVN focused its efforts on social, economic, and political restructuring within its territory. During this decade of peace, the government set about to achieve the socialist transformation of society and of the economy and the institutionalization of a "people's democracy."

The instrument entrusted by the government to achieve these changes was—and still is—the highly disciplined, all-powerful Lao Dong party, heir to the Indochinese Communist party. The Communist movement in Viet-Nam had provided major impetus to, and key leaders for, the nationalist revolution, and it is to the caliber and tenacity of this leadership that the DRVN today owes its existence. For twenty-four years, until his death on September 3, 1969, Ho Chi Minh was president of the DRVN; other veteran Communists such as Vo Nguyen Giap, Truong Chinh, Pham Van Dong, and Le Duc Tho have also held key posts in the government since its inception, providing it with continuity and stability. To this small group of senior leaders has been added a rising new generation—bureaucrats, economic planners, leaders of the guerrilla war in the south—who have already assumed membership in the ruling elite of the DRVN. They also hold commensurate positions in the decision-making body of the Lao Dong party, the Politburo, thus ensuring the smooth execution of party and government policy throughout the political and administrative hierarchy.

With the advent of peace, the war-devastated and overwhelmingly agrarian economy was the first target for change, since any major modifications of economic or social patterns necessarily involved the numerically predominant peasantry.

The cornerstone of the DRVN program for land reform was a law passed by the National Assembly in 1953 but not implemented until after the Geneva Conference. It provided for a redistribution of land-holdings based on a population classification decree dividing the rural population into five categories: Landlord, rich peasant, middle peasant, poor peasant, and landless laborer. Land was to pass from rich (landlord) to poor (landless), but such distinctions were often difficult to ascertain and led to arbitrary decisions. Agricultural reform cadres were sent out to villages to supervise mass trials supposedly directed against landlords and oppressive elements. Often inept and over-zealous, the cadres initiated public trials by "People's Land Reform Tribunals" and encouraged harsh sentences, including the death penalty, for rich and middle peasants as well as landlords.

The wave of terror which followed finally culminated in peasant uprisings in the fall of 1956. Troops had to be called out in several provinces to quell disturbances, and the government moved to halt the land reform program and make restitution to the injured. The party secretary-general, Truong Chinh, was made a scapegoat for the mishandled situation and resigned in favor of Ho Chi Minh, whose personal prestige gave impact to the extensive government-sponsored "mistakes correction" campaign. By the time it was stopped, however, the land reform program had already achieved its underlying goal: It had succeeded in destroying the rural landlord class as a political force and in changing the pattern of land ownership by greatly reducing and equalizing the size of landholdings.

Not until 1958 did the government resume a strong economic program. A Three-Year Plan (1958–1960) was initiated with priority given to increasing food production and spurring the formation of agricultural cooperatives. North Viet-Nam was always a rice-deficient area, and by streamlining and mechanizing farming techniques and utilizing collective efforts, the DRVN hoped to vastly improve agricultural output as well as to make the productive efforts ideologically more acceptable. While most peasants engaged in some sort of cooperative effort, they showed reluctance to join the larger or "higher" cooperatives. Furthermore, agricultural cadres found it difficult to cope with managerial technical problems encountered by even the average eighty-five-member cooperative, much less those of hamlet or village size. By 1960, however, the DRVN felt the move toward modernization and socialist transformation of agriculture had advanced enough to warrant a shift toward industrialization in the subsequent Five-Year Plan.

The Three-Year Plan had also focused on developing light industry and enlarging state control over the means of production. This achieved, the DRVN launched an ambitious Five-Year Plan (1961–1965) giving priority to the development of state-owned, heavy industry in order to make the leap from "socialist transformation" to "socialist construction." By the end of the Five-Year Plan, though, the party's economic goals were sharply modified by the difficulties brought on by American bombing raids. The primary goal became that of protecting industrial plants whenever possible by dispersing them throughout the countryside, and of coping with disruption of transportation and communication by encouraging local economic self-sufficiency. Although the DRVN, unlike South Viet-Nam, has the industrial resources to support a good measure of industrialization, it became clear that any massive industrialization program would have to be postponed until the end of the war.

By 1960 a major renovation of the constitution was required to keep pace with the economic and social changes instituted by the regime. After various drafts had been submitted for widespread public discussion and revision, a new constitution was adopted by the National Assembly on December 31, 1959. Election machinery was set in motion and on May 8, 1960, elections were held throughout the DRVN for delegates to a new National Assembly. The new Assembly met in July and formally sanctioned the reorganization of the government hierarchy at all levels, as well as electing officers for the executive and legislative branches.

These political changes culminated in an all-important Third National Congress of the Lao Dong party held in September 1960. The party congress was presented with a draft constitution providing for a highly centralized party infrastructure, hierarchical in form and rigid in discipline. The problems of "residual bourgeois influence" were discussed, the first Five-Year Plan was delineated, and the party assumed the task of leading the DRVN to socialism while shifting the "forefront" of the struggle for national reunification to the south. This paved the way—some three months later—for the formation "somewhere in South Viet-Nam" of the National Front for the Liberation of South Viet-Nam.

The following land reform law, adopted on December 4, 1953, was put into effect several years after its promulgation. It had the underlying purposes of eliminating "class enemies" who might serve as a focus for antigovernment sentiment in the countryside, and of modifying traditional class relationships based on land ownership. Its implementation was so mishandled that the program was finally stopped, but not until a peasant revolt in the fall of 1956 necessitated governmental intervention at all levels.

Agrarian Reform Law [December 4, 1953]*

Art. 1—The aim and significance of the Agrarian Reform are defined as follows:

—To abolish the appropriation of land by the French colonialists and imperialist aggressors of Viet Nam, to wipe out the feudal system of land ownership by the landlord class.

—To set up a system of peasant land ownership.

—To liberate the productive forces in the countryside in order to give a strong impetus to agricultural production and to pave the way for industrial and commercial development.

—To improve the peasants' living conditions, increase the people's strength and that of the Resistance.

—To give a powerful incentive to the Resistance, to complete the task of national liberation, consolidate people's democracy and develop national reconstruction.

Art. 2—Land and property belonging to the French colonialists or other imperialist aggressors will be confiscated in their entirety.

Art. 3—As for the properties of traitor or reactionary landlords or despots, their land, their draught animals, farm implements, surplus food stock and surplus housing will be confiscated in whole or in part according to the gravity of their crimes.

That part of the above-mentioned properties which are not confiscated will be subject to requisition without compensation.

Art. 4—As regards progressive personalities, landlords who took part in the Resistance and landlords not in the category of despots, the following procedure has been decided: Requisition-by-purchase of all the land presently in their possession, as well as the draught animals and the farm implements attached thereto. Their other properties will not be affected. The purchase price paid for the land will be equal to its average annual production value. The purchase price of the draught animals and farm implements will be based on local market values. The purchase price will be paid in special Treasury bonds redeemable within ten years, bearing an annual interest rate of 1.5 percent.

. . . Art. 7—All debts owed to the landlords by the working peasantry

* *Source:* Democratic Republic of Viet-Nam, *Agrarian Reform Law* (Hanoi: Foreign Languages Publishing House, 1955), pp. 1–58.

as well as by various strata of the poor population in the countryside are cancelled.

. . . Art. 9—Communal land and rice-fields, various categories of semi-communal, semi-private land and land belonging to various communities are confiscated without compensation.

Art. 10—Land belonging to religious communities, Catholic or Protestant missions, Buddhist congregations and members of religious institutions will be requisitioned with or without compensation according to specific cases. Land which has been validly acquired will benefit from requisition-by-purchase.

Art. 11—Protection will be given to industry and commerce with a view to encouraging production and developing the national economy. Industrial and commercial enterprises belonging to landlords will not be affected. . . . Other land and property belonging to landlord-industrialists or landlord-merchants or to industrialists or merchants who at the same time are landlords will be subject to requisition-by-purchase.

. . . Art. 13—The rich peasants' system of farming will be maintained. Their land, draught animals, farm implements and other properties will not be affected.

. . . Art. 21—. . . All the lands and properties confiscated as subject to expropriation without compensation or to requisition-by-purchase will be distributed to the peasants. . . .

. . . Art 26—The distribution will be carried out on the basis of the following principles: Priority to families which urgently need land; allotment to be made taking into consideration the present owner, the quality and situation of the land; distribution to be in proportion to the total number of members of each family and not to the able-bodied persons in each family. . . .

Art. 27—During the distribution, the interests of the middle peasants must be considered. In case land presently cultivated by a middle peasant is to be withdrawn, a portion of that land will be left with him; that portion added to his own property may slightly exceed the average amount of land alloted during the distribution but must not exceed the average land holding of other inhabitants of the commune.

. . . Art. 31—Beneficiaries become owners of the land that has been distributed to them without having to pay anything either to the State or to the former owner. . . .

Art. 32—During the whole period of carrying out Agrarian Reform, Committees for Agrarian Reform at the national, zonal and provincial levels will be set up.

Under the guidance of the Administrative institutions, Committees for Agrarian Reform will be entrusted with the task of implementing the

Agrarian Reform Law and directing the practical work of mass mobilization for its realization.

. . . Art. 34—The determining to which social class a person belongs must be in conformity with the government regulations drawn up for the purpose.

The social classification of each person will be decided by the Council of Peasant Delegates. The persons concerned have the right to attend the meeting and participate in the discussions. . . .

. . . Art. 36—In every locality where mass mobilization for the implementation of agrarian reform is being carried out, a Special People's Court will be set up with the following mission: 1—To try traitors, reactionaries, village despots and all of those who oppose or sabotage the agrarian reform. 2—To settle disputes concerning lands, rice-fields and other properties relating to the agrarian reform. 3—To settle all claims concerning decisions of social classification. . . .

Arbitrary arrest or killing of culprits without trial are strictly forbidden. . . .

The extract below was written by Ho Chi Minh, president of the DRVN, before the peasant uprisings of 1956, but it indicates his awareness that difficulties were mounting.

Ho Chi Minh: Letter to the Peasants and Cadres on the Successful Completion of Land Reform in the North [August 18, 1956]*

. . . Land reform is a class struggle against the feudalists; an earth-shaking, fierce, and hard revolution. Moreover, the enemy has frenziedly carried out sabotage work; a number of our cadres have not thoroughly grasped the land-reform policy or correctly followed the mass line; the leadership of the Party Central Committee and of the Government is sometimes lacking in concreteness, and control and encouragement are disregarded. All this has caused us to commit errors and meet with shortcomings in carrying out land reform: in realizing the unity of the countryside, in fighting the enemy, in readjusting the organization, in applying the policy of agricultural taxes, etc.

The Party Central Committee and the Government have rigorously reviewed these errors and shortcomings and drawn up plans resolutely to correct them with a view to uniting the cadres and the people, stabilizing the countryside, and promoting production.

* *Source:* Ho Chi Minh, *Selected Works* (4 vols., Hanoi: Foreign Languages Publishing House, 1962), Vol. 4, pp. 191–192.

We have to correct such shortcomings as: not relying fully on the poor and landless peasants, not uniting closely with the middle peasants, and not establishing a sincere alliance with the rich peasants.

The status of those who have been wrongly classified as landlords or as rich peasants should be reviewed.

Party membership, rights, and honor should be restituted to Party members, cadres, and others who have been wrongly convicted.

With regard to landlords, we should abide by the eight-point regulation when dealing with them, pay attention to those landlords who have taken part in the Resistance and supported the revolution or those whose children are enrolled in the army or working as cadres.

Wherever land area and production output have been erroneously estimated, a readjustment is required.

The correction of errors should be resolute and planned.

What can be corrected immediately should be dealt with without delay. What cannot be corrected forthwith should be done in combination with the checking-up operation.

It is necessary to further the achievements we have made, and at the same time resolutely to right the wrongs committed.

At present, *the people* have become masters of the countryside; they should therefore be closely united, enthusiastically engage in production, develop and consolidate the mutual aid teams, etc., in order to become wealthier day after day and to contribute to the enriching of our people and the strengthening of our country. . . .

While North Viet-Nam has not introduced agricultural communes on the scale found in the People's Republic of China, there has been a steady move toward elimination of the private sector in agriculture, as well as in industry, and the government has encouraged the formation of cooperatives at all levels. Despite the difficulties encountered in the push toward cooperation, the DRVN, in an ambitious Five-Year Plan presented at the Lao Dong party congress of 1960 by Nguyên Duy Trinh, vice-premier and minister of state for economic planning, decided to shift the emphasis to industrialization, to lay the "material and technical foundations of socialism."

Nguyên Duy Trinh: The First Five-Year Plan (1961–1965) for the Development of the National Economy [September 1960]*

Following the re-establishment of peace, we have, in a co-ordinated way, carried through land reform and economic restoration, paying attention to the maintenance of a firm grip on the leadership of agriculture and trade and striving to stabilize the economic and political situation in countryside and town. In the Three-Year Plan period, we have closely co-ordinated socialist transformation and socialist construction, laying stress on socialist transformation and have actively mobilized the masses to struggle for the solution of the problem "who will win," between socialism and capitalism. In the conditions of a backward agricultural economy ravaged by a protracted war, we have firmly grasped the key link of the economic task which consists in striving to restore and develop agriculture, at the same time speeding up the restoration and development of industry and handicrafts, giving due attention to the production of consumer goods and making a step forward in developing production of means of production. The decision of our Party regarding the restoration and development of agriculture and industry in the last few years was in complete accordance with the situation of the North. On the one hand, it has helped to meet the present needs of the national economy, on the other it has prepared conditions for socialist industrialization in the years to come. We have attended to the simultaneous development of economy and culture so that they stimulate each other in their development. We have attended to the socialist ideological education of Party members and masses, to the constant improvement of the people's life, to the promotion of the revolutionary enthusiasm and labour capacity of the masses, to the speeding up of socialist transformation and socialist construction, and to the emulation drive for technical improvement, higher labour productivity, reduction of production costs, increased production and the practice of economy. By constantly strengthening its leading role and using the people's democratic dictatorship to carry out the historic tasks of the proletarian dictatorship, our Party has led the masses in struggle to win great success and to ensure the daily more predominant position of socialism. . . .

The movement for agricultural co-operation is rapidly developing; many new co-operatives have been set up, the majority of which still have only a semi-socialist character, their consolidation not keeping pace with

* *Source: Third National Congress of the Viet Nam Workers' Party* (Hanoi: Foreign Languages Publishing House, 1960), Vol. 2, pp. 24–26, 28–29, 33–35.

their expansion. Besides weaknesses in economic management work, ideological education in the co-operatives is still inadequate; the socialist consciousness of a rather high proportion of co-operative members is still low, many do not really consider the affairs and interests of the co-operatives as their own, they easily become pessimistic and waver when production encounters difficulties. The policy of State purchasing of agricultural products and foods, an important link for the achievement of economic alliance between workers and peasants, and a means of strengthening their political alliance, is not being correctly implemented by many co-operatives and co-operative members, including a number of Party members. Among the cadres, there are still manifestations of lack of thorough understanding of the State policy concerning the management of food supplies. The peasants' worries have not been adequately dealt with; their tendency to keep their paddy for themselves is still a serious problem. Our peasants are very good people; they have firm confidence in the leadership of the Party; but they have not shed all the ideas and habits of the old system of doing business individually, which prevailed particularly among the upper middle peasants. We understand very well that this negative side is not essential and can be remedied. The movement for agricultural co-operation cannot avoid twists and turns, but through these trials it will be strengthened and become firmer. The point is that our leadership work should be satisfactorily carried out and first of all the ideological education of the peasants should be enhanced. . . .

In the First Five-Year Plan period, after socialist transformation has won a victory of a decisive character, we must switch over to socialist construction as the central task, achieve initial socialist industrialization, lay the preliminary material and technical foundations of socialism, and at the same time complete socialist transformation, transforming the economy of the North into a socialist economy.

As regard the fundamental tasks of the First Five-Year Plan, the Central Committee holds that it is necessary:

a) To strive to develop industry and agriculture, to take the first step in the priority development of heavy industry, at the same time striving to develop agriculture all-sidedly, to develop light industry and the food industry, to develop actively communications and transport, to expand State trade and co-operative trade, to make preparations to forge ahead and transform our country into an industrial, agricultural, socialist country.

b) To complete the socialist transformation of agriculture, handicrafts, small trade, private capitalist industry and commerce; to consolidate and expand the State economic sector; to strengthen the relations between the systems of ownership by the whole people and collective ownership; to extend socialist relations of production to the whole national economy.

c) To raise the cultural level and socialist consciousness of the people; to promote the training and fostering of cadres for economic construction and skilled workers; to raise the capacity of the cadres, workers and working people in economic management; to intensify scientific and technical work, the prospecting of our natural resources and basic research with a view to meeting the requirements of socialist economic and cultural development.

d) To improve further the material and cultural life of the working people so that our people have adequate food, clothing, better health, more housing and education; to develop welfare facilities; to bring into being a new life in countryside and town.

e) Hand in hand and in co-ordination with economic development, it is necessary to consolidate national defence, to strengthen public order and security, to protect our work of building socialism in the North.

These five tasks are closely related to each other; they embody the requirements of the well-ordered, all-sided, speedy and proportionate development of socialist economy and culture in the North in the First Five-Year Plan period, with a view to consolidating the North, making it an ever steadier base of the people throughout the country in their struggle for national reunification.

The following editorial appearing in *Hoc Tap*—the leading theoretical monthly in Hanoi, published by the Lao Dong party—discusses the difficulties encountered in moving a backward, agricultural country toward "social transformation" in the socioeconomic sphere. It also touches on coping with the wartime problems of manpower scarcity, disruption of transportation, and increased demands for foodstuffs and materiel for an expanded army.

Hoc Tap: *Strengthen Leadership over Labor* [July 1966]*

For more than 10 years, thanks to the correct leadership of our party and the efforts of our people, the labor situation in our country has undergone major changes which reflect the great vitality of the socialist regime. . . . The absolute majority of peasants and other small producers have entered the cooperativization path. Unemployment in the cities and partial unemployment in the rural areas have been basically eliminated. Social labor has been initially brought to branches and localities.

*Source: Editorial in *Hoc Tap* (Studies) (Hanoi), No. 7 (July 1966).

The number of laboring people in industry, communications and transportation, basic construction, the cultural branches and the public services in increasingly high, while the percentage of agricultural labor in all of social labor has decreased. The force of skilled labor is increasingly large. Millions of people in the delta have left to participate in the development of economy and culture in the mountainous areas. The political, ideological, technical and cultural standards of the laboring people have been improved steadily. The material life of the people has been insured. In particular, the living standards of the peasants have been improved markedly.

Nevertheless, since socialist industrialization has just been carried out, these changes are only the first step. The present situation is as follows: Manual labor still represents as much as 90 per cent of social labor, the number of persons engaged in agriculture is very large, and the social labor output is very low. This is due to North Vietnam's economic backwardness during the transition to socialism.

On the other hand, this situation also reflects our shortcomings, such as failing to attach importance to equipping laboring people with production tools of all kinds. . . .

One of the main tasks of the labor problem during the transition to socialism must involve eliminating the old system of labor division and achieving a new one. . . .

To take North Vietnam to socialism without passing through the capitalist development period—along with carrying out the socialist revolution concerning production relations, ideology, and culture—we must achieve step by step the new division of social labor and gradually shift agricultural labor to the industrial branch and other branches (while continually and strongly developing agricultural production). . . .

Technical backwardness is the cause of the poorly developed division of labor and the very low labor output in our country. But we must pay more than a little attention to the effect of labor division on technical revolution, because "in production which is based on manual labor, techniques can make progress only in the form of labor division."*

In view of the characteristics of North Vietnam, along with developing the central-level economic branches, we must develop local economy strongly, especially local industry, in order to step up the new division of labor. . . . The labor task in wartime must provide manpower for production and combat and contribute to increasing labor output in all

* V. I. Lenin, "The Development of Capitalism in Russia," *Collected Works* (Hanoi: Su That Publishing House, 1962), Vol. 3, p. 547. [Footnote in the original.]

branches. . . . Only by increasing labor output can we satisfy the present great needs of production and combat and, at the same time, strengthen our economic and national defense potential. . . .

As the war is creating very great manpower demands, we must extol the labor duty of each citizen to the fatherland and mobilize everybody to participate in production and combat and in serving the fighting. In particular, the strong force of youths and women must be developed to a higher degree. . . .

To enable the labor task to develop strongly its effect on the common revolutionary struggle of the nation, the important thing is to strengthen the leadership of the party and the state over the labor task. First of all, leading echelons of the party and the state must understand the important role, duties, and trends of the party's labor task and study thoroughly the economic and labor problems of their branches and localities in order to improve their management of and leadership over labor. . . .

As in all other revolutionary tasks, we must rely on the masses to carry out the labor tasks. Therefore, we must make everyone understand the duties and trends of the party's labor task so that they will satisfactorily implement policies on the mobilization, divisions, use and improvement of labor. . . .

In 1959 a new constitution was framed to govern only the overtly Communist regime in the north, a regime engaged in the struggle to "bring the north towards socialism" and achieve reunification with the south. Unique to the constitution is its description of the economic and social system, excerpts from which are included below. The constitution outlines a political and administrative structure as well, which provides for a unicameral legislature, the National Assembly, charged with enacting laws, choosing the president and vice-president, approving the presidential choice for prime minister, and formulating national economic policy. The National Assembly's Standing Committee is given the task of exercising legislative functions while the Assembly is not in session, thereby serving as the continuous, decision-making body of the legislature. Executive power is vested in a president with strong powers, while the prime minister and the Council of Ministers are accorded clearly subordinate roles. The constitution also provides for local administration organized in a uniform pyramidal structure.

Constitution of the Democratic Republic of Viet-Nam
[December 31, 1959]*

. . . In the new stage of the revolution, our National Assembly must amend the 1946 Constitution in order to adapt it to the new situation and tasks.

The new Constitution clearly records the great revolutionary gains in the recent past, and clearly indicates the goal of struggle of our people in the new stage.

Our State is a people's democratic State based on the alliance between the workers and peasants and led by the working class. The new Constitution defines the political, economic and social system of our country, the relations of equality and mutual assistance among the various nationalities in our country, and provides for the taking of the North towards socialism, the constant improvement of the material and cultural life of the people and the building of a stable and strong North Viet Nam as a basis for the struggle for the peaceful reunification of the country.

The new Constitution defines the responsibilities and powers of the State organs and the rights and duties of citizens, with a view to developing the great creative potentialities of our people in national construction and in the reunification and defence of the Fatherland. . . .

Under the clearsighted leadership of the Viet Nam Lao Dong Party, the Government of the Democratic Republic of Viet Nam and President Ho-Chi-Minh, our entire people, broadly united within the National United Front, will surely win glorious success in the building of socialism in North Viet Nam and the struggle for national reunification. . . .

Chapter II. Economic and Social System

. . . Art. 11. In the Democratic Republic of Viet Nam, during the present period of transition to socialism, the main forms of ownership of means of production are: state ownership, that is, ownership by the whole people; co-operative ownership, that is, collective ownership by the working masses; ownership by individual working people; and ownership by the national capitalists.

Art. 12. The State sector of the economy, which is a form of ownership by the whole people, plays the leading role in the national economy. The State ensures priority for its development.

All mineral resources and waters, and all forests, undeveloped land, and

* Source: Constitution of the Democratic Republic of Viet-Nam (Hanoi: Foreign Languages Publishing House, 1960).

other resources defined by law as belonging to the State, are the property of the whole people.

Art. 13. The co-operative sector of the economy is a form of collective ownership by the working masses.

The State especially encourages, guides and helps the development of the co-operative sector of the economy.

Art. 14. The State by law protects the right of peasants to own land and other means of production.

The State actively guides and helps the peasants to improve farming methods and increase production, and encourages them to organize producers, supply and marketing, and credit co-operatives, in accordance with the principle of voluntariness.

Art. 15. The State by law protects the right of handicraftsmen and other individual working people to own means of production.

The States actively guides and helps handicraftsmen and other individual working people to improve their enterprises, and encourages them to organize producers' and supply and marketing co-operatives in accordance with the principle of voluntariness.

Art. 16. The State by law protects the right of national capitalists to own the means of production and other capital.

The State actively guides the national capitalists in carrying out activities beneficial to national welfare and the people's livelihood, contributing to the development of the national economy, in accordance with the economic plan of the State. The State encourages and guides the national capitalists in following the path of socialist transformation through the forms of joint State–private enterprise, and other forms of transformation.

Art. 17. The State strictly prohibits the use of private property to disrupt the economic life of society, or to undermine the economic plan of the State.

Art. 18. The State protects the right of citizens to possess lawfully-earned incomes, savings, houses, and other private means of life.

Art. 19. The State by law protects the right of citizens to inherit private property.

Art. 20. Only when such action is necessary in the public interest, does the State repurchase, requisition or nationalize with appropriate compensation means of production in city or countryside, within the limits and in the conditions defined by law.

Art. 21. Labour is the basis on which the people develop the national economy and raise their material and cultural standards.

Labour is a duty and a matter of honour for every citizen.

The State encourages the creativeness and the enthusiasm in labour of workers by hand and brain. . . .

The revised platform of the Lao Dong or Workers' party, presented at the party's Third National Congress in 1960, placed the party squarely in the mainstream of Communist party dogma and discipline. The Preamble described the DRVN as "a member of the powerful socialist camp." The Lao Dong party, organized on the principle of democratic centralism, postulated "collective leadership" as its highest goal. At the national level, power was vested in the national congresses, although it is, in fact, exercised by the Central Executive Committee and, more particularly, in the Politburo elected by it. Below are excerpts from the Preamble.

Revised Platform of the Lao Dong Party [September 15, 1960]*

Preamble. The Viet Nam Workers' Party is the party of the Vietnamese working class and the organized vanguard and highest organization of the working class. The party is composed of the most enlightened, progressive, exemplary and gallant persons among workers, agricultural laborers, revolutionary intellectuals, and other laboring people who are the most ready to make sacrifices and who voluntarily join the party ranks to struggle. The Party represents the interests of the working class and at the same time represents the interests of the laboring people and all the people. The objectives of the party are the completion of the national people's democratic revolution and the achievement of socialism and communism in Viet Nam. The Viet Nam Workers' Party makes Marxism-Leninism the ideological foundation and magnet of all its activities. The party pays special attention to the teaching of Marxist-Leninist principles inside the party and among the people on a wide and permanent basis, considering this teaching the first and main starting point in the party building task and one of the decisive conditions of the success of the revolution. The party applies the Marxist-Leninist principles to the realities of the Vietnamese revolution in a correct and creative manner and combats all manifestations of experimentalism and dogmatism. The party protects Marxist-Leninist principles and combats all revisionist arguments.

To achieve its objectives and platform, the Viet Nam Workers' Party over the past 30 years has done its utmost to develop the patriotic tradi-

* *Source: Nhan Dan* (Hanoi), September 15, 1960.

tion of the working class and the people in conjunction with the international proletarian spirit, to develop the tradition of gallant struggle, unity, and uniformity of the party, and to consolidate and build the party into a strong and stable Marxist-Leninist party. Thanks to this effort, in 1945 the party led the August revolution to success and founded the DRV[N]. Later it led the protracted and gallant resistance to final victory. The north has been completely liberated from the imperialist yoke, has permanently wiped out feudalism, and carried out the slogan "land to the tiller."

At present Viet Nam is still temporarily partitioned into two zones: the north is advancing toward socialism, while the south has become a new-style colony of the U.S. imperialists. . . .

To fulfil its responsibilities during the transition to socialism in the north, the party must lead the socialist transformation of agriculture, handicrafts, small trade, and capitalist industry and trade, develop state economic elements, achieve socialist industrialization through the rational priority development of heavy industry, and at the same time endeavor to develop agriculture and light industry, in order to build at high speed a balanced and modern socialist economy and closely associate industry with agriculture.

Along with the transformation and development of the economy, the party must step up the revolution in the ideological, cultural and technical fields, unceasingly improve the living conditions of the people, and continually raise the people's level in all fields. The party must reinforce the people's democratic state, consolidate national defense, maintain order, and continually stress the necessity to heighten revolutionary vigilance.

The party must step up the economic and cultural development of ethnic minorities and achieve complete and true equality among races. The party must increasingly consolidate and develop the united people's front on the basis of the worker-peasant alliance; strengthen unity among classes, races, religious and political parties, and patriotic and socialist-supporting personalities; and mobilize all the people's forces for the construction of socialism in the north and the struggle for national reunification.

To fulfil the responsibilities of the national people's democratic revolution in the south the party advocates a patient struggle against all policies of the U.S. imperialists and their lackeys aimed at partitioning our country forever and enslaving . . . our people, and against their aggressive policies, in order to liberate the south from imperialist and feudal rule, to achieve national independence. . . . To fulfil these responsibilities, the southern people must endeavor to build a worker-peasant-army-man bloc and set up a large front on the basis of the worker-peasant alliance. They must also unite all classes, races, religious, patriotic political parties, and all persons who oppose the U.S. imperialists and their lackeys. On this basis they must carry out the appropriate fighting measures to achieve national reunification and advance the revolution.

Though having different objectives and strategies, the revolutions in the two zones are closely related and interdependent. The revolution in the north exerts the most decisive influences on the development of the entire revolution in Viet Nam and the task of achieving national reunification. . . .

At the Third National Congress of the Lao Dong party, Le Duc Tho presented a detailed and frank discussion of party problems and policies, in conjunction with an exposition of the revised party platform. In the excerpts below he discussed errors in executing land reform, difficulties in educating cadres and members, and the importance of party-government relationships.

Le Duc Tho: Report on Amendment of the Party Platform [September 6, 1960]*

. . . From the organizational viewpoint, the admission of members coming from the peasantry, the petite bourgeoisie, and the intellectuals—who brought with them the bad influence of nonproletarian thoughts—complicated the ideological struggle aimed at unifying the party ranks and preserving the proletarian character of the party. But the history of party building proved that this admission was necessary and did not bring about the loss of the party's proletarian character. . . .

It was thanks to the above line on party building that the Vietnamese working class—though small—was able to build a large, strong, and mature political party and—through this party—exercise its leadership over the revolution; that the party—though its working class members were in the minority so that they had to ally with poor and contract peasants to form the majority and though at a certain moment the total number of party members was greater than that of the working class—continued to have all the qualities of a party of the working class; and that our party—which was the party of the working class and at the same time the national party—had wide relations with various people's strata and enjoyed considerable prestige among the people and that in consequence

* Source: Nhan Dan (Hanoi), September 7, 1960.

the leader of the party and the working class [Ho Chi Minh] was at the same time the national leader. . . .

After the August revolution and at the outset of the resistance, we achieved a fundamental strong point: we formulated, in time, the policy of transforming the party into a party having a strong mass character, of actively increasing party members, and of courageously training and promoting cadres. In a few years, party membership increased from less than 10,000 to hundreds of thousands and party organizations were set up almost everywhere. The number of cadres increased rapidly, too. Basing ourselves on longstanding cadres and using them as a core, we courageously trained young workers, peasants, and petite bourgeois students of the national salvation movement into cadres and promoted them. Without so doing, our party would have been unable to fulfill the new and heavy revolutionary responsibilities of that time. . . .

While courageously developing cadre ranks, we did not—to a certain extent—keep a firm hold on the class line in the policy toward cadres and did not clearly formulate qualifications for the selection of cadres. On the one hand, we did not fully realize the fundamental good points of cadres of worker and peasant origin and did not train and promote them. On the other hand, we lacked positive measures for educating and transforming cadres coming from the petite bourgeoisie and intellectuals.

However, it is partially due to the influence of the above mistakes that at present—in the phase of socialist revolution—there appear a number of weak points in our party: party members' ideological and dialectical level on the whole is low; the class standpoint of many cadres and party members is vague and their thinking methods are subjective and unilateral; the total number of party members coming from the working class and the peasantry is too small, and there are—beside the majority of good party members—a number of party members who are lazy, who are not eager to set an example, and whose party consciousness is low. . . .

To correct mistakes and errors efficiently, we must discover their origins. Our party was born in a backward agricultural country where small production was predominant. The majority of its members—coming from the petite bourgeoisie—were trained during the national democratic revolution. Thus their national and democratic spirits were high. But their class consciousness was not much strengthened. Therefore, besides proletarian thoughts, which are leading thoughts, petite bourgeoisie thoughts were rather deeply rooted in the party.

Since the reestablishment of peace, party activities in cities have developed. The struggle between socialism and capitalism has been desperate and complex. Bourgeois thoughts have constantly exerted a certain influence upon the party. Yet during the first year of this new revolutionary phase, we were slow in intensively educating cadres and party members about socialism and in strengthening their working class standpoint.

Moreover, remnants of feudal thoughts in a backward agricultural country still survive in many party members. Thus, errors committed inside the party in the fields of standpoint and ideology first have their deep origin in unfirm class standpoints. Up to now—especially during the past few years—our party has paid attention to strengthening the working class standpoint of cadres and party members and criticizing their nonproletarian standpoint and thoughts. This task has achieved good results. But this is still insufficient. At present, in many comrades and at various levels, socialist consciousness is low, a working class standpoint is not yet firm, there is no clear distinction between proletarian and nonproletarian viewpoints in a number of cases, and our manifestations of individualism, bureaucratism, commandism, and paternalism are rather general. . . .

It is necessary to connect school training with on-duty training, reorganize the network of party schools, and draw up plans enabling almost all middle- and high-ranking cadres within five or six years to attend party schools in order to study basic dialectical problems systematically. On the other hand, it is necessary to improve on-duty training to make it suitable and efficient. What is important is that each cadre and party member shows his eagerness to study, regards study as an inescapable duty and requirement, and overcomes all difficulties and takes advantage of all opportunities to study. . . .

To develop democracy and strengthen centralization, one of the most important things to do now is to strengthen further collective leadership. . . . Collective leadership insures the correctness of the party policies and line by concentrating the views and experiences of party members and the masses, the reduction of subjective and unilateral errors, the development of the sense of responsibility, the eagerness, and the creativeness of party members, and the strengthening of party unity.

In the past, though often hampered by many objective difficulties, our party did its best to have major policies discussed and decided by an appropriate body. Since the reestablishment of peace—especially after the 10th congress of the party Central Committee in 1956, where manifestations of despotism and commandism were severely criticized—democratic and collective activities in the party have made progress. But collective leadership in the party has been affected by many shortcomings. . . .

In compliance with the principle of democratic centralization, we must also correctly solve the relations between party members and party organizations so that party activities are both democratic and disciplined. Party members are masters in the party. . . .

We must eliminate despotism and commandism in a number of leading organs and cadres, who refuse to listen to and study the views and experiences of party members and low-ranking cadres, and who do not encourage party members and cadres to criticize and examine their tasks. . . .

The preamble of the party statute once more stresses the mass policy of the party. Past experiences show that it is very urgent to make every party member understand this problem—especially now that the party has assumed the leadership of the administration.

1—Our party is the vanguard troop of the working class. At the same time, it must be part and parcel of the working class and take root deeply among the working class and laboring people. The people draw their strength from the fact that they are led by a vanguard party. The party draws its invincible strength from its close relations with the masses.

Our party has traditionally entertained good relations with the masses. . . .

After the disclosure of errors committed during land reform, there were comrades who were against mass mobilization, maintaining that mass mobilization would lead to great and "leftist" mistakes. . . . In fact, errors committed during land reform were not caused by mass mobilization, but on the contrary by the fact that, in many cases, our cadres failed to fully mobilize the masses and fell into bureaucratism and commandism. . . .

Revolution is the work of the masses. The revolution led by our party is precisely a large and continual mass mobilization.

2—As of now, it is necessary to mobilize the masses more and more widely . . . in order to push forward socialist construction. . . . To attain this goal, it is necessary to resolutely remove thoughts and attitudes which are contrary to the mass policy and which are still prevalent in the party. . . .

Thus during the agricultural cooperativization movement and the movement for improving farming techniques, a number of cadres did not understand the worries of the persons who were slow in supporting the movements, did not patiently try to convince the masses, did not set a good example, and did not use the realities to educate the masses. Instead they often forced the masses to do what they liked and even criticized and manifested their scorn for the above persons. . . .

It is necessary to strengthen party control and supervision over government cadres and organs, maintain strict discipline, and administer appropriate treatment to bureaucratic elements who have caused serious harm to the party and government. . . .

One of our party's shortcomings is the fact that the dialectic and ideological standards of party members are still low, that party members have not fully developed criticism and self-criticism, and that there has been no possibility to recapitulate and clearly define a number of problems relating to the party's history because party members had to carry out underground activities for a long period of time and because our country is still divided. This shortcoming has, to a certain extent, affected the party's unity and uniformity. . . .

What deserves consideration in this section is the problem of inner-party struggle—which involves criticism and self-criticism—and the problem of relations between this struggle and the party's unity and uniformity.

However, a number of comrades are very afraid of the inner-party struggle: they believe that this struggle will impair unity. . . . In short, the tendency "to take it easy" and to "consider tranquillity as the most important thing" has become prevalent in many party committees and organizations.

The form to be taken by the ideological struggle in the party is criticism and self-criticism. We must clearly distinguish methods of struggle against the class enemy in society from the methods for carrying out inner-party struggle. Except for a very small number of counterrevolutionary and opportunist elements which should be pitilessly denounced and expelled from the party ranks, the criticism carried out against comrades who have—through lack of self-enlightenment—failed to realize the mistakes they have committed but who are amenable to reason and ready to correct mistakes must have a friendly and educational character, conform to the slogan: "To save the man by curing his disease," and aim at insuring unity among comrades. . . .

Self-criticism has not been developed to the same extent as criticism. In addition, criticism of high echelons by low echelons has not been developed to the same extent as criticism of low echelons by high echelons. This is due principally to the fact that many leading cadres at all levels have indulged in bureaucratism and paternalism, preferred praise to criticism, shown severity toward others and indulgence for themselves, and are deeply concerned about their individual interests, prestige, and positions. . . .

The leading role of the party is the decisive factor of all successes of the revolution; this is proved by the history of the 30-year revolutionary struggle of our people. The present difficult and complicated revolutionary responsibilities require a further strengthening of the leading role of the party.

Enemies of socialism know this. Thus, they have concentrated their attacks mainly on our party's leadership. . . .

Many comrades, whose political enlightenment was weak, were slow in discerning the enemy's plot, showed their weakness and flabbiness faced with the enemy's attacks and with erroneous thoughts in the party, and did not courageously protect the truth and the party. A few comrades were so worried and disturbed that they were unable to differentiate right from wrong and had misgivings about party leadership. . . .

The party is the highest organization of the working class and the main instrument of the proletarian dictatorship. . . . The clear realization and the correct settlement of the leading relations of the party over other organizations in the proletarian dictatorship network have a very important significance.

It is necessary to strengthen the unified centralized leadership of the party over all branches and activities of the government and the masses in order to associate closely and step up the activities of various branches in accordance with party lines. . . . And on the other hand, the government machinery and various mass organizations are essential parts of the proletarian dictatorship network and are chains linking the party with the masses in one field or another. Therefore, all tendencies to slight the role of these organizations, to think that the party and government organs are one, and to cause the party to carry out tasks of government organs and mass organizations are wrong.

As our party has understood that the problem of government is the basic problem of the revolution, our party has given full attention to consolidating this government and maintaining its leadership over this government so that the latter is continually a faithful instrument of the working class and laboring people. Our party has struggled against all plots aimed at dividing this leadership. The government machinery has fulfilled its glorious responsibilities because it has been continuously placed under the correct leadership of the party.

But at present, faced with the heavy responsibilities of the government during the new revolutionary phase and in order to consolidate the leadership of the party over the government, we must continue the struggle to eliminate a number of erroneous tendencies.

First, there are party committees which exert loose leadership over a number of government organs, do not keep a firm hold on the situation, and do not supervise and closely lead the application of Central Committee policies. . . .

Second, there are party committees which do the work of the government organs, intervene in the affairs of government organs, and are unable to utilize and develop the role of government organs. There are party committees, cadres, and party members who slight the government and who do not correctly carry out the instructions and decisions of higher government organs. . . .

We must eliminate both the above two erroneous tendencies in order to establish a correct leading relationship between the party and government organs. The party must exert a firm leadership over government organs so that the will of the working class and the people and party policies and lines are fully reflected in all activities of these organs. The party leads the government. This means that, on the one hand, party committees must carefully study the situation, study how party policies and lines are applied by government organs, then, through professional groups or a certain procedure, cause government organs to carry out party policies and lines correctly.

On the other hand, party committees must send their core cadres to work in government organs so that leading organs of the party, to the necessary extent, are enclosed inside leading organs of the government. Professional groups and responsible party members in government organs must obediently follow the leadership of party committees and at the same time, must collaborate with personalities and cadres outside the party and respect their functions and rights. . . .

After entering the new revolutionary phase, we have developed all aspects of our activities which have become more complex. Socialist construction requires the party to exert comprehensive leadership and, especially, to study hard in order to go deeply into economic and cultural leadership. . . .

A number of persons still entertain the view . . . that the party is able to lead only politics and not culture, science, and techniques because the party is not versed in these matters. There are cadres and party members who also regard culture, science, and techniques as a mystery, dare not study and lead them, and even regard them as beyond their competence to lead. . . .

Party basic organizations—that is, party organizations in basic units— play a very important role. Party basic organizations form the foundation of the party and link the party and its leading organs with the masses of workers, peasants, intellectuals, and other laboring people. Basic organizations are the places where collective leadership and supervision over, and education and training of, party members are carried out. They are the starting points for the elections of leading organs of the party from the bottom upward. . . .

In an important report to the Third National Congress in 1960, Le Duan, the party's powerful first secretary, assigned to the south the "direct role" of liberating South Viet-Nam from domination by the United States, thus officially shifting responsibility for the liberation movement to the south.

Le Duan: Political Report of the Central Committee of the Lao Dong Party [September 1960]*

. . . The two revolutionary tasks in the North and in the South belong to two different strategies: Each task is designed to meet the concrete requirements of each zone in the conditions of the division of our country into two zones. But these two tasks have an immediate common goal—the achievement of peaceful reunification of the Fatherland, the resolving of the contradiction common to the whole country, i.e., the contradiction between our people and the U.S. imperialists and their henchmen. To solve this common contradiction is the responsibility of our people throughout the country, but in conditions in which each zone has its own strategic tasks, what must be the correct positions and responsibilities of the revolution in each zone?

Looking at the matter from an overall viewpoint, the North has become a common base of the revolution throughout the country, since it has completed the task of national democratic revolution, gained independence and established the people's democratic power. The more vigorously the North advances to socialism and the more its strength is enhanced in every respect, the more this benefits the revolutionary movement for the liberation of the South, the development of the revolution throughout the country and the preservation and consolidation of peace in Indo-China and the world. . . .

In short, by actively taking the North towards socialism, we create conditions for the revolution in the South to develop vigorously and to win Victory, for the revolution throughout the country to advance, for the full deployment of the strength of the Vietnamese revolution itself combined with the strength of the whole socialist camp and that of the movement for peace and national independence, with a view to isolating and finally vanquishing the most cruel and dangerous enemy of our people, the U.S. imperialists, to achieving national reunification and building a peaceful, unified, independent, democratic, prosperous and strong Viet Nam. It is clear that the task of socialist revolution in the North is the most decisive task for the development of the whole revolution in our country, for our people's cause of national reunification.

. . . Defining the positions and responsibilities of the revolution in the North as being those of firmly grasping the duty of maintaining peace, building socialism, and promoting the revolution in the South means at the same time to define clearly the position and responsibilities of the

* *Source: Third National Congress of the Viet-Nam Workers' Party* (Hanoi: Foreign Languages Publishing House, 1960), Vol. I, pp. 40–45.

revolution in the South as being those of having the direct duty of over-throwing the rule of the U.S. imperialists and their henchmen and of liberating the South, thus completing the tasks of the national people's democratic revolution throughout the country. That is the only correct line for the achievement of peaceful national reunification. The U.S. imperialists and their henchmen are the sworn enemies of our people; they do not want our country to be reunified in peace. . . . Only by overthrowing their rule in the South can we have conditions for the peaceful reunification of our Fatherland. . . .

The South must play a direct role in executing the task of liberating the South from the domination of the U.S. imperialists and their hench-men, and has the capacity to fulfill this splendid task. . . . For the revo-lution in the South is carried out in conditions of the continuous weaken-ing and isolation of the U.S. imperialists and of the vigorous development of the forces of socialism, national independence, peace and democracy in the world. . . .

The Socialist revolution in the North and the national people's demo-cratic revolution in the South belong to two different strategies, but since they have an immediate common goal—the achievement of national re-unification—they are closely connected, and influence and encourage one another in their simultaneous progress. We must understand clearly that the task of socialist revolution in the North is the most decisive task for the development of the whole revolution in our country and for the cause of national reunification, and at the same time understand clearly the direct, decisive effect of the revolution in the South upon the libera-tion of the South and the achievement of peaceful national reunifica-tion. . . .

III. Government and Politics in the Republic of Viet-Nam

In 1947 the French government officially abandoned its half-hearted attempts to negotiate with the DRVN and espoused the policy of sup-porting a rival Vietnamese national regime conciliatory to France. The former emperor of Viet-Nam, Bao Dai, who was chosen to head a newly unified State of Viet-Nam, formally granted "independence" in the Elysée Agreements of March 1949. This grant of independence was hedged to such an extent—France retained direct control over foreign relations and the armed forces as well as important financial powers—that the State of Viet-Nam never became a rallying point

for Vietnamese nationalists. The war against the Viet Minh was run
by the French and remained, in the eyes of most Vietnamese, an issue
of colonial reconquest versus national resistance.

French control over the State of Viet-Nam's governmental activities was eliminated as a significant factor in the armistice of 1954.
French military forces had proved unable to destroy the Viet Minh
and were, in fact, being defeated on all fronts when France came to
terms with the DRVN at the Geneva Conference. France yielded to
American pressure to let the State of Viet-Nam manage its own affairs
and quickly withdraw its military forces, even before the 1956 dead-
line. For the first time, the United States could now deal directly
with the Vietnamese government rather than channeling aid through
France. On October 23, 1954, a letter from President Eisenhower to
Ngo Dinh Diem, the new, American-supported premier, promised "to
make a greater contribution to the welfare and stability of the government of Viet-Nam" by an enlarged "program of American aid given
directly to your government."

Such overt American backing enabled Diem to gain ascendancy
over the fragmented and independently operating forces and groups
sharing local power in South Viet-Nam: The army; the sectarian military groups; the Catholic Church and its refugee movement; important foreign interests, such as the Banque d'Indochine; and finally the
chief of state, the emperor Bao Dai. The sects were defeated by force
of arms, culminating in the "Battle for Saigon" in the spring of 1955;
the army was won over by a variety of coercive and persuasive methods; foreign economic power was curbed by agreement and intimidation; Catholic political leaders were co-opted into the government
and refugee resettlement programs were given priority; and the emperor was deposed as chief of state by a referendum held on October
23, 1955. On October 26, Ngo Dinh Diem proclaimed the Republic
of Viet-Nam (RVN) designating himself as its first president. Elections were then held for a constituent National Assembly which approved a constitution ratified by President Diem on October 26, 1956,
one year after the proclamation of the Republic.

The central, dominating political experience for South Viet-Nam
since Geneva has been the rule of Ngo Dinh Diem. It lasted some nine
years, shaped the political process in South Viet-Nam to this day, and
subsequent events all had roots in this turbulent period. The hopes of
most non-Communist Vietnamese, as well as their American allies,

were pinned of necessity on this nearly unknown mandarin, and his fall marked the end of any real civilian authority in South Viet-Nam.

The government of Ngo Dinh Diem began auspiciously, extending its authority over the cities and large towns in both the central and southern regions of Viet-Nam. Massive infusions of American aid permitted the resettlement of nearly a million refugees from North Viet-Nam, many of them in new and model villages reclaimed from formerly Viet Minh-dominated areas. Agricultural production, the important rubber industry, and other light industry and commerce were restored. However, the government failed to mount effective programs for economic development and administrative reform, and—most crucial in an agrarian and land-hungry country—never implemented, at the grass-roots level, its various ambitious and highly publicized projects for land reform.

Coupled with its inability to meet the agricultural aspirations of the peasantry and to create a viable urban economic system, was the government's increasing insensitivity to the social and political problems engendered by the years of warfare and economic instability. Indeed, through bureaucratic ineptness and increasingly severe repression of all forms of dissent, Ngo Dinh Diem and his powerful brother and "political councillor," Ngo Dinh Nhu, succeeded in alienating and driving into opposition practically every segment of the population. Young military officers mounted a coup d'état on November 11, 1960, and issued a manifesto declaring President Diem guilty of dictatorial rule and nepotism and "incapable of saving the country from Communism and protecting national unity." This coup failed, but in the ensuing years, the government had bloody clashes with students, intellectuals, and the important Buddhist movement. The regime was finally overturned by the army, and both Diem and Nhu killed, on November 1, 1963.

The government in Saigon has been dominated by military leaders since 1963. The first military triumvirate—Generals Duong Van Minh (chief of state), Tran Van Don, and Ton That Dinh—ruled through a Revolutionary Military Committee; when this proved cumbersome, military and political manipulations changed the complexion of the military junta. A military coup on January 30, 1964, ousted the Minh government and put General Nguyen Khanh in charge. His government survived for over a year, despite several political crises, but the Armed Forces Council finally asked him to resign on February 21,

1965. A civilian government headed by Premier Phan Huy Quat ruled briefly, but Quat handed the reins back to the military on June 21. The new South Vietnamese government was headed by Air Marshal Nguyen Cao Ky as premier and General Nguyen Van Thieu as president. A Constituent Assembly, elected on September 11, 1966, drafted a new constitution describing the purposes and formal structure of the regime. The constitution was promulgated on April 1 of the following year, and elections were set for the new government. The Constituent Assembly rejected seven presidential slates including one headed by the popular exiled General Duong Van Minh, and the ticket of Thieu and Ky, as president and vice-president respectively, won the election held on September 3, 1967; they received about 35 percent of the some 418 million votes cast. General Thieu as president took charge of the new government. Since 1963, this military-dominated government along with the National Front for the Liberation of South Viet-Nam (or the Provisional Revolutionary Government of the Republic of South Viet-Nam, formed in June 1969) have been the major competitors for power in South Viet-Nam.

In 1955, Ngo Dinh Diem, newly appointed president of the RVN, outlined the problems confronting his government following the 1954 partition of Viet-Nam and how he dealt with one particularly pressing one—armed rebellion against his efforts to take control of his country's armed forces and administrative bureaucracy. The national army's rout of the Binh Xuyen forces (a criminal syndicate, usually referred to as a "sect," which operated and policed gambling and prostitution in Saigon and Cholon) paved the way for President Diem's subsequent consolidation of power.

Ngo Dinh Diem: Message to Viet-Nam's Friends in the Free World Following the Victory over the Binh Xuyen [May 1955]*

If the policy pursued and the war waged in this country during the last ten years have retained your attention, the events of the last few days have, I think, done so still more. Various views have been held in the United States, France and other countries. I think it is my duty, as

* Source: Major Policy Speeches by President Ngo Dinh Diem (Saigon: Press Office, Presidency of the Republic of Viet-Nam, 1956), pp. 7–9.

head of the Government, but especially as a Vietnamese, to acquaint you with the real facts in which thousands of my compatriots have struggled in order to defend what you yourselves defend at home: Independence, Liberty, Democracy. . . .

When I had to assume office, ten months ago, the legal authority of my country still had no control over the command of its army. The Chief-of-Staff of that army was an officer of the French Army.

And to this army had been welded armed bands—called sects—some of which, from the day they had "rallied," had no other concern than that of setting themselves up as feudal powers.

Our security services had been placed in the hands of an armed band which had the monopoly of the most gigantic gambling and prostitution organizations of Asia.

. . . It was obviously not under such conditions that a Government responsible for the fate of millions of non-communist Vietnamese was going to face Communism.

Such was not either what hundreds of thousands of refugees, whom you have aided, have abandoned North Viet-Nam for.

Such was not the independence which the Vietnamese desired.

There can be no independence in shame. For over nine months, I have endeavoured to convince the opponents of my Government of the necessity for Viet-Nam to achieve the unity of its army, administration and policy.

The only nationalism which could and can be conceived for a Viet-Nam expected by the world not to bow to Communism, demands the end of all trace of the colonial regime, but also of feudalism, injustice and deception.

And such nationalism would be without soul if it was condemned never to achieve its flowering in democracy.

Several military Chiefs like General Trinh Minh The, General Le Van Ty, General Nguyen Thanh Phuong, and General Nguyen Giac Ngo are in accord with me. But such is not the case with the Binh-Xuyen leaders who utilized the funds of the security services to organize commandos inside our very capital. During the same time, with the scandalous resources at their disposal, they have acquired considerable properties: Rubber-plantations, transport and hotel businesses, big stores, opium traffic, smuggling, control of the fish and charcoal trade. . . . Nothing escaped their greed.

My Government was faced with this alternative, and any other Government would have had to solve the same problem:

Either to retreat from one concession to another, which represented what a common euphemism would call the solution of compromise, and which would have been, considering the demands of the Binh-Xuyen, that of abdication;

Or to defend the essential, that is the unity of the national institutions of Viet-Nam without which there would be no democracy, but simply disorder and so on, until the final disintegration.

What made the difficulties greater was that, under the terms of Conventions signed by the French High Command with the sects, it had been stipulated that these would be disbanded as soon as their existence was no longer necessary.

It had been further stipulated that the French High Command would have the control of the arms detained by the sects or lent to them.

Yet since 1954, and in spite of the cessation of hostilities in Indochina, the sects have not been disbanded.

I have been reproached for having failed in the mission entrusted to me, but which I also claim as mine, that of achieving national unity. . . .

Peace ceased to prevail in Saigon only from the moment the Binh-Xuyen had mortar-shelled the Government located in the heart of the town itself.

The Vietnamese army reacted in the manner you know.

Today peace has returned to Saigon. I am glad for my compatriots, but also for the foreign, especially the French, residents.

The Vietnamese population has expressed in various demonstrations what it disapproved of and what it wished for.

Its choice is seemingly undisputable. It has solemnly condemned all that was contrary to national independence and freedom.

It will determine its destiny by democratic means, principally by elections which must be prepared for at once.

Henceforth, the politicians of my country will know that one can no longer govern by allying oneself with reactionary forces, under one cover or another.

The Vietnamese people no longer accept to be deceived. . . .

The following excerpt first appeared in a series of articles in Saigon's weekly English-language newspaper, the *Times of Viet-Nam,* on October 6, 13, 20, 1956. The writer, Phuc Thien, sought to explain the president's political philosophy, which was based on an amalgam of French and Vietnamese theories later entitled "Personalism" and espoused by Diem's brother and chief advisor, Ngo Dinh Nhu.

Phuc Thien: Ngo Dinh Diem's Political Philosophy [October 1956]*

The great issue that splits the world today, as it has split it for centuries, is a philosophical one: materialism versus spiritualism. What is President Ngo Dinh Diem's stand on this issue? In his message to the Constituent Assembly, on April 17, 1956, speaking of the search for a solid foundation on which to base Viet Nam's political life, President Ngo Dinh Diem said: "Such a basis can only [be] a spiritualist one, a line that the human being follows in his innermost reality as in his community life, in his transcendent vocation as in his free pursuit of intellectual, moral and spiritual perfection."

President Ngo Dinh Diem's *Weltanschauung* is also essentially an ethical one. He judges men and things from a moral standpoint. For him a thing is either good or evil. He does not admit of compromise on this point. In an interview granted to A. T. Steele, he said: "Our approach is an ethical one. Communism is evil, so we reject it."†

Because President Ngo Dinh Diem believes Communism is evil he rejects neutralism with equal force. He can accept neutrality as a policy, but he cannot accept neutralism as doctrine, because in the face of communism, it is a doctrine of no-choice. In the same interview he said: "If an ideology is false, we don't put it on the same level as others. Hence we do not accept neutralism as a doctrine."

President Ngo Dinh Diem intensely dislikes and despises the hypocritical attitude of those who seek to further the communist ideology under the cover of some apparently noble cause. Thus he rejects cooperation with the communists. . . .

From general ideas we come to society. What kind of society does President Ngo Dinh Diem want? A society in which human dignity and progress are combined. In his message to the Assembly referred to above, President Ngo Dinh Diem said categorically: "We affirm our faith in the absolute value of the human being whose destiny is greater than time."

President Ngo Dinh Diem rejects both absolute individualism and absolute state power. Speaking of the efforts of the various democratic countries to reconcile the demands of collective discipline and social justice with those of individual liberty [in his address to the Constituent Assembly], President Ngo Dinh Diem points out that these efforts reveal

---

* *Source: Ngo Dinh Diem of Viet-Nam* (Saigon: Press Office, Presidency of the Republic of Viet-Nam, 1957), pp. 12, 14.

† *Herald Tribune* (New York), August 6, 1956. [Footnote in the original.]

a personalistic tendency. "Viet Nam welcomes gladly the teaching born of the experience of these democratic States." In addition to the negative liberties of a political nature, it is recognized that the human being has positive freedoms, a number of freedoms of an economic and social nature. At the same time the State, organized on a more democratic basis, is given wider, more stable and more effective power to bring positive assistance to the citizen against the massive dangers of materialist civilization, and to guarantee to him the right to live and exercise his liberties.

The National Revolutionary Movement represented an attempt by leaders in the Diem government to create a mass party. It was run in the south by Tran Chanh Thanh, minister of information, and in the center, where it was without real competition, by another Diem brother, Ngo Dinh Can. It often worked in conjunction with an elitist, quasi-secret, political organization, the Can Lao, organized by Diem's brother Ngo Dinh Nhu. The National Revolutionary Movement's program of action, published early in 1956, attempted to generate support for the government from all segments of the population.

Program of Action of the National Revolutionary Movement [January 28, 1956]*

The domestic policy proposed by the Movement for National Revolution seeks the achievement of a pacific and total national revolution in order to attain two fundamental objectives:

1. The establishment of a true democracy. Opposed to the Viet-Cong regime which utterly destroys liberty in order to exploit the people and to oblige them to serve the leaders of the Communist Party, the Republic of Viet Nam will proclaim and guarantee the democratic liberties which will benefit all social strata of the nation without distinction of sex, religion or profession.

In order to guarantee a real and concrete possession of these liberties, it is necessary on the one hand to accelerate social progress in order to assure to each the minimum economic conditions necessary for the enjoyment of their political rights, and on the other hand, to render incapable of harm traitors, agents of colonialists, communists and feudalists who are enemies of independence, liberty and democracy.

2. National reconstruction, development of economic prosperity in order to raise the standard of living of the population, particularly of the workers and the disinherited strata of the nation.

* Source: Times of Vietnam (Saigon), January 28, 1956, p. 5.

In order to attain these two fundamental objectives the Movement for National Revolution will fight for the realization of the following program of action which is composed of three parts: political, economic and financial, cultural and social. . . .

Democratic liberties. In contrast with the communist regime, the Republic of Viet Nam will establish and guarantee the democratic liberties which all the social strata of the nation, excepting traitors, communist agents and feudalists, will be able to enjoy.

Political groups will be able to conduct their activities freely, the only condition being the respect for the superior interest of the nation. The organizations in the service of the communists, colonialists and rebels will have the benefit of the protection of the law. . . .

Administrative reorganization. The administrative machine must be reorganized on all echelons:

Rotten elements, incapable personnel, saboteurs, communist agents and spies will be discharged and, depending upon the case, tried. Capable and honest people having the spirit of sacrifice and a sense of responsibility must be [advanced]. . . .

Agriculture. The peasant must be the owner of the land which he cultivates. The agrarian reform already begun must be carried out with determination and rapidity. Each family of peasants must possess a minimum plot of land, farm implements and draught animals indispensable to his work.

Rents must be lowered, usury banished. At the same time agricultural credit must be widely distributed. In contrast to the Viet-Cong, whose agrarian revolution is designed to exploit the work of the peasants by organizing "kolkhoses" and to expropriate systematically without indemnity all landed property, the Republic of Viet Nam must assure to the peasant the ownership of his land and the fruits of his harvest. The Republic of Viet Nam respecting the right of property should purchase the land of large land-owners paying them in shares of industrial enterprises created by the State.

Labor. Workers will enjoy the freedom of unionizing, social insurance and the participation in the administration and the sharing in the profits of the enterprises in which they work in conformity with the saying "Social progress is the emancipation of the workers."

Contrary to the Viet-Cong, the Republic of Viet Nam must insure to the workers the freedom of forming or joining labor unions and the freedom to strike in order to enable them to defend their interests. . . .

The army will be democratized. The integration of all armed groups in the framework of the National Army must be carried out; the Republic of Viet Nam tolerates no private army on its territory. . . .

Problem of reunification of the country. The reunification of the country cannot be realized except by free, honest elections with sufficient guarantees of security for the voters during and after the elections.

Free elections will be held soon in Free Viet Nam. Our people will have to continue the fight for free elections in the North. . . .

The family, foundation of the Vietnamese society, must be respected and protected. Adequate measures must be taken to permit mothers to fulfill their familial mission as well as their professional obligations. . . .

All slavish culture and all work contrary to good morals must be abolished. At the same time, a national and scientific culture must be established and popularized to reach all strata of the nation. Anti-communist cultural activities, or those exalting the national reconstruction, must be stimulated and encouraged.

At school as well as outside the school the youth must be given intellectual, moral and physical training and must become accustomed to the collective life. Civic instruction must be vulgarized in order to foster the spirit of independence, the democratic spirit and the spirit of determination in the fight against the enemies of the people and of the nation. . . .

The following letter by Nguyen Tran, chief of My Tho Province, to President Diem concerns the policy directives of Diem's brother and political advisor Ngo Dinh Nhu to chiefs of provinces in 1958. At that time, questions of security in the countryside were beginning to become important, and Nguyen Tran disagreed, as diplomatically as possible in this letter, with Nhu's emphasis on military and security measures rather than on winning over the people.

Nguyen Tran: Letter to Ngo Dinh Diem [1958]*

To the President of the Republic:

First of all may I tell you about the directives given by the Political Advisor on the morning of March 27, 1958. . . .

These directives may be summed up principally as follows:

1. *Vis-à-vis the population:* We often discuss the question of holding on to the masses, that is, to act in such a way that the masses like us and help us maintain security. In truth, the population wants only one thing: not to be bothered, to be left alone in order to attend to their needs. They cannot like us because they have to pay us taxes, etc. The main thing is to protect our basic ground forces; as for assuring the security

* *Source:* Unpublished document given personally to one of the authors in April 1962 by Nguyen Tran.

of the population, that seems to be very difficult because three armed communists would be sufficient to spread terror. It is a question of knowing how to protect our basic ground forces. As for the question of whether the population loves or hates us, that has no importance. We have a good cause and that is why we must fight.

2. *Vis-à-vis the communists:* The policy which up to now has consisted of destroying the communist organizations seems erroneous for it is not possible to arrest all the communists. They are like a seven-headed hydra; as soon as one head falls, another takes its place. Nor should we pose the question of re-educating communists; that would only be a waste of time without obtaining important results.

The new policy to apply consists of three points: ESPIONAGE, COUNTERESPIONAGE, and INDIRECT METHOD.

Espionage will permit us to know the communist organizations; counterespionage will consist of our agents infiltrating into communist ranks in order to know their plans for action, to impede their realization and to sow suspicion among them. The indirect method consists of indirectly destroying the communist organizations through arrests made under noncommunist pretexts. . . . It would be better not to arrest communists but to try to identify them and follow their movements. To arrest them would be to lose the channel of information. In case of war we would arrest them before their plans could be carried out.

As for my request to give our cadres some good weapons to improve their firepower and consequently raise their morale, the Political Advisor objected that this is unnecessary. Valuable weapons in the hands of our cadres would tempt the communists to kill them in order to get the arms, as happened to Nguyen-van-Hinh's light battalions armed with carbines.

When these three points have been achieved, there will be no need for national guards and communal police.

Mr. President of the Republic,

Without doubt the principles developed by the Political Advisor are praiseworthy. Carrying them out will doubtlessly help us achieve important results. I will do my best to enforce them. However, in putting them into practice there are other factors which I tried to bring to the attention of the Advisor. Since certain points then escaped me, I would like to bring them here to your attention as well as that of the Political Advisor.

My only intention is to make use of the experience which I have gained during my four years of fighting under your aegis in order to present to you some aspects of the problem, stating our possible recourses.

Vis-à-vis the population: As the Political Advisor has very well stated, the population is not inclined to like us. They are actually prejudiced against us. The people of today are not like they were ten years ago. Although most of them only wish to be left alone to do their work and not be bothered, quite a few have risen like dough as a result of the ferment of the revolution. Having forged their maturity in fire and blood, they are deeply aware of the problems of existence. The sight of those women and children who braved French tanks and cannons during the resistance, of National Army troops at the time of occupation of territory evacuated by the communists in accordance with the Geneva Agreement, who sometimes even now demonstrate to demand negotiations with the North or general elections to reunify the country, is enough to prove to us that the population is no longer passive. The motive which makes them so little afraid of death or authority can be sought in their awareness of a class struggle which the communists have taught them will result in their final victory. Made fanatic by Marxist propaganda, they have faith in their historic and redemptive mission. "We have nothing to lose and everything to gain," is the appeal of the Communist Party Manifesto of 1847, which has had the strength to shake mankind.

Many intellectuals chose Hanoi rather than Saigon during the time of enforcing the Geneva Accords, like others who, now living in the South, look toward the North, because they are under the spell of an extremely attractive theory, and it will be too late when they will be exposed to reality.

The example of a good half of mankind—including at least half of our people—fallen in the clutches of communism is a painful experience which should be thought about.

I am far from overestimating the appeal of communism since in Khanh-Hoa and Dinh-Tuong formerly, and now in Saigon and Cholon, I have always won over communism, not only in the sphere of action but also as concerns theory. For example: The numerous high-ranking communist cadres, members of district committees, provincial committees and even regional committees of South Vietnam who, convinced of the errors of Marxism, deserted their party to fight communism in our own ranks. It is because I have always fought communism that I understand its strength as well as our own. . . .

Our village councils of notables, our national guards, communal police and those soldiers who are from the lower classes and influenced by it, would surely refuse to fight for us if the people were against us.

These are the words I have heard from the mouth of the people: "Government officials keep far away from us; they will flee if danger comes just as many others have before them, and hand us over to the communists; for us to fight communism under these conditions would be to seek death."

On the other hand, as the communists have infiltrated practically all of our organizations, as the Political Advisor himself has admitted, it is almost impossible to protect our organizations if we don't try to gain the support of the masses to help us in this purpose.

The conferences of province chiefs, called together a great many times this past year to study the situation in the countryside have unanimously arrived at this conclusion: "If the countryside is not secure it is because we have not been able to hold on to the masses."

It follows from all that preceded that the question of holding on to the masses is not a question of simple demagoguery but a question of life and death, and above all a goal which is not unattainable if one knows how to delineate it in all its importance, mobilize all means, utilize all methods and endure all sacrifices to achieve it.

Vis-à-vis the communists: The number of communist agents in South Vietnam is truly high. As the Advisor admitted, we will never succeed in arresting them all. But . . . we can at least destroy their organizations. . . .

The act of no longer arresting communists but only watching them and having our agents infiltrate their ranks is difficult to do . . . The enemy has more opportunity to infiltrate our ranks than we do his because our organizations are official whereas his are secret. . . . Communist organizations have a closed structure, members of various cells of the same organizations are not supposed to know what the others are doing. Our agents who succeed in infiltrating wouldn't learn much. To learn something they would have to infiltrate the higher echelons, such as district or provincial committees. . . .

The problem of maintaining security in the countryside, discussed above, became much worse following the establishment of the National Front for the Liberation of South Viet-Nam by dissident southern groups and the outbreak of full-scale warfare in the south (see Part IV below). The NLF made a strong effort to win the support of the local population and to prevent the establishment of effective governmental authority in the villages. In order to deprive the NLF of peasant support and prevent contact between insurgent forces and the local population, peasants were brought together in groups to live in areas protected by government troops. This government program is discussed below by Bui Van Luong, minister of the interior, in a speech to the Saigon Lions Club.

Bui Van Luong: Strategic Hamlets [May 22, 1962]*

Why do we use the phrase "Strategic Hamlets?" The correct usage of this phrase has not been adopted by either private or public officials. Some refer to them as "fighting hamlets," others "agrovilles," while still others call them "concentration hamlets." The official term "strategic hamlets" should be used.

Strategic hamlets are different from agrovilles, the latter being set up in troubled areas for the purpose of concentrating the people and realizing various undertakings on a larger scale. Strategic hamlets are being built from the lowest echelons of the nation and the concentration of these people is based on the principle of short distance moves for a few isolated families.

Strategic hamlets are the most efficient means of solving the important problems we now face.

The conception of these strategic hamlets is a revolutionary one, aimed at replacing the present system of work by creating a new system. The cadres will have to have a revolutionary spirit, in order to protect this new system.

The most urgent problem in Viet Nam at present is the military problem, which presents itself in two ways: The enemy always hides in the jungles or mixes with the populace in order to infiltrate into our weak spots and attack us when we are unaware. We continually do our best to seek out the enemy, but nine times out of ten we miss them and hurt innocent people instead.

Our army has failed to find the enemy after many operations, the main reason being that the villagers dare not inform the army of the enemy's position for fear of reprisals. Therefore, out of ten missions we are able to meet the enemy only once, and even then with little success because of lack of important information. The other nine times we encounter traps or ambush, and our men fall prey to snipers.

We have always talked of how we could combat the enemy if we had tanks and airplanes to organize large scale operations. This is true, but every time we have moved into an area with full battalion strength, the enemy, being informed in advance, can avoid us. This results in our soldiers becoming tired and frustrated.

The villagers are dissatisfied because they are subjected to two pressures: That of the government by day, and the communists by night.

* *Source*: Speech printed in the *Vietnam Press* (French edition, Saigon), May 23, 1962, and reprinted in Roy Jumper and Nguyen Thi Hue, *Notes on the Political and Administrative History of Viet Nam* (Saigon: Michigan State University Viet Nam Advisory Group, June 1962), pp. 184–187.

Both the army and the people are dissatisfied.

This dissatisfaction results from our present war strategy, where we try to find the enemy who always eludes us. Therefore, we are trying to avoid these problems by creating strategic hamlets as a revolutionary military means and technique. Establishing these hamlets means a complete change in tactics to combat the enemy. We would defeat the enemy if they would engage us in battle.

We have failed to meet the enemy, we found, because our army has adopted the same tactics as the French Expeditionary forces. If we can adopt a new strategy to turn the tide, we can succeed and bring victory to our side.

The district chiefs are directly responsible for the creation of these strategic hamlets under the guidance of provincial offices.

In principle the responsibilities are as follows:

—Instead of having to find the enemy, tactical forces responsible for combating the enemy should concentrate their strength to protect areas where strategic hamlets are being established.

—Provincial areas responsible for combating the enemy will, when informed of enemy concentration, attack immediately, but avoid harming the populace.

Consequently, military protection will exist where strategic hamlets are being built. And we can build strategic hamlets when we find a *system cohérent de protection* from tactical area down to district level.

The security services in each area will have to keep a clear list of all known communist followers (those who are in the jungles) and relatives of Viet Cong cadres who went to North Viet Nam.

Organizing groups will be responsible for dividing the population into separate divisions: Women, young men, oldsters and children.

Social cadres will organize lectures for the people concerning the idea of strategic hamlets.

Soldiers, civil guards and *dân vê* will train the young men to protect these hamlets.

The aims of the strategic hamlets are security and self-sufficiency in administrative and military affairs.

Members of the hamlet committees do not receive an allowance or a salary, but they are permitted to exploit the public rice fields or organize fish breeding, in order to obtain the income necessary for their support.

The government will lend needed weapons to the hamlets for six months. The para-military forces of the hamlets are to arm themselves by taking weapons from the enemy. The government will supply ammunition only.

There are difficulties, to be sure, in the building of strategic hamlets:

1. Communist properties: In strategic hamlets there are often a number of families whose relatives have been forced to follow the Viet Cong. Parents are given three weeks to appeal to their sons to surrender to the government with their guns. Failing this, the families are moved elsewhere. Their land and houses are put under the responsibility of the hamlet committee.

2. Lands taken by the Viet Cong from landowners and from the government for distribution to its followers: The Viet Cong has rented such lands to the peasants at low rates. For instance, if the rent was formerly 40 giạ of paddy, the Viet Cong charges 30 giạ, but actually takes only 15. The remaining 15 giạ is deposited with the peasants for the use of the Viet Cong troops when they happen to move through the area. The Viet Cong troops then consume more than the remaining 15 giạ upon their return, leaving the poor peasant with nothing.

How can this problem be solved?

In principle, the law must be applied by returning the land to the original landowners. But such a step would alienate the people. To do otherwise would make the landowners unhappy. Therefore, we must solve the problem by applying the law and showing respect for private property, keeping the status quo and recalculating the rentals. This would satisfy the landowner and would not alienate the people when we establish the strategic hamlets.

The purpose of the strategic hamlet program is the bringing of security to the people in order to apply the law according to the spirit of the constitution, the spirit of personalism, and of common progress, which are the solutions to the problem, as well as the idea of the revolution of personalism and social progress.

Up to now, we have been taking care of the tree, while the Viet Cong destroyed the roots; with strategic hamlets these revolutionary roots will stay firmly in the ground.

Therefore, the hamlet committee should be an *elected* one and not by nomination, in order to show the people that there is a revolution. There will be difficulties in our choice because there is still some hesitancy in the people, and a lack of experience, in those energetic ones, in both administrative organization and fighting tactics against the enemy. But, being able to realize the basic revolution is an advantage to us. . . .

The following statement is representative of the views of young, militant monks who projected the Unified Buddhist Church into political activities in the Republic of Viet-Nam. The author, Thich Nhat

Hanh, was one of the leaders of the Buddhist anti-Diem protest movement begun in 1963.

Thich Nhat Hanh: The Political Role of the Unified Buddhist Church [1967]*

The idea of Buddhism as a national religion did not take shape in the 1940's but much earlier—in the days of the Truc Lam Zen sect on Mount Yen Tu. But the idea crystallized during the hardship and suffering that the Buddhists had to endure under the French occupation and the regime of President Ngo Dinh Diem. The campaign to overthrow the Ngo Dinh Diem regime in 1963 not only succeeded in mobilizing the people to the defense of Buddhism but also awakened the nationalistic consciousness of the masses. In every Buddhist the idea of Buddhism and nationalism are intertwined and cannot be easily separated. Many non-Buddhist elements also took part in the Buddhist campaign, not because they wanted to support the Buddhists but because they realized that the Buddhist campaign was consistent with the people's aspirations.

After the November 1, 1963, revolution, which overthrew the regime of President Ngo Dinh Diem, the prestige of Buddhism reached its apex and attracted many intellectuals, students, and youth. However, at this stage Buddhism was not yet prepared to respond fully to this enthusiastic support. Most of the monks had not been trained to shoulder Buddhism's new mission. They had been trained to recite the sutras, to meditate, and to preach, and now became embarrassed at the role of responsible leadership suddenly thrust upon them. The number of monks and laymen with sufficient ability and experience to exercise leadership was small, while the need for responsible leaders became pressing. The intellectuals, artists, writers, students, politicians, workers, trade-union officials, and farmers who were inclined to support Buddhism were many but they lacked leadership. Throughout the French occupation, which lasted for nearly one hundred years, Buddhism did not have many opportunities to send its monks to study abroad nor did it have any facilities to train social workers and cultural cadres. Those who later served in the Buddhist cultural and social institutions were mostly dedicated laymen who volunteered, rather than cadres trained by the Buddhist Church itself. Furthermore, the Church lacked the financial means to meet the considerable expense of sending a monk abroad to study.

* Source: Thich Nhat Hanh, Vietnam: Lotus in a Sea of Fire (New York: Hill and Wang, 1967), pp. 45–49.

A shortage of qualified men was therefore inevitable. The Buddhist leaders were forced to take on people of lesser ability, who claimed to be Buddhists but actually were not. Moreover, in 1964 and 1965, remnants of the former Can Lao party of Ngo Dinh Nhu resumed their accustomed activity and caused a great deal of difficulty for the new Unified Buddhist Church. The Church had to meet their sabotage, reprisals, and attempts to return to power, and this alone consumed much of its energy. In addition, there were opportunists who managed to slip into the entourage of the Church leaders and traffic with the influence of the Church. Their influence on the monks was to account for many of the latter's mistakes. . . .

The Buddhists of Vietnam desire to mobilize the potential force of their religion in order to rebuild their society, and consequently they have carried Buddhism into every domain of life: culture, economics, politics, and social welfare. Such a revolutionary effort naturally requires time for its realization. In the process, the Buddhist leaders have made mistakes because they have had to face new difficulties arising from the outside and at the same time to solve internal crises that inevitably accompany any radical change. . . .

As is common to any church organization, both conservative and progressive elements are present in the Buddhist Church. The former are slow to respond to the need for actualizing Buddhism, while the latter desire to speed up the reorganization of the Church in order to take a more active part in the life of the society. The young monks belong to the latter element, grouped as they are about the Church's cultural and social institutions but lacking key positions in the Church itself. The influence of their thought and action is strong among the population, however. They have a greater awareness of the issues that Vietnam has to face, in economics, culture, education, and social welfare, and are anxious to make use of the potential resources of Buddhism in order to solve these problems. The young monks naturally have the support of the intellectuals and younger generation. However, this support is not the Church's support. Conservative dogmatism and fear of change have always hindered progress. The real issue is how the Buddhist Church can get on with its internal revolution while fulfilling its duty toward society. . . .

IV. War and Peace: The Struggle for Reunification

By the time the war against the French had ended in 1954, Viet Minh guerrillas controlled many districts in rural South Viet-Nam, where they had built a base of power following their eviction by the French from Saigon in August–September 1945 (during the post-World War II British occupation). Following the Geneva Conference in 1954, most DRVN military units were withdrawn to the North in compliance with the provisions for the partition of Viet-Nam at the seventeenth parallel. The remaining political and military personnel, mainly southerns, became targets of the Diem regime's anti-Communist campaigns. When it became clear that the countrywide elections slated for 1956 would not be held, these southern-based guerrillas no longer felt bound to the DRVN policy of "peaceful reunification." Instead, they joined with dissident sectarian forces—also hounded by the RVN army—to embark on a program of organized terror against selected targets, primarily rural government officials, teachers, and other local leaders. A climate of violence and repression slowly permeated the countryside.

In September 1960, the Lao Dong party congress held in Hanoi called for the active development of a people's national revolution in the South. Within three months, the dissident southern groups "spontaneously" created a united front coalition, and the National Front for the Liberation of South Viet-Nam (NFLSV or NLF), which officially came into existence in December 1960. Unlike most front organizations, the NLF initially consisted of an actively functioning military structure and very little political substructure. Over the next few years, additional member organizations were joined to the NLF and a hierarchical administrative framework was fashioned. At the grassroots level, villages in NLF-controlled and -dominated areas were administered by liberation committees operating as a shadow government. Intensive indoctrination efforts were carried out at all levels and for all segments of the population—to win over the enemy, convince wavering villagers, exhort the guerrillas, and consolidate NLF support within a cohesive, productive militant organization.

The stated objective of the NLF is the ultimate reunification of Viet-Nam, under the sponsorship of an NLF-dominated government in the south. The initial NLF manifesto contained a ten-point program calling for the restoration of normal relations between the two zones prior to reunification, thus implying that a separate government will exist in the south for some time to come. An elaborate political program issued by the NLF in August 1967 proposed a step-by-step reunification to be brought about by negotiations between the two zones "without foreign interference." As the sole legitimate representative of the southern people, the NLF refused to share power with the "illegitimate" Saigon regime, although they agreed in principle to the idea of a coalition government for the south. The NLF appears to place greater priority upon attaining power in the south than upon the reunification of Viet-Nam.

The most dominant member of the NLF coalition has been the People's Revolutionary party (PRP), formally established on January 1, 1962, following a congress of the followers of Marxism-Leninism in the south. The congress, held in late December 1961, established the PRP, passed its platform, and assigned it the role of vanguard to the southern revolution. It is a self-acknowledged Marxist-Leninist party, the "revolutionary party of the working class in South Viet-Nam," with close ties to the Lao Dong party in Hanoi, and its formation probably represented a shift to overt Communist hegemony within the NLF.

For a time in 1968 the NLF ostensibly shared political power with another front organization, the Viet-Nam Alliance of National, Democratic, and Peace Forces. During the NLF's so-called Tet (lunar New Year) offensive of February 1968, "alliance" committees of various interest groups were formed in "liberated" urban areas. Although the offensive failed to achieve permanent military gains, these groups merged into an urban-based Viet-Nam Alliance of National, Democratic, and Peace Forces which presented itself as a middle group between the NLF and the Saigon government. The Alliance attracted neither a substantial internal following nor any international standing, especially after the NLF began attending the Paris peace talks in May 1969 as the representative of the southern revolutionary forces. Another political change occurred in June 1969 when the NLF was presumably superceded as the "sole genuine representative" of the southern Vietnamese by the formation of a Provisional Revolutionary Government (PRG). Leaders of the provisional government, however, were NLF stalwarts: Huynh Tan Phat, vice-president of the NLF, headed the government, and Mrs. Nguyen Thi Binh, leader of the NLF delegation to the Paris peace talks, retained her post with a change of title to minister of foreign affairs.

The opening of the Paris peace talks in 1969 did not put an end to the destructive war which had raged intermittently over South Vietnamese territory for more than ten years and had even brought bombs to the heart of North Viet-Nam. Full-scale war in the south began even before the fall of the Diem regime in 1963. The NLF, with increasing DRVN aid, had capitalized on political instability in the RVN to launch a drive to take over in the south by force. Primarily to forestall the collapse of the RVN, the United States agreed to assume direction of the war and began in 1965 a large-scale infusion of American military might. The DRVN matched the American military by increasing the infiltration of VPA troops in large units. For the DRVN and the NLF, the year 1965–1966—during which both sides escalated the war enormously—was a period of great anxiety. As it became apparent that, with the arrival in 1965 of American ground forces in full strength, the NLF could no longer achieve a quick military victory, both its political and military tactics were debated carefully. At the same time, the DRVN began to give serious thought to the possibility of negotiations.

With their assumption of a greater role in the war effort, both the United States and the DRVN also began to participate in diplomatic efforts, and the search for a settlement became an issue for international negotiations. Although only Vietnamese documents are included below, the reader must not lose sight of the American—and international—initiatives and responses. While it is impossible to ascertain how decisions were reached in the closed councils of the DRVN and the NLF, careful scrutiny of their public pronouncements will help to indicate the general evolution of policy. For example, it is possible to trace how the DRVN position moved slowly from rigid insistence on withdrawal of U.S. troops to permanent and unconditional halt in the bombing of North Viet-Nam as a primary condition for holding peace talks.

A turning point in the war was reached in the winter-spring campaign of 1968, when DRVN and NLF forces demonstrated the ability to mount coordinated, large-scale assaults on major urban areas throughout South Viet-Nam, including Saigon, Cholon, and Hué. The American public was made painfully aware of the tenuous military situation in Viet-Nam and became disillusioned with the progress and purpose of the war. Increasingly widespread attacks on his war policy and leadership led President Lyndon B. Johnson to announce, on March 31, that he would limit American bombing of North Viet-Nam and not run for re-election. This overture found a favorable but conditional response in the DRVN. Hanoi announced on April 3 that

DRVN representatives would hold preliminary talks with American negotiators but only to discuss the cessation of all bombing of North Vietnamese territory. Finally, only a few days before a U.S. presidential election brought in a Republican administration to deal with the Vietnamese war, President Johnson declared a complete bombing halt. The DRVN agreed on November 1, 1968, to meet for substantive peace talks and to permit the seating of delegations from the NLF and the RVN. An unexpected delay occurred when the RVN refused to attend without official assurances that the DRVN would not take advantage of the bombing halt, but on January 25, 1969, the four protagonists in the war sat down to peace talks. Four years and two days later, on January 27, 1973, a tenuous peace was brought to the war-weary Vietnamese by the signing in Paris of the "Agreement for the Cessation of War and the Re-establishment of Peace in Viet-Nam."

The following excerpts are from the original version of the NFLSV's initial manifesto issued in English on February 4, 1961, by the Vietnamese News Agency (VNA) in Hanoi, apparently for foreign distribution. A later enlarged version was distributed on February 11 by the Liberation News Agency of the NFLSV. The NFLSV (or NLF) was formally organized at an unknown place in South Viet-Nam on December 20, 1960, by individuals and groups in opposition to the regime of Ngo Dinh Diem.

Manifesto of the National Front for the Liberation of South Viet-Nam [February 4, 1961]*

. . . The NFLSV undertakes to unite all sections of the people, all social classes, nationalities, political parties, organizations, religious communities, and patriotic personalities, without distinction of their political tendencies, in order to struggle and overthrow the rule of the U.S. imperialists, and their stooge, the Ngo Dinh Diem clique, realize independence, democracy, peace and neutrality, and advance toward peaceful reunification of the fatherland. The program of the NFLSV includes the following 10 points:

1. To overthrow the disguised colonial regime of the U.S. imperialists

* *Source:* Vietnamese News Agency (Hanoi), in English, February 4, 1961.

and the dictatorial Ngo Dinh Diem administration, lackey of the United States, and to form a national democratic coalition administration. . . .

2. To bring into being a broad and progressive democracy, promulgate freedom of expression, of the press, of belief, of assembly, association and movement, and other democratic freedoms; to grant an amnesty to all political detainees, dissolve all concentration camps dubbed "prosperity zones" and all "resettlement centers," abolish fascist law 10-59[1] and other anti-democratic laws.

3. To abolish the economic monopoly of the United States and its henchmen, protect homemade products, encourage home industry; . . . to help North Vietnamese people who had been forced or enticed to go south . . . to return to their native places if they so desire; and to provide jobs for those among them who want to remain in the South. . . .

4. To carry out land rent reduction, guarantee the peasants' right to till their present plots of land, and redistribute communal land in preparation for land reform. . . .

5. To eliminate the enslaving and depraved U.S.-style culture; to build a national and progressive culture and education, eliminate illiteracy, open more schools. . . .

6. To abolish the system of American military advisors, eliminate foreign military bases in Viet Nam and build a national army defending the fatherland and the people. . . .

7. To guarantee the right of equality between men and women and among different nationalities, and the right to autonomy of the national minorities; to protect the legitimate interests of foreign residents in Viet Nam; to protect and take care of the interests of overseas Vietnamese.

8. To carry out a foreign policy of peace and neutrality; to establish diplomatic relations with all countries which respect the independence and sovereignty of Viet Nam.

9. To reestablish normal relations between the two zones as a first step toward peaceful reunification of the country. . . .

10. To oppose aggressive wars and actively defend peace. . . .

The document below, a broadcast in Vietnamese by Radio Hanoi to South Viet-Nam, replies to contentions by the United States and the Republic of Viet-Nam that the NFLSV was formed on Hanoi's orders and lacked substantive roots in the south. It appears aimed at reassuring Hanoi's allies in South Viet-Nam in the face of American peace initiatives.

---

[1] This law empowered military courts to give the death sentence to persons found guilty of crimes against the security of the state.

The NFLSV—The Only Genuine Representative of the South Vietnamese People [January 27, 1966]*

By making a great furor about the so-called peace campaign and by issuing a series of deceptive statements—such as the 30 December 1965 statement of Dean Rusk, the 3 January 1966 communique of the White House on the U.S. 14 points, Johnson's 12 January 1966 State of the Union message, and so forth—the White House ring-leaders have tried to make people believe erroneously that the United States is filled with a genuine desire for peace. . . . One of the signs of the Johnson clique's stubbornness is their impudent distortion of the NFLSV policy, their denial of its front role in leading the South Vietnamese people, and their refusal to recognize the front as the only genuine representative of the South Vietnamese people. . . .

To fight and defeat the U.S. imperialists, the South Vietnamese people must have a political organization to provide leadership. Such an organization must come out not from the subjective desire of anyone but must be in accordance with the urgent and objective requirements of the masses of people. Such an organization must concentrate on the people's aspiration and set forth guidelines to realize these aspirations. Such an organization must represent the just rights of the people and enjoy the people's recognition, support, and obedience. Such an organization is the NFLSV.

Born more than five years ago, the front has clearly displayed its political prestige and obvious power. The front has gained control of four-fifths of South Vietnamese territory and 10 million people. The front's prestige is immense and even extends to areas which are still temporarily oppressed by the U.S. imperialists and their henchmen. The front's stands and policies have always been carried out voluntarily by the broad masses of people. The front's international position has widened continuously. The front has official representations in 11 countries. The front banner has flown on the five continents—and even in the United States.

From the political, legal, and sentimental viewpoints, it is clear that the NFLSV is the sole genuine representative of the South Vietnamese People. As the only genuine representative of 14 million people of South Viet Nam, the NFLSV is fully entitled to settle the internal affairs of the South Vietnamese in accordance with the front program—one which is consistent with the national interests and with the world people's struggle for peace, democracy, and social progress. . . .

* *Source:* Radio Hanoi, January 27, 1966.

The following document builds upon the earlier NFLSV Manifesto by elaborating a statement of policy objectives in the economic and political fields, including the goals of reunification and resumption of normal relations with North Viet-Nam. The program was adopted by an extraordinary congress of the NLF convened by its Central Committee in mid-August 1967.

Political Program of the National Front for the Liberation of South Viet-Nam [August 1967]*

The South Viet Nam National Front for Liberation lays down the following specific policies:

(1) To set up a broad democratic and progressive regime. To abolish the disguised colonial regime established in South Viet Nam, . . . overthrow the puppet administration, . . . repudiate the puppet "national assembly" . . . and abolish all anti-national and anti-democratic laws, including the "constitution," enacted by the U.S. imperialists and the puppet administration. To hold free general elections and elect the national assembly . . . in accordance with the principle of universal, equal, direct suffrage and secret ballot. To set up a national union democratic government including the most representative persons among the various social strata, nationalities, religious communities, patriotic and democratic parties, patriotic personalities, and forces which have contributed to the cause of national liberation.

(2) To build an independent and self-supporting economy and improve the people's living conditions. To abolish the U.S. imperialists' policy of economic enslavement and monopoly. . . .

(3) To enforce the land policy and carry out the slogan: "land to the tillers." To confiscate the lands of the U.S. imperialists and their lackeys, the diehard cruel landlords, and allot those lands to the landless or land-poor peasants. To confirm and protect the ownership of the lands allotted to peasants by the revolution. The state will negotiate the purchase of lands from landlords who possess land upward of a certain amount varying with the situation in each locality, and allot these lands to the landless or land-poor peasants. The recipients will receive the lands free of charge, and will not be bound by any condition whatsoever. In areas where the required conditions for land reform do not yet obtain, land-rent reduction will be carried out.

(4) To build a national democratic culture and education. . . .

* *Source: Peking Review,* No. 39 (September 22, 1967).

(5) To guarantee the rights of workers, laborers and civil servants and care for their livelihood.

(6) To build up the South Viet Nam Liberation Armed Forces. . . .

. . . (12) To welcome puppet officers and men and puppet officials back to the just cause, and show leniency and give humane treatment to enemy army people who cross over and prisoners-of-war.

To Restore Normal Relations Between North and South Viet Nam and Proceed Toward Peaceful Reunification of the Fatherland

The South Viet Nam National Front for Liberation holds:

(1) The reunification of Viet Nam will be realized step by step through peaceful means and on the principle of negotiations between the two zones with neither side using pressure against the other and without foreign interference.

(2) Pending the reunification of the country, the people in both zones will make joint efforts to oppose foreign invasion and defend the fatherland and at the same time endeavor to expand economic and cultural exchanges. . . .

To Apply a Foreign Policy of Peace and Neutrality

(1) To establish diplomatic relations with all countries regardless of their social and political system. . . . To join no military alliance and accept no military personnel or military bases of foreign countries. . . .

At its second conference, held July 30 and 31, 1968, the Viet-Nam Alliance of National, Democratic, and Peace Forces announced its political program. The announcement was timed for a high point in the development of NLF objectives following the NLF's Tet and spring offensives, when the Vietnamese began to sense the United States' failure to crush by force the extension of the Viet Minh revolution to South Viet-Nam.

Political Program of the Viet-Nam Alliance of National, Democratic, and Peace Forces [July 30–31, 1968]*

. . . The political program includes the following points:

1—National salvation: Unite all patriotic forces and individuals in resolutely opposing the aggressive war, overthrowing the lackey puppet regime, setting up a national coalition government, and regaining independence, democracy, and peace.

* *Source:* Liberation Radio (clandestine), to South Viet-Nam, August 15, 1968.

. . . The Viet Nam Alliance of National, Democratic, and Peace Forces advocates the regaining of independence and sovereignty for South Viet Nam, demanding that the U.S. government end the war, withdraw all the troops of the United States and its allies from South Viet Nam, dismantle all U.S. military bases, and respect Viet Nam's independence and sovereignty as stipulated by the 1954 Geneva agreements on Viet Nam. South Viet Nam's national independence and sovereignty and territorial integrity must be recognized and respected by all the governments in the world. The Viet Nam Alliance . . . is ready to discuss these problems with the U.S. Government.

The South Viet Nam National Front for Liberation, a patriotic force having made great contributions to the tasks of mobilizing, organizing and leading the anti-aggression struggle during the past years, cannot be absent from the settlement of problems concerning South Viet Nam. The Viet Nam Alliance . . . advocates contacts and debates with the NFLSV in order to cooperate with it in regaining national independence, restoring peace, building the country, and bringing a free and happy life to all the people.

On the basis of the united action of patriotic forces and individuals participating in the national liberation task, including the patriotic individuals in the lackey administration and army, it is necessary to set up an enlarged democratic, national coalition government composed of representatives of people of all strata—nationalist, religious, and political groups, progressive political parties, and patriotic notables. . . .

2—National reconstruction: To build South Viet Nam into an independent, free, democratic, peaceful, neutral, and prosperous state.

(1) Political regime: To eradicate all vestiges of the colonial regimes old and new in South Viet Nam; to overthrow the entire lackey, puppet administration. . . .

(2) Economic regime: To build an independent, self-governing economy, which will not be subordinated to the U.S. imperialists or any country. . . .

To respect and protect the citizens' right of ownership of the means of production and other property. . . .

To carry out an equitable and rational agrarian reform, create bases to develop agriculture and reduce rent. On the basis of negotiation, and based on a certain limit of acreage, the government will buy surplus acreage from landlords, and parcel it out to peasants who have no land or not enough land to cultivate.

To recognize the ownership of land which the NFLSV has parceled out to peasants for the needs of the resistance. As for the land of absentee landlords which the NFLSV has parceled out to peasants, it will be re-examined according to the political attitudes of these landlords to find a reasonable solution.

To respect the legal ownership of land by churches, pagodas, and holy sees; to encourage the management of plantations growing industrial crops and fruit trees; to restore and develop the handicraft industry and commerce; to carry out a policy of free trade. . . .

(3) Foreign relations: To carry out a foreign policy of peace, non-alignment with any bloc, and nonaffiliation with any military alliance; to establish relations with all nations, regardless of their diplomatic regimes, on the principle of equality, mutual respect for one another's independence, sovereignty, and territorial integrity, nonintervention in one another's internal affairs, and peaceful coexistence; to attach special importance to friendly relations with our neighboring countries, Cambodia and Laos; to develop friendly relations with nationalist countries in Asia, Africa, and Latin America; to positively support the national independence movement conducted by the peoples of various Asian, African, and Latin American countries. . . .

3—The problem of national reunification: The governments of the south and the north will conduct negotiations conducive to the peaceful reunification of the fatherland. To reunify the country is an earnest aspiration and sacred duty of our people. At present, our country has in fact two different political systems in the south and north. National reunification cannot be achieved overnight. Therefore, the south and the north should hold talks on the basis of equality and respect for the characteristics of each zone, in order to proceed toward the peaceful reunification of the country.

Since the country has not yet been reunified, it is necessary to establish economic, cultural, and postal relations and to allow movement between the two parts of the country. . . .

In the present period of desperate struggle, the Viet Nam Alliance . . . constantly sides with the NFLSV, in order to fulfill the glorious national salvation talk and to restore independence, freedom, and peace to the people.

The following excerpts are from the official policy statement of the Provisional Revolutionary Government formally created in South Viet-Nam between June 6 and 8, 1969, as the rival to the Republic of Viet-Nam. This text, broadcast by the National Liberation Front, includes a statement of objectives similar to those provided in the 1967 statement by the NLF.

Program of Action of the Provisional Revolutionary Government of South Viet-Nam [June 10, 1969]*

1—To lead the armed forces and the entire people to unite as one man, step up military and political struggle, defeat the U.S. imperialists' agressive war and their attempts to "Vietnamize" it, demand that the United States enter into serious talks with the Provisional Revolutionary Government of the Republic of Viet Nam at the Paris conference on Viet Nam on the basis of the 10-point over-all solution put forward by the South Viet Nam National Front for Liberation, and compel the U.S. Government to withdraw totally and without conditions from South Viet Nam. . . .

2—To abolish the disguised colonial regime established by the United States imperialists in South Viet Nam, to overthrow the entire structure of the puppet administration, to abolish the constitution and all antinational and antidemocratic laws. . . .

3—. . . The Provisional Revolutionary Government is prepared to enter into consultations with the political forces representing the various social strata and political tendencies in South Viet Nam that stand for peace, independence and neutrality, including those persons who, for political reasons, have to live abroad, with a view to setting up a provisional coalition government on the principle of equality, democracy and mutual respect. The provisional coalition government will organize general elections in order to elect a constituent assembly, work out a democratic constitution fully reflecting the interests and aspirations of the entire people, and set up a coalition government reflecting national concord and a broad union of all social strata. . . .

. . . 7—To carry out a land policy consistent with the specific conditions of South Viet Nam, to improve the living conditions of peasants, to restore and develop agricultural and industrial production, to encourage industrialists and traders to contribute to the development of industry, small industry, and handicrafts, to protect the right of ownership of means of production [and] other property of the citizens in accordance with the laws of the state.

. . . 9—To encourage, welcome and properly reward those officers and men of the puppet army and police and those functionaries of the puppet administration who cross over to the side of the people. . . .

. . . 11—To re-establish normal relations between South and North Viet Nam, to guarantee freedoms of movement, of correspondence, of

* *Source: New York Times,* June 12, 1969.

residence, to maintain economic and cultural relations according to the principle of mutual benefit and mutual help between the two zones. The two zones will reach agreement on the status of the demilitarized zone and work out modalities for movements across the provisional military demarcation line.

The reunification of the country will be achieved step by step, by peaceful means, through discussions and agreement between the two zones, without constraint from either side.

12—To win the sympathy, support and aid of all countries and progressive people in the world, including the American people, for national salvation.

To actively support the national independence movement of the Asian, American and Latin American peoples struggling against imperialism, colonialism and neocolonialism.

To achieve active co-ordination with the American people's struggle against the U.S. imperialists' war of aggression in Viet Nam, to actively support the just struggle of the Afro-Americans for their fundamental national rights. . . .

The introduction of American ground forces in 1965 completely changed the complexion of the war and set off lively debates in Hanoi and within the NLF about the possibilities of modifying strategy and tactics to meet the new military situation. Here, General Vo Nguyen Giap of the VPA, long an advocate of guerrilla warfare, delineates in great detail the weakness of the American enemy and the problems it faces.

Vo Nguyen Giap: The People of the Entire Country Are Determined to Fight and Vanquish the American Aggressors [January 1966]*

. . . The dispatch of an expeditionary corps for direct invasion of our country is itself subject to weaknesses so fundamental that they cannot surmount them.

First, the more troops the U.S. imperialists bring in to invade our country, the clearer they expose their faces as aggressors and their lackeys as countrysellers, thus making the contradiction between the American imperialists and our nation ever sharper and fiercer. . . .

Second, the U.S. imperialists deploy their troops to invade our country at a time when the strategy of their "special war" has basically gone

* *Source: Nhan Dan* (Hanoi), January 16, 17, 18, 1966; transmitted by the VNA (Hanoi), January 31, 1966.

bankrupt. . . . Though they may bring in hundreds or thousands of troops, they still cannot avoid being driven into a defensive strategic position which compels them to scatter their forces . . . thereby making it hard for them to regain the initiative they long for.

Third, due to the unjust character of its war, the U.S. expeditionary corps is fighting without an ideal and hence has low morale. On the southern battlefield it has to cope with a people's war; the strategy and tactics based on their bourgeois military outlook are of no use. The organization, composition, and training of the American army in general are not fit to tackle our entire people's revolutionary war; it does not take into account the great difficulties encountered in a strange terrain and climate, and the considerable demands in the fields of supply and logistics.

Fourth, the purpose of the U.S. imperialists' introduction of troops into the south is to prevent the collapse of the puppet army and administration and to create new conditions for the consolidating and strengthening of their puppet forces; the U.S. imperialists, however, directly invade the southern part of our country at a moment when the puppet army and administration are seriously decaying. In such a situation, the more active the U.S. aggression is, the more isolated and divided the puppet army and administration will become, and the greater the contraditions between the US. imperialists and their henchmen will grow; thus, those who are in the ranks of the puppet army and administration but still have some national feeling will become more conscious and return to the people's side in greater numbers. Consequently as the U.S. imperialists build up their military forces, not only will they be unable to retrieve the predicament of the puppet army and administration, but they will also accelerate the latter's collapse and annihilation. . . .

Fifth, having started the war in the south, the U.S. imperialists are being condemned ever more strictly by the peace-loving people of the world.

In spite of weaknesses in equipment and techniques and in the economic field, we have absolute political and moral superiority, a correct line of leadership, the strength of the people's unity, the invincible people's war, and the strong sympathy and support of the peoples throughout the world. . . .

First, we have the party's correct revolutionary line. This line is the condensed expression of the clever and creative combination of Marxist-Leninist general principles with the concrete realities of our country's revolution. This is the line of the people's national democratic revolution progressing toward socialism, befitting the case of a country which was once a colony and semifeudal state. . . . In the light of this line, the

Vietnamese nation was the first among the colonies to rise up and defeat the mighty army of an imperialist power, the French imperialists, to liberate itself. The northern part of our country is also the first state to take the path of socialism in Southeast Asia. . . .

Second, we are united in a bloc of all the people against the U.S. imperialists and for national salvation. The north and south are of one mind in their determination to defeat the U.S. aggressors and their lackeys. . . . Today our people in the south have the National Liberation Front, an organization with a broad base and a correct line and program and enjoying high prestige at home and abroad. . . .

Third, we have the invincible people's war and the experience to lead this struggle. If one can say that at present in the military field, apart from the great invention of the atomic weapon, there is a greater invention, the people's war, then one can safely say that the Vietnamese people have contributed to the devising and the efficient wielding of such an invincible weapon. People's war in our country has developed in the historical, political, and social conditions of Viet Nam and achieved a very high standard with an extremely varied content. People's war in our country has developed according to the general law of revolutionary war, but also to the specific laws of the Vietnamese society and battlefields. Therefore, it is a nationwide and comprehensive revolutionary war, and at the same time it is a revolutionary war waged by a small nation on a small territory inhabited by a small population, having an underdeveloped economy, relying on the strength of its people's unity in the struggle, which will finally knock out an enemy originally many times stronger than itself.

People's war in Viet Nam in general is a revolutionary armed struggle developing on the basis of the masses' political upsurge. Hence the revolutionary masses' boundless strength has pervaded the revolutionary armed forces and given them an extraordinary capacity to fight and win. Moreover, the outstanding characteristic of the people's war in our country at the present stage is that in the midst of the fighting, armed struggle and political struggle are very closely coordinated and are mutually helpful and interacting. Thus the slogan "mobilize the entire people, arm the entire people, and fight the aggressors on all fronts" has become a most lively and heroic reality. . . .

Armed struggle in the south has another characteristic: In guerrilla warfare or in regular warfare, the revolutionary armed struggle is fully capable of solving the question of outdoing an enemy equipped with modern weapons, like the U.S. Armed Forces. In the south, not only the regular army but also the regional army and the militia and guerrillas can wipe out American and puppet troops and foil their most modern tactics. . . .

Fourth, we enjoy the warm sympathy and wholehearted support given us by the peoples of the brother socialist countries and the progressive peoples throughout the world, including the Americans.

In the following article, published in the Lao Dong party's journal Hoc Tap, the correct way of meeting the challenge of better-equipped American troops is presented by the late commander of the North Vietnamese troops in the southern battlefield, General Nguyen Chi Thanh. He appears to criticize the more orthodox theorists among the military and those who would overestimate the enemy's strength.

Nguyen Chi Thanh: The South's Ideological Task [July 1966]*

In a situation where the U.S. forces increase abruptly, as far as the method of viewing things is concerned, beside the correct ideas there may appear erroneous tendencies. First, one may have a conservative spirit and fail to identify and discover the new factors. As a result, one would devote himself to working in accordance with the "old customs." Second, one may be incapable of analyzing the new concrete situation so as to formulate correct and creative opinions. As a result, one turns his attention to looking for the new factors in the formulas that exist in books, and mechanically copying one's past experiences or the experiences of foreign countries, and then applying to the live revolutionary realities a "forced love," in accordance with a dogmatic tendency. For instance, on learning that the enemy has just increased his troop strength, and without conducting a prior inquiry and studying the practical situation, one hastily jumps to such conclusions as: how many phases our revolutionary war has and which phase we are in; to annihilate one puppet battalion, we must have a troop superiority of two to one, and therefore, to fight and annihilate one American battalion—which is better equipped, which has a troop strength that is double that of a puppet battalion, and whose American officers are better than puppet officers—we must have a superiority in strength of at least seven to one or nine to one, and so

* *Source: Hoc Tap* (Hanoi), No. 7 (July 1966). Reprinted in Patrick J. Mc-Garvey, ed., *Visions of Victory: Selected Vietnamese Communist Military Writings, 1964–1968* (Stanford, Cal.: Stanford University, Hoover Institution on War, Revolution, and Peace, 1969), pp. 67–70; reprinted here by permission of the Hoover Institution on War, Revolution, and Peace.

forth. In fact, this is but a kind of "divination" not a scientific calculation, and usually the "diviners" are inclined to take regressive steps.

Therefore, in exerting leadership over the war in any situation, especially at times when the situation has just changed or changed abruptly,
it is necessary simultaneously to pay great attention to reasoning and experiences and to fully base oneself upon the realities, To repeat exactly
what belongs to history in the face of a new reality is adventurism.

Let us cite another example: It would be impossible for one to evaluate correctly the military capability of friend and foe if one failed to
fully see the important effect of our Southern people's political struggle.
Thus, it is possible that because of a method of viewing things that is
detached from reality one would pose and settle in an old-fashioned manner the question of relations between the delta and the mountainous region and between the rural areas and the cities in the Southern revolutionary war. To cite still another example: It is impossible to evaluate
the combat capability of a U.S. infantry division in abstract terms, because an abstract evaluation can only lead to a vague or erroneous conclusion. On the contrary, it is necessary to place it in a concrete situation,
in concrete locations, at concrete times, and in close contact with a concrete adversary. Speaking in terms of simple theory, a U.S. infantry division usually consists of about 15,000 troops and can annihilate one regi-
ment of the adversary in one battle. Yet why is it that in the Southern
part of our country throughout the last dry season, although Americans
had nearly six divisions and a very strong air force, they could not completely annihilate one company of the liberation armed forces; and why
is it, on the contrary, that tens of U.S. battalions were completely annihi-
lated by the liberation armed forces? How could that be? . . .

It would be impossible to understand why the United States and its
henchmen, though having as many as 700,000 troops, were defeated by
the armed forces and people in the South during the dry season if we
did not see clearly that the U.S. military activities on the Southern battlefield were fraught with contradictions bearing on their strategy, tactics,
and combat organization and command, which thus threw the Americans
and their henchmen into deep confusion. There are two reasons for their
confusion: first, they themselves were already very confused; second,
their adversary, the Southern armed forces and people, knew how to continuously sharpen their contradictions, thereby making them more confused.

First of all, the U.S. military forces and activities in the South are
directed by its political line, about which there are three important and
noteworthy points: first, it is unjust; second, the Americans had experienced bitter failure twice in the past ten years; and, third, they do not

believe now, and cannot believe, that they can get the better of us military. Thus, naturally, the enemy's strategy has inevitably been passive for three reasons: First, the Americans had to introduce their army into the Southern battlefield, an act which they previously regarded as inadvisable, which they wanted to avoid, but which they had to engage in reluctantly; second, the U.S. Army plunged into the South at a time when the American-directed puppet armed forces and administration had suffered heavy defeats and were wretched, while their adversary was much stronger than before, both militarily and politically; and third, when the U.S. Army came to the South, they wanted, by this means or another, to fight and settle the war quickly. Yet they failed, and therefore had to prolong the war. What contradictions!

As a result, there were many contradictions in U.S. tactics. For instance, while the Americans were fighting on the ground they had to rely on their air force to settle the war. If they wanted to develop the effect of the air force there should have been clear battlefronts and targets. Yet there was no front, and the targets were scattered and unclear. Thus if the air force's theoretical effect were ten, in actual combat this effect would remain only one. The Americans relied on artillery and mechanized equipment while their army had to perform assault tasks. If the Americans relied on army troops whose combat morale was low, how could these troops launch strong assaults, encircle tightly, divide rapidly the forces of the adversary, pursue actively the forces of the adversary, fight the battle rapidly and neatly in order to annihilate the adversary, and so forth? What contradictions!

In a statement made public on March 22, 1965, the NLF affirmed its determination to fight for and insist on the unconditional withdrawal of American troops, in the face of U.S. bombing of North Vietnamese territory and intensification of the war in South Viet-Nam.

Statement by the Central Committee of the National Front for the Liberation of South Viet-Nam [March 22, 1965]*

Facing the present situation of utmost gravity, the South Viet Nam National Front for Liberation deems it necessary to reaffirm once again its steel-like and unswerving stand to carry out the war of resistance against U.S. imperialists.

* *Source: We Will Win* (Hanoi: Foreign Languages Publishing House, 1965), pp. 8–22.

1. The U.S. imperialists are the saboteurs of the Geneva Agreements, the most brazen war-monger and aggressor and the sworn enemy of the Vietnamese people. . . .

2. The heroic South Vietnamese people are resolved to drive out the U.S. imperialists in order to liberate South Viet Nam, with a view toward national reunification. . . . On behalf of the 14 million valiant South Vietnamese people, the South Viet Nam National Front for Liberation solemnly declares: The South Vietnamese people and their armed forces are resolved never to loose hold of their arms so long as they have not reached their goals of independence, democracy, peace and neutrality. . . . All negotiations with the U.S. imperialists at this moment are utterly useless if they still refuse to withdraw from South Viet Nam all their troops and all kinds of war materials and means and those of their satellite countries, if they still do not dismantle all their military bases in South Viet Nam, if the traitors still surrender South Vietnamese people's sacred rights to independence and democracy to the U.S. imperialists and if the South Viet Nam National Front for Liberation—the only genuine representative of the 14 million South Vietnamese people— does not have its decisive voice.

3. The valiant South Vietnamese people and the South Viet Nam Liberation Army are resolved to accomplish to the full their sacred duty to drive out the U.S. imperialists so as to liberate South Viet Nam and defend North Viet Nam.

4. The South Vietnamese people express their profound gratitude to the wholehearted support of the peace-and-justice-loving people all over the world and declare their readiness to receive all assistance including weapons and all other war materials from their friends in the five continents. . . .

The South Viet Nam National Front for Liberation has always relied mainly on its own strength and capability, but it is ready to accept all assistance both morally and materially, including weapons and all other war materials from all the socialist countries, the nationalist countries as well as all the international organizations and peace-loving people the world over. Besides, the Front reserves for itself the right to buy weapons and war material from other countries to strengthen the potential of its self-defense war. . . . If the U.S. imperialists continue to commit U.S. combat troops and those of their satellites to South Viet Nam and continue to extend the war to North Viet Nam and Laos, the South Viet Nam National Front for Liberation will call on the peoples of various countries to send youth and armymen to South Viet Nam to side with the South Vietnamese people in annihilating the common enemy.

5. To unite the whole people, to arm the whole people, continue to

march forward heroically and be resolved to fight and to defeat the U.S. aggressors and the Vietnamese traitors. . . .

In the following well-known statement, the premier of the DRVN outlined Hanoi's four basic conditions for a settlement. Like the NLF statement above, it emphasized the requirement of complete U.S. troop withdrawal and recognition of the NLF as the legitimate power in South Viet-Nam.

Pham Van Dong: Report to the DRVN National Assembly [April 8, 1965]*

. . . The unswerving policy of the DRVN Government is to respect strictly the 1954 Geneva agreements on Viet Nam and to implement correctly their basic provisions as embodied in the following points:

1—Recognition of the basic national rights of the Vietnamese people— peace, independence, sovereignty, unity, and territorial integrity. According to the Geneva agreements, the U.S. Government must withdraw from South Viet Nam U.S. troops, military personnel, and weapons of all kinds, dismantle all U.S. military bases there, and cancel its military alliance with South Viet Nam. It must end its policy of intervention and aggression in South Viet Nam. According to the Geneva agreements, the U.S. Government must stop its acts of war against North Viet Nam and completely cease all encroachments on the territory and sovereignty of the DRV.

2—Pending the peaceful reunification of Viet Nam, while Viet Nam is still temporarily divided into two zones, the military provisions of the 1954 Geneva agreements on Viet Nam must be strictly respected. The two zones must refrain from entering into any military alliance with foreign countries and there must be no foreign military bases, troops, or military personnel in their respective territory.

3—The internal affairs of South Viet Nam must be settled by the South Vietnamese people themselves in accordance with the program of the NFLSV without any foreign interference.

4—The peaceful reunification of Viet Nam is to be settled by the Vietnamese people in both zones, without any foreign interference. This stand of the DRVN Government unquestionably enjoys the approval and support of all peace and justice-loving governments and peoples in the world. The government of the DRV is of the view that the stand ex-

* *Source:* Radio Hanoi, April 13, 1965.

pounded here is the basis for the soundest political settlement of the Viet Nam problem.

If this basis is recognized, favorable conditions will be created for the peaceful settlement of the Viet Nam people, and it will be possible to consider the reconvening of an international conference along the pattern of the 1954 Geneva conference on Viet Nam.

The DRV Government declares that any approach contrary to the aforementioned stand is inappropriate; any approach tending to secure U.N. intervention in the Viet Nam situation is also inappropriate. Such approaches are basically at variance with the 1954 Geneva agreements on Viet Nam.

From 1965 to 1968, the question of the bombing of North Viet-Nam became the single most important stumbling block to negotiations. The DRVN softened its stand perceptibly, from Pham Van Dong's "four points," requiring complete U.S. troop withdrawal and recognition of the NLF prior to talks, to Foreign Minister Nguyen Duy Trinh's statements, first that there "could" be talks, and then that there "will" be talks, if the bombing ceases.

On February 8, 1967, President Lyndon B. Johnson wrote a letter to President Ho Chi Minh proposing a cessation of U.S. bombing in North Viet-Nam and a halt in further augmentation of U.S. forces in South Viet-Nam provided that infiltration of North Vietnamese troops in the south by land and sea be stopped, too. President Johnson also suggested bilateral discussions in either Moscow or Rangoon. In his forceful reply, on February 15, 1967, President Ho made no reference to the infiltration issue but reiterated a willingness to negotiate only after the United States stopped unconditionally all bombing raids. Prior withdrawal of all U.S. troops and recognition of the NLF were no longer required for the initiation of talks.

When President Johnson limited bombing unconditionally to certain areas in the north, the DRVN responded by agreeing to preliminary talks; when the United States halted all bombing, the DRVN agreed to political talks involving also the NLF and the Saigon regime.

Nguyen Duy Trinh: Interview with Australian Journalist Wilfred Burchett [January 28, 1967]*

. . . *Question:* The United States has spoken of the need for dialogue or contact between itself and the DRV. Would you comment on this statement?

Answer: The United States has made such statements, but in its deeds it has shown the utmost obduracy and perfidy and continues the escalation, stepping up and expanding the aggressive war. If it really wants talks, it must first halt unconditionally the bombing raids and all other acts of war against the DRV. It is only after the unconditional cessation of U.S. bombing and all other acts of war against the DRV that there could be talks between the DRV and the United States.

The four-point stand and the correct attitude of the DRV Government enjoy, we are sure, ever stronger approval and support from all peace-loving and justice-loving peoples and governments in the world. If the United States refuses to listen to reason, it will further unmask itself as an obdurate aggressor. The Vietnamese people are determined to fight until total victory to defend the north, liberate the south, achieve the peaceful reunification of the fatherland, and contribute to the maintenance of peace in this area and in the world. . . .

Ho Chi Minh: Letter to Lyndon B. Johnson [February 15, 1967]†

On February 10, 1967, I received your message. This is my reply.

Viet Nam is thousands of miles away from the United States. The Vietnamese people have never done any harm to the United States. But contrary to the pledges made by its representatives at the 1954 Geneva Conference, the United States Government has ceaselessly intervened in Viet Nam, it has unleashed and intensified the war of aggression in South Viet Nam with a view to prolonging the partition of Viet Nam and turning South Viet Nam into a neocolony and military base of the United States. For over two years now, the U.S. Government has with its air and naval forces carried the war to the Democratic Republic of Viet Nam, an independent and sovereign country.

The U.S. Government has committed war crimes, crimes against peace and against mankind. In South Viet Nam, half a million U.S. and satellite troops have resorted to the most inhuman weapons and the most bar-

* *Source:* VNA (Hanoi), January 28, 1967.
† *Source: New York Times,* March 22, 1967.

barous methods of warfare, such as napalm, toxic chemicals and gases, to massacre our compatriots, destroy crops and raze villages to the ground.

In North Viet Nam, thousands of U.S. aircraft have dropped hundreds of thousands of bombs, destroying towns, villages, factories, roads, bridges, dikes, dams and even churches, pagodas, hospitals, schools. In your message, you apparently deplored the sufferings and destructions in Viet Nam. May I ask you: Who has perpetrated these monstrous crimes? It is the U.S. and satellite troops. The U.S. Government is entirely responsible for the extremely serious situation in Viet Nam.

The U.S. war of aggression against the Vietnamese people constitutes a challenge to the countries of the Socialist camp, a threat to the national-independence movement and a serious danger to peace in Asia and the world.

The Vietnamese people deeply love independence, freedom and peace, but in the face of the U.S. aggression, they have risen up, united as one man. Fearless of sacrifices and hardships, they are determined to carry on their resistance until they have won genuine independence and freedom and true peace. Our just cause enjoys strong sympathy and support from the peoples of the whole world, including broad sections of the American people.

The U.S. Government has unleashed the war of aggression in Viet Nam. It must ease this aggression. That is the only way to the restoration of peace. The U.S. Government must stop definitively and unconditionally its bombing raids and all other acts of war against the Democratic Republic of Viet Nam; withdraw from South Viet Nam all U.S. satellite troops; recognize the South Viet Nam National Liberation Front; and let the Vietnamese people settle themselves their own affairs. Such is the basic content of the four-point stand of the Government of the D.R.V., which embodies the essential principles and provisions of the 1954 Geneva Agreements on Viet Nam. It is the basis of a correct political solution to the Viet Nam problem.

In your message, you suggested direct talks between the D.R.V. and the United States. If the U.S. Government really wants these talks, it must first of all stop unconditionally its bombing raids and all other acts of war against the Democratic Republic of Viet Nam. It is only after the unconditional cessation of the U.S. bombing raids and all other acts of war against the D.R.V. that the D.R.V. and the United States would enter into talks and discuss questions concerning the two sides.

The Vietnamese people will never submit to force; they will never accept talks under the threat of bombs.

Our cause is absolutely just. It is hoped that the U.S Government will act in accordance with reason.

Nguyen Duy Trinh: Speech at Hanoi Reception for Mongolian Delegation [January 2, 1968]*

. . . The U.S. imperialist gang is planning to take the Viet Nam problem to the United Nations Security Council. It must be immediately pointed out that the United Nations has no right to intervene in the Vietnamese problem and that the United Nations Security Council has no right to discuss the Viet Nam problem. Any resolution of the Security Council on the Viet Nam problem is completely worthless.

The position of the Viet Nam people is very clear. It is the four points of the DRV Government and the political program of the NFLSV. These are the bases for settling the Viet Nam problem.

The U.S. Government constantly leads public opinion to believe that it wants to talk to Hanoi but receives no reply. If the U.S. really wants to talk, then, as clearly stated in our 28 January 1967 declaration, the U.S. must first of all unconditionally end the bombing and all other acts of war against the DRV. After the U.S. unconditionally ends the bombing and all other acts of war against the DRV, the DRV will talk to the U.S. about the problems concerned.

The DRVN Government: United States Restricted Bombing of North Viet-Nam [April 3, 1968]†

. . . The Vietnamese people's struggle for independence and freedom has entered a new phase. U.S. defeat is obvious. The United States must put an end to its aggressive war against Viet Nam and must withdraw all U.S. and satellite troops from South Viet Nam so that Viet Nam's internal affairs may be solved by the Vietnamese people themselves.

The Vietnamese people's stand of peace and independence is the four points of the DRV Government and the political program of the NFLSV. It embodies the fundamental principles and main provisions of the 1954 Geneva agreements on Viet Nam and is a correct basis for a political solution of the Viet Nam issue. . . .

The DRV Government has on many occasions stated: Talks between the DRV and the United States will begin after the latter has proved

* Source: Nhan Dan (Hanoi), January 2, 1968.
† Source: Radio Hanoi, April 3, 1968.

that it has actually ended unconditionally the bombing and all other war acts against the DRV. . . .

Recently, in face of the extremely dangerous situation with no way out faced by the United States in South Viet Nam and the heavy defeat of the war of destruction against North Viet Nem, in face of the great political, social, and financial difficulties caused by the Viet Nam aggressive war, and in face of the increasingly powerful pressure of world public opinion and U.S. progressive opinion, President Johnson has had to declare a restricted bombing of North Viet Nam.

This is a defeat and at the same time a shrewd trick of the U.S. Government aimed at placating public opinion. In reality, the U.S. Government is still sending more US. troops to South Viet Nam and endeavoring to strengthen the puppet army. They are asking for more allocations to continue the Viet Nam aggressive war. In reality, the United States is still continuing to bomb an important part of the DRV territory, from the 17th to the 20th parallels, and is still refusing to end unconditionally its bombing and all other war acts against the entire DRV territory.

It is clear that the U.S. Government has not correctly and fully responded to the just demand of the DRV Government, of U.S. progressive opinion, and of world public opinion.

However, on its part, the DRV Government declares its readiness to send its representatives to make contact with U.S. representatives to decide with the U.S. side the unconditional cessation of bombing and all other war acts by the United States against the DRV so that talks could be begun.

The DRVN Government: The Level, Place, and Time of the Formal Talks between the DRVN and the United States [May 3, 1968]*

As is known, for a correct solution of the Viet Nam problem, the Vietnamese people have adopted an unswerving position, namely the four points of the Government of the Democratic Republic of Viet Nam and the Political Programme of the South Viet Nam National Front for Liberation. . . .

One month has passed since the Government of the Democratic Republic of Viet Nam issued the above-mentioned statement [of April 3, 1968]. Preliminary contacts which are to lead to talks between the two sides should have been held. But the U.S. Government has deliberately resorted to dilatory manoeuvres.

* Source: Vietnam Courier (Hanoi), No. 163 (May 6, 1968).

In the face of such a situation, the Government of the Democratic Republic of Viet Nam is of the view that formal talks between Hanoi and Washington should be held without delay. The Government of the Democratic Republic of Viet Nam has decided to appoint Minister Xuan Thuy as its representative, with a view to ascertaining with the U.S. side the unconditional cessation of the U.S. bombing raids and all other acts of war against the Democratic Republic of Viet Nam, and then discussing other problems of concern to both sides. The Government of the Democratic Republic of Viet Nam welcomes the French Government's willingness to let Paris serve as the site for talks . . . and considers that Paris, like Phnom Penh or Warsaw, is a suitable place for formal talks between the two sides. These formal talks will begin on May 10, 1968, or a few days thereafter.

The U.S. government must positively respond to the goodwill attitude of the Government of the Democratic Republic of Viet Nam, and stop all dilatory manoeuvres so that formal talks may start at an early date. . . .

The DRVN Government: Participation of the NLF and the Saigon Regime in the Peace Talks [November 4, 1968]*

. . . Under the clearsighted leadership of the South Viet Nam National Front for Liberation, our Southern compatriots have been fighting with extraordinary gallantry, inflicting heavy failures on the enemy, winning ever greater victories, especially since the general offensives and simultaneous uprisings of Spring 1968. . . .

Confronted with a desperate situation in Viet Nam and tremendous difficulties arising from the Viet Nam war, and under the pressure of world and American opinion, the U.S. Government has been forced to announce a total cessation of air, naval and artillery bombardment against the Democratic Republic of Viet Nam. . . .

After the unconditional ending of U.S. bombardment on the entire territory of the Democratic Republic of Viet Nam, the Government of the Democratic Republic of Viet Nam will discuss with the U.S. side "other problems of concern to the two sides" with a view to a political solution to the Viet Nam problem. In agreement with the Central Committee of the South Viet Nam National Front for Liberation, the Government of the Democratic Republic of Viet Nam declares its readiness to participate in a conference whose attendance will comprise representatives of the Democratic Republic of Viet Nam, the South Viet Nam

* Source: Vietnam Courier (Hanoi), No. 189 (November 4, 1969).

National Front for Liberation, the United States and the Saigon administration. The Saigon administration's attendance at the said conference does not involve recognition of that regime by the Democratic Republic of Viet Nam. . . .

The following speech, released in Washington by the South Vietnamese Embassy, represents an effort by the South Vietnamese government to dispel the impression that it wished to avoid negotiating a peace settlement with the NLF. On May 8, 1969, the NLF had submitted at Paris a ten-point peace proposal offering to enter a provisional coalition government—a "broad union of all social strata, political forces, nationalities, religious communities"—prior to holding general elections in South Viet-Nam. Here, President Thieu puts forth his own proposal for elections.

Nguyen Van Thieu: Free Elections in Viet-Nam [July 10, 1969]*

To move the negotiations forward, I feel that a major initiative is needed. To that effect, we are willing to make, as another act of goodwill, a comprehensive offer for the political settlement of this conflict.

Both sides in this struggle have said that the internal affairs of South Viet Nam should be decided by the South Vietnamese themselves, in a free and democratic fashion.

The only way for the people of South Viet Nam to exercise their right to self-determination, to participate in public affairs and to determine the future of the country is through elections in which they can genuinely express their choice, free from fear and coercion.

In this spirit, free elections can be based on the following principles:

(1) All political parties and groups, including the National Liberation Front, which is now bearing arms against us, can participate in the elections, if they renounce violence and pledge themselves to accept the results of the elections.

(2) To make sure that the elections would be conducted in all fairness, an electoral commission could be set up in which all political parties and groups, including the N.L.F., now fighting against us, could be represented.

The electoral commission will assure equal opportunities in the campaigning to all candidates.

It will also enable all political parties and groups to participate in

* Source: New York Times, July 11, 1969.

watching the polls to see that people vote absolutely freely, and in watching the counting of the ballots to see that they are honestly counted.

(3) An international body is to be established to supervise the election and to make sure that the elections are held under conditions fair to all.

(4) We are prepared to discuss with the other side the time-table and the modalities under which the elections will be held.

(5) There will be no reprisals or discrimination after the elections.

(6) The Government of Viet Nam declares that it will abide by the results of the elections whatever these results may be. We challenge the other side to declare the same. . . . There is an obvious connection between free elections, supervised withdrawal of non-South Vietnamese forces, and an end to violence and terrorism.

Today I renew the offer of private talks with the N.L.F., without preconditions. . . .

The second Indochina war was ended in Viet-Nam on January 27, 1973, with the signing in Paris of the "Agreement for the Cessation of War and the Re-establishment of Peace in Viet-Nam." Signature of the accord by North Viet-Nam, the Provisional Revolutionary Government, South Viet-Nam, and the United States ended the military stalemate that had existed since 1970. North Viet-Nam agreed to a ceasefire without obtaining assurances of a coalition government in the south in which the PRG would play an influential, if not decisive, role. The United States agreed to withdraw its forces and end its bombing of North Viet-Nam without obtaining a guarantee of the continued existence of an independent and sovereign non-Communist regime in South Viet-Nam. Both North Viet-Nam and the United States agreed that the future of South Viet-Nam should be decided as a result of a political contest among the Vietnamese.

A compromise of their conflicting objectives had been reached in October 1972, and a summary of their agreement was broadcast by the DRVN government late that month. A settlement of the war was not reached at that time, however, presumably because of objections raised by South Viet-Nam's President Nguyen Van Thieu, which the United States tried to meet by seeking modifications of the agreement. Further talks between the DRVN and the United States broke down in December, and Hanoi and Haiphong were subjected to the heaviest American bombing of the war before the talks were resumed again in January. While the United States claimed that the final document had been improved greatly over the October text, North Viet-Nam's chief negotiator, Le Duc Tho, said the two were "basically the same."

The details of the October agreement remain secret, but it is clear that a compromise between it and the final agreement was reached on such issues as the number of international ceasefire observers, a description of the Council of Reconciliation, and South Viet-Nam's sovereignty. The agreement reached in January 1973 provides for 1,160 ceasefire observers from Canada, Hungary, Indonesia, and Poland; it avoids the implication that the Council of Reconciliation, which is charged with responsibility for working out South Viet-Nam's political future, has either the potential to be a coalition government or is a body without a governmental role; and it refers both to "the sovereignty of South Viet-Nam" and to "the independence, sovereignty, unity and territorial integrity of Viet-Nam." As the United States' chief negotiator, Henry A. Kissinger, put it, the settlement "depended on the relative satisfaction and therefore the relative dissatisfaction of all the parties concerned." A summary of the October agreement is presented below. Northern and southern views on the future of Viet-Nam are provided in statements by Mr. Tho and President Nguyen Van Thieu.

North Vietnamese Statement on the Secret Negotiations with the United States [October 26, 1972]*

Following years of a glorious resistance war of our armed forces and people in both zones, the United States had to stop in October 1968 the bombardments against the Democratic Republic of Viet-Nam and accept the holding of a four-party conference on Viet-Nam in Paris. That situation opened up prospects for restoring peace in Viet Nam.

The Nixon Administration chose, however, to embark on the path of "Vietnamization of the war" and negotiation from a position of strength. As a result, the U.S. war of aggression in Viet-Nam dragged on, was intensified and expanded, and the Viet-Nam peace negotiations could not make any progress.

Over the past four years the valiant and undaunted Vietnamese people have stepped up their just struggle on the military, political and diplomatic fronts, and have recorded unprecedented victories, especially in the

* *Source:* Radio Hanoi, October 26, 1972. Printed in the *New York Times,* October 27, 1972 (full text of the final Viet-Nam peace agreement and protocols printed in the *New York Times,* January 25, 1973).

spring, thus inflicting a very important setback on the Vietnamization policy.

At the same time, the Government of the Democratic Republic of Viet-Nam has constantly shown its serious attitude and goodwill in the search for a peaceful solution to the Viet-Nam problem on a basis guaranteeing the Vietnamese people's fundamental national rights and the South Vietnamese people's right to self-determination.

In full agreement with the Provisional Revolutionary Government of the Republic of South Viet-Nam, the Government of the Democratic Republic of Viet-Nam has held private meetings with the U.S. Government with a view to a peaceful settlement of the Viet-Nam problem. But till September 1972, the negotiations on the Viet-Nam problem had remained without result.

With a view to making the negotiations progress, at the private meeting on October 8, 1972, the DRVN side took a new, extremely important initiative: It put forward a draft Agreement on Ending the War and Restoring Peace in Viet-Nam, and proposed that the Government of the Democratic Republic of Viet-Nam, with the concurrence of the Provisional Revolutionary Government of the Republic of South Viet-Nam, and the Government of the United States of America, with the concurrence of the Government of the Republic of Viet-Nam, immediately agree upon and sign this agreement to rapidly restore peace in Viet-Nam.

In that draft agreement, the DRVN side proposed a cessation of the war throughout Viet-Nam, a cease-fire in South Viet-Nam, an end to all U.S. military involvement in Viet-Nam, a total withdrawal from South Viet-Nam of troops of the United States and those of the foreign countries allied with the United States and with the Republic of Viet-Nam, and the return of all captured and detained personnel of the parties.

From the enforcement of the cease-fire to the installation of the government formed after free and democratic general elections, the two present administrations of South Viet-Nam will remain in existence with their respective domestic and external functions.

These two administrations shall immediately hold consultations with a view to the exercise of the South Vietnamese people's right to self-determination, achieving national concord, insuring the democratic liberties of the South Vietnamese people and forming an administration of national concord which shall have the task of promoting the South Vietnamese parties' implementation of the signed agreements and organizing general elections in South Viet-Nam within three months after the cease-fire comes into effect.

Thus the Viet-Nam problem will be settled in two stages in accordance with the often-expressed desire of the American side: The first stage will include a cessation of the war in Viet-Nam, a ceasefire in South Viet-Nam, a cessation of the United States military involvement in South Viet-Nam and an agreement on the principles for the exercise of the South Vietnamese people's right to self-determination; in the second stage the two South Vietnamese parties will settle together the internal matters of South Viet-Nam. The DRVN side proposed that the Democratic Republic of Viet-Nam and the United States sign this agreement by mid-October 1972.

The above initiative of the Government of the Democratic Republic of Viet-Nam brought the negotiations on the Vietnam problem, which have dragged on for four years now, onto the path to a settlement. The American side itself admitted that the draft Agreement on Ending the War and Restoring Peace in Viet-Nam put forward by the DRVN side was indeed an important and very fundamental document which opened up the way to an early settlement.

After several days of negotiations, on October 17, 1972, the Democratic Republic of Viet-Nam and the United States reached agreement on almost all problems on the basis of the draft agreement of the Democratic Republic of Viet-Nam except for two unagreed issues. With its goodwill, the DRVN side did its utmost to remove the last obstacles in accepting the American side's proposals on the two remaining questions in the agreement.

In his October 10, 1972, message to the Premier of the Democratic Republic of Viet-Nam, the President of the United States appreciated the goodwill of the Democratic Republic of Viet-Nam and confirmed that the formulation of the agreement could be considered complete. But in the same message, he raised a number of complex points. Desirous of rapidly ending the war and restoring peace in Viet-Nam, the Government of the Democratic Republic of Viet-Nam clearly explained its views on this subject. In his October 22, 1972, message, the President of the United States expressed satisfaction with the explanations given by the government of the Democratic Republic of Viet-Nam. Thus by October 22, 1972, the formulation of the agreement was complete.

The main issues of the agreement which have been agreed upon may be summarized as follows:

1. The United States respects the independence, sovereignty, unity and territorial integrity of Viet-Nam as recognized by the 1954 Geneva agreements.

2. Twenty-four hours after the signing of the agreement, a cease-fire shall be observed throughout South Viet-Nam. The United States will stop all its military activities and end the bombing and mining in North Viet-Nam.

Within 60 days there will be a total withdrawal from South Viet-Nam of troops and military personnel of the United States and those of the foreign countries allied with the United States and with the Republic of Viet-Nam. The two South Vietnamese parties shall not accept the introduction of troops, military advisers and military personnel, armaments, munitions, and war material into South Viet-Nam.

The two South Vietnamese parties shall be permitted to make periodical replacements of armaments, munitions and war material that have been worn out or damaged after the cease-fire, on the basis of piece for piece of similar characteristics and properties. The United States will not continue its military involvement or intervene in the internal affairs of South Viet-Nam.

3. The return of all captured and detained personnel of the parties shall be carried out simultaneously with the U.S. troops' withdrawal.

4. The principles for the exercise of the South Vietnamese people's right to self-determination are as follows:

The South Vietnamese people shall decide themselves the political future of South Viet-Nam through genuinely free and democratic general elections under international supervision.

The United States is not committed to any political tendency or to any personality in South Viet-Nam, and it does not seek to impose a pro-American regime in Saigon.

National reconciliation and concord will be achieved, the democratic liberties of the people insured.

An administrative structure called the National Council of National Reconciliation and Concord, of three equal segments, will be set up to promote the implementation of the signed agreements by the Provisional Revolutionary Government of the Republic of South Viet-Nam, and the Government of the Republic of Viet-Nam, and to organize the general elections the two South Vietnamese parties will consult about the formation of councils at lower levels.

The question of Vietnamese armed forces in South Viet-Nam shall be settled by the two South Vietnamese parties in a spirit of national reconciliation and concord, equality and mutual respect, without foreign interference in accordance with the postwar situation.

Among the questions to be discussed by the two South Vietnamese parties are steps to reduce the military numbers on both sides and to demobilize the troops being reduced.

The two South Vietnamese parties shall sign an agreement on the internal matters of South Viet-Nam as soon as possible and will do their utmost to accomplish this within three months after the cease-fire comes into effect.

5. The reunification of Viet-Nam shall be carried out step by step through peaceful means.

6. There will be formed a four-party joint military commission and a joint military commission of the two South Vietnamese parties.

An international commission of control and supervision shall be established. An international guarantee conference on Viet-Nam will be convened within 30 days of the signing of this agreement.

7. The Government of the Democratic Republic of Viet-Nam, the Provisional Revolutionary Government of the Republic of South Viet-Nam, the Government of the United States of America and the Government of the Republic of Viet-Nam shall strictly respect the Cambodian and Laos peoples' fundamental national rights as recognized by the 1954 Geneva agreements on Indochina and the 1962 Geneva agreements on Laos, i.e., the independence, sovereignty, unity and territorial integrity of these countries. They shall respect the neutrality of Cambodia and Laos. The Government of the Democratic Republic of Viet-Nam, the Provisional Revolutionary Government of the Republic of South Viet-Nam, the Government of the United States of America and the Government of the Republic of Viet-Nam undertake to refrain from using the territory of Cambodia and the territory of Laos to encroach on the sovereignty and security of other countries. Foreign countries shall put an end to all military activities in Laos and Cambodia, totally withdraw from and refrain from reintroducing into these two countries troops, military advisers and military personnel, armaments, munitions and war material.

The internal affairs of Cambodia and Laos shall be settled by the people of each of these countries without foreign interference.

The problems existing between the three Indochinese countries shall be settled by the Indochinese parties on the basis of respect for each other's independence, sovereignty and territorial integrity and noninterference in each other's internal affairs.

8. With the ending of the war, the restoration of peace in Viet-Nam will create conditions for establishing a new, equal and mutually beneficial relationship between the Democratic Republic of Viet-Nam and the United States. The United States will contribute to healing the wounds of war and to postwar reconstruction in the Democratic Republic of Viet-Nam and throughout Indochina.

9. This agreement shall come into force as of its signing. It will be strictly implemented by all the parties concerned.

The two parties have also agreed on a schedule for the signing of the agreement. On October 9, 1972, at the proposal of the U.S. side, it was agreed that on October 18, 1972, the United States would stop the bombing and mining in North Viet-Nam; on October 19, 1972, the two parties would initial the text of the agreement in Hanoi; on October 26, 1972, the foreign ministers of the two countries would formally sign the agreement in Paris.

On October 11, 1972, the U.S. side proposed the following change to the schedule: On October 21, 1972, the United States would stop the bombing and mining in North Viet-Nam; on October 22, 1972, the two parties would initial the text of the agreement in Hanoi; on October 30, 1972, the foreign ministers of the two countries would formally sign the agreement in Paris. The Democratic Republic of Viet-Nam agreed to the new U.S. schedule.

On October 20, 1972, under the pretext that there still remained a number of unagreed points, the U.S. side again put forth another schedule: On October 23, 1972, the United States would stop the bombing and mining in North Viet-Nam; on October 24, 1972, the two parties would initial the text of the agreement in Hanoi; on October 31, 1972, the foreign ministers of the two countries would formally sign the agreement in Paris.

Despite the fact that the U.S. side had changed many times what had been agreed upon, the DRVN side, with its goodwill, again agreed to the U.S. proposal while stressing that the U.S. side should not under any pretext change the agreed schedule.

Thus by October 22, 1972, the DRVN side and the U.S. side had agreed both on the full text of the Agreement on Ending the War and Restoring Peace in Viet-Nam and on the schedule to be observed for the formal signing of the agreement on October 31, 1972. Obviously, the two sides had agreed upon an agreement of extremely important significance, which meets the wishes of the peoples in Viet-Nam, the United States and the world.

But on October 23, 1972, contrary to its pledges, the U.S. side again referred to difficulties in Saigon, demanded that the negotiations be continued for resolving new problems and did not say anything about the implementation of its commitments under the agreed schedule. This behavior of the U.S. side has brought about a very serious situation, which threatens to jeopardize the signing of the Agreement on Ending the War and Restoring Peace in Viet-Nam.

The so-called difficulties in Saigon represent a mere pretext to delay the implementation of the U.S. commitments, because it is public knowledge that the Saigon administration has been rigged up and fostered by the United States. With a mercenary army equipped and paid by the United States, this administration is a tool for carrying out the Vietnamization policy and the neocolonialist policy of the United States in violation of the South Vietnamese people's national rights. It is an instrument for the United States to sabotage all peaceful settlement of the Viet-Nam problem.

The above shows that the Nixon Administration is not negotiating with a serious attitude and goodwill in order to end the war and restore peace in Viet-Nam. All it is doing, in fact, is to drag out the talks so as to deceive public opinion and to cover up its scheme of maintaining the Saigon puppet administration for the purposes of continued war of aggression in Viet-Nam and Indochina. The Nixon Administration must bear before the people of the United States and the world responsibility for delaying the signing of the agreement and thus prolonging the war in Viet-Nam.

The Government of the Democratic Republic of Viet-Nam deems it its duty to bring the present situation with respect to the private meetings between the Democratic Republic of Viet-Nam and the United States to the notice of our countrymen and fighters throughout the country, and peoples in the world and the United States so that the truth may be known. This information is in the interest of peace and will in no way affect the negotiations, the two parties having agreed upon the text of the agreement and the schedule for its signing.

While pointing to the above situation, the Government of the Democratic Republic of Viet-Nam strictly holds to the undertaking between the Democratic Republic of Viet-Nam and the United States to the effect that no change should be brought to the agreed text of the agreement and that the date scheduled for its signing is October 31, 1972.

The Government of the Democratic Republic of Viet-Nam strongly denounces the Nixon Administration's lack of goodwill and seriousness. It firmly demands that the United States Government respond to its goodwill, keep its commitments and sign on October 31, 1972, the agreement whose text has been agreed upon with a view to ending the war, restoring peace in Asia and the world, thus meeting the desire of the Vietnamese people, the American people and the people around the world.

Countrymen and fighters throughout the country: We want peace in independence and freedom. We are animated with goodwill, but the U.S. imperialists still nurture the design of conquering the southern part of our country, turning it into a new-type colony and a military base of the United States, and perpetrating the partition of our country. We had rather sacrifice everything rather than submit. Nothing is more precious than independence and freedom!

For the independence and freedom of our fatherland, for peace, national independence, democracy and socialism in the world, we are fighting and defeating the U.S. imperialist aggressors. Ours is a position of

victory, of initiative, which is unceasingly improving. The position of the
U.S. imperialists and their lackeys is one of defeat, passivity and decline.

More than ever, our countrymen and fighters throughout the country
are enhancing their resolve to unite as one man, to brave all hardships
and sacrifices, to do their utmost to carry out President Ho Chi Minh's
sacred testament to persist in and step up the fight on the three fronts—
military, political and diplomatic—until these lofty objectives have been
achieved, to liberate the South, to defend and build the Socialist North
and to proceed to the peaceful reunification of the country. Our people
are determined to fight shoulder to shoulder with the fraternal peoples
of Laos and Cambodia and inflict a total defeat on the U.S. imperialist
aggressors and their lackeys.

Our people's patriotic struggle against the U.S. aggression is a just
one. The strength of our unity is invincible. We have traditions of valiant
and undaunted struggle against the aggressors. Moreover, our people enjoy the sympathy and great support of the fraternal Socialist countries
and the progressive people around the world.

We will win!

The Government of the Democratic Republic of Viet-Nam calls on the
Government and peoples of the Soviet Union, China and the other fraternal Socialist countries, of the peace- and justice-loving countries, the
international organizations, the American people and the peoples around
the world which have been wholeheartedly supporting the Vietnamese
people's patriotic struggle against the U.S. aggression, to wage a resolute
struggle to urge the U.S. Government to carry out immediately what has
been agreed upon between the United States and the Democratic Republic of Viet-Nam so as to rapidly end the war and restore peace in
Viet-Nam.

The Government of the Democratic Republic of Viet-Nam calls on
all brothers and friends around the five continents to extend even stronger
support and assistance to the Vietnamese people's just struggle until total
victory.

The Vietnamese people will win!

The three peoples of Indochina will win!

Le Duc Tho: The Return of Peace to Viet-Nam [January 24, 1973]*

Dear friends, the struggle of the Vietnamese people for independence
and liberty has lasted nearly 30 years. In particular, the resistance in the

* *Source:* Statement made at a press conference in Paris, January 24, 1973;
full text of the press conference printed in the *New York Times,* January 25,
1973.

last 13 years with its many trials was the most difficult in the history of our people's struggle against foreign invasion over several centuries.

It is also the most murderous war in the history of the movement of national liberation of the oppressed peoples throughout the world.

Finally, this war has deeply stirred the conscience of mankind.

The negotiations between our Government and the Government of the United States of America for a peaceful settlement of the Vietnamese problem have lasted nearly five years and have gone through many particularly difficult and tense moments.

But we have overcome all obstacles and we have at last reached the agreement on ending the war and restoring peace in Viet-Nam.

This agreement will be officially signed in Paris in a few days.

The just cause triumphs over the evil cause. The will to live in freedom triumphs over cruelty.

The conclusion of such an agreement represents a very big victory for the Vietnamese people. It is the crowning of a valiant struggle waged in unity by the army and the people of Viet-Nam on all fronts, at the price of countless sacrifices and privations.

It is a very big victory for the fighting solidarity of the peoples of the three countries of Indochina who have always fought side by side against the common enemy for independence and liberty.

It is a very great victory for the Socialist countries, the oppressed peoples and all the peace-loving and justice-loving peoples throughout the world, including the American people, who have demonstrated their solidarity and given devoted assistance to the just struggle of our people.

The return of peace in Viet-Nam will be greeted with immense joy by our people. At the same time, it will answer the hope which has so long been harbored by the American people and the peace-loving peoples in the world.

With the return of peace, the struggle of the Vietnamese people enters a new period. Our people, lifting high the banner of peace and of national concord, is decided to strictly apply the clauses of the agreement maintaining peace, independence and democracy and heading toward the peaceful reunification of its country.

It will also have to rebuild its war-devastated country and consolidate and develop its friendly relations with all the peoples of the world, including the American people.

Heavy tasks still await us in this new period. But the Vietnamese in the North as in the South, at home as abroad, rich in their traditions of unity and perseverance in struggle, following a just policy, strengthened by the close solidarity of the peoples of Laos and Cambodia and benefiting from strong aid from the Socialist countries and all the peace-loving countries of the world, will be able to smooth out all difficulties and victoriously accomplish their tasks.

At a time when peace is dawning on our country, in the name of the Government and people of Viet-Nam we wish to address our warm thanks to the Socialist countries, to the governments of many countries and to the peoples of the entire world for the sympathy they have shown toward the just struggle of the Vietnamese people and for the active help given in all fields.

In the past years, how many fighters for peace in many countries have known repression and prison, and certainly even sacrificed their lives in the fight they carried out to support the resistance of the Vietnamese people. These noble internationalist feelings and these sublime sacrifices occupy forever a place in our hearts.

The signature of the "Agreement for the Cessation of War and the Re-establishment of Peace in Viet-Nam" is only a first victory, because the task of strictly applying the agreement is important.

Anxious to maintain peace, independence and democracy and heading toward reunification of the country, the Vietnamese people will act in a unified manner to insure the correct and serious application of the clauses of the agreement which will be signed in a few days, and at the same time it will show vigilance towards reactionaries who try to sabotage the agreement.

But we must say that the situation in our country and in the world is developing in an extremely favorable way for the cause of the Vietnamese people.

We have the conviction that the dark designs of the reactionary forces in the country and abroad to obstruct the application of the agreement, or to sabotage it, can only fail.

The Vietnamese people has, therefore, every reason to believe in the victorious accomplishment of its tasks in the new period. No reactionary force will be able to slow down the march forward of the Vietnamese people.

Nguyen Van Thieu: The Viet-Nam Peace Agreement
[January 24, 1973]*

To all my compatriots, soldiers and government cadres:
You probably remember on October 24 I talked to you . . . regarding the signing of a peace in Viet-Nam. Today my talk will deal with the

* *Source:* Radio broadcast by President Thieu in Saigon, January 24, 1973; excerpts printed in the *New York Times,* January 25, 1973.

same thing. My talk goes to all of you—to our religious, political and social leaders, to our soldiers, our police, to all the people in the villages, our civil servants and veterans.

After three months of negotiating between the United States and Hanoi, and after much bombing, we finally have results today.

Today . . . an agreement on peace for Viet-Nam has been reviewed for the last time and will be officially signed [by] all parties participating in the Paris peace talks on Viet-Nam on January 27 and a ceasefire will come into effect at 8 A.M. Saigon time on Sunday, January 28.

After 18 years of savage fighting, the Communists have been forced to stop the conflict because they cannot beat us by force or by violence.

Our people have truly destroyed the Communist troops that have come from the North and we have valiantly fought the forces that are in the South.

Viet-Nam will remain two zones and will be reunified through peaceful means. The Communists have been forced to recognize two Viet-Nams.

North Viet-Nam will respect the sovereignty and independence of South Viet-Nam. Up to now the Communists have not been successful in carrying out their plans and have been forced to recognize that in the South there is one legal government and that is the legal Government of South Viet-Nam.

There will not be a two-part government in South Viet-Nam. The Communists have failed to win their demands for neutralism in the Communist way and to overthrow the President of Viet-Nam and abolish the legal institutions of Viet-Nam.

The Communists have failed and will fail in their demand to disband the Vietnamese Army and pull down the structure of Government in Viet-Nam. They have failed and will fail to make the South Vietnamese people accept a coalition government in South Viet-Nam.

The Communists demanded that we recognize the Provisional Revolutionary Government of South Viet-Nam. But they have failed in this respect and no longer pursue this demand because they know we will never accept two governments in South Viet-Nam.

In South Viet-Nam there is only one legal government, established and elected by the people of South Viet-Nam. The Communists have been made to recognize the sovereignty of South Viet-Nam and that the South Vietnamese people will decide their own fate by elections and through negotiations with the Liberation Front.

As long as there are foreign troops in South Viet-Nam, the sovereignty and independence of South Viet-Nam cannot be respected.

All these things which the Communists have been made to respect are in the ceasefire agreement.

In regard to the participation of members of the National Liberation Front in the Government of Viet-Nam—this will be discussed and negotiated between the South Vietnamese Government and the Front.

The signing of the agreement means the beginning of peace. But it does not mean peace.

It is not that we are overly suspicious. It is because we have had plenty of experience with the Communists in this regard and we don't place too much trust in their signature.

Even if there is an agreement between the South Vietnamese Government and the National Liberation Front it remains to be seen if the Front will carry out the terms of the agreement.

If an election is agreed on by the Republic of Viet-Nam Government and the Liberation Front, it remains to be seen whether the Front will accept the result of the election.

Although I cannot guarantee there will be a true peace in Viet-Nam, I shall see to it that peace will come.

This is only the beginning of the end of the Communist aggression by force. Another phase will now come and it is going to be a political phase. This political struggle is inevitable.

The political struggle phase, although not as bloody, will be as tough and dangerous as the military struggle phase.

If South Viet-Nam still exists after 17 long years of hard struggle then South Viet-Nam will not be lost to the Communists.

As long as the 17 million people of South Viet-Nam, as long as the Government, as long as the Constitution, and as long as the people and cadres remain, then the Republic of Viet-Nam will survive.

We are determined to step into the new phase of the struggle with strength. Only in this way will we win.

SIX

*L*aos

by ROGER M. SMITH

Prior to 1945, a political entity called Laos did not exist; during the next twenty-five years attempts were made to cement a Laotian union of formerly autonomous states under a single leadership. The task of those Laotians who have had visions of a nation-state has been made difficult by strong, persisting regional loyalties to the former petty kingdoms of Luang Prabang, Vieng Chan, Xieng Khouang, and Champassac, and rivalries among leading families within these areas. To add to the difficulty, factional leaders, members of old princely and aristocratic families or ambitious army officers and businessmen, in vying for power and control of the government, often sought achievement of their goals through appeals for help to one or another foreign power. Instead of a concern for social, economic, and political development within the framework of the constitutional monarchy, which was established in 1947, most of the leaders of Laos were noted for their interest in maintaining traditional patterns and in protecting their positions and privileges as an elite group.

The attempt by France at the end of World War II to reassert its colonial rule over Laos stimulated, among some of the elite, the idea of a Lao nation, which in turn led in 1945 to the formation of the *Lao Issara* (Free Laos) movement. It did not take root among the people, probably in large part because French rule of Laos rested very lightly on the country: Traditional life in Laos, unlike in Viet-Nam, was left largely undisturbed by the French. Moreover, many of the elite, including those in the royal house of Luang Prabang and others associated with the hereditary prince of Champassac, welcomed the resumption of France's authority and were ready to work with the French toward a gradual transference of political power to Lao leadership.

When France displayed its willingness to negotiate independence and, in 1949, granted Laos autonomy within the French Union, the Lao Issara, which in 1946 had fled into exile in Thailand, dissolved itself, and most of its members returned to Vieng Chan to seek participation in the government. Among those who refused to do so was Prince Souphanouvong, cousin of King Sisavangvong and half-brother of Princes Phetsarath and Souvannaphouma, leading members of the Lao Issara. Joining with members of other anti-French resistance groups, Souphanouvong chose a revolutionary course in pursuit of complete independence, and, with assistance from the Viet Minh, he formed the *Pathet Lao* (Lao Nation) movement through which he mounted an armed resistance to continued French rule.

There was also an absence of agreement on the future of Laos among those who returned to the country in 1949. Some, especially many from Vieng Chan and Champassac, favored a close association with Thailand in order to impede continued French influence and to gain security against an expected westward expansion of the Vietnamese. Still others feared both Thailand and Viet-Nam and hoped that an independent Laos could exist as a neutral buffer state, protected by the great powers. This conflict of views continued throughout the 1950's and 1960's and, in consequence, the chances of the contending groups reaching agreement on a common program were never very great. The opportunities for achieving a consensus on Laos's future were made still more elusive by the association of the Pathet Lao with the Vietnamese who, many of the Lao elite believe, have used the movement to further their own policies aimed at expansion into and eventual takeover of Laos.

After independence was gained in 1953 and the Franco-Vietnamese war was brought to a close by the Geneva Conference in 1954, very little was heard from the Laotian elite about the future character and objectives of the Laotian state. On the contrary, the political process was almost entirely concerned with the attempts of rival leaders, including army officers, to gain ascendancy in and control of the government. A notable exception among them was Prince Souvanna-phouma, an advocate of neutrality in foreign affairs and of reconciliation among all Laotians, who became increasingly influential as a skillful and tireless mediator among his countrymen. It was Souvannaphouma, as prime minister, who negotiated the Vieng Chan agreements of 1956–1957 with the Pathet Lao, which were designed to bring them into the national fold.

Although these agreements were not fully implemented, because of conservative opposition to and fear of Pathet Lao influence and aggressiveness, Souvannaphouma was called upon in 1960 and again in 1961–1962 to work out a resolution of the differences among the contending groups in Laos. As a result of this latter effort, which was sanctioned by an agreement reached among Souvannaphouma, Souphanouvong, and Prince Boun Oum in Zurich in 1961 and endorsed by the major powers and North Viet-Nam who, in 1962 at Geneva, also lent their signatures to a guarantee of Laos's neutrality, Souvannaphouma was able to form a government of national union in which Pathet Lao and right-wing forces were balanced by neutralists of whom he was the leader. The formation of the coalition government, however, did not succeed in restoring peace to Laos. Mutual distrust and behind-the-scenes efforts by the factions to undermine each other not only prevented Souvannaphouma from executing the few agreements they had reached, but by the mid-1960's had resulted in the collapse of the coalition: The Pathet Lao group withdrew from Vieng Chan to its northeastern stronghold in Sam Neua, from where, with North Vietnamese support, they battled the Laotian government for control of the country; meanwhile, under pressure from the army, Souvannaphouma and his neutralist group gravitated toward alignment with the American-supported, right-wing forces.

By the late 1960's, the control of the war in Laos, which grew out of the long-standing rivalry between conservative forces in the Vieng Chan government and the left-wing Pathet Lao, had virtually passed out of Laotian hands. After the Geneva Conference in 1954, Lao leaders on both sides had sought foreign support and in the process had fallen under the influence and control of their patrons for whom the unity of Laos and its future political development are matters of distant concern. During the 1950's, the assistance rendered by North Viet-Nam and the United States was confined largely to political support and advice, economic aid, and military training and equipment for the Pathet Lao and the Vieng Chan government, respectively. The United States also sought a direct hand in the political fortunes of its clients and, in 1958 and 1960, helped them to undermine Souvannaphouma's efforts as prime minister to effect a reconciliation with the Pathet Lao. Both powers intervened more directly in Laos after 1963, as a consequence of the intensification of their war in Viet-Nam. American intervention was determined by the United States' interest in protecting the Mekong valley, including the Vieng Chan plain and the Thai Korat plateau, from Vietnamese expansion and in halting the flow of war materiel from North Viet-Nam through eastern Laos to South Viet-Nam. North Vietnamese actions were aimed at protecting the Laotian "Ho Chi Minh trail" and, through the Pathet Lao, extending its influence and control throughout northeastern Laos and, ultimately, gaining influence in the Vieng Chan government.

In pursuit of its ends in the 1960's and early 1970's, the United States increased its support of the Laotian army, formed a guerrilla force of Méo tribesmen to carry the fight into Pathet Lao strongholds, and launched fighter and bomber attacks on eastern Laos. As premier, Prince Souvannaphouma was reluctant to give his approval of these acts. He had little choice, however, for after mid-1964 his freedom of action was severely limited by the army. Ironically, he remained in office throughout the 1960's and early 1970's with the backing of the United States, who apparently believed that he would have the best chance of removing all forms of intervention at the conclusion of the Indochinese war. At the same time, however, by supporting the Laotian generals and, thereby, assuring its own freedom to intervene in Laos, the United States virtually doomed all of Souvannaphouma's efforts to negotiate with the Pathet Lao.

North Viet-Nam, which was reported to be employing some forty thousand troops to guard the "Ho Chin Minh trail," sought to stiffen the Pathet Lao forces, whose strength in the early 1970's was estimated at twenty-five thousand men. In addition, North Vietnamese troops themselves carried out attacks in the Plain of Jars and in the southern Bolovens plateau region, and on nearly every occasion demonstrated their ability to overrun the Mekong valley. They chose not to, however, probably because of North Viet-Nam's primary objectives in South Viet-Nam and because of the risk, in attacking, say, Vieng Chan, of stirring direct intervention by American and Thai forces in Laos and, potentially, in North Viet-Nam as well. The Vietnamese have, in effect, chosen the Pathet Lao leaders and they continue to advise and counsel them on all matters. Training has been provided for almost all of the top leadership, who have also been assisted in creating and maintaining an army, an administrative apparatus, a party, and political and mass organizations which work among the people. There seems to be no question of Pathet Lao dependence upon North Viet-Nam. As a result, the Pathet Lao leaders appear to be as limited as Souvannaphouma is in trying to compromise the differences which have divided the Lao for so long.

A major change in the positions of the United States and North Viet-Nam on Laos took place in 1972 as a consequence of the evolution of events in neighboring Viet-Nam. As the two powers approached an agreement on peace in Viet-Nam, both urged the Vieng Chan government and the Pathet Lao to seek a cease-fire and to revive the provisions of the 1961 Zurich agreement, which called for the establishment of a government of national union. Negotiations between the two sides finally resulted, on February 21, 1973, in the signing of a peace accord which left the Pathet Lao in control of about two-thirds of the country and provided that the remaining part be administered by a coalition government consisting of an equal number of representatives from the Vieng Chan government and the Pathet Lao. The neutrality of Laos was also reasserted by the agreement, and all foreign governments were called upon to withdraw their forces from the country. Implementation of this new accord, however, was delayed by right-wing elements in the Vieng Chan government who objected that it opened the way for the assumption of political paramountcy by the Pathet Lao. Concessions to their position were made in a protocol to the agreement, signed by the two sides on September 14, but right-wing fear and suspicion of the Pathet Lao have persisted.

To complicate matters still further, there are a number of other factors which work against the development of a Lao state. Laos's geography and its social and ethnic composition present formidable obstacles to those among her leaders who may have visions of nation-building. Laos is landlocked and covered by tortuous, heavily forested mountains and narrow river valleys. There are no railways, and the few roads are, for the most part, poor and many are impassable during the rainy season from June to November. The Mekong River, which forms most of the Laos-Thailand boundary, acts in some measure to bind the country together, for it is a major artery for the transport of both goods and people between the royal capital in the north, Luang Prabang, and Savannakhet in the south. But throughout much of the country, communication is hampered by the inaccessibility of villages, great linguistic diversity, vast socioeconomic differences between a tiny elite and the mass of the people, and by the persistence of a patrimonialism which encourages regional rather than national loyalties.

Among Laos's people, the politically, economically, and culturally dominant lowland Lao comprise slightly less than half the population. Most of them are settled along the Mekong River plain where they practice wet-rice cultivation. Here, too, are found the royal capital, Luang Prabang, the seat of government, Vieng Chan, and most of the country's major commercial centers. Most of the rest of the population is made up of several upland and mountain tribal groups: The *Lao Theung* (formerly called *kha,* or slave), a seminomadic people believed to be of Indonesian stock, who dwell in the upland regions of the south where they engage in slash-and-burn agriculture; the *Lao Thai,* who live higher up in the hills, mostly in the northern and northeastern parts of the country; and the *Lao Som* (including the Méo and Yao), who live on the mountain tops and whose aggressiveness and cultivation of opium poppies place them in a special position.

The difficult time that lies ahead for Laos is made all the more inevitable by this, as yet, unresolved problem of relations between the ruling plains people and the hill-dwelling political minorities. In their numbers and in the extent of territory they cover, the tribal peoples from an especially grave problem. Because of the lowland Lao attitudes toward them, they have lacked access to government services and, with the exception of a few Méos, have been prevented from participating in the government in a way which their numbers would normally dictate. One explanation offered for Lao Theung and Méo participation in the Pathet Lao movement is that it offers them hope of gaining a position of autonomy if not equality in any future Lao state. This aspiration for greater autonomy is also said to account partially for the willingness of other Méos to fight on the side of the royal government. Without doubt, these peoples will demand and expect to play a new and meaningful role in the country's affairs when the war is over. So, too, will the lowland Lao people, whose welfare in the past has not generally weighed very heavily in the concerns of the political leadership.

The kind of relationship that any future Laotian government establishes between itself and the people is a major problem that could

result in a resurgence of political rivalry and its inevitable consequence, foreign intervention. In the early 1970's, there were two, competing systems of government in Laos. The Royal Laotian Government
related to the people through administrative and technical bureauc-
racies, the military, and the American economic and technical aid
mission, which had taken on direct responsibility for the welfare of
the increasing number of refugees fleeing from the fighting toward
the Mekong River. Almost all accounts of Laos have indicated that
the typical Lao is unaware of his place in this system, although he is
linked to the government through the village headman, the government school teacher, the health official, and, sometimes, through the
abbot of the village Buddhist monastery, the local military commander,
and the National Assembly deputy from the district. In contrast is the
system offered by the Pathet Lao, which modifies the traditional structure by adding a series of committees extending from the villages up
through a Central Committee located in Sam Neua. The key element
in the contest between the Vieng Chan government and the Pathet
Lao has been the link between villager and government—the village
headman and other local officials—and it was against this link that
the Pathet Lao was directing its attack, seeking either to eliminate
him physically, force him to leave the village, or bring about his re-
orientation to serve as a link for the rebel government. Although hardly
mentioned in contemporary accounts of the situation in Laos, these
links had in the late 1960's and early 1970's begun to spend even more
time in urban centers than they had traditionally. This, as well as the
violence directed against these persons by the rebels, was a sure sign
that an opposing elite, the Pathet Lao, had begun to exert its influence.[1]

I. The Past

The major problem confronting Laos today is, as it has been during the past twenty-five years, the absence of national unity and political stability. The persistence of this problem has been due in part

[1] For further details, see T. H. Stanton, *Conflict in Laos: The Village Point
of View,* Southeast Asia Development Advisory Group Paper, No. 21 (New
York), June 15, 1967.

to the existence of conflicting international interests—American, Chinese, French, North and South Vietnamese, Russian and Thai—in Indochina; the clash among them in Laos emphasizes that the kingdom has existed as a unified and stable state only when a condition of relative stability has prevailed among neighboring states, making the existence of a buffer state desirable. Tenacious regional concerns and petty rifts among rival leaders in Laos have been equally important, however, in impeding the development of a national consciousness, and in driving the rivals to seek outside support of their struggles for power.

On three occasions during the 1950's and 1960's, the political leaders of Laos have sought and reached agreement on the issues which have divided them. The following documents—the declaration of the Laotian government on the 1954 Geneva accord, the Vieng Chan agreements of 1956–1957, and the Zurich agreement of 1961—are the products of these efforts. None of these agreements was fully implemented, either because the leaders' mutual suspicions and ambitions overshadowed their concern for the country's welfare, or because their decisions were undermined by forces acting from without. Nevertheless, the documents do illustrate the means which the Laotian leaders felt were necessary to effect national reconciliation and to establish a national government.

Declarations by the Royal Government of Laos on the Final Declaration of the Geneva Conference on Indochina [July 21, 1954]*

The Royal Government of Laos.

In the desire to ensure harmony and agreement among the peoples of the Kingdom.

Declares itself resolved to take the necessary measures to integrate all citizens, without discrimination, into the national community and to guarantee them the enjoyment of the rights and freedoms for which the Constitution of the Kingdom provides;

Affirms that all Laotian citizens may freely participate as electors or candidates in general elections by secret ballot;

* *Source:* Documents No. 7 and No. 9, dated July 21, 1954, in *Further Documents relating to the discussion of Indo-China at the Geneva Conference, June 16–July 21, 1954* (London: H.M. Stationery Office, 1954), Cmd. 9239, Misc. No. 20, pp. 41–42.

Announces, furthermore, that it will promulgate measures to provide for special representation in the Royal Administration of the provinces of Phong Saly and Sam Neua during the interval between the cessation of hostilities and the general elections of the interests of Laotian nationals who did not support the Royal forces during hostilities.

. . . The Royal Government of Laos is resolved never to pursue a policy of aggression and will never permit the territory of Laos to be used in furtherance of such a policy.

The Royal Government of Laos will never join in any agreement with other States if this agreement includes the obligation for the Royal Government of Laos to participate in a military alliance not in conformity with the principles of the Charter of the United Nations or with the principles of the agreement on the cessation of hostilities or, unless its security is threatened, the obligation to establish bases on Laotian territory for military forces of foreign Powers.

The Royal Government of Laos is resolved to settle its international disputes by peaceful means so that international peace and security and justice are not endangered.

During the period between the cessation of hostilities in Viet Nam and the final settlement of that country's political problems, the Royal Government of Laos will not request foreign aid, whether in war material, in personnel or in instructors, except for the purpose of its effective territorial defence and to the extent defined by the agreement on the cessation of hostilities.

The Vieng Chan Agreements of 1956–1957

Joint Declaration of the Royal Laotian Delegation and the Pathet Lao Forces Delegation [August 5, 1956]*

. . . After the study of the internal and external situation, the two Parties have by common consent recognised that there exists, since sometime, a lessening of tension in the world as well as within the Kingdom.

Considering these internal and external situations, the two Parties are agreed to adopt the foreign policy repeatedly stated by His Royal Highness the Crown Prince and His Highness the Prime Minister Souvanna Phouma and according to which the Royal Government is resolved to follow the path of Peace and Neutrality; to sincerely apply Pandit Nehru's

* *Source:* Annexure 7 in *Third Interim Report of the International Commission for Supervision and Control in Laos, July 1, 1955–May 16, 1957* (London: H.M. Stationery Office, 1957), Cmnd. 314, Laos No. 1, pp. 54–56.

5 principles of peaceful coexistence; to keep good relations with all countries, in particular, with neighbouring countries; to desist from adhering to any military alliance; [and] to allow no country to establish military bases on the Lao territory apart from those foreseen in the Geneva Agreement.

Such a policy is in conformity with the interests of the entire Lao People.

In order to create a good atmosphere for the negotiations and favourable conditions for the integration of all Lao citizens in the National Community, the two Parties have acknowledged the necessity of proceeding with the cessation of all hostile acts in the two provinces of Sam Neua and Phong Saly.[2] Pending the complete settlement of all the questions concerning the two Parties, the troops of each side must respectively remain in their present position. They must not undertake any provocative or encroaching activities; they must not increase their strength in the two provinces in men as well as in armament.

The Royal Government Delegation assure the "Pathet Lao" Forces Delegation that the Royal Government will once again make an official declaration to be widely publicised among the population, on the following points:

The Government guarantees to all Lao citizens the democratic rights and freedom such as freedom of speech, press, publication, movement, association. . . .;

The Government declares itself in favour of recognising the voting and eligibility rights of all Lao citizens of both sexes;

The Government has abolished all requisitions, servitudes, "kouang lam" system, used under the colonialist regime, thus enabling each citizen to live by his own labour and the wealth of the Nation in conditions of respect of the Laws in force in the Kingdom.

The two Parties agree that all the political organisations of the "Pathet Lao" such as the front (Neo Lao Haksat), the youth, women, peasants and other organisations can undertake their activities in the legal forms as the other political parties; that there be a guarantee of the civic rights for the "Pathet Lao" and former participants of the resistance without discrimination; that the "Pathet Lao" cadres and those of the former participants of the resistance be able to take part in the administrative and technical functions at all levels according to their qualifications and after arrangement between the two Parties.

[2] The agreements reached at Geneva in 1954 between France and the Viet Minh had provided that Sam Neua and Phong Saly were to serve as regroupment areas for Pathet Lao forces; thereafter, the administration of these provinces was controlled by the Pathet Lao.

Regarding the elections and the formation of a National Union Government, the question is still under study.

As for the peaceful settlement of the question of the two provinces, the two Parties have reached an agreement on the principle of placing the administration of the two provinces under the higher authority of the Royal Government and reorganising its system identically with that of the other provinces of the Kingdom; [and] the "Pathet Lao" troops under the High Command of the Royal Government and organising them identically with those of the Royal Army.

The other details are under study.

The two Parties agree to set up a Joint Political Commission and a Joint Military Commission entrusted with the study and the settlement of the pending questions to seek the means to implement the agreements already reached. In case of need, His Highness the Prime Minister and His Highness Prince Souphanouvong will meet to endeavour in settling the questions under dispute.

The two Parties are in agreement in taking note that the negotiations have achieved happy results. The latter enabled such an understanding between the two Parties that there is already a unanimity of opinion on several points. That is an important victory of the will for Peace, Unity and Independence of the Lao People, of the Royal Government and of the "Pathet Lao" Forces. . . .

Joint and Final Declaration of the Delegation of the Royal Government of Laos and the Delegation of the Pathet Lao Forces [August 10, 1956]*

Following the signature of the Joint Declaration of August 5, 1956, the Delegation of the Royal Government and the Delegation of the Pathet Lao Forces have further agreed to the following points:

(1) To organise complementary elections throughout the Kingdom by free and secret ballot as it obtains unto this day and with a view to increasing the number of deputies in a manner that the number would be in harmony with that of the electors in conformity with the Draft Electoral Law filed in the Office of the National Assembly by the Royal Government.

(2) Setting up of a National Union Government with the participation of the Representatives of the Pathet Lao Forces.

It has, moreover, been decided that the Mixed Political and Military Commissions are to meet at the earliest in order to lay down the modali-

* *Source:* Annexure 8, in *ibid.,* pp. 56–57.

ties for the implementation of the accords in principle as per the Joint
Declaration of August 5, 1956, and the present Declaration. . . .

*Agreement on the Measures to Be Taken for Implementation of the
Cessation of Hostile Acts* [October 31, 1956]*

. . . Art. 1. (A) The High Command of the Royal Armed Forces and
the High Command of the Fighting Units of Pathet Lao shall issue to all
the units placed under their command a joint order prescribing the correct and strict implementation of the August 5, 1956, Joint Declaration
relating to the cessation of hostilities.

The terms of this joint order shall be as follows:

The troops of both Parties shall remain *in situ* in conformity with the
Joint Declaration of August 5, 1956, cease all attacks and all acts of
provocation which could lead to a resumption of hostilities or disputes;

cease all acts of infiltration, encroachments, all disputes over territory,
all attempts at occupying new positions. Forbid all reinforcements in men,
armament and various equipment to all posts and garrisons of both
Parties;

cease all provocations, all insults, all vilifying propaganda against one
or the other Party.

(B) The joint order envisaged above must be drawn up within a time-
limit of three days after the signature of this Agreement.

Art. 2. (A) After the signature of this Agreement, two Joint Military Teams shall be created, one for the Province of Phong Saly and one
for the Province of Sam Neua.

(B) Each Joint Military Team shall include representation and personnel from each Party. . . .

(C) Each Joint Military Team shall have at its disposal a signal group
consisting of five persons and a trans-receiver set. The personnel and
equipment of the signal groups shall be provided by the Royal Armed
Forces, so that the Joint Military Team utilises them jointly for liaison
with the Joint Military Commission.

(D) The Joint Military Teams shall be mobile teams depending on the
Joint Military Commission which has its seat in Vientiane.

Art. 3. The Joint Military Teams shall have the following powers
and duties:

(A) Propagate the Joint Declaration of August 5 and 10, 1956, as well
as the Joint Order regarding the cessation of hostilities to the units of the
two Parties who are facing each other, in order that they satisfactorily

* *Source:* Annexure 10, in *ibid.,* pp. 57–59.

understand its terms and create between them a spirit of mutual understanding and of national unity.

(B) Prevent all resumption of hostile acts and settle all incidents in case incidents should occur.

(C) Receive the orders from the Joint Military Commission in order to execute them. Report on the results obtained and submit the measures to be adopted in the event of hostile acts occurring so that the Joint Military Commission examines and takes a decision.

(D) Each Party must assume the security and maintenance of the Joint Military Teams operating in its zone, safeguard the honour and prestige of delegates of the other Party and give to the Joint Military Teams all facilities for the accomplishment of their mission. The High Command of the Royal Armed Forces shall, as far as possible, place at the disposal of the Joint Military Teams the necessary transport.

Art. 4. In case of violation of the present Agreement, the disciplinary sanctions taken against the defaulters by the Party concerned shall be notified to the other Party. . . .

Agreement of the Joint Political Committee on the Question of Peace and Neutrality [November 2, 1956]*

The Joint Political Commission, consisting of the Political Delegation of the Royal Government and the Political Delegation of the Pathet Lao Forces . . . met at Vientiane from September 25, 1956, to seek appropriate measures for implementation of the principles agreed upon by His Highness Prince Souvanna Phouma, Prime Minister of the Royal Government and His Highness Prince Souphanouvong, Representative of the Pathet Lao Forces on August 5 and 10, 1956.

. . . The two Parties acknowledge that following the signature of the two Joint Declarations of August 5 and 10, 1956, our country sent a Royal Laotian Government's Delegation on a courtesy visit to the People's Republic of China and to the Democratic Republic of Vietnam and achievement of a policy of peace and neutrality is of great importance and is closely connected with the destiny of our fatherland. The two Parties unanimously acknowledge that it is necessary to promote further the achievement of the policy of peace and neutrality so that it actively progresses in all the spheres, with all the countries of the world, without any distinction of the different political regimes, in particular with neighbouring countries, and have agreed upon the following measures of implementation:

* *Source:* Annexure 11, in *ibid.*, pp. 60–61.

(1) Foster friendly relations and establish diplomatic relations in accordance with the five principles of peaceful co-existence with all countries so as to guarantee the policy of peace and neutrality resolutely followed by our country.

In so far as it particularly concerns the immediate neighbouring countries who have already proposed to establish diplomatic relations with our country, we shall commence doing it right now and shall strive to achieve it as early as possible.

Besides, if other countries would wish to maintain good relations with our country, the latter would be glad to accept them also.

(2) Pending the establishment of diplomatic relations with the above-mentioned countries, steps shall be taken for mutual recognition, economic and cultural exchanges with the said countries, sending of delegations to make courtesy visits to those countries and at the same time welcome their delegations which will come to visit our country.

(3) At a time when we do not have as yet the possibilities of sending our ambassadors to the afore-mentioned countries, we shall nevertheless accept that those countries set up their embassies in our country.

(4) In order to improve the standard of living of our people and lay the foundation for an independent economy and culture for our country, we shall endeavour, right from 1957, to get the assistance of all countries which would have the goodwill to help unconditionally our country, that is to say, on an equal footing in conditions of respect of the sovereignty of our country, without any political or economic string and without any control or supervision on the use of that aid.

(5) Our country is resolved not to adhere to any military alliance and not to permit any country to set up their military bases on Laotian territory, apart from those envisaged in the Geneva Agreement. At the same time, our country shall resolutely resist any interference whatever in the internal affairs of our country, so as to safeguard the national sovereignty and the independence.

(6) The present agreement will enter into force with effect from the date of its signature. After the signature of this agreement the two Parties must diffuse it among the people through all the means of propaganda which they have at their disposal. . . .

Agreement on the Measures for the Guarantee of Civic Rights
[December 24, 1956]*

. . . The two Parties unanimously acknowledge that the members of the Pathet Lao, the persons connected with the Pathet Lao Forces and the ex-participants of the resistance throughout the country have contributed largely to the fight for national independence, that consequently the guarantee for civic right, non-discrimination and non-reprisal vis-à-vis the members of the Pathet Lao Forces, persons connected with the Pathet Lao Forces and ex-participants of the resistance all over the country, without any distinction as to their being civilians, military personnel or cadres of this service or that rank are quite in conformity with the spirit and reason, since they will contribute to the national reconciliation and the unification of the fatherland in conformity with the aspirations of the entire people.

Starting from this spirit of sincere co-operation, the two Parties are unanimously in agreement to lay down as follows the measures for the implementation of the principles enunciated above:

(1) The United National Front called "Neo Lao Haksat" and the organisations of youth, women, peasants and others which constitute the political bodies of the Pathet Lao Forces and ex-participants of the resistance shall have the right to exercise their legal activities throughout the country like the other political parties, as it is stated in the Joint Declaration of August 5, 1956, by fulfilling the necessary formalities prescribed by the Law of the Kingdom with regard to political parties.

The Royal Government shall give the assurance that it will grant all facilities to the Neo Lao Haksat and to the said organisations for fulfilling all the formalities according to the regulations, for setting up their offices and branches, for publishing their newspapers, and for acquiring the legal capacity as it is stipulated in Article 8 of the Law No. 48 of January 13, 1950, relating to associations.

(2) The Royal Government shall guarantee fully to all members of the Pathet Lao Forces, persons connected with the Pathet Lao Forces, and to the ex-participants of the Resistance throughout the country the

* *Source:* Annexure 12, "Agreement between the Political Delegation of the Royal Government and the Political Delegation of the Pathet Lao Forces relating to the measures for the guarantee of civic rights, of non-discrimination and of non-reprisal for the members of the Pathet Lao Forces and ex-participants of the resistance throughout the country and the measures for the integration of the Pathet Lao cadres and ex-participants of the resistance in the administrative and technical services of the Kingdom at all levels," in *ibid.*, pp. 62–66.

use and exercise of all the rights which the Laotian citizens possess with regard to democratic freedoms such as individual freedom, freedom to speak, write and publish, freedom of movement, freedom of association and meetings, freedom of belief and electoral freedoms, envisaged in the Constitution of the Kingdom and in the Joint Declaration of August 5, 1956.

(3) The members of the Pathet Lao Forces, the persons connected with the Pathet Lao Forces and the ex-participants of the resistance throughout the country shall enjoy all the equal civic rights in the national community in the political as well as economic and legal aspects. All activities of discrimination, division and reprisals between Laotian citizens, without any distinction as to their being members of the Pathet Lao Forces, or persons connected with the Pathet Lao Forces, or ex-participants of the resistance throughout the country, shall be formally prohibited.

(4) In future, it shall be forbidden, under any pretext to indict before the Tribunal or before any body for administrative discipline about activities or assaults connected with the military, political or administrative activity indulged in from March 9, 1945, to this day, by any civilian or military person belonging to the Royal Government or any civilian or military person, member of the Pathet Lao Forces or connected with the Pathet Lao Forces or ex-participants of the resistance throughout the country, to the exception of offences of common law.

(5) All acts assuming a character of discrimination, reprisal or prohibition opposed to the members of the Pathet Lao Forces, persons connected with the Pathet Lao Forces and ex-participants of the resistance throughout the country, in the free exercise of democratic freedoms and their civic rights, as stipulated in points 2 and 3 above and all prosecution, arrest, slander relating to the subject matter embodied in point (4) above, shall be considered as violations of the present agreement and suits shall be filed before the Tribunal as acts of national division, acts of sabotage of the unity of the fatherland and as infringements of democratic freedoms and civic rights of the people.

If the afore-mentioned acts entail material damages, the culprits shall be liable, besides the penalties of imprisonment and fines, for the restitution and damages in conformity with the civil code in force in the Kingdom.

If the acts in question are directed against any person or involves [sic] human life, the culprits shall be tried according to the penal code in force in the Kingdom.

(6) The Royal side shall give the assurance that it will take into consideration the clauses of the present agreement to make of it a law for

the guarantee of democratic freedoms for the people, for non-discrimination and non-reprisals against the members of the Pathet Lao Forces, persons connected with the Pathet Lao Forces and ex-participants of the resistance throughout the country.

(7) The Pathet Lao cadres and ex-participants of the resistance shall be integrated in the administration and the various technical services of the Kingdom at all levels, without discrimination and on an equal footing, in all the spheres together with the officials at the various levels of the administrative and technical services in the Kingdom.

As regards the administrative cadres and the cadres and personnel of various technical services, at different levels formed by the Pathet Lao Forces, the Royal Government will consider their period of service in the ranks of the resistance as periods of service in the Royal administration, and will endeavour to integrate them with the functions, ranks and specialisations which the Pathet Lao Forces have entrusted them with, so that they be able to enjoy in all the spheres the same rights as the officials of the Royal Government of the same rank, except in certain individual cases where it might not be possible to integrate them in the said ranks and functions, and in which case the Royal Government will integrate them in other services with equivalent ranks and functions.

As regards the Pathet Lao cadres who were formerly functionaries or mandarins (officials) of the Royal Government, their period of service in the ranks of the resistance shall be taken into account as being the period of service in the Royal administration; they will benefit of promotions in the minimum time; and if by their merit in the resistance they have benefited of a promotion to a higher rank, or if they had to change their branch or specialisation, the maximum efforts shall be made so that they preserve the rank and function which they occupy at the moment. In certain individual cases where it would not be possible to maintain for them that rank and that function, they shall have an equivalent rank and function.

(8) The diplomas (Brevets) and certificates delivered by the Pathet Lao Forces shall be considered as equivalent to the diplomas and certificates corresponding to those of the Royal Government. With regard to distinctions, decorations and medals conferred by the Pathet Lao Forces, these can be preserved at home, throughout the Kingdom, so as to constitute a souvenir and a proof of merit towards the fatherland for those who hold them.

(9) The Delegation of the Pathet Lao Forces will send to the Joint Political Commission the list and curriculum vitae of the cadres of the Pathet Lao and ex-participants of the resistance throughout the country who shall be integrated in the administration and various technical ser-

vices at all echelons, so as to facilitate the scrutiny for postings or appointments of these cadres individually.

(10) In order to facilitate the return to Vientiane and in the various provinces of the cadres of the Pathet Lao and ex-participants of the resistance all over the country, the Royal Government will take upon itself to help them in the field of supplies, security and transport in the course of their journey in a suitable manner according to their functions and ranks.

(11) A Joint Administrative Sub-committee, consisting of two representatives of each Party and depending on the Joint Political Commission, shall be created with the task of classifying the functions, ranks and specialisations for the cadres of the Pathet Lao and ex-participants of the resistance who have to be integrated in the administration and technical services at all echelons and to propose them for the decision of the Joint Political Commission. The Royal Government will base itself on the decisions of the Joint Political Commission with regard to the functions, ranks and specialisations of cadres of the Pathet Lao and ex-participants of the resistance to adopt decrees for the corresponding postings. This Sub-committee shall be wound up after the successful completion of its duties.

(12) The present agreement will enter into force with effect from the date of its signature. The two Parties undertake the obligation of giving it wide publicity through all the means of propaganda of which they dispose so as to make it known to the entire people and to issue orders to the agents, competent and responsible for all the ranks and services so that they implement rigorously, each in his sphere, the present agreement. At the same time, Joint Political teams shall be created with the task of going on the spot to publicise and make the people understand thoroughly all the signed agreements so as to maintain and further strengthen day by day the spirit of national reconciliation. . . .

Joint Communiqué of Prince Souvannaphouma and Prince Souphanouvong [December 28, 1956]*

His Highness Prince Souvanna Phouma, Prime Minister of the Royal Laotian Government and His Highness Prince Souphanouvong, Representative of the Pathet Lao Forces, have, since November 7, 1956, been exchanging views on the implementation of the Joint Declarations of August 5 and 10, 1956, which have fixed the main principles related to

* *Source:* Annexure 13, in *ibid.,* pp. 66–67.

the final settlement of the Laotian problem in conformity with the Geneva Agreement.

. . . The two Princes are agreed on the necessity of wide publication and a sincere implementation of the agreements on details which have been signed in order to answer to the expectations of the whole people.

Regarding the pending matters and in particular
—the guarantee of the democratic freedoms of the people,
—the general supplementary elections,
—the settlement of the question of the administration in the two provinces, [and]
—the settlement of the military problem,
the two Princes are agreed to note that the two Delegations to the Joint Political Committee and to the Joint Military Committee have discussed these matters in detail and that the views of the two Delegations are very close to each other; the two Princes are, therefore, agreed on the necessity for the two Delegations to increase their efforts in order to reach a conclusion as early as possible.

On the question of general supplementary elections, the two Princes are agreed that the Electoral Law which will soon be worked out by the National Assembly should guarantee to all citizens of both sexes the right to elect and be elected in conformity with the principles of equal, direct, free and secret ballot and include measures for the guarantee of justice and the impossibility of frauds, in conformity with the spirit of the Constitution of the Kingdom.

In order to enable the co-operation between the two Parties to achieve National unity and facilitate the settlement of the pending questions, the two Princes are agreed on the expansion of the present Government before the holding of the general supplementary elections. The coalition government, to which the Pathet Lao Forces will be adequately represented, will thus constitute a symbol of the national reconciliation on the bases of a proper policy aiming at building up a pacific, democratic, united, independent and prosperous Laos. The coalition government will have to receive the confidence of the National Assembly in accordance with the Constitution.

Once the coalition government is formed, the Pathet Lao Forces will function as a political organisation named "Neo Lao Haksat" which will undertake its activities according to law like all other political parties.

On the question of the two provinces, the two Princes are agreed that immediately after the formation of the coalition government, the administration as well as the fighting units in the two provinces of Phong Saly and Sam Neua, be placed under the authority of the coalition government and reorganised according to the normal pattern in the Kingdom.

As to the details for the concrete implementation they will be entrusted by the coalition government to Joint Political and Military Committees which will reach agreement in conformity with the spirit of the Joint Declarations of August 5 and 10, 1956, to hasten the settlement in a reasonable manner satisfying the two Parties and in compliance with the aspirations of the whole people.

Finally, the two Princes are agreed to meet again as soon as necessary. . . .

Joint Communiqué of Prince Souvannaphouma and Prince Souphanouvong [November 2, 1957]*

In the higher interest of the nation, in order to comply with the deep aspirations of the people, for the peace and for the general reconciliation between all the Laotians, in conformity with the recommendations of the Geneva Agreement and in implementation of the joint declarations of 5 and 10 August 1956, the joint communique of 28 December 1956 and various agreements reached. . . .

The Prime Minister of the Royal Government and the Representative of the Fighting Units of the Pathet Lao agree on the formation, by enlarging the present Cabinet, of a Government of a large National Union comprising previous members of Pathet Lao. The presentation of the new Government will be preceded by the official handing over to the Royal Government of the Provinces of Phongsaly and Sam Neua and the Fighting Units of the Pathet Lao.

As regards the political programme of the new Government of National Union, the Prime Minister of the Royal Government and the Representatives of the Fighting Units of the Pathet Lao agree to adopt the policy of the present Government as contained in the speech made by H.H. Prince Souvana Phouma on [8]th August 1957.[3]

---

* Source: Annexure 14, "Joint Communique," in Fourth Interim Report of the International Commission for Supervision and Control in Laos, May 17, 1957–May 31, 1958 (London: H.M. Stationery Office, 1958), Cmnd. 541, Laos No. 1, pp. 57–58.

[3] The unification and reconciliation of all Laotians by the implementation of all agreements with the Pathet Lao; the building of an independent national economy by increasing production, by exploiting resources more efficiently, and by the acceptance of unconditional foreign aid; and the improvement and expansion of the Laos's foreign relations, especially with Laos's neighbors, were the main objectives set forth by Prince Souvannaphouma in his investiture speech made to the National Assembly on August 8, 1957. For the complete text of his speech, see ibid., pp. 37–51.

The Prime Minister of the Royal Government and the Representative of the Fighting Units of the Pathet Lao agree to admit the Neo Lao Haksat as a political party which will enjoy the same rights and which will be subject to the same obligations as the other political parties legally formed in the Kingdom, as soon as the formalities of its creation are completed in conformity with the laws and regulations in force.

The Prime Minister of the Royal Government and the Representative of the Fighting Units of the Pathet Lao agree to re-establish effectively the Royal administration in the provinces of Phongsaly and Sam Neua and to integrate the officials and the combatants of the Fighting Units of the Pathet Lao in conformity with the modalities to be determined by the political and military committees; this integration will entail the de facto and de jure disappearance of the Fighting Units of the Pathet Lao.

Regarding the combatants of the Fighting Units of the Pathet Lao, The Royal Government undertakes to integrate them all in the National Army. Within the limits of the budget provisions, those who wish to continue their services in the Army will enroll themselves in the active service of the National Army, in accordance with the conditions determined by the regulations in force. Those who would wish to leave the service in order to return to their homes will be integrated in the reserves of the National Army. The Royal Government agrees to provide them, as well as their families, with necessary means of transport so that they would return to their villages, as well as all facilities in order to enable them to earn their livelihood.

The Representative of the Fighting Units of the Pathet Lao agrees to hand over to the Royal Government the totality of the war equipment, more particularly the arms and ammunition held by the Fighting Units of the Pathet Lao.

Regarding the civil employees of the Fighting Units of the Pathet Lao who fulfil the conditions required by the rules pertaining to Public Service, the Royal Government agrees to appoint them to suitable posts in the various administrative and technical services of the Kingdom according to the modalities of implementation which will be determined by the Political Committee.

The Prime Minister of the Royal Government and the Representative of the Fighting Units of the Pathet Lao admit by common consent that the agreement on the cessation of hostile acts signed on 31 October 1956 no longer fulfils the needs of the changed situation. The present situation demands that the cessation of hostile acts be more effective. With this aim, the Military Committee will determine urgent measures aiming to realise immediately the absolute cease-fire and will increase the number and the means of the mobile sub-committees.

The Prime Minister of the Royal Government and the Representative of the Fighting Units of the Pathet Lao recognise that the difficulties of implementation still exist and the general reconciliation yet remains a complex task. As there is complete agreement on principles they consider that the time has come to settle in every small detail through settlement under negotiation the practical methods of implementation. Substantial progress has been already made by the political and military committees since the recent resumption of talks. The agreement at present under discussion deals more specially with the steps of a practical nature to be adopted for the de facto re-establishment of the royal administration in the provinces of Phongsaly and Sam Neua and for the integration of the officials and combatants of the Fighting Units of the Pathet Lao. These texts will bring the talks to an end. The Prime Minister of the Royal Government and the Representative of the Fighting Units of the Pathet Lao recommend therefore to the two committees to continue actively and resolutely their task and expect from them that the settlement under negotiation be terminated in the earliest possible time.

The Prime Minister of the Royal Government and the Representative of the Fighting Units of the Pathet Lao are satisfied with the results of their present talks which seem to augur the complete and early success of the general reconciliation.

The Prime Minister of the Royal Government and the Representative of the Fighting Units of the Pathet Lao are firmly confident of the goodwill, sincerity and the efforts of the two Parties and hope that the talks will end very soon in final agreements. . . .

Agreement on the Re-establishment of the Royal Administration in the Provinces of Sam Neua and Phongsaly [November 2, 1957]*

. . . The Political Delegation of the Royal Government and the Political Delegation of the Fighting Units of the Pathet Lao . . . affirm that the formation of a Government of National Union, the settlement of the administrative and military problem and the integration of the members of the Fighting Units of the Pathet Lao into the National Community are to be considered as necessary phases for the reestablishment of the National Unity and constitute at the same time the implementation of the clauses of the Geneva Agreement, the Joint Declaration of 28 December

* *Source:* Annexure 15, in *ibid.,* pp. 59–62.

1956 and the previous agreements approved by the National Assembly in its session of 29 May 1957.

The two Delegations affirm, besides, that the national reconciliation constitutes the basis for peace, for the safeguard of Democracy, Independence and progress. Imbued with this idea, the two Delegations have agreed on the following:

Art. 1. From the date of publication of the Declaration of handing over of the two Provinces to the Royal Government, the two Provinces shall effectively be placed under the dependence of the Kingdom. All the laws in force in the Kingdom shall be applied there. They shall be governed by the Constitution and the laws of the Kingdom.

Art. 2. In order to show the good faith of the two Parties, the administration of the Provinces of Sam Neua and Phongsaly shall be ensured by officials of the Royal Government and former officials of the Fighting Units of the Pathet Lao in the conditions determined as under:

—The province of Sam Neua shall be headed by a Chaokhoueng of the the Royal Government; the province of Phongsaly shall be headed by a former official of the Fighting Units of the Pathet Lao.

The Chaokhoueng of Sam Neua shall be assisted by a former official of the Fighting Units of the Pathet Lao; the Chaokhoueng of Phongsaly shall be assisted by an official of the Royal Government.

—The Chaomuong, the officials of the khoueng and Muong offices as well as the officials of the other services shall be nominated, for half of the strength, among the former officials of the Fighting Units of the Pathet Lao. Their posting shall be announced by the Royal Government on the Proposals of a special commission.

The duties of chaomuong of the chief town of Sam Neua shall be ensured by a former official of the Fighting Units of the Pathet Lao. The functions of chaomuong of the chief town of Phongsaly shall be ensured by a functionary of the Royal Government.

The strength and ranks of the officials are those already fixed by the Government who is at liberty to modify them, by reduction or increase, according to the needs of the service.

Temporarily the tasseng and naibans shall continue to assure their duties till new regular elections. These shall take place within a maximum delay of three months with effect from the date of handing over of the two provinces to the Kingdom.

Art. 3. In conformity with paragraph 3 of the above article 2, the two Delegations shall appoint a Special Commission which will receive the former officials of the Fighting Units of the Pathet Lao and distribute them in the various services according to a list, to be provided by the Delegation of the Fighting Units of the Pathet Lao.

Art. 4. The officials who previously belonged to the cadres of the Kingdom, shall be reintegrated in their original cadre. If they have changed their situation the Government shall endeavour to maintain them in their new position provided that they possess the required ability.

Their services done outside the cadres of the Kingdom shall be considered by the Royal Government as effective services in respect of their rights to pension.

Their promotion shall be subjected to the rules which govern presently the amelioration and revision of the Public Service regulation.

Within the cadre of the regulations on the Public Service in the Kingdom, the officials and the agents formed by the Fighting Units of the Pathet Lao shall be as far as possible maintained in the present duties.

Art. 5. During the period of three months corresponding to the period of integration of the members of the Fighting Units of the Pathet Lao into the national community, the Government shall take into account their present situation. They shall not be transferred except for health reason or on their request.

Art. 6. Prior to their joining duty the former officials of the Fighting Units of the Pathet Lao integrated into the cadres of the Kingdom shall take an oath of fidelity to the King and the Constitution.

Art. 7. The former officials of the Fighting Units of the Pathet Lao who will not wish to be integrated in the cadres of the Kingdom and who want to return home as free citizens shall receive as well as their families aid and assistance from the Government so that they can rejoin their native village. The Government shall help them in the first instance, in finding means of existence.

Art. 8. Prior to the Government of National Union being presented to the National Assembly for a vote of investiture, the head of the Fighting Units of the Pathet Lao shall make a declaration of handing over to His Majesty the King the provinces of Phongsaly and Samneua as well as the military units and officials.

Art. 9. The Prime Minister of the Royal Government gives its accord for the functioning of the patriotic front called Neo Lao Haksat with all the rights, freedoms and responsibilities enjoyed by the other political parties formed in the territory of the Kingdom on the condition that the statutes of the Neo Lao Haksat are in conformity with the laws at present in force.

Art. 10. After the formation of the Government of National Union, the Government shall institute in each of the two provinces a commission charged with the handing over of the services to the Chaokhoueng,

Chaomuong and head of the technical services as specified in Articles 2 and 3 of this Agreement.

The handing over of the services shall be carried out on the basis of the provisions of the article 8 above.

Art. 11. After the handing over of the services, the commission shall proceed to the installation of the officials of the cadres of the Kingdom and the former officials of the Fighting Units of the Pathet Lao nominated and appointed by the Government, informing them that they shall henceforth exercise legally their duties pending the publication of the ordinance or decree sanctioning their new status.

After the installation of the officials an effective handing over of the services including all registers and records shall be done. The taking over of registers and records shall be recorded by administrative minutes.

The handing over of the services at the level of the Muong shall take place in similar conditions.

Art. 12. Movable and real estates held by the Fighting Units of the Pathet Lao shall be handed over to the Government, compensations and subventions in favour of the populations of the two provinces will be the responsibility of the Government according to the rules at present in force.

Art. 13. The transportation up to their place of origin of the persons assembled by the Fighting Units of the Pathet Lao in the provinces of Phongsaly and Sam Neua shall devolve upon the Government on proposal by an ad hoc commission.

Art. 14. The Government shall ensure the publication of this agreement in the whole of the Kingdom so that everybody, officials, policemen, soldiers, populations, be informed of the integration of all the Laotians into the national community and the return to the peace through reconciliation.

Art. 15. This agreement shall enter into force with effect from the date of its signature.

Art. 16. The Government shall prepare supplementary elections which shall take place in the whole of the Kingdom within a period of four months. . . .

Military Agreement on the Integration of the Fighting Units of the Pathet Lao Forces into the National Army [November 2, 1957]*

. . . Art. 1. The Royal Government undertakes to integrate the Fighting Units of the Pathet Lao into the National Army by taking over the entire personnel of these units and the entire equipment held by them.

* *Source:* Annexure 16, in *ibid.,* pp. 63–67.

Within the limits of the budget provisions, the combatants of the Fighting Units of the Pathet Lao who wish to continue their service in the Army shall enrol themselves in the active service of the National Army in conformity with the clauses of the present agreement. Those who wish to leave the service and return home shall be integrated into the Reserves of the National Army.

Art. 2. The combatants of the Pathet Lao Fighting Units integrated into the National Army in conformity with the clauses of the present agreement shall be treated without discrimination. They shall enjoy the same moral and material rights as their colleagues in the National Army, within the limit of the rules in force in this army.

Art. 3. (A) Taking into account the ceiling limit of the budgetary strength of the National Army in 1957 and in 1958, the strength of the combatants of the Pathet Lao Fighting Units which can be integrated into the National Army cannot be more than 1,500 (Officers—NCO's—Rank and file). The distribution of the strength which is to be integrated according to the ranks shall be worked out in conformity with the clauses of Article 9 below.

(B) The units newly formed from the Pathet Lao Fighting Units shall be organised according to the norms in force in the National Army. During the transition period, pending a perfect understanding and collaboration between the various units, the combatants of the Pathet Lao Fighting Units shall remain grouped in units created at the time of the integration. Nevertheless, transfers in the National Army can be decided by the General Staff of the Armed Forces in order to obtain more control in the matter of administration and command.

(C) The units composed of Pathet Lao Fighting Units shall be posted in the Military area of their origin, that is if these units consist of a majority belonging to that region.

(D) The cadres and the specialists of the Pathet Lao Fighting Units integrated into the National Army shall be posted in the new units formed from the Pathet Lao Fighting Units in conformity with the strength rosters of the National Army and the budgetary strength of this army. The remaining shall be integrated in the National Army as far as possible.

(E) The General Staff of the Armed Forces shall appoint a certain number of cadres and specialists who shall collaborate with the integrated cadres and specialists as soon as the operations of the integration are carried out, in order to create harmony between the units of the National Army and those of the new formation in the matter of command and administration.

Art. 4. The cadres and the troops of the Pathet Lao Fighting Units who shall not be integrated, shall be put in the position of the Reserves of the National Army, relieved from military service and sent to their homes in conformity with the clauses of the present agreement. During the releasing operation and till they reach their selected destination they shall be dependent on the National Army. They shall be in possession of an individual certificate of release, worked out on the model used in the National Army.

Art. 5. The rightful claimants of the combatants of the Pathet Lao Fighting Units who sacrificed their life shall be entitled for the assistance from the Royal Government and their widows to pensions, pensions to orphans or parents in the conditions determined by the rules in force regarding military pensions in the Kingdom. The combatants of the Pathet Lao Fighting Units disabled or wounded during the war shall be entitled to the same moral and material assistance as those disabled or wounded during the war in the National Army.

Art. 6. In order to avoid any incident, all kinds of forces of the National Army stationed in the provinces of Phongsaly and Sam Neua shall remain in their positions until the end of the period fixed by the present agreement for the completion of the operations of integration of the Fighting Units of the Pathet Lao. After this period the responsibility for guarding the frontiers and for the security in the provinces of Phongsaly and Sam Neua shall devolve, on the high authority of the Royal Government, and upon the command of the National Army. This command will be empowered to take in these two provinces as in the other provinces of the Kingdom, measures in conformity with the law and fit to ensure the defence of the territory of the Fatherland, the safeguard of the National independence, the security of the properties and the life of the population and the respect of the Royal Government's authority.

Art. 7. In order to facilitate the operations of integration and the transportation of the released personnel and their families to their selected destinations, the Fighting Units of the Pathet Lao shall assemble at the four following centres:

Province of Phongsaly . . . Ban Nam Saleng, Muong Khoua.
Province of Sam Neua . . . Sam Neua, Saleui.

Art. 8. The period for assembling and integration is fixed at 60 days with effect from the day of the formation of the Government of National Union. The operations of assembling, of normal preparation, of integration, of handing over of arms and equipment, the moves of the Fighting Units of the Pathet Lao shall be within the limit of 60 days, compulsory time limit. Serious incidents shall be settled by the Royal Government.

Art. 9. (A) After the signature of the present agreement and the formation of the Government of National Union, the Joint Military Sub-Committees shall be posted in the four regroupment centres. The International Commission will have access to these centres.

(B) 1. The handing over to the representatives of the High Command of the National Army of the list of the personnel, arms, equipment, registers, arms, depots, ammunition, tools and other means shall be carried out by the representatives of the Fighting Units of the Pathet Lao on the same day on which the official handing over of the administration of the two provinces to the Royal Government will take place.

2. In order to organise the reception of the combatants of the Fighting Units of the Pathet Lao and the movement of the released personnel, a detailed list will be supplied to the Joint Military Sub-Committees in each of the four regroupment centres, basing on the above said overall list, and taking into account the strength of the Fighting Units of the Pathet Lao to be integrated in each centre.

(C) The actual handing over of the arms and equipment will be carried out in stages, in the presence of the members of the International Commission for Supervision and Control in Laos.

(D) The released personnel will be handed over to the Joint Military Sub-Committee. They shall benefit of the means of transport and will be in possession of individual certificate of release on the model in use in the National Army. The release shall take place in stages in accordance with the delays necessary to integration operations.

(E) The military personnel of the Fighting Units of the Pathet Lao who will be integrated in the active service of the National Army will be handed over to the Joint Military Sub-Committee on presentation by the Pathet Lao Command in conformity with the strength rosters of the National Army.

The formalities of integration fulfilled, the Joint Sub-Committee will inform the Joint Military Committee which will fix the date of the ceremony of the handing over of the integrated units to the National Army. The ceremony of handing over will be held by corps and the oath taking will be held in the traditional way. After the ceremony, the movements of the integrated units will be decided by the General Staff of the National Army.

(F) Arms and equipment will be taken over by the Joint Military Sub-Committees of regroupment centres.

(G) All the integrated and released military personnel of the Fighting Units of the Pathet Lao will be dependent on the Pathet Lao from the day of signature of the present agreement to their arrival at the regroupment centres. From the day of their arrival in the regroupment centres

(Ban Nam Saleng—Muong Khoua—Sam Neua—Ban Saleui) they as well as their families will become the responsibility of the National Army until they reach their homes.

Art. 10. Priorities will be given to the old people, ladies, children, to the disabled combatants, to the wounded or sick for their transport by plane, vehicles, boats or pirogues to their place of destination.

The Royal Government and the High Command of the National Army shall take all appropriate measures so that the movements of the detachments of the Fighting Units of the Pathet Lao directed towards their homes are carried out in all security. The utilisation of the routes and the access to the quarters at the halting places put at the disposal of these detachments shall be prohibited to armed persons.

The Royal Government shall issue orders to the military and administrative authorities as well as to the National Police for the strict implementation of the present agreement so that the authorities give their help and accord facilities to the home-bound combatants of the Fighting Units of the Pathet Lao as well as to their movement and the means of earning their livelihood in conformity with the modalities implemented as regards the military men released from the National Army. The regional authorities, Khoueng and Muong shall give them all facilities and shall take appropriate steps for the reception, means of road transport so that the detachment of the released men and their families reach their homes with all facilities and in security.

Art. 11. (A) Four military sub-committees shall be formed in order to implement the agreement reached and to ensure the security and to facilitate the operations of integration. Besides, they shall ensure the transport and transfers of the military personnel and of the released Pathet Lao Fighting Units who are admitted in the Reserves as well as the transfer of their families until they reach their homes.

(B) The Joint Military Committee shall institute the teams which are deemed necessary for the help, protection and security during the travels and all facilities for the soldiers under transfer till they complete their journey.

Art. 12. The implementation of the present agreement within the time limit determined in Article 8, realises entirely in a military point of view, the settlement foreseen in the Article 14 of the Geneva Agreement on the cessation of hostilities in Laos.

Art. 13. The present agreement shall be widely published in the Kingdom of Laos.

Art. 14. The present agreement shall come into force on the date of the formation of the Government of National Union. . . .

The Zurich Agreement of 1961

The Agreement among Princes Souvannaphouma, Boun Oum, and Souphanouvong [June 22, 1961]*

As agreed between them on 18 June last, the three Princes, Souvanna Phouma, Boun Oum and Souphanouvong, being the high representatives of the three parties in Laos, met at Zurich on 19 June and thereafter to discuss the problem of achieving national concord by the formation of a Government of National Union. The three Princes discussed successively the political program of the provisional Government of National Union and its immediate tasks.

With regard to these two matters, the three Princes agreed as follows:

I. Political Program. The Kingdom of Laos is resolved to follow the path of peace and neutrality in conformity with the interests and aspirations of the Laotian people and with the Geneva Agreements of 1954, in order to build a peaceful, neutral, independent, democratic, unified and prosperous Laos. A provisional Government of National Union will be formed, which will give effect to this policy of peace and neutrality, by carrying out the following political program:

Domestic Policy:

(1) To implement the cease-fire agreement concluded between the three parties concerned in Laos and to see that peace is restored in the country.

(2) To give full effect to democratic freedoms for the benefit of the people and to abrogate all provisions contrary to such freedoms; to bring back into force the law on the democratic freedoms of citizens and the electoral law approved by the National Assembly in 1957.

(3) To preserve the unity, neutrality, independence and sovereignty of the nation.

(4) To ensure justice and peace for all citizens of the Kingdom with a view to appeasement and national concord without discrimination as to origin or political allegiance.

(5) To bring about the unification of the armed forces of the three

* *Source:* "Joint Communique of the Three Princes on the Problem of Achieving National Concord by the Formation of a Government of National Union," *International Conference on the Settlement of the Laotian Question, 1961–1962* (London: H.M. Stationery Office, 1962), Cmnd. 1828, Laos No. 1, pp. 13–14. (The international conference was held in Geneva, May 12, 1961, through July 23, 1962.)

parties in a single National Army in accordance with a program agreed between the parties.

(6) To develop agriculture, industry and crafts, to provide means of communication and transport, to promote culture and to concentrate attention on improving the standard of living of the people.

Foreign Policy:

(1) Resolutely to apply the five principles of peaceful coexistence in foreign relations, to establish friendly relations and to develop diplomatic relations with all countries, the neighboring countries first and foremost, on the basis of equality and the sovereignty of Laos.

(2) Not to join in any alliance or military coalition and not to allow the establishment of any foreign military base on Laotian territory, it being understood that a special study will be made of what is provided in the Geneva Agreements of 1954; not to allow any country to use Laotian territory for military purposes; and not to recognize the protection of any alliance or military coalition.

(3) Not to allow any foreign interference in the internal affairs of Laos in any form whatsoever; to require the withdrawal from Laos of all foreign troops and military personnel; and not to allow any foreign troops or military personnel to be introduced into Laos.

(4) To accept direct and unconditional aid from all countries that wish to help Laos build up an independent and autonomous national economy on the basis of respect for Laotian sovereignty.

(5) To respect the treaties and agreements signed in conformity with the interests of the Laotian people and of the policy of peace and neutrality of the Kingdom, in particular the Geneva Agreements of 1954, and to abrogate all treaties and agreements which are contrary to those principles.

II. Immediate Tasks. The provisional Government of National Union will carry out the following immediate tasks:

(1) Formation of a Government delegation to take part in the International Conference on the settlement of the Laotian question.

(2) Implementation of the cease-fire and restoration of peace throughout the country.

(3) Fulfilment of the undertakings entered into on behalf of Laos at the International Conference on the settlement of the Laotian question and faithful execution of the agreements concluded between the three parties concerned in Laos.

(4) Release of all political prisoners and detainees.

(5) Holding of general elections to the National Assembly for the formation of the definitive Government.

(6) During the transitional period, the administrative organs set up during the hostilities will be provisionally left in being.

As regards the formation of the Government of National Union the three Princes agreed on the following principles:

(1) The Government of National Union will include representatives of the three parties and will be provisional.

(2) It will be formed in accordance with a special procedure by direct designation and nomination by His Majesty the King, without reference to the National Assembly.

Exchanges of views on this matter will be continued between the three Princes at further meetings, in order to achieve national reconciliation as soon as possible. . . .

II. The Present

Prince Souvannaphouma has played a central role in the evolution of politics in Laos since 1951. A member of the cadet branch of the royal family, Souvannaphouma was prime minister on several occasions during the 1950's and has occupied that position continually since 1962. During much of his public life over the past two decades he has tried to effect a reconciliation among the country's contending factions, including especially the rebel Pathet Lao movement, one of whose leaders is his half-brother, Prince Souphanouvong. His efforts have not been rewarded with success, but the reasons for this have less to do with his skill and patience as a mediator than with the clash of foreign powers in Laos over which he has been unable to exert control.

For many years, Prince Souvannaphouma's view has been that "the Lao problem as a whole is *an internal problem and exclusively a national problem*" whose solution awaits the cooperation of all Laotians. His belief that foreign interference has impeded this solution is illustrated by his comments in the following documents.

Souvannaphouma: Laos, Vanguard of the Free World
   [March 1, 1960]*

If I have chosen as the subject of my talk the implementation in Laos of the Geneva Accord of July 20, 1954, it is that the difficulties . . . my

* *Source:* Speech at l'Académie Diplomatique, Paris, March 1, 1960 (full text in *France-Asie,* N.S., 18 [November–December 1960], 164:1427–1434).

country has known for more than five years stem from its clauses. For the peace hastily concluded on the banks of Lake Leman has not arrested the spilling of blood. Unfortunately, my country occupies a strategic position in Southeast Asia. It appears first and essentially as a passageway in tormented relief giving access from the North to the South, East and West. Burma, Thailand, Cambodia . . . have their entrées. The Republic of Viet-Nam itself, in contact with its neighbor in the North by a very narrow band of territory, is protected on its flank by this bastion. Such a key position is, naturally, an important stake and certain of our neighbors have tried for a number of years to lay their hands on it.

In the pursuit of this end they have found auxiliaries in the midst of the Laotian people. The fact that these agents constitute only a weak minority should not conceal the danger they represent. Members today of the Neo Lao Haksat . . . they were once participants in the nationalist and anti-colonialist Lao Issara Movement, which was born in 1945 and lasted until 1949. The Viet Minh-Pathet Lao collusion was officially established at Geneva. It was, however, demonstrated in 1948 when a tiny minority of the Lao Issara broke away and chose to ally itself with the foreign Viet Minh. In 1949, the majority of the Lao Issara, convinced of the French intention to accord independence to Laos, returned to the Kingdom. Under the name of the Pathet Lao, the dissidents continued a struggle, which the rebirth of independence deprived of all popular support.

In 1950, the Viet Minh radio announced the constitution of a "Pathet Lao Government," but the news passed almost unnoticed for the persons composing this "government" had lost contact with the Laotian people. Some months later, the same radio proclaimed that this "government" had proceeded to the election of a "National Assembly," which had decided to establish a "National Front," invest a "Resistance Government," and create a "People's Liberation Army." It should be noted that at this time the influence of the Pathet Lao was practically non-existent in Laos. Its soldiers, mixed with some elements of the Viet Minh guerrillas who operated in the Kingdom under conditions made very precarious by the overt hostility of the people, occupied themselves by producing sterile propaganda. . . .

In April 1953, regular Viet Minh troops violated the Kingdom's frontiers and occupied most of Phong Saly and Sam Neua (Houa Phan) provinces. Repulsed by Franco-Lao forces, they were able to maintain only scattered guerrilla elements. In December 1953, General Giap's divisions unfurled a new attack and the Franco-Lao garrison at Sam Neua fell back. The invasion was then retired only to be renewed in 1954 in an attack on Luang Prabang, which King Sisavang Vong refused to abandon. The city was saved and the Viet Minh troops returned to their bases in Tonkin; but like the high tide, they left their traces behind them: A population intimidated by this display of force and, especially, their influence in Phong Saly and Sam Neua which, except for a few heroically defended posts and some other positions established with difficulty, were not reoccupied by the Franco-Lao army.

Thus, thanks to the Viet Minh, the Pathet Lao established its administration over this part of the national territory and expanded rapidly its troop strength by the forced recruitment of young men. The Geneva Conference took note of the adversary's implantation, despite the Royal Government's opposition.

The accords signed at Geneva on July 20, 1954, are difficult for the three Indochinese states.

The one which concerns Laos is essentially an armistice convention which imposed the following conditions:

The regroupment and evacuation from the national territory of Viet Minh and French troops except, with regard to the latter, the personnel required to provide instruction to the Lao army and to maintain two military bases;

The regroupment of the "Unités Combatants Pathet Lao" in a sector of each of the Kingdom's twelve provinces, and then, while awaiting a political settlement, their assembly in two sectors of Phong Saly and Sam Neua provinces, which are connected by a corridor;

The limitations of arms, munitions and military equipment imports for the Laotian armed forces, except as would be required for the defense of the country; and

The supervision of the implementation of the armistice by an International Commission composed of representatives of India, Canada and Poland.

The settlement of the problem posed by the minority Pathet Lao was provided for by means of a general election which, conforming to the Constitution, should have taken place in November 1955. Until their reintegration into the national community, the Pathet Lao units were to benefit from a special representation in the Royal Administration in the two northern provinces. . . .

In addition, Laos agreed not to join any accord with other states if this obliged her to participate in a military alliance not in conformity with the principles of the Charter of the United Nations or with those of the cease-fire. As long as the security of the Kingdom was not threatened, the installation on its territory of foreign military bases, except for those expressly reserved for French troops, was not authorized.

It will not have escaped you that the Geneva texts were dangerously lacking in precision. I emphasize "dangerously," for history has demonstrated in super abundance the advantage which those who are on the other side of the barricade have derived from imprecision The application of the Geneva accords very quickly reinforces this opinion. In effect, if the evacuation of Lao territory by foreign troops took place in the time provided, the integration of Pathet Lao elements into the national community reveals itself as an enterprise requiring a long effort. Assured of positions acquired in the north, the Pathet Lao claimed not only the right to retain them, but to reinforce them. The administrative retreat awarded them by the Geneva accords in Phong Saly and Sam Neua constituted the first stage of their plan to extend their domination over the entire country. In order to attain this end, the usual arms—untiring patience, attrition of the nerve and morale of the adversary, and, if need be, the use of force —were to be employed. It has been the honor of the Lao people to have been able to prevent the enemies of their liberty and tradition from using successively or simultaneously, during five years, any of their means of subversion.

The negotiations between the Royal Government and the Pathet Lao leaders have become well known for their vicissitudes. Despite the efforts of the International Control Commission, despite the goodwill of the Royal Government, the carefully prepared meetings without fail ran aground on the claims of the Pathet Lao. Meanwhile, skirmishes between the national army and the dissidents multiplied. Helped by their Viet Minh allies, our adversaries agreed to some concessions in order to show they were not intractable, but they refused systematically to enter into any discussion. It was because of this that the legislative elections took place in December 1955 without Pathet Lao participation.

But while the dossiers concerning the peace that failed in Laos grew in thickness, the war knew no respite. The blood flowed in the two martyr provinces which "like an ax split China and the Democratic Republic of Viet-Nam." The guerrillas weighed heavily on the people and it was sad to encounter so frequently on the streets of the capital very young children deprived of their limbs by the explosion of a mine. I could not erase this pitiful sight from my thoughts, when early in 1956, I was recalled to the premiership of the government. Before the National Assembly, I pledged myself to pursue negotiations. Faithful to my policy of neutrality approved by the Parliament and in the interest of creating the best climate possible for talks with the Pathet Lao, I undertook goodwill visits to Hanoi and Peking. Upon my return to Vientiane, I opened new talks which—sanctioned by certain positive results such as establishment of a ceasefire— continued until November 18, 1957, the date when a Government of

National Union, in which the Pathet Lao participated, presented itself to the National Assembly and obtained its investiture.

The dispositions which permit the constitution of this government included:

The dissolution of the Pathet Lao and the creation of a legal party, the Neo Lao Haksat;

The plans for supplementary legislative elections on May 4, 1958;

The integration in the armed forces of 1,500 men, that is, two battalions of the "Pathet Lao Combat Units." . . .

The full return to the Royal Government of the administration of Phong Saly and Sam Neua provinces, which the Geneva conference had called for three years earlier; and

The Pathet Lao agreed that all disagreements with the Royal Government would be settled by negotiation.

On May 4, 1958, the supplementary elections took place without incident throughout the country. The political solution prescribed at Geneva was achieved. It was this which led the International Control Commission to decide on July 19 to adjourn *sine die*.

Thus—it seems to me useful to emphasize this strongly—international observers along with the Royal Government and the Neo Lao Haksat were in agreement on the complete achievement of the objectives laid down by the Geneva accord. On June 19, I wrote to the Prime Minister of the Democratic Republic of Viet-Nam, Mr. Pham Van Dong, a letter, which included the following passages:

"The Kingdom of Laos has taken all measures necessary to assure the strict application of its engagements, so much with regard to the application of the Geneva accords as with regard to the political and military arrangements relative to the situation of the former Combat Units of the Pathet Lao. . . .

"I know well your concern to seek all possible guarantees for the maintenance of peace. One of the best resides in the loyal application of the five principles of foreign policy found in our common declaration signed in Hanoi, August 29, 1956, to which was joined, more precisely, the solemn engagement taken at Geneva by the Royal Government."

The letter ended with the following paragraph:

"One is obliged to admit that the evolution of Southeast Asia, like the world, runs the risk of unwelcome repercussions for peace and that the assistance of the United Nations would be useful for Laos at any given moment. For this reason, the Royal Government, member of the United Nations, would naturally be disposed to envisage in case of need, the intervention on its territory of this body. The United Nations would be the sole judge of the means it would employ."

It goes without saying that I hoped very much that my country would never be obliged to call upon the United Nations for assistance and that I, along with all my compatriots, hoped that my country would know the benefits of a long peace. Alas! this hope was disappointed. Rejected by the opposition from participating in the formation of the government after the May 4, 1958, elections, the members of the Neo Lao Haksat underwent successive and growing difficulties concerning the integration of their 1,500 combatants. On November 18, 1957, at that time the two provinces were returned to the King, their leader said:

"I declare, as the High Representative of the Pathet Lao Combat Units, to remit officially the two provinces of Sam Neua and Phong Saly, with the administration, all troops, civil servants and war material of the Pathet Lao Combat Units, to His Majesty the King, from this moment.

"All of the administration, all troops and all civil servants will respect and defend the Nation, the Religion, the Monarchy and the Constitution and will perform their duties and exercise their responsibilities like all other citizens of the Kingdom."

Despite this proclamation, one of the two ex-Pathet Lao battalions returned to the maquis and, favored by the terrain, regained the frontier of the Democratic Republic of Viet-Nam. The guerrilla war was revived, fed and largely supported by Hanoi, and events took a sufficiently dramatic turn that the Royal Government appealed to the U.N. A subcommittee of the Security Council came to Laos and the Royal Government put at its disposition everything to facilitate its investigation. But the resolution of the western members of the Security Council already constituted a measure of intimidation against the adversaries of the legal authority of Laos. . . . The Democratic Republic of Viet-Nam forces withdrew, leaving—according to a new familiar tactic—the Lao rebels to pursue their subversive activities. In support of this action, Radio Peking and Radio Hanoi charged that the Royal Government had violated the Geneva accord by authorizing the use of its territory by foreign forces and by nourishing aggressive projects vis-à-vis its neighbors.

But it is easy, for those of good faith, to convince themselves of the truth:

The Lao army consists of 25,000 men. Is it reasonable to assume that it seeks war with the Democratic Republic of Viet-Nam, which, in violation of agreements it signed, has not stopped reinforcing its troops?

The maintenance of two French bases had been authorized by Geneva. Only one—at Seno—exists and its forces are far from the 3,500 authorized. No other foreign power, at any moment, has ever been authorized to undertake any military activity in Laos; and

The Royal Government has remained faithful to its agreement not to join any military alliance not in conformity with the principles of the United Nations Charter or with those of the cease-fire.

This evidence did not prevent certain states from calling for the return to Laos of the International Control Commission. The belief that it had fulfilled all of its obligations led the Royal Government to reject formally this demand. The position, that I expressed on June 19, 1958, i.e., before the events necessitating the intervention of the United Nations, to the Chairman of the International Commission, remains the same.

"The Royal Government is convinced that it should take full advantage of the situation which has evolved. This will bear fruit only under conditions permitting it to develop further. In order to obtain results, one must not continually focus on the situation which existed in 1954, but consider the situation as it exists at present.

"It is true that the Geneva Conference met in 1954 to find a solution to the problem of re-establishing peace in Indochina. There is no longer an Indochina, from the political point of view. The element which was common to the three states in 1954 was the presence of foreign troops. This common element has now disappeared with the application of the Accords.

"The Kingdom of Laos has taken all necessary measures to put its engagements into effect. . . . A law has been passed by the National Assembly on October 18, 1957, guaranteeing democratic liberties . . . to all citizens of the Kingdom. . . .

"Considering that all aspects of the Accords relative to the attributions of the International Commission in Laos have been executed, the Royal Government has decided to request the cessation of that body's activities.

"This request responds, moreover, to the very pronounced opinion . . . of the Lao people who feel that the maintenance without good reason of an international control body is an attack on the sovereignty and independence of the State."

Following this, the International Commission made its own decision to suspend its activities in the Kingdom *sine die*. The Royal Government understands its situation, for our country has known too many ordeals, too many of its sons have fallen for the achievement of its pledge at Geneva, so that any return to the past is inconceivable. With the unfailing help of its friends, the Royal Government is more than ever determined to preserve its policy of neutrality with the objective of maintaining its independence and the defense of its democratic liberties.

446

Souvannaphouma: North Vietnamese Interference in Laos [1968]*

The history of North Vietnamese interference in the internal affairs of Laos is not recent. For more than twenty years that country, communist in its beliefs and actions, has considered the Kingdom of Laos as a natural area of expansion for its political and ideological ambitions. The North Vietnamese Worker's Party (Lao Dong) has recently evinced a particular interest in the unity of action in the struggle of the States of the old Indochinese Federation against imperialism. For a Marxist party, such "unity" has a particular and very clear significance.

For the purpose of its interference in the Lao affairs, the Hanoi government found a faithful and totally devoted ally: the Lao Communist Party, the Neo Lao Hak Xat, a minority without a following among our people who remain very much attached to their way of life and customs, to the Buddhist religion, to the present House and hereditary Monarchy and have little sympathy, moreover, for theories in which they see nothing related to the history and conditions in their own country. There is no working class in Laos, as there is no industry. There are no large land-owners. Over 85 percent of the inhabitants own their land and have more land to cultivate than they need. The Kingdom covers 230,000 square kilometers of fertile land with a population of less than 3 million people. Under these conditions one cannot talk of inhuman capitalism or the exploitation of man by man, this according to the classic definition by Karl Marx. Laos is undoubtedly an under-developed country in the modern sense of the term; but this state of under-development is not the result of the so-called "scientific" conditions which the Communists like to invoke in order to explain history. Furthermore, the Lao people by an overwhelming majority reject the panacea offered by the Neo Lao Hak Xat and its North Vietnamese protector, which is imposed in the portions of the country under military occupation, and where the Neo Lao Hak Xat and the North Vietnamese are experimenting and brutally molding the "Lao society of tomorrow."

The common beliefs of the Neo Lao Hak Xat and of the North Vietnamese explain the conduct of the Hanoi government towards Laos. The Lao Communist Party, nothing in itself, has no armed forces, no war materiel, no financial resources and cannot hope to survive without the support of the North Vietnamese battalions. Souphanouvong, the leader of the Neo Lao Hak Xat, cannot hope to find any effective support other

* *Source:* Prince Souvannaphouma's "Forword" to *White Book on the Violations of of the Geneva Accords of 1962 by the Government of North Vietnam* (Vientiane: Ministry of Foreign Affairs of Laos, 1968), pp. 5–8.

than from North Vietnam, since the popular base of his Marxist revolution is non-existent in his own country. When he fought against French colonialism before his conversion to Marxism, he commanded more popular respect.

In order to save the Neo Lao Hak Xat, the Hanoi government is now engaged in a more blatant interference in Lao internal affairs. The Indochinese war might have, perhaps in the name of the anti-colonialist struggle, served as a cover to the collusion between the North Vietnamese Communists and the Lao Communists. But the Geneva Accords of 1954 indicated specific boundaries. Furthermore, Laos has been independent since 1949. The Indochinese Federation no longer exists, and the former States are all independent and sovereign nations. Thus no valid argument can be advanced in support of the North Vietnamese interference in our affairs, except by pretending that the revolution of which the Hanoi government has become the champion, allows it to flout international rules of conduct, laws and morality.

However, being a democratic country, with a parliamentary system governed indirectly by a constitutional monarchy, the Kingdom, with its successive governments, rather than outlaw the Communist Party as it could have done, allowed the Neo Lao Hak Xat to become a legal party. We prefer to allow our small group of Marxists to express their opinions freely, and in the open, rather than conduct the struggle by more violent means, such as guerrilla warfare, clandestine subversion and civil war.

The internal agreements concluded to that effect clarify rather well the positions of the Lao political parties. While ratifying on the international level a Neutrality which represented the true wishes of the Lao people, the Geneva Accords of 1962 were signed by a tripartite government in which the Neo Lao Hak Xat had a large representation in comparison with its modest following on the internal scene. The 1962 Accords, guaranteed by 13 powers, were in our eyes to end external interference and [signal] the beginning of an era of peace and work which could not have failed to have had the best influence in Southeast Asia and in world affairs.

However, after their signature, the Accords were violated by the Hanoi government. While strong North Vietnamese forces were still present in the Kingdom, a number of North Vietnamese civilian specialists assigned to Khang Khay, at my request, did report to the control points. This is all that the Hanoi government has admitted by way of North Vietnamese presence in Laos. This is their official position when answering accusations of interference.

Even if this comes as a shock this should not surprise us. The Hanoi government is primarily concerned with protecting the fundamental objectives of its Marxist revolution and those of its Neo Lao Hak Xat friends. The conversations now taking place in Paris between the North Vietnamese and the Americans are one additional proof to our contentions, and no matter how absurd and cynical they may be, the fiction maintained by the North Vietnamese confirms once more that Marxist affairs have their own special definitions and meanings, and that black can be white, just as white can be black.

In any case, today there are at least 4 North Vietnamese divisions in Laos, operating alongside the Neo Lao Hak Xat. The Ho Chi Minh Trail has become the Ho Chi Minh Road. Day and night, North Vietnamese troops and convoys use it to go to South Vietnam. (We call the attention of the international audience that this road runs through Laos for several hundred kilometers.)

In these conditions, when we speak of North Vietnamese interference and aggression against our country, we are not merely speaking of myths but of known and proven facts, verified by the International Control Commission, denounced by the British government and by a body of international journalists. The North Vietnamese weapons, aircraft, dead, defectors, and wounded counted on Lao soil are not fiction. The 600,000 refugees coming from the Neo Lao Hak Xat areas cannot all be liars and the facts they report cannot honestly all be doubted.

Thus, the North Vietnamese aggression against Laos, a sovereign country, a neutral state, and a member of the United Nations is unquestionable. Many times we protested against these violations of international usage and of the Geneva Accords. In newspapers, by diplomatic notes, at the United Nations, by representations made to the Co-Chairmen of the Geneva Conference of 14 nations and to the International Control Commission, Laos continuously attempted to draw the attention of the world opinion to a war forgotten because it does not have the dramatic scope of the Vietnam War, but which is nevertheless destroying our country little by little, decimating our families, ruining our economy, and which has delayed our social development by 20 years.

. . . We hope that from now on the world will be willing to admit that the Vietnam War also extends to Laos, and that this has been the case for the past 20 years, and that it is escalating on a daily basis as a result of the ambitions of the Hanoi government to see the Kingdom of Laos one day become a satellite of North Vietnam and eventually serve as a base for further conquests.

Souvannaphouma: Letter to Chou En-Lai [November 28, 1967]*

Mr. President,

As you well know the situation in Laos is far from being satisfactory. In certain aspects it is even very dangerous. The war here continues more and more strongly; the aggression that our Kingdom is undergoing grows daily and the Lao people have come to the point where they ask themselves two basic questions. What significance does our statute of neutrality have? What does the guarantee by the thirteen nations represent—those nations which at Geneva in 1962 solemnly accepted the declaration of neutrality of the Kingdom of Laos?

This situation, Excellency, is due to foreign aggression. In spite of the energetic denials of the aggressor, who is one of the signatory powers for the 1962 Accords, troops coming from [North Viet-Nam] have for more than twenty years lent their support to the [Neo Lao Haksat].

This has been proven in indisputable fashion by all sorts of accounts —by the International Commission of Control, the British Government made it known, by [North Vietnamese] prisoners captured with their war material during battle which their units were carrying out on Laotian soil, by Laotian refugees (who number five hundred thousand) who come from the [Pathet Lao] zones. In short, no one can deny that the Hanoi government is supporting by arms a Lao political party which paradoxically has representatives in the Tripartite Government which is at present responsible for the affairs of the Kingdom.

This, then, is the fundamental fact which explains that Laos, five years after the Geneva Conference (1962), still remains a dangerous spot of tension for all of Southeast Asia and for the world. The fault and the responsibility—I regret to say—fall totally on the Hanoi government which does not wish to admit and to carry out sincerely the principles of pacific co-existence and which, on the other hand, given the reason of its own war against the Saigon government and the United States of America, needs this strategic route known throughout the world as the Ho Chi Minh Trail. This trail crosses a good deal of Laotian territory (several years ago the Hanoi government termed this trail "pure imperialistic invention").

The Accords of 1962 have been violated by one of their principal signatory powers. Our government hasn't failed to raise the necessary and legitimate protests and to alert world opinion. I have personally on several occasions before the UN brought this matter up, but the Hanoi govern-

* *Source:* Annex A, No. 22, in *ibid.,* pp. 79–83.

ment has remained deaf and immovable. It has continued to support and to re-supply the [Neo Lao Haksat] in spite of the 1962 Accords, knowing that the [Neo Lao Haksat] is nothing without its political and military support.

Your Excellency can be certain that the [Neo Lao Haksat], left to itself, would rejoin the national community and the most serious of our problems would be removed and settled. This is to say once again that one of the two trouble spots in Southeast Asia is deliberately supported by the Hanoi government. In these conditions, Excellency, there can be no question of peace. The Laotian people for more than 20 years have suffered quite cruelly. They now have the right to rest, to peace, and above all, to the respect of other people although they are among the smallest and most fragile; I would even say because they are small and fragile.

We love peace and tranquility, but we are forced to note that in this world everything depends, in the long run, on the great powers. Thus, the Laotian problem cannot be resolved by Laos itself. If, through prolonged opposition from those forces which are fighting in Southeast Asia, our destiny suddenly became tragic, this could also embroil the destiny of other powers in the chaos. This is my thought in full to ask of these powerful nations who have already engaged their honor and given their signature for the respect of the 1962 Accords, that they should arrange that these Accords be sincerely and fully respected—that is, if they truly wish to re-establish world peace.

Excellency, the People's Republic of China is a great power. It has respected the 1962 Accords and we are very grateful. This is the proof that it agrees with the stipulations of the Accords that it has signed five years ago and that it intends to respect our statute of neutrality. This is all that we ask of the thirteen signatory powers of the Geneva Agreement.

Mr. President, in calling your attention to the present situation in Laos, a situation which could lead to internal and international complications, I wish to save the peace. I wish also to save my people. Beyond the differences between our political regimes there is, I strongly believe, a community of view and aspiration between our two peoples towards peace. Based on that it seems to me that this appeal of the Lao Kingdom could be heard by one of the great nations of the world.

Please accept, Excellency, the assurances of my highest consideration.

Signed: Prince SOUVANNA PHOUMA

The *Pathet Lao* (Lao Nation), the name commonly used to designate all parts of the Lao Communist movement, was formed in 1950 by Prince Souphanouvong with assistance from the Viet Minh. Operating through several organizational structures (including the Neo

Lao Haksat, or Lao Patriotic Front, which was founded in January 1957 as a legal political party), all of which are supported by North Viet-Nam, the Pathet Lao in the early 1970's controlled much of northern and eastern Laos. Its success has been attributed to the dedication of its leaders, who include members of both the Lao elite and minority groups, and to its centralized organization, whose control extends through party and army cells to the remotest villages.[4] In its competition with the government for popular support and loyalty, the Pathet Lao has stressed the unity of all groups, allegiance to traditional symbols (including the monarchy), internal reform, neutrality in foreign affairs, and hostility toward the United States, which the Pathet Lao describes as the principal cause of destruction and suffering in Laos.

After the collapse of the tripartite national union government in 1963, the leaders of the Pathet Lao retired to their stronghold in Sam Neua and engaged the Souvannaphouma government in an armed struggle for control of Laos. Several attempts were made by the two forces after 1963 to negotiate their differences, but none was successful until early 1973 when they agreed on the terms of a cease-fire and the establishment of a new coalititon government. The Pathet Lao's view of, and proposed solution for, the Laotian problem are set forth in the following documents.

Action Program of the Neo Lao Haksat [April 10, 1964]*

. . . 1. To strengthen the union of all Lao people without distinction of social condition, sex, age, ethnic origin, religion, or political affiliation. The national monolithic block also includes representatives, members of the royal family, patriotic intellectuals, monks and other religious partisans of peace and neutrality as well as all organizations and persons who, while they

---

[4] According to a Laotian government report in 1957, "The Pathet Lao propagandist knows how to present himself as a friend who helps and advises and works with his own hands. He acts disinterestedly, shows honesty and enthusiasm and knows how to get along with a minimum of comfort. The success of his work lies in those qualities and in the fact that he is always there. . . ." (quoted in Bernard B. Fall, "Informal Communications in Southeast Asia" [Washington: mimeo., 1960], Pt. 2, pp. 32–33).

* Source: Resolution of the Second Neo Lao Haksat Congress, April 6–12, 1964, in Programme d'Action du Neo Lao Haksat (Editions du Neo Lao Haksat, n.d.), pp. 9–15.

were constrained by coercion to follow the American imperialists and their valets, now opt for peace and neutrality, associate themselves with the growth and the consolidation of the alliance and mutual assistance between the Neo Lao Haksat and the patriotic neutralist forces, with a view to making Laos a truly peaceful, neutral, independent, democratic, unified and prosperous country.

2. To lead an energetic and persevering fight against the imperialist American aggressors and the traitors in their pay, demanding that they execute correctly and integrally the Geneva accords, the joint Zurich and Plain of Jars communiques and the other accords undertaken among the three parties; to safeguard and consolidate the tripartite Government of National Union, setting about at the same time to achieve its political program with a view to re-establishing peace, achieving national concord and reinforcing the independence of the country; to demand immediately that the American imperialists and their valets withdraw their troops, military personnel and war material, cease all introduction of new arms and war material, and all forms of interference in the internal affairs of Laos under any form, abolish all their existing military bases and undertake not to construct new ones in Laos; to demand the immediate cessation of repressive operations against the people in Savannakhet and attacks against the freezone, the retreat of troops to their positions when the 1962 Geneva accords were signed, the integral execution of all agreements signed by the three parties, particularly the formation of a mixed police force, and the immediate neutralization of Vientiane and Luang Prabang with a view to the resumption of normal activities by the National Union Government, and the resumption of tripartite negotiations seeking solutions to all problems of national interest.

3. To realize the policy of peace and neutrality that was recognized by the 1962 Geneva Accords, abide firmly by an independent foreign policy based on the five principles of peaceful co-existence, establish diplomatic relations with all countries on the basis of equality, receive unconditional aid from all the countries wishing to help Laos in its national construction, on the basis of recognition of and respect for the sovereignty and national independence of Laos; to support all movements fighting for peace, democracy and social progress; to support energetically the national liberation movement of Afro-Asian and Latin American peoples, and contribute actively to the defense of peace in Southeast Asia and in the world.

4. To intensify the appeal for unconditional aid from all countries with a view to building our autonomous and independent economy under the management of the tripartite National Union Government; to eliminate the vestiges of the repressive regime of loans and corvées called "Kuang lam," the monopolization of lands as well as the private monopoly of

investments, business and commerce, and at the same time to help the people augment production, the exploitation of agriculture, intensify commercial exchange, develop handicrafts and industry, fight against speculation and the black market, corruption, stealing and wasting public goods, and the monopolization of products of prime necessity; to revalue the Kip and stabilize the price of foodstuffs; to suppress all taxes and all fines which are irrational and unjust; to apply a tax policy which is appropriate and just; to give to the peasants the maximum of assistance for the development of agriculture and livestock, encourage and assist them especially in the improvement of agriculutral techniques and the protection of crops with a view to permitting them to increase their annual revenue; to assist the workers to find work, improve their living standards, institute a social security system so as to enable them to contribute to the restoration and growth of the national economy; to aid businessmen and industrialists, encourage them to invest in enterprises which will profit the national economy and raise the standard of living; to give to students and young people the conditions which will favor their development; and to assist intellectuals, civil servants and all those preoccupied with literature and the arts to find employment suited to their capacities and to enable them to devote these capacities to the service of the people and the country.

5. To form a national army and a unified police corps to defend national independence and assure public security; to establish the principle that the army and police should be in close touch with the people and be ready constantly to come to their assistance; to stop all acts of repression and exactions against the people; to guarantee the full play of political rights to soldiers and policemen; to assure them a regular monthly salary; to abolish the practice of corporal punishment; and to adopt a policy of assisting invalided and wounded soldiers as well as the families of soldiers killed in battle.

6. To assure all citizens the exercise of human rights and democratic liberties conforming to the law of 1957, with a view to permitting all Lao to devote themselves to the edification of the country; to liberate all political detainees, guarantee the security of life and well being of all citizens, end discrimination and reprisals against the patriots and progressive organizations in the Savannakhet area and, in particular, in the city of Vientiane.

7. To respect and preserve the throne, edify and consolidate national unity, and carry out a policy of concord and national unification; to achieve the solidarity of all ethnic groups and their equality before the law; to assist them to improve their conditions of existence, cultural level and common progress; to combat all maneuvers aimed at dividing the

different ethnic groups; and to defend the legitimate interests of all foreign residents in Laos.

8. To achieve the legal equality of the two sexes, assist Lao women to develop their capacities in order to permit them to overcome their backwardness in the common evolution of the nation; and to assist pregnant women and mothers, and protect children.

9. To develop a progressive national culture; to attach a particular importance to public instruction and develop primary, secondary and professional education as well as adult education, aiming at making everyone, including especially the ethnic minorities, able to read and write; to preserve and develop the good traditions of our people against the infiltration of the rotten and the evil culture of the American imperialists and their consorts; to fight against social plagues, gambling, backward and retrogressive practices; to respect freedom of belief, fight against sabotage and division of the different religions, assure respect for the monks and other clergy, the protection of temples, pagodas and other religious monuments; to develop public health and spread the practice of hygienic and prophylactic rules; to develop fully curative and prophylactic measures against sicknesses; and to organize social assistance and come to the aid of the people at times of disasters and natural and other calamities.

10. At the present time when the American imperialists and their valets persist in their efforts to annihilate the Neo Lao Haksat and other patriotic forces in order to transform Laos into a new type of colony and a base for their aggression in Southeast Asia and to reduce the Lao to slavery, it is important that all Lao harness themselves to the task of defending and consolidating the liberated zones, to reinforce the Neo Lao Haksat from all points of view, to contribute to the consolidation of other patriotic forces and to remain ready to crush all attempts at aggression and attack against the liberated zone. It is important that all cadres and combatants of the Nea Lao Haksat fulfill their obligations and perform well their immediate tasks in order to improve the people's conditions of living, build the liberated zone and make it a base of solid help for the national struggle against the American imperialists and their valets for the achievement of a truly peaceful, neutral, independent, democratic, united and prosperous Laos.

The Neo Lao Haksat Position and the Solution to the Problem of Laos [October 13, 1965]*

Faced with the incessant aggravation of our country's situation, and in order to complete victoriously the fight against the American imperialists for national salvation, the National Political Conference affirms that *the unalterable position of the Neo Lao Haksat and the Patriotic Neutralist Forces as well as that of all our people* is:

1. To safeguard resolutely the peace, neutrality, sovereignty, independence, unity and territorial integrity of our country on the basis of strict respect for and correct execution of the Geneva Accords of 1962 and the tripartite accords of Zurich of 1961 and of the Plain of Jars of 1962;

2. To fight persistently in order to check the American imperialistic intervention and aggression under whatever form in our country;

3. To guarantee to the Lao people the right to settle for themselves their own affairs by means of peaceful negotiations among the interested parties without the interference of the American imperialists; and

4. To fight with perseverance for the application of the political program of the tripartite Government of National Union, which seeks promotion of a peaceful, neutral, independent, democratic, unified and prosperous Laos.

In the light of this steadfast position, the National Political Conference affirms that *the fundamental solution to the problem of Laos at the present time* is:

1. To remove from Laos all of the troops, military personnel, camouflaged military organizations, arms and war material of the American imperialists and their satellites, which were introduced illegally into Laos; to liquidate all American military bases on Lao territory;

2. To cease completely all aggressive acts by the American imperialists against Laos and, first of all, to halt immediately the attacks by the American air force and pro-American troops on the zone controlled by the Lao patriotic forces;

3. To put an end to all collusion among the valets of the U.S.A.—Vientiane, Bangkok and Saigon—and to the utilization of Thai and South Vietnamese territories as spring boards for interference in Laos;

4. To undertake seriously and in a spirit of understanding and of reciprocal concessions tripartite negotiations in order to settle all litigious

* *Source: Manifest de la Conférence Politique Nationale d'Alliance entre le Neo Lao Haksat et les Forces Neutralistes Patriotiques, 13 Octobre 1965* (Editions du Neo Lao Haksat, October 1965), pp. 14–15.

problems among the interested parties with a view to stabilizing step-by-step the situation of the country; and

5. To restore the organization and principle of tripartite unanimity of the Government of National Unity of Laos established on the basis of the Accords of Zurich of 1961 and of the Plain of Jars of 1962.

The Five Points of the Neo Lao Haksat [March 6, 1970]*

For many years now the US imperialists have carried out a policy of unceasing intervention and aggression in Laos in an attempt to turn it into a new colony and a military base of the United States in Southeast Asia.

In defiance of its obligations under the 1954 Geneva agreements and the 1962 Geneva agreements on Laos, the United States has trampled upon the independence and sovereignty and undermined the peace and neutrality of Laos. Over the past eight years, its intervention and aggression in Laos have grown ever more brazen. The United States, through a military putsch, has toppled the National Union Government which received investiture from the King and recognition from the 1962 Geneva agreements on Laos, and rigged up a stooge administration headed by Prince Souvanna Phouma and following a so-called policy of "peace and neutrality" by the agency of that administration, it has conducted a "special war" in Laos, it has launched bombing raids against the Laos territory, and used the Lao puppet army for repeated nibbling attacks on the areas under the control of the Lao Patriotic Forces.

True to the Lao people's aspirations for a peaceful, independent, neutral, democratic, unified and prosperous Laos, the Lao Patriotic Front has always correctly implemented the 1962 Geneva agreements on Laos. In close alliance with the Lao Patriotic Neutralist Forces, it has exercised along with the people its legitimate right of self-defense, it has resolutely fought against the US "Special war," it has opposed the nibbling attacks of the Americans and their stooges, it has inflicted on them fitting blows, and has recorded increasing victories.

While fighting against the US intervention and aggression, the Lao Patriotic Front has repeatedly demonstrated its good will with regard to a peaceful settlement of the Lao problem. . . .

Yet the United States and the Vientiane Administration have ignored all reasonable and logical proposals made by the Lao Patriotic Front. Since notably Nixon took office as President of the United States, the

* *Source:* Statement of the Neo Lao Haksat Central Committee, March 6, 1970 (broadcast by Pathet Lao Radio, March 9, 1970).

United States has intensified the war in Laos with even greater obstinacy.

The United States has brought more US and Thailand military personnel, weapons and war materiel into Laos; it has strengthened the puppet army and the special forces under Vang Pao's[5] command; it has launched repeated nibbling attacks against many places controlled by the patriotic [forces] from the north to the south of the country. It has also put in action a modern air force for saturation bombings against the territory of Laos, thus perpetrating extremely barbarous crimes against the Lao people.

Beginning August, 1969, it mustered about fifty battalions of puppet troops and Thailand mercenaries, conducted operation "Kukiet" to nibble at the Plain of Jars–Xieng Khouang area. Meanwhile, it launched several nibbling operations against the liberated zone in central and southern Laos. What is particularly serious, since February 17, 1970, the United States has used B-52's and planes of the types for mass bombings against the Plain of Jars–Xieng Khouang, area, as well as against central and southern Laos, destroying hundreds of villages and savagely massacring the civilian population.

But the armed forces and people, resolved to defend the liberated areas, have smashed the nibbling attack of the United States and its agents in the Plain of Jars–Xieng Khouang area as well as other places. They have wiped out an important part of the US command . . . and dealt a heavy blow at the "prestige" of the US Air Force.

To cover up the Nixon Administration's "escalation" of the war in Laos, the United States and the Vientiane Administration have launched a campaign of slander against the Lao Patriotic Front and the Democratic Republic of Vietnam. At the same time, they have resorted to deceitful allegations about "peace" in an attempt to fool US and world public opinion which is condemning the Nixon war of aggression in Laos.

The Nixon Administration's attempt to "escalate" the aggressive war has brought about the present tension in Laos, and poses an extremely serious threat to peace and security in Indochina and Southeast Asia.

In face of the tension in Laos, the Lao Patriotic Front affirms the necessity of ending the US war and finding a political solution to the Lao problem.

The position of the Lao Patriotic Front is: The peaceful settlement of the Lao problem must be based on the 1962 Geneva agreements on Laos and on the actual situation in Laos. In more concrete terms:

1. All countries respect the sovereignty, independence, neutrality, unity

---

[5] Major-General Vang Pao, a Méo, is commander of the irregular Méo forces financed and advised by the United States.

and territorial integrity of the Kingdom of Laos, as provided for in the 1962 Geneva agreements on Laos. The United States must put an end to its intervention and aggression in Laos, stop escalating the war, completely cease the bombing of the Lao territory, withdraw from Laos all US advisers and military personnel as well as all US weapons and war materiel, and stop using military bases in Thailand and Thailand mercenaries for purposes of aggression against Laos. It must stop using Lao territory for intervention and aggression against other countries.

2. In accordance with the 1962 Geneva agreements, the Kingdom of Laos refrains from joining any military alliance with foreign countries, and from allowing foreign countries to establish military bases in Laos and to introduce troops and military personnel into its territory.

The Kingdom of Laos follows a foreign policy of peace and neutrality, establishes relations with other countries in accordance with the five principles of peaceful coexistence, and accepts aid with no political conditions attached from all countries. With the other Indochinese countries, it establishes friendly and good neighbour relations on the basis of the five principles of peaceful coexistence and of the principles of the 1954 Geneva agreements on Indochina and the 1962 Geneva agreements on Laos.

With regard to the Democratic Republic of Vietnam and the Republic of South Vietnam, it respects Vietnam's independence, sovereignty, unity and territorial integrity. With regard to the Kingdom of Cambodia, it respects the latter's independence, sovereignty, neutrality and territorial integrity within its present borders.

3. To respect the throne, to hold free and democratic general elections, to elect a national assembly and to set up a democratic government of national union truly representative of the Lao people of all nationalities, to build a peaceful, independent, neutral, democratic, unified, and prosperous Laos.

4. During the period from the restoration of peace to the general elections for setting up the national assembly, the parties concerned shall, in a spirit of national concord, equality and mutual respect, hold a consultative political conference composed of representatives of all Lao parties concerned in order to deal with all the affairs of Laos, and set up a provisional coalition government. The parties shall reach agreement on the establishment of a security zone to ensure the normal functioning of the consultative political conference and the provisional coalition government, free from all attempts at sabotage or pressure by forces from inside or outside Laos.

5. The unification of Laos shall be achieved through consultations between the Lao parties on the principle of equality and national concord.

Pending this unification, no party shall use force to encroach upon or nibble at the areas controlled by another. The pro-American forces must withdraw forthwith from the areas they have illegally occupied, and resettle in their native places those people who have been forcibly removed from there. At the same time, they must pay compensations for damages caused to them. Each party pledges itself to refrain from discrimination and reprisals against those who have collaborated with another party.

The above-mentioned position of the Lao Patriotic Front for the settlement of the Lao problem meets the Lao people's earnest aspirations and is consistent with the interests of peace and security in Indochina, Southeast Asia and the world. It is the just basis of a solution to the Lao problem.

The Lao problem must be settled among the Lao parties concerned. To create conditions for the Lao parties concerned to meet, the United States must, as an immediate step, stop escalating the war, and stop completely the bombing of Lao territory without posing any condition.

The Lao people deeply aspire for independence, freedom and peace. If the United States obdurately persists in its aggressive schemes, the Lao Patriotic Front, the Lao Patriotic Neutralist Forces and the Lao people are resolved to fight on till total victory.

The Lao Patriotic Front earnestly calls on the Laos people of all nationalities to closely unite around the military alliance between the Lao Patriotic Front and the Lao Patriotic Neutralist forces, to heighten their vigilance, to stand ready and resolved to smash all military plans and deceitful schemes of the United States and its agents with a view to defending the liberated zone, safeguarding their fundamental national rights and contributing to the preservation of peace in Indochina and Southeast Asia.

The Lao Patriotic Front calls on the peace and justice loving governments, the American people and the world's peoples strongly [to] support the Lao people's just struggle, and resolutely demand that the United States stop its war of aggression in Laos, and, as an immediate step, put a complete end to the bombing of Lao territory.

With the broad sympathy and strong support of the world's peoples, the entire Lao people, closely united, are sure to defeat the US aggressors and their agents, and successfully build a peaceful, independent, neutral, democratic, unified and prosperous Laos.

The Pathet Lao's call in March 1970 for "a consultative political conference . . . in order to deal with all the affairs of Laos" was its first proposal in five years for resumption of a search for a negotiated solution to the Laos problem. But progress toward a solution, which

was sought in direct talks between representatives of the Pathet Lao
and the Vieng Chan government, was hindered by their inability to
agree on the conditions for a cease-fire: The Pathet Lao demanded a
halt to American bombing, and the Vieng Chan government insisted
that a cease-fire could be established only when foreign forces, by
which it meant North Vietnamese troops, were withdrawn from Laos.
The influence of the United States and North Viet-Nam, thus, continued to be a determining factor in Laos's politics, and it was only
when these two powers began in 1972 to resolve their differences in
South Viet-Nam that their allies in Laos were able to move toward
an accommodation. The solution which the Pathet Lao and the Vieng
Chan government finally devised was reached on February 21, 1973,
and is reprinted below.

*An Agreement on the Restoration of Peace and Reconciliation
in Laos* [February 21, 1973]*

In response to the supreme desire of His Majesty the King and the
earnest aspirations of the people of all nationalities throughout the country, who want to end the war as soon as possible and restore and safeguard lasting peace, in order to achieve national concord and unification
and build Laos as a country of peace, independence, neutrality, democracy, unity, and prosperity, and to diligently contribute to improving
peace in Indochina and Southeast Asia on the basis of the 1962 Geneva
agreement on Laos and the present reality in Laos, the Vientiane Government side and the Patriotic Forces side have agreed on the following
provisions:

Art. 1. A. The desires of the Lao people to safeguard and exercise
their cherished fundamental national rights—the independence, sovereignty, unity, and territorial integrity of Laos—are inviolable.

B. The 9 July 1962 communiqué on the neutrality of Laos and the
1962 Geneva agreement on Laos are the correct basis of the policy for
peace, independence, and neutrality of the Kingdom of Laos. The parties
concerned in Laos, the United States, Thailand, and other foreign countries must strictly respect and implement this agreement. The internal
affairs of Laos must be conducted by the Lao people only, without external interference.

C. To achieve the supreme objective of restoring peace, enhancing
independence, implementing national concord, and restoring national uni-

* *Source: New York Times,* February 22, 1973.

fication, and due to the present reality in Laos, which has two zones under the control of the two sides, the internal problems of Laos must be solved on the spirit of national concord and on the basis of equality and mutual respect, with neither side trying to swallow or oppress the other side.

D. To safeguard national independence and sovereignty, implement national concord, and restore national unification, the people's various rights and freedoms must be absolutely respected—for example, privacy, ideology, speech, press, writing, assembly, establishing political organizations and associations, candidacy and elections, traveling, living where one wants, and establishing business enterprises and ownership. All acts, regulations, and organizations that violate these rights and freedoms must be abolished.

Art. 2. Beginning at 1200 on 22 February 1973, a cease-fire in place will be observed simultaneously throughout the territory of Laos. This includes:

A. Foreign countries must completely and permanently cease the bombing against the territory of Laos, all acts of intervention and aggression in Laos, and all military involvement in Laos.

B. All armed forces of foreign countries must completely and permanenently cease all military movements in Laos.

C. The armed forces of all sides must completely cease all military movements encroaching upon one another both on the ground and in the air.

Art. 3. As soon as the cease-fire goes into effect:

A. It is definitely forbidden to commit small encroachment attacks or threats by army or air forces against the territory temporarily controlled by the other side.

B. It is definitely forbidden to commit any military acts that antagonize the other side, including the movement of bandits . . . and armed air reconnaissance. In case a particular side wants to transport food supplies across the territory under the control of the other side, the committee for implementation of the agreement must discuss and lay down a clear-cut procedure for this.

C. It is definitely forbidden to carry out mop-up, intimidation, and suppression drives against the lives and property of the people or to discriminate against those who participated with the opposite side during the war. The people who were forced to evacuate from their native land during the war must be assisted to freely return to their domiciles to earn their living in accordance with their desires.

D. It is forbidden to bring into Laos military personnel of any type, regular forces or irregular forces, and all kinds of weapons and war means of foreign countries, as mentioned in the 1954 and 1962 Geneva agreements. In case it is necessary to replace damaged or out-of-order weapons and war means, the two sides will discuss this and come to an agreement among themselves.

Art. 4. Within 60 days at the latest after the establishment of the National Provisional Coalition Government and the National Political Coalition Council, the withdrawal of all military personnel and regular and irregular forces from Laos and the dissolution of all military and paramilitary organizations of foreign countries must be completed. The special forces organized, armed, trained, and commanded by foreign countries must be disbanded, and their bases, military positions, and strongholds must be completely dismantled.

Art. 5. The two Lao sides will repatriate all persons, regardless of nationality, who were captured or detained because they collaborated with one side or the other in the war. The repatriation will be carried out in accordance with the principles agreed upon by the two sides and be completed within 60 days at the latest after the establishment of the National Political Coalition Council. Following the completion of the repatriation of captured personnel, each side will have the responsibility to provide the other side with information on those reported missing during the war in Laos.

Art. 6. General free and democratic elections are to be carried out to establish the national assembly and permanent national coalition government, which are to be the genuine representatives of the people of all nationalities in Laos. The principles and procedures of the general elections will be discussed and agreed upon by the two sides. Pending the general elections, the two sides must set up a National Provisional Coalition Government and a National Political Coalition Council within 30 days at the latest after the signing of this agreement, to implement all the agreements signed and to administer national tasks.

Art. 7. The new National Provisional Coalition Government is to be composed of representatives of the Vientiane Government side and the Patriotic Forces side, in equal proportions, and two intellectuals who advocate peace, independence, neutrality, and democracy, who will be agreed upon by both sides. The Prime Minister must be a person who is not a member of the representatives in the Government. The National Provisional Coalition Government is to be set up in accordance with special procedures by royal decree of His Majesty the King. It will perform its duties in accordance with principles unanimously agreed upon by both sides. It will have the responsibility to implement all agreements reached and the political program agreed upon by the two sides—for example, in implementing and maintaining the cease-fire, permanently safeguarding peace, completely implementing popular rights and freedoms, implementing the policy for peaceful foreign relations and for independence and neutrality, for coordinating all economic development plans, expanding culture, and accepting and distributing all aid materials from all countries aiding Laos.

Art. 8. The National Political Coalition Council is to be an organization of national concord and to be composed of representatives of the Vientiane Government side and of the Patriotic Forces side in equal proportions, as well as intellectuals who advocate peace, independence, neutrality, and democracy, whose number will be determined by the two sides. It will perform its duties in accordance with principles unanimously agreed upon by both sides. It has the responsibility to consult with and express views to the National Provisional Coalition Government on major problems relating to domestic and foreign policies, to support and assist the National Provisional Coalition Government as well as the two sides in implementing the agreements signed, to bring about the realization of national concord, to scrutinize and endorse the electoral [sic] coalition government in holding general elections to establish the national assembly and the permanent national coalition government. The procedures in detail on the establishment of the National Political Coalition Council will be discussed and argeed upon by the two sides and will be sent to the National Provisional Coalition Government to be forwarded to His Majesty the King for his decree of appointment. The abolition of the National Political Coalition Council must go through the same procedures as its establishment, as mentioned above.

Art. 9. The two sides agree to neutralize the royal capital of Luang Prabang and the city of Vientiane and to take all measures to guarantee the security of the National Provisional Coalition Government and the National Political Coalition Council so they may carry out their tasks effectively, and to prevent all acts of sabotage or threats from any force from within or without.

Art. 10. A. Pending the establishment of the national assembly and the permanent national coalition government, in the spirit of Article 6 . . . of the joint Zurich communiqué of 22 June 1961, the two sides will maintain the territories under their temporary control, and will endeavor to implement the political program of the National Provisional Coalition Government, as agreed upon by both sides.

B. The two sides will promote the establishment of normal relations between the two zones, and create favorable conditions for the people to move about, make their living, and carry out economic and cultural exchanges with a view to consolidating national concord and bringing about national unification at an early date.

C. The two sides acknowledge the declaration of the United States Government that it will contribute to healing the wounds of the war and the postwar reconstruction in Indochina. The national coalition government will hold discussions with the United States Government in connection with such a contribution regarding Laos.

Art. 11. The implementation of this agreement is the responsibility of the two sides concerned in Laos. The two sides will immediately establish a commission for implementation of the agreement, comprising representatives of both sides in equal proportions. This commission will begin functioning immediately after the cease-fire goes into effect. It will perform its tasks in accordance with the principles unanimously agreed upon by both sides.

Art. 12. The International Commission for Control and Supervision, which was established in accordance with the 1962 Geneva agreement on Laos, is composed of the representatives of India, Poland, and Canada, and is chaired by India. It will continue to perform its duty in accordance with its rights and principles of work as provided for in the . . . Geneva agreement mentioned [above].

Art. 13. The Vientiane Government side and the Patriotic Forces side pledge to implement this agreement and to continue discussions in order to effect all the provisions already agreed upon and to settle the other pending problems concerning them, in the spirit of equality and mutual respect with a view to ending the war, to restore and safeguard lasting peace, achieve national concord, create national unity in order to proceed to build a peaceful, independent, neutral, democratic, united, and prosperous Laos. . . .

III. The Future

Political power in Laos is based on regional and family loyalties and alliances, and its pace has been set by the clash of personalities and factional interests. Those who hold power belong to an older generation, initiated into public affairs during the French colonial period; they have dominated the command posts of authority since then because of their wealth and the influence of tradition. However, in the late 1960's, a new generation of leaders, constituting a new constellation of the Luang Prabang, Vieng Chan, Xieng Khouang, and Champassac clans, began trying to make its voice heard. Composed of men who have received their education since World War II and who are eager to share in the power of their elders, this group is interested in the development of a political system based on national interests and problems. Many of them are looking ahead to the time when peace will be restored in Laos and they will have to contest for power not only with the older leaders but with the Pathet Lao as well.

One of these men is Chao Sopsaisana, who in the early 1970's was vice-president of the National Assembly. An active rightist, he was a founding member of the Committee for the Defense of the National Interests, formed with American help in June 1958 to oppose the growth of Pathet Lao influence in the governmnt. In December 1959 he joined with General Phoumi Nosavan and others in a coup which deposed Phoui Sananikone from the premiership and set the stage for the clash of rightists and neutralists in 1960. By 1969, still having been denied access to the councils of power, he had turned his attention to the future: He and other ambitious and conservative younger members of the Assembly formed the Parliamentary Group for the Implementation of the Geneva Accords, which they hoped to transform into a national political party. The issues on which the Parliamentary Group has tried to develop positions include corruption in government, the need for action on crucial rural problems, and the threat posed to Laos by North Viet-Nam. Chao Sopsaisana's views on the latter subject are contained in the following document.

Chao Sopsaisana: The Threat Posed to Laos by North Viet-Nam [July 1970]*

In any conflict, and even before the end of the hostilities, belligerents—who are potential winners and losers—try to explore the future situation of their . . . countries. The Kingdom of Laos, a victim in a war it neither sought nor deserved, is no exception to this rule. In addition, however, Laos also must take into account that its "after-the-war period" depends upon two different elements: The fight it wages on its own territory against a North Vietnamese invader, and the fight in South Viet Nam between Saigon and Hanoi—two conflicts which have a common factor: North Viet Nam.

This leads some observers to the conclusion that the end of one of these

* *Source:* Chao Sopsaisana, "Laos after Viet Nam," *Pacific Community,* 1 (July 1970), 4: 707–716. Reprinted by permission of the journal publishers; copyright 1970 by *Pacific Community,* the Pacific News Commonwealth, the Jiji Press, Ltd., Tokyo.

conflicts will bring the end of the other. Such a hazardous conclusion is favored by an international public opinion which continues to regard the two situations as a single one, seeing them linked by North Viet Nam which, at the same time, fights in South Viet Nam and intervenes in Laos. This is true. But in Viet Nam, one deals . . . with a civil war between two opposing states . . . with a single population, officially and internationally separated by agreement between the two sides at the Geneva Conference in 1954.

Laos is a neutral, sovereign and independent country under the aegis of 13 nations which, in 1962, in Geneva, thanks in part to continuous and persevering efforts in this direction by Prince Souvanna Phouma, . . . recognized its status and took the engagement to respect it and to have it respected. In Laos one is facing a real aggression, characterized by invasion, a permanent violation of international agreements by a country which signed them, which is encouraged in the continuation of its aim of hegemony by the silent complicity or indifference, in all ways guilty, of the other signatories to the agreement.

One can admit that the Vietnamese population, artificially split into two parts, aspires to reunification. This aspiration would be legitimate if it was not motivated by interests which are more ideological than national. My aim here is not to analyse, interpret or criticise problems of a country with which my own country has no affinities other than those created by geographical propinquity. But on the other problem, one seeks in vain for an historical explanation or a moral justification for the aggression against the Kingdom of Laos of which Hanoi is guilty. Certainly, there are Communists in Laos, a minority united by the leftist "Neo Lao Haksat" party, and the help they receive from Hanoi is along the line of Communist logic—a logic which, as one knows, evades all ethical concepts. For, indeed, there are facts, tragic ones, which prove that under the cover of a so-called "war of liberation," communists in Laos practice a bloody, ruthless terrorism which has nothing in common with the "happiness of the people" they claim as their motivation. This terrorism has a powerful accomplice in Hanoi, under the aberrant pretence of helping a brotherly party which in Laos has never been anything more than a handful of rebels, whose activities would have stopped since a long time by the regular forces of Vientiane if not for Hanoi's intervention in Laotian affairs.

It is necessary to have a look at the past to better understand the problem. After the 1962 Geneva Agreements on Laos, North Viet Nam which was also a signatory to these agreements, dampened the help it had given until then to Laotian Communists, who had been reintegrated by the Geneva Conference into the national community and had a place in the

Provisional Government of National Union established on that occasion. There are two explanations as to why Hanoi wanted to show at that time some discretion in dealing with Laotian affairs. First, to give the ink on the agreement time to dry with Hanoi seemingly willing to respect it. Secondly, the fact that at that time North Viet Nam was not yet engaged in the South Viet Nam war, and thus did not have to use Laos for infiltration into South Viet Nam.

As discreet as it was, Hanoi's help to Laotian Communists was nevertheless efficacious and permitted the Neo Lao Haksat to build a better structure and to consolidate its position during the political battle which followed the establishment of the Provisional Government of National Union. Laotian Communist leaders, headed by the "Red Prince," Tiao Souphanouvong, thus hoped to gain control of power through partial and, later, general elections.

On their part, this was not from any care for the aspirations of the Lao people, their loyalty to the monarchy, and their religious fervor. The "agrarian reform," spearheading any Communist propaganda, was not necessary in a country like Laos where demographic density makes it an under-populated nation: three million inhabitants for a territory which is twice as big as North Viet Nam. So that, little by little, the Neo Lao Haksat was losing ground and, upon the orders of Hanoi, left the legal political scene—where it was a loser—to enter into a rebellion where the Communists were to wage a "war of liberation." For Hanoi, this was striking a double blow. The Lao Communist Party, which had been on the point of being absorbed into legality and democracy, survived, even if it was in a condition of dissidence. It suits North Vietnamese interests that rebellion centres and troubles exist as so many cancers serving Hanoi's policy. Moreover, a "war of liberation" authorised North Viet Nam— from the viewpoint of international Communist solidarity—to deliver all material help to the Neo Lao Haksat and its military organ, the Pathet Lao.

As viewed from Hanoi, from then on, North Vietnamese intervention into Laotian affairs, forbidden by the Geneva Agreements of 1962, was simply "aid to a brotherly party, fighting for the happiness of the people and for the liberation of its country." This was the situation in 1964. It had taken another dimension which went beyond the frame of the signed agreements: The increasingly active intervention of North Viet Nam in Laos, its presence at the side of a rebellion which fought against "imperialism." That word is a latch-key of Communist dialectics which permits all excesses in the name of the people. The intervention could only be approved by the Communist world, and especially by the Soviet Union and People's China, both being in addition anxious to cater to their interests and to their prestige with an ally as ambitious and dynamic as North Viet Nam.

Rebellion was rising again stronger than in the period before 1962 and, this time, was little inclined to return to a legality where it had received only painful defeats. The battlefield again became the stage, the more interesting for Hanoi in that it now permitted it—under the cover of help to neighbouring Communists, who would be grateful in the future if the situation turned to their advantage—the use of Laotian territory for maintaining the flow of men and material into South Viet Nam, where North Viet Nam is now directly engaged. The Viet Nam affair, a focus of world attention, had priority over the Laotian affair which is considered by some people as being only an accidental extension of the Viet Nam war which, according to them, would soon be resolved after the end of the hostilities in Viet Nam. We will come back to this error of judgment.

Whatever the case, North Viet Nam, at the time, held the cards. Its Communist conscience was appeased (was it not coming to the aid of a brother party?). The road to South Viet Nam was opened. The signatories to the 1962 Agreements were immobilised (even passively compliant). They did not intervene (probably persuaded, also, that order would be restored in Laos after the solution of the Viet Nam problem). There was the complicity of the Polish delegation on the International Commission of Control and Inspection for the application of the Geneva Agreements (which vetoes especially any attempt to control and thus any chance to denounce violations by Hanoi of these agreements). Everything, then, favoured the realisation of North Vietnamese plans.

I have mentioned the inaction of the countries which signed the Geneva Agreements, depositary of the independence, sovereignty and neutrality of the Kingdom of Laos. This deplorable passivity on the part of nations which took the solemn engagement to maintain peace in that part of the world does not inspire much belief that these same nations will show more efficacy when, the Viet Nam problem being solved, the Laos problem must be dealt with. One must not forget that, for the time being, the real war, for the North Vietnamese leaders, is in South Viet Nam. Laos—where their politico-military apparatus is already set up, ready to function fully when the time will be appropriate—does not specifically interest them. Why? Because, if Hanoi is the winner in South Viet Nam, then the whole of the Indochina peninsula is menaced and in the long run forced to be pro-Communist, if not Communist. Or if North Viet Nam is the loser, but having lost only what it coveted—the South—and finding itself back again in its 1954 positions—it still has won a real advantage in Laos: A war of liberation in the image of the one waged by the Viet-cong, the true instrument of Hanoi's expansionist ambitions.

Freed by the end of hostilities in South Viet Nam, whatever the result, all of the North Vietnamese forces, all the actions of Hanoi kept in re-serve for this eventuality, then concentrate upon Laos, where North Viet-namese Communists hold stronger positions than they had in 1954 or in 1962. In this situation, how could one for a single moment imagine that Hanoi will be ready to lose, in the case of a defeat in the South, the only benefit it gained from the conflict or, in the case of a victory, to abandon a key position in Indochina which at the same time has a direct frontier with Thailand where the guerrilla war Hanoi foments develops at a pace which justifies the fears of the Thai Government? Finally, to believe in a simple withdrawal from Laos by North Vietnamese units and the political staff, for the only reason that all will have been solved in South Viet Nam, is to forget Hanoi's dream to make the whole of Viet Nam, Laos and Cambodia a great Indochina Communist Federation. This is an ambition that the North Vietnamese Communists have had for many years and which they have no reason whatsoever to abandon. Moreover, this federa-tion answers a vital need of North Viet Nam and is not inspired by ideology only; there are economic and demographic considerations.

The ideological fight which, as I have said, explains everything and permits everything, cloaks aspects of the North Viet Nam desire for hege-mony over the whole of the Indochina peninsula which are much more practical and also a reflex of self-defence towards its colossal neighbour, China, and against the eventual territorial claims of China on Viet Nam. The history of North Viet Nam which was invaded several times by Chinese hordes, justifies the apprehensions of Hanoi's leaders. But, in addition to the fact that an Indochina politically and militarily grouped into a single bloc could incite an ambitious China to some caution, it could bring to North Viet Nam a number of economic advantages which explain the pursuit of this dream and the policy towards the other nations of Indochina: The rice granaries of South Viet Nam and its vast planta-tions of *Hevea;* the underground riches of Laos—notably tin, iron, and coal—its forests, and land which is not cultivated for lack of inhabitants, but where manpower from North Viet Nam, an over-populated country with 19 million inhabitants, would be ready to establish itself quickly; the forests, agriculture and fisheries in Cambodia. Here are so many strong reasons for Hanoi not to change an inch on its policy.

Menaced with asphyxia within its narrow confines, backed up against a China which casts a massive and alarming shadow, North Viet Nam—potentially weakened in all fields by a war which has lasted a quarter of a century—places all its hopes on a federation it would obviously control. One understands better, then, North Viet Nam's refusal of the proposal by Prime Minister Prince Souvanna Phouma, at the beginning of last February, to neutralize the Plain of Jars and to have it jointly reoccupied by the rightist neutralist forces, whose leader he is, and the leftist neutralist, pro-North Vietnamese forces. In exchange for the acceptance by Hanoi of a neutralization of the Plain, the Prince promised to "close his eyes" to the use by North Vietnamese troops of the famous Ho-Chi-Minh trail on Lao territory, seized by the North Viet Nam command to send units and material towards South Viet Nam.

This determination by Hanoi to reject any possibility of an eventual pre-solution of the Laotian problem gives the irrefutable proof that the North Viet Nam Government has long-term plans regarding the Laotian Kingdom. If not, why refuse any proposal likely to end the fighting in Laos without compromising in any way the struggle in South Viet Nam, since Hanoi continued to possess its main road of infiltration? All this demonstrates that, contrary to what a world opinion, badly informed and more sensitised to the Viet Nam than to the Laos problem, believes, North Viet Nam at the same time wages two wars which are very different from each other, despite the fact that they are fought on the same chess-board —the Indochina peninsula, which the North Vietnamese Communists one day hope to absorb completely.

Waiting for the realisation of this dream, if it is ever to be realised, Hanoi deems it necessary to consolidate its positions in Laos. The offensive which it launched at the end of last February, and which permitted it to reoccupy the important strategic centre of the Plain of Jars, is a recent proof of this fact. Who can still pretend, in this situation, that the key to the Laotian problem lies in a solution to the Vietnamese problem? How to believe, without being unrealistic or naive, that North Viet Nam can abandon its interests in Laos once hostilities end, one way or the other, between South and North Viet Nam? No, the "after-the-war period in Laos" has nothing to do with the after-the-war period in Viet Nam. For Hanoi, the Kingdom of the "Million Elephants," which has common frontiers with six countries (North Viet Nam, South Viet Nam, Cambodia, Thailand, Burma and China) is and will remain the "bolt" to lock its Indochina strategy.

Events in Cambodia add weight to this opinion. North Viet Nam, which is in the process of probably losing in Cambodia an important card in its Indochina game, will need Laos more than ever whatever arrangements or agreements come from contacts which have been initiated between Prince Souphanouvong, leader of the Communist left, and Prince Souvanna Phouma, head of the Laotian Royal Government. The latter, besides, has wisely decided to wait until the situation in Cambodia clarifies—in other words he is waiting to know the orientation given to his government by the Cambodian Prime Minister, General Lon Nol—before pursuing these contacts. For nothing is yet decided definitely in Cambodia.

All the experts on Communist affairs in Southeast Asia agree that the withdrawal from Phnom Penh of the diplomatic missions of North Viet Nam and of the Provisional Revolutionary Government of South Viet Nam will not automatically entail the departure of North Vietnamese and Vietcong units from their sanctuaries in Cambodian territory. The stake is too important to Hanoi's strategy. The bases in Cambodia are too important to its war in South Viet Nam. . . .

What is true is that, in wanting to woo Hanoi's favour with the commendable aim of avoiding for his country a war similar to the one in which Laos is a victim, Prince Sihanouk—by giving some mutual privileges (hospitals, rest centres, bases for withdrawal, etc.) which did not constitute by themselves any dangers at the time for Cambodia—showed a real lack of perspicacity, or at least an astonishing candor for a politician of his importance. For, after all, nobody ignores nowadays that for the Communists, whoever they are, the smallest gesture of good will is always considered by them to be a gesture of weakness. To give them a little is to incite them, to encourage them to want more. The Laotian Communist Party (Neo Lao Haksat) does not ignore this fact as it is little by little absorbed by the North Vietnamese. Does not the message sent last March to Prince Souvanna Phouma by Prince Souphanouvong, which hinted at resuming the dialogue between Laotians, denote to some degree the desire of Laotian Communists not to disengage themselves completely but at least to keep a certain distance from Hanoi? Or, in any case, some independence when dealing with Laotian affairs? After all, Prince Souphanouvong intends to stay, while it is still possible, a "valid interlocutor." He forgets only that, as long as there are North Vietnamese forces in Laos, he will be for the great majority of the Laotians only a spokesman for Hanoi.

North Vietnamese units in Laos fight Laotian troops and wage a real war of aggression which has nothing to do with the war North Viet Nam wages in South Viet Nam. There is no question whatever here of "privileges" or even of real military bases which could motivate a global strategy. One deals here with an attempt simply to annex Laos, with the aim of consolidating the famous "bolt" I mentioned before. In contrast to Cambodia, Laos is not a victim of "concessions" it made to Hanoi or of a double-dealing policy. Nothing in the attitude of Prince Souvanna Phouma's government could cause North Vietnamese leaders to suppose that they benefited in Laos from a kind of tacit complicity. There was here no false equilibrium, such as the one established in his country by Prince Sihanouk.

Prince Sihanouk could believe that in using a "see-saw" or "swing" policy, he avoided for Cambodia a complete engagement on one side or the other, keeping open the possibility of an eventual complete disengagement from one or the other. This could succeed for him when he ousted from Cambodia American officials and refused American aid, not so much to please Communists (despite the fact they were delighted) but rather to avoid displeasing them, believing that any annoyance on their part could be a pretext to indulge in the kind of excesses they commit in Laos. Prince Sihanouk probably hoped that, in exchange, Hanoi would keep Cambodia away from the Indochina conflict.

It should not be forgotten that, in matters of relations between States, Communists do not proceed on the same criteria as those used by the Free World. In the anti-American measure taken by Prince Sihanouk— which incidentally was not at all irreversible—North Vietnamese and the Vietcong did not see a simple "road accident" between Cambodia and the United States, but a real and total disengagement from imperialism. Being doctrinaire and thus lacking sensibility for the nuances of a policy in which they wanted to see only the aspects which agreed with them, Vietnamese Communists decided that it could amount only to an overture on the part of the Cambodian Government towards Socialist countries. The conjuncture appearing to them to be favourable, it is under this pretext that they transformed the initial privileges which had been given to them by Prince Sihanouk into important military bases, from which nowadays nearly 40,000 North Vietnamese and Vietcong operate on South Vietnamese territory.

If it is true that, since the "coup" in Phnom Penh, these units are menaced by isolation, and lack of supply lines in particular, and thus limited in their action, it is also true that, after the call to rebellion launched from Peking by Prince Sihanouk, the new Cambodian situation will become politically more favourable to Hanoi in the proportion that this rebellion develops. It will divide the country, and will re-establish the position of the Red Khmers who had until now but little importance.

Until these last days, one could wonder about the degree of sincerity of Prince Souphanouvong when he sent, last March, a message to Prince Souvanna Phouma which many observers considered to be a prelude to a pre-solution between Laotians. A propaganda manoeuvre or not, there was then a not negligible possibility of resuming a dialogue. The deposition of Prince Sihanouk and, more certainly, his declared intention to join the guerillas of his country, have changed all the elements of the problem—in Cambodia of course, but also in Laos. There is no more question here of the Neo Lao Haksat renewing its contacts with Vientiane, if it ever had this intention. On the contrary, one can expect a gradual hardening of the attitude of the Laotian Communists. The clandestine radio of the Pathet Lao (Communists) has already totally rejected, in an editorial which was not subject to interpretation, the answer of Prince Souvanna Phouma to the message of Prince Souphanouvong.

One must recall that, in the meanwhile, the Cambodian affair had erupted. Military operations in the famous Plain of Jars, which can be considered as a barometer for political developments in Laos, have resumed on a larger scale than ever. One could believe for a time that the evacuation by Royal forces was an answer to the condition put by the Neo Lao Haksat, which declared that it would engage in talks only if—among other conditions—the Plain of Jars was again its undisputed fief. This evacuation, which seemed to have effectively begun, coincided also, it is true, with the American policy of disengagement in Indochinese countries. One can take as certain, anyway, that it constituted a gesture of good will on the part of the Laotian Government, which effectively wished to create conditions likely to facilitate a solution in Laos.

A few weeks were sufficient, later on, to give a new dimension to the war in Laos which is now unquestionably linked to the Cambodian affair. It indeed suits Hanoi, and also all Indochinese Communists, that when he leads a "war of liberation" in Cambodia—which will not fail to be a copy of the wars by the Vietcong and the Pathet Lao—Prince Sihanouk has his rear positions secure in Laos. Moreover, is not the publicly announced summit conference . . . in China [the "Summit Conference of the Indochinese Peoples," April 24–25, 1970]—where the ex-chief of the Cambodian State, the president of the Laotian Communist Party, the Foreign Minister of the P.R.G. (Vietcong) and the chief of the Lao-Dong Party (North Vietnamese Communists) were to meet—the alarming proof of the preparation in Indochina of a new and common Communist strategy? Does not one find there a rough draft of the famous "Indochinese Communist Federation" Hanoi has been wanting for 30 years?

Can one believe that, with this particularly favourable situation for North Viet Nam and its allies of any kind, the Communists will let pass this historic chance to affirm their solidarity? No! A new situation is now being established. In the same way that, according to some people, the United States cannot win the war in Viet Nam without winning the war of Indochina as a whole, one can also foresee that Hanoi will realize Indochinese Communist unity only by regrouping, under its control, in a kind of "United Front," the four Indochinese Communist parties.

The Cambodian affair is an opportunity. And it is probably for this reason that the North Viet Nam delegation to the Paris Conference rejected the French proposal to hold talks between all concerned countries "so as to create a zone of neutrality and peace in Indochina." Hanoi, thus, continues to cast its alarming shadow over the whole of the Indochinese peninsula. Its uncompromising attitude, explained by its political aims and, as I mentioned at the beginning of this article, by its economic interests, will oblige menaced countries in this part of the world one day to face a dramatic choice. Will they have to follow, so as to honour international agreements they are the only ones to respect, a policy of "Neutrality in War" or, so as to have at last a chance of survival, apply the principle of "neutral engagement in peace"? The answer lies in Hanoi . . . as well as in Peking.

SEVEN

Cambodia

by ROGER M. SMITH

On March 18, 1970, the Cambodian National Assembly by unanimous vote deposed Prince Norodom Sihanouk as chief of state, and by this unexpected action they brought to a close an era of peace and relative political stability. For nearly twenty years, Sihanouk had dominated Cambodia's public life, as king, prime minister on several occasions, chief of state, and as the country's foremost politician. So pervasive and salient was his influence in the political life of his country that, for many foreigners, he was the personification of Cambodia itself.

Sihanouk's removal from power was unanticipated. The widespread popular support that he seemed to enjoy made a coup a remote possibility in the minds of most observers. But among the elite there had always existed rancor born out of Sihanouk's unwillingness to share political authority. Their growing resentment and the military's demoralization—caused by inadequate equipment, manpower, and training at a time when the Viet Cong and the North Vietnamese were becoming increasingly brazen in their use of Cambodian soil—contributed to Sihanouk's dénouement in 1970.

From the beginning of his rule, two of Prince Sihanouk's principal preoccupations had been the securing of national unity and the retaining of Cambodia's newly won independence (November 1953). A keen student of his country's history, Sihanouk was aware of how, in the past, rivalries among Cambodia's leaders had been exploited by her neighbors, Viet-Nam and Thailand, who were quick to play off one faction against another for their own ends. The prince believed that internal cohesion and a neutral policy in Cambodia's external relations formed the edges of the sword that could most effectively ward off threats of intervention by rival foreign powers and a subsequent demise of Cambodian independence. A people in whom was awakened a consciousness of a common destiny, a magnificent historical past, and the numerous ethnic ties binding them together would, he reasoned, be invulnerable to the machinations of foreign powers. By assuming a neutral posture in Cambodia's foreign relations, he hoped to eliminate a potential cause for internal political divisiveness as well as to keep in check the hostile intentions of Thailand and Viet-Nam. Moreover, he gambled that the big powers would realize that it was in their interests to keep Cambodia neutral, thus restraining aggressive actions by the Thais and the Vietnamese.

One of the most significant of Sihanouk's attempts to cultivate a sense of community among the Cambodian people was to make possible their active participation in the political process. To this end, in early 1955 he proposed a number of constitutional reforms to make elected representatives more directly responsible to the people. But at the same time, the reforms would strengthen Sihanouk's authority and power as king. In the statement of these reforms Sihanouk included a strong criticism of the obstructionist attitudes of Cambodia's elite, embodied in its party system. To his rivals it appeared that in erecting direct lines of communication between the throne and the masses he was not only involving the peasantry in political action, but he was also depriving the elite of a leadership role and eliminating the need for him to be accountable to them. The proposed revisions of the constitution understandably evoked strong elitist opposition, and Sihanouk sought to dissolve the opposition by abdicating the throne in favor of his father, Prince Norodom Suramarit, in 1955 in order to don political habit. One of his first acts in his new role was to found the *Sangkum Reastr Niyum* (People's Socialist Community), which he envisioned would accommodate all political interests and thus remove the basis for political parties. He also instituted the National Congress, a biannual forum at which the country's political leaders met with the people to discuss national problems.

By and large, these strategies had their desired results. In the 1950's, neutrality enabled Cambodia to avoid being drawn into the troubles which were rending Laos and Viet-Nam. Factional politics, if not completely eliminated, were submerged in the Sangkum. Moreover, Sihanouk was adept at playing rival groups against each other and in cultivating support among the people, to whom he portrayed himself as the only person capable of leading them without succumbing to the partisan demands of rival interest groups. In the early 1960's, however, the currents of both international events in Indochina and politics in Cambodia underwent a marked change and so, too, did the prince's views and strategies.

First, the threat of a generalized conflict in Indochina began to loom ever larger. The war in Viet-Nam and Laos was growing in intensity, and there was now a danger that it would spill over into Cambodia. From the end of the first Indochina war in 1954 until this time, foreign threats to Cambodia had appeared remote or, at least, had not endangered seriously the country's security. The increasing magnitude of the external threat led Sihanouk in mid-1965 to seek closer association with North Viet-Nam and China: He traded, in effect, Cambodia's moral and political support of North Viet-Nam's cause for its agreement to honor the border between Cambodia and Viet-Nam. The effects of this modification in his neutral policy, however, were not those he intended. Far from remaining content with Sihanouk's diplomatic support, the North Vietnamese made increasing use of Cambodian territory as a sanctuary from which to attack South Viet-Nam. Moreover, they interfered in Cambodia's internal affairs by providing political and materiel support to the *Khmer rouge* (Red Khmers), an armed rebel movement started in 1967 by a group of young elite who had been ousted from positions of political power. The Cambodian army of thirty-two thousand poorly trained and ill-equipped men was incapable of halting either the Vietnamese incursions or their attempts at subversion. Furthermore, by sanctioning in 1969 an illicit trade in Cambodian rice and supplies with the North Vietnamese, the prince appeared to be disregarding the elite's efforts to bring the country's economy and finances under control.

On the domestic front, latent political rivalries found new channels of expression in the National Assembly, where legislation proposed by Sihanouk and the National Congress was frequently obstructed or emasculated. It was, no doubt, for this reason that in 1959–1960, Prince Sihanouk began to draw into government some of the increasing numbers of younger men who had recently completed their education abroad, mostly in France. By according them status and a share in the allocation of power, he hoped not only to counter the older elite but also to create a new group on whose loyalty he could depend. By 1962, several of these men, who were referred to collectively as the "young intellectuals," were ensconced in government and legislative positions of considerable power, from which they began to chart a new course for Cambodia's development. Among other things, this course was aimed at establishing greater state control over the economy and restricting dependence on foreign imports and capital. The young intellectuals were also influential in turning Cambodia more toward the socialist camp in her foreign relations, and they revealed their sympathies for the cause of North Viet-Nam and the National Front for the Liberation of South Viet-Nam. It was in part a consequence of their increased influence that Prince Sihanouk was motivated in 1963 to renounce American economic, technical, and military assistance. The older elite became less willing to cooperate with the prince, as their own status declined and their interests were placed in jeopardy by Sihanouk's backing of their young antagonists.

Their opportunity to retaliate first occurred in 1966, when it had become clear that, as a result of the young intellectuals' policies, Cambodia's economy was stagnating. Foreign investment capital was no longer available in the amounts required to maintain the momentum of development that had been built up prior to 1963. Foreign reserves were fast melting away. Consequently, the government was unable to honor the promises which the prince continued to make to the people. This situation, coupled with mounting unemployment (especially among recent university and high-school graduates), mismanagement and corruption in the state-controlled manufacturing and trading concerns, the inability of the government to meet the army's materiel needs, and a succession of poor rice harvests, provided the elite with grounds for an attack on Sihanouk and the young radicals.

Confronted with obvious economic problems for which there was no quick or easy solution, Prince Sihanouk, under strong pressure from the right, once again granted a voice to the old guard. They counselled a return to a mixed economy, and demanded that Sihanouk allow the free play of politics in the 1966 national legislative elections. To this he agreed: For the first time since 1955 he did not endorse any of the candidates. The result was an overwhelming victory for the old guard and the removal from government office of most of the young intellectuals. Sihanouk tried to placate his young supporters by creating for them an official opposition known as the "Counter-Government." This was a poor substitute for the power they had so recently enjoyed, however, and when the prince rejected their demand that he restore them to office, they resorted to armed rebellion. Instead of slowing the move to the right in Cambodian politics, the action of the intellectuals had only spurred rightist efforts toward extensive economic reform and the erosion of Sihanouk's personal control over the country's fortunes.

In the face of increasing opposition from his ministers and a rapidly deteriorating security situation, Prince Sihanouk sought a compromise solution. Without altering his position vis-à-vis the Vietnamese, for he feared that a confrontation with them would plunge Cambodia into war, he tried to bring diplomatic pressure on them by making overtures to the West, in effect, patching up his disintegrating policy of neutrality. He also relinquished, in mid-1969, much of his power to a so-called "Government of Salvation" headed by General Lon Nol, one of his trusted advisors who, however, had become disenchanted with Sihanouk's policies, and by Prince Sisowath Sirik Matak, one of Sihanouk's cousins. Neither of these moves was to prove successful in checking the deterioration of his power.

Diplomatic relations with the United States, ruptured in 1965 as a result of a series of American and South Vietnamese attacks on Cambodian frontier villages, were restored in 1969, and several other Western nations announced their recognition of Cambodia's borders. The much-sought-after guarantees of Cambodia's independence and territorial integrity did not accompany these declarations, however; the Vietnamese presence in the country expanded, and consequently American and South Vietnamese attacks on Cambodia continued unabated.

Internally, Lon Nol and Sirik Matak quickly gathered the reins of power and moved to introduce extensive economic reforms. The *riel,* still set at the rate established for it in the early 1950's by the French, was devalued; banking regulations were relaxed to attract foreign investment capital; in December the abolition of state industries was proposed. The National Assembly, meanwhile, charged Sihanouk's entourage with enriching themselves at the country's expense by trading illicitly with the Vietnamese in eastern Cambodia.

Prince Sihanouk left Cambodia in January 1970 for medical treatment in France. During his absence the government mounted a propaganda campaign to impress upon the populace the seriousness of the Vietnamese threat, and they announced plans to increase the army's size by 25 percent. Both of these moves were opposed by Sihanouk. Phnom Penh was astir with rumors of an impending crisis.

On March 11, demonstrations by thousands of students, Buddhist monks, and soldiers in mufti led to the sacking of the North Vietnamese and Provisional Revolutionary Government embassies. Official sponsorship of these acts was probably inspired by North Viet-Nam's failure to heed the Cambodian government's demand that Vietnamese troops be evacuated from the eastern frontier region. Sihanouk's response to these events came in a cable to his mother, the dowager queen,[1] on March 12, in which he charged the rightists with scheming to shear him of his authority and to throw Cambodia into the arms of an imperialist power. He said he would return to ask the people and the army to choose between him and his opponents. But when he refused to receive government envoys to discuss a compromise, the die against him was cast. On March 18, the National Assembly, by unanimous vote, withdrew its confidence in Prince Sihanouk as chief of state, and he and all members of his entourage were forbidden to return to Cambodia.

Over the years, Prince Sihanouk had come to count on his own indispensability. Time and again he had stepped aside from political power only to be persuaded by popular demand to resume leadership in the face of a new crisis, real or staged. That he was able to hold the reins for so long was due to his charismatic qualities, great energy, imagination, courage to take calculated risks, and to his respected position as former king and father of independence. His political maneuvers that had long maintained him in power also contributed to his downfall, for they had in the end alienated both the right and the left. But his dénouement may not have occurred at this particular time were it not for the growing deterioration of Cambodia's economy and security, which provided his rivals among the elite with sufficient stimulus and justification to unite in disposing of him.

After Sihanouk's ouster, the second Indochinese war was extended by the South Vietnamese and the Americans into Cambodia with the

[1] King Norodom Suramarit, Sihanouk's father, died in April 1960. A successor suitable to Prince Sihanouk was not available, and the throne was left vacant. Sihanouk was nominated as chief of state in June 1960.

approval of the Lon Nol government. In a further step to affirm its power, the government abolished the monarchy and proclaimed the Khmer Republic on October 9, 1970. The government, however, soon revealed its ineptness in coping with the spread of the Vietnamese Communists throughout the country and the development of a National United Front of Kampuchéa, a rebel group led by several of the former young intellectuals. In trying to take the bull by the horns in international politics, rather than sparring with it, the Lon Nol government led the country into a nightmare in which the North Vietnamese could openly support dissident elements. Thus, by 1973 Cambodia was being torn asunder by wars fought on two fronts, international and domestic. Ironically, the unpopularity of the Lon Nol government had also pushed the radical rebels and Prince Sihanouk, at the head of a government-in-exile in Peking, into the same camp, whereas formerly it was against the prince's policies that they were dissenting.

By 1973, it appeared that the government, its authority restricted virtually to Phnom Penh and its environs, was not viable and could exist only so long as American bombers carried on the offensive for it. The morale of the poorly trained Khmer army had sunk to a new low, as corruption at the higher ranks had made itself felt sorely at the bottom and the soldiers fought against overwhelming odds a war many of them did not understand. Whole villages were reported to have been razed and rice fields abandoned as terrified peasants fled the bombing to a capital already overcrowded with refugees. Transportation of food and other necessities between towns had been slowed, and the arrival of new shipments of vital goods into the country was sporadic and unpredictable, for convoys of trucks from Cambodia's only seaport, Kompong Som (formerly Sihanoukville), or of ships along the Mekong River from South Viet-Nam had to pass through territory under the control of the rebels.

I. The Personalization of Power

From 1945 to 1954, the evolution of Cambodian politics was marked by ferment, uncertainty, and disorder. Much of this was stirred by a conflict between King Norodom Sihanouk and the Democrat party, the chief political body of the time, over the question of how independence should be sought, who should lead the struggle for it, and who would shape the country's future after it was won. The impasse between them was not resolved until 1953 when Sihanouk, who favored negotiation with France rather than an armed rebellion, assumed charge of the government, dissolved the parliament, and took upon himself a mandate to achieve independence and establish political stability within two years.

Once independence was attained in November 1953, as a result of Sihanouk's "royal crusade," and peace and stability were restored by the 1954 Geneva Conference on Indochina, the king considered various ways to prevent a return to the "anarchy of parties," while restoring constitutional rule. As a result of a referendum in February 1955, which confirmed the people's trust in his leadership, and his own growing conviction that only his direct participation in politics could prevent a disruptive Democrat victory in new elections for the National Assembly, the king proposed a number of constitutional reforms to ensure that elected representatives would be held directly responsible to the people. Sihanouk's proposed reforms, excerpts from which are presented below, would also have enhanced greatly his own authority as king.

Norodom Sihanouk: Constitutional Reforms [February 1955]*

The People will no longer choose their representatives according to Party labels, but will require that candidates stand for election as individuals and not as party nominees. The new system will suppress the proliferation of parties and noisy, deceptive and costly electoral campaigns, the sequels to which are a very heavy burden on the People.

In order to relieve present abuses, the King proposes the revision of the present representative system according to the following new principles:

a) the *Khums*, the traditional administrative districts of the Kingdom, will replace the artificially constituted electoral districts;

b) each *Khum* will elect its own representative who will be its *Mékhum* and its deputy in the legislative assembly;

c) only those persons who have resided in the *Khum* continuously for three years may be candidates; and

d) the *Mékhum*-deputy of the *Khum* will draw his compensation and

* *Source:* "Corrective Study of the Constitution Accorded by H.M. the King of Cambodia in 1947," *France-Asie*, 11 (May 1955), 108: 654–663. Reprinted with permission of *France-Asie*.

emoluments, not from the national budget, but from the *Khum* budget or, if one does not exist, from the *Khet* budget. The *Mékhum*-deputy of the *Khum,* elected for five years, will be removable at any time by the People, provided that they address to the King a petition to this effect signed by at least three-quarters of the *Khum* electors.

These remedies will cure the ills of the present system, for

a) the deputy coming from the *Khum* and from an electoral district reduced to the *Khum* will know thoroughly the needs of the small districts he represents;

b) the People will no longer be deceived by candidates who come from afar, i.e., the cities, who know nothing of local needs and who often disappear from their electors' sight once they are elected; and

c) the representative of the People . . . will never be able to conduct himself as their master for he will be obliged, at the end of each month, to come to draw his salary and benefits in his *Khum;* he will, therefore, remain their servant. . . .

[Under this system] there will be several hundred deputies. At first glance, there might seem to be a major inconvenience resulting from the requirement of having to pay this large number of deputies. But this inconvenience would be quickly eliminated by the following dispositions, which would constitute the advantages dreamed of by Our People:

a) the popular representative is already paid as *Mékhum;*

b) in place of equating the parliamentary salary of the People's representatives with that of an *Oudam Montrei hors-classe,* a modest salary will be added, such that the total compensation of a representative will not exceed the emoluments of a *Kromokar,* for example. This salary will remove from the list of candidates those who are not interested in the well-being of the People, but only in their own;

c) the great number of People's representatives will guarantee that the voice of the popular assembly will be the authentic voice of the People . . . ;

d) the great number of deputies will maintain the liberty of the various tendencies of national opinion and, thus, will constitute the best obstacle to the dictatorial endeavors of a party; and

e) the greater the number of popular representatives, the closer will be their contact with the People and the wider the spread of their control of the country. The affairs and complaints which will be submitted by the People will receive more complete and rapid attention, for substantive inquests would be conducted by the representatives.

The People will be able to control easily the activities of the civil servants. The efforts made by the King in the past to cure the faults found in the midst of the national administration have failed. In consequence, He presents the following enlargement of the People's powers:

a) seeing that the financial burden of maintaining them is supported by the People, it is necessary to consider all State employees as the employees of the People;

b) as the employer . . . the People will have the right, under certain guarantees of equity, to discharge from the administration those officials they proclaim unworthy of serving in the administration; and

c) the Royal Government will recruit, name and employ the civil servants. But the People will have the power to oversee them and terminate their services. The King thinks that there will thus be a strong chance that the "chosen ones" will do better in the future.

In other respects the former parliamentary system presents a lacuna: Heretofore, the representatives constituted only an assembly and therefore resided only in Phnom-Penh and the *Khets* were neglected, whereas the People, the affairs of the *Khet, Srok,* and *Khum* were of more immediate and vital importance than the affairs treated in the capital. The King thus accords a supplementary power to the People and their representatives. The old system permits the National Assembly to oversee only the government. The new system will permit the People to oversee the provincial administration at all levels.

The great number of representatives will endow the new system of popular representation with two stages:

First stage: Each *Khet* will have a *Khet* Assembly composed of representatives of all the *Khums* in the *Khet.* The *Khet* Popular Assembly will authorize the *Khet* budget and will establish the regulations, taxes and privileges of special interest to the *Khet.* It will follow the management of provincial affairs by the *Chauvaykhet, Chauvaysroks,* and all civil servants. At the same time, its members, who will also be *Mékhums,* should assist the *Chauvaykhet* and the administration in the execution of the law, regulations and government directives in the respective *Khums.*

Second Stage: In Phnom-Penh, in place of the National Assembly, there will be a Popular Assembly of the Kingdom, which will be composed of representatives of all the *Sroks* of the *Khets* in the Kingdom. The Popular Assembly of the Kingdom will vote the laws of the Kingdom, the national budget and will oversee the Royal Government.

The King's reform in favor of popular representation conceives of mixed powers giving the legislature a foothold on the executive, thus moving beyond the democratic systems of most other countries. In doing this, the King intends that Cambodian democracy shall profit from the good sense, wisdom, clairvoyance and the spirit of justice of the Khmer People. It is therefore a bold reform which should find, as in all democratic systems known in the world, a counter-weight susceptible of assuring equilibrium, stability and, consequently, permanence to the new system.

Our People themselves have found and expressly indicated this counter-weight: It is the King's influence, and the People have asked the King to take the direction of the government and administration of the country and the edification of national laws, in intimate cooperation with the mass of the People and their representatives.

But in homage to the total confidence which His People have expressed in Him, the King must not deceive the People and must tell them frankly that He is not in a position to embrace all activities and responsibilities. In order to serve the country well, the King needs the active aid of the People.

Moreover, the King is persuaded that the People, rid of their intermediaries, are capable of managing well the affairs of the country. In this management, the King, in order to respond to the requirements of the People as a counter-weight for the democratic system, should play the role of Guide of the People and of the Chief of the Executive, it being understood that in the executive as in the legislature the People alone should have the last word. Therefore, the King will choose and name the members of the government. However, on the demand of the Popular Assembly of the Kingdom, He will revoke automatically the members of the government who are judged by this Assembly to be unworthy of continuing their ministerial functions.

If the King alone chooses the members of government, it is for the following two reasons:

a) the Popular Assembly includes only men who come from the *Khums*. As a man from Phnom-Penh cannot pretend to know the needs of *Khum* Baphnom as well as the inhabitants of that *Khum,* so it is preferable to confide in the King the care of recruiting, in the service of the People, men whom the King knows possess the experience and the capability needed in order to constitute the government of the country. Moreover, the People have always accepted and even called upon the King to choose the ministers; and

b) this power residing in the King is only one part of the counter-weight. . . . The other part of the counter-weight assumed by the King . . . will consist of the following dispositions:

1. The power to request a second reading of legislative acts. . . . If, after the second reading, the Popular Assembly maintains the same position which the King cannot approve, the dispute will be resolved by the Crown Council, the highest constitutional body . . . , which chooses the Sovereigns and Regents of Cambodia. However, in order to guarantee the

spirit of democratic justice, the Crown Council may deliberate on only two disputes each year. In case the Crown Council is unable to resolve the dispute, the Popular Assembly will be dissolved and its members returned to their electors, who are the supreme judges. Thus, if the electors should re-elect and return the same representatives to the Popular Assembly, the King will be obliged to consider the opinion expressed by the Assembly as that of the People. The King will then promulgate the disputed bill into law;

2. The power to dissolve the Chamber of Deputies, which is granted to the King by Our Constitution, will be limited to the circumstances cited above. The King, however, will have the right to return to his electors this or that individual popular representative. This action will be accompanied by a message explaining the King's motives to the electors, who will then organize new elections in the *Khum* in order to choose their representative who, moreover, could be the former representative. This system is fully democratic, since the People and not the King will be the supreme judge of the matter. If the King has the right to return the deputies to their electors, the deputies, by a three-quarter majority, will have the right to remove the King's ministers;

3. The King will be the final interpreter of the constitution. This disposition is only a correction of an anomaly which exists in Article 101 of the constitution. In effect, this constitution was granted by the King to His People. Since the King is considered as the Father of the Constitution, it is only logical that the duty of interpreting it should revert to Himself; and

4. The King designates the provincial governors who, however, being members of the Royal Government, may be removed on the simple demand of $\frac{3}{4}$ or $\frac{4}{5}$ of the popular representatives.

This constitutes all of the King's powers. None of these royal powers is unlimited. None is exclusive. All are limited and depend finally on the verdict of the People, whom the King has made Supreme Judge of all and even of the King who considers Himself only as First Representative of the People.

Finally, governmental stability shall be assured by the following new disposition: There will be only one Royal Government. If the People ask for the removal of the Chief of Government, the King will satisfy their demand automatically, but will retain the other members of the Government. These members may be removed one by one on the request of the People, but the Government will always remain the same. The King will appoint new members of the Government. There will no longer be Cabinets of X . . . , Y . . . , or Z. . . . There will only be the Royal Government, whose members may change without the Government changing.

The reform which the King has the honor to present to Our People, conforming to the needs newly but clearly and powerfully expressed, contains certain original ideas.

But the King is convinced that they respond point by point to the real needs of Our People.

The failure of democracy in Cambodia arose, in My Opinion, from the blunders of the men to whom the King confided the task of implementing Our Constitution. They brought to the Khmer People French constitutional dispositions which did not satisfy the French people, who have known democracy for a long time.

I do not mean by that that it almost deprived Our People of the liberties, rights and powers they all merited as much as other peoples on earth. But, in creating democracy here, one did not take into account the peasant qualities of Our People: Good sense, courage, honesty, wisdom, religiousness—qualities which make Our People strong and which should assure their future.

Why not permit the People to exercise directly the powers as theirs? Why give these powers to persons who possess none of the fundamental qualities of Our People and who, because of that, cannot represent them but make them lose faith in their representatives and their government? From this comes the anarchy we have known and which we still experience.

I add, moreover, that the absolute Monarchy is not to be revived. The King is not infallible. As it is useful to utilize Him, so it is necessary to limit His useable powers like His responsibilities.

Inasmuch as the People have total confidence in Me, I do not have the right to deceive them into accepting a system which does not, in My Opinion, satisfy all popular needs. In order to repay what would be only a small part of the immense debt of recognition that I have contracted vis-à-vis My People, who have always defended me against the disloyal intrigues of certain politicians, I have devoted several days of work in order, today, to be able to present to them in all honesty the present reform measures, which, in My Opinion, constitute the best solution to our problems. Our People are free to adopt or reject, as they wish, the present reforms.

In all honesty, I believe I have found a solution, unusual perhaps, but susceptible to making Our People a free and sovereign People, conscious of their responsibilities, a happy People who will no longer be deceived.

The spirit and the letter of My Reform seem to Me to be more democratic and "socially" more advanced than that of the old system. The only powers that I permit Myself to reserve to the King have for their aim that of facilitating, in guiding them, the exercise by the People of their sovereign powers and of assuring, by guarding against intrigues, corruption and the maneuvers of demagogues, the stability and the prosperity of the Regime which is, I dare to assert, one of the most advanced democratic regimes among the free countries of the present world.

Our People, therefore, will choose between the direct exercise of sovereign powers which devolve upon them and the exercise of their powers by the intermediary of deputies elected according to the old system.

If they adopt by referendum the first solution, Our Constitution, which will have been amended according to the reform presented here, will permit them, in general elections, to choose their representatives without seeing the reappearance of the parties, which in their petitions they have denounced as being so inconvenient.

If they choose the second solution, i.e., the *status quo ante,* it will be My Duty to order the integral application of the old system, in spite of My fear of seeing the same conflicts reappear, the same lack of understanding between the People and their representatives, the same incompatibility between the deputies and the King, ending in the same crisis, aggravated in an incalculable way.

With the reform, there would be at least a 90 percent chance that the People and the King would be happy and would live together without constraint, because the reform would put the People and the King side by side, hand in hand, thus uniting their responsibilities as their destinies.

Thus, the destiny of the Nation and the Country will have no fissures.

I remain persuaded that all Khmers of good will, animated by the spirit of justice and by a disinterested love of the country, will opt courageously for the end of political chaos and for the advent of a democracy more in conformity with the genius of our race, more pure and also more just.

NORODOM SIHANOUK

P.S. We have omitted, in this study, noting the replacement of the Council of the Kingdom by a People's Consultative Council. This Council, whose members (numbering 20) will be chosen by the Popular Assembly of the Kingdom from a list, presented by the King, of 40 names of personalities who have much experience in the affairs of the Kingdom, would have the following attributions:

a) elaboration of proposed laws and regulations on the request of the Popular Assembly of the Kingdom and the *Khet* Assemblies;

b) technical or political advice on all deliberations of the Popular Assemblies or the Royal Government;

c) regulation, on appeal, of administrative matters in dispute; and

d) obligatory advice on cases of recall, removal and revocation of members of the government or civil servants.

Also, We have omitted noting that the Supreme Court, provided for by the Constitution, would be abolished and its attributions transferred to the Popular Assembly of the Kingdom (thus completing the sovereign powers of the People).

N. S.

According to his advisors, King Sihanouk's proposed constitutional reforms were received badly "by politicians, certain civil servants and some 'bourgeois aises,' who have been in the habit of using their knowledge to deceive others." This opposition convinced him that only by stepping down from the throne, which by custom is above politics, and becoming an active participant in the political arena, could he work effectively toward his announced objectives. On March 2, 1955, therefore, King Norodom Sihanouk abdicated in favor of his father, Prince Norodom Suramarit. Sihanouk explained his action in the following radio broadcast to the nation on March 15.

Norodom Sihanouk Explains His Abdication [March 15, 1955]*

Compatriots,

I abdicated at the moment when, having succeeded in winning Cambodia's independence, the people restored to the King through a free referendum all democratic powers. I wanted by this abdication to demonstrate to our statesmen the importance of their mission in the service of the Nation. . . . I wanted to give to our youth and more particularly to our students proof that the Monarch of Cambodia, in working for the Country and the Nation, was not motivated by a desire to be "His Majesty the King," especially attached to his throne, enjoying indefinitely its display and grandeur, its prerogatives and pomp, as was asserted by certain politicians in their propaganda and commentaries.

Moreover, I wanted to set an example for our government servants who thought that, since I was already on the throne and thus enjoyed all of the inherent advantages of royalty, I amused myself by giving counsel merely by words and clamour: Let's not aspire to grandeur! Let's not aspire to power! Let's not aspire to riches!

I hope that in abandoning my reign, my crown and my throne, my sacrifice will help to call the attention of our elite to the great importance of raising our Nation from its present state, which prompts foreigners to

* *Source:* "Message of H.R.H. Samdech Upayuvareach Norodom Sihanouk," *Agence Khmère de Presse,* No. 1455 (March 15, 1955), pp. c/1–c/5.

say that we do not know how to conduct ourselves with the dignity and courage required by the statute of independence. Moreover, I should like to see these same elite take on the determination to assure the defense and safety of the little people so that they may escape the abuse which they suffer at the hands of the leaders, for the people have made me a part of their sorrows and have declared to me formally that they would succumb ineluctably if those who have administrative charge of them refuse to purify themselves and abolish injustice.

When I assigned myself the duty of fighting against foreign domination, . . . royal authority was necessary in order to facilitate my task and to lead victoriously this fight for the benefit of my country. In order to win this struggle, I needed my legal title of representative of my country and of the whole Khmer nation, for if I could not speak as King of Cambodia, it would be possible to claim that I did not represent all of Cambodia, but only a clan or a part of national opinion.

The problem needing resolution today differs from the problem of independence.

This problem concerns social order. . . .

In order to resolve this internal problem, I feel that I must sacrifice myself in order to serve as an example and to give proof of my convictions.

. . . This social problem, which consists of coming to the aid of the little people, the poor people, the people in the countryside, imposes on a statesman who is determined to serve and succor them the obligation of living constantly in intimacy with them, for it is only in this way that he will be able to see clearly for himself the abuses which they suffer in the villages, districts, provinces and the cities.

If I remained on the throne, shut up in my palace, what affection could I bring to my people? I would know little of either their situation or the abuses of which they were the victims. I should be incapable of discerning truth from falsehoods, black from white, just from unjust, truth from calumny, for the Sovereign occupies too elevated a rank for the people to be able easily to come to see him frequently. Even if the people were able to obtain an audience with the King, their sorrows would not be exposed in all their details to the Sovereign for, on the one hand, they would always be accompanied by those who serve the Palace and they would believe themselves to be liable to reprisals. How would the Monarch be able to know what became of the people when they left the Palace?

On the other hand, the Palace swarms with a crowd of big and little mandarins among whom schemers creep like veritable leeches, living only on blood, fastening themselves to the legs of the elephant. Under these conditions, it is impossible for the Sovereign to search for justice for the people, for, on the one side, they would hardly dare to "tell all" to the

Monarch and, on the other, there are always certain high personalities who seek only the right occasion to give the King advice which is not always necessarily in the interests of the modest people.

During the fourteen years of my reign, I never stopped searching for the means of resolving the problems which interest the people and of relieving them of their unhappiness and sorrow, but I must confess to them that great obstacles have stood in my path, preventing me from carrying through successfully, as I have wished, the mission I assigned myself on their behalf.

I am now orienting myself in another way in order to relieve the ills of my people, a way not followed by many Sovereigns of other countries. I shall now travel in the countryside every year in order to make direct contact with the people.

If I were to remain King, however, it would be necessary on each of these journeys, to notify the administrative authorities in advance so that they could make preparations. They would organize the official cortege, mobilize the military forces and the police, put the provinces and districts in order, all according to a carefully devised program. There . . . would be many tribunes and triumphal arches decked with the national colors, troops rendering military honors, and gatherings of civil servants, clergy and inhabitants—all impeccably ranged. After his discourse, it would hardly be possible for the Sovereign to establish contact with the people and to gather the information he desires, for on occasions of this sort the government officials have already taken the necessary precautions in order that everything appears to be proper and correct. Moreover, the program of the royal tour would not permit the Sovereign to tarry and he would be obliged to hasten on his journey.

Another obstacle which prevents the Sovereign from devoting the time necessary to be in contact with his people resides in the fact that the King is the representative of his country vis-à-vis the world and as such the duties of his office impose on him the obligation of receiving a never-ending train of Ambassadors, Ministers, Statesmen, and high personalities of foreign countries.

Because the country has acquired full independence and is recognized today by more than forty powers, the King's time is entirely taken up by the audiences he must accord the personalities of these powers coming to visit our country. He must organize and offer banquets, receptions, ballets in their honor, and, in consequence, he does not find any moment of free time to move about the country.

It is because of all these obstacles that I believed it would be impossible to remain on the throne and to be capable of relieving the suffering of the people.

It is because of this that I have decided definitely to abandon the throne, its display and pomp, forever, and to dedicate myself, body and soul, to the service and well-being of my people.

As for the obstacles thrown up by politicians and foreigners in the Sovereign's path in order to prevent him from leading his people toward their goal, I am in a position to evade them by no longer depending on royal ways and means. I have formed a partnership with the people who have confidence in me in order to open up a new way which will lead them to power, rights, sovereignty, liberty and justice, according to the provisions of a new law which I have elaborated for this purpose.

If I persevere in my efforts, it is because I know perfectly the feelings of our people in their present circumstances. At the same time, I know that ninety percent of our humble compatriots have confidence only in me and are asking me to pursue the fight until democracy triumphs.

I am persuaded that this will come about only when our people will have acquired the powers that have been defined by the new law which I have prepared; when they will be truly sovereign; when the administration will be correct and clean; when the National Government will really search for concrete results for the Nation; when the foreigner will no longer try to take over the soul of the Nation, which is composed of the independence, liberty and sovereignty of the people; when the foreigner will no longer find it possible to buy politicians; when the country, relieved of all its maledictions and its disasters, will know once again the grandeur and prosperity of yesteryear conforming to the wishes of the whole Nation.

As you see, this social problem is of great importance and requires that I sacrifice without regret my throne and my life. In the service of the Nation, I dare to try my hand in this supreme effort. I should try to undertake it with all my energy, for if luck should favor me, I would be able, perhaps, to assist our people in attaining their aims according to their aspirations. Perhaps then the people would see an end to their sufferings and miseries and no longer would the elephants crush them, the tigers carry away their wives and children, the crocodiles snap at them, and the leeches suck their blood.

I am not sure of being able successfully to lead this enterprise, which is still more arduous than the winning of independence. But even supposing that this effort were not crowned with success, I would not be dissatisfied were I to succumb to my task, for I would be at peace with myself, destiny having decided that I leave a name in the history of my country.

In this terribly important effort I am proposing to undertake, I have no intention of opposing any political party or any government official by name or anyone in particular.

I believe that what I should search for is the realization of the union of all our compatriots, the moment when all of the people really hold in their hands all power.

The aim of my fight seeks only the suppression of abuses, reprehensible acts and injustices and is far from constituting an opposition or a sanction against anyone or any party.

I hope that my abdication—on the subject of which I permit myself to renew my solemn promise before the Nation, before history, before religion and before the world that I refuse categorically to return to the throne whatever the turn of circumstances—will have the effect of persuading all my compatriots that I do not have any intention of rising up against anyone.

When my people have achieved success, at that moment I will refuse any other charge. I have no other aim but to lead them to happiness. If one supposes that I wish to become Prime Minister or President of the National Assembly, would it not be better for me to become King again? Besides, when I was King no one harassed me or rebelled against me.

On the basis of my formal refusal to hold on to any power, be it royal, governmental, political or military, I permit myself to make a gift of my person to the country and to religion in order that my services find employment wherever there is a mission that does not have the character of governmental power, as, for example, the defense of popular, religious, educational, cultural and military interests before the Sovereign and the Government, or any services that it is believed may be entrusted to me in diplomacy abroad, either to represent our Kampuchea or to negotiate with foreign powers through conferences and so on. I suggest this because I have a certain renown in the world and because I am accustomed to negotiations and official relations with international powers, foreign ambassadors and world statesmen, and also because I am possessed of a demeanor and of a suitable bearing enabling me to represent the Nation with dignity before the world's powers according to the aspirations of the clergy, the elite and the people.

Still, it is for the people to decide as they wish on what I have just said.

This message contains all the particulars destined for my compatriots on my principal objectives and the essential points of my ideal derived from my abdication.

To all my compatriots whom I love as much as my own life—religious persons, men of the people, military and youth—I extend the sentiments of affection to all without distinction.

NORODOM SIHANOUK

Within a month of his abdication, Sihanouk announced the establishment of the *Sangkum Reastr Niyum* (People's Socialist Community). It was publicized as a rallying point for all Cambodians wishing to vote into office men who would be faithful to the throne and who would put into effect a modified version of Sihanouk's proposed reforms. As conceived by Sihanouk, it was not a political party; it was to be above petty factionalism, and its only requirement for membership was nonmembership in a political party. It would provide the organizational base for implementing popular participation in politics.

In actuality, the Sangkum only remotely resembled the people's movement that Sihanouk had envisioned. The elite, whose perennial challenge of Sihanouk's programs had given him the idea of the Sangkum in the first place, readily deserted their own parties to join it. Once part of the organization, they dominated its committees and controlled its operations. The masses were denied meaningful participation, and the elite had free rein to use the Sangkum as a means to further secure their control of the government.

Statute of the Sangkum Reastr Niyum [April 1955]*

Art. 1. There is formed among all Cambodians who accept the present statutes, a Community of Citizens known as the People's Socialist Community ("Sangkum Reastr Niyum"), with its headquarters in Phnom-Penh.

Art. 2. It is composed of companions who have freely responded to the appeal which has been addressed to them.

Art. 3. Its organization is directed to the formation of a cadre of volunteers constituted for common, responsible and disinterested action, with a view to the realization of the Union of the children of the Khmer Fatherland, a union [now] compromised by the proliferation of Political Parties, the birth in Cambodia of a true socialist and egalitarian democracy, and the Fatherland's return to its great past. The Community will try to assure this return by giving a true meaning to the Trinity: Nation—Religion—King, which can survive and render service to the Fatherland only if state institutions search for their inspiration among the mass of the People and function under their real, direct and continuous supervision in their real and permanent interests. The Community is directed equally at honoring the moral qualities and at raising the standard of living of the people by promoting their social, economic and cultural progress.

* *Source: Statut de Sangkum Reastr Niyum* (Phnom Penh), 1955.

Art. 4. The practical definition of the Community and its program of action are presented below:

Our Community is not a political party.

Our Community is the symbol of the hopes of the little people who are the True People of Cambodia, our beloved Fatherland.

Our Community is a National Gathering, which combats injustice, corruption, extortion, oppression and treason, which imperil the People and the Country.

Our Community defends the National Union by the return of the good traditions which made the country grand during its glorious past. These traditions are the communion of the People with their two natural protectors: Religion and the Throne.

Our Community intends to promote the PEOPLE'S SOCIALIST REGIME which gives to the True People—to the great mass of the little people who symbolize the Khmer Nation—Sovereignty, National Powers to be exercised directly by the People at [all] levels, in conformity with the spirit of the Constitution and with the dispositions conceived for the People and bestowed by Preah Bat Samdech NORODOM SIHANOUK.

. . . Art. 6. In order to be admitted into the People's Socialist Community, Cambodians should:

1st—Not belong to any political party;

2nd—Not have incurred any conviction depriving them of their civil rights (convictions for political acts excepted);

3rd—Bring all of their zeal and devotion to bear upon the realization of the objectives laid down in . . . the present statutes;

4th—Give proof of respect for the discipline of the Community, established by its internal rules, and manifest their disinterest by orienting their activities, not towards the goal of succeeding to power and of serving their personal interests, but towards the realization of the People's aspirations.

Art. 7. The title of Companion is lost:

1st—By resignation;

2nd—By disciplinary dismissal.

Art. 8. Any Companion who resigns must first advise the Secretary of the Central Committee. . . .

Art. 9. The exclusion of a Companion will be carried out by the Central Committee if he is convicted:

1st—Of sabotaging or trying to sabotage the spirit or the work of our Community, or of disobeying or trying to disobey the Community's discipline;

2nd—Of having acted or suffered conviction for acting in such a way as to blemish his honor.

. . . Art. 12. The People's Socialist Community is composed of the Central Committee, the Groups, and the Congresses.

Art. 13. The [Central] Committee, designated by the National Congress for a one-year term, which may be renewed, is made up of a President, a Secretary-General, three Deputy-Secretaries, a Treasurer, two Deputy Treasurers, five Political Counsellors, [and] three Commissioners. The Congress elects the President and the 15 other members of the Committee. The Central Committee takes its decisions by voting. In the case of a tie vote, the vote of the President is decisive. . . .

Art. 14. The Supreme Counsellor [President], who is in principle a personality who has rendered eminent and indisputable service to Cambodia and who is recognized as a veritable national hero, has the task of assuring strong cohesion among the Members of the Community and of inspiring, should the occasion arise, the national action of the Community.

Art. 15. The Secretary-General, assisted by his deputies, is charged with the administration of the Community. He also conducts all investigations which interest the Community and assures the coordination of its different bodies. He receives instructions concerning the management of the Community from the National Congress and the President. Investigation committees are constituted by the Secretary-General in order to furnish the Central Committee with data on which its actions may be based.

. . . Art. 19. The Groups constitute the organs of rallying and common action. They include the *Khum* Groups, *Srok* Groups, and the City or Provincial Capital Groups.

Art. 20. Each Group is directed by a committee of between 5 to 20 members, depending on the importance of the *Khum, Srok* or City, elected by secret vote for one year, by the Companions of the Group. The Committee of the Group appoints its Executive Board, consisting of a Director and two Members.

Art. 21. A Delegate is named by the Central Committee of the Community to each City or Provincial Capital Group to coordinate the particular action taken by the Groups with the general action of the Community. The Delegate advises the Group Committee on matters concerning the administration of the Group. With the Delegate, a Treasurer named by the Central Committee is responsible for the [Group's] funds. His advice must be sought on all expenditures and on all request for funds.

Art. 22. There are two kinds of Congresses:

—The Provincial Congresses;

—The National Congress. . . .

Art. 23. Each Provincial Congress convenes the representatives of all the *Khums* in the province. Every quarter, each of the Provincial Congresses meets separately to discuss questions concerning the activities of the assemblage. This convention seeks a consensus of opinions and confirms the designation of the candidates in general or special elections, designation made by the people of the *Khum, Srok,* or City.

Art. 24. The National Congress meets, in ordinary session, at least once a year and, in special session, any time when there is a need for it and on the convocation of the Secretary.

The National Congress is composed of delegations of the people from the *Khums, Sroks,* and Cities or Capitals of the Provinces. The number of delegates from the *Khums, Sroks,* and Cities or Provincial Capitals will be established, for the first Congress, by the founding members and, for other Congresses, by the decision taken by the previous Congress.

Phnom-Penh, 22 March 1955
The President
NORODOM SIHANOUK

Prince Sihanouk viewed himself not only as the father of Cambodia's independence but as its saviour as well. He was firmly convinced that his country's destiny was inextricably tied to his own. From time to time he deemed it necessary to remind the Cambodian people that his actions were taken in the best interests of the country and that he was the sole figure on which they could focus their respect, loyalty, and affection. The following excerpts from *Neak Cheat Niyum* (The Nationalist), one of several state journals of which the prince was editor, provide an example.

Neak Cheat Niyum: *The Evolution of Cambodian Democracy*
[August–October 1960]*

When, in 1947, His Majesty Norodom Sihanouk, King of Cambodia, granted a democratic constitution to the Khmer Nation, certain circles were critical of him. They said, "The Cambodian people did not ask for so much and, moreover, we are absolutely unprepared to enjoy the rights enjoyed by the citizens of a western-style liberal 'Democracy.' " Strictly speaking, this criticism was easily justified and was justified as much by the disastrous functioning of the first elected assemblies as by the no less disastrous management of the governments which emanated from them. However, as long as French authority remained absolutely sovereign, the repercussions on the life of the Nation were limited.

* *Source: Neak Cheat Niyum* (Phnom Penh), August 21, September 4, October 2, 1960.

But, in 1952, it became evident that this parliamentary democracy, left to itself, was absolutely incapable, not only of leading but also of supporting the fight for independence undertaken by the King. And one knows that H.M. Norodom Sihanouk, recognized by all the people as the symbol of the Nation, had to dissolve the National Assembly in order to lead by himself, with the aid of a few collaborators whom he chose, the Royal Crusade for independence.

It seems inconceivable, with the passage of time, that certain Khmer politicians, of whom many were sincere, haggled over and sometimes refused in the name of democracy their support of the Sovereign, while the liberation of the territory and national unity were at stake. How should one judge the attitude of these isolated men, having lost all contact with the people and always pretending to speak in their name? Where else could they find joined the symbol of national unity and the collective will to fight for a well-defined goal, which was the independence of the nation, but in the King himself with whom the people identified themselves.

This situation is not unique to Cambodia for there is hardly any country in Asia or Africa which sought its liberation from direct colonial tutelage without a unanimously respected leader whom the people recognized. . . . The necessity of a leader in certain circumstances, moreover, is not unique to under-developed and 'colonized' countries, but is equally true in the most modern western countries when they face dangers which menace their existence. . . .

But in under-developed, ex-colonized nations the situation is something else. The personal authority of a leader, having led the fight for independence, maintains itself intact at the end of the struggle—if it is victorious —even reveals itself as being indispensable in order to preserve the unity of the Nation and to begin the work of national edification. . . .

Here *it is certain* that without the presence and the will of Prince Norodom Sihanouk, Cambodia, inevitably, would have known a period of anarchy followed by the alienation of all or part of its national independence.

It is in the fight for independence that the people recognize their leader, especially if this leader remains at their side during the darkest days and shares their trials. This leader is unique. No force in the world can ever impose a leader on a nation and no personality can ever impose himself as their leader without the unanimous accord of the people of the nation. . . .

This uncontested authority acquired by a national leader in the direction of the fight for independence is irreplaceable when it becomes a question of organizing the State, of planning and implementing an economic program, and of instilling in the people the courage and faith necessary to support a great, even unbounded, effort. . . .

The disappearance of the leader of Independence may often be catastrophic for the stability of the new state and for its economic and social development. . . .

If it is a question of an imposed leader (most often by foreigners) these persons would have no other means to assure his power than dictatorship and police oppression, and these would be temporary, for civil war would then become inevitable. But from this fight against dictatorship may come a truly popular leader, recognized by all the people. One may say, therefore, that a national leader is always a strong personality, but that, on the contrary, a "strongman" is not always necessarily a popular leader. . . .

Contrary to a dictator, to a "strongman," the national leader is especially careful to remain in close and constant contact with the people. One governs with a police apparatus, the other with the confidence of the people. One imposes, the other explains, persuades, leads by his example.

Without doubt a national leader cannot always escape the temptation to totalitarianism, all the less because he knows that the people would accept it without a murmur—during the first years—and that he never lacks "counselors" to encourage him in this direction. But a national *and* *popular* leader is also a political educator of his people. All his efforts tend, not only to convince the people but to lead them to participate in the political life of the nation, towards the development of democratic institutions adapted to the nation's particular psychology and the proper functioning of these institutions. This veritable "mise au point" of democracy is without doubt the most thankless task which awaits a popular leader but it is also the most noble. . . .

Cambodia has the immense fortune of having at its head a national and popular leader in the person of Samdech Sahachivin [Lord Comrade]. The people know it. May the handful of intellectuals set in a sterile and negative opposition understand it, too!

There is no doubt that the notion of a unique, or dominant, party is one which Western liberal democrats find it very difficult to accept. Let's remind ourselves that, when the fifth legislative elections (1958) assured for the Sangkum all of the seats in the Assembly, certain foreign circles did not hesitate to criticize this unanimity by "counseling" [sic] that some seats first be reserved to the opposition. In effect, for an important number of westerners the percentage of votes harvested by the Sangkum is too great to be believable. Those who witnessed the elections or the referendums are able to affirm that the secrecy of the ballots was respected and that the counting of the ballots was conducted honestly, but there are always the skeptics, the clever ones, who say with a smile, "There is always trickery!" It is inconceivable for the majority of westerners in Cambodia, with their own world carefully preserved, that a political "party" could obtain 98 per cent of the votes. . . .

People have always needed and, moreover, searched for a political framework. If it is a question of a people of a nation which desires to leave rapidly its state of under-development this need becomes an imperious necessity.

In western democracies this political framework, an intermediary between central power and the people, exists. It is constituted by the parliaments taken together and by the political parties and groups which, alternatively, assume the charge of power. This system has its partisans and its adversaries, and functions in an acceptable way in materially developed countries which have a long democratic tradition behind them. . . .

As for the young states which have just gained independence and which must progress at a forced march in order to make up for lost time, a political framework which includes multiple parties can be catastrophic. We have had experience, limited happily by the creation of the Sangkum by Samdech, with confusion degenerating into anarchy during the first years of Cambodian democracy, when parties, more numerous each month, faced each other. We also saw what difficulties Indonesia, for example, faced following the quarrels among many political parties, and the measures taken under "guided democracy" in order to remedy that state of affairs.

For the peoples of Asia and Africa, for whom the awakening is one of the most important events of the century, if it is not the most important, a *homogeneous* and *efficacious* political framework is a vital, an absolute necessity. Some nations have found this framework in a fascist dictatorship, while others have established a people's democracy, i.e., a communist dictatorship. But many people have *refused the totalitarian formula* and are searching for a liberal but nonetheless efficacious formula, generally a socialism adapted to national conditions. It cannot be denied, however, that in all the States which have just rediscovered their independence the political example of the former power dominates, and, today, some communist nations . . . attract a part of the intellectuals who have been trained abroad. These external factors play an important role in this search for a "national" formula and obstruct—sometimes in a happy way but more often destructively—the authentically national and popular evolution, conforming to traditions, to economic reality, and especially to the psychology and aspirations of the masses and their natural leaders.

In all countries subjugated to foreign rule . . . the fight for independence and the expression of nationalism crystallized itself as a general rule in a dominant party . . . directed by a powerful personality recognized by all of the people. We have a perfect example in the history of the reconquest of our independence and also in that of most of the countries which have liberated themselves from the colonial yoke during the past fifteen years. The necessity of a dominant party is affirmed, moreover, not only in the fight for independence but also in the case of a nation having liberated itself from economic subjugation or emerging quickly from an archaic and under-developed state.

In truth, a dominant or unique party is indispensable not only in the fight for political independence, but still more, after the acquisition of independence, for its definitive consolidation and for the economic and social edification of the Nation.

It is erroneous to assert an absolute equality: A unique party equals a totalitarian regime. Without doubt, a totalitarian regime is always founded on a unique party, but it also follows the liquidation by force of other parties and groups, which is not the case of democratic regimes building themselves around a dominant party and its leader.

A true totalitarian party founds itself on an ideology by which it judges, in the case of communism, the happiness of the entire human race, or in the case of fascism and of nazism, that of the chosen people. The goal to be attained is fixed once and for all and any means may be used to achieve it.

By contrast, the dominant party in an under-developed country has for its essential goal the return of political independence, . . . the economic and social development of the liberated country and especially the formation of a political and administrative elite. The dominant party is not an end in itself but a means by which the country may achieve development. It is only an indispensable temporary formula which leads, . . . and in this sense it takes on the aspect of an official political school.

Finally, a unique party permits the free application of a unique political economy. That is perhaps its principal advantage for an under-developed country.

When the choice of an economic and social development policy has been made . . . only a unique party animated by a strong personality is able to pursue it to the end, without reticence, tergiversations, and misgivings about the past. It is thus difficult, if not impossible, to imagine that a two-, five- or ten-year economic plan may be realized without the unconditional help of a solid dominant political party, assisted by all of the people who furnish it with its framework. . . .

The Sangkum Reastr Niyum did not exist formally before 1955 and, notably, during the period of the struggle for national independence. But it can hardly be denied that the rallying of the people around the King, His Majesty Norodom Sihanouk, in the Royal Crusade for Independence, anticipated the Sangkum of today. In fact the necessity of a "party" of Independence did not impose itself and, besides, could not have imposed itself, for the throne had taken the leadership of the national liberation movement. . . .

With Independence acquired, His Majesty Norodom Sihanouk thought that a western style parliamentary democracy could preside over the consolidation of independence and the political, economic and social edification of the Nation. The result was not expected. The political parties, without constructive programs and before becoming more than a credulous clientele of ambitious men, began, with the encouragement of foreigners, to contend for power, and the new independence was threatened. The reconstruction and the development of the country were on the brink of death.

The reconstitution of the national union which had assured the success of the Royal Crusade for Independence became a question of life or death for the Kingdom. His Majesty Norodom Sihanouk abandoned the throne in order to devote himself to this task by creating the Sangkum Reastr Niyum. In truth, only Prince Norodom Sihanouk, having the full support of the people, was able to rally all political forces of good will which were adrift, with their leaders wandering along paths which had little to do with the national interest.

The profound originality of the Sangkum Reastr Niyum is, undeniably, that it is not a political party but a Community, the gathering in a great national movement of all authentically Khmer forces around an uncontested leader and a well-defined political, economic and social program, which seeks Cambodia's progress from its state of under-development to one where it is aligned with the world's modern nations.

The Sangkum is in no way an authoritarian "party" which gives its carefully chosen members rights over the mass of the people. It claims no other profession than respect for the Constitution, the Monarchy and Neutrality. It does not seek to eliminate by terror or interdiction the political parties, which respect the law, but it does try to persuade their members to rally to the Sangkum.

We said earlier that a dominant party may be an official political school. Undeniably, the Sangkum is this political school, not only for those who participate directly in the Nation's political life: Members of government, parliamentarians, civil servants, but also for all the people who, a few years ago, had no political education and were easily misled by demagogues.

The role of political educator of the people is perhaps the most noble task of the Sangkum and the Prince. The permanent care of educating the masses politically is affirmed in the periodic National Congresses where *all* opinions may be expressed freely. It appears still more clearly perhaps in the speeches and messages which the Prince, President of the Sangkum and the Chief of State, addresses to the people each week . . . in which all problems are *discussed* with a frankness and sincerity which is disconcerting to foreigners.

The National Congresses and the veritable political conferences . . . of Samdech Sahachivin have borne fruit. The people now follow with increasing interest the political life of the Nation and the international situation. . . .

Finally, one should admit that its quality as dominant party has permitted the Sangkum to achieve a great number of things. It is only thanks to the union in the midst of the Sangkum that Samdech Sahachivin has been able to carry on campaigns for the development of education, for the water policy, for the enhancement of manual labor. . . . Several parties sharing power among them would have had neither the means nor the indispensable will in order to achieve this unanimity of effort, but rather their efforts would have been dissipated. . . . We see already the lack of cooperation among small political opposition groups; what would have been the result of the rivalries among strong political parties one dares not imagine.

II. Foreign Policy

The formulation and execution of Cambodia's foreign policy after 1955 was clearly Prince Sihanouk's forte. Advised primarily by Penn Nouth and Son Sann, two trusted senior civil servants who frequently served as ministers of state, the prince determined that only through a policy of neutrality could Cambodia preserve her newly won independence, protect her territorial integrity against what he believed were the imperialistic ambitions of her traditional antagonists—Thailand and Viet-Nam—avoid the consequences of a confrontation between the cold-war powers on her territory, and preserve her freedom of action in, and possibly exert some influence upon, international events.

The first two of the following three documents provide succinct statements on Cambodia's foreign policy during the years immediately after independence was achieved in 1953. The third, the "Law of Neutrality," was adopted by the National Assembly at Sihanouk's insistance in 1957 in an effort to convince the major powers that Cambodia was serious about her neutral stance.

Early Statement on Foreign Policy [July 1954]*

. . . The Royal Government of Cambodia will not join in any agreement with other States, if this agreement carries for Cambodia the obligation to enter into military alliances not in conformity with the principles of the Charter of the United Nations, or, as long as its security is not threatened, the obligation to establish bases on Cambodian territory for the military forces of foreign powers.

A Definition of Cambodia's Neutrality [1956]†

The neutrality of Cambodia was defined well in January 1956 by Prince Norodom Sihanouk during the second National Congress. He determined that Cambodia is neutral because:

1) it does not accept any offensive or defensive military pact with anyone and it refuses to be protected by any international defense organism;
2) it does not tolerate the presence of foreign troops or commands on its territory;
3) it does not grant any military base to any foreign country, not even to a friendly country; and
4) politically, it agrees to enter into friendly and diplomatic relations with all Powers and Governments who respect its sovereignty, integrity and its ideal of peace.

Finally it chooses not to make a decision regarding those countries which are divided politically (Viet-Nam, Korea, Germany).

Law of Neutrality [September 11, 1957]‡

1. The Kingdom of Cambodia is a neutral country.
2. Cambodia abstains from any military or ideological alliance with foreign countries.

* Source: Further Documents Relating to the Discussion of Indo-China at the Geneva Conference, June 16–July 21, 1954 (London: H.M. Stationery Office, 1954), Cmnd. 9239, Misc. No. 20, p. 14.

† Source: Gouvernement Royal du Cambodge, Cambodge (Phnom Penh: Ministère de l'Intérieur, 1962), p. 70.

‡ Source: Law 232-NS, September 11, 1957, printed in Réalités Cambodgiennes (Phnom Penh), September 21, 1957.

3. Cambodia will not undertake any aggression against any foreign country.

In the case of foreign aggression Cambodia reserves to itself the right

    a) to defend itself with arms;

    b) to call upon the United Nations; or

    c) to call upon a friendly power.

Throughout the late 1950's and early 1960's, the principal foreign-policy concern of Prince Sihanouk and his advisors was to preserve a balance between the major powers in Indochina. A confrontation between them, the prince believed, would lead inevitably to the victory of one over the other, with a consequent shift in the balance of power in the area and a renewed threat to Cambodia's security. With an American-supported victory in Viet-Nam, Cambodia would find herself completely surrounded by countries solidly in the Western camp. Thus firmly entrenched in the peninsula, the United States might cease to regard Cambodia as being of strategic importance to her, and she would no longer be likely to restrain the Thais and the South Vietnamese from encroaching upon Cambodia. On the other hand, according to Sihanouk, a Communist victory in Laos would open a direct land route between Cambodia and North Viet-Nam. Such an event, of more immediate danger to Cambodia, would probably hasten the conclusion of the war between North and South Viet-Nam in the former's favor. A united, Communist-dominated Viet-Nam, released from the burdens of a costly civil war, would then be free to direct its efforts against Cambodia.

It was this view of events in Indochina that led Sihanouk in 1959 to propose an arms moratorium in, and an internationally guaranteed neutrality of, Laos. In 1960 at the United Nations he again proposed the establishment of a neutral buffer zone in Indochina, this time suggesting the zone include Cambodia as well as Laos. As a result of another suggestion, made by the prince in early 1961, thirteen nations having an interest in Laos met in Geneva and, in 1962, agreed to recognize Laos's neutrality. Sihanouk's efforts to gain similar assurances for Cambodia, however, were made in vain. Largely because of his inability to win major power commitments to Cambodia's defense, Prince Sihanouk sought, in the mid-1960's, an accommodation with North Viet-Nam. In so doing, the prince altered significantly the course of Cambodia's foreign policy.

The following documents portray Prince Sihanouk's position on Cambodia's foreign policy, his appeal to the major powers to consider Cambodia's case, and his effort to persuade the Vietnamese Communists to moderate their stance in order to end the war in Viet-Nam and Laos.

Norodom Sihanouk: Cambodia's Foreign-Policy Position [September 26, 1961]*

. . . We are well aware that Cambodia's survival as a free and sovereign nation depends entirely on preserving equilibrium and friendship with these two blocs. The day we find ourselves facing only one all-powerful bloc, the days of our independence—perhaps even of our very existence—will be counted. This is why we are absolutely sincere when we say that we want the United States and our other Western friends to preserve and maintain their influence, their position in our area.

Norodom Sihanouk: Cambodia Seeks an International Guarantee of Her Neutrality and Independence [September 3, 1962]†

I have the honor to call Your Excellency's attention particularly to the very serious threat that has for years been hanging over my country, which has constantly been subjected to threats, plots, sabotage, blockades, and aggression by neighboring powers that are very much stronger militarily, concerning whose annexationist aims there is no longer any doubt. Territorial claims supported by the use of armed forces, the crossing of frontiers, flights over our territory, and its recent occupation by foreign troops cause me to fear that, in a short time, an insoluble situation will be created which could lead to an international conflict with unforeseeable consequences.

Cambodia can no longer endure this constant provocation and aggression, or the official or unofficial accusations made repeatedly by these same neighbors to the effect that it is encouraging and promoting subversion in their countries; this is not and has never been true.

Sincerely desiring peace, but resolved to defend its honor and what remains of its national territory after numerous "amputations," Cambodia

* Source: Address of H.R.H. Prince Norodom Sihanouk, Chief of State of Cambodia, to the Asia Society, New York, September 26, 1961 (New York: Permanent Mission of Cambodia to the United Nations, 1961), p. 18.

† Source: Letter to President John F. Kennedy (Department of State, Press Release, No. 532 [September 3, 1962]; italics in the original).

sees no other reasonable solution of this situation than to claim for itself the benefit of the international protection provisions that have been granted to Laos. . . .

Today, before making decisions of prime importance in order to protect its existence, Cambodia requests of Your Excellency's Government and the other powers which met last month in Geneva *the official recognition and guarantee of its neutrality and territorial integrity*. It is ready to accept any appropriate control for that purpose. . . .

I take the liberty of suggesting that Your Excellency be good enough to take an active interest in our fate and agree that an international conference on Cambodia be held as soon as possible in a large neutral capital or city of your choice. . . .

Norodom Sihanouk: For a New Indochina [February 26, 1965]*

. . . We should try, as much for ourselves as for other threatened Asian nations, to stop the process of a war whose flames embrace our whole continent. This war will destroy our development efforts of the past several decades. It will sow suffering and ruin. . . . *It is a question, therefore, of our conference helping to make the chances for peace prevail over those for war.*

It is a question, not of persuading our peoples of the utility and necessity of the solution that we are going to specify . . . but of persuading other nations, especially the Western nations—beginning with the people of the U.S.A.

It is a question, finally, of our acting in such a way that all men of good will in the world, all governments on earth, recognize the very grave and real danger of extermination stemming from U.S. imperialism, which, its amour-propre and pride deeply wounded, threatens humanity.

In résumé, it is necessary that our Conference succeed in securing the support of world opinion so that it can bring pressure to bear on the U.S.A. until it agrees to put an end to the war and to bring, *with our collaboration,* a peaceful solution to the problem of Indochinese independence, the crux of which is found in South Viet-Nam. . . .

Honorable delegates and very dear friends, you will perhaps permit me,

* *Source:* Address prepared for presentation at the plenary session of the Indo-China People's Conference, Phnom Penh, February 25, 1965 (text in *Neak Cheat Niyum* [Phnom Penh], February 26, 1965; italics in the original). Prince Sihanouk did not deliver this address, for shortly before the conference opened, the United States introduced combat troops into South Viet-Nam and began bombing targets in North Viet-Nam; and the North Vietnamese informed Sihanouk they were not amenable to the course he intended to propose.

in my capacity as an Indochinese citizen . . . to present some personal views . . . on the way in which certain of our decisions should be elaborated.

First, there is *the tone and the form* of the resolutions on which we will be called to vote.

Whatever the griefs each of us has formulated against American imperialism and whatever the gravity of the faults and even the crimes which have been committed to the detriment of our peoples and our countries, whatever the legitimate anger that this imperialism has stirred in our hearts, I believe in all honesty that our cause . . . will be so much better understood and admitted by others and will impress the American people if our resolutions are free from polemic, attack or injury and contain only objective considerations, constructive propositions, expressed as much as possible with calm and moderation, with neither hate nor passion, in carefully considered terms. . . .

In this fashion, the imperialists will understand that we are concerned to influence world opinion, which could not fail to approve our stand and to exercise appropriate pressure to *render Indo-China to the Indochinese* and restore to our peoples the peace that has been denied them. . . .

As for the propositions that we are going to adopt, it goes without saying that the delegations of North and South Viet-Nam will compose the solutions for Viet-Nam while the Laotian delegation will present its solution for Laos. . . .

But I believe I should express our opinion that if we wish to obtain the disengagement of the U.S.A. and the "free world" from Laos and South Viet-Nam and end this unhappy war *without waiting for an armed settlement* . . . it is absolutely necessary to offer, in exchange for total disengagement, *solid guarantees* which do not appear to the "free world" as bitter derision.

It is the fear of being duped, I cannot emphasize this too much, which makes public opinion, in the United States as well as in Great Britain, Australia, even in France and several other countries, hesitate to bring real pressure on Washington to make it accede to the demand that I, General DeGaulle and other leaders have presented with a view to providing a reasonable solution to the Indochina problem—which is essentially the problems of South Viet-Nam and Laos.

What might these guarantees be? First of all, we should proclaim that we all accept *the convocation of a new international conference* which would re-examine with all interested and concerned powers the details of the Indochinese problems.

It is certainly necessary that we reclaim a "return to the sources," i.e., *respect for the [Geneva] accords of 1954 and 1962.*

But this return and this respect cannot be assured by simple exchange of words or even by diplomatic notes.

We once tried to resolve the problem of recognition and guarantee of our territorial integrity by a simple exchange of diplomatic correspondence in order not to inconvenience the Americans who dreaded an eventful confrontation with China. This attempt was a complete failure. Not only did it come to naught, but it enlarged the gap of misunderstanding and distrust between the "interlocutors." Nothing will do, we are persuaded, but *direct and general conversations.*

It is true, as is often remarked, that the Geneva accords of 1962 on Laos were violated by certain of their signatories shortly after being signed. But it would be profoundly unjust to conclude from that that the contacts made at Geneva were useless. The proof of this is that we have at least been able to prevent a generalized war from breaking out in Laos and that the accords continue to form a valuable base for the solution of present problems.

It is only at Geneva, in the course of an international conference on Cambodia, Laos and South Viet-Nam, that we will find an acceptable solution to these problems.

I repeat again that everything that constitutes the basis of the 1954 and 1962 accords should be rigorously preserved, for example, the prohibition of all foreign bases in South Viet-Nam and Laos, the reunification of Viet-Nam by means of popular and democratic consultation, etc.

But it is necessary to recognize that there are aspects of these accords which are out of date or which have been proven by experience to be ineffective and have not contributed to restoring peace, independence and unity among the countries or the peoples concerned.

It is thus necessary, if one has good faith, if one is sincerely devoted to the cause of these countries, to re-examine these accords and to adapt them to the exigencies of the new situation, to the evolution of events.

One will tell me without doubt and with reason that it is the Americans and the British who are the most strongly opposed to and practically the only opponents of a return to Geneva. I would reply that we can only overcome their reticence and resistance by announcing in advance that we are ready to discuss at Geneva the question of *guarantees,* which I would qualify as essential.

First, it is important, in my humble opinion, that we specify that we are all in accord on the *true neutralization of Laos,* as well as the *authentic-*

neutralization of South Viet-Nam, at least until the period of popular consultation leading to *its reunification with North Viet-Nam.*

This neutralization itself will signify nothing for our American adversaries and the "free world" if it is not *seriously guaranteed* as much by the East as by the West.

It would have meaning only if, 1) it comprises *total and simultaneous disengagement* by the West and the East from the countries concerned, and 2) it comprises an *efficacious and impartial international supervision* of the countries concerned by an International Control Commission (ICC) which should have *more powers, personnel and means* in order to fulfill its responsibilities.

Our brothers of the NLF, the Patriotic Front of Viet-Nam, and the Neo Lao Haksat will, without doubt, assure us that it is useless to search for a disengagement by the East for, they will say, the socialist powers have never interfered in the affairs of Laos and South Viet-Nam.

We do not have any reason to doubt their word. But, since the East has no fear of being reproached about Laos and South Viet-Nam, it should not feel any embarrassment about approving the disengagement clause and that of an efficacious supervision.

Apropos of the supervision of Laos, we, Khmers, had at Geneva in 1962 a small but friendly "altercation" with certain representatives of the big socialist powers. They said they could not understand why we Cambodians, known for our jealous concern for our independence, could advocate for Laos the status of "international protégé" and desired close supervision (by the ICC) of our neighboring brother Kingdom.

One of these high representatives even asked . . . why we could not accept that Laos was "as independent as Cambodia."

I now have the opportunity, before our Laotian brothers, to do away with this regrettable misunderstanding.

First, let me recall that *my country has always claimed for itself a generalized, permanent and efficacious supervision of its territory,* including *its cities, ports, and airports.*

On the other hand, Cambodia is the only Indochinese country which has taken vis-à-vis the ICC a clear, consistent and unequivocal attitude. We have very firmly insisted on its maintenance in our country and we have furnished it on every occasion with the freedom and the means for desirable investigations. . . .

If we act in this way, it is simply because we wish *to preserve our independence and our freedom,* which the ICC helps us to maintain; it is to show our adversaries that we have *nothing to hide* and to thwart their Machiavellian plan to carry the war to us under false pretexts.

Are we wrong to wish too strongly for the same peace, the same inde-

pendence for Laos. It is this which provokes animosity against us from those who do not sincerely desire it for Laos, including certain Laotian personalities.

At Geneva no one—our Laotian brothers less than others—took our suggestions into consideration. And now, the *results are known.* Lacking a real guarantee of its neutrality by the big powers and lacking an impartial and efficacious supervision, this country has been deprived of a correct application of the Geneva accords, which have been constantly violated. Some people have even charged my country and my humble person with responsibility for the present unhappiness of the Laotian people. . . .

That said, we, Khmers, are ready to associate ourselves with the desiderata of our Indochinese brothers, even if their points of view are not persuaded by our convictions, for *solidarity,* for us, is not and never will be a vain word.

We will ask only to disengage our responsibility in case the resolutions voted by the Conference should prove to be inoperative. For we cannot be ignorant of the fact that the Americans will not soon put down their arms and the "free world" will not support us efficaciously if we content ourselves here with calling for the departure of American troops without indicating our conception of the independence, peace and neutralization of Laos and South Viet-Nam, and their preservation in the future.

For its part, Cambodia will call again, for itself, in the course of these debates, for the reconvening of a Geneva conference, which would seek international guarantees of its neutrality and territorial integrity and a general supervision of its territory, cities and ports. . . .

III. The End of an Era

Throughout the 1960's, Prince Sihanouk made a number of decisions that were to result in the alienation of the political and military elite: He terminated American aid programs and nationalized the banks and foreign trading firms, which brought about a decline in Cambodia's economic fortunes; and he sought an accommodation with Hanoi to assure Cambodia's independence and territorial integrity in the future, which led the Vietnamese Communists to increasingly use Cambodian territory as a sanctuary from which to attack South Viet-Nam. In consequence, Cambodia was drawn into the Viet-Nam war.

As a result of the elite's loss of confidence in his leadership, Prince Sihanouk was deposed on March 18, 1970, by the unanimous vote of the National Assembly. His place as the principal political leader of Cambodia was assumed by General Lon Nol and Prince Sisowath Sirik Matak, the premier and deputy premier, respectively, of the "Goverenment of Salvation."

The reasons for Prince's Sihanouk's deposition are given in the following document, written by Sirik Matak in answer to an article Sihanouk published in the October 1970 issue of *Foreign Affairs*.

Sisowath Sirik Matak: The Reasons for the Deposition of Prince Sihanouk [January 20, 1971]*

To understand the meaning of the events which took place in Cambodia during 1970 and which have greatly modified the fate of the Khmer nation, it is necessary to look back and to consider the political situation of the country during these last few years. Indeed the deposition of Prince Sihanouk, the defensive war against North Vietnamese and Vietcong Communist aggressors, and finally the change of the regime with the proclamation of the Republic are events which constitute a logical and unavoidable ending of pre-existing causes.

First . . . it must be recalled what Prince Sihanouk's regime consisted of and how this regime—a dictatorship deriving from a feudal monarchy —gradually stirred up a feeling of revolt among the Khmer people and has rendered irresistible their aspiration towards liberty. For fifteen years, since 1955, when his political and unique movement of "The Sangkum" was created, Prince Sihanouk ruled Cambodia as a despotic master, taking for himself all powers and not tolerating any form of opposition against his personal dictatorship. Besides, in 1960, he made himself Head of State, soon after the death of his father King Suramarit, thereby creating a vacancy in the throne which only favoured his ambitions and his craving for power.

During the ten years that preceded the historical event of 18th March 1970, marking the legal deposition of Prince Sihanouk, the Khmer people had been living under the sign of systematic destruction of rights and liberties theoretically recognised by the Constitution of 1947. Year after year, Prince Sihanouk kept on ignoring this Constitution and established instead in practice the reign of his own convenience. Freedom of expression and any possibility of opposition in legal forms then disappeared completely while a heavier and heavier oppression was befalling our country. The

* *Source:* Press release of the Government of the Khmer Republic, January 20, 1971, published in *Khmer Information Bulletin* (Bangkok: Embassy of the Khmer Republic), 1 (March 2, 1971), 1.

Head of State, in fact, arrogated to himself every right, keeping for himself all powers of decision in every field, while refusing to consult the Government and the Parliament both of which he reduced to an acclamatory role.

Under such circumstances no criticism was allowed, and any opinion different from his was considered by Prince Sihanouk as a personal offense or a crime of lèse-majesté. He thus found a method permitting him to neutralise pitilessly all Khmer citizens who, in increasing number, showed some disapproval against his dictatorial policy. He denounced these citizens in public as traitors, some of them accused of being "Blues" (or pro-Americans) and the others of being "Reds" (or pro-Communists). This method permitted the former Head of State to exert an implacable repression against all those who did not unconditionally approve his policy which became more and more contrary to national interest and popular aspirations.

Those who were designated as "Reds" were systematically persecuted by him, whereas they were generally unhappy citizens who wished only a little more social justice and an improvement of their standard of living. During the last three years of his despotic rule, namely 1967–1969, Prince Sihanouk had thousands of "Red Khmers" . . . executed and in order to intimidate, he himself announced the executions he had ordered in this or that province.

Finally it must be recalled that at the time of Prince Sihanouk's destitution, numerous political prisoners were in jail where some of them had been for years. That was why in Phnom-Penh alone 486 political prisoners were freed on the 2nd April 1970 following a decision of the Government of Salvation which had been formed in 1969 and had been so called by Prince Sihanouk himself.

In the economic field, the regime of dictatorship imposed upon the country since 1955 caused the most disastrous consequences. Having no knowledge of economic affairs as he himself admitted, Prince Sihanouk wanted however to direct the national economy according to his whims without taking into account the advice of experts. An out and out policy of nationalization which he had decided himself at the end of 1963, aggravated even more an already precarious economic and financial situation. The main result of this policy was a stagnation in the field of development while unbridled corruption took place everywhere, as Prince Sihanouk had appointed as managers of State Enterprises members of his entourage who found it a good opportunity to enrich themselves quickly at the expense of state finances.

Nor were things going well in the social field, Prince Sihanouk having preferred to practice demagogy rather than to make essential reforms which would have made possible the improvement of the very low standard of living of the people. Hence no progress had been achieved under his regime. All those achievements which he boasted of in his speeches were mainly accomplished for purposes of prestige, meant to impress foreign visitors without bringing any actual improvement to the standard of living of the population. Indeed, all the figures and statistics relating to the economic situation of the country were faked by the Prince himself who distorted the truth in a manner which suited him most. With the use of such methods in the economic and social fields the results could only be deplorable, and Cambodia in reality lagged considerably behind other non-Communist countries of the area during these last ten years.

But another very grave reason was added to all previous ones which finally caused the fall of Norodom Sihanouk. Not only did he impose upon the country a regime of dictatorship accompanied by a generalised corruption, but the former leader of Cambodia also practiced a policy of treason against national interest for the benefit of Vietcong and North Vietnamese Communists, whom he had allowed, since the beginning of the 60's, to use Khmer territory for military purposes against South Vietnam, in total contempt of our neutrality which was not compatible with the presence of foreign forces (Vietcong and North Vietnamese) in our border areas. As a matter of fact, the presence of these Vietnamese Communist forces in Khmer territory had steadily increased year after year. Apart from the occasional and relatively limited infiltrations at the beginning, large scale military occupation took place in all our border provinces with South Vietnam during these last few years from the northern high region of Rattanakiri to the southern sea coast province of Kampot. These militarily occupied portions of our territory had in fact become actual sanctuaries which the Vietcong and North Vietnamese used as bases of attacks against South Vietnamese territory, thereby provoking frequent border incidents with American and South Vietnamese forces.

The large scale military occupation by the Communists became so considerable that Prince Sihanouk himself was finally alarmed, and he denounced them publicly for the first time at the end of 1968. Since then, and up to his legal deposition in March 1970, he kept on denouncing in numerous speeches, articles and press conferences, this occupation as well as the continuing increase of the Vietcong and North Vietnamese infiltrations which were going on so speedily that the former Cambodian Head of State had to reveal in October 1969 that the total Vietnamese Communist forces installed in Khmer territory at that time were up to 50,000 men. However, he did nothing to obtain the withdrawal of these foreign forces which should never have penetrated into our territory as they had done for years in flagrant violation of the 1954 Geneva Agreements due to Prince Sihanouk's connivance.

This connivance gradually became a real treason of national interest, destroying at the same time the Khmer neutrality. In fact, the Vietnamese Communist forces had in Cambodia, in addition to their sanctuaries, multiple facilities in the logistic field. Their supply in arms and ammunitions, medicine and foods, etc., was secured from our port of Kompong Som, used these last years almost exclusively for this purpose.

In short, Cambodia became by the will of Prince Sihanouk, but against the will of its people, a country becoming more and more involved in the Vietnamese conflict on the Communist side. And it is precisely against this situation, which is absolutely incompatible with the maintenance of real independence and neutrality, that the Khmer people had reacted at the beginning of this year.

While Prince Sihanouk, concerned with his physical health, left for France at the beginning of the year 1970 to undergo a dietetic treatment in a specialised clinic, Khmer opinion was more and more preoccupied with the increase of North Vietnamese and Vietcong military occupation and with the threat against our territorial integrity. On March 8th, 1970, the first popular anti-Vietcong demonstrations broke out in the province of Svay-Rieng. On the 11th and the 16th March, similar demonstrations took place in Phnom-Penh, while everywhere people demanded the departure of foreign forces. Informed of the situation, Prince Sihanouk—who was then in Paris—reacted by condemning these demonstrations in the most violent terms and by siding openly with the Vietnamese Communists against his own countrymen. Acting in accordance with the general feeling and the popular sentiment which had so strongly been expressed, the National Assembly and the Council of the Kingdom met in joint session and preclaimed on March 18th, 1970, the deposition of Prince Sihanouk by a unanimous vote.

Meanwhile, the Government of Salvation had, on the 12th March, asked the North Vietnamese and the so-called "provisional revolutionary government" [PRG] of South Vietnam (Vietcong) to withdraw all their forces illegally stationed in Khmer territory by the 15th of March. At the same time, it proposed to have talks in order to settle this question of withdrawal of Vietnamese Communist forces peacefully. On the 16th March, the first meeting between a Khmer delegation and the representatives of North Vietnam and of the P.R.G. took place but to no avail, the communist side having systematically avoided any discussion on the main issue, i.e., the question of withdrawal of North Vietnamese and Vietcong forces. Notwithstanding this disappointing result, the Government of Salvation proposed to hold another meeting between the two parties on the 27th March.

But this meeting could not take place because North Vietnam and the P.R.G. decided the "de facto" rupture of relations with Cambodia by withdrawing on that day all the personnel of their diplomatic missions in Phnom-Penh. Two days later, on the 29th March, Vietnamese Communist forces began attacking—without declaration of war—our defense forces in several provinces and launched an offensive against Phnom-Penh. It must be noted in this connection that the . . . aggression started almost immediately after the failure of the attempts made by the Vietcong and the North Vietnamese on the 26th and the 27th March to organize riots in some areas (Kompong-Cham and Takéo) and to send misled demonstrators in a march on the capital.

The series of events which followed this aggression are well known to the world, because a great number of correspondents of the international press—whose entry into Cambodia was strictly forbidden under the Sihanouk regime—came to Cambodia where they have been freely admitted since the beginning of April 1970. These correspondents could then verify that there was no civil war in Cambodia, contrary to the claims made by the propaganda campaigns led by the Asian Communists and by Peking-based Prince Sihanouk. They could also verify that our country was a victim of a brutal and naked aggression by the Vietnamese Communist forces, an aggression against which we were not prepared to resist. That is why, and considering the enormous disproportion of forces and means, we had to appeal for help from friendly countries on the 14th April, in conformity with the provisions of our Constitution which provide such a recourse in case of a grave external threat against our independence.

Since then, friendly countries, particularly the United States and South Vietnam, have given us effective military aid, while other friendly countries (Australia, New-Zealand, Indonesia, Japan, Thailand, Republic of Korea, Republic of China, etc.) have helped us either in the diplomatic and economic fields or by humanitarian and medical assistance. All these aids, which were very much appreciated by the Khmer people, have effectively supported the great efforts made by us to resist the North Vietnamese and Vietcong Communist aggression, particularly by helping our defense forces which have increased considerably thanks to the tens of thousands of volunteers who answered immediately the Government's appeal.

Today, thanks to this great number of volunteers and to the equipment provided by friendly countries, we now have a defense force of more than 180,000 men, which will be increased to 260,000 at the beginning of 1971.

This new army hastily recruited in an atmosphere of patriotic enthusiasm of our people and our youth has already proved its worth by inflicting heavy losses and severe defeats on the North Vietnamese and Vietcong invading forces. This army which is the army of the Khmer people working in close cooperation with the population, is aware that it is fighting for a just cause, and this conviction certainly explains its high morale. The Khmer national armed forces fight in fact to drive the Communist invaders from our territory, to liberate regions now still occupied by them, to preserve our independence and our territorial integrity, and to defend the Khmer Republic proclaimed on the 9th October in accordance with the aspirations of our people and our youth.

These aspirations were expressed in an irresistible manner for more liberty immediately after the fall of Norodom Sihanouk's dictatorship. In short, our forces are fighting to insure the future of the Khmer people as free, neutral and independent people.

This bright future which we want to secure for our nation, after the disastrous years we have endured, up to this year, is the object of the constant preoccupations of our Government and our elite. First in the political field, we envisage this future only under the sign of democracy and liberty. The establishment of a Republican regime in Cambodia is in conformity with this aspiration, and the new Constitution which is being drafted now to replace that given in 1947 by Prince Sihanouk—Constitution that he himself has never respected but has violated on every occasion—will consecrate the rights of Khmer citizens and the fundamental principle of sovereignty of the people exercised through their democratically elected representatives.

Like the advent of the Republican regime, our new Constitution is going to mark a complete and definite rupture with the past, in particular with the dictatorial regime we have suffered for fifteen years, and which was marked by the concentration of all powers in the hands of only one man on whom everything depended. The Khmer people no longer want to experience this intolerable situation. That is why the Constitution which we will adopt before long will have as its guiding principle the objective of never permitting only one man to assume all powers as had done the former Head of State. Of course, we are not pretending to reach perfection as far as our new institutions are concerned. We are at least determined to do everything in our power to make our country a true democracy—which has not been the case for centuries—so that our Republic which is the youngest in the world, may occupy an honorable place in the community of freedom-loving nations. This is our ambition, and we will spare no effort to achieve it.

In the economic field, we chose a wide scale liberalization of the main sectors of financial and commercial activity. We have suffered the disastrous consequences of the nationalizations ordered without any discernment by Prince Sihanouk since the end of 1963. A period of six years within this system caused stagnation, then a dangerous regression of our economy deprived of foreign investments which Prince Sihanouk's policy of nationalization completely banished from our country. At the same time, any initiative or interest in free enterprise disappeared, and this unavoidably resulted in the deterioration and the stagnation of our economy.

Of course, Prince Sihanouk always tried to make the external world believe that our economy and the standard of living of our people were in constant progress. But the truth was different, and it is precisely due to the deplorable economic situation in which the country found itself last year that the former Head of State was compelled to entrust the Salvation Government, formed in August 1969, with the ungrateful task of improving an economy which collapsed after six years of nationalization and squandering of state finances by Prince Sihanouk and his entourage.

Reorganizing the whole economy of Cambodia on a new basis and in accordance with our possibilities is one of the main tasks which we have to undertake in the future. All the decisions made by the Salvation Government since the beginning of the year (1970) even before the fall of Sihanouk's regime have this objective as their aim. At the same time, we are determined to come out of the harmful economic isolation in which Prince Sihanouk kept Cambodia for many years. With this in mind, we have become members of important international organizations such as the IMF [International Monetary Fund] and the Asian Development Bank. For the same reason, we wish to welcome foreign investments which are indispensable to our economic development, which will be made possible thanks to our measures of liberalization as well as to the setting up of a free zone at our Kompong Som seaport.

On the other hand, we consider regional cooperation in the economic field as a very important means to promote our progress in the future, at a time when common efforts are necessary for all South East Asian countries who want to raise the standard of living of their population in order to better secure their independence in the face of the Asian Communist threat. We will therefore participate in any form of regional cooperation between countries of our region and particularly with our nearest neighbours.

Finally, in the social field, we have to fulfill an enormous task whose importance will determine our future. We must completely reorganize the fabric of our society which has just conquered its liberty and come out of a very long period of feudal despotism under a retrograde monarchy which has for centuries smothered every attempt towards progress and liberty. Prince Sihanouk's dictatorship has prolonged for fifteen years this deplorable situation. The indispensable reorganization which we have already undertaken this year starts at the village level.

Our people are essentially composed of peasants, as Cambodia, economically speaking, has mainly an agricultural vocation. The major objective of our Government is to make our rural population (80% of the total population) participate as much as possible to the development of agriculture, which is the key to the improvement of their standard of living. Of course, the task is immense in a country like ours, which lacks an adequate infrastructure, and where everything remains to be done to change the living conditions of the inhabitants of the villages and to associate them closely to the efforts made on the national level. It is to achieve this objective that we have already set up a new ministry, the Ministry of Community Development, entrusted with the fundamental task of reorganizing rural life with the essential participation of the rural population.

However, it is obvious that our projects and our efforts are now seriously handicapped by the Communist aggression which compels us to mobilise all our forces and resources to repel the Vietcong, North Vietnamese and the Pathet Lao hordes and to adjust ourselves temporarily to a war economy. But we also know that the difficulties which our country is going through at present will come to an end when we are able to repel the foreign invaders. In any case these difficulties should not prevent us from preparing from now on our future as a free people.

In 1973, a People's United Resistance Movement (*Mouvement d'Union de Lutte du Peuple*) or MULP (formed in 1970), mounting a revolutionary war with the support of North Viet-Nam and the National Front for the Liberation of South Viet-Nam, claimed control of two-thirds of Cambodia. Acting in the name of the National United Front of Cambodia (*Front Uni National du Kampuchéa*) or FUNK, which is under Prince Sihanouk's ostensible leadership, the MULP seeks to replace the Khmer Republic with a democratic socialist regime in which "the people are the source of all power." Among the MULP's leaders are several of the former "young intellectuals," including Khieu Samphan, Hou Yuon, and Hu Nim, who joined the maquis in the late 1960's. On May 3, 1970, a congress of the FUNK, meeting in Peking, adopted the following political program.

Political Program of the National United Front of Cambodia [May 3, 1970]*

. . . The Cambodian society . . . will be rid of all defects impeding its rapid and full bloom. . . . The FUNK declares that "power is, and will always be, in the hands of the progressive, industrious and genuine working people who will ensure our motherland a bright future on the basis of social justice, equality and fraternity among all Khmers." The people are the source of all power.

The democratization of Cambodian society is being carried out in the liberated zone at present and will be carried out in the whole country in the following ways:

—Guarantee to all Cambodians, except traitors, . . . the freedom of vote, . . . of standing for election, . . . of speech, the press, opinion, association, demonstration, residence, travel at home and going abroad, etc. Safeguard the inviolability of the person, property, wealth and privacy of correspondence.

—Guarantee effective equality to both sexes. . . . Encourage by all means the cultural and professional development of women to enable them fully to participate in the common struggle. . . .

—Buddhism is and will remain the state religion. But the FUNK recognizes and guarantees the freedom of all other religions and beliefs. . . .

—Look after with the greatest solicitude the needs of our disabled servicemen and the families of our fighters who gave their lives for the country, and reserve a privileged treatment for them.

. . . —See to it that the legitimate rights and interests of minority [groups] . . . are respected.

The FUNK is dedicated to building and developing an independent national economy by relying principally on the resources and productive forces of Cambodia. This economic policy finds concrete expression in:

—Freeing the national economy from persons who engage in profiteering, smuggling, blackmarketeering and inhuman exploitation of people.

—Protecting and guaranteeing the rights of ownership of land and property in accordance with the laws of the state.

—Confiscating the land and property of traitors who are active accomplices in the pay of the American imperialists and who have committed crimes against the people. The land and property seized will be distributed among the needy peasants.

* Source: Programme Politique du Front Uni National du Kampuchéa (FUNK) (Peking?), May 1970?

—Guaranteeing to the peasants the right of ownership of the land they cultivate. Establishing a fair system of land rent and interest rates on loans.

—Helping the peasants resolve the agrarian problem through a fair solution of unreasonable debts.

—Helping the peasants increase production. . . . Protecting and developing cooperation and the good customs of mutual aid in the countryside.

—Ensuring conditions for secure and rational farm management and the economical marketing and transportation of products.

—Encouraging the formation of trade unions. Guaranteeing security of employment and reasonable remuneration to the working classes. Improving working conditions. Ensuring a system of social insurance.

—Developing the industrialization of the country and carrying out a rational industrial policy so that production will meet the principal needs of the people. . . .

—Encouraging the national bourgeoisie to set up and manage well enterprises beneficial to the people. . . .

—Helping artisans raise and diversify their production and ensure the sale of their products on the best terms.

—Developing means of transportation and communications.

—Safeguarding the interests of students, intellectuals and civil servants; providing employment for those "without occupation" and the unemployed in accordance with their ability and helping them develop further their ability to serve the country.

—Maintaining the nationalization of the banks and foreign trade.

. . . —Encouraging and developing exports, limiting imports to products necessary to the national economy. Protecting national products from foreign competition.

—Safeguarding the purchasing power of the *riel* and improving the public finance.

. . . The policy of the FUNK concerning education and culture is based on the following points:

—Develop the good traditions of the Angkorian civilization.

. . . Build a national culture based on patriotism and love for work well done and love of art. Protect historical relics and monuments.

—Khmerize gradually the curricula for education, including higher education.

—Adopt the national language as the sole official language in the public services.

—Adapt the programs and methods of education to the needs of the country.

—Encourage and assist scientific research and experimentation. . . .

—Promote research in our national history, which is often distorted by foreign authors, and include it in educational programs.

—Ensure continuous education through regular school terms or vocational training.

—Develop pre-school education. . . .

—Ensure free education and provide scholarships for needy children and youth.

—Ensure and support an extensive political, civic and cultural education among the people and the youth. Help every citizen realize his duties to himself, to society and to the people. Instill actively the ideas of public interest and service to the community. . . . This political, civic and cultural education should be carried out at all levels [of government], in factories, shops, cooperatives, in the capital, provinces, districts, villages and families. Develop the ideas of morality, honor, national dignity, patriotism, mutual aid, usefulness of collective labor, the sense and nobleness of rendering sacrifices for the people's cause, the spirit of working conscientiously and practicing economy, and respect for public property.

The foreign policy of the FUNK is one of national independence, peace, neutrality, non-alignment, solidarity and friendship with all peace-loving and justice-loving peoples and governments. The FUNK maintains relations of friendship and cooperation with all countries according to the five principles of peaceful coexistence and the spirit of the United Nations Charter regardless of their political system and ideology. It will not participate in any military alliance, nor does it allow any foreign country to set up military bases or station troops and military personnel on Cambodian territory for the purpose of aggression against other countries. The FUNK does not accept the protection of any country or of any military alliance. In the common struggle against American imperialism, the FUNK pursues a policy of friendship, militant solidarity and cooperation with Laos and Viet Nam according to the principle that the liberation and the defense of each country are the affair of her own people and that the three peoples pledge to do their best to support one another according to the desire of the interested country on the basis of mutual respect. In addition, Cambodia is ready to make concerted efforts with Laos and Viet Nam to make Indo-China genuinely a zone of independence, peace and progress, where each nation preserves its integral sovereignty with the sympathy and support of the peoples and governments of the socialist countries, non-aligned countries and peace-loving and justice-loving countries in the world, including the American people. . . .

EIGHT

The Philippines

by DAVID WURFEL

The Philippine political system has been reputed to be the most
Americanized in Asia. However, Philippine politics cannot be understood without taking full account of pre-Western cultural traditions.
The Americanisms are not usually as profound as they appear, nor was
the Spanish impact of much greater significance. Early American commentators were impressed with the Latin manners of the elite, which
at the turn of the century were certainly very pronounced, but today
only a handful of Filipinos speak Spanish at home, and genetically
Chinese influence is much greater than European. Among the formal
institutions of government only the rendering of justice—in the civil-
law tradition—retains any important Spanish imprint.

The Philippine economy also reflects variety in the cultural heritage.
The prevalence of large land holdings is seen by some as a consequence of Spanish grants, though most of the large holdings today
were probably acquired since the turn of the century. The long-standing dominance of some segments of the economy by the Chinese took
place in spite of Spanish or American policy. Alongside the Chinese is
a rapidly growing group of dynamic Filipino entrepreneurs, unabashed
exponents of a free-enterprise philosophy, similar to America's in the
1870's.

The economy of the Philippines is one of the three largest in South-
east Asia. The population of over thirty-five million is second only to
Indonesia's and the per capita income is about equal to Thailand's.
Like the rest of Southeast Asia, the Philippine economy is predomi-

nantly agricultural, relying heavily on three export crops: lumber, copra, and sugar. The rate of industrialization by the standards of the region is rapid, however.

There is more historical continuity in the politics of the postwar Philippines than is the case for other countries in Southeast Asia. Only in the Philippines did one constitution mold the course of political events for more than thirty years. Not until 1970 were concrete steps taken toward constitutional revision by the election of a new constitutional convention. The first break in the continuity of political institutions was the failure of President Ferdinand Marcos in 1973 to use the procedures for ratification of the new constitutional draft that were prescribed in the 1935 constitution still in force.

Philippine independence in 1946 was declared in the midst of smoldering peasant rebellion in Central Luzon. Conditions worsened in the next four years so much that some feared the success of a revolution led by the People's Liberation Army (*Hukbong Mapagpalaya ng Bayan*) or Huks, which in 1950 called for the overthrow of the government. But improved leadership, American aid, factional quarrels among the Huks, and the resiliency of Philippine society helped create more peaceful conditions by the time Ramon Magsaysay was elected president in 1953. Magsaysay opened a new era in Philippine politics, based largely on his own charismatic appeal, and hope for progress reached a new high. In both political and economic terms, however, he failed to realize his full potential before his life was ended by a tragic airplane crash in 1957. His vice-president and successor, Carlos Garcia, returned to the "old politics," but nevertheless he was elected to the presidency in his own right. Garcia was defeated in 1961 by Diosdado Macapagal, who attempted to emulate Magsaysay. But Macapagal's promises to "clean up the graft," on which he based his campaign, were so inadequately fulfilled that he himself was defeated in the face of corruption charges four years later. He had taken a major economic step in ending foreign-exchange controls, but while one source of corruption was thus dried up, tariffs and the "need" to evade them contributed to a growing problem of smuggling. Ferdinand Marcos, elected to the presidency in 1965, fared only slightly better in his attempt to deal with this problem during his administration. Nevertheless, due to the notable success of certain of his projects, such as road building, and to his political skill, Marcos became the first man to win re-election to the presidency of the Republic. His re-election, however, was marked by a sharp decline in the integrity of the electoral process, and his second term was scarred by increasing social tension and protest. On September 23, 1972, Marcos imposed martial law on the Philippines.

The Philippines is often described as a very dynamic nation, and rightly so. Movement, however, is not all upward. Social scientists observe different signs and portents that can lead to contradictory conclusions.[1] It is this mixed picture that the following documents—the voices of Filipinos speaking individually and collectively—will present.

I. Ideology and Values

The late senator Claro M. Recto was a harbinger of the Filipino nationalist renaissance in the 1960's. One of the most respected in-tellectuals among political leaders of his day, he was not afraid of saying things that might earn him the epithet "anti-American," at a time when others were. In this 1951 speech Recto explains, with very slight exaggeration, why Filipinos were then seldom regarded as full-fledged nationalists by their Asian neighbors.

Claro M. Recto: Our Lingering Colonial Complex [1951]*

Our peculiar situation has been heightened by the unique circum-stances in which we attained our independence. The other liberated Asian nations have been spared the ambiguities under which we labor; they faced issues that were clear-cut; blood and tears, exploitation and subju-gation, and centuries of enmity divided the Indonesians from the Dutch,

---

[1] One conclusion, which is by no means typical of the views of experienced observers of Filipino politics, is the result of a very extensive Rand Corporation study: "We have found that much of the bleak view of the country's prospects rests on misperceptions: Crime is not mounting, the economy is growing re-spectably, and the polity appears stable" (H. A. Averch, F. H. Denton, and J. E. Koehler, *A Crisis of Ambiguity: Political and Economic Development in the Philippines* [Santa Monica, Calif.: Rand, 1970], R-473-AID, p. vii).

* *Source:* From Renato Constantino, ed., *Recto Reader* (Manila: Recto Me-morial Foundation, 1965), pp. 8–10; reprinted by permission of Rafael R. Recto, Recto Law Offices, Rizal, The Philippines.

the Indians and the Burmese from the British, the Vietnamese from the French; and their nationalist victories were not diluted by sentiments of gratitude, or by regrets, doubts, and apprehensions.

But an intensive and pervasive cultural colonization, no less than an enlightened policy of gradually increasing autonomy, dissolved whatever hatreds and resentments were distilled in the Filipino-American war, and, by the time of the enactment of the Jones Law, promising independence upon the establishment of a stable government, an era of goodwill was firmly opened. . . . A system of temporary trade preferences, under which our principal industries were developed, cemeted the relationship with the hard necessities of economic survival, for it was belatedly realized that the same system of so-called free trade had made us completely dependent on the American market. The vicissitudes and triumphs of the common struggle against the Japanese Empire completed the extraordinary structure, and it was not at all strange or unexpected that, when our independence was finally proclaimed, it was not so much an act of separation, as one of "more perfect union."

Great numbers of Filipinos, therefore, pride themselves in professing fealty to America even without the rights of Americans. Their gaze is fixed steadily and unwaveringly on the great North American Republic, which is to them the alpha and the omega of human progress and political wisdom. . . . We are afflicted with divided loyalties. We have not yet recovered from the spell of colonialism.

The flagstaffs that still stand, two by two, in front of our public buildings, are the symbols of this psychological phenomenon, this split personality, of our nation. Too many of our people, in their heart of hearts, profess allegiance not only to the Republic of the Philippines, whose sun and stars wave alone in this fourth year of our independence, but unconsciously also to the United States of America, whose stars and stripes may have been hauled down in fact but not in spirit, and which, by an optical illusion induced by long habit, are imagined to be still flying from the empty flagpole.

Emmanuel Pelaez, at one time a close advisor of President Magsaysay, was among those Filipino leaders who had on occasion been subject to Senator Recto's scathing criticism. But by the 1960's his increasingly nationalistic utterances reflected the tenor of the times. Still, he was prone to accentuate the positive, to avoid the use of ridicule or violent attack, as did others whose nationalism was dubbed "moderate." In 1963 Pelaez spoke as vice-president on "our national identity," the search for which was a major theme in Filipino intellectual life.

Emmanuel Pelaez: Our National Identity [1963]*

Let us rid ourselves of such hackneyed notions as the Philippines serving as a bridge between East and West, the Philippines as the show-window of American democracy in Asia, the Philippines as a bastion of the free world in the Western Pacific, and so forth.

The Philippines is what it is, and it cannot help being what it is: the result of an age-old and still continuing inter-penetration of races and languages and cultures.

We are proud to be what we are, but we do not consider ourselves necessarily better or worse off than our neighbors. The Arabs and the Hindus, the Chinese and the Japanese, the Spaniards and the Americans have each left their mark upon us.

But whatever foreign influences we may have absorbed over the centuries, ours is essentially and basically a Malay nation.

One of the benefits of American political tutelage in the Philippines, capped by an uncoerced grant of independence, was the widespread acceptance of democratic values. Most Filipinos explain these values as a correlate of Christianity. President Ferdinand Marcos, in his response to the award of an honorary doctorate at the University of Michigan in 1966, linked them as well to private enterprise.

While Filipino political incumbents tend to paint a rosy picture of the political scene, especially when speaking abroad, the evident pride Marcos showed in Philippine democracy, made him typical of many educated Filipinos of his generation. His pride existed then despite an incessant barrage of criticism against the many ills of Philippine democracy from the country's Congress, the press, and college campuses.

Ferdinand Marcos: Democracy in the Philippines
[September 19, 1966]†

The Philippines is the proving ground for democracy in the world today. . . . A truly meaningful democratic experiment in a setting of un-

* *Source:* Emmanuel Pelaez, *Government by the People* (Quezon City: published privately by the author, 1964); reprinted by permission of Emmanuel Pelaez.

† *Source:* Address given at the University of Michigan, Ann Arbor, September 19, 1966; mimeographed copy in possession of the author.

derdevelopment is taking place and with a good chance of succeeding.

For many of you, probably, the word "underdevelopment" is just another piece of abstract political jargon. But for us in Asia, the meaning of the word is apprehended viscerally. . . . It means damp hovels made of packing crates in which families of eight or ten seek nightly shelter; it means children who are crippled for life by diseases they contract the moment they leave the womb; it means people who lose the power of sight without understanding a line of print; it means, above all, personal despair. . . .

In such a setting, can the abstractions of democracy have any meaning? Can notions like freedom, equality, and human dignity carry any personal significance? The answer is, yes.

To explain this, allow me to recall with you a few things about Philippine history. We were, during our period as a Spanish colony, absorbed into the mainstream of western thought. . . . The idea that the individual person carries within himself the full meaning and measure of existence, and therefore, also the full range of moral choice and responsibility, was inevitable in the Christianization of the Philippines. The political implication of this idea—that the state exists for man and not man for the state—was also inevitable.

When the Philippines revolted against Spain in 1896 and established the First Philippine Republic, the premises of its political and social life rested firmly on democratic principles. These are reflected not only in the constitution of the First Republic but also in the writings of its most vigorous proponent—Apolinario Mabini. . . .

The First Philippine Republic, as you know, was crushed by American arms and once again we became a colony. But not before the Philippines had fought a long and bitter war against the Americans. . . .

It is to the credit of America that her colonial record in the Philippines was enlightened. America made an honest attempt to train the Filipinos for self-government, to raise the level of education, and to improve the health and physical well-being of our people. . . .

During the American period in our history, we inherited the American ideals of democracy. These ideals were not merely grafted but were assimilated by Philippine democracy. These were the American ideas of individualism and self-reliance.

The system of public education instituted by the Americans in the Philippines propagated among other things the idea that every citizen has the opportunity to rise to whatever heights he aspired for; the only limits recognized are inborn talent and natural ability.

The economic consequence of these ideas was private enterprise. For the Filipino, private enterprise is an extension of the idea of individual

freedom; hence, for him, private enterprise and democracy are inseparable.

When finally America withdrew from the Philippines, we had a stable
democratic society with private enterprise as the chosen mode of economic development.

The stability of our democracy is a fact. In a region where authoritarian rule, political and military coups, armed insurrection are facts of
political life, the Philippines has not deviated from the path of democracy. Even while we were recovering from the devastation of the last
world war, beset at the same time by communist subversion, we maintained an unbroken record of constitutional representative government.

These are, I will admit, decided advantages over our Asian brothers
whose histories were shaped in a somewhat different way. But what is
worth noting is that democracy and democratic institutions have worked
in the Philippines during the process of its economic development.

To be sure, our record in economic development is not miraculous.
The falterings that a permissive system like ours tolerate would probably
appall a completely rational planner. But we look upon these as inevitable
consequences of our national decision to hew to democracy and private
enterprise.

It is the price we pay for freedom and it is a burden that we gladly
bear. . . .

Former Senator Raul Manglapus, an unsuccessful third-party presidential candidate in 1965, is a self-conscious intellectual much concerned with ideology in a political milieu where such men are rare.
Long a leader in the Catholic reform movement, Manglapus has
moved toward what he calls "Christian socialism." But in this speech,
delivered at a conference in Singapore in early 1967, he showed a new
openness to both Marxism and other Asian ideologies—reflecting, perhaps, the gradual Asianization of Filipino intellectual life. In 1973 he
was able to bring together Filipinos of differing ideologies in his leadership of the anti-Marcos movement in the United States.

Raul Manglapus: Ideology for Asian Revolutionaries [1967]*

Nationalism in the Philippines, as in Asia, must go about seeking alliances with relevant ideology that will speed social revolution. As we have
said, the French Revolutionary ideology was never relevant and the

* *Source: Solidarity* (Manila) 3 (March 1968), 3:8–9.

American revolutionary spirit has lost its steam—and its lustre. The example of Japan is hardly useful to the rest of Asia. . . .

The prospects of quick social revolution are undeniably there in the Russian, the Chinese and the Cuban examples. And it is idle to warn people who have never led lives of real human dignity about the loss of freedom and even about the necessary initial cruelties, including mass murders, under communism.

There are other possible allies for nationalism that do not demand the sacrifice of freedom, that do not limit themselves to a purely materialistic evaluation of the universe, in order to achieve justice for all. Socialism, for instance, is a faith of many hues and many sources. Today Christian Social thought is a worthy, and I might add, an increasingly friendly competitor to Marx in claiming the allegiance of those who hope to bring about social justice without violent social upheaval. . . .

Democratic socialism and Christian social ideology are two peas in the same pod. They meet on common ground in humanism, in a new non-atheist humanism, which means faith in the ability of man to render justice to man, without losing sight of his destiny in the bosom of God. A humanism, combining a passion for the fullness of this life with a concern for eternal happiness—this could certainly be born in any major faith in Asia today. It can find roots in Buddhism, Islam, Hinduism as well as in Christianity. . . .

Where will Asian nationalism find its ally? Is the new humanism ready? Or will it continue to lose by default?

Professor José Maria Sison is one of the most colorful figures of the Filipino "New Left." He was president of the most radical of Philippine student groups, Kabataang Makabayan (KM)—organized while he was a student at the University of the Philippines—and he has thus often been investigated by intelligence and security agents, as well as by the Congress. His emotional nationalism was probably typical of Filipino university students in the 1960's, but his Peking-inspired rhetoric was characteristic of only a small minority. There was, at first, little indication that the KM had been much more successful than the Students for a Democratic Society in the United States in linking middle- and upper-class students with the "masses." It was to the surprise of many, therefore, that Sison fled to the hills in 1969, thus providing new ideological impetus to the dissident movement known collectively as "the Huks."

José María Sison: Youth on the March [November 2, 1968]*

A nation that does not continually renew itself through progressive-minded and militant youth cannot possibly advance. Even a revolutionary society, say, a socialist one, would stagnate and be thereafter corrupted if the process of renewal and of continuous revolution is neglected or deliberately held back. . . .

We are living today in a world of crises, marked by rapid emergence of the new and rapid resistance of the old. Never has the world been so shaken as now. The forces of socialism and national liberation are striking down the ramparts of imperialist and local reactionary power with global sweep. We are in the midst of a radical choice. . . .

"To rebel is justified!" is the battle cry of the youth of China. There the youth came to be known the world over as the Red Guards. Millions mobilized all over China and, because of our proximity to China, we could almost hear the sound of their marches. Supported by the masses, they brought down the bourgeois academic authorities (reactionary teachers and administrators) and demanded a change in the educational system. Again, together with the masses, the Red Guards gathered enough strength to topple . . . degenerate government and party officials taking the capitalist road. . . .

We [also] see the revolutionary courage and heroism of Vietnamese youth fighting American aggression in their country. The People's Liberation Armed Forces of South Vietnam are youthful faces.

The Filipino youth have had their own share of revolutionary struggles—against the Spanish colonialists, against the American imperialists, against the Japanese fascists. A revolutionary civil war has once occurred within the living memory of many of today's youth. . . .

Youth is the best fighting age. . . . Now again young peasants are goading their elders; the youth are astir in Cotabato, Negros, Quezon, Pampanga, in many places. The youth are the vanguard of national reawakening.

The Kabataang Makabayan, the national democratic youth organization with the most profoundly articulate program and the most widespread membership in the Philippines today . . . is a movement that prepares public opinion for the advance and triumph of working people under the radiant banner of proletarian leadership. It seeks to arouse and mobilize the masses towards the achievement of a national democ-

* *Source: Philippines Free Press* (Manila), November 2, 1968; reprinted by permission of the editor of the *Philippines Free Press.*

racy that is new and progressive within the context of the most radical
advances made by mankind and the working class. It seeks to project the
ideological and political principles that can provide scientific direction
to social revolution. . . .

In schools all over the country, especially in the University of the
Philippines, there is a growing ferment manifested often by student action. In the working class movement, the young workers are reassuming
leadership. In the countryside, the youth are more articulate and critical
of the old problem of feudalism. . . .

Whatever its dectractors say, the Kabataang Makabayan on the basis
of present objective conditions has become a milestone in the long march
of national democratic revolution. Is there any Philippine youth organization now comparable in strength and achievement in the national democratic movement? The KM has made certain achievements that can
no longer be disregarded by history.

We have presented, to this point, statements of explicit values by
major actors in the political scene. Yet, implicit values, imbedded deep
within a cultural tradition that retains more of the early Malaysian
imprint than most foreign observers recognize, probably influence Filipino behavior more significantly than does formal oratory. Until fairly
recently the most crucial ingredients of Filipino political culture had
not been described or analyzed. Mary Hollnsteiner, a leading Filipino
anthropologist at the Institute of Philippine Culture, Ateneo de Manila University, has best elucidated traditional networks of obligation,
which must be understood in order to fathom the fluid nature of alliances that take the name "political party" in the Philippines. Mrs.
Hollnsteiner's work has more than scholarly significance: The transformation of implicit cultural values into explicit political ones is becoming part of the political dialogue now that Filipinos are searchng
so avidly for national identity.

Mary R. Hollnsteiner: Reciprocity in the Lowland Philippines [1970]*

While the norm of reciprocity is a universal principle of behavior, its
manifestations, the emphasis placed upon it, and the power it has to in-

* *Source:* Mary R. Hollnsteiner, "Reciprocity in the Lowland Philippines,"
in Frank Lynch and Alfonso de Guzman II, eds., *Four Readings on Philippine
Values,* IPC [Institute of Philippine Culture] Papers No. 2, 3d ed., rev. and
enl. (Quezon City: Ateneo de Manila University Press, 1970), pp. 65–88; reprinted by permission of the Ateneo de Manila.

fluence social behavior differ from one society to the next. In the Philippines, where people are so concerned about getting along with others, reciprocity is a constant consideration, and some knowledge of its operation is essential for an understanding of Philippine society.

. . . A study of reciprocity in . . . Philippine lowland communities yields a threefold classification; namely, a contractual reciprocity, quasi-contractual reciprocity, and *utang na loób* (debt of gratitude) reciprocity. Contractual reciprocity supposes a voluntary agreement between two or more people to behave toward one another in a specified way for a specified time in the future. An example of this is found in the case of a group of farmers who agree to take turns plowing one another's fields. . . .

The second type of reciprocity, the quasi-contractual, regulates balanced exchanges where the terms of repayment are not explicitly stated before the contract is made; rather, the terms are implicit in situations which the culture recognizes and defines as calling for these terms. Reciprocity comes into play automatically without any specific prior arrangement, and repayment is made in a mechanical, almost nonaffective manner. But failure to reciprocate brings censure.

. . . The third type of reciprocity, *utang na loób* reciprocity, is most consciously generated when a transfer of goods or services takes place between individuals belonging to two different groups. Since one does not ordinarily expect favors of anyone not of his own group, a service of this kind throws the norm into bold relief. Furthermore, it compels the recipient to show his gratitude properly by returning the favor with *interest* to be sure that he does not remain in the other's debt. It is a true gift in this sense. It is also a kind of one-upmanship. The type of debt created in the recipient is called *utang na loób* (literally, a debt inside oneself) or sense of gratitude.

Utang na loób reciprocity is an ancient Filipino operating principle. . . .

. . . Every Filipino is expected to possess *utang na loób;* that is, he should be aware of his obligations to those from whom he receives favors and should repay them in an acceptable manner. Since *utang na loób* invariably stems from a service rendered, even though a material gift may be involved, quantification is impossible. One cannot actually measure the repayment but can attempt to make it, nevertheless, either believing that it supersedes the original service in quality or acknowledging that the reciprocal payment is partial and requires further payment. Some services can never be repaid. Saving a person's life would be one of these; getting a steady job, especially for an unskilled laborer at a time when employment is scarce and unskilled laborers abound, might be another.

. . . One-sided *utang na loób* relationships also exist, especially where a power-status differential precludes the likelihood of equivalent repayment on the part of the subordinate party. . . . In the landlord-tenant relationship . . . the tenant knows he cannot approach anywhere near an equivalent return. As long as he fulfills his expected duties toward his landlord and shows by bringing a few dozen eggs and helping out at festive occasions that he recognizes a debt of gratitude, he may continue to expect benefits from his landlord. . . .

The *utang na loób* repayment, where it is made or attempted, is undefined in the sense that it can encompass any acceptable form within the reach of the one reciprocating. In a seesawing coordinate relationship there is an uneasiness about being on the indebted side, temporary though the position may be. This reluctance to be indebted encourages full payment with interest as soon as the opportunity presents itself.

The permanent superordinate-subordinate relationship, on the other hand, is characterized by acceptance of the relative positions and a corresponding lack of uneasiness on the part of the subordinate element about reciprocation with interest. In the former case, failure to discharge one's *utang na loób* by *repaying with interest* brings, or should bring, *hiyâ,* or shame, on the side of the guilty party; in the latter case, failure to make *partial payment* through sporadic, token gifts or services indicating recognition of the debt causes, or should cause, *hiyâ.*

. . . [As an example of] the workings of *utang na loób,* when a government official in Manila gives a person special treatment, facilitating his papers ahead of others, it becomes virtually mandatory to show one's gratitude for this service with a few pesos, or by sending special food to his house, or by taking him to dinner and perhaps to a nightclub. Obviously, the line between bribery and reciprocal giving is a thin one, and it is easy for an official to rationalize bribery in terms of *utang na loób* payment.

However, the gift is usually presented *after* the initial service is rendered, sometimes long afterwards and at an appropriate festive occasion. To give before the service is rendered would smack of bribery, while to give shortly after the service would be crass and crude. But a decent interval assuages the conscience of most highly moral individuals because the boundary between bribery and *utang na loób* reciprocity has been rather clearly marked by the lapse in time. Indeed when an outright bribe is in the offing, the usual procedure is for the parties involved to have a meaningful conversation beforehand, each sounding out the other in euphemistic language to see what the conditions will be. If this is the case, then the source of obligation is now a quasi-contract or contract and no longer *utang na loób*.

The repugnance of many non-Filipinos and many modernized Filipinos at this "handout" situation is not matched by the rest of Filipino society, simply because Filipinos rarely interpret postservice gift giving as bad. To them it is not bribery. How can fulfillment of one's social obligations, brought about through *utang na loób*, be anything but good, reasons the average Filipino. It is the system he has learned as a member of his society; it is part of his culture.

A particularly fruitful occasion for reciprocation is an election. Political leaders, cognizant of the social system, exploit it by deliberately cultivating *utang na loób* debts toward themselves so that when voting time comes, they can reclaim these by requesting the debtors to vote for them or for their candidates. In general, the debtor's sense of honor and propriety forces him to comply regardless of the quality of the candidate involved or his party. This is also true of elections in private groups— clubs, for example. A man who might perform the job better by efficiency standards may lose the election simply because his opponent has a larger group of followers, among them many *utang na loób* debtors. A vote . . . is considered a substantial repayment and is the object of a great deal of competition. Voting in accordance with an *utang na loób* creditor's request can wipe out one's debt to him, unless of course that is ruled out by the original circumstances which created that debt. (That some debts can never be fully repaid has already been mentioned.)

. . . In a society such as the Philippines, where the gap between social classes is marked, *utang na loób* reciprocity stabilizes the social system in a special manner by acting as a bridge between the separated sets. It particularizes the functional interrelationship of the upper and lower classes, that is, the rights and obligations of the upper class toward the lower class and vice versa are translated by it into a functional relationship between *this* upper-class person and *this* lower-class person. Thus, the general expectancy that the upper class will share its surplus with the lower class now becomes a particular expectancy between *this* landlord, for instance, and *this* tenant. . . .

II. Institutions and Processes

The legal framework of national politics in the Philippines is established by the constitution and a variety of implementing statutes. Because the Philippines has a unitary rather than a federal system, national legislation also determines the structure of government for provinces, cities, towns, and villages.

The Philippine constitution of 1935 (excerpts appear below) is the product of both American and Filipino political experience, but its language sometimes gives Americans a greater impression of unselective borrowing than is actually the case. The document was drafted by a constitutional convention that was authorized by the U.S. Congress and elected in 1934 by the Filipino people; the draft was approved by plebiscite in the following year. This constitution first served as the fundamental law of the domestically self-governing Commonwealth, and from 1946 served likewise for the Republic. It was amended in 1939, 1940, and 1946. In 1967 the machinery was set in motion for the calling of a new constitutional convention, which was elected in 1970 and began deliberations in 1971. For Senataor Pelaez, as for many others, "the one impelling reason for the calling of a constitutional convention is that . . . the Republic of the Philippines does not have a constitution which is truly the handiwork of the sovereign Filipino people."

Like statements of political ideology by national leaders, the constitution is often modified in practice by the implicit values of Filipino political culture. Yet, this is true, in part, of every constitution. What is noteworthy is that, to a greater extent than in most parts of Southeast Asia, Philippine governmental practices in the 1950's and 1960's actually conformed to constitutional mandates.

Constitution of the Philippines [1935]*

Art. II—Declaration of Principles

Sec. 1. The Philippines is a republican state. Sovereignty resides in the people and all government authority emanates from them.

Sec. 2. The defense of the State is a prime duty of government, and in the fulfillment of this duty all citizens may be required by law to render personal, military or civil service.

Sec. 3. The Philippines renounces war as an instrument of national policy, and adopts the generally accepted principles of international law as a part of the law of the Nation.

* Source: The Constitution of the Republic of the Philippines (Manila: Government of the Republic of the Philippines, n.d.).

. . . Sec. 5. The promotion of social justice to insure the well-being and economic security of all the people should be the concern of the State.

Art. III—Bill of Rights

Sec. 1. (1) No person shall be deprived of life, liberty, or property without due process of law, nor shall any person be denied the equal protection of the laws.

(2) Private property shall not be taken for public use without just compensation.

. . . (5) The privacy of communication and correspondence shall be inviolable except upon lawful order of the court or when public safety and order require otherwise.

. . . (10) No law impairing the obligation of contracts shall be passed.

. . . (21) Free access to the courts shall not be denied to any person by reason of poverty. . . .

Art VI—Legislative Department

Sec. 1. The Legislative power shall be vested in a Congress of the Philippines, which shall consist of a Senate and a House of Representatives.

Sec. 2. The Senate shall be composed of twenty-four Senators who shall be chosen at large by the qualified electors of the Philippines, as may be provided by law.

Sec. 3. The term of office of Senators shall be six years and shall begin on the thirtieth day of December next following their election.

. . . Sec. 5. The House of Representatives shall be composed of not more than one hundred and twenty Members who shall be apportioned among the several provinces as nearly as may be according to the number of their respective inhabitants, but each province shall have at least one Member. The Congress shall by law make an apportionment within three years after the return of every enumeration, and not otherwise. . . .

Each representative district shall comprise, as far as practicable, contiguous and compact territory.

. . . Sec. 23. . . . (3) No public money or property shall ever be appropriated, applied, or used, directly or indirectly, for the use, benefit, or support of any sect, church, denomination, sectarian institution, or system of religion, or for the use, benefit, or support of any priest, preacher, minister, or other religious teacher or dignitary as such, except when such priest, preacher, minister, or dignitary is assigned to the armed forces or to any penal institution, orphanage, or leprosarium.

Art. VII—The Executive

. . . Sec. 2. The President shall hold his office during a term of four years, and together with the Vice-President chosen for the same term, shall be elected by direct vote of the people.

. . . Sec. 5. No person shall serve as President for more than eight consecutive years. The period of such service shall be counted from the date he shall have commenced to act as President. . . .

. . . Sec. 10 . . . (2) The President shall be Commander-in-Chief of all the Armed Forces of the Philippines and, whenever it becomes necessary he may call out such armed forces to prevent or suppress lawless violence, invasion, insurrection, or rebellion. In case of invasion, insurrection, or rebellion or imminent danger thereof, when the public safety requires it, he may suspend the privilege of the writ of habeas corpus, or place the Philippines or any part thereof under martial law.

Art. VIII—Judicial Department

Sec. 1. The Judicial power shall be vested in one Supreme Court and in such inferior courts as may be established by law.

. . . Sec. 4. The Supreme Court shall be composed of a Chief Justice and ten Associate Justices and may sit either in banc or in two divisions unless otherwise provided by law.

. . . Sec. 9. The members of the Supreme Court and all judges of inferior courts shall hold office during good behavior, until they reach the age of seventy years, or become incapacitated to discharge the duties of their office.

Sec. 10. All cases involving the constitutionality of a treaty or law shall be heard and decided by the Supreme Court in banc, and no treaty or law may be declared unconstitutional without the concurrence of two-thirds of all the members of the Court.

Art. X—Commission on Elections

Sec. 1. There shall be an independent Commission on Elections composed of a Chairman and two other Members to be appointed by the President with the consent of the Commission on Appointments, who shall hold office for a term of nine years and may not be reappointed. Of the Members of the Commission first appointed, one shall hold office nine years, another for six years, and the third for three years. The Chairman and the other Members of the Commission on Elections may be removed from office only by impeachment in the manner provided in this Constitution.

Sec. 2. The Commission on Elections shall have exclusive charge of the enforcement and administration of all laws relative to the conduct of elections and shall exercise all other functions which may be conferred upon it by law. It shall decide, save those involving the right to vote, all administrative questions affecting elections, including the determination of the number and location of polling places, and the appointment of election inspectors and of other election officials. All law enforcement agencies and instrumentalities of the Government, when so required by the Commission, shall act as its deputies for the purpose of insuring free, orderly, and honest elections. The decisions, orders, and rulings of the Commission shall be subject to review by the Supreme Court.

No pardon, parole, or suspension of sentence for the violation of any election law may be granted without the favorable recommendation of the Commission. . . .

Other than the constitution itself, the Election Code was probably the most significant formal determinant of the pattern of Philippine politics. Though it did not explicitly encourage a two-party system, as is done in some Asian countries, the code certainly gave no encouragement to third parties. In fact, until 1951 straight-ticket voting and majority-party control of local boards-of-election inspectors even made it difficult for a strong, stable second party to emerge. In 1951 a split in the majority Liberal party made possible revisions in the code which helped to make Philippine elections more honest and fair. In any case, local cultural patterns may be more important than the formalities of election administration.[2]

Section 98 of the code states that only literate Filipino citizens over twenty-one are entitled to vote. But the list of disqualifications is more meaningful, for, in practice, only those who cannot write out candidates' names on their ballots are deprived of franchise. Because candidates' names are not printed on the ballot the means of illegally marking ballots are numerous, as attested by the code's "rules for appreciation of ballots." The ability to mark a ballot is essential for an effective system of vote-buying—an extremely widespread practice in the Philippines.

Much of the Election Code deals, in fact, with the control of material inducements in campaigns. It is an exercise in futility, however,

[2] See Carl H. Landé, *Leaders, Factions and Parties: The Structure of Philippine Politics* (New Haven, Conn.: Yale University, Southeast Asia Studies, Monograph Series, No. 6, 1965).

for section after section of prohibitions merely catalogue actual practices, and candidates' expense statements have traditionally been a farce of underreporting.

But the prevalence of vote buying and other excessive campaign expenditures are not inconsistent with measured praise of free elections in the Philippines. Often the major spender loses. Yet election costs do restrict the field, just as in the United States.

The Election Code was suspended following the imposition of martial law in September 1972.

The Philippine Election Code [June 21, 1947]*

Art. II—Candidacies and Eligibility of Candidates

. . . Sec. 29. Disqualification on account of violation of certain provisions of this Code. Any candidate who, in an action or protest in which he is a party, is declared by final decision of a competent court or tribunal guilty (a) of having spent in his election campaign more than the total emoluments attached to the office for one year; or (b) of having solicited or received any contribution in connection with his election campaign from any of the corporations or entities mentioned in section forty-seven, or from any of the persons mentioned in section fifty-six; or (c) of having violated any one of sections forty-nine, fifty, fifty-one, shall be disqualified from continuing as a candidate, or, if he has been elected, from holding the office. . . .

Art. III—Contributions and Other Practices

. . . Sec. 43. Statements by candidates. Within thirty days after the holding of the election, every candiate shall file with the Commission on Elections, for such action as it may deem proper, a statement, complete as of the date next preceding the date of filing, which shall contain (1) a lists of the contributions received by him or by another with his knowledge and consent, from whatever source, to help or support his candidacy or to influence the result of his elections together with the name and address of the contributor; (2) a statement of the expenditures made by him or by another with his knowledge and consent, in aid or support of his candidacy or for the purpose of influencing the result of the election,

* *Source:* Republic of the Philippines, Office of the President, *Laws and Resolutions,* 1st Cong., Republic Act No. 180, *The Revised Election Code,* approved June 21, 1947 (Manila: Bureau of Printing, 1948).

together with the name of the person to whom such expenditure was made. . . .

. . . Sec. 46. Prohibited collections of funds. It shall be unlawful for any person to hold balls, beauty contests, entertainments or cinematographic, theatrical, or other performances, during two months immediately preceding a regular or special election, for the purpose of raising funds for benefit purposes or for an election campaign, or for the support of any candidate. . . .

Sec. 47. Prohibited contributions. It shall be unlawful for any corporation or entity operating a public utility or which is in possession of or is exploiting any natural resources of the nation to contribute or make any expenditure in connection with any election campaign. . . .

Sec. 49. Unlawful expenditures. It is unlawful for any person to make or offer to make an expenditure, or to cause an expenditure to be made or offered to any person to induce one either to vote or withhold his vote, or to vote for or against any candidate, or any aspirant for the nomination or selection of a candidate of a political party, and it is unlawful for any person to solicit or receive directly or indirectly any expenditure for any of the foregoing considerations. . . .

Sec. 51. Prohibition regarding transportation, food and drinks. It is unlawful for any candidate, political committee, voter or any other person to give or accept, free of charge, directly or indirectly, transportation, food, or drinks during a public meeting in favor of any or several candidates and during the three hours before and after such meeting, or on registration days, or on the day preceding the voting and on the day of the voting; or to give or contribute, directly or indirectly, money or things of value for such purposes. . . .

. . . Sec. 53. Deadly weapons. It is unlawful to carry deadly weapons in the polling place and within a radius of thirty meters thereof during the days for registration, voting and canvass. However, in cases of affray, tumult or disorder, any peace or public officer authorized to supervise the elections may carry firearms or any other weapons for the purpose of preserving order and enforcing the law. . . .

Sec. 54. Active intervention of public officers and employees. No justice, judge, fiscal, treasurer, or assessor of any province, no officer or employee of the Army, no member of the national, provincial, city, municipal or rural police force, and no classified civil service officer or employee shall aid any candidate, or exert influence in any manner in any election or take part therein, except to vote, if entitled thereto, or to preserve public peace, if he is a peace officer. . . .

Sec. 55. Soliciting contributions from subordinates prohibited. Public officers and employees holding political offices or not belonging to the classified civil service, though they may take part in political and electoral activities, shall refrain from soliciting contributions from their subordinates for partisan purposes. . . .

Sec. 56. Active intervention of foreigners. No foreigner shall aid any candidate, directly or indirectly, or take part in or influence in any manner any election. . . .

. . . Sec. 86. Prohibition of political activity. No member of the board of election inspectors shall engage directly or indirectly in partisan political activities or take part in any election except to discharge his duties as such and except to vote. . . .

. . . Sec. 93. Official watchers of candidates. (a) During the registration of voters, voting and counting of the votes, and, in general, at all meetings of the board of inspectors, the watchers appointed by the candidates shall have the right to stay in the space reserved for them within the polling place . . .

(b) The watchers shall have the right to witness and inform themselves of the proceedings of the board, to take notes of what they may see or hear, to file a protest against any irregularity which they believe may have been committed by the board of inspectors, to obtain from the poll clerk a certificate as to the filing of such protest or of the resolution thereon, and to read the ballots after they have been read by the inspectors, without touching them, but they shall not speak to the inspectors, or to the voters, or among themselves in such manner as to interrupt the proceedings. . . .

. . . Sec. 98. Qualifications prescribed for a voter. Every citizen of the Philippines, whether male or female, twenty-one years of age or over, able to read and write, who has been a resident of the Philippines for one year and of the municipality in which he has registered during the six months immediately preceding, who is not otherwise disqualified, may vote in the said precinct at any election. . . .

Sec. 99. Disqualifications. The following persons shall not be qualified to vote:

(a) Any person who has been sentenced by final judgment to suffer one year or more of imprisonment, such disability not having been removed by plenary pardon.

(b) Any person who has been declared by final judgment guilty of any crime against property.

(c) Any person who has violated his allegiance to the Republic of the Philippines.

(d) Insane or feeble-minded persons.

(e) Persons who cannot prepare their ballots themselves. . . .

. . . Sec. 149. Rules for the appreciation of ballots. In the reading and appreciation of ballots the following rules shall be observed:

1. Any ballot where only the Christian name of candidate or only his surname appears is valid for such candidate, if there is no other candidate with the same name or surname for the same office. . . .

2. A name or surname incorrectly written which, when read, has a sound equal or similar to that of the real name or surname of a candidate shall be counted in his favor.

. . . 4. When in a space in the ballot there appears a name that is erased and another clearly written, the ballot is valid for the latter.

. . . 9. The use of nicknames and appellations of affection and friendship, if accompanied by the name or surname of the candidate, does not annul such vote, except when they were used as a means to identify their respective voters.

. . . 18. Unless it should clearly appear that they have been deliberately put by the voter to serve as identification marks, commas, dots, lines, or hyphens between the name and surname of a candidate, or in other parts of the ballot, traces of the letters "t," "j," and other similar ones, the first letters or syllables of names which the voter does not continue, the use of two or more kinds of writing, and unintentional or accidental flourishes, strokes, or stains, shall be considered innocent and shall not invalidate the ballot.

. . . 23. Any ballot which clearly appears to have been filled by two distinct persons before it was deposited in the ballot box during the voting is totally null and void. . . .

Amendments to the Philippine Election Code [1951]*

. . . Sec. 75. Appointment of election inspectors and poll clerks. . . . The Commission on Elections shall . . . appoint a board of election inspectors for each election precinct, to be composed of a chairman and two inspectors and a poll clerk. . . . The chairman and his substitute shall be appointed by the Commission on Elections. . . .

Sec. 76. Representation of parties in the board of inspectors. The appointment of one inspector and his substitute shall be proposed by the party presenting candidates for election which polled the largest number of votes in the next preceding presidential election and the other inspec-

* *Source:* Republic of the Philippines, Office of the President, *Laws and Resolutions,* 2d Cong., Republic Act No. 599, *An Act to Amend Certain Sections of the Revised Election Code* (Manila: Bureau of Printing, 1951).

tor and his substitute shall be proposed by the party also presenting candidates for election which polled the next largest number of votes in the Philippines. The Commission on Elections shall appoint the poll clerks in each election precinct, who shall be public school teachers. . . .

. . . Sec. 124. Official ballots. . . . Each ballot shall contain the names of all offices to be voted for in the election, allowing, opposite the name of each office, sufficient space or spaces within which the voter may write the name or names of the individual candidate voted by him. . . .

. . . Sec. 135. Manner of preparing the ballots. The voter, on receiving his ballot, shall forthwith retire to one of the empty voting booths and shall there fill his ballot by writing in the proper space for each office the name of the person for whom he desires to vote. . . .

It shall be unlawful to prepare the ballots outside the voting booth or to exhibit their contents to any person, or to erase any printing from the ballots, or to intentionally tear or deface the same or put thereon any distinguishing mark. It is likewise unlawful to use carbon paper, paraffin paper, or other means for making a copy of the ballot or make use of any other means to identify the vote of the voter.

The Revised Administrative Code determines the governance of provinces and municipalities in the Philippines, both of which have had their own elective officials since long before independence. Until 1956, however, there were no regular elections at the village, or barrio, level. Village administration, what there was of it, was handled by an appointed barrio lieutenant.

One of the most significant accomplishments of the Magsaysay administration was a move toward greater village autonomy. Since 1956 barrio lieutenants have been elective and have been given increased powers. Republic Act No. 2370, officially known as the Barrio Charter, was passed in 1959 to further develop and expand barrio government. For the first time the barrio council in each village was given the power to tax. In later legislation the barrio lieutenant was promoted to "captain" and given a small salary.

The growth of village self-government and the heightened political awareness of the villagers associated with it was probably the most fundamental change in the Filipino political system during the Republic's second decade.

The Barrio Charter [June 30, 1959]*

Art. I—General Provisions

. . . Sec. 2. Definition and general powers of barrios. Barrios are units of municipalities or municipal districts in which they are situated. They are quasi-municipal corporations endowed with such powers as are herein provided for the performance of particular government function, to be exercised by and through their respective barrio governments in conformity with law.

. . . Sec. 4. The barrio assembly. The barrio assembly shall consist of all persons who are qualified electors, who are duly registered in the list of barrio assembly members kept by the secretary thereof, and have been residents of the barrio for at least six months.

The barrio assembly shall meet at least once a year to hear the annual report of the barrio council concerning the activities and finances of the barrio.

It shall meet also when members of the barrio council are to be elected and/or at the call of the barrio council or upon written petition of at least one-fifth of the members of the barrio assembly.

For the purpose of conducting business and taking any official action in the barrio assembly, it is necessary for a quorum, which shall consist of at least one-third of the members of the barrio assembly, to be present. All actions involving the raising of taxes, payment of compensation and solicitation of voluntary contributions shall be by a two-thirds vote of those present at the meeting there being a quorum. All other actions may be by a majority vote of those present at the meeting there being a quorum.

Sec. 5. Powers of the barrio assembly. The powers of the barrio assembly shall be as follows:

(a) to elect members of the barrio council; act upon their resignation, if presented, and fill vacancies therein by election;
(b) to provide for reasonable compensation of barrio council members when authorized by two-thirds vote of the barrio assembly;
(c) to adopt measures for the raising of funds for the barrio by taxation and by voluntary contributions;

* *Source:* Republic of the Philippines, Office of the President, *Laws and Resolutions,* 4th Cong., Republic Act No. 2370, *An Act Granting Autonomy to Barrios of the Philippines,* approved June 30, 1959 (Manila: Bureau of Printing, 1959).

(d) to adopt measures for the good of the barrio;

(e) to decide on measures submitted to it in accordance with law; and

(f) to enter into contracts for and in behalf of the barrio and to autho-
     rize the barrio council so to do.

Sec. 6. The barrio council. In each barrio there shall be organized a
barrio council which shall have as members the following:

(a) a barrio lieutenant;

(b) a barrio treasurer;

(c) four council members;

(d) vice barrio lieutenants, in such number as there are sitios in the bar-
     rios; or where there are no sitios, one vice barrio lieutenant for
     every two hundred inhabitants of the barrio: Provided, That no per-
     son shall be elected vice barrio lieutenant unless he is a resident of
     the sitio he shall represent.

Sec. 7. Election of the barrio council. The barrio lieutenant, the barrio treasurer, the vice barrio lieutenants, and the four council members
shall be elected at a meeting of the barrio assembly.

. . . All members of the barrio assembly as defined in section four shall
have the right to vote at such elections. Voting shall be by secret ballot:
Provided, That open voting may be allowed if two-thirds votes of the
qualified voters present in the meeting shall so decide. No votes may be
cast by proxy.

The members of the barrio council shall hold office for two years from
the time of their election and qualification or until their successors are
duly elected and qualified. In no case shall a member of the council be
elected to the same position for more than three consecutive terms, but
after two years shall have elapsed from the expiration of his last term
he shall again be eligible for election to the same position.

. . . Sec. 9. The municipal mayor shall exercise the power of supervision over barrio officials. . . . For minor delinquency, he may repri-
mand the offender; and if a more severe punishment seems to be desirable,
he shall submit written charges touching the matter to the municipal
council. . . . The municipal mayor may in such case suspend the officer
pending action by the council. . . .

Art. III—Powers, Rights and Duties

. . . Sec. 10. Rights and duties of members of the barrio council. The
barrio lieutenant, or in his absence or inability, the vice barrio lieutenant
designated by the barrio council, shall discharge the following duties:

(a) To look after the maintenance of public order in the barrio and to assist the municipal councilor in the performance of his duties in such barrio;

(b) To preside over the meetings of the barrio assembly and the barrio council;

(c) To organize a fire brigade;

(d) To organize and lead an emergency group whenever the same may be necessary for the maintenance of peace and order within the barrio;

(e) To approve vouchers relating to the disbursement of barrio funds;

(f) To attend conventions of barrio lieutenants; and

(g) To enforce all laws and ordinances which are operative within the barrio and to sign and enter into contracts with the approval of the barrio council. . . .

. . . Sec. 12. Powers and duties of the barrio council. The barrio council shall have the power to promulgate barrio ordinances not inconsistent with law or municipal ordinances.

Any violation of barrio ordinances duly promulgated shall be punished by a fine of not more than one hundred pesos or imprisonment of not more than fifteen days, or both such fine and imprisonment, in the discretion of the court.

The barrio council shall have the following powers, duties and responsibilities:

(a) To construct and/or maintain within its boundaries the following public works: barrio roads, bridges, viaducts and sidewalks, playgrounds and parks, school buildings; water supply, drainage, irrigation, sewerage, and public toilet facilities, and other public works and facilities, and for this purpose, to exercise the power of eminent domain with the approval of the municipal council;

(b) To undertake cooperative enterprises that will improve the economic condition and well-being of the barrio residents. Such enterprises may include stores for the sale or purchase of commodities and/or produce, warehouses, activities relating to agricultural and livestock production and marketing, fishing, and home and barrio industries, and other activities which may promote the welfare of barrio inhabitants; . . .

(d) to initiate and submit to the barrio assembly community programs of economic and social benefit to the inhabitants of the barrio;

(e) To employ or contribute to the expenses of employing community development workers under terms of agreement made with the Office of the Presidential Assistant on Community Development or with any other bureau or agency of the government; . . .

(h) To hold benefits in their respective barrios without having to secure permits from the Social Welfare Administration. The proceeds from such benefits shall be tax-exempt and shall go to the barrio general fund, unless previously set aside for a specific purpose; . . .

(l) To appropriate barrio funds to implement the decisions of the barrio assembly and for purposes herein specified.

. . . Sec. 14. Taxing powers of the barrio council and the barrio assembly. The barrio council with the approval of two-thirds vote of the barrio assembly as provided in section four hereof, may raise, levy, collect and/or accept monies and other contributions from the following sources:

(a) Voluntary contributions annually from each male or female resident twenty-one years of age or over;

(b) Licenses on stores, signs, signboards, and billboards displayed or maintained in any place exposed to public view except those displayed at the place or places where profession or business advertised thereby is in whole or in part conducted;

(c) A tax on gamecocks owned by residents of the barrio and on the cockfights conducted therein: Provided, That nothing herein shall authorize the barrio council to permit cockfights;

(d) Monies, materials and voluntary labor for specific public works and cooperative enterprises of the barrio raised from residents, landholders, producers and merchants of the barrio;

(e) Monies from grants-in-aid, subsidies, contributions and revenues made available to barrios from municipal, provincial or national funds;

(f) Monies from private agencies and individuals;

(g) An additional percentage, not exceeding one-fourth of one per cent of the assessed valuation of the property within the barrio, collected by the municipal treasurer along with the tax on real property levied for municipal purposes by the municipality and deposited in the name of the barrio with the municipal treasurer: Provided, That no tax or license fee imposed by a barrio council shall exceed fifty per centum of a similar tax or fee levied, assessed or imposed by the municipal council.

Sec. 15. Share in real estate taxes. Ten per cent of all real estate taxes collected within the barrio shall accrue to the barrio general fund, which sum shall be deducted in equal amounts from the respective shares of the province and municipality: Provided, That the municipal treasurer may designate the barrio lieutenant and/or the barrio treasurer as his deputy to collect the said taxes.

To call Philippine political parties "loose confederations of unstable factions" is only a slight exaggeration. Switching party affiliation happens frequently, both at the highest and lowest levels. Personal loyalties, built themselves on perceptions of individual self-interest, hold parties and factions together; ideology carries little weight. Political wisdom dictates that no economic interest should tie itself irrevocably to a single party.

Within this party system the most persistent competition has been between the Nacionalistas, the party of Manuel Quezon and Sergio Osmeña (the president and vice-president, respectively, of the Commonwealth of the Philippines, inaugurated on November 15, 1935), that won independence, and the Liberals, a 1946 offshoot led by Manuel Roxas, first president of the Republic of the Philippines. As organizations these two parties have remained active since independence was declared on July 4, 1946, despite a lack of any fundamental or lasting difference between them on policy or principle. Rumor of the demise of either the Liberal or the Nacionalista party, as has circulated after some crushing electoral defeats, has so far proved premature.

Groups of moderate, reform-minded young leaders have often appeared on the fringes of these two parties. On occasion they have formed their own parties to contest national elections, but these third-party attempts have never been successful. The more promising of the youthful reformers are usually assimilated by one of the two major parties. The Liberals and the Nacionalistas have survived, in fact, because of their willingness to co-opt "new blood."

There is also a third category of small party, more radical, more ideologically oriented, and thus less assimilable into the mainstream of party politics. These groups range from the Communist party, founded in 1930 but now outlawed, to more ephemeral organizations on the nonrevolutionary left. Rebellious peasants, portions of the labor movement, and uncompromising nationalists from the middle class have been their sources of strength.

The 1953 winning platform of the Nacionalista party is reproduced in full below because it is brief and because it is typical of a challenging party's appeal. (The platform of the party in power is generally so platitudinous that it is unworthy of reproduction.)˙ Corruption and fiscal extravagance were attacked; honesty and economy in government, social justice, land reform, economic progress, help for schools and veterans were promised; both nationalism and friendship with the United States were extolled. Yet since 1953 there has been more corruption, a larger budget, poorer schools, and a tendency for the rich to get richer. But, of course, no sophisticated Filipino would take a party platform at face value any more than would his American counterpart. And, since the 1953 Nacionalista platform was the one on which Magsaysay was elected, performance on campaign promises was actually somewhat better than in other administrations.

Platform of the Nacionalista Party [1953]*

For six years, a wasteful, corrupt, ineffiecient and undemocratic administration has battered on the people. The compelling, imperative need of the hour is to CHANGE IT. Therefore, as soon as we receive the mandate of the nation, we pledge to:

I. Create a body of special prosecutors fully empowered to indict, for trial and punishment, all erring officials and all those who have conspired, abetted in, and profited by the commission of corrupt acts and practices, of deliberate infractions of law intended to guarantee free and clean elections and of culpable violations of the Constitution;

II. Cleanse and streamline the government by removing all useless, incompetent and corrupt officials, emancipating the public service from nepotism and political lameducks, strictly and properly implementing the provisions of the Constitution on the civil service and eliminating duplication or overlapping of functions;

III. Bring about a real balanced government budget by curtailing lavish expenditures, eliminating deficit spending, establishing a scientific long-term program of public works, particularly in the undeveloped regions of the country, in lieu of the pork barrel system, and enforcing our tax laws without discrimination;

IV. Restore immediately the privilege of the writ of habeas corpus and adopt whatever measures are necessary fully to safeguard the rights secured to the people by the Constitution;

* Source: Nacionalista Party Platform, 1953 (Manila: published by the party, n.d.).

V. Maintain an independent judiciary, and eliminate the present pernicious practice of designating special prosecutors and special judges to try particular cases;

VI. Readjust the character of our economy from its present predominantly colonial agricultural status to a progressively industrial system, thus removing unemployment and accelerating the attainment of economic independence and sound national prosperity; as to rice and other food products, encourage and promote full production so as to be able not only to supply adequately the needs of the people but to export them as well; carry out a sound program of economic development of all undeveloped regions, with special attention to Mindanao and Sulu;

VII. Remove present limitations on our economic freedom of action contained in existing executive agreements and trade arrangements under the Bell Trade Act;[3]

VIII. As the best means to combat and eradicate communism, effect land reforms through legislative and executive action, to bring into realization the principle declared in the Constitution that the State should concern itself with insuring the well-being and economic security of all the people so that every Filipino shall have a home and a farm which he can call his own;

IX. Eliminate restrictions on the freedom of self-organization by workers and on free collective bargaining;

X. Insure the purity and freedom of election, by establishing a scientific electoral census and a special tribunal to hear and decide presidential electoral protests and properly and strictly implementing, by executive action, all elections laws;

XI. Secure additional benefits for our veterans and war widows and

[3] The Bell Trade Act (1946) provided that after the end of duty-free trade in 1954, the Philippines and the United States would begin levying tariff on the imports of the other at 5 percent of regular duty, with a 5 percent increase each year until the full duty is reached in 1974. It was criticized as retarding Philippine industrialization because it would be so long before any tariff protection could be raised against American imports. It was amended in 1955 to provide that the speed at which U.S. tariffs were increased would be slowed while Philippine tariffs were raised more rapidly.

orphans and guarantee the honest disposition of all aids extended by the United States;

XII. Improve and elevate our educational standards, and implement adequately and effectively the constitutional provisions regarding national language and optional religious instruction in the schools of the nation; and provide proper health facilities for adequate medical care to the humblest citizen without interference to the free practice of the medical profession;

XIII. Encourage and provide opportunities to Filipinos abroad to participate in the political activities and economic development of the Republic and see to it that the diplomatic and consular representatives of the Philippines give adequate attention and protection to the Filipinos in their respective jurisdictions;

XIV. Propose constitutional amendments to prevent encroachment by any of the three coordinate departments of the government in the functions of the other and to make the government ever responsive to the needs and sentiments of the people; and

XV. Secure and maintain our freedom of action in the field of foreign relations, obtain just reparations from Japan as a prerequisite to the ratification of the Japanese Peace Treaty, improve and strengthen the ties of friendship existing between the Philippines and the other nations of the free world particularly those of Asia and the United States, and contribute to the cause of world freedom and peace through the United Nations Organization.

Bill of Economic Rights.   We will strive for the immediate recognition and wide-spread acceptance of the following rights of the common man:

1. The right of every Filipino to obtain a stable job proportionate to his aptitude;

2. The right of every Filipino laborer or employee, in the office and shop, the factory, the forest, the mine and the field to join a trade union of his free choosing, and to receive a wage that will not only enable him to live, but to live adequately, and permit him to acquire food, shelter, clothing, recreation, education for his children, and some savings;

3. The right of every Filipino laborer who so desires to own as much land as he can till; and to count upon government assistance in securing implements, tools, animals, seeds and scientific advice which he may need;

4. The right of every Filipino family to be protected against the fear

and worry of illness, accident, disability, unemployment, old age and death;

5. The right of every Filipino family to own and enjoy undisputed possession of a decent and sanitary home where it can live in peace and security;

6. The right of every Filipino to acquire a good education;

7. The right of every Filipino farmer, trader, merchant and business-man, large or small, to be free to trade on a market free from all unfair competition and domination by monopolists, native or foreign;

8. The right of every Filipino to modern medical care and to the op-portunity to achieve, sustain and enjoy health; and

9. The right of all Filipinos to obtain, individually or collectively, full and quick justice in all their grievances and complaints.

We will execute a more liberal and expeditious plan for the disposition of our public agricultural lands, and make lots of convenient sizes avail-able to discharged members of our armed forces, to government employ-ees, and to the laboring class.

We will embark on a large-scale campaign to purchase, sub-divide and distribute large landed estates to their tenants at cost. Meanwhile, we will encourage and aid the farmer and the tenant to raise minor crops or en-gage in household industries so as to augment their earnings from the cultivation of the major crop.

What We Believe In [*is as follows:*]

1. We believe that the only form of government that can in fact and practice promote the well-being of the people is a constitutional democ-racy, in which each man, woman and child is guaranteed freedom of reli-gion, freedom from fear, and freedom from want;

2. We believe that this is the age of the common man; that property rights are subordinate to human rights, and that man is not free politi-cally if he be not free economically;

3. We believe that the problem of peace and order must be solved quickly; that it requires a scientifically conceived humanitarian solution;

4. We believe that the highest tribute we can pay to the memory of the illustrious heroes of our country—Rizal, Mabini, Bonifacio, Del Pilar, Luna, Lopez-Jaena, Quezon, Abad Santos and others—is to actively con-tinue in practice the principles and ideas they set to achieve for the good of the Filipino people;

5. We believe that nothing we can do for our veterans and guerrilleros and their orphans and widows will ever be too much;

6. We believe that we owe the United States of America an abiding

debt of gratitude, and that we must forever preserve our friendship with
that country;

7. We believe that the government is the faithful servant, and not the
cruel and thoughtless master, of the people; that government must be
clean, honest, simple, efficient and progressive, ever alert, not only to safeguard, but also to promote and preserve the freedom of the people—all
the people;

8. We believe that our youth, who will in due time take our places in
the councils of the nation, are entitled to, and must have, an increasing
voice in government;

9. We believe that the invaluable role that the Filipino woman plays
in the life of this nation must be given due and increasing appreciation,
and that the law must recognize and uphold her rights and grant her a
greater and fuller participation in public affairs, national and international; and

10. We believe in serving only one master—our country; in following
only one voice—the voice of the Filipino people.

The *Lapiang Manggagawa,* or Workers' party (the only Filipino
political party which regularly uses a Tagalog name), represents the
extreme left within the spectrum of legal, organized politics. The president of this third party is Cipriano Cid, a labor leader with much experience, who was active in the Democratic Alliance.

The document below is not a formal party platform, but, as a major
address by the party's secretary-general delivered at the nation's leading university, it must be recognized as authoritative. Ignacio Lacsina,
who made the speech in 1965, is a bright and very articulate young
attorney who organized, early in his career, his own trade union, but
was forced out of it in a factional fight. Lacsina and other *Lapiang
Manggagawa* leaders were imprisoned under martial law in 1972.

Ignacio Lacsina: The Lapiang Manggagawa [March 26, 1965]*

. . . We of the Lapiang Manggagawa consider ourselves not the Third
Force, but the emerging decisive alternative to the one and only ruling
force in our society—the landlord-comprador sector. To us, the Liberal
and Nacionalista parties, as well as the motley contenders for the title
of Third Force, are nothing but competing factions of this ruling sector.
All these factions are at peace with the prevailing, American-designed

* *Source:* Speech delivered at a convocation/open forum at the University of
the Philippines, Diliman, Quezon City, March 26, 1965 (mimeo).

social order, and the contest consists in proving which one can best protect and advance it. We of the Lapiang Manggagawa are not a party to this contest. Our concern is to put an end to the conditions which make this senseless contest inevitable.

Indeed the situation today is upsetting in the extreme. Both the Liberal and the Nacionalista parties have evidently fallen completely, as never before, in the hands of reaction. . . .

However, while it is extremely upsetting, this situation need not surprise us at all. All these so-called parties from the NP [Nacionalista party] down to its latest splinter are merely acting according to the iron logic of the interests they commonly represent—the interests not of the Filipino people but of the ruling landlord-comprador sector of society— the same sector which treacherously usurped the leadership of the Katipunan Revolution from Andrés Bonifacio,[4] . . . and later totally betrayed the same Revolution to American imperialism at the turn of this century. . . .

This alliance for the exploitation of our people is today anchored upon a complex of so-called treaties, . . . and other instruments of American domination in this country. Viewed in their proper light, these are not treaties between the Filipino people and the United States; these are acts of conspiracy between the Filipino landlord-comprador sector and American imperialism.

It was this view of the forces at work in our society which moved us to found the Lapiang Manggagawa in February 1963.

Now, how do we differ from the landlord-comprador parties?

Fundamentally, the points of difference are these:

First, we represent not the landlord-comprador sector, but the great mass of its victims.

Second, the interests we represent are not linked submissively but opposed unconditionally to those of imperialism, American or otherwise.

Third, we want to expand democracy, to give it economic and social content for all our people, not to restrict its substance for the aggrandizement of a few.

In brief, we reject the exploitation of man by man no less than the exploitation of one nation by another.

Mr. Cipriano Cid, the president of our party, declared at its founding convention: "The Katipunan and the Lapiang Manggagawa are in fact one. . . .

[4] Organized in the early 1890's as a secret society by Andrés Bonifacio, a clerk in Manila, the Katipunan instigated an uprising against the Spanish colonial regime in 1896. In a struggle for power and control of the revolution, Bonifacio lost to Emilio Aguinaldo.

"The Lapiang Manggagawa in 1963 seeks to launch a peaceful and democratic revolution in our social, economic and cultural life, as a people, to achieve what the Katipunan, for historical reasons, could not achieve in its time, namely, the economic and social emancipation of our suffering people."

In the pursuit of this crucial task—the unfinished task of the Katipunan Revolution—we have been deeply encouraged by the growing support of our youth, particularly the awakening students of this University. We have also been encouraged by the sympathetic response of our emancipated intellectuals and the emerging Filipino entrepreneurial sector.

Today, our immediate objective is to expose to our people the inhuman, exploitative character of the alliance between the ruling landlord-comprador sector and American imperialism. This alliance is the chief obstacle to economic and social development for the benefit of our people. It is the chain which shackles our people in bondage—to poverty, ignorance, disease and injustice.

This will prepare our people for our ultimate objective, namely, to dislodge the landlord-comprador sector from power, and thereby put an end to its treasonable alliance with imperialism.

Only the capture of national political power by the emerging forces of Filipino nationalism—the workers, the youth, the intellectuals and the entrepreneurs—can restore the honor of our country, conserve and develop its resources for the benefit of all our people, and secure to this and future generations of Filipinos the blessings of genuine independence under a regime of justice, liberty and democracy.

III. Domestic Policies

Economic development is a high-priority goal shared by all Southeast Asian nations. Philippine performance, measured by annual growth of the gross national product, has been better than average in the region. But high rates of population increase have kept the annual growth of average per capita real income below 1 percent, and averages hide gross inequalities.

Government has played a smaller role in economic development in the Philippines than anywhere else in Asia. The Four-Year Economic Program, excerpts from which follow, expected 17 percent of capital formation to come from the Philippine national government, less than the government contribution in the 1950's.

Nevertheless, ambitious development plans are still being drawn up. In the Philippines "planning" is more a projection of possible or desired growth than of government action to shape the pattern of development. Tariffs, tax, and credit policies are all difficult to enforce; thus even with the best of intentions among top political leaders the impact of such measures is uncertain. No presidential economic plan in the Philippines has ever been adopted by Congress.

In this Four-Year Economic Program (1967–1970), prepared for President Ferdinand Marcos, a 6.2 percent growth rate for the gross national product was projected, about average for the decade.

Four-Year Economic Program [1967–1970]*

This Program presents a blueprint for the development of the Philippine economy during the period from fiscal year 1967 to fiscal year 1970.

. . . The Philippine economy, despite the progress achieved in the past 20 years, continues to be essentially a dualistic economy.

At the time the country gained independence in July 1946, the economy was characterized by a colonial structure, with the majority of the population engaged in traditional agriculture and a small minority engaged in a modern sector producing primary products for exports. In the fifties, organized manufacturing developed in response to incentives proffered by the Government. Despite its impressive growth, the manufacturing base is still narrow consisting essentially of consumer goods industries dependent on imported raw materials. By 1965, two-thirds of the population earned their livelihood from agricultural activities.

. . . The basic economic problem is the inadequacy of the dualistic economy to support a rising standard of living for the country's rapidly growing population. On the one hand, the tradition-bound agricultural sector does not produce enough surplus food and basic raw materials needed for inputs to domestic industry and for exports. On the other hand, the progress attained in the modern export and industrial sector does not spread out to the agricultural sector. As a result, the population engaged in traditional agriculture, with its low income level, does not provide an adequate market to support an expansion in manufacturing activities. In the meantime, population is growing at the rate of 3.2 per cent a year.

* Source: Four-Year Economic Program for the Philippines: Fiscal Years 1967–1970 (Manila: Government of the Republic of the Philippines, September 1966).

One other major consequence of the separation between the two sectors is the substantial and growing unemployment situation. In 1965, the number of totally unemployed persons rose to nearly 950,000 or 8.2 per cent of the labor force. In addition, substantial under-employment, equivalent to nearly 550,000 of fully unemployed (based on a 40-hour week) existed.

The second basic problem of the economy is introduced by external factors, consisting of the tendency of the terms of international trade to favor industrial goods at the expense of primary export products. . . .

Arrayed against these problems are several assets of the economy. One of the most important is the high educational level in the Philippines, much higher than in many other developing countries. The rate of literacy is 75 per cent and the number of graduates from institutions of higher learning has exceeded the capacity of the economy to absorb them.

An equally important asset is the aggressive entrepreneurial class and the core of skilled labor that have been developed during the past fifteen years.

A third important asset of the country is the stable political institution which has been epitomized by the peaceful turnover of the mantle of power in consonance with the results of balloting. . . .

Finally, the export structure of the Philippines is diversified, covering a wide range of products, albeit mainly primary commodities. Thus, total exports expanded by about 12 per cent between FY 1965 and FY 1966 despite the more than 5 per cent decline in the combined export value of coconut products, sugar and abaca, three products which accounted for 58 per cent of total exports in the earlier years. . . .

Considering these characteristics of the Philippine economy, the strategy of economic development adopted in the Program consists of integrating the traditional and modern sectors of the economy and fostering the increasing use of rationality in the decision-making processes of economic activities. In this way, a more efficient allocation of resources is expected to be accomplished, bringing about larger output and more numerous job opportunities.

The integration of the two sectors will be accompanied by a vigorous policy of import substitution and promotion of even more diversified exports.

Finally, to solve the unemployment problem, the rate of investment will have to be increased. While capital formation will depend mainly on domestic effort, foreign assistance will be sought to accelerate the integration of the economy.

On the part of the public sector, this strategy means moulding the government institutions into more effective instruments for economic development and channeling a larger proportion of their resources into productive investments. The challenge to statesmanship is to be able to convince politicians that good economic performance is better politics.

On the part of the private sector, the task before them is to build on the entrepreneurship spawned during the past fifteen years, discovering and developing new methods of producing more out of available resources. The process of economic development will operate within the accepted framework of free enterprise wherein the private sector will continue to play the dominant role.

The pace of development during the plan period FY 1967–FY 1970 will depend mainly on the initiative of the private sector. To a lesser but still significant extent, the success of the Program will depend on the efficiency of the Government in accommodating economic rationality in its political decision processes and in fostering the integration of the two sectors of the economy. Given the effectiveness of these two internal factors, the rate of development will be limited only by the constraints imposed by the balance of international payments.

Over the four-year plan period, the Program aims at increasing the annual rate of growth of per capita real income from its level of 0.9 per cent in FY 1961–FY 1965 to 2.4 per cent.

Since the population of the Philippines will most likely grow at the same rapid rate of 3.2 per cent annually, real national income will have to rise by an average 5.7 per cent a year in order that the target increase in per capita income will be attained. Correspondingly, gross national product will have to rise at an average annual rate of 6.2 per cent.

At attain this objective, the rate of investment will have to increase from 14.6 per cent of gross national product in FY 1962–FY 1966 to 21.3 per cent during the plan period. For the four-year plan period, the projected investments aggregate ₱20.3 billion as compared to a total of ₱10.1 billion for the preceding four-year period and, thus, represents an increase over 100 per cent.

With the increasing tempo of economic activities envisaged in the Program, enough employment opportunities are expected to be generated to absorb the new entrants to the labor force and reduce unemployment and underemployment from 13.0 per cent to 7.2 per cent of the labor force by FY 1970. . . .

Of the total capital formation required, investments of the national Government will account for ₱3.5 billion or 17 per cent, seven-tenths of which are earmarked for infrastructure projects. These investments will mainly implement the strategy of integrating the economy's traditional and modern sectors. . . .

Probably no one is better qualified to comment on the nature of Filipino economic planning than Sixto K. Roxas, an influential investment banker and former economic advisor to President Macapagal. In this excerpt from a report to the president in 1964, he describes a situation that has not basically changed.

Sixto K. Roxas: The Problems of Public Administration for Economic Development [1964]*

. . . It is meaningless, at this stage, to talk of national planning. It is meaningless because neither the Philippine government nor any of its agencies is in any position to draw up a meaningful national plan. The whole public administration system, the whole governmental machinery as it stands, is a large, cumbersome and sticky structure that militates not only against implementing a plan, but even against formulating a meaningful plan. The "five-year plans" we have had during the whole postwar period were not really plans but merely statements of general aspirations. That there has been no concrete "implementation" of any of these plans is due not only to the fact that the implementing machinery is not geared for it, but also to a basic deficiency in the plans themselves: they have been too general and too aggregative, and thus provided nothing concrete enough to implement.

There has really been no national economic planning in this country. The government organization is not capable of it.

Planning and implementation are not so much a chain of sequences as a cycle. They reinforce and give substance to each other. If the government is not properly organized to implement a plan, it follows that it is not properly organized even to plan, if by the latter we mean a program that is substantive enough to be translated into action. "To increase production" is not a plan but a wish; "to increase the production of rice" is [not] a plan but a slightly more specific wish; it becomes a plan only when the region most suited for increased production is defined, the nature and magnitude of investments in irrigation facilities, in fertilizer, in agricultural extension, in transport and storage facilities are determined, the financial requirements are measured, the sources of finance are specified, the policies consistent with these objectives are laid down, and the agencies responsible for each thread of action in the whole scheme are mobilized and made to carry out their specific roles under an effective

* Source: Philippine Journal of Public Administration, 9 (January 1965), 1; reprinted by permission of the publishers of the Philippine Journal of Public Administration.

over-all executive coordinator. What was first a wish thus becomes a meaningful program of action which the various agencies concerned can then "implement."

While the Philippine government has always been engaged in implementing a multiplicity of individual schemes—some productive, others purely diffusive—it has never been organized to implement a scheme on a national basis, or even on a broad regional basis (e.g., a regional plan for the Central Luzon river basin) it has never been organized to draw up a plan of this coverage. The machinery that links planning at the top with execution in the field breaks down in innumerable places. Even within single departments, the activities of bureaus and units often diverge rather than merge. Since the links in the machinery are widely disconnected, the over-all planning bodies have not been able to draw from the departments and the agencies the concrete data—the stuff, as it were—that would form the content of the plan.

The problem, thus, is not one of planning alone or implementation alone. It is a problem of organization. It is a crisis of public administration, of government management, which must be met head-on if planning for economic development is to be successful in this country. It cannot be solved by continuously going through the exercise of drafting more five-year plans, of setting and re-setting targets. It can be solved only by recognizing that the first order of business is to attack the crippling bottlenecks that are built into the system and procedures of our whole governmental administrative system.

Serious attention to agrarian reform by government leaders in the Republic of the Philippines did not occur until after the Huk rebellion had reached dangerous proportions in the early 1950's. Much was accomplished during the Magsaysay administration, but even then the caution of the president and the power of the landed interests in Congress prevented any basic change in the Philippine land-tenure system. In fact, there was some indication that the percentage of share tenants was on the rise. The significant progress initiated under Magsaysay's leadership slowed to a snail's pace after his death.

Diosdado Macapagal campaigned in 1961 as a "poor boy who made good," but he made almost no mention of land reform. After he took office in 1962 he began to appreciate the seriousness of the agrarian crisis and the inadequacy of existing legislation and its implementation. In 1963, when his party faced a mid-term election for senators and local officials, Macapagal showed even greater determination than had Magsaysay in pressing for passage of the comprehensive Land Reform Code. It was finally adopted by Congress on August 8, 1963, only after the president had called the sixth special session for that purpose. The code strengthened and integrated most of the existing legislation on land redistribution, agricultural labor, tenant-landlord relations, rural credit, land settlement, land registration, and agricultural productivity. To coordinate administration of previously competing agencies, a National Land Reform Council was created to supervise the code's implementation.

But inertia was greater than impetus. For instance, authorized capitalization of the Land Bank, which was to finance the purchase of large estates for redistribution, was four hundred million pesos. By 1969 the bank was actually capitalized at less than twenty million pesos. Likewise, the law which was designed to transform over one million share tenants into lessees, on their way to full ownership, had netted less than fifteen thousand registered leasehold contracts in six years. A Senate critic of the Marcos administration's agrarian program in 1969 estimated that it would take thirteen hundred years at the existing pace to convert tenants into cultivator owners. New land reform measures proclaimed by Marcos in 1972 under martial law attempted to implement and expand upon the Code below, but the actual realization of such measures has just begun.

The Agricultural Land Reform Code [August 8, 1963]*

. . . Sec. 2. Declaration of Policy.—It is the policy of the State:

(1) To establish owner-cultivatorship and the economic family-size farm as the basis of Philippine agriculture and, as a consequence, divert landlord capital in agriculture to industrial development. . . .

Sec. 3. Composition of Code.—In pursuance of the policy enunciated in Section two, the following are established under this Code:

(1) An agricultural leasehold system to replace all existing share tenancy systems in agriculture;
(2) A declaration of rights for agricultural labor;

---

*Source: Republic of the Philippines, Office of the President, *Laws and Resolutions,* 5th Cong., Republic Act No. 3844, S. No. 542, H. No. 5222, *The Agricultural Land Reform Code 1963,* approved August 8, 1963 (Manila: Bureau of Printing, 1963).

(3) An authority for the acquisition and equitable distribution of agricultural land;

(4) An institution to finance the acquisition and distribution of agricultural land;

(5) A machinery to extend credit and similar assistance to agriculture;

(6) A machinery to provide marketing, management, and other technical services to agriculture;

(7) A unified administration for formulating and implementing projects of land reform;

(8) An expanded program of land capability survey, classification, and registration; and

(9) A judicial system to decide issues arising under this Code and other related laws and regulations.

Sec. 4. Abolition of Agricultural Share Tenancy.—Agricultural share tenancy, as herein defined, is hereby declared to be contrary to public policy and shall be abolished: Provided, That existing share tenancy contracts may continue in force and effect in any region or locality, to be governed in the meantime by the pertinent provisions of Republic Act Numbered Eleven hundred and ninety-nine, as amended, until the end of the agricultural year when the National Land Reform Council proclaims that all the government machineries and agencies in that region or locality relating to leasehold envisioned in this Code are operating, unless such contracts provide for a shorter period or the tenant sooner exercises his option to elect the leasehold system: Provided, further, That in order not to jeopardize international commitments, lands devoted to crops covered by marketing allotments shall be made the subject of a separate proclamation. . . .

Sec. 11. Lessee's Right of Pre-emption.—In case the agricultural lessor decides to sell the landholding, the agricultural lessee shall have the preferential right to buy the same under reasonable terms and conditions. . . .

. . . Sec. 34. Consideration for the Lease of Riceland and Lands Devoted to Other Crops.—The consideration for the lease of riceland and lands devoted to other crops shall not be more than the equivalent of twenty-five per centum of the average normal harvest during the three agricultural years immediately preceding the date the leasehold was established after deducting the amount used for seeds . . . and the cost of harvesting, threshing, loading, hauling and processing, whichever are applicable. . . .

. . . Sec. 49. Creation of the Land Authority.—For the purpose of carrying out the policy of establishing owner-cultivatorship and the economic family-size farm as the basis of Philippine agriculture and other policies enunciated in this Code, there is hereby created a Land Authority, hereinafter called the Authority, which shall be directly under the control and supervision of the President of the Philippines. . . .

. . . Sec. 51. Powers and Functions.—It shall be the responsibility of the Authority:

(1) To initiate and prosecute expropriation proceedings for the acquisition of private agricultural lands as defined in Section one hundred sixty-six of Chapter XI of this Code for the purpose of subdivision into economic family-size farm units and resale of said farm units to bona fide tenants, occupants and qualified farmers: Provided, That the powers herein granted shall apply only to private agricultural lands subject to the terms and conditions and order of priority hereinbelow specified:

a. all idle or abandoned private agricultural lands, except those held or purchased within one year from the approval of this Code by private individuals or corporations for the purpose of resale and subdivision into economic family-size farm units in accordance with the policies enunciated in this Code. . . .
b. all private agricultural lands suitable for subdivision into economic family-size farm units, owned by private individuals or corporations worked by lessees . . . in excess of seventy-five hectares except all private agricultural lands under labor administration.

. . . Sec. 53. Compulsory Purchase of Agricultural Lands.—The Authority shall, upon petition in writing of at least one-third of the lessees and subject to the provisions of Chapter VII of this Code, institute and prosecute expropriation proceedings for the acquisition of private agricultural lands and home lots enumerated under Section fifty-one. In the event a landowner agrees to sell his property under the terms specified in this Chapter and the National Land Reform Council finds it suitable and necessary to acquire such property, a joint motion embodying the agreement, including the valuation of the property, shall be submitted by the Land Authority and the landowner to the Court for approval: Provided, That in such case, any person qualified to be a beneficiary of such expropriation or purchase may object to the valuation as excessive, in which case the Court shall determine the just compensation in accordance with Section fifty-six of this Code.

. . . Sec. 56. Just Compensation.—In determining the just compensation of the land to be expropriated pursuant to this Chapter, the Court, in land under leasehold, shall consider as a basis, without prejudice to considering other factors also, the annual lease rental income authorized by law capitalized at the rate of six per centum per annum. . . .

. . . Sec. 60. Disposition of Expropriated Land.—After separate certificates of titles have been issued in accordance with Section fifty-eight, the Land Authority, on behalf of the Republic of the Philippines and in representation of the Land Bank as the financing agency, shall allot and sell each parcel or lot to a qualified beneficiary selected under Section fifty-five of this Code, subject to uniform terms and conditions imposed by the Land Bank: Provided, That the resale shall be at cost which shall mean the purchase price plus not more than six per centum per annum, which shall cover administrative expenses, and actual expenses for subdivision, surveying, and registration: Provided, further, That such cost shall be paid on the basis of an amortization plan not exceeding twenty-five years at the option of the beneficiary.

. . . Sec. 74. . . . To finance the acquisition by the Government of landed estates for division and resale to small landholders, as well as the purchase of the landholding by the agricultural lessee from the landowner, there is hereby established a body corporate to be known as the "Land Bank of the Philippines. . . ."

. . . Sec. 80. Making Payment to Owners of Landed Estates.—The Land Bank shall make payments in the form herein prescribed to the owners of land acquired by the Land Authority for division and resale under this Code. Such payment shall be made in the following manner: ten per centum in cash and the remaining balance in six per cent, tax-free, redeemable bonds issued by the Bank in accordance with Section seventy-six, unless the landowner desires to be paid in shares of stock issued by the Land Bank in accordance with Section seventy-seven in an amount not exceeding thirty per centum of the purchase price.

The profits accruing from payment shall be exempt from the tax on capital gains. . . .

With a consistent pattern for nearly two decades of many promises of agrarian reform and very little action, understandably unrest has increased in the Philippine countryside, especially in Central Luzon where tenancy is highest and where corrupt and inefficient reform agencies have been busiest. The Huks seem to have exploited this unrest again, though with tactics somewhat different from those of the 1950's.

The revival of Communist activity in recent years has occasionally produced red-baiting and witch-hunting. But the Philippine Senate Committee on National Defense and Security reacted differently: Chaired by Senator Manuel Manahan, a close associate of the late President Magsaysay and a third-party presidential candidate after

Magsaysay's death, this committee produced a report which is a most perceptive and enlightened analysis of the complex crisis.

The Security Problem Posed by the Huk Movement [1967]*

Almost a decade and a half after Magsaysay had smashed the communist-led Huk rebellion, the Huks appear to have recovered from their defeat and are now, according to the best available intelligence, running a sort of "invisible government" in Pampanga, in the western sector of Bulacan, and in the southern fringes of Nueva Ecija and Tarlac.

. . . From reports by persons who had come in contact with the dissidents, particularly in Pampanga and Tarlac, one would conclude that the Huks today represent a strange conglomeration of oldtime idealist-reformers, communists, farmers who are so poor they have decided to join the movement to assure themselves of three meals a day, persons with pending criminal cases in court, bandits who have joined forces with the Huks, and plain gangsters who have found it extremely profitable to operate their protection rackets "in the name of the Huk organization."

Save for Pedro Taruc, Sumulong and a few other aging Huk leaders, who had communist indoctrination under the old leadership, the Huks today are generally young, many of them hardly past their teens, and who were infants at the height of the Huk movement. It is possible some of these young Huks are sons of dissidents who had been killed in action or been captured, brought to court and sentenced to long terms of imprisonment at the compound for political prisoners at Fort Bonifacio, Rizal. In such a case, these young rebels represent the second generation Huks out to continue the struggle where their fathers left off.

As admitted by the military the Huk force today is much smaller than the rebel army of the 50's. It consists of armed Huks, 156; combat support, 136; service support of legal cadres, 850; and mass support, 30,000. In point of numbers the Huks today present no big threat to our national security. However, its strength lies in such intangibles as the people's growing apathy to the problems confronting the country, their deepening skepticism which renders more difficult the implementation of any program undertaken by the government, and their inaction in the face of the critical situation of the country.

Without the support, active or passive, of the people the Huk movement will collapse like a house of cards.

* *Source:* Republic of the Philippines, Senate, Committee on National Defense and Security, *Committee Report,* No. 1123 (printed in the *Manila Times,* June 4–8, 1967).

Despite the addition of new elements in the Huk organization, there is reason to believe that the Huk movement is in large measure an agrarian reform movement. The Huks, today as in the past, want a thorough-going, honest-to-goodness land reform that will assure them full owner-ship of their farms which they can till in freedom and dignity, relying on their inherent talent, ingenuity and industry, and in due time becoming responsible members of the community.

While the Huk leaders are either communist or have communist lean-ings, the rank and file of the organization is made up of poor, unschooled, landless tenants. The latter don't even know the difference between de-mocracy and communism, and they don't give a hoot what the rest of the world will think of them provided that they have lands of their own be-cause in their simple minds land ownership means economic stability, independence and dignity, let alone a respectable place in the community. It was this hunger for land of the peasants which the communists have exploited to win their faith and confidence.

In the political sphere the Huk challenge is primarily directed at what the dissidents claim as abuses committed by government officials and military personnel. A Huk leader said in an interview with a provincial newsman that the Huks were needed to protect the "downtrodden people of Central Luzon from being victims of injustices." He asserted that the Huks were not against the government but against the way the govern-ment was being run. He likewise denounced the shenanigans of govern-ment officials who "forgot the plight of the farmers."

Perhaps the more authentic political statement to come from a Huk leader was provided by Pedro Taruc, tagged by military intelligence as the new Huk supremo, who denied he was a communist but asserted that the Huks have a 'new government' called the "Bayung Fuerza Democ-ratica Ding Memalen" (New People's Democratic Force). The primary objective of this government, he explained, was to work for the ameliora-tion of the masses—for social justice and equality of all, rich and poor alike, before the law.

To the end that the alleged abuses by government officials would be stopped, the Huks have been participating in the local elections, support-ing candidates of their choice who would be sympathetic to their move-ment. Today, as another election draws near, people in the Huk-controlled areas pressure their candidates to get the endorsement of the Huks in order to assure their success. . . .

The local communist movement is presently intensifying the organiza-tion of new HMB[5] units in Central Luzon. . . .

[5] Hukbong Mapagpalaya ng Bayan—People's Liberation Army.

Reactivation of former HMBs has been noted not only in Central Luzon but also in other parts of the country. Former HMBs who had surrendered or captured and later on were released, pardoned or paroled, are urged by the party to rejoin the movement. . . .

Recruitment and training of new HMB members continue in Central Luzon. The sound financial position of the movement is evidently reflected in its ability to pay new HMB recruits with salaries ranging from ₱150 to ₱250. The new recruits are even promised salary increases and bonuses upon accomplishment of their missions which are usually liquidation and sabotage.

The HMBs have also sustained their limited operations such as ambuscades, raids, robberies, and other atrocities. It may be noted that as of July 1966, the HMBs successful execution of these atrocities not only serves to harass local government officials in Central Luzon but also instills fear among the people rendering the latter vulnerable to Communist exploitation.

The mass of information collected by the committee in the course of its formal investigation into the security problem posed by the present Huk movement points conclusively to the fact that the Huks have never been as strong as they are today since the defeat of their revolutionary struggle by President Magsaysay. . . .

The committee notes the existence of aversion to and dislike [of] the aggressive acts of the military in the area.

This can only mean that military commands and units operating in sensitive jurisdictions like Central Luzon must wage continuing and effective public relations and psychological warfare campaigns to improve relations with the civilian sector. . . .

The military aspect of the Huk problem is actually only one of the many factors which must be considered in dissecting the seriousness of this peril. While it cannot be denied that by defying duly constituted authority and taking up arms against the government, the Huks have become the principal responsibility of our military agencies, it is still the primary concern and obligation of the government, as a whole, to uncover all the other facets of this problem. . . .

The peasants of Central Luzon still constitute the bedrock of the Huks' growing strength and influence. Farmers by day, many have once more become fighters by night. They are the ones who can no longer afford to wait for promised government reforms or who have been coerced into rejoining the Huk cause due to government failure to provide them with adequate protection.

But the committee believes that the greater portion of the masses in Central Luzon remain hopeful and uncommitted. It is they whose hearts and minds must be won if the government must defeat the Huks and prove that democracy is better than the Huk cause and way of life.

They need justice, the protection of the law, a better and honest government they can respect and trust. They need land of their own plus the resources and facilities to make that land bountiful. . . .

For in the final analysis, even if it were only a few hundred Huks in Central Luzon who still lack, need and demand these things, it is the committee's conviction that such a demand would be just and within rights—a demand which a free and democratic government truly responsive to the people's welfare is obligated to honor. For the Huks—whether communists, bandits or reformists—are also citizens and human beings.

IV. Foreign Policy

For the first decade after independence, the image of Philippine foreign policy abroad—and the reality at home—was of close coordination with, at times subservience to, the U.S. position in world affairs. The Soviet Union even refused to recognize the Philippines on the grounds that it was not, in fact, independent—though a Soviet ambassador would probably not have been accepted in Manila in any case.

The United States granted the Philippines independence in 1946, but with a humiliation that Filipinos still vividly recall—the Parity Amendment. To ensure continued free entry into the American market for leading Filipino exports—generally considered essential for Philippine postwar economic rehabilitation—the Philippines was required to amend its constitution to give Americans equal opportunity with Filipinos in the exploitation of natural resources. At the same time a Philippine-American trade agreement was signed providing for an eight-year period of mutual free trade, followed by gradual and symmetrical imposition of full U.S. and Philippine tariffs on each other's imports. The process was to be completed in 1974.

Before the imposition of tariffs began, however, Philippine-American negotiations were reopened to revise the 1946 agreement. Senator José P. Laurel, unsuccessful Nacionalista candidate for the presidency in 1949, headed the Philippine negotiating team. James Langley was President Dwight D. Eisenhower's representative. Excerpts from the so-called Laurel-Langley Agreement of 1955 follow. Absolute quotas on certain Philippine exports were retained in Article II.

The Laurel-Langley Agreement [September 19, 1955]*

. . . Art. VI. 1. The disposition, exploitation, development, and utilization of all agricultural, timber, and mineral lands of the public domain, waters, minerals, coal, petroleum and other mineral oils, all forces and sources of potential energy, and other natural resources of either Party, and the operation of public utilities, shall, if open to any person, be open to citizens of the other Party and to all forms of business enterprise owned or controlled, directly or indirectly, by citizens of such other Party in the same manner as to and under the same conditions imposed upon citizens or corporations or associations owned or controlled by citizens of the Party granting the right.

2. The rights provided for in Paragraph 1 may be exercised, in the case of citizens of the Philippines with respect to natural resources in the United States which are subject to Federal control or regulations, only through the medium of a corporation organized under the laws of the United States or one of the States thereof and likewise, in the case of citizens of the United States with respect to natural resources in the public domain in the Philippines, only through the medium of a corporation organized under the laws of the Philippines and at least 60% of the capital stock of which is owned or controlled by citizens of the United States.

The rights provided for in this Paragraph shall not, however, be exercised by either Party so as to derogate from the rights previously acquired by citizens or corporations or associations owned or controlled by citizens of the other Party.

3. The United States of America reserves the rights of the several States of the United States to limit the extent to which citizens or corporations or associations owned or controlled by citizens of the Philippines may engage in the activities specified in this Article. The Republic of the Philippines reserves the power to deny any of the rights specified in this Article to citizens of the United States who are citizens of States, or to corporations or associations at least 60% of whose capital stock or capital is owned or controlled by citizens of States, which deny like rights to citizens of the Philippines, or to corporations or associations which are owned or controlled by citizens of the Philippines. The exercise of this reservation on the part of the Philippines shall not affect previously acquired rights, provided that in the event that any State of the United States of America should in the future impose restrictions which would deny to citizens or corporations or associations owned or controlled by citizens of the Philip-

* *Source:* United States, Department of State, *Bulletin,* 33 (September 19, 1955), 847: 466–473.

pines the right to continue to engage in activities in which they were engaged therein at the time of the imposition of such restrictions, the Republic of the Philippines shall be free to apply like limitations to the citizens or corporations or associations owned or controlled by citizens of such States.

Art. VII. 1. The United States of America and the Republic of the Philippines each agree not to discriminate in any manner, with respect to their engaging in business activities, against the citizens or any form of business enterprise owned or controlled by citizens of the other and that new limitations imposed by either Party upon the extent to which aliens are accorded national treatment with respect to carrying on business activities within its territories shall not be applied as against enterprises owned or controlled by citizens of the other Party which are engaged in such activities therein at the time such new limitations are adopted, nor shall such new limitations be applied to American citizens or corporations of associations owned or controlled by American citizens whose States do not impose like limitations on citizens of corporations or associations owned or controlled by citizens of the Republic of the Philippines.

. . . Art. X. The United States and the Philippines agree to consult with each other with respect to any questions as to the interpretation or the application of this Agreement, concerning which either Government may make representations to the other. Not later than July 1, 1971, the United States and the Philippines agree to consult with each other as to joint problems which may arise as a result or in anticipation of the termination of this agreement.

The remarkable oratory which concluded President Marcos's address to the U.S. Congress in 1966 characterized an important element in Philippine-American relations: Besides calling attention to the persistent Filipino opposition to pro-Americanism, President Marcos reminded Americans of what is expected of them by a people who fought and suffered with the United States—for a time almost as equals—in World War II. This wartime experience created a powerful emotional reservoir in the Philippines. It has spilled over most frequently in frustration at the American government's very inadequate treatment of Filipino veterans. But even in other areas of the relationship between the two peoples—once called "special"—Filipinos see Americans as being burdened with obligations which the Americans do not seem to want to admit. When American obligations remain unfulfilled, Marcos warned, the erstwhile loyalty of Filipinos turns very sour.

Ferdinand Marcos: Philippine-American Relations
[September 15, 1966]*

Let me bare my heart to you. I have come not as an enemy. I have contributed my modest share in payment of the price for the liberties and ideals which we all cherish.

It is precisely because of this that I have been hounded by loud, persistent criticism that I am much too pro-American in my policies. Perhaps I am emotionally so. For I was one of the many who gambled everything—life, dreams and honor—on a faith in and the vision of America, when all was lost as the Stars and Stripes for the first time in history was trodden to the ground in Asia. I have faith in your objectives in Asia and am deeply convinced that democracy such as ours in the Philippines can thrive in an ocean of neutrals and Communists but only if you keep true to and abide by the image of fairness that is America.

And the truth is all of Asia watches how America will treat her most loyal and steadfast ally. The whole world watches if America will mete out justice to the Filipino veterans. There are rumblings among my people. For too many of them, including some of our intellectual leaders, have long ago lost faith in your sense of fairness. Without necessarily heeding the importunings of our Communist enemies, they are harsh critics and have given up hope of American justice. They claim American policy desires only the permanence or predominance of American power in Asia regardless of what happens to the individual Asian and that you could not care less who lost his head to the tyrant provided that tyrant was your tyrant. . . .

So, upon the kind invitation of your great President, I have come to you with leave of my people. When I sought their counsel, they told me: "Go, young man of many dreams and many scars, go to your friends. Go but once and no more." I can hear them say still: "Go, without misgivings, for we know only too well the Americans' disdain for state visitors who go to their land with promises of loyalty to their ideals and global objectives but with their palms and hands stretched out for aid. Do not beg for alms or aid for we do not solicit charity.

"But tell them loyalty is not for sale. There is no price tag for faith except justice.

"Go and tell them this. If after they have heard you, they remain unmoved, then with sorrow and grief tell them we are prepared to close this unfortunate chapter of Philippine-American history. With dignity, the

* *Source:* Address to Joint Session of the United States Congress, Washington, D.C., September 15, 1966 (text in *Manila Chronicle,* October 17, 1966).

Philippines shall stand alone as we have done in the past, fighting off the terrors of our enemies. If we are overwhelmed, then Asia is lost to Communism but we would have had our share of conflict. And if we fall, we shall have fallen with pride and shall have died with honor."

But the critics were more cruel. And even the veterans scoff at our own scars in battle. One of these scars I received in trying to save an American comrade. "Where is he now?" they ask. "He is dead like many of our dreams."

Yes, my American comrade died in my arms. We were surrounded and we had to break out. He fell and as he tried to crawl to safety, I returned to him, to fall at his side—Filipino and American blood comingling in Philippine soil.

As I cradled him in my arms to a foxhole, he died with the words: "Tell them back home, you who will live, my only regret in dying is that America has failed us."

I, the Filipino, assured the American, as if this would assuage his dying. "No, America does not forget and will not fail us."

New trends in Philippine foreign policy are closely linked to a continuing search for an identity as a nation. It is ironic, however, that the following statement on national identity should come from one who was considered some years ago by Claro Recto an apostle of Americanism in the Philippines.

The development of Carlos P. Romulo's career has, in fact, paralleled in many ways the sea change in the Filipino world view. Romulo, long-time Philippine ambassador to the United States and the United Nations, was the first Asian president of the U.N. General Assembly. Often tagged in the 1940's and 1950's as a spokesman for the United States in the world arena and less than affectionately dubbed "The Little Brown Brother" by Manila wags, Romulo seemed to reassess his position in the crucible of the first Afro-Asian conference at Bandung, Indonesia, in 1955. After his return to the Philippines in 1964 he served as president of the University of the Philippines, secretary of education, and since 1968, secretary of foreign affairs. He has become increasingly sensitive to the new nationalism in the land, but without a breakdown in his communications with Americans. In fact, perhaps only one with such long and friendly ties with the United States can implement the basic changes in Philippine foreign relations which he suggests in this significant address.

Since the proclamation of martial law, Philippine foreign policy has turned simultaneously toward closer cooperation with American and Japanese capital and greater openness to trade and diplomatic contact with Communist countries.

Carlos P. Romulo: The New Filipino Ideology [January 30, 1969]*

We are embarked, it seems, on a course that will present a real test of nerve and resolve, and of our native intelligence, in the months and years ahead. . . . Indeed, what the Philippines needs at this hour is a total involvement of its citizenry in the noble enterprise of reorienting the nation's course in world politics and economy. . . . Let us sit down and, with a deep sense of urgency, forge a new Filipino Ideology that will, in effect, give sense and direction to events around us and be an enduring guide for our actions in the brave new world ahead.

From this point on it will be necessary for the leaders of this country to demonstrate the ineluctable continuity between antecedent conditions, contemporary realities, and creative needs and interests of our developing society. We must persuade ourselves, as we must our friends and neighbors, of the reasonableness of our actions, and of any changes we may undertake. In doing so we must be convinced of the rightness of our own actions, avoiding the paralysis that smugness brings.

In re-examining the military and other agreements with the United States and Western countries, on the one hand, and in wishing to establish beneficial relations with the Socialist countries in Asia and Europe, on the other hand, the Philippines is wholly motivated by the desire to attain balance and maturity in her international relations.

I consider the move a logical development in the Philippines' twenty-two year drive towards economic well-being and self-respect. . . . The treaties, pacts and agreements into which we entered, out of necessity but by a deliberate choice on our part, served to keep us under a protective umbrella while we tried to develop. Today, we realize that they served us, but not too well.

We cannot gloss over the fact of our over-dependence on one country for economic and security benefits. In the future, as an independent Asian country, we shall have ourselves only to rely upon for survival. Survival can best be assured by a policy of peace, of friendliness, and alertness to take quick advantage of economic opportunities where these present themselves, as in regional economic cooperation and trade with all countries, regardless of political differences.

*Source: Address to the Manila Overseas Press Club, January 30, 1969 (*Philippines Free Press,* February 8, 1969); reprinted by permission of the editor of the *Philippines Free Press.*

From where we are, right in the heart of Southeast Asia, the logical and respectable role would not be as an outpost of any foreign power. It is our belief that the day is past when Asia can be used for the power struggles of the large nations of the world.

The developing countries are coming together, and when they do, when they transcend the present differences that keep them apart, there will be no need for military bases, alliances, pacts and other agreements for they will then present, in themselves, in their freely working together for common growth, the best argument for peace.

It violates the principle of sovereignty and self-determination to have the national territory fragmented by foreign military bases where the state's rights and prerogatives are inoperative, in effect to allow states to exist within the state.

As if these were not enough, we have allowed other fences to be erected around us, circumscribing our freedoms, to the extent that our trade and cultural exchanges have been confined to a limited circle of countries, our professional and intellectual awareness and skills conditioned by one source of training, ideas and alternatives.

I think thereby we have not been true to the spirit of our Revolution, when our forebears sought to escape the suffocating embrace of a decadent empire, and reached outward. This restriction of growth precisely formed the basis of our Revolutionary protest. To rectify this we need, in accordance with the primal wish of the Filipino people, to expand our international relations with only national interest setting the limits of this outward thrust.

Thus the search for nationhood—for identity, order and strength— makes us reach out to other nations, but never to allow another nation to construe this as sanction for violating our integrity and our freedom. Internationalism, and our responsibilities to the world community, must be unequivocally rooted in national integrity. . . .

Hand in hand with this all-inclusive concept of nation it is our intention to erase all narrow identifications and interests and literally create a new awareness, a new identity. But this is not to be created out of nothing, for we are to draw from two historic wellsprings: (a) our cultural heritage, and (b) our Asian affinities. This is an intriguing paradox in which we deal, for by delving inwards, we may achieve an Asian identity; by retracing ancient links with Asia and forging new relations with Asian peoples we may gain a Filipino identity.

This is the point when a foreign policy of closer cooperation with our Asian neighbors, of regionalism and more intense exchanges with them, bear directly on our primordial goal of nationhood and sense of identity. But it also is an important factor in the other goals of economic pro-

ductivity and in the aspiration to become an industrialized nation, both of
which are bound up within the over-riding goal of modernization—of
ideals, values, outlook, attitudes and behavior, to permeate all levels of
national existence.

We have, in addition, slowly come to realize a growing opportunity
for some measure of leadership among the less developed countries of
Asia. This realization goes as far back as the 1950's, especially when we
first joined the Afro-Asian Conference at Bandung, and made common
cause with them. Awareness grew in the 1960's with our first tentative
moves to join regional schemes independent of sponsorship by Western
countries. But this awareness became most acute with the first state visits
undertaken by President Marcos in Southeast Asia, for these contacts
made it plain that only by coming together can the developing countries
of Southeast Asia secure their independence within competing spheres of
influence of the super-powers.

The Philippines remains viable in a forest of toppling regimes. If anything, we have become more respected, on the whole, as an Asian country and our citizens range far and wide in many fields of opportunity
abroad, steadily impressing the Filipino imprint by their good work. We
have been spared bitter disappointments and the rending shocks that
many less viable societies have experienced since the rescission of Empires.

Perhaps a measure of our vitality is, right now, our ability and our
readiness to undertake a re-examination of the entire range of our foreign
policy, without the spasms of fear and social turbulence that usually
accompany such proposals in other climes.

Let us, as Filipinos from this day on, as we essay to give shape and
substance to the Filipino out-look, work together in inscribing the new
Filipino Ideology in the hall of the nations of the world.

V. The Future

The process of internal development will determine the way of life
of future generations of Filipinos. It might, therefore, be useful to
summarize the nature of sociopolitical change in the Philippines and
its possible consequences.

American-inspired modernization had its greatest and earliest influence on the communications system. Relatively high literacy has
stimulated the growth of the press, and technology has more recently
expanded radio and television, with transistors having the widest impact. The communication explosion, advertising rapid changes in the

style of life in middle- and upper-class Manila, has raised aspirations and increased the variety and intensity of demands on the policy process.

But the capabilities of political institutions to meet these demands with policy output have not kept pace; in fact, there are recent signs of stagnation and even retrogression. Existing government services cater to those with the most influence—corrupt or otherwise—not to those with the greatest need. While government outputs and economic progress have long helped to reinforce the political system, fortunately they are not the sole source of its legitimacy.

Widespread popular participation in the system, through elections, has also been an important legitimizer. But in the last few years, cynicism about the meaning of the electoral process has grown in both city and countryside.

Great hope was placed by some in constitutional reform. However, when it becomes clear that constitutional change does not automatically produce economic and social progress, this source of hope may be lost, too.

Under these conditions, the stability of Filipino institutions is less certain than it appears. Though political practitioners tend to be more sanguine, the view below of the Filipino political future is probably characteristic of the pessimism expressed by most Filipino intellectuals. Teodoro Locsin, editor and publisher of the *Philippines Free Press,* once the most widely read English-language journal in the country, is an eloquent writer with considerable influence. Though his weekly was closed following the imposition of martial law in 1972 and he was imprisoned, Locsin's analysis is still timely.

Teodoro M. Locsin: Revolution Anyone? [February 8, 1969]*

The Philippines has been described as sitting on top of a social volcano. The question arises: Why has the volcano not erupted?

Conditions prevailing in the country today are the same as those that prevailed in Cuba just before the revolution led by Castro that overthrew the Batista regime and established a Communist dictatorship, another description goes.

* *Source:* Teodoro M. Locsin, "Revolution Anyone?" *Philippines Free Press,* February 8, 1969; reprinted by permission of the editor of the *Philippines Free Press.*

Is the Philippines just waiting for a Filipino Castro?

It is admitted that the rich few are getting richer and the poor many are getting poorer. Unemployment keeps increasing, and so do prices, without a commensurate increase in income, ensuring the ever-increasing misery of the masses—which should lead to a mass revolt against the existing social order, according to Communist belief.

Why, then, has there been no revolt of the masses?

Is it because the masses are not yet miserable enough?

When will they be miserable enough to rise in revolt?

Will they ever be miserable enough?

It may take 20 years for the Filipino people to become miserable enough to stage a successful revolution. The Huk movement was not nationwide and it was crushed. All it merited, therefore, was the designation of "rebellion." But in 20 years, the population of the Philippines will have doubled. Seventy million Filipinos living in the same area as 35 million now, with unemployment and prices continually rising, should create the necessary revolutionary situation. What is merely simmering, if it is that, should finally come to a boil. Then, as water becomes steam, the inert masses would become active, changing their condition through revolutionary action in the best tradition of dialectical materialism.

But that would be 20 years from now—perhaps.

Meanwhile, there is a kind of democracy with a mock two-party system that permits changes of administration while keeping the social system essentially the same. There is no total repression as in the countries that came under Communist rule. Leaders of the opposition are not arrested and tortured. There is no secret police. And there are elections, of course. No matter how angry the people may get with the party in power, it is always possible to throw it out of power without recourse to arms. All the people have to do is vote against it in the elections—an easy process involving no risk to the voter as a rule—and the hated regime is replaced by another. Why rise in revolt when one has the ballot with which to punish erring officials, including the President himself? Why risk being jailed or getting killed when all one has to do to express one's anger at the administration is to vote against it? With the casting of the anti-administration vote, anger is dispelled.

Because the two major parties are essentially the same, representing as they do the same economic interests, there are changes of administration but no change of government, no change of the social system. Those who vote for a new deal are cheated in every election, but what can they do about it? "That's democracy!" they are told. Have they not been allowed freely to assemble and air their grievances? Have they not exercised their right to vote against the party in power which has kept so many of them so miserable? Has their will not been given expression at the polls? The voice of the people is the voice of God—and have the people not spoken? What's there to complain about? . . .

In the Philippines, the illusion of a choice in the elections keeps the people from resorting to violence to effect change. By voting against officials who have made them suffer so much, they get some satisfaction; they are disarmed. They will become more miserable than ever under the "new" administration, which will be composed of officials they have previously kicked out of office for making them so miserable, but they can always punish them by voting against them in the next elections. There is only the appearance of change, but it will do. There is only temporary punishment of enemies of the people, but there is some satisfaction to be derived from it, and it does not matter at the moment that these same enemies of the people will eventually be restored to power by the people themselves. That's democracy, to say it once more.

There is also the institution of a free press in which the people can say anything against the administration—short of libelling individual officials—and not be sent to prison. Freedom of speech serves as a safety valve; it releases the force of popular indignation harmlessly; the people explode with words instead of violent actions. The press, free and impotent, buttresses the Establishment. It keeps alive the illusion that there is freedom—freedom to choose the government one would live under—and thus gives the Establishment a respectable appearance. At the same time, the press cannot really do anything to change the social order; it is as much of a fraud as the so-called two-party system. At best it entertains; it cannot reform. If it were not a part of the Establishment, its members would be in jail. Because it is ineffective, it is not only tolerated but also supported. If it should ever constitute a challenge to those who hold the real power in the country, it will be eliminated. As a safety valve, however, it serves the purposes of reaction. It relieves popular feeling and helps keep the people down.

And those in power know better than to push the people to utter desperation. Exploitation is leavened with concessions. The minimum wage and other labor laws make the workers' lot less awful than it would be under a regime of absolute "free enterprise." The beginning of land reform offers tenants hope of finally owning the land they till. All these do not keep unemployment and prices from rising; life is increasingly difficult for most of the people; whatever gains the economy makes in providing for the needs of the people are cancelled by the explosion in population, but the oppression is not total and the general reaction is one of anger mixed with resignation.

And, of course, for the people to be miserable is not a new condition.

Centuries of foreign rule and colonialism have made the Filipino people accustomed to being exploited and abused. It is their normal condition. When they summoned enough energy in the previous century to have a revolution, it was crushed by an ally, which proceeded to impose its own rule on them. Filipinos have grown accustomed to being oppressed by foreigners; when "independence" came and their own countrymen became their oppressors, they reacted in the same fashion. They merely suffered.

And there is the Catholic Church, the most powerful factor for keeping things as they are. It promises "pie in the sky, by and by" to the poor; the more they suffer, the greater their reward in heaven. Suffer now, enjoy later. What could be more tranquilizing? The Church is against revolution; it's for reform. And if reform does not come, that's too bad, but the Church is still against revolution. What should the people do, then?

Suffer and pray. . . .

Some Filipinos do wring their hands—over the fact that there is no sign of any significant revolutionary activity. What else can bring about real reform? The social system will never change except under pressure. But the pressure for change is constantly lowered by the various factors we have described. There will be neither revolution nor reform in the near future. Instead, there will be increasing lawlessness. And that will invite a rightist take-over of the government, followed by a suspension of civil liberties under a military dictatorship set up to keep the poor in their place and the rich in theirs.

How about the student demonstrations?

They have yet to prove that they are not a passing fancy, a fad. And if they develop into a real challenge to those in power, to the power elite, they will be met with force. Even now, they are being used, it may well be, to prepare the country for suppression of all dissent.

When that time comes—

Revolution, anyone?

Locsin's fear of repression was well-founded. On September 23, 1972, President Marcos announced the imposition of martial law throughout the Philippines. The constitution allows the president to impose martial law "in cases of invasion, insurrection or rebellion or imminent danger thereof"; Marcos justified his action on grounds of a growing revolutionary Communist movement and a sharp increase in acts of violence, which, he said, threatened the existence of the government.[6] Thousands of persons, including senators, mayors, publishers,

[6] See the *New York Times*, September 24, 1972.

professors, and priests were imprisoned for their views and political activities. After martial law became a fact, however, little was said in the tightly controlled press about the "Huk threat."

Ferdinand Marcos: Address to the Nation [September 23, 1972]*

My Countrymen:

As of the 21st of September, I signed Proclamation No. 1081 placing the entire Philippines under martial law. This Proclamation was to be implemented upon my clearance, and clearance was granted at 9:00 in the evening of the 22nd of September. I have proclaimed martial law in accordance with powers vested in the President by the Constitution of the Philippines.

The proclamation of martial law is not a military takeover. I, as your duly elected President of the Republic, use this power implemented by the military authorities to protect the Republic of the Philippines and our democracy. A republican and democratic form of government is not a helpless government. When it is imperiled by the danger of a violent overthrow, insurrection, and rebellion, it has inherent and built-in powers wisely provided for under the Constitution. Such a danger confronts the Republic.

Thus, Article VII, Section 10, paragraph (2) of the Constitution, provides:

"The President shall be Commander-in-Chief of all the Armed Forces of the Philippines and, whenever it becomes necessary he may call out such armed forces to prevent or suppress lawless violence, invasion, insurrection, or rebellion. In case of invasion, insurrection, or rebellion or imminent danger therof, when the public safety requires it, he may suspend the privilege of the writ of habeas corpus, or place the Philippines or any part thereof under martial law."

I repeat, this is not a military takeover of civil government functions. The Government of the Republic of the Philippines which was established by our people in 1946 continues. The officials and employees of our national and local governments continue in office and must discharge their duties as before within the limits of the situation. This will be clarified by my subsequent orders which shall be given wide publicity. . . .

We will explain the requirements and standards or details as soon as possible. But any form of corruption, culpable negligence, or arrogance will be dealt with immediately.

* *Source:* Radio address by President Ferdinand Marcos, Manila, September 23, 1972.

The Armed Forces is already cleaning up its own ranks. I am directing the organization of a military commission to investigate, try, and punish all military offenders immediately. For more than any other man, the soldier must set the standard of nobility. We must be courageous but we must be humble and above all we must be fair. As this is true of the soldier, it must be true of the civilian public officer. . . .

Persons who have nothing whatsoever to do with such conspiracy and operations to overthrow the Republic of the Philippines by violence have nothing to fear. They can move about and perform their daily activities without any fear from the Government after the period of counter-action is over.

The persons who will be adversely affected are those who have actively participated in the conspiracy and operations to overthrow the duly constituted government of the Republic of the Philippines by violence.

But all public officials and employees whether of the national or local governments must conduct themselves in the manner of a new and reformed society.

In addition to this, I issued General Orders for the government in the meantime to control media and other means of dissemination of information as well as all public utilities. All schools will be closed for one week beginning this coming Monday. The carrying of firearms outside residences without the permission of the Armed Forces of the Philippines is punishable with death; curfew is established from twelve o'clock midnight to four o'clock in the morning; the departure of Filipinos abroad is temporarily suspended; exceptions are those of official missions that are necessary. Clearances will be given by the Secretary of National Defense. In the meantime, rallies, demonstrations are prohibited. So too are strikes in critical public utilities.

I have ordered the arrest of those directly involved in the conspiracy to overthrow our duly constituted government by violence and subversion.

It is my intention beginning tomorrow to issue all the orders which would attain reforms in our society.

This would include the proclamation of land reform all over the Philippines, the reorganization of the government, new rules and conduct for the civil service, the removal of corrupt and inefficient public officials and their replacement and the breaking up of criminal syndicates.

Again I repeat—this is the same government that you—the people—established in 1946 under the Constitution of the Philippines.

There is no doubt in everybody's mind that a state of rebellion exists in the Philippines.

The ordinary man in the streets, in our cities, the peasants and the laborers know it. Industrialists know it. So do the government functionaries. They have all been affected by it. This danger to the Republic of the Philippines and the existence of a rebellion has been recognized even by our Supreme Court in its decision in the case of *Lansang* vs. *Garcia*, dated December 11, 1971.

Since the Supreme Court promulgated this decision, the danger has become graver and rebellion has worsened or escalated. It has paralyzed the functions of the national and local governments. The productive sectors of the economy have ground to a halt. Many schools have closed down. The judiciary is unable to administer justice. Many of our business-men, traders, industrialists, producers, and manufacturers stopped their operations. In the Greater Manila area alone, tension and anxiety have reached a point where the citizens are compelled to stay at home. Lawless-ness and criminality like kidnapping, smuggling, extortion, blackmail, armed robbery, illegal traffic in drugs, gunrunning, hoarding and manipu-lation of prices, corruption in government, tax evasion perpetuated by syndicated criminals, have increasingly escalated beyond the capability of the local police and civilian authorities.

The usually busy centers of the area such as cinema houses, super-markets, restaurants, transportation terminals and even public markets are practically deserted. Battles are going on between elements of the Armed Forces of the Philippines and the subversives in the Island of Luzon at Isabela, Zambales, Tarlac, Camarines Sur, Quezon; and in the Island of Mindanao at Lanao del Sur, Lanao del Norte, Zamboanga del Sur, and Cotabato.

If this continues even at the present rate, the economy of the country will collapse in a short time.

In one province alone—Isabela—where the Communist Party and the New People's Army have sought to establish a rural sanctuary, they are now in control of 33 municipalities out of 37. Other towns are infiltrated severely by these armed elements. In this province alone, the supposed in-visible government of the Communist Party has been organized through the Barrio Organizing Committees (BOCs), totaling 207 in twenty-five towns, compared to 161 in twelve towns in early 1971. . . .

The armed elements of the New People's Army under the Communist Party of the Philippines (Maoist faction) have increased to about 10,000, which includes regulars as well as farmers in the daytime and soldiers at night. This is an increase of 100 per cent in a short period of six months. It has increased its mass base to 100,000. Their front organiza-tions' operations have increased tremendously. Example of such a front organization is the Kabataang Makabayan (KM), the most militant organization of the Communist Party, which has increased its chapters from 200 in 1970 to 317 up to the end of July 1972, and its membership from 10,000 in 1970 to 15,000 up to the end of July this year. The Samahang Demokratiko ng Kabataan (SDK), an outspoken front organization, had also increased its chapters from almost none in 1970 to 159 at the end of July this year and has now 1,495 highly indoctrinated and fanatical members. . . .

The subversives have organized urban partisans in the Greater Manila area. They have been and still are active. They have succeeded in some of their objectives.

The violent disorder in Mindanao and Sulu has to date resulted in the killing of over 1,000 civilians and about 2,000 armed Muslims and Christians, not to mention the more than five-hundred thousands of injured, displaced, and homeless persons as well as the great number of casualties among our government troops, and the paralyzation of the economy of Mindanao and Sulu.

I assure you that I am utilizing this power vested in me by the Constitution to save the Republic and reform our society. I wish to emphasize these two objectives. We will eliminate the threat of a violent overthrow of our Republic. But at the same time we must now reform the social, economic, and political institutions in our country. The plans and orders for reform to remove the inequities of that society, the clean-up of government of its corrupt and sterile elements, the liquidation of the criminal syndicates, the systematic development of our economy—the general program for a new and better Philippines—will be explained to you. But we must start out with the removal of anarchy and the maintenance of peace and order.

I have had to use this constitutional power in order that we may not completely lose the civil rights and freedom which we cherish. I assure you that this is not a precipitate decision—that I have weighed all the factors. If there were any other solution at our disposal and within our capability which we could utilize to solve the present problem, I would choose it. But there is none.

I have used the other two alternatives of calling out the troops to quell the rebellion and suspending the privilege of the writ of habeas corpus. But the rebellion has not been stopped. I repeat, it has worsened. . . .

All other recourses have been unavailing. You are all witnesses to these. So we have fallen on our last line of defense.

You are witnesses to the patience that we have shown in the face of provocation. In the face of abuse and license we have used persuasion. Now the limit has been reached. We are against the wall. We must now defend the Republic with the stronger powers of the Constitution.

To those guilty of treason, insurrection, rebellion, it may pose a grave danger. But to the citizenry, whose primary concern is to be left alone to pursue their lawful activities, this is the guaranty of that freedom.

All that we do is for the Republic and for you. Rest assured we will continue to do so.

I have prayed to God for guidance. Let us all continue to do so. I am confident that with God's help we will attain our dream of a reformed society, a new and brighter world.

After Marcos's term of office under the 1935 constitution expired on December 30, 1973, the basis of his claim to legitimacy was the new constitution, pushed through the Constitutional Convention after the proclamation of martial law and while some of the more outspoken members of that Convention still languished in jail. This constitutional draft was "ratified" in January 1973, not by a "plebescite" as provided in Art. XVII, Sec. 16, but in village assemblies throughout the country where *viva voce* voting was held under the watchful eyes of policemen and constabulary.

While a number of articles in the new constitution are identical with the old, there is a basic shift to unicameralism and the parliamentary system, thus permitting the incumbent president—barred from further reelection under the old constitution—potentially indefinite office as prime minister. Nor is the power of the new prime minister more restricted than that of the president in the earlier document. Under the 1973 constitution the president is simply "symbolic head of state."

The Commission on Elections was retained—and enlarged—at the same time that the franchise was expanded, ironic in view of the fact that elections have not been held at all under martial law. The Commission was also given new power over political parties which may, in fact, be used.

There is also evidence in the 1973 charter that a wistful hope persisted among convention delegates that types of behavior which could not be prevented by ordinary laws, e.g., party switching, graft or corruption, might be stopped by constitutional injunction.

In the realm of culture and education there were new expressions of nationalism in the basic law of 1973. However, in the economic sphere the nationalism already embodied in laws and court decisions as of 1972 was significantly relaxed in order to allow continued large-scale American participation in the economy.

Finally, the "Transitory Provisions" in Art. XVII reveal the most obvious Marcos imprimatur. All sitting Congressmen and Convention Delegates were to be allowed to continue indefinitely in the interim

National Assembly—unless, of course, they were so bold as to oppose those not so "Transitory Provisions." But those who endorsed the Marcos plan before adoption of the new constitution were not so well treated afterwards. At the same time as he proclaimed the new charter, Marcos decided *not* to convene the interim National Assembly, exercising legislative power by decree.

Constitution of the Republic of the Philippines [1973]*

Art. VIII   The National Assembly.

Sec. 1. The Legislative power shall be vested in a National Assembly.

Sec. 2. The National Assembly shall be composed of as many Members as may be provided by law to be apportioned among the provinces, representative districts, and cities in accordance with the number of their respective inhabitants and on the basis of a uniform and progressive ratio. Each district shall comprise, as far as practicable, contiguous, compact, and adjacent territory. Representative districts or provinces already created or existing at the time of the ratification of this Constitution shall have at least one Member each.

Sec. 3. (1) The Members of the National Assembly shall be elected by the qualified electors in their respective districts for a term of six years which shall begin, unless otherwise provided by law, at noon on the thirtieth day of June next following their election. . . .

. . . Sec. 13. (1) The National Assembly may withdraw its confidence from the Prime Minister only by electing a successor by a majority vote of all its Members. No motion for the election of such successor shall be debated and voted upon until after the lapse of three days from the submittal of such motion. . . .

. . . Sec. 20. (1) Every bill passed by the National Assembly shall, before it becomes a law, be presented to the Prime Minister. If he approves the same, he shall sign it; otherwise, he shall veto it and return the same with his objections to the National Assembly. The bill may be reconsidered by the National Assembly and, if approved by two-thirds of all its Members, shall become a law. The Prime Minister shall act on every bill passed by the National Assembly within thirty days after the date of receipt thereof; otherwise, it shall become a law as if he had signed it.

(2) The Prime Minister shall have the power to veto any particular item or items in an appropriation, revenue, or tariff bill, but the veto shall not affect the item or items to which he does not object.

* *Source: The Constitution of the Republic of the Philippines* (Manila: Bureau of Printing, 1973).

Art. IX—The Prime Minister and the Cabinet

Sec. 1. The Executive power shall be exercised by the Prime Minister with the assistance of the Cabinet. The Cabinet, headed by the Prime Minister, shall consist of the heads of ministries as provided by law. The Prime Minister shall be the head of the Government.

. . . Sec. 3. The Prime Minister shall be elected by a majority of all the Members of the National Assembly from among themselves.

. . . Sec.12. The Prime Minister shall be commander-in-chief of all armed forces of the Philippines and, whenever it becomes necessary, he may call out such armed forces to prevent or suppress lawless violence, invasion, insurrection, or rebellion. In case of invasion, insurrection, or rebellion, or imminent danger thereof, when the public safety requires it, he may suspend the privilege of the writ of *habeas corpus,* or place the Philippines or any part thereof under martial law. . . .

Art. XII—The Commission on Elections

Sec. 1. (1) There shall be an independent Commission on Elections composed of a Chairman and eight Commissioners. . . .

. . . Sec. 8. A political party shall be entitled to accreditation by the Commission if, in the immediately preceding elections, such party has obtained at least the third highest number of votes cast in the constituency to which it seeks accreditation. No religious sect shall be registered as a political party, and no political party which seeks to achieve its goals through violence or subversion shall be entitled to accreditation.

. . . Sec. 10. No elective public officer may change his political party affiliation during his term of office, and no candidate for any elective public office may change his political party affiliation within six months immediately preceding or following an election.

Art. XIII

. . . Sec. 5. The National Assembly shall create a special court, to be known as *Sandiganbayan,* which shall have jurisdiction over criminal and civil cases involving graft and corrupt practices and such other offenses committed by public officers and employees, including those in government-owned or controlled corporations, in relation to their office as may be determined by law.

Sec. 6. The National Assembly shall create an office of the Ombudsman, to be known as *Tanodbayan,* which shall receive and investigate complaints relative to public office, including those in government-owned or controlled corporations, make appropriate recommendations, and in case of failure of justice as defined by law, file and prosecute the corresponding criminal, civil, or administrative case before the proper court or body.

Art. XIV

. . . Sec. 9. The disposition, exploration, development, exploitation, or utilization of any of the natural resources of the Philippines shall be limited to citizens of the Philippines, or to corporations or associations at least sixty *per centum* of the capital of which is owned by such citizens. The National Assembly, in the national interest, may allow such citizens, corporations, or associations to enter into service contracts for financial, technical, management, or other forms of assistance with any foreign person or entity for the exploration, development, exploitation, or utilization of any of the natural resources. Existing valid and binding service contracts for financial, technical, management, or other forms of assistance are hereby recognized as such.

. . . Sec. 11. The rights and privileges granted to citizens of the United States or to corporations or associations owned or controlled by such citizens under the Ordinance appended to the nineteen hundred and thirty-five Constitution shall automatically terminate on the third day of July, nineteen hundred and seventy-four. Titles to private lands acquired by such persons before such date shall be valid as against other private persons only. . . .

Art. XVII—Transitory Provisions

Sec. 1. There shall be an *interim* National Assembly which shall exist immediately upon the ratification of this Constitution and shall continue until the Members of the regular National Assembly shall have been elected and shall have assumed office following an election called for the purpose by the *interim* National Assembly. . . .

Sec. 2. The Members of the *interim* National Assembly shall be the incumbent President and Vice–President of the Philippines, those who served as President of the nineteen hundred and seventy-one Constitutional Convention, those Members of the Senate and the House of Representatives who shall express in writing to the Commission on Elections within thirty days after the ratification of this Constitution their option to serve therein, and those Delegates to the nineteen hundred and seventy-one Constitutional Convention who have opted to serve therein by voting affirmatively for this Article. They may take their oath of office before any officer authorized to administer oath and qualify thereto, after the ratification of this Constitution.

Sec. 3. (1) The incumbent President of the Philippines shall initially convene the *interim* National Assembly and shall preside over its sessions until the *interim* Speaker shall have been elected. He shall continue to exercise his powers and prerogatives under the nineteen hundred and thirty-five Constitution and the powers vested in the President and the Prime Minister under this Constitution until he calls upon the *interim*

National Assembly to elect the *interim* President and the *interim* Prime Minister, who shall then exercise their respective powers vested by this Constitution.

(2) All proclamations, orders, decrees, instructions, and acts promulgated, issued, or done by the incumbent President shall be part of the law of the land, and shall remain valid, legal, binding, and effective even after lifting of martial law or the ratification of this Constitution, unless modified, revoked, or superseded by subsequent proclamations, orders, decrees, instructions, or other acts of the incumbent President, or unless expressly and explicitly modified or repealed by the regular National Assembly.

Glossary

Abangan: Nominal Muslims in Indonesia whose real beliefs owe less to Islam than to Hinduism and Buddhism.

AMPERA: Mandate of the people's suffering (Indonesian).

Amphur: District (Thai).

Baht: Unit of Thai money (*bahts* 20 = U.S. $1.00).

Ban: Village (Thai).

Barrio: Village (Filipino).

Bogyoke: The General (Burmese title reserved for the leading military-political figure in the country).

Changwad: Province (Thai).

Chaokhoueng: Provincial governor (Laotian).

Chaomuong: District officer (Laotian).

Chauvaykhet: Provincial governor (Cambodian).

Chauvaysrok: District officer (Cambodian).

Condrodimuko: The deepest and most dreadful level of hell; to emerge from this level is to have passed the supreme test (Indonesian).

Crore: Burmese unit of measure equal to ten million.

Dacoit: Thief, murderer, or bully; *dacoity,* from which the term comes, means gang activity (Burmese).

Dân vê: South Vietnamese National police.

Duwa: A Kachin title for a leader (Burmese).

Gestapu: September 30 movement (Indonesian).

Gịa: Vietnamese unit of measure equal to about forty liters.

G.O.C.: General officer commanding.

Jakarta Charter: An earlier and more Islamic draft of the Preamble to the 1945 Constitution of Indonesia.

Jogja: Jogjakarta, Indonesia.

Kabupaten: The major level of regional government between province and village in Indonesia.

Kampuchéa: Cambodia.

Kha: "Savage" or "slave"; a term used in Laos and Thailand to designate upland peoples whose linguistic affiliation is Mon-Khmer.

Khet: Province (Cambodian).

Khoueng: Province (Laotian).

Khum: Township (Cambodian).

Kip: Unit of Lao money (in the late 1960's, *kips* 500 = U.S. $1.00).

Kromokar: Middle-ranking civil servant (Cambodian).

Kouang Lam: Forced labor (Laotian).

Kyat: Unit of Burmese money (in the late 1960's, *kyats* 4.76 = U.S. $1.00).

Lakh: Burmese unit of measure equal to one hundred thousand.

Marhaenism: Term used to indicate the social and political ideas advanced in Indonesia by Sukarno in the 1920's (adopted later as the philosophy of the PNI).

Mékhum: Mayor (Cambodian).

Merdeka: "Freedom" or "independence" in Malay and Indonesian.

MNDO: Mon National Defense Organization in Burma.

Mujahid: Arakanese Muslims who revolted against the Burmese government in 1947–1948.

Muong: District (Laotian).

Myosas: Literally "town eater"; formerly a Burmese royal term designating a prince or high official who shared in the revenues collected from a town or district; today a government official equivalent to a district officer.

Nai Amphur: District officer (Thai).

Nai Ban: Village headman (Thai).

Naikong: District officer in areas inhabited primarily by non-Lao ethnic groups.

NASAKOM: Indonesian term for the unity of nationalists, religious people, and Communists.

Ngwe-khun-hmus: Tax collector; formerly a Burmese royal term designating a revenue official.

Oudam Montrei hors-classe: Senior civil servant with the rank of cabinet minister (Cambodian).

Palay: Tagalog term for unhusked rice (Filipino).

Panca Sila Front: Anti-Communist movement established by leaders of Muslim and Christian parties in Indonesia after the coup attempt of October 1, 1965.

Pao: Minority people in the Shan state; identified by anthropologists as Toungthus.

Pendawa: The five Pendawa brothers are central figures in the stories of the Mahabharata and much of the Javanese Wayang literature.

People's Comrade Party (PCP) : A socialist group which broke away from the Burma Workers' and Peasant Party in the early 1950's.

People's Tatmadaw: People's Army (Burmese).

Peso: Unit of Filipino money (in the late 1960's, *pesos* 4.34 = U.S. $1.00).

Phoban: Village headman (Laotian).

Preah Bat Samdech: Literally "Your Royal Highness, Prince"; title used by Cambodia's Prince Norodom Sihanouk.

PRRI: Revolutionary Government of the Republic of Indonesia, the rebel government established in Central Sumatra in February 1958.

Pyithu Yebaws: Burmese term used to designate soldiers in the Burma National, Independence, or Defense Armies; also for members of the PVO.

Rai: Thai unit of land measurement, equal to approximately ⅗ acre.

Ratu Adil: Just King; Messiah (Indonesian).

Riel: Unit of Cambodian money (in the late 1960's, *riels* 54 = U.S. $1.00).

Rupee: Unit of Indian money; used in Burma during British colonial rule.

Rupiah: Unit of Indonesian money (in the early 1970's, *rupiahs* 415 = U.S. $1.00).

Samdach Preah Sanghaneayok: Supreme patriarch of one of the two Buddhist sects in Cambodia.

Samdech Sahachivin: Prince, or Royal, comrade; used to designate Cambodia's Prince, Norodom Sihanouk.

Samdech Upayuvareach: Literally "The Prince who was formerly king"; title used by Cambodia's Prince Norodom Sihanouk, indicating that he had abdicated the throne.

Sangha: Buddhist order.

Saophalong, Saophas, Sawbwas: Various spellings for titles of chiefs of the former Shan and Kayah states in Burma (*saophalong* is a formal and special designation; *saophas* is the term used in the Burmese constitution; *Sawbwas* is the term most commonly used).

Sasana: Religion, with reference to Buddhism; sometimes used to refer to Buddhist teaching.

SEALF: South East Asia Land Forces.

Sitio: Hamlet, subdivision of a *barrio* (Filipino).

Srok: District (Cambodian).

Tasseng: Township (Laotian).

Tet: Vietnamese lunar New Year.

Thadingyut: The name of the festival held at the end of the Burmese Buddhist Lent; usually translated as the "Festival of Lights" because of the carrying of candles and the showing of lights in all houses and buildings.

Viet Cong: Vietnamese Communist.

Yang di-Pertuan Agong: Paramount ruler or king (Malaysian).

Index

SOUTHEAST ASIA

Designed by R. E. Rosenbaum.
Composed by York Composition Co., Inc.
in 10 point intertype Baskerville, 2 points leaded,
with display lines in Weiss.
Printed letterpress from type by York Composition Co., Inc.
on Warren's No. 66 text, 50 pound basis,
with the Cornell University Press watermark.
Bound by Vail-Ballou Press
in Columbia book cloth
and stamped in All Purpose foil.